SOUTHEAST ASIAN AFFAIRS 2018

The **ISEAS – Yusof Ishak Institute** (formerly Institute of Southeast Asian Studies) is an autonomous organization established in 1968. It is a regional centre dedicated to the study of socio-political, security, and economic trends and developments in Southeast Asia and its wider geostrategic and economic environment. The Institute's research programmes are grouped under Regional Economic Studies (RES), Regional Strategic and Political Studies (RSPS), and Regional Social and Cultural Studies (RSCS). The Institute is also home to the ASEAN Studies Centre (ASC), the Nalanda-Sriwijaya Centre (NSC) and the Singapore APEC Study Centre.

ISEAS Publishing, an established academic press, has issued more than 2,000 books and journals. It is the largest scholarly publisher of research about Southeast Asia from within the region. ISEAS Publishing works with many other academic and trade publishers and distributors to disseminate important research and analyses from and about Southeast Asia to the rest of the world.

SOUTHEAST ASIAN AFFAIRS 2018

EDITED BY

MALCOLM COOK
DALJIT SINGH

First published in Singapore in 2018 by
ISEAS Publishing
30 Heng Mui Keng Terrace
Singapore 119614

E-mail: publish@iseas.edu.sg
Website: http://bookshop.iseas.edu.sg

The responsibility for facts and opinions in this publication rests exclusively with the authors and their interpretations do not necessarily reflect the views or the policy of the publisher or its supporters.

ISEAS Library Cataloguing-in-Publication Data

Southeast Asian affairs.
1974–
Annual
1. Southeast Asia—Periodicals.
I. ISEAS – Yusof Ishak Institute.
DS501 S72A

ISSN 0377-5437
ISBN 978-981-4786-83-6 (hard cover)
ISBN 978-981-4786-84-3 (E-book PDF)

Typeset by Superskill Graphics Pte Ltd
Printed in Singapore by Mainland Press Pte Ltd

Contents

Introduction

Daljit Singh[1]

As foreshadowed in *Southeast Asian Affairs 2017*, key developments in 2016 helped shape Southeast Asia's regional environment in 2017 and the domestic developments of the eleven countries covered in this volume.[2] As discussed by Lee Hwok-Aun, the improvements in the global economy and the wider East Asian one meant economic headwinds were positive for Southeast Asia in 2017. The beginning of the Trump administration in the United States of America has added a new source of regional geostrategic and geoeconomic uncertainty. In contrast, China's growing influence and assertiveness in the region is a source of geostrategic and geoeconomic certainty. The five-month siege of Marawi City and fears of Rohingya radicalization in Myanmar and the refugee camps in Bangladesh are a reminder that the threat of violent extremism is a structural rather than a cyclical factor. Election cycles in the region's democracies and leadership renewal cycles in the non-democracies were the most important determinants of domestic politics in most regional states.

Southeast Asia and the Great Powers

The year 2017 heralded the coming of more great power rivalry in the Indo-Pacific region, a geopolitical framework of Japanese origin but one adopted by U.S. president Donald Trump and featuring prominently in official U.S. documents like the National Security Strategy (NSS) of December 2017 and the National Defence Strategy (NDS) soon after. China's assertiveness and pressures on other countries had been leading to a pushback from the United States and its allies.

Daljit Singh is Senior Research Fellow at the ISEAS – Yusof Ishak Institute, Singapore.

There were at least two important indicators of this. The first was the Quadrilateral Security Dialogue (the Quad), an informal forum of Japan, Australia, the United States and India to discuss security challenges in the Indo-Pacific. Though not a formal military alliance and still at the discussion stage, it is likely to evolve further. Second, the NSS and the NDS for the first time describe China (together with Russia) as a strategic competitor and the most significant security challenge to the interests of the United States and its allies and friends in the region, replacing terrorism. There were also more freedom of navigation (FON) operations conducted by the U.S. Navy in the South China Sea.

The Trump Administration

Two chapters in the regional section of this volume deal with major-power policies for the region, by Joseph Liow Chin Yong and by Walter Lohman. Lohman argues that, after the early alarums and uncertainties, by the end of 2017 much more continuity in the Trump administration's security and political policies was evident than change. U.S. alliance commitments remained strong. The president had bilateral meetings in Washington with several of the leaders of Southeast Asian states and also attended the APEC leaders' meeting in Hanoi and the important meetings under the rubric of the Association of Southeast Asian Nations (ASEAN) in Manila in November. The United States remained committed to ASEAN centrality in the ASEAN-centred regional security architecture.

Although this was reassuring to many countries in the region, some unease remained. As Liow points out, the administration's "America First" approach could mean a narrower conception of U.S. interests in the region and some abandonment of America's traditional leadership role. There were worries in particular about the protectionist feature in the administration's economic policies, which Lohman also underlines, which has been generating considerable uncertainty. The U.S. withdrawal from the Trans-Pacific Partnership (TPP) was a significant setback for the United States in its competition for influence with China. As Liow points out, the TPP had been seen as a crucial expression of American commitment to the region. The Trump administration will need to have a judicious mixture of diplomatic, economic and military instruments to sustain U.S. engagement in the Indo-Pacific region. Nguyen Manh Hung's thematic chapter on Vietnam addresses Hanoi's concerns regarding the "Trump Surprise".

China's Influence

Meanwhile, China continued to advance its influence and presence through increasing trade and investment flows, the Belt and Road Initiative (BRI), and an assertive "neighbourhood" diplomacy. It was also rapidly modernizing and expanding its air and naval forces and militarizing its "islands" in the South China Sea.

Growing Chinese influence and importance is one of the most powerful cross-chapter themes in *Southeast Asian Affairs 2018*. Lee Hwok-Aun flags the growing importance of China as a regional trade partner and source of foreign direct investment. Lye Liang Fook's thematic chapter for Singapore is devoted to the strengthening of China–Singapore ties, while President Duterte has placed China, not the United States, at the centre of Philippine foreign policy. Pushpa Thambipillai notes that China's foreign direct investment in the non-oil sectors is central to Brunei's plans for economic diversification, while Oliver Tappe looks at the importance and risks for Laos of its huge railway project with China. Priyambudi Sulistiyanto and Eve Warburton both address political opposition efforts in Indonesia to play up the perceived negative effects of growing Chinese influence in Indonesia. Mary Callahan notes that growing Western criticism of the Myanmar government and military is encouraging Myanmar to seek closer relations with China.

Growing concern with China and uncertainty with the United States are behind Japan's and India's stepping up of their engagement with Southeast Asia, as Liow delineates in his chapter. Japan has signed strategic partnerships with some key Southeast Asian states involving economic and maritime cooperation and assistance, stepped up high-level diplomacy, and increased aid and investments, including for infrastructure development. It has also pledged to support the defence capabilities of the Philippine armed forces. India, too, is paying more attention to Southeast Asia, with high-level visits and cooperation in the maritime security domain. A new naval agreement was signed with Singapore. India also announced the provision of $500,000 of aid to the Philippines to help it fight terrorist groups. Liow notes that this is the first time that India has sent aid to any country to help in the fight against terrorism, signalling its intention to be a security provider in the wider Asian region.

Southeast Asian Responses

In response to the Trump administration's withdrawal from the TPP, the other eleven signatories signed a revised version of the agreement called the Comprehensive and Progressive Trans-Pacific Partnership (CPTPP), hoping that eventually the United States will rejoin. The U.S. withdrawal also gave urgency to the successful conclusion of the sixteen-nation Regional Comprehensive Economic Partnership (RCEP) to keep the flame of trade liberalization burning. However, this proved elusive by the end of 2018 because of the difficulty of harmonizing qualitatively and quantitatively different free trade agreements between ASEAN and its six Plus countries.

The year 2017 marked the fiftieth anniversary of ASEAN. Indeed, there was much to celebrate as the association had contributed much to advance peace and stability among the countries of Southeast Asia and taken important steps towards economic integration. However, as Liow points out, 2017 must also have been a year of introspection for ASEAN, as challenges had been developing to its centrality in the regional security architecture. This was due to more major-power competition, specifically with regard to South China Sea issues which had strained ASEAN unity. During the year, China and ASEAN agreed on a "framework" for a Code of Conduct and to begin negotiations for the code. Whether the code eventually agreed on will meet ASEAN's expectations is left to be seen. The emergence of the Quad as an apparently serious proposition and talk of a new Indo-Pacific strategy of the United States and some of its allies also caused unease. While many in ASEAN would quietly welcome a pushback against a perceived overbearing China, ASEAN would not want to see its centrality in major-power interactions with Southeast Asia diminished, given the fact that Southeast Asia is geographically located in the middle of the Indo-Pacific region.

Insurgencies and Terrorism

ASEAN also arguably had to face the two most dramatic developments in Southeast Asia in 2017 — the Rohingya crisis in Myanmar and the Marawi siege in the southern Philippines. Apart from the humanitarian dimensions of the two events, they portended new political and security risks for Southeast Asia and ASEAN. A common problem is that the existing peace processes to address insurgencies in southern Thailand, the southern Philippines and in Myanmar are showing more signs of strain than progress, as noted by Mary Callahan for Myanmar, Dennis Quilala for the Philippines and Pongphisoot Busbarat for Thailand.

The Politics of Southeast Asian States

Political consolidation and continuity may be broadly described as the situation in Brunei, the three Indochina states, Indonesia, the Philippines and Singapore in 2017. Malaysia, Myanmar and Timor-Leste may be classified as experiencing significant political strain or uncertainty. Thailand lay somewhere in-between: clearly, the military government had consolidated its power, but considerable uncertainty loomed on the horizon.

Political Consolidation and Continuity

Brunei marked the fiftieth anniversary of the ascension of Sultan Hassanal Bolkiah to the throne with no significant threat to the monarchy or domestic stability despite the recent downturn in prices of hydrocarbons. In Singapore, the People's Action Party retained its firm hold on the state apparatus with little or no prospect of an opposition government coming to power. However, as Shashi Jayakumar points out in his chapter on Singapore, there was some anxiety about who the next prime minister would be, since Prime Minister Lee Hsien Loong had earlier stated he would step down after the next general election, to be held by 15 January 2021, after making sure somebody was ready to take over from him.

There was also little prospect of major discontinuity or regime change in the countries of Indochina. Oliver Tappe's chapter on Laos argues that Prime Minister Thongloun Sisulith's efforts to tackle key economic and governance problems, especially illegal logging and corruption, have enhanced the ruling communist party's standing at home and the government's esteem abroad. In Cambodia, covered in two chapters by Khatharya Um and Steve Heder, respectively, long-serving Prime Minister Hun Sen, sensing a looming electoral threat to the grip on state power of his Cambodian People's Party (CPP), banned the increasingly popular opposition Cambodian National Rescue Party (CNRP) and took action against opposition leaders and members of parliament, some of whom fled abroad or joined the CPP. The National Assembly seats of those who fled or were imprisoned were distributed among some minor friendly parties in the assembly. General elections will go ahead in 2019 with the carefully crafted appearance — but without the spirit or substance — of a continuing multiparty system. Western countries criticized this as the blatant undoing of the political arrangements made under the 1991 Paris Peace Agreement, but Hun Sen had the support of China, a major economic provider, and Vietnam, which feared that a CNRP government in Phnom Penh would inflame Cambodia–Vietnam tensions by playing up the sensitive issue of Vietnamese residing in Cambodia. Also, neither China nor Vietnam would be comfortable with a freewheeling democracy, unguided by the experienced hand of Hun Sen, in their neighbourhood.

Nguyen Manh Hung, in his chapter on Vietnam, notes the consolidation of power in the hands of the Communist Party of Vietnam under General Secretary Nguyen Phu Trong, who placed his supporters in all the top positions of the Central Committee and in two key positions in the party secretariat. A powerful protégé of former prime minister Nguyen Tan Dung was removed from the politburo. Hung sees these moves as restoring the dominance of the party over the state from the ambivalent power division between the two during former premier

Dung's stewardship. Trong also mounted a vigorous anti-corruption campaign that netted senior figures from the banking sector and Petro Vietnam. Hung expects the campaign to continue, arguing that Trong has reached a point of no return: he cannot afford to let up for fear of being seen as not serious, which could affect his standing and the legitimacy of the party. Yet, persistence in the enterprise would lead to more serious and dangerous resistance. But if Trong succeeds he will become the most powerful general secretary of the party since the 1990s. The anti-corruption campaign was accompanied by steps to rebuild and strengthen the party, streamline the administration and reinvigorate the economy.

In his review of Indonesia, Priyambudi Sulistiyanto argues that during 2017 President Jokowi not only consolidated but strengthened his domestic political position. This was against expectations, because the mass demonstrations and tensions of 2016 and early 2017 against Jakarta governor Basuk Tjahaja Purnama (Ah Hok) had been seen as probably denting the president's authority. Jokowi achieved this through a mixture of constitutional means and political manoeuvres against extremist and anti-Pancasila organizations and moves to limit the impact of outspoken critics. He also energetically engaged community and religious leaders at the grass-roots level across Indonesia to put across his message of religious tolerance and the importance of Pancasila. By the end of the year, opinion polls were showing him having high levels of popular support, putting him in a strong position for the 2019 national elections. However, Sulistiyanto cautions that this still does not guarantee a win in 2019. Jokowi will need all his political skills to ensure that a coalition of forces of the sort that undid Ah Hok does not jell into a powerful anti-Jokowi force.

Eve Warburton analyses the nationalist and populist issues which could be used by opposition groups against Jokowi in the 2019 election campaigns. She maintains that a nationalist and anti-Chinese narrative could draw some public support, reminding that it was telling how public opinion shifted against Ah Hok after such an offensive mounted at the time of the Jakarta gubernatorial election campaign. Already Jokowi's detractors were framing the problem of inequality in ethno-religious terms: that foreign investments, especially Chinese investments and workers, harmed the interests of poor Muslim masses in the country and that the president was "unable or unwilling to address the gap between the poor Muslim majority and a wealthy, predominantly non-Muslim — or Chinese Christian — elite".

In Thailand the military had strengthened its hold on power and seemed determined to retain a strong influence in the governing of the country through a new constitution, under which elections are expected to be held in late 2018 or early 2019. Despite this consolidation, the titles of two chapters on Thailand also point to the underlying uncertainties: Pongphisoot Busbarat's chapter entitled "Stability without Certainties" and Prajak Kongkirati's entitled "Haunted Past, Uncertain Future". Despite the apparent stability under military rule in 2017, the tensions between the contending political groups which had led to the military coup of 2014 had not been resolved and "would continue to challenge Thailand in the immediate and long-term future", according to Busbarat. Uncertainties about the future role of the military in politics, the future of Thai democracy and the future of the pro-Thaksin forces and their leadership remained.

There were uncertainties, too, about whether Thailand will be able to balance its closer relations with China since the military coup with the improvement of relations with the United States under the Trump administration. Busbarat feels this may not be easy, because the U.S. law prohibiting full military cooperation and assistance to a foreign government that came to power through a military coup remains on the books. The new government after the elections will still face opposition from human rights and pro-democracy groups in the United States and European Union, which could colour the policies of their governments. Further, the military hopes to revive the lacklustre economy with Chinese help, and this may well require more policy concessions. Kongkirati explains how the military has been restructuring the political order to prolong its power and influence through various institutional mechanisms. He traces two models of military rule in Thailand since the 1950s.

The Philippines also saw consolidation of power by the incumbents. As Malcolm Cook shows, President Duterte and his administration finished the year in a stronger position than at its start, notwithstanding the outcry among human rights groups against the killings in the "war on drugs" and the tragic and hugely destructive Marawi conflict. Duterte's "intensely personal, brusque and often confrontational approach ... has been well received by a large majority of the electorate", says Cook, citing opinion polls that show high approval ratings across all sub-sections of the population, including among the most educated and the wealthiest. He was able to further strengthen his position in both chambers of Congress. He was also helped by good economic growth, estimated at 6.7 per cent, and his diplomatic embrace of China which led to a 40 per cent increase of tourists from China over 2016.

Political Strain or Uncertainty

The political tensions and uncertainties in Malaysia revolved mainly around the next general election, which must be held before the expiry of the term of the present government in June 2018. As Faisal S. Hazis says in his chapter on Malaysia, the country was in election mode in 2017, with rhetoric from both the Barisan Nasional (BN) government and the opposition raising the political temperature, which, according to Hazis, was having a divisive and destabilizing effect in the country. The stakes were high because the election would determine whether, for the first time since the country's independence in 1957, an opposition coalition would unseat the BN government.

Hazis considers this unlikely, because Prime Minister Najib Razak has strengthened his grip on his party, the United Malays National Organisation, and on the government, while the opposition was divided. The opposition's prospects may have brightened somewhat with former prime minister Mahathir Mohamad leading it, but Hazis feels this will not compensate for the fact that the Islamic party, Parti Islam Se-Malaysia (PAS), with its grass-roots networks in the Malay rural areas of the northern states, was no longer part of the opposition coalition, as it was in the 2013 general elections.

In Myanmar, as Mary Callahan explains in her chapter, the good feelings generated by the remarkable transformation of the country from military dictatorship to democratic civilian rule (even though the military remained an important player) dissipated under a number of challenges and failures. The most important was the violence in Rakhine State which led to the exodus of nearly 700,000 Rohingya Muslims to neighbouring Bangladesh, widely believed to be caused by disproportionate use of force by the Myanmar security forces and local Rakhine Buddhists armed by the military in response to the attacks by the Arakan Rohingya Salvation Army (ARSA). The Myanmar government, both Aung San Suu Kyi and the military, faced mounting international opprobrium, especially from Western countries and the United Nations, with renewed talk of sanctions against the country. It was like the replay of an old, familiar narrative from the days of military rule from the 1990s till 2011, happening at a time the country could ill afford this damage to its international standing, given the lack of progress in other important areas.

Perhaps foremost among them was the lacklustre economic performance because of the slow pace of reforms, as discussed by Aka Kyaw Min Maw. The economic growth rate declined in 2017 and foreign direct investment commitments were 30 per cent lower than in 2016. Then there was the failure to achieve any breakthrough in the government's negotiations with ethnic armed groups as violent conflict with insurgent groups continued in the north and northeast of the country.

Timor-Leste ended 2017 with a political impasse. A FRETILIN minority government had been unable to implement its national programme and budget because it did not command a majority in the national parliament. Rebecca Strating — in her chapter "Timor-Leste in 2017: A State of Uncertainty" — sees the likely resolution of the impasse through fresh elections in 2018, though there were concerns that if not resolved the situation could lead to a constitutional crisis.

ISEAS' Golden Anniversary

The year 2018 is the fiftieth anniversary of the ISEAS – Yusof Ishak Institute, and *Southeast Asian Affairs 2018* celebrates this golden moment in two ways. Nick Farrelly's regional thematic chapter looks at the future of Southeast Asian Studies as a discipline and the positive trend that the discipline is becoming less Western-dominated and more locally based. This is very much in line with the mandate of ISEAS. Second, the book cover is indigo blue, the colour of the Institute's logo.

Notes

1. I acknowledge the valuable comments of my co-editor Malcom Cook on an earlier draft of this introduction.
2. Authors were required to submit their chapters for editing and preparation for publishing in early December 2017 with little scope to revise them to take into consideration new developments or the unfolding consequences of changes identified. ISEAS would like to thank the authors and the readers for their appreciation of this unavoidable situation.

Acknowledgements

We would like to thank the large number of people who contributed to this volume. First, to the twenty-four authors of the book's chapters for their diligence. Special thanks to Gao Jiankang and Vandana Prakash Nair, the Institute's Research Officers who have spent the most time helping bring this book to print. On the publication side, thank you to Stephen Logan for overseeing the project and preparing the drafts for publication and to Betty Tan for assisting in this process. We would like to acknowledge the contributions of ISEAS colleagues and friends whose advice was sought and happily provided. These include Aries Arugay, Lee Hock Guan and Sean Turnell. Finally, we would like to thank for their support ISEAS – Yusof Ishak Institute Director Choi Shing Kwok, former Director Ambassador Tan Chin Tiong, Deputy Director Terence Chong, and Head of Publishing Ng Kok Kiong.

Apologies to anyone inadvertently omitted.

Malcolm Cook
Daljit Singh
Editors
Southeast Asian Affairs 2018

The Region

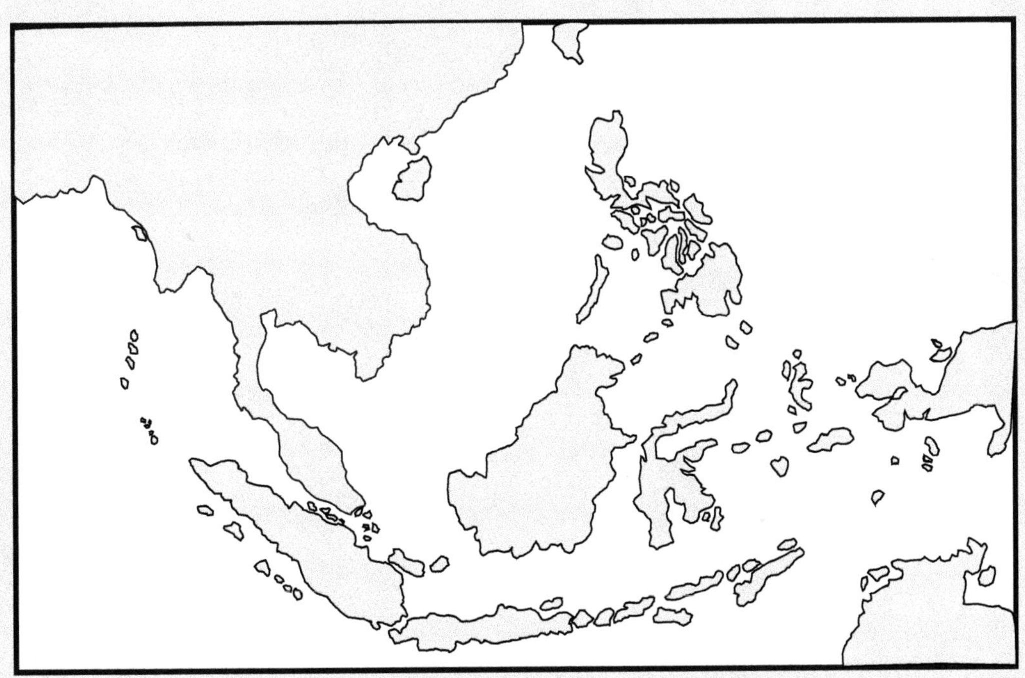

NOTES ON THE FUTURE OF SOUTHEAST ASIAN STUDIES

Nicholas Farrelly

Looking Back

When done poorly, efforts to understand and explain other cultures and societies earn justified and withering critique. Where scholarly appreciation lacks empathy, depth or context it is not a surprise that opposition should emerge. The charge of orientalism is one that still echoes through the halls of knowledge. It is a blunt rebuke to those accused of reifying the Other. Avoiding the common tendencies to essentialize complex subject matter requires skill, breadth and compassion. The political situation in which studies of human societies occur is crucial, and the difficult reality is that neutral enquiry, of the type imagined in some methodological textbooks, always proves an illusion. Academic analysis, of whatever type, should begin with an appreciation that power and knowledge sit in uneasy and permanent conversation. Knowledge of society, politics, culture, history, language and economics, in whichever disciplinary tradition, should therefore start with questions about how the world works, including through close scrutiny of scholarly practices and mentalities.

It was in such a quest, for academic and practical knowledge, that what we now recognize as Southeast Asian Studies emerged after the Second World War, just as a new region emerged from the colonial shadows.[1] The colonial machines transplanted to this region from Britain, France, the Netherlands and the United States had, in their time, devoted immense energy to research enquiries that helped secure their exploitative rule.[2] But, from the 1950s, the new nation-states of this region — wedged between China and India — found themselves the subjects

NICHOLAS FARRELLY is Associate Dean in the College of Asia and the Pacific at the Australian National University.

of a new type of concerted analytical attention. Interest in such Area Studies increased with Cold War competition between the Soviet Union and the United States, and with Southeast Asia's rolling, often violent, struggles for independence and ideological direction.[3]

During the second half of the twentieth century, a Southeast Asian core coalesced, initially, around a group of societies with relatively consistent pro-Western policies — Indonesia, Singapore, Malaysia, Thailand and the Philippines — ruled by various styles of nationalist strongmen.[4] These five countries came together in 1967 as the Association of Southeast Asian Nations, marking a key moment in nation-building and region-building projects.[5] After securing independence from Britain in the early 1980s, Brunei, an absolute monarchy, joined the grouping, and later ASEAN's numbers were bolstered by Cambodia, Laos, Myanmar and Vietnam. The newest four members of ASEAN brought their own interpretations of socialist, post-socialist and authoritarian politics to the table. Matters of ideological purity diminished in importance over time, especially as more effort was expended on crafting a common set of elite diplomatic, economic and political expectations.[6] While, in the 2000s, the United States sought to continue its general sponsorship of ASEAN unity, other countries, especially Japan and China, saw advantages in their own increasingly proactive engagements with the group. To maintain ASEAN's cherished solidarity, the notion of non-interference in domestic political affairs, especially sensitive matters of human rights, is the central pillar of the region's policy identity. It happens that Southeast Asian Studies, in its current form, is often understood to sit relatively neatly on the outline of this group of ten ASEAN members.[7]

Yet, adequately defining the shape of Southeast Asian Studies, as an academic undertaking, spatially contained, or not, is actually a heavily contested matter.[8] Certainly, in every direction, whether we consider the maritimescape,[9] or the unruly, and often mountainous, borderlands, there are problems with drawing any firm boundary around Southeast Asia.[10] National borders can prove helpful for explaining aspects of political demarcation, but they are much less useful when it comes to culture, religion, language or the lived experiences of different people living under the one national umbrella.[11] It is no surprise that in Southeast Asia, and in directly adjacent areas, significant scholarly arguments have emerged to consider alternative spatializations.[12] The Dutch historian Willem van Schendel, inspired by his experiences in Bangladesh and its borderlands, presented the most famous of these contrarian counter-arguments in 2002. He argued that the highland areas of Southeast Asia enjoyed commonalities not well explained by the delineation of national borders, or by the shape of academic Area Studies

(South Asian Studies, East Asian Studies, Central Asian Studies and Southeast Asian Studies, etc.). For van Schendel, a region he called "Zomia" could help to present a different appreciation of space, power and knowledge.[13] Zomia came to its apotheosis in James C. Scott's 2009 *The Art of Not Being Governed*, where he sought to present an "anarchist history of upland Southeast Asia" drawing on the illustrative potential of this spatial-epistemological model.[14]

Expertise and Contention

For all the value of these studies, most treatments of Southeast Asia are contained by quite conventional expectations of political and social space.[15] One of the traditional challenges for scholars of this region is the very heavy, up-front investment in linguistic and cultural acumen needed, simply as a foundation, for serious scholarly work. At the same time, most scholars of Southeast Asia maintain a parallel disciplinary personality, as an anthropologist,[16] political scientist,[17] historian,[18] economist,[19] or what have you.[20] Depending on an individual scholar's institutional backing, and the broader incentives of their university system, it can be difficult to justify any perceived overinvestment in Southeast Asia expertise. In the United States, almost all Southeast Asia specialists work within a disciplinary department, which ensures they can enjoy comparative discussions, sometimes with people who have similarly strong awareness, as Area Studies specialists, of other regions of the world. As Hirschmann put it back in 1992:

> In the past, area studies scholars tended to make their careers on the margins of their disciplines. This is no longer an option given the structure of American universities. Area studies scholars will have to publish in the prestigious disciplinary journals and make their careers in the mainstream.[21]

The situation in parts of Europe and Australia has been different, to an extent, in the sense that some of the major universities devoted to the study of Southeast Asia maintain Southeast Asian Studies as an integral part of their academic structure.[22] Yet, even those universities have now tended to re-emphasize disciplinary success as the simplest, most direct way of maintaining global prestige and academic standing.

Nowadays, the weight of Southeast Asia focused expertise is also spread across hundreds of universities in the Southeast Asian region, and, increasingly, scholars from these institutions are making a major mark on the publishing landscape.[23] It follows that academic and analytical attention, among Southeast Asians, increasingly deals with the pressing issues of their own societies, including in far-flung concerns and on under-studied topics. As Victor King explained in 2012:

> It would seem that the Western construction of Southeast Asia is being embraced, filled in, elaborated and developed by local scholars but with the hope that this endeavour can be founded on local perspectives and priorities.[24]

Southeast Asian institutions, especially in Singapore, Malaysia and Thailand, devote sizable resources to analysis of their neighbours, and to the broader Asian region.[25] Singapore offers a useful illustration of these trends, with its powerhouse constellation of the Institute of Southeast Asian Studies (renamed in 2015 ISEAS – Yusof Ishak Institute), Institute of South Asian Studies, Asia Research Institute, and East Asian Institute. Together, these institutions claim hundreds of regionally oriented specialists. They have helped to shape global discussion of regional affairs through publishing, regular events, and funding for policy-relevant and academic research. Even in countries like Myanmar and Vietnam there are specialized research and teaching institutions that deal with foreign studies, often putting a great deal of weight on the closest relationships. For both of those countries, China and Thailand are countries of specific concern.

Under these conditions, what is the future of Southeast Asian Studies? Most appraisals point to the general fragility of Area Studies, especially in those places where disciplinary knowledge has taken oxygen from previously strong centres and departments devoted to the serious study of Southeast Asia, or other regions. The reality of such study, however, is that universities now make up a shrinking component of the Southeast Asianist terrain. The modest numbers of senior scholars, and even the numbers enrolled in graduate programmes, are dwarfed, nowadays, by the other analysts, journalists, writers, thinkers and doers focused on Southeast Asia. While they may not have enjoyed a deep academic training in the subject matter, and would rarely, if ever, publish in academic forums, there is no doubting their contributions to knowledge, especially when it comes to public debate and broadening awareness.[26]

Previously, academic debates about Southeast Asia were almost all conducted in a spirit of congenial, scholarly disinterest, and far from the publics with whom such debates should have been concerned. The Internet has, like in so many other areas of life, completely changed the equation. When it comes to the ideas that matter in Southeast Asian Studies, passions, online, are often amplified, magnified. Hyperbole abounds. The future of Southeast Asian Studies will, under these conditions, look very different to what has gone before.

Disinterest versus Entanglement

Academic Southeast Asia specialists tend to seek a balance between disciplinary legitimacy and deep knowledge of particular societies, languages, politics, economies and cultures. There is a broad appreciation that professional or career penalties can follow for those who lurch too deep into esoteric expertise focused on a specific place. The balancing act model is predicated on the need to be taken seriously in disciplinary cohorts, whether anthropology, political science, linguistics, history, sociology, economics. However, the art of knowing something about somewhere still draws its defenders, especially from those who invest heavily in language knowledge. The traditional power centres in Southeast Asian Studies — Ithaca, Canberra, London, Singapore, Kyoto — have all put a strong emphasis on language skills. The priority on acquiring competency in one, or more, Southeast Asian languages shaped the study of Southeast Asia in ways that made cultural immersion a prerequisite for entry to the learned community. Learning a Southeast Asian language to a meaningful level, especially those that require mastery of a new script and sound system, usually requires years, and even senior scholars will privately often claim only modest competence in the language(s) of their key field sites. The entry price is high and it takes a significant commitment to maintain the skills that create new knowledge.

Within Southeast Asian Studies there is also tension around proximity to power. Strong critical positions, especially about government action and inaction, have been a standard part of the development of analysis in academic circles.[27] At the same time, many institutions are required, whether by habit or circumstance, to work closely with government stakeholders.[28] Previously, such work led to great consternation, especially in what is termed the "Thailand controversy". Research that could have supported American intelligence and security operations in the region, especially in highland regions of Thailand, ended up generating intense debate within, and beyond, the American Anthropological Association and other professional groups.

Among Southeast Asia specialists the situation was always complicated, partly because the political role of Southeast Asia focused knowledge has made it impossible to disentangle certain national interests from the academic knowledge business. Where governments, from places like the United States, Australia, Singapore and Japan, have made major investments in Southeast Asia knowledge, they have tended to do so based on specific judgments about strategy, policy and connection. It is naive to imagine that governments will not continue to support research which, in the big picture, helps to support their visions of security and prosperity.

It is also very healthy that there is ongoing debate about these issues and that a variety of national interest considerations, whether they are Singaporean, Australian or Indian, are given adequate consideration, both from within their own societies and from further afield. Chinese and Japanese studies of Southeast Asia are interesting to consider in this context, partly because most of their scholarship is published in Chinese or Japanese, and because the two countries continue to duel for influence in the Southeast Asian sphere.[29] In rare cases, often after much delay, this research finds its way into English or another language, but in the future it makes sense that the Chinese and Japanese will be more assertive in seeking to shape debates within Southeast Asian societies. The translation of English works into Chinese and Japanese will also still be important, although it probably matters less now that the political circumstances across Asia are shifting to reflect the ambitions of rising regional powers, rather than the once-dominant English-speaking powers. The United States could, for a time, have claimed a preeminent position when it comes to shaping global ideas about Southeast Asia.[30] This is now a much more heavily contested terrain, and also one of remarkable diversity and vitality.

From the 1980s onwards, it is clear that more Southeast Asian voices have found prominence in the study of their own societies, or adjacent societies. Their insider insights have proved invaluable in helping to diminish the predominance of voices from the outside. Their own relationships and entanglements have greatly enriched the field, offering new dimensions, often in contrast to established, centralized perspectives. Singapore has been the strongest contributor, partly because of the expansion of its universities into world-class research and teaching hubs, and also because of the consistent investment in the ISEAS – Yusof Ishak Institute. Singapore can now claim regional leadership as a knowledge broker. It attracts talent from elsewhere in Southeast Asia, and indeed from all over the world, bolstering what are impressive local capabilities. The relationship between this knowledge and Singapore's potentially precarious strategic and economic position should not be ignored. Singapore seeks to understand developments in its neighbourhood for economic, political, security and strategic reasons. In areas where there is a confluence of interests — the protection of global shipping routes is one example, and climate change adaptation is another — then it makes sense that Singapore has become a leading analytical centre. Elsewhere, Southeast Asians of Chinese descent have become prominent in academic debates.[31] Elsewhere in Southeast Asia there are other key voices on regional issues.[32] In Thailand, there is vast depth of knowledge, accumulated by scholars like Charnvit Kasetsiri, Thitinan Pongsudhirak, and Yos Santasombat. It is still striking, however, that when some compilations of influential work are made, there are relatively few Southeast Asian names.[33]

At the same time, a further positive trend is now seen outside Southeast Asia, where a significant number of the leading voices on the region are, themselves, Southeast Asian. Some examples include Thongchai Winichakul, based at the University of Wisconsin and a former President of the Association for Asian Studies;[34] Ariel Heryanto, who holds the Herb Feith Chair in Indonesian Studies at Monash University; Aim Sinpeng, a rising star at the University of Sydney; and Evelyn Goh, the Shedden Professor of Strategic Policy Studies at the Australian National University's College of Asia and the Pacific. Others are leading figures in the teaching of Southeast Asian languages, with major examples like Chintana Sandilands at the Australian National University; Saw Tun, formerly of Northern Illinois University; and Soe Tjen Marching at the School of Oriental and African Studies in London. Southeast Asian Studies increasingly finds a plurality of Southeast Asian voices.

Politics and Technology

In a broader sense, Southeast Asia remains difficult terrain for democratic sentiments, with authoritarian governments holding sway, in 2018, in most of the region's capitals. These governments have proved effective at legitimizing their long-term rule, but it would be a stretch to suggest that there is any tradition of popular votes leading to peaceful changes of government. Across the entire region the number of genuinely democratic transfers of power remain few, with a pattern of entrenched dictatorships setting the tone for most regional interaction, especially through ASEAN and other diplomatic forums. Such authoritarian domination makes Southeast Asia an unpredictably inhospitable place for researchers who seek to understand contentious local issues. Over the past generation many of the difficulties have focused on Thailand, where academics choose their words carefully if they want to maintain access to the country. In earlier periods, Myanmar blacklisted large numbers of foreign scholars and analysts. For a time, the Indonesian government was also very careful about the scope of academic activities permissible under the rule of General Soeharto. In Vietnam, Laos, Cambodia, Brunei, Singapore and Malaysia there are varying degrees of sanction for scholars who are perceived to step out of line.

For Southeast Asian Studies, maintaining long-term access is an important consideration, especially for scholars deeply invested in a particular set of issues. If access is constrained, then it can become difficult, even impossible, to maintain research productivity. In extreme cases, academics have been forced to find alternative field sites. The most famous example is Benedict Anderson who, after being banned from Indonesia under President Soeharto, went on to complete further research in both the Philippines and Thailand. Such unfortunate interruptions can help to incentivize path-breaking research work, but they also come with potential risks for informants and for others that may be caught in retribution related to research output.

The censorship of controversial ideas also remains an issue across Southeast Asia.[35] Almost every country has its "sacred" topics, whether it is the Communist Party in Vietnam, the monarchy in Thailand, or Islam in Malaysia and Indonesia. Scholars who are judged to have transgressed local boundaries could find their work dumped from bookshops or teaching curriculums. Thailand has proved an extreme example in recent times. In the past decade, its governments have banned books and blocked websites that challenge officially mandated ideas about Thai society, especially related to the royal family.

In this context, one that changes quickly, the most profound trends in Southeast Asian Studies relate to the emergence of new tools for communication and outreach.[36] It is not certain that pay-walled, traditional scholarly journals, most of which remain inaccessible to students and scholars *in* Southeast Asia, will survive the further waves of disruption on the horizon. For now, they persist due to the subsidies, usually government provided, that allow academics to write, edit, review, and read increasingly obscure discussions, heavily cloaked in the latest conceptual trends. While there are good reasons for allowing the persistence of specialist registers of language, legible only to those with the right training and background, there is little evidence that even most scholarly audiences find these academic discussions of Southeast Asia fit their needs.

The academic English required of peer-reviewed publications sets a high barrier for entry and, for now, Southeast Asian vernacular publications do not rate highly in global discussions of the field. This will change as machine translation makes it possible for the best Tagalog, Burmese, Vietnamese and Malay writers to have their thoughts understood, in a deep sense, by readers of Italian, Chinese, Arabic and, yes, English.[37] Artificial intelligence, as a new component of the global landscape of ideas, will shift expectations of expertise. Those who could comfortably accumulate knowledge in, for instance, Hmong, and then publish it in English, safe in the knowledge it would never be read by the Hmong themselves, could be in for a rude shock. The proliferation of narrative, counter-narrative and alternative narrative will make it impossible for any individual scholar to keep up. Managing knowledge about Southeast Asia will, in this future, be a more difficult task than ever before.

What the field currently lacks is the integration of knowledge that should be made possible by the new tools at our disposal. These range from the cartographic, to the linguistic, to the theoretical, to the computational. In an epistemological sense, everything is now at stake at a time when there are no simple or single academic responses to the digital cascade. So, right this minute, scholars need to look hard at their existing practices if they are planning to survive and prosper. Then, in the longer term, the academic institutions that support most Southeast Asian Studies programmes will endure their own decades of disruption. The monopoly on offering high-level credentials currently enjoyed by universities will be tested in new ways, especially as the value of mass education is queried, by students, by their parents, and by tax-paying society. The availability of student fee income to cross-subsidize worthwhile scholarly activities will, in some cases, cease entirely. How will we keep the lights on? Then, more broadly still, the expertise of scholars will come under attack from those who believe that academic knowledge has little to offer the world under conditions of fast-moving change. A small number of model-builders and theory-makers will likely do well, but many other academic researchers will never have their voices heard beyond the confines of academic discourse.[38]

Taking scholarly work to wider audiences, especially through online platforms, is one of the obvious areas where changes will continue to rapidly emerge. What might happen? Attitudes to language learning are one area where changes could intensify. Imagine what little value might be put on half-a-decade of language study when the newly sophisticated computational translation technologies announce their arrival as full-scale artificial intelligence interfaces, as voice-enabled personal interpreters and translators. Under those conditions, if everyone had access to their own pan-language communication technology, then the barriers around Southeast Asia, which are also welded in to Southeast Asian Studies, could melt away quickly. In this scenario, shifts in the usage of information will also mean that businesses, government and civil society will all be seeking competitive advantages in terms of how they understand changes in the world. The consequences of this not implausible future situation are immense for those focused on Southeast Asia, particularly at a time when Southeast Asia is rapidly changing, often most dramatically through the upwards flow of aspirational consumption. In this region alone, hundreds of millions of people will be prepared to pay to use technologies that unshackle them from language barriers.

Getting to grips with such future situations will require creativity, and a wider acceptance that the models of academic output favoured in previous decades will need to be refreshed, or even destroyed. Simply put, the audience for peer-reviewed, pay-walled content is miniscule. Not only do relatively few people have access to the content but their interest in yet another conceptually dense treatment of an obscure question, often one that few people were asking in the first place, also proves almost intolerable to sustain. Even the most notable academic arguments rarely receive attention beyond a small, expert and pedantic audience. For internal university purposes, such an audience is still often sufficient, but it is not clear taxpayers will continue to support Southeast Asian Studies expertise that does not contribute, in a more direct fashion, to the real-world challenges facing Southeast Asian societies. Increasingly, academics, of many types, devote a proportion of their time to media commentary, social media exposition, and a range of interactions with governments, business and civil society.

Challenges Unknown

To conclude, it is worth emphasizing that knowledge about Southeast Asia has been upended by the increasing wealth, connectivity and interaction within societies, and across the region. Notions, inherited from the twentieth century, that Southeast Asia is weak and requires charity no longer match local realities or ambitions. The trend in Southeast Asian Studies away from dominance by foreign scholars is very clear and will only increase in the years ahead. Southeast Asian voices about Southeast Asia now benefit from the move towards mass education which, in many societies, only began in a substantial way from the 1980s onwards. Higher levels of literacy, and greater attention to the economic benefits available to increasingly sophisticated publics, mean that the audience for analysis also continues to grow. The ongoing contest of ideas in Southeast Asia, especially where authoritarian systems of government hold sway, can only be a good thing.

Yet, there are other challenges that are much more difficult to pin down. One of the primary issues for academic Southeast Asian Studies is that so-called "professional" researchers do not, nowadays, complete much of the best analysis. "Amateurs" — a broad category, no doubt — are increasingly central to the knowledge-making enterprise. Among the many groups of non-academics making major contributions to the study of Southeast Asia, journalists are increasingly prominent, but so are people in think tanks and in civil society. Changes to the media model have encouraged many journalists, but especially those who freelance, or who are otherwise unencumbered by the preoccupations of a large news organization, to chase the kinds of deep analytical stories that academics also want to understand. With the resurgence of long-form journalism, apparent at the global scale with magazines like *The New Yorker* and *The Atlantic*, but also in the region with *The Mekong Review*, there is less demarcation between journalist and scholar than ever before. Many academics find the democratization of knowledge and knowledge production a mixed blessing, with plenty of concern that standards are in free fall.

But there are benefits, too. While it is impossible to say with certainty, the level of scrutiny applied to publicly available research work, especially Internet content, is often higher than critics would assume. While peer review has long struggled to fully justify its claims to supremacy, the form of "open review" that can occur online has obvious advantages. It can be instantaneous, updatable, and calibrated to deal with the concerns that Southeast Asians themselves have about their own societies. This is where the future of Southeast Asian Studies may not be so bleak after all. The political and economic consequences of the region's ongoing changes are yet to be properly digested, and there is a chance that the entire landscape of Southeast Asian Studies is now ripe for a major shake-up. Such a shake-up could well require a better appreciation of exactly how Southeast Asia is bustling ahead.

From this perspective, it is the linkages across Southeast Asia, the broadening of the imagined community, which is making it possible for different futures to emerge. As one example, the unprecedented velocity and intensity of travel within Southeast Asia, within national borders, but also across the region, is making it possible to imagine a different kind of future for its peoples; one where ASEAN serves as a genuine model of diversity, inclusion and, perhaps eventually, democratic instincts. These regional connections are facilitated by the massification of English language usage, and by the potential unleashed through the Internet, especially with Facebook already such an engine of information sharing. But just imagine what might come next.

In the long run, we also anticipate that artificial intelligence, automation, machine learning, and so much more, will have shifted the Southeast Asian landscape in unimaginable ways. So much has changed, so quickly, and the changes keep happening, that it makes sense to be making big efforts towards completely re-imagining the study of Southeast Asia at a time when the future of Southeast Asia is also up for grabs. While, at the international level, there are significant geopolitical uncertainties, the most important changes are actually happening, right this moment, and often without much fanfare, within Southeast Asian societies. Before long, the changing nature of work, knowledge and power will up-end most of our preconceptions. Making the best of this situation, and analysing its ramifications, will be the main job if Southeast Asian Studies wants to have a sustainable and successful future.

Notes

1. For a very useful overview of the history and politics of Southeast Asian Studies, see: Charles Hirschman, "The State of Southeast Asian Studies in American Universities", in *Southeast Asian Studies in the Balance: Reflections from America*, edited by Charles Hirschman, Charles F. Keyes, and Karl Hutterer (Ann Arbor: Association for Asian Studies, 1992).
2. For useful examples of the subsequent critiques, see: Oscar Salemink, "Ethnography as Martial Art: Ethnicizing Vietnam's Montagnards, 1930–1954", in *Colonial Subjects: Essays on the Practical History of Anthropology*, edited by Peter Pels and Oscar Salemink, pp. 282–25 (Ann Arbor: University of Michigan Press, 1999); also, Mandy Sadan, "Translating Gumlao: History, the 'Kachin' and Edmund Leach", in *Social Dynamics in the Highlands of Southeast Asia: Reconsidering Political Systems of Highland Burma by E. R. Leach*, edited by Mandy Sadan and Francois Robinne, pp. 67–87 (Leiden: Brill, 2007); Mandy Sadan, "Production of Borderland Knowledge: The British East India Company and the Public Imaginary of the Patkai Borderlands, 1824–57", in *Social Formations of South East Asian Frontiers*, edited by Sang Kook Lee and Alexander Horstmann (Amsterdam: Amsterdam University Press, 2017).
3. For some wider context it is worth considering some of the historical discussion of these issues: Vicente L. Rafael, "The Cultures of Area Studies in the United States", *Social Text* 41 (1994): 91–111; Peter J. Katzenstein, "Area and Regional Studies in the United States", *PS: Political Science and Politics* 34, no. 4 (2001): 789–91; Filomenov Aguilar, Caroline Hau, Vicente Rafael, and Teresa Tadem, "Benedict Anderson, Comparatively Speaking: On Area Studies, Theory, and 'Gentlemanly' Polemics", *Philippine Studies* 59, no. 1 (2011): 107–39.
4. One of the classic commentaries on "Southeast Asianist" comparison is: Benedict Richard O'Gorman Anderson, *The Spectre of Comparisons: Nationalism, Southeast Asia, and the World* (London: Verso, 1998).
5. Amitav Acharya, "Imagined Proximities: The Making and Unmaking of Southeast Asia as a Region", *Asian Journal of Social Science* 27, no. 1 (1999): 55–76; Donald K. Emmerson, "Challenging ASEAN: A 'Topological' View", *Contemporary Southeast Asia* 29, no. 3 (2007): 424–46.
6. Craig J. Reynolds and Hong Lysa, "Marxism in Thai Historical Studies", *Journal of Asian Studies* 43, no. 1 (1983): 77–104.
7. In one sense, for now, ASEAN and the academic field of Southeast Asian Studies match up relatively neatly. The primary exception to that neat institutional and academic match is Timor-Leste, independent for less than two decades, and still not a full member of ASEAN. Where the country is studied by academics it often fits somewhere between Melanesianist and Southeast Asianist cohorts.
8. Adequately defining and delineating Southeast Asia has proved a persistent challenge. For one of the formative contributions to the debate, see: Donald K. Emmerson, "'Southeast Asia': What's in a Name?" *Journal of Southeast Asian Studies* 15, no. 1

(1984): 1–21; and the counterpoints made in Wilhelm G. Solheim, " '"Southeast Asia": What's in a Name', Another Point of View", *Journal of Southeast Asian Studies* 16, no. 1 (1985): 141–47.

9. Donald K. Emmerson, "The Case for a Maritime Perspective on Southeast Asia", *Journal of Southeast Asian Studies* 11, no. 1 (1980): 139–45; Markus P.M. Vink, "Indian Ocean Studies and the 'New Thalassology' ", *Journal of Global History* 2, no. 1 (2007): 41–62; Barbara Watson Andaya, "Presidential Address: Oceans Unbounded: Transversing Asia across 'Area Studies' ", *Journal of Asian Studies* 65, no. 4 (2006): 669–90; Martin W. Lewis and Kären Wigen, "A Maritime Response to the Crisis in Area Studies", *Geographical Review* 89, no. 2 (1999): 161–68.
10. There are many discussions of these unruly borderlands. One good starting point is Jim Glassman, "On the Borders of Southeast Asia: Cold War Geography and the Construction of the Other", *Political Geography* 24, no. 7 (2005): 784–807; another is Oh Su-Ann, ed., *Myanmar's Mountain and Maritime Borderscapes: Local Practices, Boundary-Making and Figured Worlds* (Singapore: Institute of Southeast Asian Studies, 2016).
11. Alexander Horstmann and Reed L. Wadley, eds., *Centering the Margin: Agency and Narrative in Southeast Asian Borderlands* (Oxford: Berghahn Books, 2006).
12. Spatial considerations have been key, going right back to Russell H. Fifield, "Southeast Asian Studies: Origins, Development, Future", *Journal of Southeast Asian Studies* 7, no. 2 (1976): 151–61.
13. Willem van Schendel, "Geographies of Knowing, Geographies of Ignorance: Jumping Scale in Southeast Asia", *Environment and Planning D: Society and Space* 20, no. 6 (2002): 647–68.
14. James C. Scott, *The Art of Not Being Governed: An Anarchist History of Upland Southeast Asia* (New Haven: Yale University Press, 2009).
15. See: Ruth McVey, "Change and Continuity in Southeast Asian Studies", *Journal of Southeast Asian Studies* 26, no. 1 (1995): 1–9.
16. For instance, Andrew Walker, *The Legend of the Golden Boat: Regulation, Trade and Traders in the Borderlands of Laos, Thailand, China, and Burma* (Honolulu: University of Hawai'i Press, 1999); Charles F. Keyes, "Mother or Mistress but Never a Monk: Buddhist Notions of Female Gender in Rural Thailand", *American Ethnologist* 11, no. 2 (1984): 223–41.
17. Sorpong Peou, "Realism and Constructivism in Southeast Asian Security Studies Today: A Review Essay", *Pacific Review* 15, no. 1 (2002): 119–38.
18. Craig J. Reynolds, "A New Look at Old Southeast Asia", *Journal of Asian Studies* 54, no. 2 (1995): 419–46; Michael Aung-Thwin, "The 'Classical' in Southeast Asia: The Present in the Past", *Journal of Southeast Asian Studies* 26, no. 1 (1995): 75–91; Michael Aung-Thwin, "Continuing, Re-emerging, and Emerging Trends in the Field of Southeast Asian History", *TRaNS: Trans-Regional and -National Studies of Southeast Asia* 1, no. 1 (2013): 87–104.

19. Hal Hill, *The Indonesian Economy* (Cambridge: Cambridge University Press, 2000).
20. Nicholas Farrelly, "Reflections on Political Cultures in Thought and Action", in *Muddy Boots and Smart Suits: Researching Asia-Pacific Affairs*, edited by Nicholas Farrelly, Michael Wesley, Hugh White, and Amy King, pp. 28–39 (Singapore: ISEAS – Yusof Ishak Institute, 2017).
21. Charles Hirschman, "The State of Southeast Asian Studies in American Universities", *Southeast Asian Studies in the Balance: Reflections from America*, p. 57 (Ann Arbor: Association for Asian Studies, 1992).
22. Anthony Milner, "Approaching Asia, and Asian Studies, in Australia", *Asian Studies Review* 23, no. 2 (1999): 193–203.
23. For a few examples from Thailand, see: Thorn Pitidol, "Redefining Democratic Discourse in Thailand's Civil Society", *Journal of Contemporary Asia* 46, no. 3 (2016): 520–37; Jakkrit Sangkhamanee, "Democracy of the Desired: Everyday Politics and Political Aspiration in the Contemporary Thai Countryside", *Asian Democracy Review* 2 (2013): 5–37; Pinkaew Leungaramsri, "Women, Nation, and the Ambivalence of Subversive Identification along the Thai–Burmese Border", *SOJOURN: Journal of Social Issues in Southeast Asia* 21, no. 1 (2006): 68–89.
24. Victor T. King, "The Problem with Areas: Asia and Area Studies", *Bijdragen tot de taal-, land-en volkenkunde/Journal of the Humanities and Social Sciences of Southeast Asia* 168, nos. 2–3 (2012): 314–24; Victor T King, *Defining Southeast Asia and the Crisis in Area Studies: Personal Reflections on a Region* (Centre for East and South-East Asian Studies, Lund University, 2005); and also, Solvay Gerke and Hans-Dieter Evers, "Globalizing Local Knowledge: Social Science Research on Southeast Asia, 1970–2000", *SOJOURN: Journal of Social Issues in Southeast Asia* 21, no. 1 (2006): 1–21.
25. This situation has emerged since the publication of the provocative and enticingly argued: Ariel Heryanto, "Can There Be Southeast Asians in Southeast Asian Studies?" *Moussons. Recherche en sciences humaines sur l'Asie du Sud-Est* 5 (2002): 3–30.
26. In this context just consider the combined influence of publications like the *Mekong Review*, *The Irrawaddy*, *New Mandala*, *The Straits Times*, *Nikkei Asian Review*, *The Jakarta Post*, to name just a few. The vast quantity of vernacular language publication, which now happens at an unprecedented, indeed mind-boggling, scale must also be taken very seriously.
27. For a useful discussion of these issues in historical context, see: Peter Hinton, "The 'Thailand Controversy' Revisited", *Australian Journal of Anthropology* 13, no. 2 (2002): 155–77.
28. My own institution, the College of Asia and the Pacific, takes particular pride in its long history of helping shape Australian discussions of Southeast Asia. Within our academic community there are a broad range of ideas about how this is best achieved, including among those who seek to limit their interaction with the Australian government at any official level.

29. Yoko Hayami, "Towards Multi-laterality in Southeast Asian Studies: Perspectives from Japan", *Southeast Asian Studies: Debates and New Directions* (2006); Wang Gungwu, "Two Perspectives of Southeast Asian Studies: Singapore and China", in *Locating Southeast Asia: Geographies of Knowledge and Politics of Space*, edited by Paul H. Kratoska, Remco Rabin, and Henk Schulte Nordholt (Singapore/Athens, OH: NUS Press/Ohio University Press, 2005).
30. Grant Evans, "Between the Global and the Local there are Regions, Culture Areas, and National States", *Journal of Southeast Asian Studies* 33, no. 1 (2002): 147–61.
31. Wang Gungwu, "Southeast Asian Hua-Ch'iao in Chinese History-Writing", *Journal of Southeast Asian Studies* 12, no. 1 (1981): 1–14; more recently a new generation has emerged: Terence Chong, "Practising Global Ethnography in Southeast Asia: Reconciling Area Studies with Globalisation Theory", *Asian Studies Review* 31, no. 3 (2007): 211–26.
32. For a wide range of details and argument, see: Goh Beng Lan, ed., *Decentring and Diversifying Southeast Asian Studies: Perspectives from the Region* (Singapore: Institute of Southeast Asian Studies, 2011).
33. Hui Yew-Foong, "The Most Influential Books of Southeast Asian Studies", *SOJOURN: Journal of Social Issues in Southeast Asia* 24, no. 1 (2009): vii–xi.
34. Thongchai has written on the challenges of Area Studies in the new era: Thongchai Winichakul, "Asian Studies across Academies", *Journal of Asian Studies* 73, no. 4 (2014): 879–97.
35. Craig J. Reynolds, *Seditious Histories: Contesting Thai and Southeast Asian Pasts* (Singapore: NUS Press, 2006).
36. My own experience co-founding *New Mandala* in 2006 is relevant to these points. Along with many other new digital initiatives, emanating from institutions in Jakarta, Bangkok, Melbourne and Oxford, *New Mandala* has sought to play a constructive role in building new spaces for online interaction and debate.
37. For a discussion of the relevance of new ideas about language to our academic vocations, see: Nicholas Farrelly and Michael Wesley, "Internationalizing Minimal English: Perils and Parallels", in *Minimal English for a Global World: Improve Communication with Fewer Words*, edited by Cliff Goddard, pp. 95–112 (London: Palgrave Macmillan, 2017).
38. For some thoughts on potential models, see: Rommel Argamosa Curamin, "Towards a Poststructuralist Southeast Asian Studies?" *SOJOURN: Journal of Social Issues in Southeast Asia* 21, no. 1 (2006): 90–112.

SOUTHEAST ASIA ON THE ECONOMIC FRONT: Holding Steady, Bracing for Change

Lee Hwok-Aun

A Welcome Lull

The year 2017 passed with nothing matching the political spectacles of 2016 or the economic vagaries of 2014–15. Less drama was probably welcomed, and the Southeast Asian region, as with much of the world, waited to see the eventual outcome of Donald Trump's election and the Brexit vote, while seeking to manage economic growth amid relative stability in commodity prices and currency values, and freedom from major shocks.

Between 2016 and 2017, Southeast Asian economies increased or maintained economic growth. Investment and trade kept healthy levels, boosted by improved conditions in the world's major economies, export markets and investment sources. In 2017, prospects of new economic opportunities unfolded, as well as challenges in regional and multilateral relations. China officially launched the Belt and Road Initiative. And the Trump presidency tempered stances that previously were more hostile towards trade surpluses, and completed a cordial, non-confrontational East Asia tour in November.

An upswing in exports, alongside sustained domestic and foreign direct investment (FDI), bodes well for economic growth ahead. However, increased trade deficits with China are a regional cause for concern. Country-specific deficits in trade and the current account, which make economies dependent on capital inflows, and in government budgets, which considerably derive from infrastructure

LEE HWOK-AUN is Senior Fellow at the ISEAS – Yusof Ishak Institute, Singapore.

development, highlight the importance of facilitating prudent and productive investments and expenditures, and competitive exports.

The backdrop of macroeconomic stability and steady growth set the tone for policy considerations of a more long-term and structural nature. While each Southeast Asian country has distinct circumstances, constraints and priorities, three salient and emergent issues warrant our attention. The first revolves around structural change and the future of manufacturing. Southeast Asia faces challenges in building productive capacity, upgrading skills, promoting innovation and adapting to technological change. Second, the region also grapples with labour market issues: generating employment and wage growth, alongside societal demands to safeguard welfare and protect the vulnerable. Third, infrastructure is a burgeoning priority. Southeast Asian countries have committed to massive transportation and utility projects, which hold out potential to generate multiplier effects, but also pose challenges in project delivery and financial sustainability.

Growth Trends and Outlook

Looking back on the past three years, we can characterize 2017 as a year of steadying macroeconomic conditions, with some modest pickups. Half of Southeast Asia's economies grew slower in 2016 compared to 2015, notably Brunei (which dropped from –0.4 to –2.5 per cent), Myanmar (7.0 to 6.1 per cent), Malaysia (5.0 to 4.2 per cent) and Vietnam (6.7 to 6.2 per cent). Growth rates basically held constant in the region's other countries across both years; only the Philippines recorded a significant rise (6.1 to 6.9 per cent).

According to the latest 2017 projections at the time of writing, almost all Southeast Asian economies sustained or improved on the previous year's growth rate (Table 1). Malaysia and Myanmar rebounded from slower growth in 2016, registering 5.4 and 7.2 per cent, respectively, in 2017, while Brunei alleviated its economic contraction to –1.3 per cent. Singapore and Thailand also fared better in 2017. In general, more of the same is expected in 2018.

Most Southeast Asian countries are classified by the World Bank as lower middle income, but this very broad category can be further differentiated, and in so doing we can observe a general inverse relationship between income level and growth. Countries with the lowest incomes regionally — Cambodia, Laos, Myanmar, Vietnam — hold out prospects for more rapid growth, while Indonesia and the Philippines, further up the income rung, remain robust. Malaysia and Thailand, Southeast Asia's upper-middle-income countries, grow steadily at a slower pace, and officially high-income countries Singapore and Brunei have settled at

TABLE 1
Real Annual GDP Growth, 2008–18

	2008	*2009*	*2010*	*2011*	*2012*	*2013*	*2014*	*2015*	*2016*	*2017*	*2018*
Brunei	–2.0	–1.8	2.7	3.7	0.9	–2.1	–2.5	–0.4	–2.5	–1.3	0.6
Cambodia	6.7	0.1	6.0	7.2	7.3	7.4	7.1	7.0	7.0	6.9	6.8
Indonesia	7.4	4.7	6.4	6.2	6.0	5.6	5.0	4.9	5.0	5.2	5.3
Laos	7.8	7.4	8.0	8.0	7.8	8.0	7.6	7.3	7.0	6.9	6.9
Malaysia	4.8	–1.5	7.5	5.3	5.5	4.7	6.0	5.0	4.2	5.4	4.8
Myanmar	3.6	5.1	5.3	5.6	7.3	8.4	8.0	7.0	6.1	7.2	7.6
Philippines	4.2	1.1	7.6	3.7	6.7	7.1	6.1	6.1	6.9	6.6	6.7
Singapore	1.8	–0.6	15.2	6.2	3.9	5.0	3.6	1.9	2.0	2.5	2.6
Thailand	1.7	–0.7	7.5	0.8	7.2	2.7	0.9	2.9	3.2	3.7	3.5
Vietnam	5.7	5.4	6.4	6.2	5.2	5.4	6.0	6.7	6.2	6.3	6.3
China	9.6	9.2	10.6	9.5	7.9	7.8	7.3	6.9	6.7	6.8	6.5
India	3.9	8.5	10.3	6.6	5.5	6.4	7.5	8.0	7.1	6.7	7.4
Japan	–1.1	–5.4	4.2	–0.1	1.5	2.0	0.3	1.1	1.0	1.5	0.7
South Korea	2.8	0.7	6.5	3.7	2.3	2.9	3.3	2.8	2.8	3.0	3.0
USA	–0.3	–2.8	2.5	1.6	2.2	1.7	2.6	2.9	1.5	2.2	2.3
eurozone	0.4	–4.5	2.1	1.6	–0.9	–0.2	1.3	2.0	1.8	2.1	1.9
World	3.0	–0.1	5.4	4.3	3.5	3.5	3.6	3.4	3.2	3.6	3.7

Note: Forecasts for 2017 and 2018.
Source: IMF.

low growth trajectories, albeit for different reasons. These cross-country patterns illustrate the relative capacity to rely on factor-driven and productivity-driven growth, which underpin development policies for 2018 and beyond.

Global economic trends also weigh in. Southeast Asia's relatively open economies, with vibrant trade and investment flows, are connected to major economies of Asia and the world. Concurrent with the positive regional trends of 2017, economic growth also held steady or rose in China, Japan and South Korea, as well as the United States and Europe. Barring unforeseen economic shocks or political crises, the outlook for 2018 is for continued growth.

Consumer and business sentiment, which influence spending and investment, vary across countries and time. Such data are, of course, highly subjective, and are also mostly limited to the ASEAN-5. Nonetheless, what we can gather is instructive. In terms of political and economic outlook, survey evidence from early 2017 suggests relatively low and declining optimism in Malaysia, in contrast to higher and steady optimism in Indonesia and Vietnam.[1] The outlook turned more positive as the year progressed, as the spectre of United States protectionism abated. Thailand, Malaysia, Vietnam and Indonesia are among sixteen nations President Trump put on a list of countries against whom the United States runs bilateral trade deficits, but the form and severity of U.S. action on this matter remains unclear. Substantial export growth in electronics industries through 2017 further boosted sentiments.[2]

Trade, Investment and Public Finance

Southeast Asian economies continue to trade voluminously across borders. While varying due to geography, economic structure and export capacity, in 2016 all countries recorded relatively high or exceedingly high levels of combined trade — exports plus imports — as a share of GDP: Indonesia 37 per cent, Myanmar 43, the Philippines 65, Laos 68, Brunei 83, Thailand 123, Cambodia 127, Malaysia 128, Vietnam 185 and Singapore 318 per cent.[3]

The region has enjoyed burgeoning exports in recent years, partly abetted by weakening exchange rates of Southeast Asian currencies in 2014–15. Currency devaluations moderated in 2016. The Indonesian rupiah, Philippine peso and Vietnamese dong remained fairly stable in 2017, while the Malaysian ringgit, Thai baht and Singapore dollar sizably appreciated (by 5–10 per cent). Export demand stayed upbeat, fuelling export growth. Significantly, global prices of some key Southeast Asian commodities sustained rising trends in 2017, continuing the momentum from 2016, particularly in crude oil and palm oil (Figure 1). The

FIGURE 1
Monthly Prices of Selected Commodities, 2013–17 (current US$)

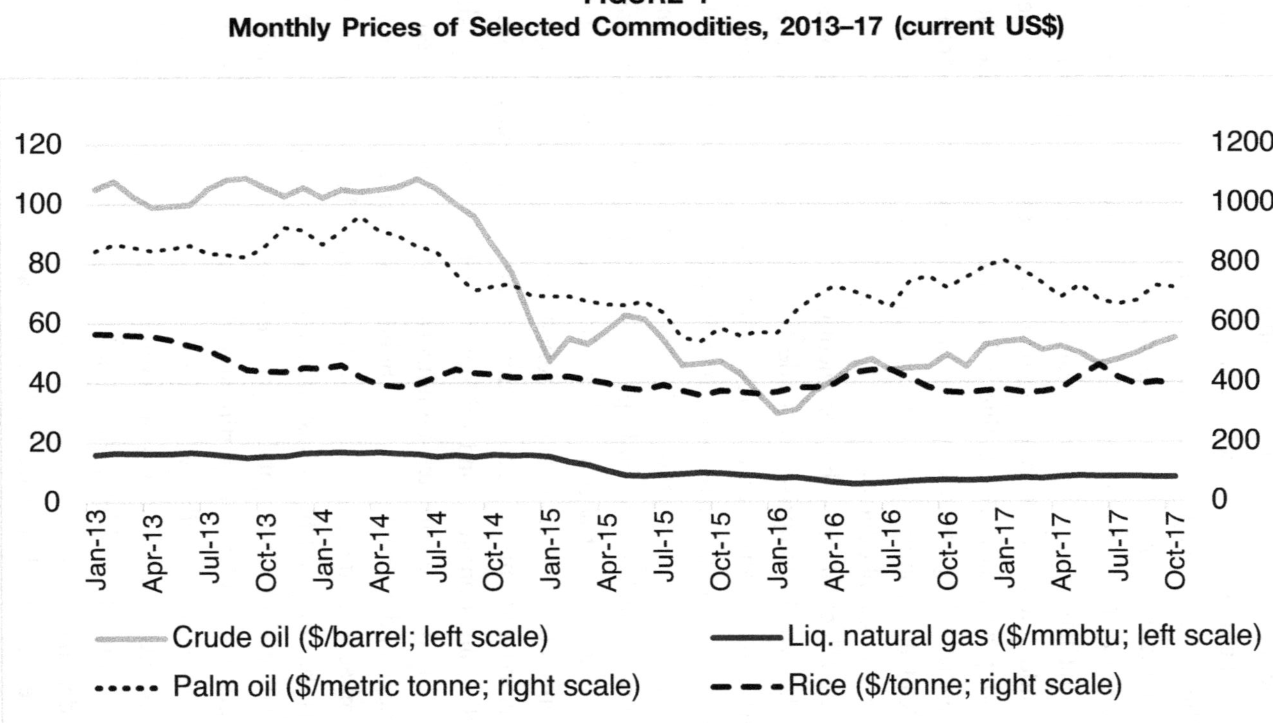

Notes: Crude oil: average of Brent, Dubai, WTI; Rice: Thailand (5 per cent broken, white).
Source: World Bank Commodity Price Data (The Pink Sheet) <http://www.worldbank.org/en/research/commodity-markets>.

overall effects on economy and society depend on the balance of exports and imports. Oil-exporting countries enjoy higher export revenues, but oil-importing countries may experience rising costs of living.

Trade balances of Southeast Asian economies reflect export strength, but reveal some regional dynamics, with higher income associated with surplus of exports over imports (Figure 2). Singapore has maintained a substantial trade surplus, while Thailand has markedly increased its trade surplus since 2012. Malaysia's trade surplus, as a share of GDP, has declined the past few years, although it remains positive. Indonesia has hovered at the break-even point, and the Philippines has been running trade deficits, with widening margins in recent years. Brunei's trade surplus has steadily decreased, fluctuating in line with oil prices, while Vietnam, in contrast, has consistently grown exports faster than imports, moving from a deficit to surplus in 2011 and continuously climbing up. Trade deficits have persisted in Laos, Myanmar and Cambodia since 2011.

The overall effect of cross-border income flows is captured in countries' current accounts, which comprise the trade balance plus remittances and other incomes received from overseas. Current accounts move in tandem with the trade balances shown in Figure 2, and do not affect the pattern of surpluses and deficits, with the exception of the Philippines and Indonesia. The copious remittances sent by overseas workers back to the Philippines exceed its trade deficit, resulting in a net positive on the current account. The converse has transpired in Indonesia, where net income outflows amount to a deficit on the current account.

Trade balance and current account deficits are not necessarily problematic, especially if they are transitory and mitigated by technological acquisition and capital inflows. In the medium term, industrialization may propel countries to import equipment and technology while building export capability, resulting in trade and current account deficits. Capital inflows counterbalance trade and current account deficits, but may not be as sustainable in the long term, and can increase exposure and vulnerability to capital flight. Persistent and large deficits increase risks. These concerns will be more pertinent to the nascent industrializing countries of Laos, Myanmar and Cambodia, which should stay vigilant to avoid persistently large deficits and avoid financial system vulnerability, and to ensure that deficits correspond with capacity-building, particularly for exports.

National destinations of Southeast Asian exports are diverse, but China has increased its presence in this space (Table 2). Land borders remain significant: Thailand is a major export destination for Laos and Myanmar; Malaysia–Singapore mutually trade in large volumes. China, more than any other country, absorbs exports from Laos, Myanmar, Indonesia and Singapore. Laos and Myanmar are

FIGURE 2
Trade Balance of Goods and Services (Exports minus imports, % GDP)

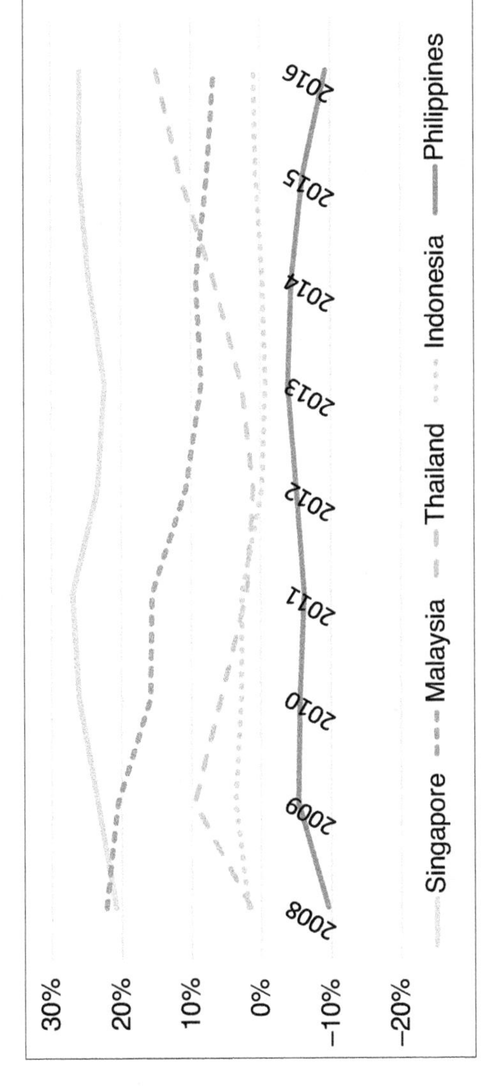

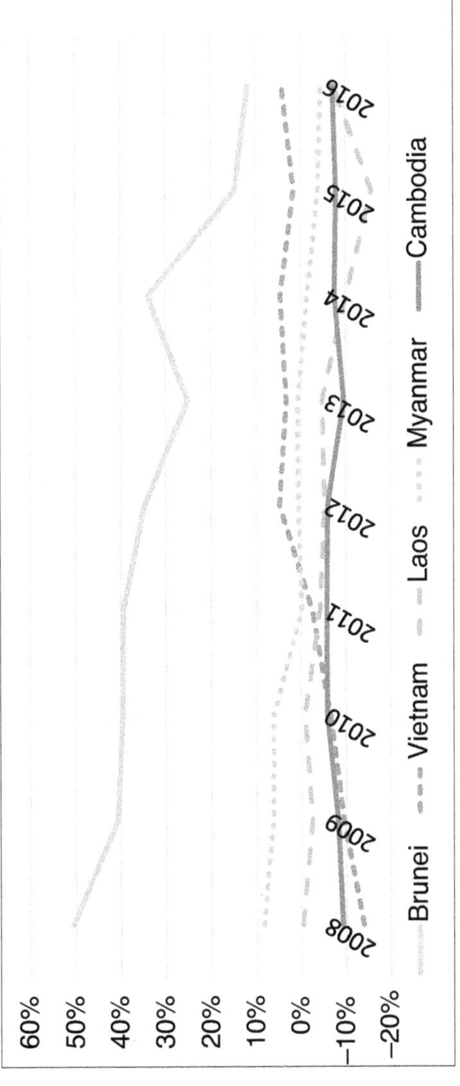

Source: World Bank.

TABLE 2
Destination of Southeast Asian Country Exports, 2016 (% total exports)

	Brunei	*Cambodia*	*Indonesia*	*Laos*	*Malaysia*	*Myanmar*	*Philippines*	*Singapore*	*Thailand*	*Vietnam*
China	1.6	6.1	12.0	40.0	13.0	41.0	11.0	14.0	12.0	10.0
Japan	37.0	8.3	11.0	1.8	8.3	5.7	22.0	4.6	8.8	8.1
USA	0.9	21.0	11.0	0.6	11.0	1.3	16.0	7.2	12.0	21.0
South Korea	15.0	1.6	5.0	0.1	3.0	2.9	3.9	4.6	2.1	5.2
Hong Kong	0.2	2.1	1.5	0.2	4.9	1.7	12.0	13.0	5.0	2.9
India	9.5	0.2	7.2	2.8	4.2	8.9	0.6	3.1	2.4	1.5
Indonesia	1.6	0.2		0.1	3.6	1.0	1.1	8.2	3.3	1.5
Malaysia	2.9	1.0	5.0	0.1		1.2	2.2	11.0	4.6	2.5
Philippines	0.4	0.2	3.7		1.8	0.3		2.1	2.2	0.8
Thailand	10.0	4.2	3.8	29.0	5.8	19.0	3.9	4.1		2.1
Singapore	3.0	0.6	8.0	0.5	15.0	7.6	6.8		3.9	1.9
Vietnam	0.8	2.3	2.2	16.0	3.1	0.7	1.4	3.6	3.7	
Australia	4.4	1.1	2.3		3.5	0.2	0.9	3.0	4.4	1.8
Germany	0.0	9.0	1.9	1.6	2.9	1.5	4.2	1.8	2.4	4.7
UK	0.9	9.5	1.1	0.8	1.1	0.6	0.9	1.0	1.6	2.6
Netherlands	0.1	3.0	2.3		2.9	0.5	3.2	2.2	1.3	2.6
Total	*88.2*	*70.4*	*78.0*	*93.6*	*84.1*	*94.0*	*90.1*	*83.5*	*69.7*	*69.2*

Source: ATLAS.

especially dependent on China, which accounts for 40 per cent of both countries' exports. China plus Hong Kong constitute the top export destination of goods and services from Malaysia, Thailand and the Philippines. The United States, Japan and European nations also sizably import from the region.

The past year was marked by the official launch of the Belt and Road Initiative, which will accelerate China's existing and prospective trade and investment in the region. This has raised concern over China's influence in the region.[4] Markedly, ASEAN's overall trade position vis-à-vis China is a deficit, which burgeoned from US$6 billion in 2010 to US$77 billion in 2017.[5] China's geographic proximity and complementary interests with Southeast Asia present opportunities to build economic ties. At the same time, there is much room to expand intra-ASEAN regional trade and investment, and the benefits of diversifying partnerships and maintaining autonomy bolster the importance and urgency of ASEAN economic integration.

Southeast Asia has maintained vibrancy in investment, the key determinant of economic growth. In 2016, investment rates generally hovered in the 22–25 per cent range, with Indonesia and Brunei exceeding 30 per cent (Figure 3). However, the relative proportions of domestic and foreign sources vary widely. Domestic investment ultimately drives the economy. FDI, while no panacea, can contribute to investment in capital-scarce countries and channel technology transfers. The share of FDI in GDP is highest in Singapore by far, followed by Cambodia, Vietnam, Laos and Myanmar. The values of these investments show uneven regional distribution. Singapore receives the mammoth share, at US$60 billion, followed by Malaysia and Vietnam at around US$12 billion.

FDI inflows to Southeast Asia clearly comprise both the high-technology, high-wage and low-technology, low-wage variants, and those in between — the Philippines, Indonesia, Thailand and Malaysia. This stratification poses country-specific opportunities and challenges. In terms of FDI sources, the established countries — Japan, South Korea, Taiwan, China, the United States and EU members — maintain prominence, but China's presence is growing here as well.[6] The ASEAN perspective stands out. The *ASEAN Investment Report 2017* reports that intra-ASEAN investment has sustained an upward trend in recent years, and in 2016 reached one quarter of total FDI inflows.[7] As with trade, the scope for expanding investment within the region remains wide and plentiful.

Turning to the public sector, the state of government finance warrants some attention (Figure 5). Southeast Asian governments have been running deficits over the past half-decade, with the exception of Singapore, which consistently registered surpluses (but is omitted from Figure 5 due to space constraints).[8] Malaysia and especially Cambodia have engineered smaller government budget

FIGURE 3
Total Investment and Net FDI, 2016

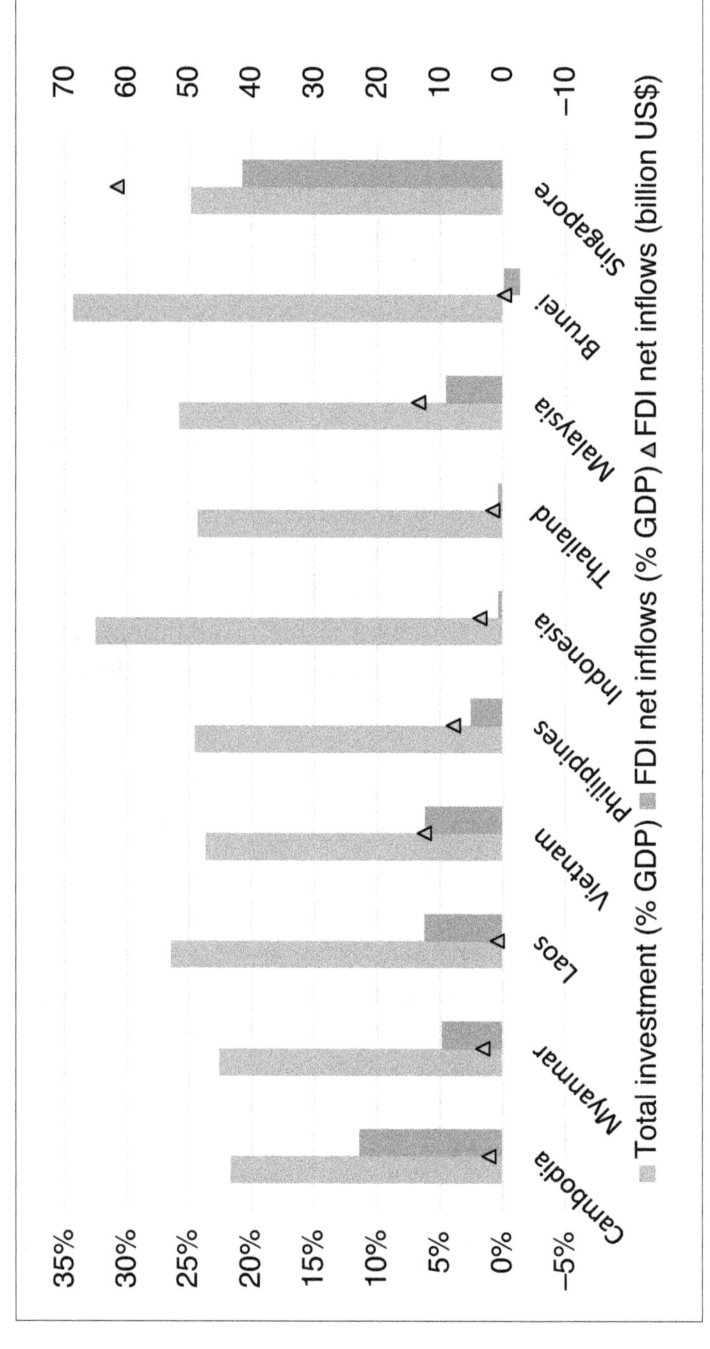

Sources: IMF and World Bank.

FIGURE 4
Net FDI Inflows (% GDP)

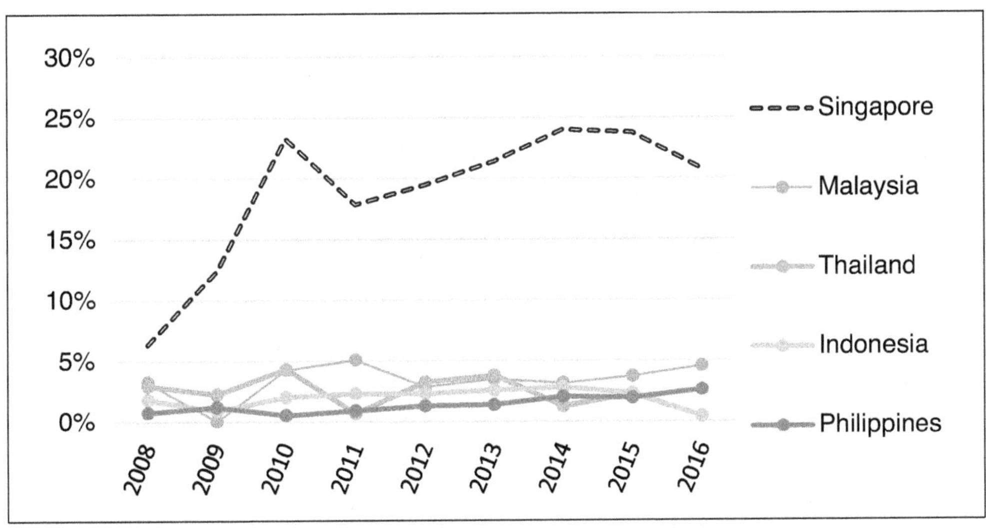

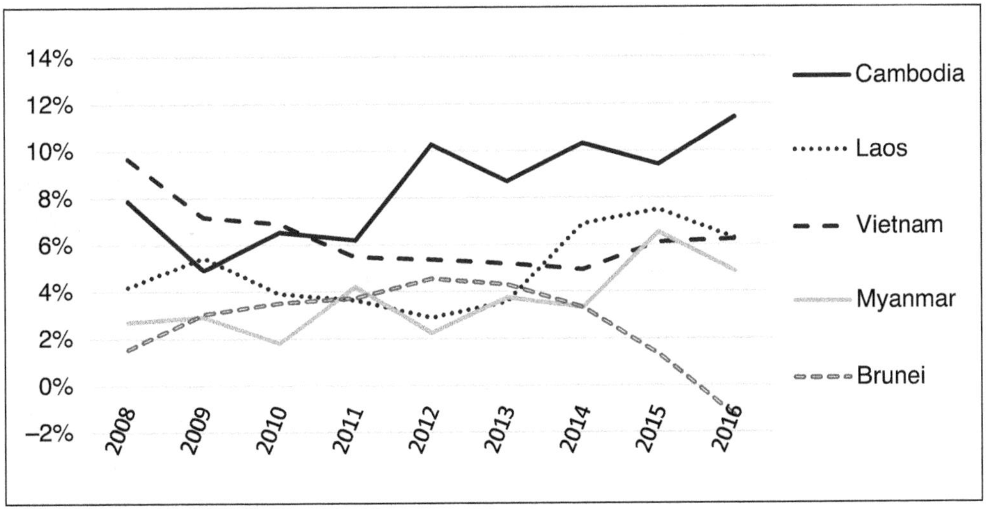

Source: World Bank.

FIGURE 5
Fiscal Balance, 2010–16 (% GDP)

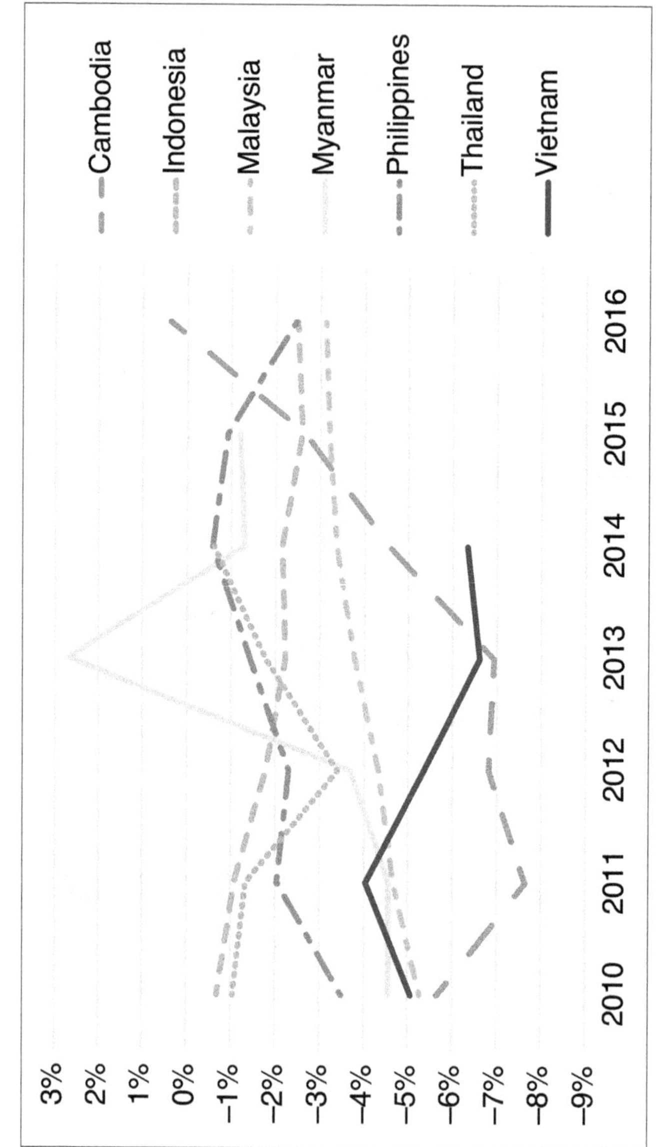

Source: CEIC.

deficits, while Indonesia has been undertaking increased deficits since 2010. The Philippines has also widened the deficit since 2014, reversing a previous downward trend.

The excess of expenditures over revenue, and accumulation of government debt (Figure 6), derives in part from infrastructure expenditures. These substantial commitments, entailing high fixed costs, have placed some strain on Indonesia and raised concern in the Philippines and Vietnam.[9] Moving forward, governments in Southeast Asia will have to be vigilant and prudent, while also looking to increase efficacy and close loopholes on the revenue side.

Structural Change and the Future of Manufacturing

Contemporary economic conditions and technological transformations have brought to light various development challenges revolving around structural change and the future of manufacturing. The Southeast Asian economic landscape spans a broad range of sectoral profiles (Table 3). Countries with large agriculture sectors, in terms of share of output and employment, and nascent manufacturing populate the region alongside countries with sizable manufacturing sectors, where the services sector has begun to dominate. For the most part, manufacturing in the region lacks home-grown technological capacity and remains dependent on FDI.

These structural features, coupled with technological change, wage growth and demands for social protection, have animated policy discourses in 2017. Manufacturing continues to be production hubs, of goods that are exportable, and the major site of technological upgrading, linkages and spillovers. Productivity levels remain low and growth has plateaued (Figure 7).

The issues correspond with the development level and sectoral makeup of the region's economies. Singapore's Committee on the Future Economy disseminated its report in February, emphasizing the need to generate high skills, digital capability, and connectivity.[10] Policy discourses have also unfolded in Malaysia, premised on lagging productivity growth and the country's aspirations to ascend to be an innovation-driven economy.[11] Cultivating manufacturing sectors that are dynamic, competitive and technologically advanced pose steep challenges for Malaysia and Thailand.[12] Regional peers also acutely face the possibility of transitioning into a services-based economy before establishing a high-productivity, high-wage manufacturing base. Southeast Asian economies at earlier stages of industrialization face a different set of challenges, oriented around more labour-intensive manufacturing.

Each country will have distinct sectoral, geographic and socio-economic factors to weigh, while, for the region as a whole, skills development, investment

FIGURE 6
Government Debt, 2010–16 (% GDP)

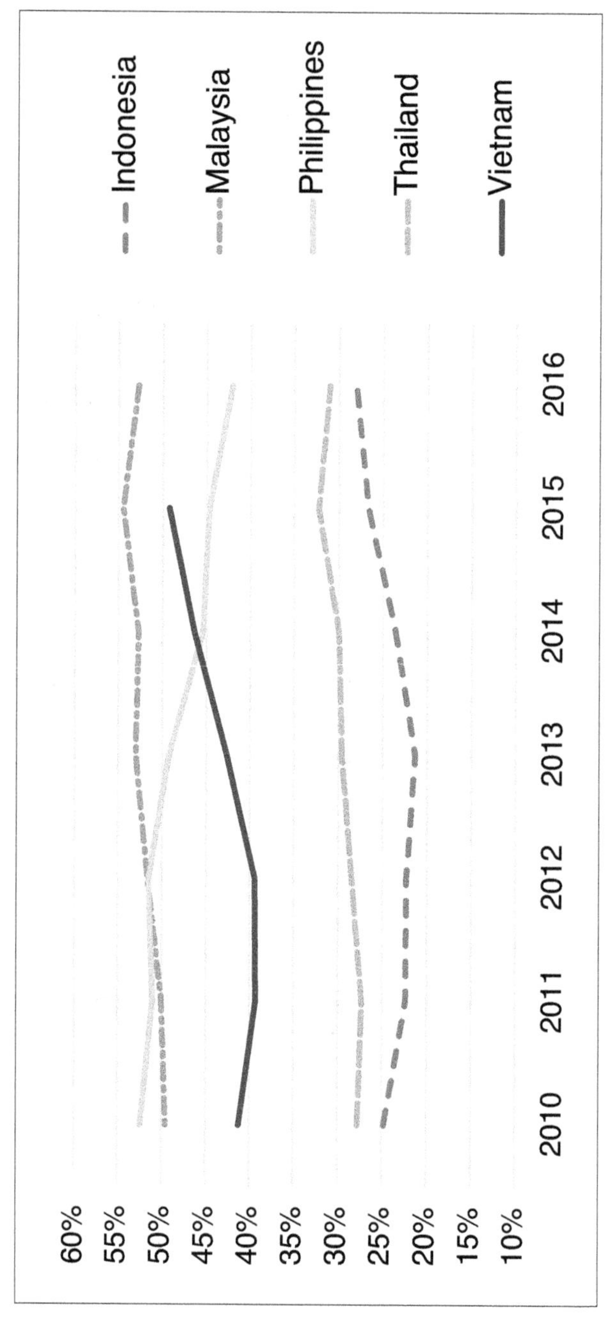

Source: CEIC.

TABLE 3
Structure of Employment and Per Capita Income, 2015

	GDP per capita[1]	*Share of GDP*				*Share of employment*		
		Agri.	*Manuf. industry*	*Non-manuf. industry*	*Services*	*Agri.*	*Industry*	*Services*
Cambodia[2]	1,025	28.6	17.3	12.5	41.5	54.1	16.2	29.6
Myanmar	1,346	26.8	20.7	13.9	38.7	n/a	n/a	n/a
Laos[3]	1,557	19.7	9.2	21.8	49.4	n/a	n/a	n/a
Vietnam	1,685	18.9	15.2	21.8	44.2	43.6	23.1	33.3
Philippines	2,616	10.3	20.0	10.9	58.8	29.2	16.2	54.7
Indonesia	3,828	13.5	21.0	19.0	43.3	32.9	22.2	44.9
Thailand	5,734	8.7	27.6	8.8	43.9	32.3	23.7	43.9
Malaysia	10,740	8.5	22.8	13.6	55.1	12.5	27.5	60.0
Brunei	32,662	0.9	14.5	53.3	31.4	0.6	18.7	80.8
Singapore	52,245	0.04	19.5	6.7	73.8	—	16.3	82.7

Notes: [1]Constant 2010 US$; [2]2010 for share of employment; [3]2011 for share of GDP
Source: World Bank.

FIGURE 7
Manufacturing Productivity (GDP per employment, current US$)

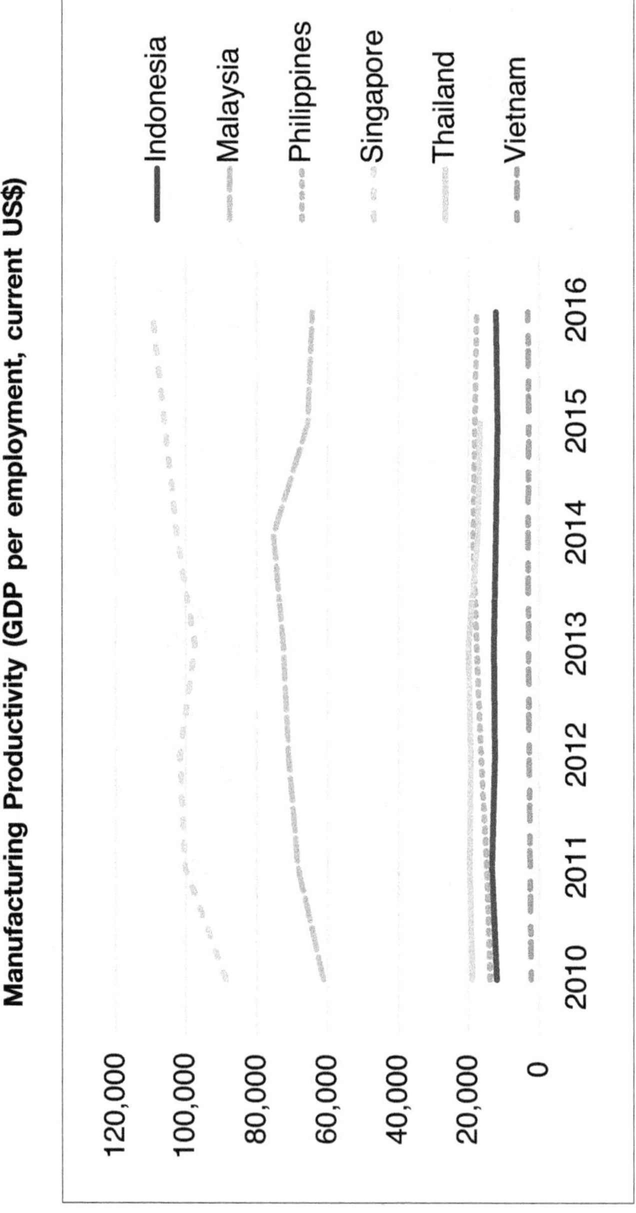

Source: CEIC.

promotion and coordination, and productivity gains are imperative for continued economic progress. Development of digital platforms, particularly e-commerce, and logistical support, also hold out potential for greater regional connectivity and market expansion relevant to all countries.

Employment and Social Protection

Intertwined with the challenges of spurring economic activity and adapting to technological change, contemporary Southeast Asia is also confronted with the need to foster employment growth, household well-being, and socio-economic security. Unemployment captures an important aspect of labour market vitality. Official statistics show that unemployment is generally not a severe problem. Figure 8 reports ILO estimates that strive to translate cross-country inconsistencies into a compatible dataset. Youth unemployment, however, is substantially higher, and an increasing concern in Indonesia, Brunei and Malaysia.

Qualitative aspects of employment are also important considerations. Labour participation and unemployment rates indicate inclination to work and possession of a job, but shed little light on the form and quality of employment. Indeed, labour participation is relatively high and unemployment low in Southeast Asia's lower-income countries, but a large proportion of the employed are classified as "vulnerable" — specifically, designated as contributing family workers and own-account workers (Figure 9).

These jobs are typically in the informal economy, where productivity and wages are lower and legal protections absent. It is difficult to coax or compel informal enterprise to formalize, and potentially disruptive if this is pursued too aggressively and abruptly. Nevertheless, such measures stand to generate further gains in terms of higher productivity, wages, and access to social protection, along with broader tax revenue bases.

Around the world, and specifically in Asia, inequality and insecurity are increasingly acknowledged as economic issues enmeshed with employment, wages and safety nets, and not just social or political concerns.[13] In the wake of the 2008–9 global financial crisis, even the International Monetary Fund and the World Economic Forum recognize that more equitable income distribution is important to sustain economic growth and mitigate socio-political volatility.[14]

In response to slow real growth in incomes, particularly wages, and in line with growing social consciousness and political pressures for interventions to mitigate market failure, social protection has become more mainstreamed in Southeast Asia. These take the form of public health subsidies, cash transfers and labour market instruments.

FIGURE 8
Unemployment, Youth and Overall

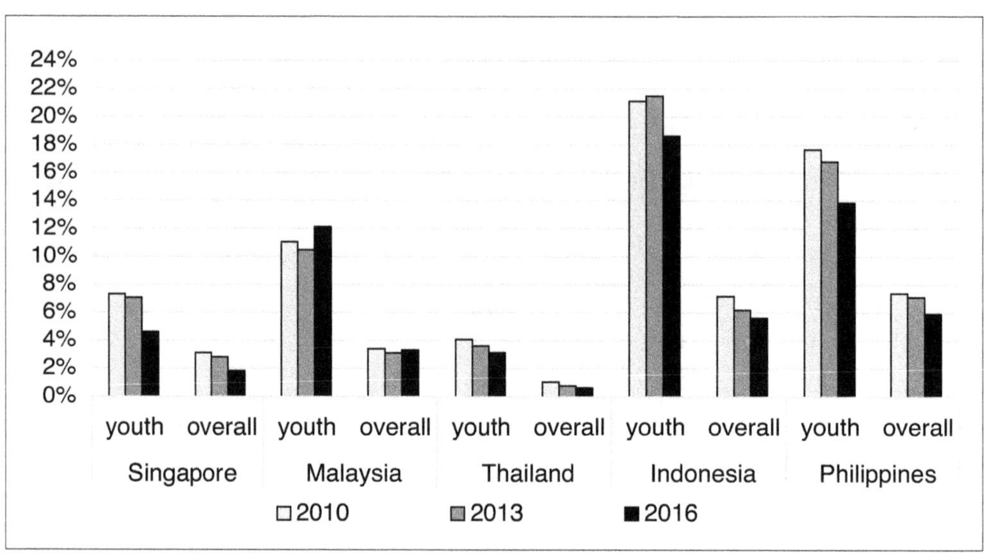

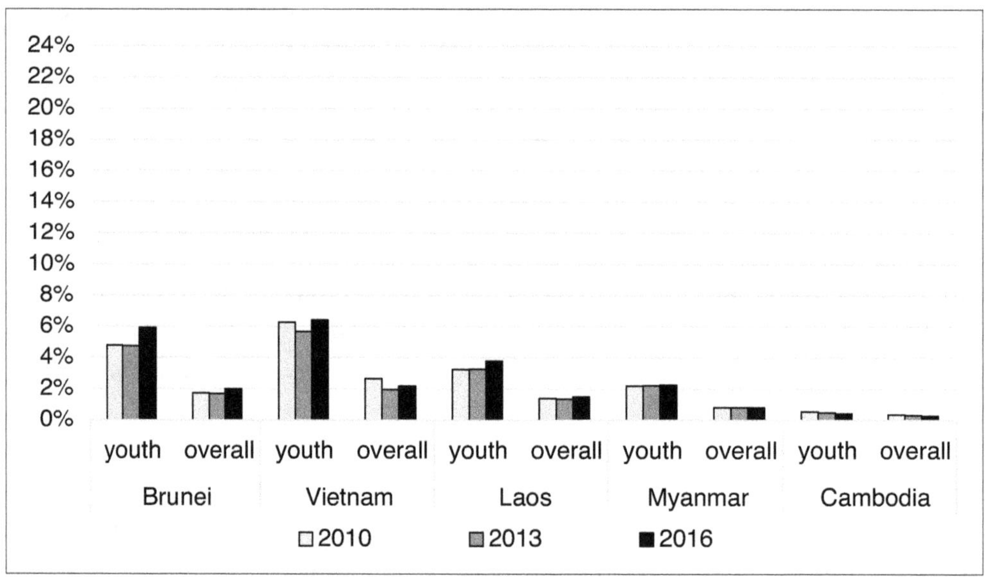

Source: World Bank.

FIGURE 9
Labour Force Participation and Vulnerable Employment, 2015

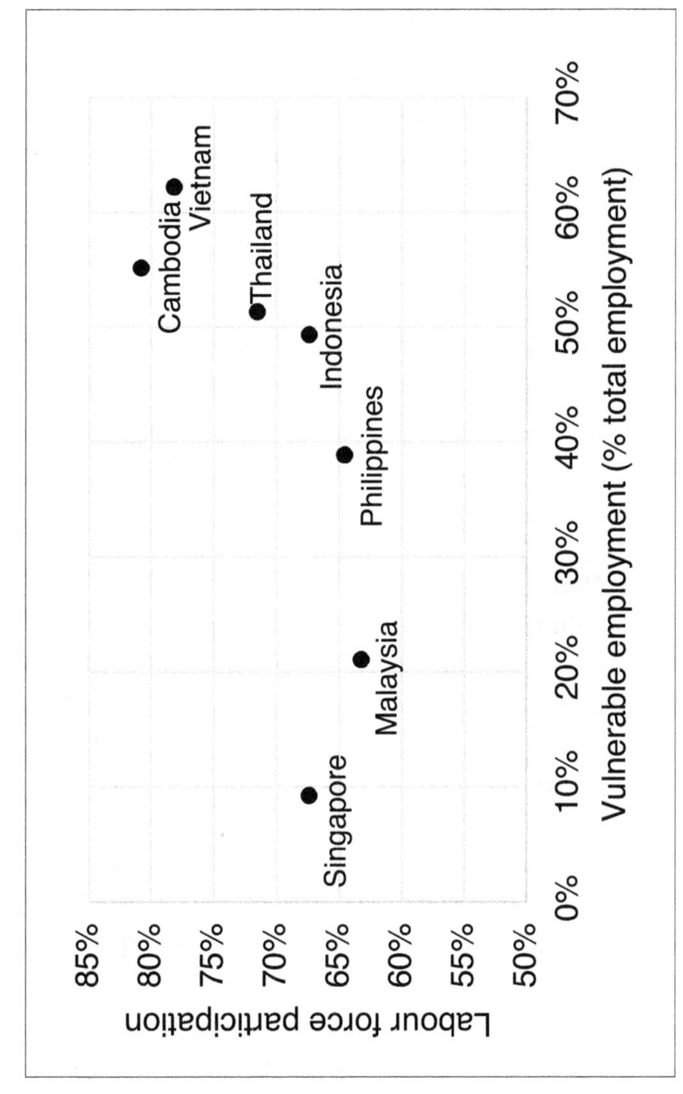

Source: World Bank.

Active revisions and growing demands for a minimum wage — a major labour market safeguard — illustrate the policy imperative of social protection. Malaysia raised its minimum wage rates by 11–15 per cent in July 2016 (from RM900 per month to RM1,000 per month in Peninsular Malaysia, and RM800 to RM920 in Sabah and Sarawak).[15] Vietnam increased the minimum wage by 7.3 per cent in 2017. Deliberations are under way in provinces of Indonesia, and Myanmar nationally, towards raising the statutory wage floor. An 11 per cent increase is scheduled to take effect in Cambodia in early 2018, on the back of large upward revisions of late. Minimum wages for garment workers have increased over 150 per cent over the past five years.[16] Social protection will assuredly grow in importance in Southeast Asia, necessitating effective policy responses.

Infrastructure

Infrastructure is another resurging priority throughout the region, in terms of basic provisions such as paved roads as well as technological advancement, for instance, high-speed rail. The composition differs across countries, from roads to railways, ports, irrigation and hydroelectric power, but massive projects aligned with national objectives are scheduled for the coming years.

Infrastructure development rides on electoral mandates and popular outreach. In Indonesia and the Philippines, Presidents Jokowi and Duterte have been especially vocal in their commitment to expanding and modernizing infrastructure. In 2017, Jokowi reaffirmed infrastructure as a top policy priority, and followed through with US$30 billion public allocations in 2017 and 2018, although the government must also muster voluminous funding from private sources.[17] Duterte's "Build, build, build" agenda, to the tune of US$180 billion by 2022, will roll out from 2018.[18] Malaysia's *Eleventh Malaysia Plan* (2016–20) designated "strengthening infrastructure to support economic expansion" as one of six strategic thrusts, and Prime Minister Najib's 2018 Federal Budget Speech highlighted a few showcase projects: the East Coast Rail Link, Mass Rapid Transit 2 (having completed the first MRT), and the Pan-Borneo Highway.[19]

With perhaps less flair, but no less significance, Thailand has projected $50 billion for infrastructure in 2017–22, with $25 billion approved for 2017 alone.[20] Vietnam has also spent heavily on infrastructure in recent years, and will continue to do so.[21] Cambodia, Myanmar and Laos have also prioritized infrastructure, on transportation as well as hydroelectric power generation. China's Belt and Road Initiative potentially impacts on these countries more than fellow ASEAN members.

The opportunities and positive implications of infrastructure development are bounteous, but such ventures are also fraught with high costs and considerable risks.[22] The extent to which Southeast Asian economies benefit from the forthcoming investments and expenditures will hinge on project design and execution. In financing, countries must strike an efficient balance of public and private sources, and make prudent decisions in direct government expenditure and loans, especially from foreign sources.

Operational integrity will also be of utmost importance to monitor work quality and check against graft. Ultimately, infrastructure development aims to improve connectivity, spur economic growth and foster poverty reduction and human development. Projects must strive for productive, equitable and sustainable outcomes for communities and the environment.

Conclusion

Southeast Asia enjoyed a smooth and buoyant passage through 2017, while internally engaged with changes and policy considerations of longer-term consequence. Economic growth stayed constant or picked up from the previous year, and macroeconomic conditions remain conducive for continued growth in 2018. Trade and fiscal deficits prevail, and may become more major concerns if they persist.

Beneath the relative calm on the surface, Southeast Asian economies were occupied handling economic challenges, in restructuring economies and reinvigorating manufacturing, in fostering income growth, equitable distribution and social protection, and in expanding and modernizing infrastructure. In all areas, judicious policy design and administrative efficacy carry a high premium domestically, while economic integration and coordination potentially yields benefits regionally. Southeast Asia has its work cut out for 2018 and beyond.

Notes

1. FT Confidential Research, "Malaysians Most Pessimistic among ASEAN-5", *Nikkei Asian Review*, 15 August 2017.
2. Kiyoshi Kusaka, "ASEAN5 Outlook Up as Export-Led Growth Continues", *Nikkei Asian Review*, 11 October 2017.
3. Figures from the World Development Indicators (data.worldbank.org).
4. Sanchita Basu Das, "Southeast Asia Worries over Growing Economic Dependence on China", *ISEAS Perspective* 2017, no. 81 (3 November 2017).
5. Tang Siew Mun, "Can China Be a Considerate Power?" *ASEAN Focus* 2017, no. 6 (November 2017).

6. Basu Das, "Southeast Asia Worries".
7. ASEAN, *ASEAN Investment Report 2017: Foreign Direct Investment and Economic Zones in ASEAN* (Jakarta: ASEAN Secretariat and UNCTAD, 2017).
8. Singapore is omitted from Figure 6 due to the somewhat misleading picture generated by its gross debt figure, which stands at an exceptionally high 112 per cent of GDP. However, this variable only includes liabilities; Singapore holds a break-even net position after including assets and, as noted in this article, the government has repeatedly run fiscal surpluses in recent years.
9. Natasha Hamilton-Hart and Günther G. Shulze, "Taxing Times in Indonesia: The Challenge of Restoring Competitiveness and the Search for Fiscal Space", *Bulletin of Indonesian Economic Studies* 52, no. 3 (2016): 265–95.
10. Committee on the Future Economy, *Report of the Committee on the Future Economy: Pioneers of the Next Generation*, February 2017 <https://www.gov.sg/microsites/future-economy/the-cfe-report/read-the-full-report>.
11. World Bank, *Malaysia Economic Monitor December 2016: The Quest for Productivity Growth* (Kuala Lumpur: World Bank, 2016).
12. V.G.R. Chandran and Evelyn S. Devadason, "Energizing the Manufacturing Sector: Can Malaysia Move Forward?" *Journal of Southeast Asian Economies* 34, no. 3 (2017): 523–51; Asian Development Bank, *Thailand Industrialization and Economic Catch-up* (Manila: ADB, 2015).
13. Asian Development Bank, *Asian Development Outlook 2012: Confronting Rising Inequality in Asia* (Manila: ADB, 2012).
14. Larry Elliot, "Rising Inequality Threatens World Economy, Says WEF", *The Guardian*, 11 January 2017.
15. "New Minimum Wage Policy to Take Effect Tomorrow", *The Star*, 30 June 2016.
16. Reuters, "Cambodia Hikes Minimum Wage for Textiles Workers by 11 pct from 2018", 5 October 2017.
17. News Desk, "Government to Spend Rp 404t on Infrastructure Projects in 2018", *Jakarta Post*, 18 August 2017; Dikanaya Tarahita and Muhammad Zulfikar Rakhmat, "Solving Indonesia's Infrastructure Gap", *The Diplomat*, 16 May 2017.
18. Rosemarie Marquez, "Making 'Build, Build, Build' Work in the Philippines", *Asian Development Bank*, 30 October 2017.
19. Malaysia, *Eleventh Malaysia Plan, 2016–2020* (Putrajaya: Government of Malaysia, 2015); Najib Razak, The 2018 Budget Speech, Parliament of Malaysia, 27 October 2017.
20. Hiroshi Kitani, "Thailand Targets Competitive Infrastructure with $50bn Plan", *Nikkei Asian Review*, 5 March 2016.
21. Karl Lester M. Yap and Nguyen Dieu Tu Uyen, "In Asia's Infrastructure Race, Vietnam is among the Leaders", Bloomberg, 23 March 2017.
22. The imperatives, constraints and pitfalls are very country-specific, including land

acquisition issues faced by Indonesia. See Siwage Dharma Negara, "Indonesia's Infrastructure Development under the Jokowi Administration", *Southeast Asian Affairs 2016*, edited by Malcolm Cook and Daljit Singh (Singapore: ISEAS – Yusof Ishak Institute, 2016).

YEAR ONE OF THE TRUMP ADMINISTRATION'S POLICY: Uncertainty and Continuity

Walter Lohman

It seems like a distant memory now, but the first year of the Obama administration was an anxious one for many American Asia watchers. Those closest to the president, people who worked on his campaign, and people heartened by his boyhood connections to the region may have been confident about his professional interest in Asia. Those not in-the-know or disinclined to take too seriously the policy implications of his personal story were uncertain. The substance of President Obama's interest was also unclear. Asia policy was not a major theme of the campaign and he seemed ambivalent about its most important element — international trade.

Secretary of State Hillary Clinton went to Asia on her first overseas trip as secretary. It was a very positive statement about American interests. During the course of the visit, however, what made the most news was a remark in reference to China that the United States had to be careful not to let human rights interfere with its broader interests. Later in the year, President Obama compounded doubts about his administration's priorities by refusing a customary meeting with the Dalai Lama. The best reading of his reluctance was that he would soon be visiting China for the first time and did not want to spoil the prospects for a productive visit; the worst was that, as his first National Security Strategy would later indicate, he saw China as a partner more than a challenge. And when President Obama made his own visit that November, it was plagued by doubt. Given his interaction with the Chinese, many critics were concerned that he had been manipulated.[1]

WALTER LOHMAN is Director of the Asian Studies Center of the Kathryn and Shelby Cullom Davis Institute for National Security and Foreign Policy at The Heritage Foundation, as well as an Adjunct Associate Professor in Georgetown University's Asian Studies Program.

It was not until the Tokyo stop of this November swing through the region that President Obama committed the United States to joining negotiations on what would ultimately become central to his Asia policy — the Trans-Pacific Partnership (TPP). Until then, it was anything but certain whether he would endorse his predecessor's initiative. Similarly, until it was finalized in 2010, suspense surrounded the future of the U.S.–Korea Free Trade Agreement (KORUS), portions of which President Obama demanded be renegotiated as the price for his support.

The point of this recounting is not to evaluate the history of the previous administration but to contextualize the Trump administration's policy. The first year of a presidency is often an uncertain one. In 2009, few could have predicted that the "Asia Pivot" — much maligned by Beijing — would emerge as the framework for the administration's approach. The clues to the Trump administration's policy priorities may be cloudier than were Obama's at the end of 2009. Among other things, this is attributable to a very slow appointment process, the president's own haphazard messaging, and a remarkably hostile relationship with the press. Yet, at the end of 2017, the outlines of the Trump administration's Asia policy began to emerge, and they did not comport with many of the impressions coming out of the 2016 election. It is best characterized by a continuity with the past that will ensure a robust U.S. leadership into the future, albeit with one important caveat. On the economy, many policies were still pending at the end of 2017, but the signals pointed to an unorthodox approach that could derail the broader effort to maintain America's position in the region.

Expectations about relationships in Asia were dire following the election. Donald Trump's scepticism about America's relationship with China had been clear for many years. His campaign rhetoric only accentuated it. Fierce criticism of China is nothing new in American politics. Going back to the debate over "who lost China" in the 1950s, presidential candidates have often featured China negatively in their campaigns. What was striking about Trump's rhetoric in 2016 was not what he said about *China*, but the criticism directed at American allies in Japan and South Korea — which he portrayed as free riders on American largesse. Yet, in all three cases, the situation at the end of 2017 was much different than expected. The relationship with China settled somewhat, but continued to roil around a number of issues. With Japan and South Korea, relationships have found solid, traditional footing.

U.S.-China Relations

With China, Trump got off to an exceptionally shaky start. His pre-inaugural phone call with the President of Taiwan, Tsai Ing-wen, and subsequent questioning of

America's one-China policy panicked Beijing and many China policy specialists in Washington. Having provoked the concern, however, the president corrected the record in a phone call with General Secretary Xi Xinping that was officially made public.[2] This and his invitation to Xi to visit him at Mar-a-Lago put things back on track. In fact, the atmospherics became so good that speculation around the Xi–Trump summit shifted from concern over a breakdown in relations to prospects for U.S.–China condominium in Asia. This prospect resounded most loudly in Taipei. If Taipei was encouraged by early signs of new thinking in Washington about the fundamentals of U.S.–China relations, it now fretted that its security would be traded away. Rumours of connections among Trump's daughter and son-in-law, the Chinese embassy and Taiwan's bête noire, Henry Kissinger, abounded. Not for the first time in U.S.–Taiwan relations, there was speculation about a "fourth communiqué" to be negotiated at Taiwan's expense.

In June, concerns began to abate. Trump made good on a $1.4 billion arms sale to Taiwan that was left pending from the Obama administration. The good news was supplemented in the winter by the confirmation of a well-known friend of Taiwan to the position of Assistant Secretary of Defense for Asian and Pacific Security Affairs. By the end of the year, Taiwan would occupy a place in the administration's National Security Strategy that it had not since 2002. The presidential document explicitly endorses America's "strong ties with Taiwan" and its "commitments under the Taiwan Relations Act".

Setting aside the sound and fury, the Trump administration ended the year with a relatively conventional diplomatic approach to China. As with his predecessors', it is founded on the three U.S.–PRC communiqués and the Taiwan Relations Act, which as a matter of law commits the United States to provide Taiwan arms of a defence character. Even the "six assurances" — the promise that President Reagan made to Taiwan in 1982 that the third U.S.–China Communiqué would not degrade U.S.–Taiwan relations — made it into U.S. official policy.[3] In terms of engagement, the president did not end high-level dialogue with China, but instead reconfigured the Obama-era Security and Economic Dialogue (S&ED) into four new distinct dialogues: the Diplomatic and Security Dialogue, the Comprehensive Economic Dialogue, the Law Enforcement and Cybersecurity Dialogue, and the Social and Cultural Dialogue.

In one area that deeply impacts U.S.–China relations — American freedom of navigation operations — the Trump administration continued a policy inherited from President Obama, but strengthened it. In 2017 the United States conducted four maritime operations to demonstrate international rights in waters claimed by China around the Spratly and Paracel Islands. The Obama administration had conducted the same number in its entire second term. The Trump administration's demonstrations were also more insistent. Earlier exercises had settled into a pattern of demonstrating rights to innocent passage within the twelve-mile territorial seas of Chinese-claimed islands. By contrast, in May 2017 the Navy challenged the very existence of a twelve-mile limit around Mischief Reef.[4] Coupled with a very persistent and vocal effort on the part of the Trump administration to secure the funding necessary to restore U.S. military readiness rates and ultimately grow the U.S. naval fleet, and its stated continuing commitment to a forward deployed navy,[5] this laid down a marker. The U.S. was emphatically demonstrating clear commitment to its long-held maritime interests in the Pacific.

U.S.–Japan Relations

With regard to U.S.–Japan relations, prospects began to turn positive very quickly after the election. Prime Minister Abe was the first foreign leader to meet the president-elect. He followed-up in February — as only the second leader after the UK's Theresa May — to hold a formal meeting with Trump. At those meetings in Washington and Mar-a-Lago, the two appeared to get along very well. Trump himself attested to the bond at an associated news conference and extended this to the relationship between the two nations. "The bond between our two nations and the friendship between our two peoples runs very, very deep", he said. Then, crucially, he alluded to Japan's Senkaku islands, "We are committed to the security of Japan and *all areas under its administrative control*."[6] Commitment to the alliance was a sentiment that carried over into the joint statement released by the two leaders at the conclusion of their meetings in Washington. That statement, in general, was thoroughly conventional. It referenced continued commitment to arrangements reached by Trump's predecessors, the 2015 U.S.–Japan Defense Guidelines, agreement on the realignment of U.S. forces on Okinawa, and the "2+2" process involving the cabinet officials responsible for foreign affairs and defence from each side.

By the time of President Trump's visit to Japan in November, he had been preceded by his Vice President, Secretary of State, and Secretary of Defense, and was calling Prime Minister Abe a "close friend". In fact, President Trump's first visit to Asia, very importantly, started in Tokyo, where Trump again emphasized the centrality of the alliance to American interests. Since 1998, when President Clinton visited China for nine days without stopping through the capital of America's most critical ally, the Japanese have worried about their place on America's priority list. Trump's interaction with Abe again proceeded with a reassuring focus on the alliance, including what he called America's "unwavering commitment to

Japan's defense through the full range of U.S. military capabilities, both nuclear and conventional".[7] The United States and Japan also seemed to have come to a meeting of minds on a strategic vision for a "free and open Indo-Pacific". Trump's reference to Japan's willingness to play a greater security role and its effort to defray the cost of U.S. forces stationed in Japan indicated his opinions about Japan's free riding on the alliance had evolved.

U.S.–South Korea Relations

As with Japan early on, when South Korean President Moon Jae-in was inaugurated in May, there was reason to be concerned about U.S.–Korean relations. Korean progressives like Moon have historically been ambivalent about their nation's relationship with the United States. They are also much more proactive in their outreach to North Korea — an inclination that has strained U.S.–Korea relations in the past. And as chief of staff to former President Roh Moo-hyun, President Moon came to office with impeccable progressive credentials. His former boss was notoriously anti-American, and an enthusiastic adherent of the "sunshine policy" approach to the North.

As the election season got under way in South Korea, Moon lived up to his associations. He seemed inclined to dialogue with the North and initially opposed the deployment of the American THAAD missile defence system. His shift on this issue and memories of his interaction with American specialists during Roh's presidency, however, led many in Washington to assume the best. On the other hand, many conservative Korean commentators expected the worst, and conveyed as much to their Republican friends in the United States. His apparent reasonableness they dismissed as a disguise. This uncertainty led to anxiety over the potential clash between a progressive president in Korea and a conservative-backed and volatile president in the United States at a time when the alliance was being pressurized by repeated North Korean provocation.

In the end, whether because he learned from the rocky relationship his former boss had with the United States, or because he was biding his time, Moon proved to be a very astute, circumspect American partner in 2017. And this, like President Abe's approach, helped create stability in South Korea's relationship with the United States. After delaying the final deployment of launchers to the THAAD missile battery in deference to an environmental impact review, Moon shifted further and actually allowed it to go forward, over the fierce objections of Beijing. American concerns that Moon would drift away from the alliance were relieved.

Also similar to Abe, personal diplomacy with Trump appeared to pay off. President Moon made Washington his first overseas trip after being inaugurated. Standing next to Moon in the White House Rose Garden, Trump said, the United States "will defend itself ... and will always defend our allies".[8] Their official joint statement was similarly conventional. It extolled the virtues of the alliance and reiterated traditional American security guarantees, including extended deterrence, and backed "regular dialogue channels". Crucially, it pledged "lock-step coordination" on the allies approach to North Korea, and agreed to joint coordination with Japan.

Throughout 2017 a number of factors came together to stabilize these three critical Northeast Asia relationships. First, an intense interest on the part of America's allies and China to stabilize relations led to very careful proactive outreach to Washington. Second, a very highly experienced and capable national security team, including National Security Adviser H.R. McMaster, Secretary of Defense James Mattis and Secretary of State Rex Tillerson, brought the president up to speed quickly and represented the United States in a highly professional, confidence-inspiring manner. Third, at the end of the day, the president of the United States proved to be a pragmatist, not an ideologue of any sort, conservative, liberal or nationalist. And although he was intent on fulfilling campaign promises, positions taken on issues not essential to his election victory, like alliance issues, turned out to be flexible.

North Korea Policy

The most immediately influential catalyst in these three relationships, however, was North Korea and its nuclear weapons programme. This issue has become the Trump administration's number one national security priority — globally. Over the course of 2017, North Korea conducted tests of two dozen missiles[9] — including intercontinental ballistic missiles capable of reaching the American mainland. The test carried out in November of 2017 demonstrated a range that leaves no corner of the United States safe.[10] In 2017, North Korea also conducted what was by far its most massive nuclear detonation. The only question among the experts was the state of North Korea's efforts to marry these two capabilities and construct a re-entry vehicle capable of delivering the missile's payload.

The constant reminders of the threat from North Korea stemmed potential differences in U.S. relations with South Korea and Japan. It has been the number one item on the agenda for all high-level diplomatic and security dialogue among the three over the last year. Even on the economic side, the North Korean threat has brought the United States and South Korea closer together than they might otherwise be. In internal Trump administration deliberations, it was the imminent threat posed by North Korea that facilitated the relatively amicable process for meeting Trump's campaign promise to renegotiate KORUS — a dispute that had the potential to upend relations. With China, the threat has frequently been cited by the president himself as key to his restraint in pressing his trade complaints. Accordingly, the threat of a breakdown with trade over China ebbed and flowed throughout the year, depending on the degree of cooperation that Trump felt he was receiving from the Chinese.

The Trump administration was left with no good options on North Korea. Inaction could lead to a fait accompli on North Korea's status as a nuclear power. In turn, passive acceptance would preclude dialogue because dialogue under such circumstances would strengthen North Korea's hand. It would call into question the very relevance of U.S. security guarantees and military presence in South Korea. Key players in the Trump administration deduce this to be Kim Jong-un's interim objective on the way to unifying the Peninsula under his leadership. On the other side of the equation, the cost of using force to prevent the further development of North Korea's nuclear and missile programmes was unacceptable — particularly to South Korea, which would be closely consulted in any such decision.

Faced with these choices, the Trump administration adopted a policy of "maximum pressure". The idea as outlined by Secretary Tillerson at the United Nations Security Council (UNSC) in April called on the international community to fully enforce UNSC resolutions relevant to North Korea, suspend or downgrade diplomatic relations with North Korea, and impose new sanctions. He also declared American readiness to sanction third party "entities and individuals supporting (North Korea's) illegal activities" contrary to UNSC resolutions.[11]

In his UNSC speech, Tillerson very dramatically called the Obama era of "strategic patience", dead. "Business as usual", Tillerson said, is not an option. Yet, the policy pursued by the Trump administration differed from that of the Obama administration's in degree, not in kind. The idea of strategic patience was developed in recognition that, on the one hand, diplomatic engagement was futile and, on the other, the cost of preventative military confrontation was far too high to contemplate. While it is true that the Obama administration did not fully absorb the first part of this equation until its second term, when it did, it developed a policy very similar to that which the Trump administration would later adopt. This was the application of multilateral and unilateral pressure, while keeping the door open to talks conditioned on North Korea's willingness to give-up its nuclear weapons programme.

The Trump administration added North Korea back to the U.S. list of state sponsors of terrorism. It has also pressed much harder on diplomatic and economic isolation, with some effect. Several capitals have expelled North Korean ambassadors.[12] Others — including Singapore, Malaysia and the Philippines — have cut off or curtailed economic relations. However, the Trump administration was as reluctant as Obama's to impose third-party sanctions on the Chinese. Spanning the two administrations, for the first time, in 2016 the United States targeted four Chinese entities and a Chinese company for evading sanctions on North Korea,[13] and in 2017 it targeted a small Chinese bank for a similar charge.[14] A list of larger Chinese banks involved with North Korea provided[15] the administration by the chairman of the House Foreign Affairs Committee went without being acted upon.

Throughout 2017, different administration officials sent different messages — some more open to dialogue with the North, some, mostly from the president himself, belligerent. To hear administration officials explain it, this was a deliberate good cop, bad cop tactic intended to drive Pyongyang to the bargaining table. It often did not feel so carefully coordinated. Yet, despite what is sometimes a very confusing communications effort, the Trump administration's policy on prospects for war with North Korea tracks a long-held American position. The president's statement at the United Nations General Assembly made clear that "if it is forced to defend itself or its allies, [the United States] will have no choice but to totally destroy North Korea". This is standard U.S. policy, and a form of classic nuclear deterrence. It came off as bellicose perhaps because of the subsequent colourful reference to Kim Jong-un as "Rocket man". Trump did not say that the United States would take military action against North Korea if it refused to give up its nuclear weapons and missile programmes, as some interpreted it.[16] In fact, what he said was expressed less dramatically by Obama's Secretary of Defense Ash Carter in 2016: "Make no mistake, any attack on America or our allies will not only be defeated, but any use of nuclear weapons will be met with an overwhelming and effective response."[17] In fairness to Trump's critics, his rhetoric did at times stray into very aggressive territory — most notably in his "fire and fury" comment in August 2017.[18] Even in this case, however, it was still unclear whether the president intended to reference a preventative attack on North Korea or a pre-emptive one. The full official context would indicate the latter.

Southeast Asia

For decades, policymakers and analysts have suggested that the most important thing in dealing with Southeast Asia is "just showing up". President Obama was very good at that. The most innovative aspect of his "Asia Pivot", in fact, was his attention to Southeast Asia. Trump continued the policy of "showing up" during his first year in office, actually becoming personally involved in the development of American relationships in Southeast Asia. In 2017 he welcomed to Washington the leaders of Malaysia, Singapore, Thailand and Vietnam. By contrast, during his first year in office, President Obama received only Philippine President Gloria Macapagal-Arroyo in Washington.

Like Obama, Trump also made a visit to Southeast Asia during his first year in office. He visited the region during November to attend APEC meetings in Danang and officials in Hanoi, as well as the ASEAN and bilateral meetings in Manila. Manila was also the site for the restart of the quadrilateral dialogue among the United States, Japan, India and Australia, which had been in abeyance since 2007.

Trump's November visit to Vietnam and the Philippines was the culmination of a year-long cabinet-level effort that began with the vice president's visit to Indonesia in April. Clearly, like the trip by the secretary of defense to Japan and South Korea only weeks after Trump's inauguration, Pence's primary mission was to reassure treaty allies in the midst of a very tumultuous time in American politics. He went to Japan, South Korea and Australia. The inclusion of Indonesia, a non-treaty ally, was an effort to demonstrate continued interest beyond Northeast Asia and formal treaty alliances to partnerships in Southeast Asia,[19] and with ASEAN in particular.[20]

The occasions of these presidential and cabinet-level visits point to the second element of the Trump administration's approach to Southeast Asia — engagement of its ASEAN-centric diplomatic and security architecture. Trump was in the Philippines for the ASEAN Summit and related events, such as the U.S.–ASEAN Leaders meeting and the East Asian Summit (EAS). Originally scheduled to depart the Philippines before the plenary session of the EAS, after what was already a near two-week trip, President Trump changed his plans just before departing Washington. He extended a day in order to attend. Ultimately, scheduling problems on ASEAN's side still prevented this, but he had made an unusual effort to accommodate the forum, and at any rate delivered prepared remarks to a leaders' luncheon prior to the plenary. Vice President Pence visited ASEAN headquarters in Jakarta. Tillerson visited in August to attend the annual ASEAN Regional Forum and associated meetings. And Mattis, in addition to advancing Trump's visit, was in Manila in October to attend the annual ASEAN Defence Ministers Meeting Plus. He also attended the Shangri-la Dialogue earlier in the year in Singapore.

This commitment to ASEAN-centric architecture has been more than a matter of gesture for the Trump administration. It is found in the administration's official policy statements. Reference to ASEAN's central role in the region appears in the joint statements marking each of Trump's meetings with leaders in Washington.[21] In a bow to continuity, those statements also reference principles from the Sunnylands Declaration that proceeded Trump's inauguration. The Trump administration explicitly endorsed the concept of ASEAN centrality in the joint statement commemorating the U.S.–ASEAN Leaders meeting in the Philippines.[22] Certainly, some of this continuity was attributable to the career foreign service officers tasked with working on these issues. Even so, they required concurrence of political staff at the White House. And it should be noted that commitment to ASEAN was also featured in the president's own remarks at the leaders meeting,[23] and it is referenced in his National Security Strategy.[24]

The collaboration between career foreign service officers and political appointees at the White House in favour of continuity appears to be at work on values issues as well. There are indications that the president's personal interest in human rights and democracy are not to be taken for granted. He has made a number of statements interpreted to imply an active negligence of them. Yet, under his leadership, other levels of government remain clearly committed to these issues.

In the case of Cambodia, even as Prime Minister Hun Sen sought to curry favour with President Trump, commending him for his aversion to interference in internal affairs,[25] members of the president's travelling party were doing precisely that in a meeting with[26] Foreign Minister Prak Sokhonn. The Americans involved in this conversation — White House Senior Director for Asian Affairs, Matt Pottinger, and Deputy Assistant Secretary of State for Southeast Asia, W. Patrick Murphy — released a statement summarizing the conversation. In it, they state, "the U.S. side forthrightly expressed strong concerns about recent steps that challenge the country's democratic progress, including restrictions on the free press, civil society, and the political opposition". They also expressed "deep concern" over the continued detention of Kem Sokha, the leader of the political opposition.[27] Two days later, when the Cambodian government dissolved Kem's political party, the White House released another statement expressing its concern and announcing the termination of assistance for Cambodia's 2018 national elections.

On Myanmar, there was much broader consistency within the administration. Following the August 2017 scorched earth effort to "cleanse"[28] Northern Rakhine State of its Rohingya minority population, the Trump administration became quite active. In testimony before the Senate Foreign Relations Committee in late October,

Patrick Murphy cited a long list of communications with "Burmese civilian and military officials at the highest levels", expressing alarm and calling for an end to the violence, often in direct diplomacy. Among those in the administration so engaged, he singled out President Trump himself, Secretary Tillerson, Vice President Pence, US Ambassador to the United Nations Nikki Haley, and National Security Advisor HR McMaster.[29] On the same day as Murphy's testimony, the State Department also announced a suspension of military engagement with Myanmar.[30]

There are a number of other indicators of the administration's broader attention to values in foreign policy. The Trump administration's decision to withdraw funding for the United Nations Population Agency (UNPA) may not sit well with many UN members. It was, however, made with an eye to values — opposition to forced abortions in China.[31] Media attention focused on the fact that the Secretary of State was not in attendance at the rollout of the department's annual human rights report. Yet, he did attend the rollout of its annual religious freedom report.[32] And, not only did he launch the annual trafficking in persons report, but he was joined by the president's daughter, Ivanka Trump, for the occasion. Each of these reports prominently featured Southeast Asian transgressions.

Trade Caveat

The wildcard in America's Asia policy in 2017 was the trade component. Unlike some of the alliance issues addressed above, these cannot be easily dismissed as issues unrelated to Trump's election appeal. That he sees trade issues as key political priorities was made clear many times. On his first full workday in office, he withdrew the United States from TPP negotiations. Since then he has chartered a course that has shaken the international trade community in Washington. The most salient initiatives include a renegotiation of NAFTA, amendment of KORUS, and appeal to several unilateral mechanisms to address what he believes to be inequities in America's international economic relationships. These include section 201 safeguard investigations likely to target Chinese and South Korean industry; a 301 investigation of Chinese violations of intellectual property rights; and rare 232 investigations concerning the national security implications of steel and aluminium imports that is aimed principally at China. The president also ordered an "Omnibus Report on Significant Trade Deficits" that targeted, among others, four Southeast Asian countries — Vietnam, Malaysia, Thailand and Indonesia.

Unlike the political/security issues, there were no signs by the end of 2017 that the president's protection-oriented approach to trade policy had evolved. He and his cabinet members often referenced an interest in negotiated new bilateral trade agreements. However, their aggressive approach to existing agreements like NAFTA and KORUS, hostility to the WTO process, and the White House's laser-like focus on trade imbalances, has kept potential trading partners in Asia at arms-length. There have been no takers in Asia for new agreements with the United States. The only solace free traders could find in 2017 was that all the above-referenced trade measures and others remained to be concluded. Some of them, in fact, were long past their due dates.

There was one silver lining in this cloud of American trade policy. Concerns about the U.S.–Japan economic relationship that had dominated so much of Donald Trump's public career and risked creating new tension in the relationship were artfully delegated to an economic dialogue co-chaired by Vice President Mike Pence and Deputy Prime Minister Taro Aso. This has allowed them to be addressed in a constructive, systematic way out of the glare of media that President Trump himself can bring to an issue. This, in turn, has allowed the U.S.–Japan relationship to focus on more immediate shared interests like the North Korean nuclear threat and the promotion of a "free and open IndoPacific" framework capable of managing the challenge to the international order presented by the Chinese. The constructive attitude of South Korea — perhaps driven by its existential need to maintain a close U.S.–Korea security relationship — has also helped keep the KORUS amendment process under the political radar in the United States.

Conclusion

All American presidents come to office with a great deal to learn. Their campaigns are not always good indicators of where they might be on issues most critical to Asia policy. That was the case with President Obama to some extent; it was the case with President Trump in 2017 to a greater extent. In many areas, however, if one can disconnect from the media frenzy that surrounds the American president, the contours of a relatively conventional Asia policy — with the exception of its trade component — emerges.

Notes

1. Helene Cooper, "China Holds Firm on Major Issues in Obama's Visit", *New York Times*, 17 November 2009 <http://www.nytimes.com/2009/11/18/world/asia/18prexy.html> (accessed 2 February 2017).

2. Statements and Releases – The White House, "Readout of the President's Call with President Xi Jinping of China", 9 February 2017 <https://www.whitehouse.gov/briefings-statements/readout-presidents-call-president-xi-jinping-china/> (accessed 2 February 2017).
3. CNA Staff Writer, "Tillerson Reaffirms US' Commitment to Taiwan", *Taipei Times*, 10 February 2017 <http://www.taipeitimes.com/News/front/archives/2017/02/10/2003664699> (accessed 2 February 2017).
4. James Kraska, "Dewey Freedom of Navigation Operation Challenges China's Sovereignty to Mischief Reef", *Lawfare*, 25 May 2017 <https://www.lawfareblog.com/dewey-freedom-navigation-operation-challenges-chinas-sovereignty-mischief-reef> (accessed 2 February 2017).
5. Joseph Dunford and James N. Mattis, "The Fiscal Year 2018 National Defense Authorization Budget Request from the Department of Defense", testimony before the Committee on Armed Services, U.S. House of Representatives, 12 June 2017 <https://armedservices.house.gov/legislation/hearings/fiscal-year-2018-national-defense-authorization-budget-request-department> (accessed 2 February 2017).
6. Julie Hirschfeld and Peter Baker, "In Welcoming Shinzo Abe, Trump Affirms U.S. Commitment to Defending Japan", *New York Times*, 20 February 2017 <https://www.nytimes.com/2017/02/10/world/asia/trump-shinzo-abe-meeting.html> (accessed 2 February 2017).
7. Statements and Releases – The White House, "President Donald J. Trump's Summit Meeting with Prime Minister Shinzo Abe of Japan", 6 November 2017 <https://www.whitehouse.gov/briefings-statements/president-donald-j-trumps-summit-meeting-prime-minister-shinzo-abe-japan/> (accessed 2 February 2017).
8. David Nakamura and Jenna Johnson, "With South Korean President, Trump Denounces 'Reckless and Brutal' Regime in North Korea", *Washington Post*, 30 June 2017 <https://www.washingtonpost.com/news/post-politics/wp/2017/06/30/with-south-korean-president-trump-denounces-reckless-and-brutal-regime-in-north-korea/?utm_term=.de85dc86ac6b> (accessed 2 February 2017).
9. Missile Threat: CSIS Missile Defense Project, *North Korean Missile Launches & Nuclear Tests: 1984–Present*, 29 November 2017 <https://missilethreat.csis.org/north-korea-missile-launches-1984-present/> (accessed 2 February 2017).
10. Bruce Klingner, "How to Stop North Korea: Use the 'Python' Strategy", *The National Interest*, 3 December 2017 <http://nationalinterest.org/feature/how-stop-north-korea-use-the-python-strategy-23463> (accessed 2 February 2017).
11. U.S. State Department, "Remarks at the United Nations Security Council Ministerial Session on D.P.R.K.", 28 April 2017 <https://www.state.gov/secretary/remarks/2017/04/270544.htm> (accessed 2 February 2017).
12. Heekyong Yang and James Pearson, "Factbox: Countries which have expelled North Korean Ambassadors after Nuclear Test", Reuters, 19 September 2017 <https://

www.reuters.com/article/us-northkorea-missiles-diplomacy-factbox/factbox-countries-which-have-expelled-north-korean-ambassadors-after-nuclear-test-idUSKCN1BU0ED> (accessed 2 February 2017).

13. U.S. Department of Justice, Office of Public Affairs, "Four Chinese Nationals and China-Based Company Charged with Using Front Companies to Evade U.S. Sanctions Targeting North Korea's Nuclear Weapons and Ballistic Missile Programs", 26 September 2016 <https://www.justice.gov/opa/pr/four-chinese-nationals-and-china-based-company-charged-using-front-companies-evade-us> (accessed 2 February 2017).
14. U.S. Department of Treasury, Press Center, "Treasury Acts to Increase Economic Pressure on North Korea and Protect the U.S. Financial System", 29 June 2017 <https://www.treasury.gov/press-center/press-releases/Pages/sm0118.aspx> (accessed 2 February 2017).
15. "Ranking U.S. Lawmaker Seeks Sanctions on 12 Chinese Banks over North Korea", Yonhap News Agency, 13 September 2017 <http://english.yonhapnews.co.kr/northkorea/2017/09/13/44/0401000000AEN20170913008800315F.html> (accessed 2 February 2017).
16. Kori Schake, "What Total Destruction of North Korea Means", *The Atlantic*, 19 September 2017 <https://www.theatlantic.com/international/archive/2017/09/north-korea-trump-united-nations-kim-jong-un-nuclear-missile/540345/> (accessed 2 February 2017).
17. "U.S. Warns 'Overwhelming' Response to Any North Korea Use of Nuclear Weapons", CBS News, 19 October 2016 <https://www.cbsnews.com/news/us-warns-overwhelming-response-north-korea-nuclear-weapons/>.
18. Peter Baker and Choe Sang-hun, "Trump Threatens 'Fire and Fury' against North Korea If It Endangers U.S.", *New York Times*, 8 August 2017 <https://www.nytimes.com/2017/08/08/world/asia/north-korea-un-sanctions-nuclear-missile-united-nations.html> (accessed 2 February 2017).
19. Statements and Releases – The White House, "Remarks by the Vice President and Indonesian President Widodo to the Press", 20 April 2017 <https://www.whitehouse.gov/briefings-statements/remarks-vice-president-indonesian-president-widodo-press/> (accessed 2 February 2017).
20. Statements and Releases – The White House, "Remarks by the Vice President at ASEAN", 21 November 2017 <https://www.whitehouse.gov/briefings-statements/remarks-vice-president-asean/> (accessed 2 February 2017).
21. Statements and Releases – The White House, "Joint Statement between the United States of America and the Socialist Republic of Vietnam", 12 November 2017 <https://www.whitehouse.gov/briefings-statements/joint-statement-united-states-america-socialist-republic-vietnam/>; Statements and Releases – The White House, "Joint Statement for Enhancing the Comprehensive Partnership between the United States of America and Malaysia", 13 September 2017 <https://www.whitehouse.gov/briefings-statements/

joint-statement-enhancing-comprehensive-partnership-united-states-america-malaysia/>; Statements and Releases – The White House, "Joint Statement by the United States of America and the Republic of Singapore", 24 October 2017 <https://www.whitehouse.gov/briefings-statements/joint-statement-united-states-america-republic-singapore/>; Statements and Releases – The White House, "Joint Statement between the United States of America and the Kingdom of Thailand", 2 October 2017 <https://th.usembassy.gov/joint-statement-united-states-america-kingdom-thailand/> (accessed 2 February 2017).

22. "Joint Statement of the ASEAN – U.S. Commemorative Summit on the 40th Anniversary of the ASEAN – U.S. Dialogue Relations", 13 November 2017 <http://asean.org/storage/2017/11/Joint-Statement-on-ASEAN-US-40th-Anniversary-ADOPTED.pdf> (accessed 2 February 2017).
23. "President Trump Remarks at ASEAN Summit", *C-SPAN*, 13 November 2017 <https://www.c-span.org/video/?437286-1/president-trump-addresses-asean-summit-manila> (accessed 2 February 2017).
24. Donald J. Trump, "National Security Strategy of the United States of America", December 2017 <https://www.whitehouse.gov/wp-content/uploads/2017/12/NSS-Final-12-18-2017-0905.pdf> (accessed 2 February 2017).
25. David Boyle, "Cambodian Strongman's Trump Outreach Falls Flat", VOA, 14 November 2017 <https://www.voanews.com/a/cambodia-strongman-trump-outreach-falls-flat/4114717.html> (accessed 2 February 2017).
26. Statements and Releases – The White House, "Deputy Assistant to the President and Senior Director for Asian Affairs, Matt Pottinger and Deputy Assistant Secretary of State for Southeast Asia, W. Patrick Murphy Meeting with Cambodian Foreign Minister Prak Sokhonn", 14 November 2017 <https://asean.usmission.gov/press-release-november-14-2017/> (accessed 2 February 2017).
27. Statements and Releases – The White House, "Statement by the Press Secretary on Setbacks to Democracy in Cambodia", 16 November 2017 <https://kh.usembassy.gov/statement-press-secretary-setbacks-democracy-cambodia/> (accessed 2 February 2017).
28. Statements and Releases – The White House, "Efforts to Address Burma's Rakhine State Crisis", 22 November 2017 <https://www.state.gov/secretary/remarks/2017/11/275848.htm> (accessed 2 February 2017).
29. Hearings, "Assessing U.S. Policy towards Burma: Geopolitical, Economic, and Humanitarian Considerations", Senate Committee on Foreign Relations, 24 October 2017 <https://www.foreign.senate.gov/imo/media/doc/102417_Murphy_Storella_Testimony.pdf> (accessed 2 February 2017).
30. Press Release – Embassy of the United States of America, "Accountability for Human Rights Abuses in Rakhine State, Burma", 24 October 2017 <https://bd.usembassy.gov/wp-content/uploads/sites/70/Statement-by-Spokesperson-Heather-Nauert-Oct-24-2017-1.pdf> (accessed 2 February 2017).

31. Nurith Aizenman, "Citing Abortions in China, Trump Cuts Funds for U.N. Family Planning Agency", NPR, 4 April 2017 <https://www.npr.org/sections/goatsandsoda/2017/04/04/522040557/citing-abortions-in-china-trump-cuts-funds-for-u-n-family-planning-agency> (accessed 2 February 2017).
32. Laura Koran, "Tillerson Skips Release of Annual Human Rights Report", CNN, 3 March 2017 <https://www.cnn.com/2017/03/03/politics/rex-tillerson-state-department-human-rights-report/index.html> (accessed 2 February 2017).

SOUTHEAST ASIA IN 2017: Grappling with Uncertainty

Joseph Chinyong Liow

The year 2017 was a significant one for Southeast Asia in many ways. It was a milestone year, marking the fiftieth anniversary of ASEAN. Formed in the cauldron of the Cold War in August 1967, ASEAN has been credited with playing an instrumental role in fostering stability and security in the Southeast Asian region over the last five decades. Expressing this celebratory mood, the ASEAN calendar for the year was predictably inundated with events to commemorate the formation of the regional organization. In terms of economics, the countries of the region continued to grow at commendable rates, buoyed in no small part by increased domestic consumption and Chinese and Japanese investments.

Yet, the celebratory atmosphere could barely conceal the uncertainties and host of challenges that confront the region, and which manifested themselves in 2017. Foremost, at the geostrategic and geoeconomic level, was the election into office in the United States of Donald Trump, who, based on his campaign rhetoric, seemed to desire a fundamental overhaul of America's role in global affairs. On the other hand, China appeared to be relentlessly expanding its economic clout and influence in the region, with the Belt and Road Initiative (BRI) leading the way. Meanwhile, under Prime Minister Shinzo Abe, Japan appears to have awakened from its slumber and has both deepened and accelerated its own engagement of the region. Together with several other major challenges, such as humanitarian crises in Myanmar and Marawi, these developments not only made for an exacting year but also reflect the increasing complexity that has come to characterize the regional strategic and economic landscape and suggest potential challenges that need to be overcome in the years ahead.

JOSEPH CHINYONG LIOW is Dean and Professor of Comparative and International Politics at the S. Rajaratnam School of International Studies, Nanyang Technological University, Singapore.

Navigating Major Power Politics

The inauguration of the mercurial Donald Trump into the White House on 20 January ushered in something of a new era in regional affairs. A product of popular dissatisfaction among the American electorate, the Trump administration cast doubt over America's continued leadership of global affairs with its "America First" approach to international diplomacy. For the region, the early portents of change were not encouraging. One of Donald Trump's first acts as president was to withdraw the United States from the Trans-Pacific Partnership (TPP), which was painstakingly negotiated by his predecessor, Barack Obama. The TPP was significant not only because of its potential to be a major driver of regional trade and prosperity but, equally important, it served as a crucial expression of American commitment to the region. That America's withdrawal from the TPP was not followed up with any concrete effort to explore alternative avenues for American participation in regional free trade arrangements occasioned further consternation. Indeed, there was little indication that the United States under Trump was interested in either American leadership or free trade. It was striking, for instance, that in a speech that otherwise had hit all the right notes, Secretary of Defence James Mattis's address at the annual Shangri-La Dialogue in June 2017 made no mention of American leadership. Moreover, the desire of the Trump administration to fundamentally recalibrate American participation in regional trade was also made abundantly clear on the occasion of the president's participation in the APEC Summit in Da Nang in November, when he railed against trade practices that disadvantaged Americans and reiterated his "America First" agenda.[1] Concomitantly, he was pleased to stand on the sidelines as the remaining eleven signatories of the TPP agreed to pursue a revised iteration of the agreement, to be known as the Comprehensive and Progressive Trans-Pacific Partnership (CPTPP). In view of his presence in Da Nang, however, APEC members were prepared to accommodate the views of the Trump administration. This led to the incorporation of "Trumpisque" language into the Da Nang Declaration through references to the "importance of non-discriminatory, reciprocal and mutually advantageous trade and investment frameworks", "unfair trade practices" and "unfair trade subsidies".[2] Additionally, members of the CPTPP also continued to hold out the prospect of America's future participation. This was clear when they expressed the hope that the United States would join in the revised agreement should it eventually come to pass.

Notwithstanding the uncertainties regarding the foreign policy trajectory and priorities of the United States under President Trump, especially on trade, Southeast Asia's relations with the United States did still manage to make headway on other counts. In an effort to assuage regional concerns, Secretary of State Rex Tillerson hosted his ASEAN counterparts in Washington DC on 4 May. During the exchange, Tillerson reiterated President Trump's promise to meet his Southeast Asian counterparts at the end of the year at the various ASEAN and APEC summits (a promise which he made good on) and established the point that the Asia-Pacific remains a top U.S. policy priority for the new administration. On their part, the meeting also offered regional foreign ministers an opportunity to obtain a first-hand view of the newly developing (at the time) Trump foreign policy, amidst headlines dominated by sabre-rattling on the Korean Peninsula and the South China Sea. Economic partnerships through the U.S.–ASEAN Connect, the Trade and Investment Framework Agreement, and the ASEAN Connectivity through Trade and Investment programmes were also discussed.[3] Prior to the Washington meeting, Vice-President Mike Pence's visit to Jakarta in April put Southeast Asia on the White House's agenda. During the trip, Vice-President Pence visited Southeast Asia's largest mosque, Istiqlal, where he also made the symbolic gesture of praising Indonesia's form of "moderate Islam", doubtless to dampen fears about President Trump's perceived harsh rhetoric towards Islam. Moreover, it was reported that $8 billion worth of energy deals were signed during the Pence visit, despite talk of the president's intention to renegotiate trade deals with Indonesia. While in Jakarta, Pence also met the ASEAN Secretary-General, Le Luong Minh, and reiterated President Trump's commitment to visit the region in November for the East Asia Summit, the U.S.–ASEAN Summit (both in the Philippines), and the APEC Summit (in Vietnam).

Prime Minister Nguyen Xuan Phuc was the first Southeast Asian leader to visit Washington, when he was hosted in the White House in May. Visits by Prime Ministers Najib Razak, Prayuth Chan-ocha, and Lee Hsien Loong followed over the course of the year. Concomitantly, President Trump's visit to the region for APEC, the U.S.–ASEAN Summit, and the East Asia Summit went some distance in calming regional anxieties of American neglect. At the same time, the unpredictability that has come to characterize the White House has also precipitated a recalibration of regional relations with other external powers. Not surprisingly, relations with China featured prominently, as did progress in engagement with Japan and India.

Southeast Asia featured prominently in Beijing's efforts to further regional economic development, trade and integration with its BRI. To that end, Southeast Asian governments were strongly represented in the BRI Summit hosted by President Xi Jinping in May, although not all regional states were represented at the level of heads of government. China's partnership with several Southeast Asian countries under the rubric of BRI, particularly Malaysia and Indonesia but also Laos and Cambodia, deepened considerably over the past year. Cambodia was the beneficiary of a slew of agreements in 2017 alone, involving the construction of hydropower facilities, a new airport, and several major road projects, all bearing the imprimatur of BRI.[4] Meanwhile, bilateral discussions took place between China and Singapore on the latter's role and contribution to BRI projects in terms of funding and technical expertise.

The expansion of China's interests and presence in the region via BRI-linked projects was, however, not without problems and criticism. Local environmental groups in Cambodia and Laos have expressed concerns over the large-scale hydroprojects spearheaded by Chinese state-owned enterprises, while Prime Minister Najib Razak has had to fend off accusations that he was "selling" Malaysian interests to China. Indeed, China's BRI is arguably potentially most extensive in Malaysia, where it is supporting a variety of port projects, but also a highly-visible, ergo publicly significant, US$12.8 billion East Coast Rail Link from Port Klang through Kuantan to Pengkalan Kubor at the tip of the Thai border with Peninsular Malaysia. Both countries have further committed to spending a combined US$50 billion on BRI infrastructure projects over the next ten years. Opponents have criticized the lack of transparency and oversight of such large projects, yet it also points to the enormous clout China has in Malaysia that they can lead such strategically important projects.[5] Meanwhile, China's extensive interests in hydropower projects has also created diplomatic problems among Southeast Asian states, with Thailand, Cambodia and Vietnam vehemently protesting the expansion of the Laotian hydropower programme on grounds of its potential adverse effect on the flow of the Mekong river.

On the diplomatic and security front, China and ASEAN made progress on a "framework" for a Code of Conduct in the South China Sea. The two-page document was agreed at the meeting of the foreign ministers of ASEAN and China in August. Following the adoption of the "framework" at the 20th ASEAN–China Summit later in November, the leaders agreed to begin negotiations on the Code of Conduct. While optimists see the "framework" as a step towards the holy grail of a legally binding Code of Conduct, it should be noted that the document itself provided no such guarantees.[6] Furthermore, consensus on the "framework" barely veiled the continual challenge that the South China Sea presents for ASEAN unity, and this has come to be expressed in the all-too-familiar internal debates over the contents of statements that follow the conclusion of ASEAN meetings. By that token, criticisms of how ASEAN statements did or did not address the South China Sea issue under Manila's chairmanship in 2017 was notable given the fact that the Philippines is not only one of the claimant states but, more to the point, was the beneficiary of a major international tribunal decision on the South China Sea which ruled in its favour (against China) in July 2016 on a case brought before it by the previous administration under Benigno Aquino III.[7] Having seen ties with the Philippines improve under the presidency of Rodrigo Duterte, China has now turned its attention to Singapore, ASEAN Chair for 2018, and efforts — both oblique and direct — have been made to influence how the ethnic Chinese-majority island-state might shepherd regional discussions on the South China Sea during the course of its chairmanship.[8]

Under Prime Minister Shinzo Abe, Japan has been making a strong play for influence in Southeast Asia as well. Japan has already signed strategic partnerships with key Southeast Asian states such as Vietnam, Indonesia and Malaysia, which tie economic partnerships with maritime security. As the region fretted over the impending inauguration of Donald Trump in January, Prime Minister Abe made a highly significant trip to Southeast Asia that included stops in the Philippines, Vietnam and Indonesia (and Australia) in January. In the Philippines he pledged to provide 1 trillion yen (US$8.7 billion) in aid and investments to the Philippines over five years for the purpose of improving the country's infrastructure.[9] This followed on from the US$1.85 billion of Japanese investment pledged to President Duterte — mostly to develop the automotive industry in the Philippines — on the occasion of his October 2016 trip to Tokyo.[10] In addition, Japan has also pledged to support efforts to improve the defence capabilities of the Philippine Armed Forces. Doubtless with concern over increasing Chinese assertiveness in mind, both leaders also released a joint statement that established their mutual interest in freedom of navigation and the application of international law (via UNCLOS) in the South China Sea. Maritime security featured prominently in Abe's stops in Hanoi and Jakarta as well, as the Japanese prime minister offered to enhance mutual cooperation towards the objective of improving the maritime security capabilities of both states. In Indonesia, President Joko Widodo reiterated an earlier invitation (first made in October 2016) to Japan for it to work on the Jakarta–Surabaya rail project.[11] Abe's visit to Southeast Asia was reciprocated by the visits of several regional leaders to Japan. These included a visit by his Vietnamese counterpart, Nguyen Xuan Phuc, in June that resulted in the signing of several cooperation frameworks to provide for technical assistance and commercial ventures, and by Prime Minister Hun Sen of Cambodia in August, when he sought US$800 million in infrastructure investments, including a sky train project.[12]

Relations with India have in recent years received a boost from Prime Minister Narendra Modi's efforts at making stronger inroads into ASEAN. Against this backdrop it is notable that between Prime Minister Modi, President Pranab Mukherjee and Vice-President Hamid Ansari, Indian leaders have visited all ten ASEAN members, even as India and ASEAN celebrated five years of strategic partnership in 2017. Substantial progress was also made on the bilateral front. In November, a visit by the Defence Minister of Singapore resulted in the conclusion of a new naval agreement aimed at boosting maritime security cooperation, an arena where the Indian Navy has gradually been playing a more active role in recent years. Apart from furthering India's efforts to interact more with Southeast Asian states in the maritime security domain, at the bilateral level this agreement completes the trifecta of defence engagement which began with the 2007 Air Force Bilateral Agreement and 2008 Army Bilateral Agreement. Several months earlier, in July, India announced the provision of financial assistance amounting to $500,000 to the Philippines, to aid Manila in its fight against Islamic State–affiliated terror groups in the troubled Mindanao province.[13] This marked the first time that India dispatched aid to another nation to help it fight terrorism, marking an important development in New Delhi's attempts to burnish its credentials as an emerging security provider in the wider Asian region. India also expressed its concern at the Marawi situation and used this crisis to enhance anti-terror and de-radicalization partnerships with the Philippines. Relations with Vietnam, New Delhi's longstanding strategic partner in Southeast Asia, were also strengthened in 2017 with the designation of that year to be "Friendship Year" between India and Vietnam.

Korean Peninsula

The year 2017 witnessed a marked escalation of the Korean Peninsula crisis as the DPRK regime embarked on a series of nuclear and missile tests, in its search for an intercontinental ballistic missile capability that, when perfected, would place just about every major U.S. city within its range. While peripheral to the resolution of this increasingly intractable conflict, ASEAN was nevertheless still looked to by the conflict parties, including both the United States and the DPRK, to play something of an active role. In April the DPRK appealed to ASEAN to persuade the United States to take a softer stance in order to avert a nuclear holocaust, just as the United States confirmed the THAAD defence system in South Korea was operational. On the other hand, ASEAN foreign ministers were urged to cut ties with and strengthen sanctions on the DPRK by U.S. Secretary of State Rex Tillerson during the ASEAN–U.S. meeting in Washington DC in May.

The collapse of the Six Party Talks in 2009 left the ASEAN-led ASEAN Regional Forum (ARF) as the remaining diplomatic institution that engages all the major actors involved in the Korean Peninsula (apart from UN-related organizations). On 5 August, alongside the ARF, ASEAN foreign ministers issued a rare standalone statement expressing concern over developments in the region. This included a call for "the complete, verifiable, and irreversible denuclearisation of the Korean Peninsula in a peaceful manner".[14] Without outright condemning the DPRK, it noted the threat to peace and urged the DPRK to comply with UN Security Council resolutions. Cambodia was reportedly unhappy with the document that went ahead anyway.[15] The ASEAN defence ministers repeated the call for peace and for the DPRK to comply with Security Council resolutions in their 23 October statement.[16] As the situation worsened, with repeated DPRK tests, ASEAN registered its heightened concerns with collective condemnation of the nuclear and missile tests. Meanwhile, the DPRK's foreign minister, Ri Yong Ho, met four of the other Six Party Talks nations (excluding the United States) at the ASEAN Regional Forum meeting in Manila, just as new UN sanctions were being announced.[17] In return, the United States proposed suspending DPRK membership from the ARF and also urged the Philippines to rescind its invitation to the DPRK before the forum.[18] At the end of August, South Korea held its first Conference on ASEAN–Korea Partnership, where it welcomed ASEAN taking a more proactive role in addressing the crisis.[19]

One of the few countries with an embassy in Pyongyang, Malaysia's relations with the DPRK soured over the murder of Kim Jong-nam, the half-brother of Kim Jong-un, in Kuala Lumpur on 13 February. The murder and subsequent investigations triggered tit-for-tat exchanges between the governments of the DPRK and Malaysia. Following the cancellation of DPRK visas and the expulsion of the DPRK ambassador on 4 March by Malaysia, Pyongyang retaliated by barring Malaysian nationals from entering or leaving the country, which was only resolved on 30 March. Malaysia further banned its citizens from travelling to the DPRK in September, and halted all imports from the DPRK in October.

The Regional Trade Agenda

The withdrawal of the United States from the TPP cast doubt on the future of the regional trade agenda. While Southeast Asia was not collectively represented in the TPP, by dint of the membership of four regional states — Vietnam, Malaysia, Singapore and Brunei — and the prospect of Indonesian and Thai participation in future, the TPP was nevertheless viewed as a major driver of the next cycle of economic growth and prosperity for the region. The TPP was also welcomed for establishing the "gold standard" in free trade agreements, not only in terms of tariff and non-tariff reductions but, significantly, on issues of labour relations and intellectual property rights. The American withdrawal prompted the remaining eleven signatories to scramble to rescue the agreement. In the event, all eleven declared at the sidelines of the November APEC Summit their intention to advance a Comprehensive and Progressive Agreement for Trans-Pacific Partnership, or CPTPP. Essentially a revised TPP according to the joint ministerial statement, the CPTPP nevertheless differed from its predecessor on at least two counts. First, it suspends twenty provisions from chapters primarily dealing with services, procurement, and intellectual property rights that had hitherto been inserted at the insistence of the United States; and, second, it emphasized that members should be allowed to prioritize "country-specific" circumstances and conditions when making trade policy decisions.[20] Significantly, it has also been calculated that Southeast Asian signatories are likely to gain most from the CPTPP — Malaysia (2 per cent of GDP), Vietnam and Brunei (1.5 per cent), and Singapore (1 per cent).[21]

The Regional Comprehensive Partnership (RCEP) for Asia was flagged as a priority deliverable for ASEAN's fiftieth anniversary year. Needless to say the matter of the conclusion of the RCEP gained greater strategic and economic urgency in the wake of the U.S. withdrawal from the TPP and the need to boost waning enthusiasm for free trade globally. With the inclusion of India, China and Indonesia, the RCEP would be the world's most populous free trade agreement, covering roughly half the world's population and over a third of its GDP. The value of RCEP is further attested to by the fact that while ASEAN has "Plus One" trade deals with all the Plus Six countries, these involve different levels of agreement, both qualitatively and quantitatively. Nevertheless, harmonizing these will not be straightforward, especially as several Plus countries continue to be unenthusiastic about opening their markets to the other major economies, particularly India and China (who also lack a free trade agreement between them).

Ministerial level talks were held in May in Hanoi and September in Pasay City, Philippines, while the seventeenth to twentieth negotiating rounds took place in February/March in Kobe, May in Manila, July in Hyderabad, and October in Incheon. The Hyderabad round saw agreement on the *RCEP Key Elements for Significant Outcomes by End of 2017*, that aims to narrow the areas within which agreement can be reached. Nevertheless, ASEAN struggled to meet its target of concluding the agreement in 2017; with differences over the percentage of goods respective countries are willing to liberalize proving to be an especially stubborn stumbling block.[22] Even as negotiations are now carried over into 2018, it is unlikely that agreement and ratification by all sixteen nations can be achieved before 2019; meaning implementation would start from 2020 at the very earliest.[23]

While Southeast Asia made piecemeal progress in economic integration efforts with the broader Asia-Pacific and East Asian regions, intraregional integration proved more difficult. Specifically, efforts to further advance the ASEAN Economic Community (AEC) continued to face a host of obstacles. At the end of 2015, ASEAN declared that the AEC had been "established" according to the timeline set by regional leaders in 2007 with the Cebu Declaration, but the AEC itself had not yet been "realized" because of the need at the time to defer 105 of 506 measures that the organization set for itself as a target for the realization of an AEC.[24] While progress has been made on tariff reductions over the years, policy harmonization across member states and reductions in non-tariff barriers have proven considerably more challenging.

The Rohingya Issue

The year 2017 saw the worsening of one of the most tragic humanitarian crises in recent history. Following insurgent attacks by the Arakan Rohingya Salvation Army (ARSA) on three border police posts in October 2016 in Rakhine State, the Myanmar military waged an intensive (and extensive) operation to weed out militant elements among the estranged Muslim Rohingya community, the consequence of which was a mass exodus of Rohingya across the border to Bangladesh amidst mounting allegations of indiscriminate violence and human rights abuses on the part of Myanmar soldiers.

To be sure, the Rohingya problem is not new. Yet, the recent violence serves as a reminder of just how intractable the problem has become, particularly in terms of how deep-seated animosity between Buddhist and Muslim communities in Myanmar have been amplified, as well as how difficult the search for solutions would be even after transition to a democratically elected government. This last point is worth repeating given the tendency among Western media sources (and some governments) to believe that the problem could be resolved once democracy was simply allowed to flourish. In considering the role that the democratically elected National League for Democracy (NLD) government under Aung San Suu Kyi's leadership can play, it bears recalling that constitutional changes enacted in 2008 effectively place the Tatmadaw (Myanmar military) in charge of all security affairs in Rakhine State, to wit, conflict resolution can only derive from close cooperation between the elected government and the military. To that effect, any move by the civilian government to overtly criticize the military would likely have an adverse effect.

While clearly a domestic issue that bedevils Naypyitaw, the re-ignition of the Rohingya problem also posed challenges for ASEAN. The Rohingya crisis cast a pale shadow over the 30th ASEAN Summit in Manila, and mention of it was noticeably absent from both the formal agenda as well as the twenty-five-page Chairman's Statement. This absence was almost certainly in observance of the organization's principle of non-interference. The Rohingya crisis posed particularly challenging problems for leaders of Muslim-majority countries in Southeast Asia, where popular opinion was vitriolic against Naypyitaw's handling of the humanitarian situation and demands for a robust response on the part of their governments especially vociferous. Indonesia's president, Joko Widodo, and foreign minister, Retno Marsudi, both held talks with Aung San Suu Kyi, highlighting that stability in Myanmar was vital not only for the country itself but also for the region. Malaysia went a step further in its expression of disapproval of the management of the crisis, with Prime Minister Najib Tun Razak equating Myanmar's treatment of the Rohingya to "genocide". On its part, Myanmar responded by alleging Najib was using the Rohingya crisis to further his own political interests.[25] Malaysian foreign minister Anifah Aman expressed concern at the lack of initiative on the part of Myanmar to find a viable solution to the conflict, stating that: "though the Myanmar government has given its assurance to implement measures to solve the problem, the recent incidents of violence as widely reported by the media show that little, if any, progress has been achieved".[26] He also warned that failure to address the problem adequately would cause an influx of refugees to other states within ASEAN and increase the possibility of these displaced individuals being recruited by extremists, negatively affecting the security and stability of the region.

Malaysia's robust position on the Rohingya crisis created something of a crisis for ASEAN in September. On the occasion of the UN General Assembly in New York, a statement was issued by the foreign secretary of the Philippines, Alan Peter Cayetano, in his capacity as ASEAN Chair and purportedly representing the collective views of ASEAN foreign ministers, that they were "concerned over the recent developments in the Northern Rakhine State", and broadly denouncing "all acts of violence which resulted in loss of civilian lives, destruction of homes and displacement of large numbers of people".[27] Malaysia was quick to clarify that the statement issued did not reflect Kuala Lumpur's position on the crisis. Instead, the Malaysian foreign minister proceeded to release a statement declaring that Malaysia would be disassociating itself from the ASEAN Chairman's words for reasons that it did not specifically mention the Rohingya as one of the communities affected by the violence. Despite the fact that both Anifah and Cayetano's statements reproved the ARSA attack on Myanmar's security personnel on 25 August which triggered the recent violent spell in Rakhine state, it was this disagreement that seized the headlines and drew attention once again to the matter of ASEAN's unity, or lack thereof.[28]

The Seige of Marawi City

While terrorism had been a security challenge particularly for the maritime states of Southeast Asia for some years, matters gained greater urgency in 2017 when the risk of ISIS (the Islamic State of Iraq and as-Sham) establishing a foothold in the region found acute expression in the southern Philippines. On 23 May, Muslim militants who claimed affiliation with ISIS swarmed over Marawi City in the main southern Philippine island of Mindanao, easily overrunning police and government forces in the process. Initially led by the Maute Group, a militant organization which had earlier claimed allegiance to ISIS, the militants comprised not only Filipinos but also fighters from Indonesia, Malaysia, Singapore, Yemen and Saudi Arabia. President Duterte swiftly placed the area under martial law, while security officials and media confidently predicted that the siege would be brought to an end by Philippine Independence Day on 12 June.[29] In the event, five months of intensive urban warfare ensued, far longer than Manila had predicted or was prepared for, and the siege was only declared ended on 23 October. Needless to say, the siege has staggered the Philippines and underscored broader concerns that terrorists continue to harbour ambitions to make the southern Philippines an area and base for operations in Southeast Asia. In that respect, the situation in the southern Philippines has become both a cause and a consequence of radicalization across the region.

In mid-July, ASEAN began flying out its ASEAN relief items stored in the hub in Subang (Malaysia) under the ASEAN Coordinating Centre for Humanitarian Assistance on Disaster Management (AHA Centre).[30] The AHA Centre was set up in 2011 in Jakarta to facilitate regional and international collaboration in times of crisis, and included an Emergency Rapid Assessment Team (ERAT) that aimed to provide dozens of rapidly deployable experts to a specific area in times of disaster. The deployment for Marawi was completed with the support of the Malaysian government, which mobilized its military aircraft to expedite the mission. The extent of support from the AHA Centre included more than six hundred tents for families, family kits and three thousand personal hygiene supplies, six hundred kitchen sets and four filtration units for water to cater for the population displaced by the violence.[31] This effort proved a concrete expression of the ASEAN declaration of One ASEAN, One Response, signed last September at the 28th ASEAN Summit to achieve a more effective and cohesive response to disasters. Upon the conclusion of the Marawi siege, the 11th ASEAN Defense Ministers' Meeting (ADMM) saw officials reaffirming their commitment to work together on countering all forms of violent extremism. ASEAN member-states also expressed full support for the Philippines' efforts to address the security and humanitarian situation and acknowledged the need for enhanced regional cooperation.[32]

Assistance did not come only from ASEAN. China immediately rendered assistance by way of almost US$12 million of military equipment in June.[33] In October it delivered heavy equipment to the Department of Public Works and Highways to be used for the major rehabilitation effort of Marawi City.[34] Despite the anti-U.S. rhetoric of President Duterte, American assistance was swiftly extended to — and readily received by — the Philippine government to help counter the militants in Marawi. This included an initial aid package of at least US$13.5 million worth of weapons and equipment dispatched in late May, followed by twenty-five combat rubber raiding craft and thirty outboard motors to assist the Philippine Armed Forces in its counterterrorism efforts. In January, a Raven tactical UAV system was delivered and in July the United States transferred two C-208 Cessna surveillance aircraft to the Philippine Air Force for operations in Marawi. Grey Eagle drones were also supplied, and they proved crucial in the provision of intelligence information necessary for the Philippine military forces to regain control of the city. Further to that, the United States also deployed more than a hundred soldiers to advise and train local troops for the fight against the Muslim extremists in Marawi.[35]

Conclusion

The year 2017 was one of celebration for Southeast Asia as it commemorated the fiftieth anniversary of the formation of ASEAN. But, in many ways, it was also a year of introspection. Shifts in the geopolitical configuration in the region, prompted in no small part by the change in government in the United States, set in motion dynamics that quickly challenged ASEAN in terms of how they threatened to alter the strategic, economic and diplomatic landscape in the region. ASEAN pursued a diversified engagement strategy in response, and this will necessarily be its approach for the foreseeable future in order for the small states in the region to avoid having to choose sides.

Even so, these efforts are likely to come under increasing pressure in the coming years on at least three counts. First, the revival of the Quadrilateral Dialogue featuring the United States, Japan, India and Australia — ironically, as a sideshow to the November ASEAN Summit — suggests impending pressure on ASEAN as it seeks to reinforce its regional role on the notion of ASEAN Centrality. Second, the new strategic focus among these regional powers on the "Indo-Pacific" that accompanies the revival of the "Quad" raises the question of where Southeast

Asia fits into this geopolitical concept, not to mention the geostrategic thinking of its proponents, in terms of priorities. Third, with China having consolidated its domestic politics, it is widely expected that Beijing will now return its attention to pressing its interests in the region more assertively, and this will doubtless have consequences for Southeast Asia. All said, developments in 2017 point to the fact that the coming years will require ASEAN to attend to challenges emanating not only from within the region but also as a result of the centrifugal forces hastened by great power politics taking place in its neighbourhood.

Notes

1. Kevin Liptak and Dan Merica, "Trump Delivers 'America First' Speech at Asia-Pacific Economic Summit", CNN, 10 November 2017 <http://edition.cnn.com/2017/11/10/politics/donald-trump-apec-vietnam-trade/index.html>.
2. Joseph Chinyong Liow, "Is US Engagement back on Track in East Asia?" *Straits Times*, 14 November 2017.
3. U.S. State Department, "Secretary Tillerson Meets with the Foreign Ministers of the Association of Southeast Asian Nations", 4 May 2017 <https://www.state.gov/r/pa/prs/ps/2017/05/270657.htm>.
4. May Kunmakara, "Minister: BRI Great for Economy", *Khmer Times*, 9 November 2017.
5. "Malaysia's Biggest Railway, China's Biggest Coup?" *Nikkei Asian Review*, 9 August 2017 <https://asia.nikkei.com/Politics-Economy/International-Relations/China-begins-works-of-largest-railroad-in-Malaysia?page=2>.
6. Raul Dancel, "Framework of South China Sea Code Skirts Thorny Issues with China", *Straits Times*, 3 August 2017.
7. Paterno Esmaquel II, "ASEAN 2017: A Wasted Opportunity for the West Philippine Sea", *Rappler*, 20 November 2017 <https://www.rappler.com/newsbreak/in-depth/188948-asean-summit-2017-philippines-assessment-south-china-sea>.
8. Greg Torode, "China Leaning on Singapore to Keep ASEAN Calm over South China Sea: Sources", Reuters, 8 August 2017 <https://www.reuters.com/article/us-asean-china-singapore-analysis/china-leaning-on-singapore-to-keep-asean-calm-over-south-china-sea-sources-idUSKBN1AO17D>.
9. Leila B. Salaverria, "Japan Pledges $8.7B in Aid, Investments", *Inquirer.net*, 14 January 2017 <https://globalnation.inquirer.net/151632/japan-pledges-8-7b-aid-investments>.
10. Further deals were secured by President Duterte during his trip to Japan in early November.
11. The significance of this gesture lay in the fact that Japan had earlier lost out to China in its bid for the contract to build the Jakarta–Bandung rail project in 2015, which has since been confronted with several delays and ballooning costs. Heru Asprihanto

and Eveline Danubrata, "Indonesia, Japan Discuss Maritime Security, Railway Project", Reuters, 15 January 2017 <https://www.reuters.com/article/us-indonesia-japan/indonesia-japan-discuss-maritime-security-railway-project-idUSKBN14Z0P9>.

12. "In Japan, Hun Sen Guarantees 'Peace, Security' for Investors", *Cambodia Daily*, 9 August 2017 <https://www.cambodiadaily.com/news/in-japan-hun-sen-guarantees-peace-security-for-investors-133386/>.
13. Indrani Bagchii, "In a First, India Gives Rs.3.2 Crore Aid to Philippines in Fight against ISIS", *Times of India*, 12 July 2017.
14. "Foreign Ministers' Statement on the Developments in the Korean Peninsula", 5 August 2017 <http://asean.org/storage/2017/08/ASEAN-Statement-on-the-Developments-in-the-Korean-Peninsula-FIN-5-Aug-2017.pdf>.
15. "Cambodia Upset over ASEAN Standalone Statement on North Korea", *GMA News Online*, 6 August 2017 <http://www.gmanetwork.com/news/news/nation/620849/cambodia-upset-over-asean-standalone-statement-on-north-korea-diplomat/story/>.
16. "Joint Declaration of the ASEAN Defence Ministers on Partnering for Change, Engaging the World", 23 October 2017 <http://asean.org/storage/2017/10/11th-ADMM-Joint-Declaration-as-of-23-Oct-20172.pdf>.
17. "A Rare Round of Diplomacy from North Korea's Top Diplomat", *New York Times*, 7 August 2017.
18. "US Secretary of State Not Planning to Meet with N. Korean Foreign Minister at ASEAN Regional Forum", *The Hankyoreh*, 4 August 2017 <http://english.hani.co.kr/arti/english_edition/e_northkorea/805563.html>.
19. Richard Heydarian, "Time for ASEAN to Play a Role", *New Straits Times*, 12 October 2017.
20. Pradumna B. Rana and Ji Xianbai, "TPP's Resurrection: Will It Be Finally Ratified?" *RSIS Commentary*, no. 219 (17 November 2017). Rana and Ji suggest that the second difference was "as opposed to the neoliberal thinking and beliefs on free trade and market forces which were embedded in the TPP".
21. Ibid.
22. "ASEAN Economic Ministers Move to Accelerate Trade Talks", *Nikkei Asian Review*, 6 September 2017 <https://asia.nikkei.com/Politics-Economy/International-Relations/ASEAN-economic-ministers-move-to-accelerate-trade-talks>.
23. "RCEP's Strategic Opportunity", *ISEAS Perspective* 2017, no. 76 (16 October 2017) <https://www.iseas.edu.sg/images/pdf/ISEAS_Perspective_2017_76.pdf>.
24. Jayant Menon and Anna Cassandra Menendez, "(Re)realizing the ASEAN Economic Community", *East Asia Forum*, 24 August 2017 <http://www.eastasiaforum.org/2017/08/24/rerealising-the-asean-economic-community/>.
25. "Rohingya Issue: Najib's Remarks Rile Myanmar", *Straits Times*, 21 January 2017.
26. "Wisma Putra Summons Myanmar Ambassador over Crisis in Rakhine State", *The Star*, 5 September 2017.

27. A. Gunanasagaran, "Malaysia Dissociates from ASEAN on Rohingya Crisis", 25 September 2017 <http://www.theaseanpost.com/article/malaysia-dissociates-asean-rohingya-crisis>.
28. Ibid.
29. Mikas Matsuzawa, "End of Marawi Siege Eyed on Independence Day as Maute Further Weakens", *Philippine Star*, 9 June 2017.
30. Prashanth Parameswaran, "ASEAN Deploys Terror Aid to Philippines amid Marawi Crisis", *The Diplomat*, 25 July 2017 <https://thediplomat.com/2017/07/asean-deploys-terror-aid-to-philippines-amid-marawi-crisis/>.
31. Jil M. Caro, "ASEAN Relief Body Donates Equipment for Residents Displaced by Marawi Conflict", *Business World Online*, 22 June 2017 <http://www.bworldonline.com/content.php?section=Nation&title=asean-relief-body-donates-equipment-for-residents-displaced-by-marawi-conflict&id=148629>.
32. Parameswaran, "ASEAN Deploys Terror Aid".
33. "China Gives $16 Million in Weapons to Help Tackle Marawi Siege", *Straits Times*, 29 June 2017.
34. Lou Antonio, "Heavy Equipment from China Turned Over to DPWH to Fast Track Marawi Recovery, Report from the Government of Philippines", 12 October 2017 <https://reliefweb.int/report/philippines/heavy-equipment-china-turned-over-dpwh-fast-track-marawi-recovery>.
35. Ibid.

Brunei Darussalam

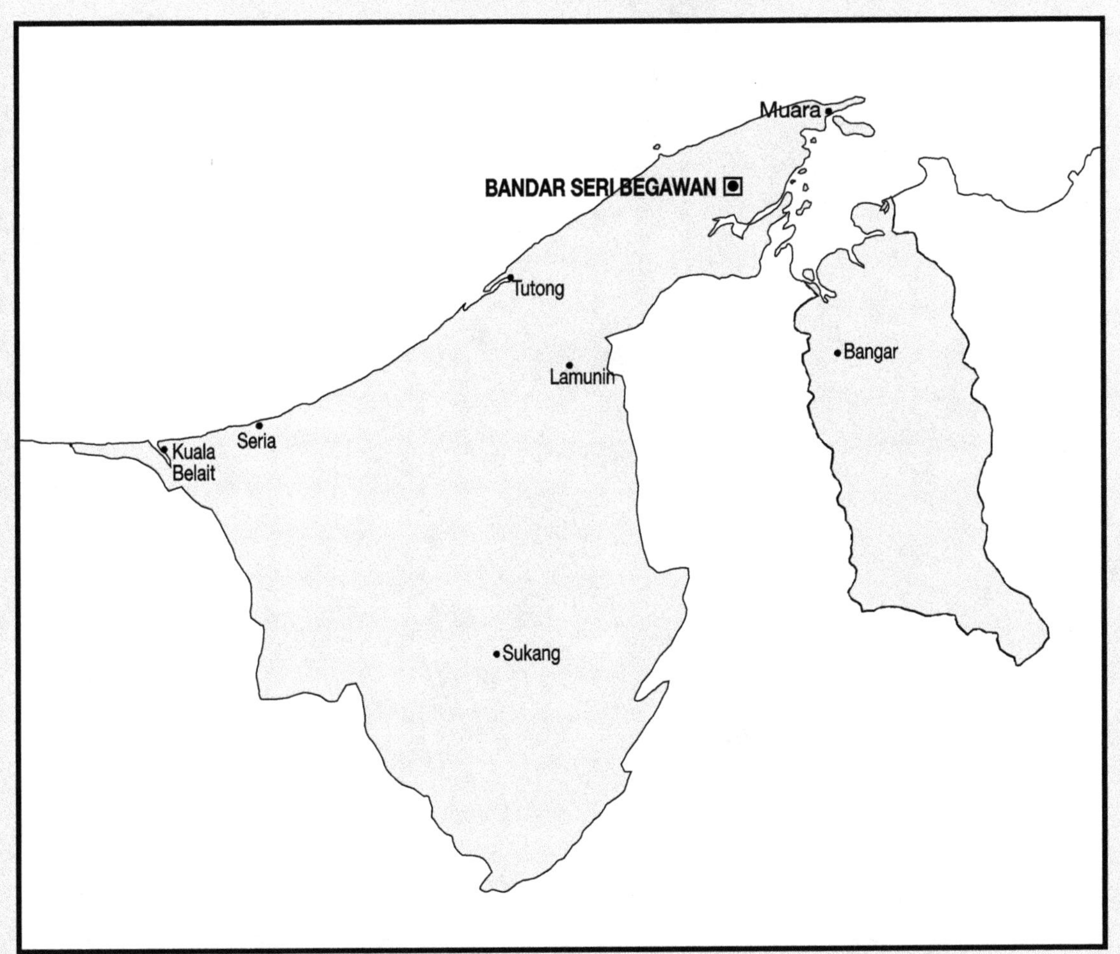

BRUNEI DARUSSALAM: The "Feel-Good Year" Despite Economic Woes

Pushpa Thambipillai

Introduction: Taking Stock

To the outside observer, Brunei may have appeared to be quiet and off the busy track of newsworthy happenings in 2017. However, with the dawn of 2017, residents were reminded of the special year, the fiftieth year of the reign of Sultan Haji Hassanal Bolkiah, who commemorated his ascension to the throne in 1967 on the abdication of his father, the late Sultan Haji Omar Ali Saifuddien. Several events were staged to mark the occasion, organized not only by the government but also by community-based organizations and business groups. The economic recovery that had been projected the previous year did not materialize, as global oil prices were still low. However, prices were slightly higher in 2017 than in 2016, providing some financial relief for the national economy. With a few "cuts" in certain areas of expenditure, the government was still able to offer the usual perks of a "welfare" state. Improving the economic performance was the government's prime concern throughout the year. Although the sultanate did not host any major international meetings, there were opportunities for the exchange of high-level visits, while maintaining its external responsibilities in regional and global affairs.

The pulse of Brunei's socio-political and economic environment can be assessed from the sometime forceful or, at other times, subtle indicators in the Sultan's numerous speeches. A number of *titah* (official speeches or statements

---

Pushpa Thambipillai is Associate Fellow at the ISEAS – Yusuf Ishak Institute. She was formerly a Senior Lecturer at the Faculty of Business, Economics and Policy Studies, Universiti Brunei Darussalam.

of the Sultan) are referred to in this article, which provide an understanding of Brunei in 2017.

The National Economy, Painfully Slow Growth

The sultanate fared only slightly better in 2017 compared to the previous three years; in fact, its economy was the worst performer within ASEAN. Being a small state, with only about 422,600 people,[1] Brunei has enjoyed a high per capita income, sustained by its hydrocarbon resources. However, it has registered a steady decrease since 2013, from a high of B$56,000 to B$37,000 in 2016, though still making it the second wealthiest in ASEAN (US$1≈B$1.35). However, its growth rate has been dismal. Being heavily dependent on its hydrocarbons for 60 per cent of its GDP, for about 90 per cent of its export income, and on the public sector for employment, it has not fared well in boosting its economic growth. Brunei's economy has been largely government driven, including a major stake in the oil and gas industry. Its long-term plan for Vision 2035 (a blueprint for the state's political, economic and social development) foresees the economy being private sector led as a diversified economic environment emerges. From the vantage point of 2017, there appears to be a difficult process ahead, even though government policies and reforms supporting the services and industries sectors are incrementally being introduced.

The effects of the economic slow down have been noticeable in many sectors. According to the Population Census of 2016, although there was an increase in the population, it was as a result of the growth rate of citizens and permanent residents, while the temporary residents' share had declined by an average of 5.8 per cent between 2011 and 2016. "Temporary residents" refers to non-citizens who are legally employment in the public and private sectors. It is evident that there has been an impact on foreign labour across various sectors, including the hydrocarbon industry, which reduced oil production during the price slump period of 2014–16. It also affected the economies of the supply chain in that sector. The construction industry also felt the adverse effect, as government expenditure and allocations for projects were reduced, except for the mega projects already allotted under the Five Year Development Plan 2012–17.[2]

Global oil prices showed an improvement of 10 per cent over the previous year, reaching an average of US$51 per barrel in Q2 (second quarter) of 2017. Prices for liquefied natural gas (LNG) had increased by about 30 per cent, but part of the country's gas exports had been negotiated earlier under fixed terms. The sultanate's crude oil production in 2017 was still below optimum, while LNG production increased. The growth rate for Q2 2017 at constant price (year-on-year) showed a positive rate of 0.7 per cent, while during Q1 2017 it was –1.7 per cent.[3] Slightly higher prices for oil exports in Q2 contributed not only to higher income but also generated greater expenditure, thus lifting the growth rate for that quarter to surpass that of 2016, where it stood at –2.5 per cent. Fortunately, Brunei's inflation rate was low. Besides, the government's support system for essential items like petrol, rice, sugar, housing for civil servants and free health care/education for its citizens was a helpful feature, despite the varying performance of the national economy.

The Sultan, concerned about the slow pace of economic growth, called for efforts to attract more foreign investment, and at the same time urged local business interests to increase their productivity and seek export markets. He advised every ministry and department to encourage the growth of enterprises under their jurisdiction, focusing especially on the non-hydrocarbon sectors.[4]

Budget Allocation, a Reduced Outlay

The 13th Legislative Council, which convened in March 2017, was presented with a reduced national budget for financial year April 2017 to March 2018. The proposed budget of B$5.3 billion was B$300 million lower than the 2016/17 budget of B$5.6 billion. The reduced revenue from oil exports was the main cause for the reduced expenditure. The national income was projected at only B$3.45 billion, the oil and gas sector accounting for about 77 per cent of it. Thus, a budget deficit of B$1.85 billion is expected for the fiscal year.[5]

Some of the high-profile infrastructure projects allocated under the Tenth Development Plan did influence the economy's buoyancy. These included the upgrading of the waterfront areas around the Brunei River and Bandar Seri Begawan (as part of the Bandar Seri Begawan Master Plan), the Sungai Kebun Bridge over the Brunei River, linking the city to Sungai Kebun in Mukim Lumapas (reducing a formerly 60-minute trip to a mere 15 minutes), the ongoing thirty-kilometre Temburong Bridge[6] linking Brunei-Muara to Temburong (enabling travellers to bypass Limbang that divides Brunei in two), completion work on the international airport extension, construction of highways, and a number of educational and training institutions that were either newly built or renovated. On the whole there seemed to be more streamlining of national policies and infrastructure construction stemming from the economic situation.

MSMEs, Economic Drive and Policy Revamp

The structural overhaul of business policies and practices that began in 2016 was continued into 2017, focusing on the local micro and small businesses and potential foreign investment. The Department of Energy and Industry at the Prime Minister's Office (PMO) has become the focal point for introducing reforms in energy (including upstream and downstream activities) and in industrialization targeting MSMEs (micro, small and medium enterprises). While the energy sector has had a longer history in the sultanate, it is the manufacturing sector that has been targeted under economic diversification.

The World Bank study mission to Brunei Darussalam in June 2017 reported improvements in the country's pro-business policies. It recommended the need for "maintaining consistent communication with the private sector".[7] However, the business environment still lagged behind neighbouring states. For instance, for Starting a Business, the overall score was 84, and it earned low rankings for Registering Property, Protecting Minority Interests, and Trading across Borders.[8] The World Bank team's assessment of Brunei saw the country cited in the *Doing Business 2018* report as the most improved economy in the world for the third successive year: Brunei moved up 16 places from the previous year to rank 56th among 190 economies. In fact, since 2014 Brunei had improved by 40 places, from 105th to 56th (in comparison, Singapore ranked 2nd, Malaysia 24th, and Thailand 26th in the latest report).[9]

The *Global Competitive Report 2017–2018* of the World Economic Forum (WEF) also recognized Brunei as the most improved economy in ASEAN, moving to 46th out of 137 economies (an improvement of 12 places from the previous report).[10] The WEF's Global Competitiveness Index measures the facilitation process of foreign direct investment (FDI) into Brunei. Several actors contributed to the improvement, including the Ease of Doing Business Secretariat at the Energy and Industry Department, PMO.[11] The Steering Committee is headed by the Minister of Energy and Industry. The PENGGERAK committee, chaired by Prince Al-Muhtadee Billah, Crown Prince and Senior Minister at the PMO, regularly reviews the progress of reform agendas. Another of these is FAST (FDI Action and Support Centre), whose task is to coordinate various investment-related agencies to facilitate fast-track processes to evaluate and approve projects. A number of task forces have been promoting pro-business plans. For instance, cooperation between government and professional bodies has resulted in revisions to the Building Guidelines, Companies Act and Insolvency Order. And it has not only been the foreign investor who has been feted, but also the local. An innovative body, the six-member Competition Commission of Brunei Darussalam was established in August 2017; it is mandated to promote business competition in Brunei through enforcement of the Competition Order 2015.[12] The order seeks to deter market manipulation and cartels, create a better business environment, lower the cost of doing business, attract more FDI, and improve consumer welfare. It may take a few more years for the results of the various reform policies to be realized.

Cross-border Trade and Investments

Trade

The increase in export volume in 2017 and the slight improvement in the oil prices may contribute positively to the national accounts in 2017. For the first eight months of 2017, both total trade and trade balance increased by about 10 per cent compared to the same period in 2016. The export price of crude oil in August 2017 was US$52 (it was US$47 in August 2016). The export price of LNG had also increased in 2017. Brunei's main export partners were Japan (31 per cent of exports), Malaysia (15 per cent), Australia (11 per cent) and China (8 per cent). Imports were from China (31 per cent), Singapore (18 per cent), Malaysia (14 per cent) and the United States (6 per cent).[13]

Investment

Detailed data on current FDI is not available. The latest published data for 2015 shows a net inflow of only BN$238 million, as there was a considerable outflow from the manufacturing and wholesale/retail sectors. This followed a "good" year when it recorded about BN$900 million of FDI in 2014. Based on media reports on investment activities, there has been an actual inflow as a result of previous years' commitments. A joint venture enterprise, the Muara Port Company, consisting of Darussalam Assets and Guangxi's Beibu Gulf Holding, took over the management of Muara Port in February 2017. The Muara Container Terminal is also expected to become more efficient. An MOU with the Chinese company will result in the construction of a Logistics Park near Muara Port.[14] This will enhance the facilities at the port, thereby attracting further foreign investments; for example, in the development of shipping and other logistical support systems to meet the increased demand in trade.

Over the past three years, China has been the lead foreign investor, with several high-profile infrastructure projects. Hengyi Industries has been constructing the basic infrastructure on Pulau Muara Besar while jetties and a four-lane, 2.7-kilometre bridge linking it to the mainland are being completed. Hengyi's largest commitment for the year is the crude oil refinery and aromatics cracker plant on Muara Besar. Through the implementation agreement (by the joint venture between Hengyi Industries and the Brunei government), Hengyi will commit

US$3.445 billion (Phase I) for the refinery and petrochemical project, which will be completed in the next two years.[15] Once operational, exports of refined products are expected to begin in late 2019.[16] Phase II, with an investment of US$12 billion, will provide for increased crude refining capacity and increased production of paraxylene and ethylene, which will be ready in 2022.[17] Another Chinese enterprise, China Fortune Land Development International, CFLD (Singapore), the Brunei Government, and Darussalam Assets have signed an MOU for the development of a special economic zone utilizing CFLD's expertise in creating a "model of new industry city" to be located at Jerudong. The public–private partnership is expected to stimulate Brunei's knowledge-based economy and contribute to its economic transformation process.[18]

Brunei Fertilizer Industries (BFI) has signed an engineering, procurement and construction agreement to build an ammonia and urea plant with a projected investment of BN$1.8 billion, boosting investments in the downstream gas industry sector. BFI (with the major investment from Turkey) is expected to create about a thousand jobs during the construction phase and another two hundred during the operational phase. The plan will produce fertilizer for export beginning in 2021.[19]

Another joint venture company from Turkey, Western Foods and Packaging Sdn Bhd (WFP), has established a manufacturing plant at the Serasa Industrial Site to produce margarine (from imported palm oil) and other edible products for export. With halal certification from the Brunei Islamic Religious Council, it hopes to fill a niche market amongst Muslim consumers. Other downstream industries producing pastries, biscuits and foodstuffs are also planned. By-products such as chicken feed, soap and detergent are projected for manufacturing at a later date. WFP has contributed to local employment; of the current 75 employees at the margarine plant, 72 are locals; the company's target is 200 employees.[20]

Similar to the Turkish investors in Brunei, Russia has also been amongst the "new" entrants to the Brunei scene, exploring potential business opportunities. In 2017, several Russian delegations representing the IT, oil and gas and food sectors visited the sultanate. One of the results was the signing of letters of intent between BAG Networks (Brunei) with two visiting IT-related companies that will cooperate in Brunei's digital programmes. The Brunei Malay Chamber of Commerce and Industry and the visiting Odinstovo Chamber of Commerce and Industry signed an agreement for partnership in the hydrocarbon and food industries.[21] To facilitate better linkages, Brunei and Russia have agreed for "Mutual Exemption of Visa Requirements for Holders of Ordinary Passports", which allows for visits of up to fourteens days[22] (Bruneians enjoy visa-free travel to major partner countries like the United States, United Kingdom, Japan and China). Other multi-sector investments were from long-standing partner Japan, while Singapore and Taiwan invested in the emerging agro-food and services industries.

An investment abroad from Brunei is the UBD-FPT Global Centre in Da Nang, Vietnam, officially inaugurated in November 2017 by the Sultan as Chancellor of Universiti Brunei Darussalam (UBD) during his APEC summit visit. It represents the first UBD campus outside the country, and the first overseas campus established in Vietnam by an ASEAN university.[23] Since 2012, UBD has cooperated with FPT University, a private IT-oriented institution with three campuses and several branches in foreign countries.[24] Instructors from UBD will teach English language courses in the Vietnamese campus. In addition, there will be exchanges of staff and students from various Brunei institutions.

Tourism

In addition to the establishment of halal food industries, pharmaceutical manufacturing and e-commerce, the local economy has also seen an improvement in the tourism sector. The in-bound market has expanded to include more travellers from Malaysia and other ASEAN countries, China and some from as far away as Russia. However, it still lacks product variety and the professionalism of services compared to neighbours like Sabah and Sarawak. Tourism as a potential source of revenue is being considered within the limits of its MIB-oriented (Melayu Islam Beraja, or Malay Islamic Monarchy) national culture.

The establishment of the Ministry of Primary Resources and Tourism (under a restructuring of the cabinet in 2015) had provided a dedicated department to plan and implement tourist-related policies. In Q2 2017 there were 65,747 arrivals by air (a 25 per cent increase year-on-year from Q2 2016) and 1,026,769 by land and cruise ships. Due to its proximity, the largest source of visitors was Malaysia (22 per cent), followed by China (16 per cent), Indonesia, the Philippines and Singapore (25 per cent). Improved connectivity by the national carrier and other air linkages, the increasing popularity of the "half-day stopover" by cruise ships, and excitement around the special year of 2017 have all had a positive impact on tourism. With the possibility of global economic recovery, the prospects seem brighter for Brunei's tourism industry.[25] Brunei is also a source for outbound tourists, who command a high level of purchasing power. Popular destinations are Malaysia, Singapore and Jeddah, which offers *haj* and *umrah* visits to Islam's holy sites. Bruneians form the fifth-largest group of visitors to Malaysia.[26] The Pan Borneo Highway that aims to link Sarawak and Sabah is under construction in Sarawak. Whether Brunei will be directly linked to the highway has yet to be decided; nevertheless, the highway linking the two Malaysian states will inevitably see benefits for Brunei in terms of trade and tourism in the future.

Socio-Political Environment: Riding the Wave

Golden Jubilee

The "hype" had been built up since early in the year for the fifty-year celebrations of the Sultan's ascension to the throne. The usual gaiety of the national day celebrations in February and the monarch's birthday in July were eclipsed somewhat by the grand expectations for October 2017. The thousands of residents who had been anticipating the "mother of all celebrations" were not disappointed by the packed two weeks of intense festivity. The bulk of expenditure for the events came from the government; however, business groups and individuals also contributed. The various gatherings also provided ample opportunities for public expressions of loyalty to the monarch, who often participated with his royal entourage.

In a *titah* during the Royal Audience Ceremony at the palace prior to the Golden Jubilee Royal Procession in the capital on 5 October, Sultan Haji Hassanal Bolkiah extolled the "close ties between the sovereign and the people, with no boundaries in between" and declared "my history is also the history of the people and the nation". He referred to the mutual obligation that "a sovereign is obliged to rule with fairness while the people are obliged to show their loyalty in return.... The sovereign is responsible for solving the problems of his people, while the people are obliged to be responsive towards their sovereign."[27] On the same occasion, the Crown Prince, in a moving speech, paid tribute to his father, stating that "the people are enjoying high standards of living, as a result of the developments personally made by my father through the government".[28] On behalf of all, the Prince pledged undivided loyalty and support to the Sultan.

Related to the celebrations was the official opening of the Sungai Kebun Bridge linking Bandar Seri Begawan across the Brunei River to the water village of Sungai Kebun and beyond to Lumapas. Amidst a procession of decorated boats and fireworks, the Sultan opened the 0.75-kilometre Raja Isteri Pengiran Anak Hajah Saleha Bridge, named after his wife. Built at a cost of B$139 million, it reduces travel time between Lumapas and the capital, and is expected to spur socio-economic activities in the surrounding areas. The traditional small-boat operators are still available as a mode of transportation to other destinations in the water villages.

The recently completed waterfront project was another infrastructure project officially designated for a meet-and-greet-the-Sultan session. The Sungai Kedayan

Eco Corridor was completed under the Tenth National Development Plan. About eight old villages bordering Sungai Kedayan had to make way for the landscaped area adjacent to the picturesque Omar Ali Saifuddien Mosque. The park was named Taman Mahkota Jubli Emas in recognition of the celebrations and the personal involvement of the Crown Prince in this iconic symbol of modern development which promotes the cultural identity of the city.[29] Bandar Seri Begawan has not performed well on the 2017 Economist Intelligence Unit's Global Liveability Ranking, attaining 100th position out of the 140 cities ranked as most liveable.[30] It may rank better in subsequent rankings, given the recent construction of new infrastructural and leisure outlets.

Administration

State administration was "business as usual" throughout the year. There were regular reminders by the leadership of economic adjustments to be made in response to changes in the domestic and global economy. Political stability, terrorism, commitment to the prescribed religious norms and strengthening of the MIB ideology were often the focus of speeches and meetings.

Despite the attention given to the success of the jubilee year, other domestic issues were also addressed. New members were appointed to the thirty-three member Legislative Council (LegCo) to replace the previous one that was dissolved in August 2016. While the Ex-Officio Members (Prime Minister and Ministers) remained the same as in the previous year, there were changes in the appointed list of members, notably in the category of "titled persons", "persons who have achieved distinction" and the district representatives.[31] The persons of distinction included one Chinese member (as in the previous assembly) and three women. Noteworthy was the appointment of three young leaders active in business (a member of the APEC Business Advisory Council, the environment (the founder of Green Brunei), and societal issues (the president of the Brunei Aids Council), adding weight to relevant issues of interest to the younger generation. Brunei's LegCo is a fairly new institution (reinstituted in 2004) and operates within the hereditary monarchical system; it is, thus, not the venue for controversial debate. Its main mission is to disseminate the national budget and review the various ministries' proposed programmes and expenditure. The Sultan, as is the practice, delivered his address at the opening of the 13th Assembly on 6 March 2017, providing an overview of various policy initiatives in the socio-economic development of the state.[32] During the last two years, the speaker of the LegCo has enlivened and highlighted the role of the assembly, in order that it not be forgotten once the assembly session ends. As a high-ranking official, the speaker is actively engaged in meeting local and foreign visitors who call on him.

The annual Civil Service Day, which often extols various public sector agencies and their service programmes, was witness this year to some oblique rebukes from the chief guest. The Sultan referred to the "good civil servant" as an honest and trustworthy person, not someone who misused authority for personal interests or to slander others.[33] He repeated the theme on another occasion, reminding those entrusted with rank or authority not to abuse it or oppress others.[34] It left observers wondering about the cause and the target of his comments. The Prime Minister's Office announced a minor cabinet change, effective 1 December 2017. The serving Minister of Health was replaced. There were also transfers or dismissals of a few senior civil servants. This was the first cabinet reshuffle since 2015.[35]

Brunei Darussalam's Islamic faith is based on the teachings according to *Ahli Sunnah Wal Jama'ah*, as prescribed in the state constitution. Speaking at the Knowledge Convention 2017, the monarch warned that action would be taken against those who spread distorted views on Islamic practices. He mulled the idea of setting up legal procedures to block the opinions of those who questioned certain established practices.[36] He again made similar observations during his broadcast to the nation on the eve of Maulud Nabi.[37]

Security

Unity and stability was at the forefront of the administration's concern, even though the general public did not feel any disruptive effects in their daily lives. It was reported that four Indonesian nationals were deported for "terror links", including possession of materials on IS (the so-called Islamic State) and, in one case, having direct contact with an IS member overseas.[38] In the meantime the police and armed forces continued their duties in providing essential safeguards to the state and its peoples. With carefully crafted defence diplomacy, ASEAN's smallest armed forces (Royal Brunei Armed Forces – RBAF) has not only built up close ties with its friendly partners, it has also played an important part in the fast-track development of the RBAF itself, undertaken by the revamped Defence Academy and Training Institute. The RBAF has also become a most visible presence in cases of natural disaster and in search and rescue operations.[39]

As part of cooperation with external partners, the Royal Brunei Navy ship KDB *Daruttaqwa* participated in the "First ASEAN Maritime National Exercise" in Pattaya Bay, Thailand with ships from the Thai navy and twenty-four other navies. The exercise was held in conjunction with the ASEAN International Fleet Review

2017 to commemorate ASEAN's fiftieth anniversary.[40] Brunei is also a member of the Information Fusion Centre hosted by the Singapore Navy at the Regional Maritime Security (MARSEC) Centre, which supports the regular exchange of information.[41] As part of the longstanding Brunei–U.S. defence partnership, the 23rd Cooperation Afloat Readiness and Training exercise (CARAT) saw the participation of the RBAF and about a hundred U.S. sailors over a five-day training stint.[42]

External Ties

Policy Areas

The foreign affairs team of the Sultan — as the Minister of Foreign Affairs and Trade — and the Minister of Foreign Affairs and Trade II have promoted the essential external commitments throughout 2017. Participation at the United Nations, OIC (Organisation of Islamic Cooperation), APEC and ASEAN were, as usual, given priority. The Sultan has never missed a summit of APEC, ASEAN or the East Asia Summit. In 2017 he had several opportunities to interact with other regional and dialogue partner leaders. Celebrations of ASEAN's 50th year entailed participating in the various meetings and summits hosted by the Philippines. Regional integration, including at the sub-regional level of BIMP-EAGA (Brunei Indonesia Malaysia Philippines – East ASEAN Growth Area), were promoted.

In keeping with its commitment, Brunei has continued to send its personnel to join the International Monitoring Team in Mindanao. To date, thirteen missions have completed their tours of duty since operations began in 2004, made up of 144 RBAF and 8 RBPF (Royal Brunei Police Force) personnel.[43] On another front, a replacement team of 30 RBAF peacekeeping personnel assumed its duties in Lebanon under UNIFIL (UN Interim Force in Lebanon). Brunei forces there have been operating with the Malaysian Battalion under a special embedding arrangement.[44] The two external attachments provide invaluable exposure for Brunei military personnel.

At the UN and OIC, Brunei delegates spoke out against terrorism and violence. The Ministry of Foreign Affairs and Trade issued a short "Statement on the Humanitarian Situation in Rakhine State", stating that it was concerned over the humanitarian situation there and was willing to work with Myanmar to explore ways for Brunei Darussalam to provide humanitarian assistance and that Brunei Darussalam was prepared to offer financial assistance to alleviate the situation of those affected.[45] At a specially convened OIC leaders' meeting in Istanbul in mid-December following President Trump's announcement that the United States would move its embassy from Tel Aviv to Jerusalem, the Sultan joined other leaders in expressing opposition to the move. The Sultan called for a negotiated settlement of the Jerusalem and Palestine issue, and reiterated Brunei's support for existing UN resolutions on the matter.[46]

Bilateral Relations

In recognition of the Philippines being ASEAN Chair during ASEAN's fiftieth anniversary and of it hosting the special summit, the Sultan paid a state visit to the country. The visit focused on Brunei–Philippine socio-economic and security relations. President Rodrigo Duterte expressed his appreciation of Brunei's role in the decades-long Mindanao peace process between the government of the Philippines and the Moro Islamic Liberation Front. It has also been people-to-people relationships throughout the past decades that have laid the strong foundation in ties; the Sultan was appreciative of the more than 23,000 Filipino nationals contributing to Brunei's development.[47]

The Sultan's state visit to China followed his officiating at the China ASEAN Expo (CAEXPO) in Nanning, where Brunei was accorded the "Country of Honour" for 2017. Following his keynote address, the Sultan interacted with leading business personnel from China. The 14th CAEXPO celebrating ASEAN's 50th anniversary attracted the largest Brunei delegation ever, comprising 119 local companies. Several senior ministers and leading public/private sector officials were also in attendance to promote the sultanate's products and services and to seek new links. In Beijing, the Sultan and President Xi Jinping witnessed the signing of a number of MOUs promoting cooperation in infrastructure construction, defence, health, and in jointly promoting cooperation in the Maritime Silk Road Initiative.[48] Observers often point out that Brunei is one of the aggrieved parties in the expanding maritime claims of China in the South China Sea. China's actions have so far not encroached on to Brunei's maritime territory, though there could be tension in the future. Brunei's leadership insists on "quiet diplomacy"; the government is characteristically non-confrontational and has supported ASEAN's approach of a negotiated Code of Conduct to address the multiple claims in the South China Sea.

Another close partner is Singapore, with which there were several occasions in 2017 for strengthening ties. The Golden Jubilee of the currency interchangeability pact between the two countries (in effect since June 1967) was celebrated in Singapore during a state visit by Sultan Hassanal Bolkiah in July 2017. A special edition fifty dollar note for both countries was issued. The Sultan and Prime Minister Lee Hsien Loong also opened an exhibition titled "Abode of Peace and the Lion City: A Brunei–Singapore Exhibition" at the Singapore Philatelic Museum, organized by curators of agencies from the two states. It showcased items from Brunei's royal regalia, material from the museum department, philatelic items, currency notes and coins from both countries.[49] The exhibition continues till February 2018, while a second part of the exhibition focusing on Singapore runs in Brunei from November 2017 till April 2018.[50] The currency agreement (among others) and frequent exchange of visits at various echelons of the government and non-government sectors have sustained the trust and opportunities for investment, trade and cooperation in several areas. On a visit to the sultanate in October 2017 for the anniversary celebrations of the Sultan's accession to the throne, Prime Minister Lee took the opportunity for a "jungle visit" to meet up with Singapore Armed Forces personnel on training in Temburong, one of the features of the long-established Brunei–Singapore military relations.

With Malaysia, Brunei has strong socio-economic and security relations. Cooperation in combatting terrorism and drug trafficking has continued, and military personnel from the two nations have working relations under the UNIFIL and IMT. Brunei's Deputy Minister of Defence was an observer at the signing of the Trilateral Cooperation Agreement between Indonesia, Malaysia and the Philippines on joint maritime and air patrols in the Sulu Sea to combat piracy and militancy in the area.[51] There are also regular contacts between members of the royalty from both countries. The Brunei royalty was at the wedding of the Sultan of Johor's daughter and at the Southeast Asia Games in Kuala Lumpur, where members of the royalty participated in the equestrian and polo matches. Some of the Malaysian royalty and government leaders have visited Brunei during the Sultan's birthday and golden jubilee celebrations. Prime Minister Najib Razak visited Brunei for the 21st Annual Leaders' Consultation. They reviewed, among other things, cooperation under way between PETRONAS and PetroleumBRUNEI, ongoing demarcation of land borders and issues related to the Pan Borneo Highway.[52] There is no indication, yet, whether the highway will connect through Brunei or will bypass it.

One of the more visible "new" partner countries for Brunei is Russia. Several delegations from Russia visited Brunei, exploring cooperation in the economic, military and education sectors. The two leading universities in Brunei — Universiti Brunei Darussalam and Universiti Islam Sultan Sharif Ali — have signed agreements with St Petersburg University and Moscow Islamic Institute, respectively, for academic cooperation and student–staff exchange. The first Brunei student under a Russian scholarship embarked on a Masters in Business Management at the Higher School of Economics in Moscow.[53] Brunei and Russia also signed an MOU in military cooperation during a visit to Moscow by Brunei's Deputy Minister of Defence and a delegation to attend the Sixth Moscow Conference on International Security organized by Russia's Ministry of Defence. Earlier in May 2016 Brunei and Russia had signed an MOU on military-technical cooperation at Sochi during the ASEAN–Russia Summit.[54] The Russian Navy from the Pacific Fleet visited Brunei in October 2017 during the Jubilee celebrations. The recently concluded visa-free travel arrangements between Brunei and Russia is expected to encourage more exchanges between the two countries[55] and more Russian tourists visiting Brunei.

Other bilateral interactions included the visit of King Salman of Saudi Arabia, the first Saudi ruler to visit the sultanate (although two decades earlier he had visited as the Governor of Riyadh). The King was on a two-week visit through Asia, and Brunei was accorded a day's stopover. Brunei and Saudi Arabia have a long historical relationship. This relationship is continually strengthened through education, tourism and religious pilgrimage of Bruneians to Islam's holy sites. Another notable visitor was the United Kingdom's Prince Charles, who arrived with Camilla, Duchess of Cornwall in Brunei in early November as part of their extended trip though Southeast Asia and India. The couple's itinerary included meetings with the Sultan (on a belated Golden Jubilee call) and a visit to the British Garrison in Seria.

Conclusion

Brunei successfully concluded a busy year in its political history, celebrating the fiftieth anniversary of the reign of Sultan Haji Hassanal Bolkiah, currently one of the world's longest-serving monarchs. The sultanate hosted one of the grandest celebrations, with the participation of residents and a number of foreign leaders and tourists. The economy was still teetering, due to the low returns on oil, its major export. Foreign investment has slowly been moving in due to opportunities afforded in the construction of infrastructure and niche industries in the halal sector. There is optimism that 2018 will be economically more promising for Brunei as oil prices are predicted to rise. And there have been encouraging indications that young Bruneians are pursuing self-employment and venturing into businesses rather than being dependent on the public sector. There has also been a marked increase in social entrepreneurship among the youth. Education and training were being adapted to meet employers' expectations for new skills.

The Golden Jubilee celebrations also helped to promote greater solidarity in upholding the national MIB ideology. Numerous religious activities ensured that the country stayed close to its Islamic identity, one which is zealously guarded against alternative interpretations. As head of the religion in the state, the Sultan's numerous *titah* often included religious inspiration. He has reminded his subjects that "there is no other priceless blessing than enjoying peace, stability and unity. Hence all must pray to Allah the Almighty for such blessings to be everlasting and continue to flourish."[56] As the Abode of Peace, on the external front, too, Brunei upheld its peaceful and obligatory responsibilities as a member of the international community.

Notes

1. A Population and Housing Census was conducted between May and September 2016 to update information obtained by the 2011 Census. In 2017 the Department of Economic Planning and Development of the Prime Minister's Office released the *Preliminary Report, Population and Housing Census Update 2016*. The population had increased from 393,372 to 422,678 between 2011 and 2016. The report showed an annual growth rate of 1.4 per cent; lower than the 1.7 per cent rate registered during 2001–11.
2. The Minister of Development alluded to the slowdown in his speech at the annual meeting of PUJA.
3. Department of Economic Planning and Development, Prime Minister's Office, Brunei Darussalam, "Gross Domestic Product, Second Quarter 2017" <http://www.depd.gov.bn>. See, also, Asian Development Bank, *Asian Development Outlook 2017 Update* <http://www.adb.org> (Manila: ADB, 2017).
4. See the Sultan's *titah* on the occasion of his seventy-first birthday, *Borneo Bulletin*, 16 July 2017.
5. *Borneo Bulletin*, 8 March 2017. The budget is about 5.4 per cent lower than that of the previous year.
6. Considered the longest in Borneo, when completed the Temburong bridge will stretch over thirty kilometres, including portions over the land at both ends and spanning the inner Brunei Bay area. Several companies have been assigned various aspects of this major project. See <http://www.xinhuanet.com/2017-04-20> for "aerial pictures of the construction area of China's Temburong Bridge Project in Brunei".
7. See the World Bank team's comments to the media: *Borneo Bulletin*, 2 July 2017.
8. Detailed information is provided in *Doing Business 2018: Reforming to Create Jobs* <http://www.doingbusiness.org/reports/global-reports/doing-business-2018>. The Brunei country tables are available on page 75 of the report. The previous year's ranking is available in "Economy Profile: 2017 Brunei Darussalam", in *Doing Business 2017: Equal Opportunity for All* (Washington, DC: World Bank, 2017).
9. <http://www.worldbank.org>.

10. <http://www.wef.org>.
11. The Ease of Doing Business Steering Committee and the Energy and Industry Department of the Prime Minister's Office held a three-day workshop in September 2017 to consider reform options to improve business practices of SMEs. *Borneo Bulletin*, 29 September 2017.
12. See PMO News, 5 August 2017 <http://www.pmo.gov.bn>. Details on the Competition Order 2015 are available at <http://www.depd.gov.bn>.
13. "Brunei Darussalam International Merchandise Trade Statistics, August 2017" <http://www.depd.gov.bn>.
14. There is no information on the percentage share of investment by Guangxi Beibu and Darussalm Assets in the Muara Port Company. It can be assumed that Beibu will have a large financial and managerial input in the company. For further information on Darussalam Assets, see <http://www.da.com.bn>.
15. The implementation agreement was signed between Hengyi Industries Sdn Bhd, the Energy and Industry Department at the Prime Minister's Office, and the Brunei Economic Development Board. See *Borneo Bulletin*, 28 March 2017.
16. Hengyi Industries International Pte Ltd, based in Singapore, was established in October 2017 to facilitate the sourcing of raw materials and other commercial support activities for Hengyi's operations in Muara Besar. See *Borneo Bulletin*, 17 October 2017.
17. The agreements with the Chinese companies were signed in Nanning after the state visit of the Sultan to China where he met with President Xi Jinping in Beijing in September 2017. See Azaraimy HH, "Brunei Companies Ink Five Key Agreements with Chinese Firms". *Borneo Bulletin*, 16 September 2017. The Sultan also visited The China–ASEAN Expo (CAEXPO), held in Nanning, 12–15 September 2017.
18. *Borneo Bulletin*, 4 May 2017.
19. *Borneo Bulletin*, 27 August 2017.
20. See Danial Norjidi, "Prince Opens Joint Venture Margarine Plant", *Borneo Bulletin*, 19 November 2017, and other related news items from the *Bulletin*.
21. *Borneo Bulletin*, 3 August 2017 and 4 August 2017.
22. The agreement was signed on 8 November 2017 on the sidelines of the APEC Summit in Vietnam. Russia was represented by its Foreign Minister Sergey Lavrov and Brunei by Pehin Lim Jock Seng, Minister at the Prime Minister's Office and Minister of Foreign Affairs and Trade II.
23. See *Borneo Bulletin*, 11 November 2017 for further details.
24. FPT University is a private information technology university established in 2006 by the FPT Group, or the Corporation for Financing and Promoting Technology.
25. Further information is available from the Tourism Development Department, Ministry of Primary Resources and Tourism.
26. According to the Malaysian High Commissioner to Brunei Darussalam, the number of Brunei visitors to Malaysia is expected to reach at least 1.5 million by the end

of 2017; in 2016 it recorded 1.4 million. See *New Straits Times*, 22 November 2017.

27. *Borneo Bulletin*, 6 October 2017.
28. Ibid.
29. Rokiah Mahmud, "A Beacon of Bandar's Revitalisation", *Borneo Bulletin*, 24 October 2017; Hakim Hayat, "His Majesty Launches Taman Mahkota Jubilee Emas", *Borneo Bulletin*, 24 October 2017. The displaced villagers from 168 water village houses, comprising 563 residents, were relocated to new housing schemes elsewhere in Kampong Ayer before the start of the Eco Corridor project.
30. *Borneo Bulletin*, 19 August 2017. The consolation was that it ranked third in Southeast Asia after Singapore and Kuala Lumpur, which were in the top league.
31. Detailed information is available at <http://www.pmo.gov.bn>.
32. "Titah KDYMM *Sempena Majlis Pembukaan Rasmi Mesyuarat ... Ketiga Belas...*, 6 March 2017". From <http://www.pmo.gov.bn/titah>.
33. The Sultan's *titah* at the 24th Civil Service Day. See <http://www.rtbnews.rtb.gov.bn> 22 November 2017.
34. The Sultan's *titah* on the occasion of Prophet Muhammad's birthday celebrations, broadcast over Radio Television Brunei <http://www.rtbnews.rtb.gov.bn> 30 November 2017.
35. <http://www.rtbnews.rtb.gov.bn> 29 November 2017. In a surprise move, Sultan Haji Hassanal Bolkiah announced a major reshuffle to the cabinet and list of deputy ministers on 30 January 2018. The Sultan retained his portfolio as Prime Minister, Minister of Defense, Minister of Finance, Minister of Foreign Affairs and Trade, while the Crown Prince remained as Senior Minister in the Prime Minister's Office. A number of senior ministers, including those in the Finance, Foreign, Energy and Industry, Education and Communications ministries were replaced. Of significance was the reappointment of the Special Adviser to His Majesty (who had left the cabinet a few years earlier), who will also be a minister in the Prime Minister's Office, and the reappointed Minister for Energy and Industry, who had served several years earlier. Source <http://www.rtbnews.rtb.gov.bn> 30 January 2018.
36. Azlan Othman, "Distorted Views on Islamic Practices Must be Stopped", *Borneo Bulletin*, 3 November 2017.
37. <http://www.rtbnews.rtb.gov.bn> 30 November 2017.
38. *Borneo Bulletin*, 7 April 2017. The operation against the suspects was conducted earlier in February.
39. Certain new policies for the Officer Cadet School as well as cooperation with other domestic and foreign institutions were proposed by the Sultan during the Sovereign's Parade ceremony in September 2017. He reminded the graduates of various sacrifice that would need to be made to ensure the nation's strong resilience. *Borneo Bulletin*, 1 September 2017.
40. *Borneo Bulletin*, 22 November 2017.

41. For further information on MARSEC, see <http://www.mindef.gov.sg>.
42. Further details are available in *Borneo Bulletin*, 7 November 2017.
43. *Borneo Bulletin*, 16 September 2017.
44. *Borneo Bulletin*, 29 August 2017.
45. "Statement on the Humanitarian Situation in Rakhine State", 14 September 2017 <http://www.mofat.gov.bn/Lists/PressRoom/news>.
46. *Borneo Bulletin*, 14 December 2017.
47. "Joint Statement between the Republic of the Philippines and Brunei Darussalam on the State Visit of His Majesty Sultan Haji Hassanal Bolkiah Mu'izzaddin Waddaulah, Sultan and Yang Di-Pertuan of Brunei Darussalam to the Republic of the Philippines", 27 April 2017 <http://www.mofat.gov.bn/Lists/PressRoom/news>.
48. The Sultan's state visit to China was from 12 to 14 September 2017. See *Borneo Bulletin*, 13–14 September 2017.
49. *Straits Times*, 6 July 2017.
50. "The Abode of Peace and the Lion City: A Brunei–Singapore Exhibition" was launched in Bandar Seri Begawan by Prince Haji Al-Muhtadee Billah together with Singapore's visiting Deputy Prime Minister Teo Chee Hean. See *Borneo Bulletin*, 6 November 2017. DPM Teo led a team of younger political leaders to Brunei for a four-day working visit, the fifth in the Young Leaders Programme that began in 2013 and includes an annual exchange of visits hosted in turn by the two states. See *Straits Times*, 3 November 2017.
51. *Borneo Bulletin*, 20 June 2017.
52. "Joint Statement on the 21st Annual Leaders' Consultation", 23 November 2017 <http://www.mofat.gov.bn/Lists/PressRoom/news>.
53. See *Borneo Bulletin*, 26 April 2017, 19 September 2017 and 7 November 2017.
54. *Borneo Bulletin*, 28 April 2017.
55. *Borneo Bulletin*, 19 November 2017.
56. "Titah KDYMM Smperna Hari Ulang Tahun Keputeraan", 15 July 2017 <http://www.pmo.gov.bn>; Azlan Othman, "Boosting FDI, SMEs Key Growth Strategy: Sultan", *Borneo Bulletin*, 16 July 2017.

Cambodia

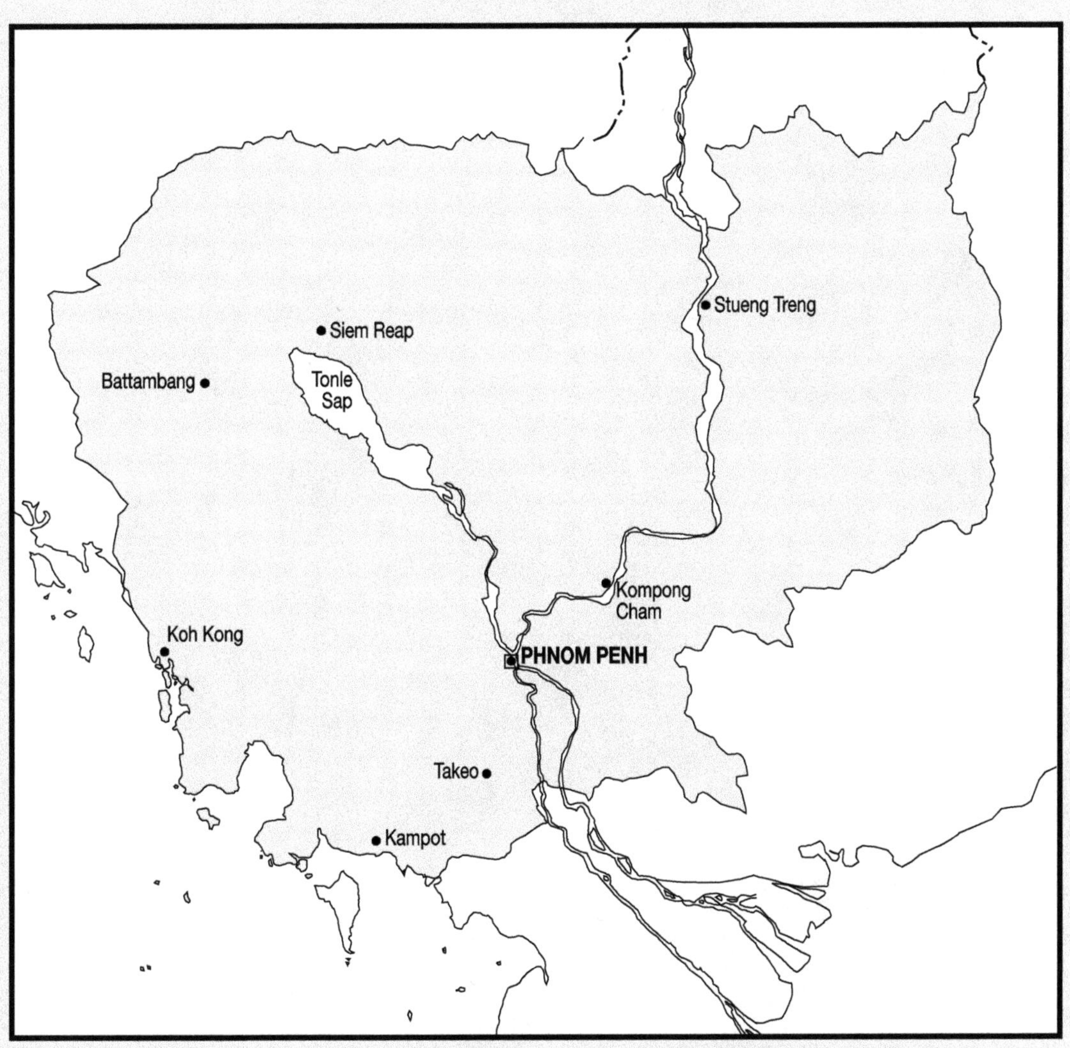
Stueng Treng
Siem Reap
Battambang
Tonle Sap
Kompong Cham
Koh Kong
PHNOM PENH
Takeo
Kampot

CAMBODIA 2017:
Plus ça change...

Khatharya Um

While election years in Cambodia are always eventful, 2017 proved to be even more so than expected. While the months leading to the June commune elections brought the customary machinations and jitters, it was the post-election developments that dashed whatever hope for political change may have been engendered by the results of the last two elections. As the ruling Cambodian People's Party (CPP) moved to consolidate its power in anticipation of the forthcoming elections in 2018, the country spiralled away from whatever measure of political openness may have been achieved in recent years. While election-related violence is not unprecedented, as forecast in the frequent references to "colour revolution" and imminent eruption of "social chaos", the crackdown against regime opponents in the months following the June elections was wholesale and decisive. The consequences affect not only the upcoming 2018 elections but potentially the next electoral cycle as well. The hoped-for democratic transition into which the international community had poured massive financial and political investment over the last quarter of a century appears more elusive than ever.

Still smarting from its precarious win in the 2013 elections, the CPP was confronted with yet another disconcerting outcome in the 2017 commune elections. Despite the ruling party's efforts to turn the political tide, the Cambodian National Rescue Party (CNRP) successfully secured 5,007 council seats (to the CPP's 6,503) and 489 out of the 1,646 commune chief seats, a tenfold increase from their win in the 2012 elections. Though short of the 60 per cent that the party had projected, the CNRP did secure 44 per cent of the vote, compared to the CPP's 51 per cent. This narrowing margin is significant because it reveals not

---

KHATHARYA UM is a political scientist, Associate Professor and Chair of Asian American and Asian Diaspora Studies at the University of California, Berkeley.

only a wide base of support for the opposition in urban centres but, even more significantly, an erosion of the CPP's political control in rural areas that have been the party's traditional base, where the majority of Cambodians live and where the ruling party has long-established political infrastructure. At 85 per cent of registered voters, voter turnout was impressively high, an indicator of popular optimism about the prospect of change, bolstered in no small part by the earlier performance of the opposition party, despite the preponderant power and repressive grip of the CPP.

These shifting terrains are not lost on the CPP. While transgressions against civil society and fundamental freedoms, particularly of expression and assembly,[1] have been unrelenting, the violent measures taken by the ruling party against its political opponents reached a new height in the months surrounding the June elections. Arrests and imprisonment of activists and members of the CNRP, many charged with participating in the 2014 popular demonstration that the government has labelled an "insurrection", preceded the commune elections in June. The systematic attack escalated after the elections, spurred no doubt by the CNRP's notable performance at the polls, culminating in the late-night arrest and imprisonment of Kem Sokha, head of the CNRP, on 3 September 2017, in disregard of his parliamentary immunity. Citing as evidence a 2013 speech he made to the Cambodian community in Australia in which he mentioned receiving advice from American experts, Kem Sokha was charged with treason, accused of plotting and conspiring with "foreign elements" to overthrow the government, and, through the CNRP, of inciting a "lotus revolution" in Cambodia.[2] Earlier, the government had introduced a law stipulating that parties cannot be headed by someone with a criminal record, which had already forced CNRP president Sam Rainsy, who is facing multiple charges and a $1 million fine for libel against Hun Sen, to resign in an effort to save the party.

With Sam Rainsy in exile, Kem Sokha's imprisonment essentially decapitated the party. Fearing their own arrest, a number of CNRP officials and party supporters have fled the country, many to Thailand. Others defected to the CPP. The final move to destroy the opposition came on 16 November when the Supreme Court issued a decree to dissolve the CNRP under the charge of attempting, with American support, to destabilize the government through a "colour revolution". The government also imposed a five-year ban on political activities of the 118 senior CNRP members, which essentially undercut the possibility of any party-led mobilization for the upcoming 2018 elections and beyond. Amidst rumours of his leaning towards the CNRP, Nhek Bun Chhay, head of the Khmer National United Party (KNUP) and a former royalist commander who fought against

Hun Sen's forces in 1997 but who broke away from FUNCINPEC last year to form KNUP, was stripped of his bodyguards and his position as adviser to the government (a rank equal to that of deputy prime minister) for not being "loyal to the government". Besides the CPP and CNRP, KNUP was the only other party to secure a commune chief position in the June elections.

In what the regime termed "a slight correction on democracy for the common public good",[3] the dissolution of the CNRP was followed by amendments to the election laws to allow for the redistribution of the party's electoral seats in the National Assembly, Senate, communes, and district councils to other parties. Once a rival, but now aligned with the CPP, the royalist party, FUNCINPEC, which had advocated the redistribution of CNRP seats, was catapulted from its politically insipid status by an exponential gain of over a third of the National Assembly seats through the reallocation.[4] In 2013 the party had won less than 4 per cent of the vote and was unable to secure a single assembly seat. In the Senate, remnants of the Sam Rainsy party who regrouped under the newly minted Candlelight Party were allowed to retain their seats. With the lion's share of the commune seats going to the CPP, the ruling party now controls over 95 per cent of seats at the commune level,[5] along with the majority control of over 55 per cent of the National Assembly.

The redistribution of CNRP seats — which Phil Robertson, deputy director of Human Rights Watch–Asia, describes as "a looting of democracy" — essentially nullified the will of 44 per cent of registered voters who cast their ballots in June. Calling the amended laws "unconstitutional", legal analyst Yoeurng Sotheara noted: "the constitution says the National Assembly should represent the people.... It's no longer representative if the seats of the opposition party which supporters voted for ... are distributed to parties they don't support.... the government doesn't have the authority to redistribute the will of the people."[6] Evoking the need to defend national interests, a twelve-man working group has been tasked with looking into constitutional amendments, alluding to the likelihood of additional changes, which does not bode well for the rapidly shrinking democratic space. Concern about the fairness of the upcoming elections in 2018 was reinforced by the resignation of the three CNRP representatives from the National Election Committee (NEC), including the vice chair of the committee, and their replacement with members from minor parties.

Combined, the imprisonment, flight, exile and ban on political activities of the CNRP leadership and the defection of party members has effectively neutralized the only viable oppositional force for the upcoming 2018 elections. FUNCIPEC's renewed rapprochement with the CPP and resulting political resurgence are suggestive of a familiar replay of the 1990s political theatre in which an uneasy alliance was expediently forged between the CPP and its weaker non-communist ally to give a veneer of multiparty democracy in Cambodia that was necessary and sufficient for regime legitimation in the eyes of the international community. This newly found symbiosis notwithstanding, the CPP has already admonished FUNCINPEC for its attempt to solicit Chinese aid for the 2018 elections in contravention of a recently passed law that prohibits parties from accepting foreign funds. With the party dismantled and banned from political activities and with most of the leadership in exile, a faction of the former CNRP led by Sam Rainsy has announced the launch of the Cambodian National Rescue Movement (CNRM) to continue mobilizing for regime change, a move that has been rejected by Kem Sokha, who insists on the legitimacy of the CNRP and its three million voter–supporters.

In the concerted campaign to undercut the political strength of the opposition and ensure an uncontested win at the national polls in 2018, the regime also tightened control over the media, rights organizations and activists, further silencing dissent. While the independence of the media has always been compromised by state surveillance and censorship, the forced closure of the English-language newspaper *The Cambodia Daily*, curtailment of the in-country operations of the U.S.-funded Voice of America (VOA) and Radio Free Asia (RFA), and the cessation of operations of fifteen local stations that aired their programmes and those of the CNRP were unprecedented developments. As it was with the $6.3 million tax bill levied against *The Cambodia Daily*, VOA and RFA also faced potential tax liabilities and licensing issues, and were compelled to close their Cambodia offices. Two former RFA reporters, Oun Chhin and Yeang Sothearin, were arrested in November and detained at Prey Sar prison for engaging in espionage, charged with providing "a foreign state with information which undermines national defence",[7] for which each could face up to fifteen years in prison. According to RFA, the men had not been in the station's employment since the termination of its Phnom Penh–based operations in September. Similarly, the government ordered the closure of the U.S.-funded National Democratic Institute and the prompt departure of its foreign staff for allegedly failing to register the organization in accordance with Cambodia's NGO Law. Rights organizations such as the Cambodian Human Rights and Development Association (ADHOC), the Cambodian League for the Promotion and Defense of Human Rights (LICADHO), the Committee for Free and Fair Elections (COMFREL), and the Cambodian Center for Human Rights (CCHR) founded by Kem Sokha in 2002 also came under scrutiny. Rights activists, particularly those working on labour and land disputes, continue to be in the crosshairs of the state that seeks to emphasize stability and growth amidst political turmoil.

International Relations

The attack on the CNRP not only neutralizes oppositional forces, thus calling into question the possibility of a free and fair election in 2018, but also destabilizes U.S.–Cambodia relations that were already on unsteady ground, particularly given the accusation of U.S. complicity in the supposed CNRP "colour revolution". Denouncing the "meritless and politicized allegations" used to justify the dissolution of the CNRP, and noting the "unnecessary damages" to U.S.–Cambodia relations, the Trump administration stated "it is becoming increasingly evident to the world that the Cambodian government's restrictions on civil society, suppression of the press, and banning of more than 100 opposition leaders from political activities have significantly set back Cambodia's democratic development and placed its economic growth and international standing at risk".[8] Citing concern that "next year's election will not be legitimate, free or fair",[9] the United States withdrew the two-year $1.8 million grant to Cambodia's National Election Committee that it had pledged in April. The U.S. Senate also passed a unanimous motion urging the listing of key Cambodian officials on the Specially Designated Nationals list, a move that could mean the freezing of assets and curtailment of business relationships with American companies. On 6 December the United States announced that it would be imposing visa restrictions on individuals involved in "undermining democracy in Cambodia", and made the lifting of the ban contingent on the reinstatement of the opposition and reversal of the regime's political course. U.S.–Cambodia relations were also rocked by the temporary stall of the deportation programme, affecting some 1,900 Cambodians in the United States with felony convictions or undocumented status, though Cambodia's Ministry of Foreign Affairs and International Cooperation attributed this moratorium to protests from the Cambodian diaspora and some congressional members. The programme has since resumed.

The European Union (EU) was equally condemning of the deteriorating political situation in Cambodia and what Commissioner Karmenu Vella described in his address to the European Parliament as "a significant step away from the path of pluralism and democracy enshrined in Cambodia's constitution and supported over more than two decades by Cambodia's international partners including the European Union".[10] In her meeting with the Cambodian Foreign Minister Prak Sokhonn on 20 November, High Representative Mogherini insisted that EU development cooperation and assistance to Cambodia, including trade preferences under the

EU's Everything But Arms (EBA) scheme, are predicated on the country's respect for human and labour rights. In December, the EU suspended its funding support for the 2018 elections, noting that "an electoral process from which the main opposition party has been arbitrarily excluded cannot be seen as legitimate".[11] The European Parliament has also passed a resolution calling for visa restrictions and the freezing of assets of Cambodian officials, as well as a temporary suspension of preferential trade access under article 19 of the EBA. In November, Sweden announced that it would not provide new aid to Cambodia except to support education and research. Concerns were also registered by the Inter-Parliamentary Union, which called for a fact-finding mission to Cambodia, and by ASEAN Parliamentarians for Human Rights (APHR), which insists that "anyone who thinks genuine, participatory, and inclusive elections are still possible in 2018 under these circumstances is gravely mistaken. The international community's engagement with Cambodia, including monitoring of the elections, should be conditional upon the restoration of democracy...".[12] The Geneva-based International Commission of Jurists, in turn, expressed concern over the "weaponization" of the country's judicial system in the CPP's campaign against its political opponents and critics. Rhona Smith, UN Special Rapporteur on Human Rights in Cambodia, underscored that what distinguishes "rule of law" from "rule by law" is respect for human rights, fairness, justice and public participation. At a UN forum, Kem Monovithya, a spokeswoman for the banned Cambodia National Rescue Party and daughter of jailed CNRP leader Kem Sokha, urged member states and signatories of the Paris Peace Accord to request a fact-finding and monitoring mission to Cambodia and to "review Cambodian membership at the UN".[13] The latter issue drew harsh admonishment from the Phnom Penh regime, citing the importance of protecting "national interests".[14] In the face of international pronouncements that under these circumstances the 2018 elections will not be free and fair, and the consequent withdrawal of aid, Prime Minister Hun Sen has defiantly declared that the elections will proceed as scheduled — 25 February for Senate seats and 29 July 2018 for the national election — pointing out that "the Cambodian constitution or around the world doesn't state one country needs another country's president or the U.N. Secretary General to acknowledge its election is legitimate".[15]

Limits of Sanctions

Despite its dismissive attitude, the Hun Sen regime is not oblivious to international opinion, particularly with an economy that is reliant on external, essentially Western, markets. With the EU the destination of an estimated 50 per cent of Cambodia's total exports, mostly in sugar and garments, preferential trade access is important, accounting for some $5 billion. Combined, the United States and the EU absorb some 60 per cent of Cambodia's exports, markets that cannot easily be replaced by China, which only imported $609 million of goods from Cambodia in 2016,[16] or by regional partners with much smaller markets and whose economies are more competitive than complementary. Additionally, the EU also provides development assistance to Cambodia — totalling nearly $170 million in 2016 — for projects in agriculture, education, governance, administration and electoral reform and in support of the Extraordinary Chambers of the Courts of Cambodia (ECCC).

Sanctions, however, have their limitations, not the least of which is the frequent subordination of international principles to the imperatives of realpolitik. Demand for accountability has been less than consistently applied by Western countries and by the donor community at large. In fact, Cambodia was granted and allowed to retain its EBA preferential trade status over the last decade, effectively spurring the exponential development of the sugar industry, despite widespread land disputes and forced evictions linked to economic land concessions that the European Parliament had found to have displaced over 400,000 Cambodians.[17] In 2016, members of the EU Parliament and civil society groups had also called for the withdrawal of tariff preferences for Cambodia because of negative social and environmental impacts and violations of labour and other rights. The same concerns about the unravelling of democratic processes and regime repression of political opposition have also been raised in the past, all with little enduring impact. At present, the EU is also engaging countries such as Myanmar and Vietnam that have yet to embark on democratic reforms. Finally, while the EU may be willing to issue public rebuke of state repression, they are more challenged in their ability to arrive at a consensus on what constitutes viable concrete action, given some states' concern that removal of preferential trade access would only adversely impact the 700,000 low-wage garment workers and not the leadership, and without any assurance of meaningful change.

The paramount nature of realpolitik is evident in the varied responses to developments in Cambodia. Despite American condemnation of the violent crackdown, President Trump did not raise human rights concerns during the ASEAN Summit in Manila in November. International outcry in general, including from the West, was relatively tempered. The circumspection of Asian governments, including ASEAN with its member states' spotty records and policy of non-interference, was notable though not unexpected. Tokyo's expressed concern about the dissolution of the CNRP was offset by Japanese Minister of Foreign Affairs Kazuyuki Nakane's assertion that Japan will continue its assistance to the NEC while "keep[ing] dialogue" with the Cambodian government.[18] Besides the EU, Japan is the biggest funder of the upcoming elections. On 7 August the Japan International Cooperation Agency (JICA) signed an agreement with Cambodia to provide a Japanese official development assistance loan (ODA) of up to 23.502 billion yen (approximately US$208 million) for the Sihanoukville Port New Container Terminal Development Project.

Tokyo's policy stance is likely informed by China's expanding influence in the region. While the West is an important market, China is not only Cambodia's largest source of international aid but also of foreign investment, amounting to ten times the size of U.S. investment, which accounts for only 3 per cent of the country's total foreign investment capital. It is also Cambodia's largest trade partner and a major source of foreign tourists, on whom the country remains highly dependent. Significantly, Chinese aid is also directed to critical sectors. With high economic growth and an annual increase of 20 per cent in electricity demand, the Cambodian government has given priority to the development of hydropower. The six operational hydroelectric plants account for 47 per cent of available electricity in Cambodia.[19] The seventh and biggest hydropower dam, the Lower Sesan II in northeastern Cambodia, is scheduled to be fully operational in 2018. With the exception of the Lower Sesan II project — which is a joint venture between Chinese, Cambodian and Vietnamese companies, with China holding 51 per cent control — all hydropower projects in Cambodia have been fully financed by Chinese companies.[20] In addition to almost US$2 billion in concessional loans, Chinese firms had also committed to investing an additional $7 billion in Cambodia for infrastructural projects, including a highway connecting Phnom Penh with Cambodia's main port, Sihanoukville. In recent years, Chinese investment has also extended beyond largely infrastructural projects to real estate, as investors seek additional safety nets in the event of an economic bust.

Even more than the size and sectoral importance, Chinese aid is not tied to human rights or other aspects of social accountability. As Cambodian government spokesman Phay Siphan puts it, "the Chinese always support us in economic growth and they never interfere in our decisions".[21] Undoubtedly seizing the opening provided by the retraction of Western aid as an opportunity to also lure Cambodia away from Vietnam's sphere of influence, China was quick to affirm its commitment to "support Cambodia's efforts in maintaining political stability"[22] and to extend aid to the NEC in the form of some 60,000 polling booths and 15,000 ballot boxes for the 2018 elections, which sent a clear and bolstering signal to the Hun Sen regime that it can proceed on its political course with relative impunity.

Chinese support is, by no means, uncalculating or unconditional, nor is its economic presence without adverse consequences. As part of the One Belt, One Road initiative backed by the Asian Infrastructure Investment Bank (AIIB) and the Silk Road Fund, these development projects are critical aspects of China's strategic calculus to enhance its influence among regional states in Asia. This deployment of soft power is important given China's economic and strategic interests in Southeast Asia, which is projected by the World Economic Forum to have the world's fifth-largest economy by 2020, and through which the planned maritime Silk Road will pass. With growing economies and populations, the infrastructural needs of ASEAN member states are vast, making China's economic backing indispensable to the Southeast Asian countries, and the latter an economically and geopolitically important site for Chinese investment. With China's territorial claims and undeterred expansion in the South China Sea (despite the unfavourable ruling of the Arbitral Tribunal in 2016) a source of contention and concern in the region, the support of some ASEAN member states is critical for China. With Cambodia's support, for which it was rewarded with a generous aid package, China was able to block any mention of the South China Sea in the joint communiqué of the 45th ASEAN Foreign Ministers Meeting in Phnom Penh. Despite the disconcertion of some regional states over Cambodia and Laos' pro-China position, the importance of Chinese goodwill is not lost on an ASEAN that is feeling the uncertainty of America's Asia policy, as evidenced by the conciliatory tone of the statement issued at the conclusion of the November summit in Manila.

Though Chinese aid has been indispensable, Chinese projects have also been controversial. While they may have brought electrification to some 79 per cent of the villages, as reported by the Ministry of Mines and Energy, and enabled the reduction of the country's dependency on costly imported electricity, the Chinese-financed hydropower plants in Cambodia have also engendered mass displacement. The Lower Sesan II project alone affects 860 mostly indigenous minority families who were forced to abandon their ancestral villages. Despite the government offer of compensation of $6,000 or five hectares of land per family, many are reluctant to relocate because of their cultural and spiritual rootedness and because some of the resettlement sites are yet to be cleared for cultivation or are prone to inundation. Some 60 families have refused the government compensation and were given until the end of December to accept the deal, after which time the government will no longer compensate them for their losses.[23] Experts have also warned against the adverse impact of the dams on the ecosystem and fish migration routes that, in turn, affect fish supplies. In response to widespread concern about the social and environmental impacts of these projects, Prime Minister Hun Sen commented that "there is no development in the world that does not affect environment; it's just small or big impact only", arguing that "this project will provide great benefit to socio-economic development and poverty reduction, especially in the northeastern region".[24]

Growth, Development and Social Justice

With economic growth of 7 per cent, the Hun Sen regime has stood on the platform of peace and development. With signs of slowing down in the construction and textile export sectors, continued growth is contingent on an expected rise in other manufacturing exports and robust tourism. This rests on Cambodia being able to maintain or even increase its competitive edge and to diversify its export manufacturing sector, and on a stable social and political environment. Uncertainties in the past had adversely impacted business confidence. In the agricultural sector, growth remains hindered by poor infrastructure and difficult access to markets, rural indebtedness and landlessness.

As Transparency International country director Preap Kol noted, however, "for a growth of a country like Cambodia to be sustainable, development of economy should ideally go hand in hand with development of social justice and democracy". Though growth has been impressive, the challenges to sustainable and inclusive development — improved land administration, natural resource management, good and equitable public service delivery, transparency, and overall good governance — remain to be effectively addressed. Disparity between the rich and poor and between urban and rural areas persists. While the poverty rate continues to fall and the country has reached lower-middle-income status with a per capita gross national income of $1,079 in 2015, over 28 per cent of the population continues to live in economic precarity. With the living wage a major catalyst in the mass labour protests of 2013 that resulted in violent clashes and deaths of protesters, the government has been particularly attentive to this issue, especially as it pertains to the garment and footwear industries that employ over 700,000 workers and generate a revenue of $7 billion annually. Though wages for workers in the footwear and textile industries had jumped 150 per cent over the past five years — from $61 per month in 2012 — they are struggling to keep up with the cost of living. Currently at $153, the government has recently promised another 11 per cent increase by next year. Though it will improve workers' living conditions, there is also concern, shared by the unions, that this minimum wage increase would reduce the country's competitiveness in the global labour market.

In the rural areas, where 80–90 per cent of the population resides, the inequities and dislocations of development continue to register. Land disputes and forced displacement continue to plague many communities. Among many peasant protests, nearly a hundred villagers from Banan and Bavel districts of Battambang demonstrated in front of Prime Minister Hun Sen's home and the Ministry of Land Management to protest against the illegal occupation of their social land concessions by government soldiers. In many forested regions, such as the northeastern province of Rattanakiri, the creation of largely foreign-owned export plantations and illegal logging continue to destroy the country's rapidly shrinking forestland, upon which many communities, including a large number of indigenous minorities, rely for their livelihoods. A recent international survey revealing a 30 per cent increase in forest cover loss between 2015 and 2016[25] has been heatedly contested by the government. Protests by villagers and activists — such as the one mobilized to stop illegal logging in the Preah Roka Wildlife Sanctuary, a 223,287-acre national park that has been designated as a protected refuge for endangered wildlife — are numerous, despite the violent consequences that they engender. Forest defenders have underscored the importance not only of stepped-up efforts to stop illegal logging in Cambodia but also of the EU and the United States to terminate their timber export agreements with countries such as Vietnam where illegally felled timber has reportedly been exported.

In Phnom Penh, development has also seen to the demolition of one of the capital's historic landmarks, popularly known as the "White Building". The land was purchased by Arakawa, a Japanese developer, with plans to build an $80-million twenty-one-story complex. Constructed in the 1960s as an affordable housing project, it was home, in its derelict state, to 493 families, some 25 of which had refused to be relocated. Meanwhile, six years after the early morning demolition of their homes, 11 evicted families of the yet-to-be-resolved Borei Keila development controversy are still awaiting fair compensation for their losses. While the government has moved to address the problems of illegal logging and corruption, the initiatives, though important, have not amounted to systemic reform. Pointing to regime failings as the basis for popular dissatisfaction[26] reflected in the June electoral outcomes, PM Hun Sen has called for officials to "bathe and clean themselves".

Migration

For many of Cambodia's land poor and landless, migration is the only viable option. According to government records, 116,000 have migrated to Thailand through official channels over the last decade. Other estimates place migrants currently working across the border at closer to one million, of which an estimated 500,000 are undocumented. Labour exploitation and abuses persist. The passing of a new law in Thailand that penalized both undocumented workers and their employers saw to the mass return exodus of over 8,000 Cambodian migrant workers in June, 10–15 per cent of whom were reported to be minors.[27] Though the official cost of a passport is $100 ($200 for expedited processing), migrants often have to pay much more to an agency — as high as over $800 — a sum that few can afford, given the menial work and earnings they stand to secure in Thailand. Despite the Ministry of Labour's plan to legalize more migrant workers through the issuance of travel documents in Thailand, the cost and lack of personal documents remain major obstacles to the registration effort, which is scheduled to continue until the end of 2017. At home, the Cambodian government has tightened its own immigration policies with a more stringent review of identity cards and residency papers. As of October, these measures stand to affect some 70,000 migrants, the majority of whom are ethnic Vietnamese, prompting Vietnam to urge the Cambodian government to guarantee the legal rights of those "waiting for their legal documents to be completed". With the 7 January anniversary in view, this immigration policy and general pivoting towards China are testing Cambodia–Vietnam relations in unprecedented ways.

Conclusion

As this chapter goes to print, the anniversary of the Veng Sreng demonstrations in which some fifty thousand protesters took to the streets calling for regime change came and went unceremoniously, as fear effectively silenced critique. The outcry of earlier months against the dismantling of a meaningful multiparty democratic system enshrined in the Paris Accords had fizzled. Back-door diplomacy and economic pressure may continue but are unlikely to reverse the course of a regime moving unapologetically towards shedding any pretence at political liberalization and democratic reform in a "descent into outright dictatorship", as the ASEAN Parliamentarians for Human Rights chairman put it.

That the hope for a democratic transition for Cambodia is more elusive now than ever should not come as a surprise. Arguably, the stage was set twenty-four years ago when the international community endorsed a fait accompli presented not by the will of the Cambodian people but the right of force, when the CPP stared down the international community and walked away with the election they did not win and proceeded to rule for the next two decades: "Their dreams of democracy wilted. They blinked."[28] Thus began a performance politics in which all participated, with Cambodia presenting a façade of political openness with elections and their predictable outcomes that are sufficient to nurse the justification of continued aid. Democracy was exchanged for purported stability, with liberalization success measured against the infernal days of the Khmer Rouge. Indeed, the ability of the Hun Sen regime to consolidate power — political, military, economic — in a single party and its willingness to exercise force unflinchingly have effectively prevented the possibility of war. It has not, however, been able to foster peace, just governance or equitable access to basic rights — to freedom from fear; to education, jobs and life opportunities; or to equal protection under the law — for the majority of the Cambodian people. Whatever liberalization we may have witnessed over the last two and half decades have largely been economic. While it did move the country out of the cloister of the socialist economy, it has also engendered a widening of socio-economic gaps and the unrelenting disenfranchisement of millions of Cambodians in the process.

With the Western gaze fixed on the geopolitical balancing game in East Asia — pivoting around China and North Korea — Cambodian leadership is once again astutely playing the China wildcard. It is unlikely that the country's autocracy and violent crackdown on opponents and dissent are going to provoke more than symbolic condemnation by the international community. This much is evident and is not lost on the ruling regime, or on the Cambodian people. If anything, recent developments affirm that rule of and by force is effective, made even more so by its seeming impunity. With the CNRP refraining, to prevent bloodshed, from calling for mass protest, the only resolution is a political one, which is not unimaginable. In previous impasses the Hun Sen regime had eased its grip, with entry bans lifted and detainees released at the eleventh hour. Whether this will happen in time to make any difference to the electoral outcomes in 2018 remains to be seen. With the gains and losses of the recent elections a looming reminder of possibilities and challenges, the stakes are indeed very high.

Notes

1. See Amnesty International, "Cambodia 2016/2017" <https://www.amnesty.org/en/countries/asia-and-the-pacific/cambodia/report-cambodia/>.
2. Ben Sokhean and Leonie Kijewski, "PM Accuses Kem Sokha–founded NGO of Serving Foreign Interests, Says It 'Must Close', *Phnom Penh Post*, 27 November 2017.
3. Andrew Nachemson, "Cambodia: From Pet Project to Problem Child", *Phnom Penh Post*, 27 November 2017.

4. Prak Chan Thul, "Cambodia's Hun Sen Warns His Party It Could Still Lose Election", Reuters, 22 November 2017.
5. Leonie Kijewski and Khouth Sophak Chakrya, "CPP Big Winner in Local Seat Reallocation", *Phnom Penh Post*, 4 December 2017.
6. Mech Dara and Andrew Nachemson, "Breaking: National Assembly Passes Election Law Amendments to Allow CNRP Seat Distribution", *Phnom Penh Post*, 16 October 2017.
7. Mech Dara and Yesenia Amaro, "Ex-RFA Reporters Provisionally Charged with 'Espionage' Sent to Prey Sar", *Phnom Penh Post*, 20 November 2017.
8. Mech Dara and James Reddick, "US Withdraws Election Funding Following CNRP Dissolution", *Phnom Penh Post*, 17 November 2017.
9. Amy Sawitta Lefevre and Prak Chan Thul, "Cambodia Faces U.S., EU Action after Banning Opposition", Reuters, 16 November 2017.
10. <https://eeas.europa.eu/delegations/cambodia/37658/speech-commissioner-karmenu-vella-european-parliament-urgency-debate-banning-opposition_en>.
11. Reuters, "EU Suspends Funding for Cambodian Election", 12 December 2017.
12. See APHR statement, 13 October 2017 <https://aseanmp.org/2017/10/13/asean-parliamentarians-condemn-moves-to-eliminate-opposition-in-cambodia/>.
13. Voice of America, "UN General Assembly Urged to Review Cambodia Membership", 22 December 2017.
14. Mech Dara and Andrew Nachenson, "Kheng Seeks Constitutional Ban on Individuals Harming Cambodia's 'Interests' ", *Phnom Penh Post*, 29 December 2017.
15. Neou Vannarin, "Hun Sen: CNRP Dissolution, NEC Resignations, and Aid Cuts Will Not Affect 2018 Election", Voice of America, 23 November 2017.
16. David Hutt, "Why the EU is Dallying over Possible Cambodian Sanctions", *Forbes*, 3 November 2017.
17. See European Parliament resolution on Cambodia, 26 October 2012 <http://www.europarl.europa.eu/meetdocs/2009_2014>.
18. Daphne Chen, "Japan 'Expresses Concern' over CNRP", *Phnom Penh Post*, 22 November 2017.
19. Terence Chong, "The Politics behind Cambodia's Embrace of China", *ISEAS Perspective* 2017, no. 59 (2 August 2017).
20. *China Daily*, "Chinese Investment in Energy Creates New History for Cambodia: Cambodian Minister", 10 October 2016.
21. Reuters, "China's Big Money Trumps US Influence in Cambodia", 11 September 2017.
22. Neou Vannarin, "Hun Sen: CNRP Dissolution, NEC Resignations, and Aid Cuts Will Not Affect 2018 Election", Voice of America, 23 November 2017.
23. Phak Seangly, "Relocation Site for Sesan Villagers Flooded", *Phnom Penh Post*, 2 November 2017.

24. Xinhua, "Chinese-Built Biggest Dam in Cambodia to Start Operation in November", 25 September 2017.
25. See <https://earthobservatory.nasa.gov>.
26. Van Roeun and Ben Paviour, "Wary of Losing Votes, Hun Sen Makes Rare Call for Reform", *Cambodia Daily*, 27 June 2017.
27. Leonie Kijewski and Yon Sineat, "Voices from the Border", *Phnom Penh Post*, 14 July 2017.
28. Paul Millar, "Why the West was Doomed to Fail in Cambodia", *Southeast Asia Globe*, 1 January 2018.

CAMBODIA–VIETNAM: Special Relationship against Hostile and Unfriendly Forces

Steve Heder

Comprehensive Relations with a Military Pillar

Vietnam–Cambodia relations are described officially as "comprehensive"[1] and indeed have political, economic, security (military and police), cultural and other facets. Politically, there are close and tightening links between the two countries' ruling parties, symbolized by the fact that in a speech to the Communist Party of Vietnam (CPV) Congress in January 2016, General Ngo Xuan Lich, about to be promoted to Minister of Defence, placed the Cambodian People's Party (CPP) as second among the foreign political organizations with which the CPV was strengthening bilateral cooperation, behind only that of Laos.[2] The comradeship entails general efforts "to closely coordinate and to strengthen the exchange of information and experiences in party-building work"[3] and the two sides speak of it as a "special relationship",[4] the formulation used to describe the relationship between Cambodia and Vietnam (and Laos and Vietnam) from 1979 to 1990.[5] During an April 2017 visit to Phnom Penh to meet with Cambodian Prime Minister Hun Sen, Vietnamese Prime Minister Nguyen Xuan Phuc described links as flourishing, declaring that "especially in the recent years and months, Vietnam–Cambodia relations have been very much more familial, affectionate, trusting and intimate".[6]

Within this framework, the Vietnam–Cambodia military ties embodied in the links between the Vietnam People's Army (VPA) and Royal Cambodian Armed Forces (RCAF) are characterized as a "main pillar".[7] This is a realm in which the Vietnamese believe they can and should continue to have a very special place, rooted in their unique role in militarily toppling Pol Pot's Democratic Kampuchea

Steve Heder is honorary Research Associate at the School of Oriental and African Studies of the University of London.

in January 1979 and directly building Cambodia's security forces for a decade thereafter.[8] In bilateral contexts with a military flavour, Hun Sen has been prone to affirm that "without the help of Vietnam, Cambodia would absolutely not be where it is today".[9]

Two overarching themes of VPA–RCAF cooperation are that, historically, "always at the most difficult times, there has been only Vietnam helping Cambodia",[10] and that, currently, the VPA is ready to assist the RCAF "in all circumstances",[11] including at any time "when the CPP is encountering difficulties".[12] Hun Sen has described bilateral relations like one of "lips and teeth", with a basis in a "political relationship" between the two countries' armed forces.[13] In historical Asian Communist parlance, the notion of a lips and teeth relationship has referred to one of militant solidarity in wartime against a common enemy.[14]

Combating "Hostile" and "Unfriendly" Forces

In policy terms, current VPA–RCAF relations are pursuant to a 2014 CPV Central Military Commission policy resolution,[15] according to which VPA forces combine preventing political change away from CPV rule in Vietnam itself with cooperating closely with the RCAF.[16] In January 2016, the Director of Vietnam's National Defence Academy explained that helping make Cambodia strong with regard to its domestic "political security" helps "protect the security of Vietnam."[17]

This puts security force relationships at the core of Cambodia–Vietnam mutual assistance to realize the CPP–CPV objective of ensuring that what in Khmer are labelled "unfriendly forces" (កម្លាំងអមិត្រ or កម្លាំងអមិត្ត)[18] and what in the official Vietnamese translation are labelled "hostile forces" (*thế lực thù địch* or *lực lượng thù địch*) are unable to use the territory of one against the other.[19]

For the CPV, "hostile forces" include those accused of attempting to use the issues of "democracy and human rights" to form political organizations and develop civil society to promote "radical" democratic tendencies to destabilize political security, bring about "peaceful evolution" and overthrow the CPV's monopoly leadership position.[20] Hostile forces' tactics are said to include calling for a depoliticization of the VPA and public security forces by ending CPV control over them,[21] demanding "religious freedom" for minority groups and others,[22] accusing the government of failing to protect national interests,[23] and doing something to precipitate war.[24]

In Cambodia, the phrase "unfriendly forces" has been used particularly by CPP senior security force commanders when referring to the opposition Cambodian National Rescue Party (CNRP) since its foundation in late 2012 through to its

November 2017 dissolution and the banishing of its 118 leading political figures from politics for five years by Cambodia's Supreme Court.[25] The CNRP has been so stigmatized for allegedly refusing to give Hun Sen and the CPP their due for their services in the cause of the nation,[26] creating instability in the national society,[27] generating political turmoil via demonstrations and strikes to destroy public order and national security,[28] and ultimately for allegedly "colluding with foreign imperialism", that is, the United States, to use demonstrations to make a "colour revolution" to overthrow the government. These were the contentions presented in late October 2017 as the immediate justification for a pre-emptive strike against the CNRP to prevent a national catastrophe[29] and they were the underlying basis for the Supreme Court decision. They had also been the grounds put forward in September 2017 in support of the arrest for alleged treason of CNRP President Kem Sokha,[30] replacement for the self-exiled founding party leader Sam Rainsy, who has opted since November 2015 to remain outside Cambodia to avoid his own arrest.[31]

Linked over the years to the characterization of the CNRP as an unfriendly force have been statements by Hun Sen and other Cambodian officials that the CNRP was wrongly alleging that the government had violated Cambodia's national interests by ceding Cambodian territory to Vietnam,[32] and that the CNRP was acting in such a manner as to provoke either internal class war or external war with Vietnam,[33] both of which Hun Sen has said would follow from the CNRP taking power by defeating the CPP in elections.[34]

CNRP as Electoral Threat

Voting trends in Cambodia's 2013 National Assembly elections and the 2017 commune elections, in which the CPP lost a considerable portion of its previous vote tallies to the CNRP, made a future CNRP election triumph appear a possibility, perhaps in the next National Assembly elections, scheduled for July 2018.[35]

After the 2013 vote and both before and after the 2017 vote, the CPV has signalled trepidation about this prospect and its desire to have the CPP fend it off. Reporting on the CPP's 2015 Congress, Vietnamese media revealed concerns that its vote share had "significantly decreased" in 2013 due to a decline of popular confidence in the party, and that unless it learned the lessons of this setback, its survival would be at stake.[36] In a November 2015 meeting with a CPP Central Committee official, the head of the CPV's Central Office advised it to adopt "proper strategy and tactics" in order to win "bigger achievements" by successfully organizing commune and national elections.[37] In a December 2015 meeting with

Cambodia's Deputy Prime Minister and National Defence Minister Tea Banh in Hanoi, CPV General Secretary Nguyen Phu Trong indicated that to do so, the CPP would have to exercise more disciplined leadership.[38] During Vietnamese President Tran Dai Quang's meeting with Hun Sen a year later, the president affirmed "a consistent policy of always supporting the CPP" and appreciated Cambodia's "steadfastness … in not allowing any hostile force to use its territory to undermine the peace, security and stability" of Vietnam, but counselled the Prime Minister to carry out "preventative work, not allowing extremist forces to provoke national animosity or to break up or sabotage the relations of cooperation and friendship" between the two countries.[39]

Three days after the CPP setback in the 2017 commune elections, the official CPV newspaper quoted "observers" as saying that although the results showed that the electorate supported peace, stability and development, the CPP "still had much work to do in order to realize its commitments before the voters" in the run-up to national elections.[40] The CPV manifested worries about the CPP's ability to maintain political stability and social order in Cambodia and indicated support for its efforts to do so.[41] However, in early August 2017, a CPP Central Committee official told CPV counterparts that the CPP was still encountering "not a few difficulties" in the wake of the commune election and would have to confront "not a little destructive resistance from hostile forces" as the National Assembly vote approached.[42]

Security Force Relations

It is in this context that the Vietnam–Cambodia security pillar takes on psychological and potentially operational significance as an armed alliance against political change that would bring hostile forces of unfriendly elements to power in Cambodia. At October 2015 talks between a Cambodian defence ministry secretary of state and a Vietnamese deputy defence minister, the two concurred that they faced a danger of outside powers using their "soft power" to interfere in their countries' internal affairs,[43] and that they needed to further strengthen defence relations to prevent this.[44] In separate talks with the Vietnamese official, Hun Sen specified that new security threats were arising due to attempts by counter-revolutionary forces to use a "colour revolution" to overthrow his government, and that therefore the militaries of both countries needed to be highly vigilant in order to defeat their dark schemes.[45]

To assist in ensuring their defeat, from 2014 to 2016, Vietnam gave Cambodia at least US$29 million in defence aid.[46] Much of the aid focuses on a direct twinning between VPA and RCAF or Cambodian Ministry of National Defence organs and units, the better to build close military cohesion and solidarity.[47] Other VPA aid for the RCAF is devoted to construction of training facilities inside Cambodia.[48] This compliments VPA education of RCAF personnel inside Vietnam, some of which dates to as far back as 1980. Since that year, Cambodia has sent nearly 17,000 military personnel for training in Vietnam, of whom 10,230 have finished their courses since 2002.[49] In 2017, 300 more were to undergo long-term training and more than 1,000 short-term training.[50]

Police-to-police relations are similarly designed to ensure their "long-term durability" and effectiveness in promptly defeating the negative activities of hostile forces.[51] As with the military, this has included construction of training facilities inside Cambodia.[52] Also in that year, it was agreed that 600 Cambodian police would go to Vietnam for study.[53] Some of these presumably followed in the footsteps of previous waves who had attended the People's Security College II, from which almost 6,000 Cambodian police have graduated as of July 2015, including 2,227 since 2004.[54] A new round of police cooperation to "ensure the security of both countries" was agreed in February 2017,[55] and in a late July 2017 meeting, the Vietnamese side praised the two countries' police forces for having coordinated and intensified their struggle to defeat "all plots of hostile forces and targets acting detrimentally to the interests and security of each country."[56]

Historical Factors

Profound historical factors have encouraged Vietnamese acceptance of the CPP's view of the political threat posed by the CNRP. One is that Sam Rainsy, Kem Sokha and other CNRP or CNRP-affiliated figures often use the historical and still widely heard Khmer-language term Yuon,[57] originally the customary name applied to peoples ruled by predecessor polities of today's Vietnam and to those polities themselves, to refer to Vietnamese today, despite the fact that official and many other Vietnamese nowadays object to it because they consider it derogatory and to have racist connotations.[58] Another factor is calls CNRP figures have made for what they present as the rightful restoration to Cambodia of historically Khmer realms in what is now southern Vietnam, or alternatively for political autonomy for ethnic Khmer areas there or at least full respect for Khmer minority human rights.[59] The historical narrative and legal argumentation on which the territorial claims rely are hotly contested in official and other Vietnamese circles,[60] as in some recent Western scholarship,[61] and autonomy for Khmer areas is anathema to the Vietnamese government, which denies that it is violating Khmer minority rights.[62]

What Vietnamese authorities see as a dangerously irredentist tendency is concretized in a history of rejection by the CNRP or CNRP-affiliated figures of the legality or at least the validity of treaties and other agreements relating to these issues made between 1979 and 2011, to the accuracy of the placement of border markers pursuant to those texts, and to the actual situation of administrative control on the ground where border markers are placed (see below). Another provocative issue is CNRP opposition to the presence among the various historical and recent Vietnamese communities in Cambodia of the many it says are illegal migrants and/or have been illegally voting in elections.[63] While the CPP has also been addressing what it too characterizes as in significant part an illegal immigration problem by, inter alia, deportations,[64] the CNRP is widely understood to be much more determined to "send all the Yuon to Vietnam".[65]

2015 Crises Previewing an Unwanted Future

Two 2015 crises previewed other things that could happen on a larger scale if the CNRP were to take power. The first was an outflow of Vietnamese Montagnard "national minorities" into Cambodia seeking recognition as refugees by a Cambodian government determination process advised by staff of the United Nations High Commissioner for Refugees (UNHCR). The second was dealing with CNRP challenges to the two governments' handling of the delineation and demarcation of the Cambodia–Vietnam border.

By March 2015, Vietnamese security forces were becoming increasingly concerned about what they feared was a "situation of political turmoil in Cambodia" in the wake of the 2013 national elections. Initially, they saw these "internal disturbances" as having led negative repercussions on security and order particularly in border areas due to the flight of Montagnards claiming religious and political persecution in Vietnam. Their immediate reaction was to concentrate VPA Border Defence Forces and other security personnel to try to prevent what they deemed illegal departures.[66] They asserted these were the result of instigation by Montagnard exiles who wanted to use it as a cover for an armed separatist insurgency under the banner of a Front Uni de Lutte des Races Opprimées (FULRO)[67] or by "domestic and foreign hostile forces" generally to foment an illegal overthrow of the local CPV regime via bogus "peaceful evolution" means or simply violent unrest.[68]

They also pushed to step up existing cross-border cooperation[69] between Vietnamese and Cambodian authorities and security forces against "hostile forces".[70] This was in line with CPP policy that influxes of Montagnards are the result of plots by "unfriendly circles" to wreck Cambodia–Vietnam relations and destroy CPV rule in Vietnam, which the two parties must prevent.[71] Thus, on the Cambodian side, there was a reported deployment of almost a thousand troop reinforcements in Rattanakiri province by the end of April 2015.[72] Cambodian soldiers told journalists that this was at the request of the Vietnamese.[73]

In September 2015, a Vietnamese media account highlighting successes by Vietnamese border security forces in stemming the flow of Montagnard asylum seekers into Cambodia attributed these successes to the deployment of Vietnamese military reinforcements and improved Cambodian cooperation.[74] Further cooperation from this point to 2017 between Cambodia's General Department of Immigration and Vietnamese authorities meant that among the hundreds of Montagnards who nevertheless managed to make it into Cambodia after late 2014,[75] the majority were more or less forcibly returned to Vietnam, except for those who eventually fled onwards to Thailand.[76] Those who remained in Cambodia as of October 2017 faced the same fate, even though the UNCHR judged that they had strong claims to be bona fide refugees and thus had a right to non-refoulement.[77]

Direct 2015 confirmation to the CPV that the CNRP was a "hostile force" came with its increasingly activist allegations of Vietnamese violations of Cambodian sovereignty.[78] This included trips by CNRP parliamentarians to locations where they insisted this was happening, such as a part of Kampong Ro district in Svay Rieng province.[79] This dispute related to land on which Hun Sen had said in 2012 that Vietnamese had been resident on what the two governments agreed was the Cambodian side both of the frontier and of where they had placed a border marker.[80] The placement seems to have been at precisely the right spot as indicated by the French colonial-era maps that the government and CNRP alike agreed with Vietnam should divide the two sovereign territories.[81] However, a map produced by authorities of the bordering Vietnamese province of Long An had included territory beyond the marker as under its administration.[82] Vietnamese authorities admitted there was a problem of Vietnamese families cultivating land already demarcated as Cambodian.[83]

In acting in this manner, the Vietnamese side was claiming a right to administer the area based on its interpretation of a 1995 joint press release by the two governments,[84] which the Cambodian side agreed in principle was applicable in this locality.[85] This 1995 document provides that each government can continue to exercise management in places where their nationals have been residing on the wrong side of the agreed delineation of the border, until some future date at which time all delineation and demarcation issues between the two sides have been resolved, which was not the case in 2015[86] (and is still not the case now).[87]

A CNRP visit led by parliamentarians to the site on 28 June 2015 resulted in an altercation with Vietnamese villagers and security forces on the Cambodian side of a watercourse that Long An province was using as its administrative boundary.[88] Vietnam implausibly maintained the clash had occurred deep in its territory and praised Long An Border Defence Forces, local militia and farming families for having repulsed an incursion by Cambodian "extremists". It called upon the Cambodian government to prevent further such activities.[89]

Meanwhile, activist CNRP parliamentarians announced on 7 July 2015 plans to lead a large group of Cambodians back to the same place on 19 July.[90] Two days later, the then editor of the *Khmer Times* newspaper, T. Mohan, published a lengthy article citing what appeared to be government security sources as being concerned about machinations by what the article characterized as "local traitors" among politicians and the possibly imminent dispatch of CIA agents disguised among other things as reporters and students to carry out a "colour revolution" to overthrow the Cambodian government. The article maintained that to achieve this end, the plotters would not only pretend to be promoting democracy and human rights, but had already "upped … the escalation of border tensions with Vietnam", taking advantage of deep anti-Vietnamese sentiments among Cambodians. It suggested that the CNRP border trip of 28 June had been "intended to provoke a fight" with Vietnam as part of a scheme to ignite the colour revolution. It mentioned CNRP leaders Sam Rainsy and Kem Sokha by name and implied that there was evidence of official foreign backing for their treasonous plotting, because some in the "opposition party had openly said that they had been undergoing training in the United States and elsewhere on the various strategies of unseating an incumbent prime minister".[91] Other English-language newspapers in Cambodia have published reports characterizing Mohan as a "CPP-friendly businessman"[92] and containing purported leaks of correspondence suggesting connections between him and RCAF military intelligence.[93]

On 19 July, a CNRP parliamentarian-organized convoy carrying some 1,800 people left Phnom Penh for Kampong Ro, where Svay Rieng and Long An government forces had coordinated the deployment of security forces to maintain "security" and "order".[94] The number in the group increased to as many as 2,000 because people had joined it along the route,[95] and grew further to 2,500 because villagers joined in as it neared the frontier,[96] cheering it wildly on.[97] Only about 800 went as far as the watercourse that was the Vietnamese administrative boundary, and the security forces deployed along it insisted only 100 could go on to the border marker.[98] Further advance to the border marker by any more than a few over the limit of 100 was blocked by a mixed force of Cambodian police,[99] gendarmes and other military personnel with firearms and local para-police carrying clubs. Those allowed through were watched from a distance by armed Vietnamese[100] Border Defence Forces and villagers.[101] After they returned to the watercourse, the CNRP led an exit from the area, were given a heroes' farewell as they proceeded, and then travelled by convoy back to Phnom Penh.[102]

The Cambodian government immediately decried the event as part of a CNRP-led "insurrectionary", "anarchist" and "extremist" movement.[103] A Vietnamese commentary spoke of a conspiracy by such extremists trying their best to oppose the Cambodian government and of the need to "resolutely smash the forces taking advantage of border problems" to undermine Cambodia–Vietnam friendship.[104]

On 21 July 2015, the Phnom Penh court suddenly convicted and sentenced eleven CNRP activists to prison terms for "insurrection" in connection with a demonstration in the capital a year before that had ended in violent clashes between protesters and government para-police. Amnesty International, in calling for the convictions to be quashed, noted that several of those sent to prison had also "been involved in recent CNRP activities to raise awareness of what they allege are efforts by Viet Nam to encroach on Cambodian territory".[105]

Two days later, Hun Sen presided over a meeting of nearly five thousand security force commanders. He warned that CNRP parliamentarians causing serious problems on the border with Vietnam would be arrested, regardless of parliamentary immunity.[106] He reportedly issued instructions that commanders must prevent a "colour revolution" in Cambodia, which government-aligned media explained meant CNRP plans to spark mass demonstrations to overthrow the government.[107] Editorializing on the convictions the same day, T. Mohan said the acts for which they had been prosecuted "could have had dangerous consequences" for Cambodia–Vietnam relations.[108] The eleven remain in prison.

On 15 August 2015, Hong Sok Hour, a senator from the Sam Rainsy Party, a precursor to the CNRP, was arrested for having posted online a mistranslation of a passage in a 1979 Cambodia–Vietnam treaty wrongly suggesting that it provided for "dissolution" of the border between the two. This was characterized by Hun Sen as an act of treason, and the senator was subsequently convicted and sentenced to prison for forgery and intent to generate "serious disturbance of the security of society".[109] A CPP spokesperson declared that Hong Sok Hour wanted "to lead the people to revolutionize against the legitimate government",[110] and a government spokesperson added that he was trying to get people to become "angry and rebel" as part of the same colour revolution plot as the eleven insurrectionists.[111]

The next month, Tran Cong Truc, former head of Vietnam's Government Border Committee, published an article praising Hun Sen's "tireless efforts to neutralize every resistant and destructive ploy to distort the border and territorial issues between the two countries used by Cambodia's opposition political forces in order to resist and destroy him, deceive the masses, and garner votes". He particularly decried the Cambodian opposition's use of "political tricks" related to border and territorial issues to gain seats in the 2013 elections. However, he said, Hun Sen had been handling "quite convincingly" what he called the "culmination" since June of CNRP's efforts to "incite social unrest", thereby stabilizing Cambodian society. He added that even if some "extremist opponents" were still "provoking extreme nationalism", the "experienced politician" Hun Sen could be relied upon to successfully run Cambodia's complex multiparty system, including via necessary "radical" measures to deal with the "scourge" of ultra-nationalism, such as prosecutions of figures like SRP Senator Hong Sok Hour.[112]

In follow-up articles published in early October 2015, Tran Cong Truc specified this meant that Cambodia "needed to appropriately punish troublemakers like Um Sam-an", a CNRP parliamentarian who had led expeditions to the border, but who by this time was out of Cambodia. Tran Cong Truc denounced Um Sam An and other CNRP figures as reactionary "traitorous elements" conspiring to disrupt not only Cambodia–Vietnam relations but also "causing political and social instability" in Cambodia.[113]

Um Sam An was arrested immediately upon his return to Cambodia in April 2016 for having previously posted on Facebook allegations that the maps being used by the Vietnamese and Cambodian governments to locate the border were inauthentic, and that the latter was guilty of a sell-out of land to Vietnam. He was convicted and sentenced to prison in October 2016 for inciting social instability and anti-Vietnamese discrimination.[114] Like the eleven CNRP "insurrectionists", he remains in prison. (Hong Sok Hour, however, was released on 25 October 2017 by royal pardon at Hun Sen's request after the senator wrote to the Prime Minister expressing regret for disseminating what he said was an inaccurate text and praising Hun Sen's handling of border matters.)[115]

Towards Showdown with the CNRP

The 2015 handling of the Montagnard and CNRP border activism crises did not pre-emptively resolve the potentially much larger and more serious ones that could come about if the opposition were to win National Assembly elections in July 2018. Both the CPP and CPV had reasons to fear that the polls could not only end CPP political hegemony but also open the floodgates for Montagnard asylum seekers, for CNRP border challenges and for CNRP facilitation in Cambodia of anti-CPV activities among Montagnards and also ethnic Vietnamese.

In January 2017, a Vietnamese government website published an article hailing Vietnam–Cambodia cooperation and criminal proceedings in Cambodia against Sam Rainsy, Hong Sok Hour, Um Sam An and the eleven CNRP activists. However, it expressed concern that the CNRP was nevertheless "aggressively moving into border areas" to do campaigning for elections in 2017 and 2018, and that meanwhile anti-CPV "reactionary exile organizations", especially FULRO, might again be increasing their presence in Cambodia.[116]

Highlighting the notion of a Montagnard threat, a Cambodian government-aligned online outlet accused Sam Rainsy in February 2017 of treason, basing this on his having signed a cooperation agreement with the U.S.-based anti-CPV Montagnard Foundation that allowed this organization to operate from inside Cambodia.[117] Hanoi has long maintained that the foundation is a terrorist organization threatening Vietnam's national security by fomenting secessionism among Central Highlands Montagnards.[118] Seeming to confirm Vietnamese fears, in April 2017 Sam Rainsy called for the non-refoulement of Montagnard asylum seekers, describing them as refugees facing human rights–violating punishment once back in Vietnam.[119]

As regards ethnically Vietnamese "hostile forces", just after the commune elections, a CPP spokesperson recalled long-standing CPP allegations[120] that Sam Rainsy had once made an agreement with an anti-Communist "Free Yuon Movement" based in the United States, allowing it a presence in Cambodia.[121] Earlier, the Vietnamese Ministry of Public Security had deemed Viet Tan, another U.S.-based anti-CPV movement, a "terrorist organization", specifying it had a history of using Cambodia as a base for operations against Vietnam.[122] Viet Tan confirmed a 2017 presence in Phnom Penh by reporting that on 2 September a member of its Central Committee who was one of four Viet Tan members then in-country had been the victim of an acid attack that it alleged was carried out by Vietnamese government security forces.[123]

Joint RCAF-VPA concern about a possible resurgence of CNRP border activism was apparent during a March 2017 meeting in Cambodia between a VPA regional commander[124] and RCAF Commander-in-Chief Pol Saroeun, who felt it was still necessary to reassure Vietnam that "if any individual accuses the Royal Government of having ceded land to Vietnam, they will be arrested and thrown in jail".[125]

It is thus no surprise that at a Phnom Penh ceremony on 27 November 2017, a senior Cambodian defence ministry officer denounced the defeated "poisonous schemes, plans and activities of the CNRP, which was colluding with foreigners to overthrow" the government, and Vietnam's military attaché declared that Vietnam would continue to be Cambodia's "comrade-in-arms", vowing once more that the two countries would maintain their friendship regardless of what circumstances might arise in Cambodia. Government-friendly media affirmed that this signalled Vietnam's support for the arrest of Kem Sokha, dissolution of the CNRP and related recent measures.[126] During 21 December 2017 discussions with Hun Sen about the "victorious suppression" of the purported threat of a CNRP colour revolution, Vietnam's deputy minister of national defence reaffirmed that his country fully backed Cambodia in doing whatever it needed to do to prevent "social instability". In line with Hun Sen's request for strengthened bilateral opposition to any ongoing attempts at colour revolution,[127] the Vietnamese official agreed with the Cambodian defence ministry to further "intensify cooperation" during 2018.[128]

Common Interests, Not Master–Supplicant

All this points to a conclusion that keeping the CNRP out of power, if necessary by eliminating it from the contest for power, is a strongly shared CPP–CPV common interest that lies at the core of their comprehensive relationship and is most concretely manifest in the relationship between their security forces. However, this and other CPP–CPV common interests do not add up to Vietnamese domination of Cambodia, as is shown, inter alia, by Cambodia's refusal to toe Vietnam's line on the South China Sea.[129]

Thus, assertions like that by overseas Cambodian activist Chham Chhany that Hun Sen's recent moves to "smash the CNRP" have been because "he wanted to please the Yuon" wrongly posit a master–supplicant relationship.[130] The reality is that the CPP has had an increasingly urgent interest in convincing the CPV that the CNRP is a one-and-the-same "unfriend" of Cambodia and a "hostile force" vis-à-vis Vietnam, but the CPV has needed no convincing. Thus, a more persuasive analysis of their relations comes from Merle Pribbenow, a long-term observer of Vietnam's security forces and their relations with Cambodia: "Vietnam shares and supports Hun Sen's view of the CNRP" and "clearly has some influence on the Cambodian government and on the Cambodian military/security apparatus", but "does not have any meaningful level of control over Hun Sen and the CPP" nor "anything that approaches control over" its security forces.[131]

This reflects the fact that although Vietnam was originally able to dominate the regime it created and nurtured in Cambodia from 1979 to 1989, it lost its once almost totally decisive leverage in the late 1980s to early 1990s.[132]

Current Cambodia–Vietnam relations are the result of an evolution away from dependency into a reasonable fit with political scientist Brantly Womack's model of "mature asymmetry"; that is, a stable relationship "between units confident of the acknowledgment of their basic interests by the other and in which the management of the relationship is institutionalized". Although Vietnam is in the stronger position, and the two sides do not have identical interests and perspectives on all issues, Cambodia's autonomy is recognized and respected by Vietnam in the context of consensus on other crucial areas of common concern.[133] This outcome is also in line with what historian Liam Kelley has suggested the bottom-line objective of pre-colonial Vietnamese political projects and diplomacy vis-à-vis Cambodia have been: not necessarily conquest, absorption, mass colonization or mass cultural Vietnamization, but having in power there Khmer leaders who agree with their Vietnamese counterparts on who their common enemies are and who are willing and able to fight them.[134] That the CPV most definitely now has in today's CPP Cambodia.

Notes

1. <https://www.dap-news.com/kh/ព័ត៌មានក្នុងប្រទេស/24591.html>; <http://vtv.vn/viet-nam-va-the-gioi/doan-dai-bieu-dang-cong-san-viet-nam-tham-chinh-thuc-campuchia-20150608181235385.html>.
2. <http://www.baomoi.com/Dai-hoi-Dang-XII-doi-moi-the-che-kinh-te-la-nhiem-vu-uu-tien/c/18507522.epi>.
3. <http://www.baomoi.com/dong-chi-truong-thi-mai-tiep-doan-dai-bieu-campuchia/c/20983552.epi>.
4. <http://www.baomoi.com/viet-nam-campuchia-giu-vung-tinh-huu-nghi/c/20980965.epi>.
5. Speech by Nguyen Ho, Ho Chi Minh Domestic Service, 9 January 1979; Hoang Van Thai, "On the Special Relations of Cooperation among the Three Indochinese Nations", *Tap Chi Cong San*, January 1982; speech by Vo Chi Cong, VNA, 30 April 1990.
6. <http://www.qdnd.vn/qdndsite/vi-vn/61/43/quan-doi/bo-truong-bo-quoc-phong-campuchia-tham-chinh-thuc-viet-nam/392537.html>.
7. <http://www.qdnd.vn/qdndsite/vi-vn/61/43/quan-doi/bo-truong-bo-quoc-phong-campuchia-tham-chinh-thuc-viet-nam/392537.html>.
8. <http://www.quansuvn.net/index.php?topic=4304.120>;
<http://www.dap-news.com/2011-06-14-02-39-55/99609-2015-09-22-08-07-20.html>.
9. <http://www.baomoi.com/quan-he-tot-dep-ben-vung-viet-nam-campuchia-mai-mai-nhu-dong-mekong-noi-lien-hai-nuoc/c/22582332.epi>; <http://www.baomoi.com/thu-tuong-hun-sen-cam-on-viet-nam-khi-tro-lai-binh-phuoc/c/22582102.epi>.

10. <http://www.baomoi.com/nhung-luc-kho-khan-nhat-chi-co-viet-nam-giup-do-campuchia/c/22579231.epi>.
11. <http://www.dap-news.com/2011-06-14-02-39-55/85529-----mou---0.html>; <http://www.baomoi.com/khong-the-luc-thu-dich-nao-chia-re-duoc-quan-he-campuchia-viet-nam/c/21130217.epi>.
12. <http://www.baomoi.com/chu-tich-nuoc-tran-dai-quang-tiep-thu-tuong-campuchia-hun-sen/c/21130838.epi>.
13. <http://www.baomoi.com/thu-tuong-hun-sen-viet-nam-va-campuchia-nhu-moi-voi-rang/c/21140704.epi>.
14. Womack, Brantley, *China and Vietnam: The Politics of Asymmetry* (Cambridge: Cambridge University Press, 2006), pp. 162–73.
15. <http://bit.ly/2njxcrn>.
16. <http://qk7.qdnd.vn/vi-vn/118/337/doi-ngoai-quoc-phong-quan-khu-7-bao-ve-to-quoc-va-hoi-nhap-quoc-te/390691.html>.
17. <http://www.baomoi.com/Khong-ai-co-quyen-nhan-nhuong-ve-chu-quyen-lanh-tho/c/18512637.epi>.
18. <https://www.dap-news.com/kh/ព័ត៌មានក្នុងប្រទេស/8174.html>.
19. <http://www.baomoi.com/khong-the-chia-re-tinh-doan-ket-viet-nam-campuchia/c/22805345.epi>.
20. <http://www.qdnd.vn/chong-dien-bien-hoa-binh>.
21. <http://www.tapchicongsan.org.vn/Home/xay-dung-dang/2017/42980/Canh-giac-voi-am-muu-thu-doan-phi-chinh-tri-hoa-luc.aspx>.
22. <http://laodong.com.vn/chinh-tri/loi-dung-van-de-ton-giao-de-chong-pha-viet-nam-39334.bld>.
23. <http://www.dautruongdanchu.com/2017/03/thu-oan-nguy-hiem-cua-chien-luoc-dien.html>.
24. <http://www.tapchicongsan.org.vn/Home/Binh-luan/2017/43499/Xay-dung-Chien-luoc-ket-hop-quoc-phong-an-ninh-doi-ngoai.aspx>.
25. <http://www.phnompenhpost.com/national-post-depth-politics/death-democracy-cnrp-dissolved-supreme-court-ruling>.
26. <http://kpt-news.com/local-news/28089-2013-05-18-06-24-00.html>.
27. <http://edition.bayontv.com.kh/bayontv-national-news/24791-2014-04-11-04-23-01.html>.
28. <http://vodhotnews.com/25285>.
29. <http://m.freshnewsasia.com/index.php/en/localnews/68795-2017-10-27-11-58-35.html>.
30. <http://www.phnompenhpost.com/national/sokha-arrested-treason-accused-colluding-us-topple-government>.
31. <http://www.phnompenhpost.com/post-weekend/sam-rainsy-faces-arrest-warrant>.
32. <https://www.cambodiadaily.com/news/in-sweeping-address-pm-defends-border-work-93682/>.

33. <https://www.dap-news.com/kh/ព័ត៌មានក្នុងប្រទេស/29375.html>.
34. <http://www.dap-news.com/2011-06-14-02-39-55/99631-2015-09-22-13-06-45.html>; <https://www.cambodiadaily.com/news/hun-sen-says-sam-rainsy-no-different-than-pol-pot-97014/>.
35. Vannarith Chheang, "Cambodian Power Shift in 2018?" *ISEAS Perspective* 2017, no. 53 (17 July 2017).
36. <http://vtv.vn/tin-tuc/dai-hoi-dang-toan-quoc-dang-nhan-dan-campuchia-20150130182944126.htm>.
37. <http://vov.vn/chinh-tri/doan-ban-doi-ngoai-tw-dang-nhan-dan-campuchia-lam-viec-tai-viet-nam-450312.vov>.
38. <http://vov.vn/chinh-tri/tong-bi-thu-tiep-bo-truong-quoc-phong-campuchia-458875.vov>.
39. <http://www.baomoi.com/chu-tich-nuoc-tran-dai-quang-tiep-thu-tuong-campuchia-hun-sen/c/21130838.epi>.
40. <http://www.baomoi.com/lua-chon-hoa-binh-on-dinh-va-phat-trien/c/22472701.epi>.
41. <http://www.baomoi.com/kinh-te-campuchia-tren-da-tang-truong-kha-quan/c/22592656.epi>.
42. <http://www.baomoi.com/thanh-uy-ha-noi-va-dang-nhan-dan-campuchia-trao-doi-kinh-nghiem-cong-tac-kiem-tra-giam-sat/c/22981785.epi>.
43. <http://www.thanhnien.com.vn/chinh-tri-xa-hoi/thuong-tuong-nguyen-chi-vinh-viet-nam-campuchia-chu-trong-quan-he-quoc-phong-khu-vuc-bien-gioi-622706.html>.
44. <http://baophapluat.vn/thoi-su/viet-nam-campuchia-doi-thoai-chien-luoc-quoc-phong-233138.html>.
45. <http://www.thanhnien.com.vn/chinh-tri-xa-hoi/thuong-tuong-nguyen-chi-vinh-viet-nam-campuchia-chu-trong-quan-he-quoc-phong-khu-vuc-bien-gioi-622706.html>.
46. <http://en.baomoi.com/Source/VOV-News-English/118.epi>; <http://www.baomoi.com/campuchia-khanh-thanh-toa-nha-so-chi-huy-bo-tu-lenh-tang-thiet-giap-do-viet-nam-vien-tro/c/21889156.epi>; <http://en.baomoi.com/Source/VOV-News-English/118.epi>.
47. <http://baotintuc.vn/thoi-su/quan-doi-viet-nam-tai-tro-kinh-phi-xay-benh-xa-cho-campuchia-20150228134948544.htm>.
48. <http://hanoimoi.com.vn/Tin-tuc/Doi-ngoai/806659/viet-nam-giup-do-quan-doi-campuchia-xay-dung-ha-tang-dao-tao>.
49. <http://www.khmertimeskh.com/news/32577/vietnam-and-cambodia-military-ties-mature/>.
50. <http://www.baomoi.com/dai-tuong-ngo-xuan-lich-du-le-trao-bang-tien-si-cho-can-bo-cao-cap-quan-doi-hoang-gia-campuchia/c/22255356.epi>.
51. <http://www.baomoi.com/bo-cong-an-coi-trong-tang-cuong-hop-tac-voi-chinh-phu-campuchia/c/21070424.epi>.
52. <https://www.cambodiadaily.com/news/hanoi-funded-police-academy-inaugurated-in-kompong-speu-76366/>.
53. <http://kpt-news.com/local-news/general-news/23293-2015-01-17-04-27-14.html>.

54. <http://cand.com.vn/thoi-su/doan-Bo-Noi-vu-Vuong-quoc-Campuchia-lam-viec-tai-Cao-dang-aNNd-ii-359948/>.
55. <http://www.baomoi.com/baotintuc.vn-bao-tin-tuc-ttxvn-tin-tuc-ttx/p/294.epi>.
56. <http://www.baomoi.com/an-ninh-viet-nam-campuchia-hop-tac-triet-pha-nhieu-chuyen-an/c/22810443.epi>.
57. "The Provocateur" <https://www.cambodiadaily.com/weekend/>.
58. <http://www.vanchuongviet.org/index.php?comp=tacpham&action=detail&id=17477>; <http://danlambaovn.blogspot.com/2014/02/sam-rainsy-con-co-moi-cua-trung-cong.html>.
59. <https://www.cambodiadaily.com/news/k-krom-mark-66-years-since-cochinchine-pact-85037/>; <http://www.phnompenhpost.com/national/cnrp-clings-anti-vietnamese-rhetoric>.
60. <http://www.baomoi.com/ky-4-nha-nguyen-thuc-thi-va-bao-ve-chu-quyen-tren-vung-dat-nam-bo/c/23095818.epi>; <http://giaoduc.net.vn/quoc-te/khong-ai-co-the-lat-lai-hiep-uoc-bien-gioi-viet-namcampuchia-post159767.gd>.
61. Brian A. Zottoli, "Reconceptualizing Southern Vietnamese History from the 15th to 18th Centuries: Competition along the Coasts from Guangdong to Cambodia" (PhD dissertation, Department of History, University of Michigan, 2011); Liam Kelly, "Revisiting the Vietnamese Annexation of Cambodia" (1–8) <https://leminhkhai.wordpress.com>.
62. <http://www.baomoi.com/doan-dai-bieu-uy-ban-dan-toc-quoc-hoi-viet-nam-tham-campuchia/c/19749837.epi>.
63. <https://www.cambodiadaily.com/news/parties-diverge-over-leniancy-for-immigrants-116972/>.
64. <http://www.khmertimeskh.com/5085566/vietnam-alarm-documents-purge/>.
65. <https://www.cambodiadaily.com/news/kem-sokha-says-theres-no-racism-in-cambodia-95426/>.
66. <http://www.bienphong.com.vn/tang-cuong-ngan-chan-vuot-bien-trai-phep-o-tay-nguyen/30468.bbp>.
67. <http://bienphong.com.vn/baobienphong/news/bdbp-dak-lak-mot-nam-voi-nhieu-cai-moi/29064.bbp>.
68. <http://congankontum.gov.vn/hdccat/xay-dung-luc-luong-ca/52912-mot-so-kinh-nghiem-trong-cong-tac-dan-van-o-vung-dong-bao-dan-toc-thieu-so-cua-luc-luong-cscd.html>.
69. <http://bienphong.com.vn/baobienphong/news/bdbp-dak-lak-mot-nam-voi-nhieu-cai-moi/29064.bbp>.
70. <http://www.vietnamplus.vn/tang-hop-tac-luc-luong-vu-trang-dak-nong-va-tinh-mundulkiri/321153.vnp>.
71. <http://www.dap-news.com/2011-06-14-02-39-55/99609-2015-09-22-08-07-20.html>.
72. <http://www.phnompenhpost.com/national/troops-sent-ratanakkiri-border-area>.

73. <http://www.phnompenhpost.com/national/soldiers-say-main-mission-stopping-refugees>.
74. <http://www.baomoi.com/Vong-tay-rong-mo/c/17433759.epi>.
75. <http://www.phnompenhpost.com/national/seven-asylees-fly-out>.
76. <https://www.cambodiadaily.com/second2/govt-slammed-plans-send-montagnards-vietnam-134230/>.
77. <http://www.khmertimeskh.com/5084745/172-montagnards-deported/>.
78. <http://vodhotnews.com/26721>.
79. <http://vodhotnews.com/29773>.
80. "Main Statement by Samdech Akka Moha Sena Padei Techo Hun Sen Prime Minister of the Kingdom of Cambodia on 'Demarcation of Land Boundary and Maritime Delineation between the Kingdom of Cambodia and the Socialist Republic of Vietnam': The Plenary Session of the National Assembly, 9 August 2012", np, nd, p. 67.
81. Border map analysis done by Cambodian non-governmental organization, in the author's possession.
82. <https://www.longan.gov.vn/chinh-quyen/Pages/ban-do-hanh-chinh.aspx?InitparamUrl=/BanDo/DatDai/BanDoHanhChinh/HuyenMocHoa/XaBinhHoaTay>.
83. <http://www.conganlongan.gov.vn/laca/ch12/189.prt>.
84. "Thông cáo báo chí", *Nhân Dân*, 17 January 1995.
85. <http://www.dap-news.com/2011-06-14-02-39-55/95557-2015-07-20-09-34-22.html>.
86. <http://giaoduc.net.vn/quoc-te/viet-nam-nen-kien-tri-hop-tac-voi-campuchia-tuyen-truyen-giai-thich-ve-bien-gioi-post162184.gd>.
87. <https://www.dap-news.com/kh/[illegible]/54283.html>.
88. <https://www.youtube.com/watch?v=gIYVq7DhS7M>.
89. <http://tuoitre.vn/tin/chinh-tri-xa-hoi/phan-tu-qua-khich-campuchia-lam-7-nguoi-viet-bi-thuong/20150701/phan-tu-qua-khich-campuchia-lam-7-nguoi-viet-bi-thuong/769539.html>.
90. <http://kampucheathmey.com/kpt/?p=35040>.
91. <http://www.khmertimeskh.com/news/12989/what-is-the-political-end-game-of-the-vn-border-dispute-/>.
92. <https://www.cambodiadaily.com/archives/cpp-friendly-businessman-launches-newspaper-58610/>.
93. <http://www.phnompenhpost.com/national/portions-leaks-verified-nine>.
94. <http://baotintuc.vn/thoi-su/viet-nam-va-campuchia-phoi-hop-giu-gin-an-ninh-trat-tu-bien-gioi-20150720183849198.htm>.
95. <http://vodhotnews.com/30914>.
96. <https://www.cambodiadaily.com/news/despite-obstacles-cnrp-activists-reach-border-88874/>.
97. <http://www.phnompenhpost.com/national/point-no-resolution>.
98. <http://baotintuc.vn/thoi-su/viet-nam-va-campuchia-phoi-hop-giu-gin-an-ninh-trat-tu-bien-gioi-20150720183849198.htm>.

99. <https://www.cambodiadaily.com/news/authorities-in-svay-rieng-wont-talk-about-thugs-at-border-89004/>.
100. <https://www.cambodiadaily.com/news/despite-obstacles-cnrp-activists-reach-border-88874/>.
101. <http://cand.com.vn/thoi-su/lien-quan-den-cot-moc-chu-quyen-203-viet-nam-campuchia-phoi-hop-giu-gin-an-ninh-trat-tu-bien-gioi-khong-de-xay-ra-tranh-chap-358971/>.
102. <http://www.phnompenhpost.com/national/point-no-resolution>.
103. <http://vodhotnews.com/30917>.
104. <http://phapluattp.vn/thoi-su/chinh-tri/dua-tren-can-cu-phap-ly-ro-rang-khong-the-phu-nhan-569511.html>.
105. <https://www.amnesty.org/en/latest/news/2015/07/cambodia-quash-insurrection-ruling-against-opposition-activists-following-unfair-trial/>.
106. <https://www.cambodiadaily.com/news/pm-hosts-mass-meeting-of-armed-forces-89310/>.
107. <http://www.dap-news.com/2011-06-14-02-39-55/95757-2015-07-23-07-58-54.html>.
108. <http://www.khmertimeskh.com/news/13629/impunity--ngos-and-lango/>.
109. <https://www.hrw.org/news/2015/10/01/cambodia-drop-case-against-opposition-senator>;
110. <http://www.khmertimeskh.com/news/14527/rule-of-law-vs-political-expediency/>.
111. <https://www.cambodiadaily.com/news/govt-spokesman-says-senator-wanted-color-revolution-92099/>.
112. <http://giaoduc.net.vn/quoc-te/ts-tran-cong-truc-vai-loi-nhan-gui-thu-tuong-hun-sen-post161725.gd>.
113. <http://giaoduc.net.vn/quoc-te/campuchia-can-trung-tri-thich-dang-nghi-si-phan-dong-um-sam-an-post162183.gd>; <http://giaoduc.net.vn/quoc-te/viet-nam-nen-kien-tri-hop-tac-voi-campuchia-tuyen-truyen-giai-thich-ve-bien-gioi-post162184.gd>.
114. <https://www.cambodiadaily.com/news/opposition-lawmaker-sentenced-facebook-posts-119092/>.
115. <http://www.freshnewsasia.com/index.php/en/localnews/68545-2017-10-25-08-16-30.html>.
116. <http://www.baobinhphuoc.com.vn/Content/cau-tra-loi-danh-thep-cho-bon-pha-hoai-tinh-doan-ket-viet-nam---campuchia-303110>.
117. <http://www.freshnewsasia.com/index.php/en/localnews/47280-facebook-5.html>.
118. <http://www.mofa.gov.vn/vi/nr040807104143/nr040807105001/ns050819141225/The%20book%20%20-%20Achievements%20in%20protecting%20and%20promoting%20human%20rights%20in%20Vietnam.doc/view, 2005>.
119. <https://www.dap-news.com/kh/ព័ត៌មានក្នុងប្រទេស/34171.html>.
120. <http://www.phnompenhpost.com/national/srp-denies-link-free-vietnam-movement>.
121. <https://www.dap-news.com/kh/ព័ត៌មានក្នុងប្រទេស/41400.html>.

122. <http://www.baomoi.com/bo-cong-an-thong-bao-ve-to-chuc-khung-bo-viet-tan/c/20512757.epi>.
123. <http://www.ttdq.de/node/3441>; <http://www.rfa.org/vietnamese/in_depth/vietnam-opponent-acid-attacked-09182017140214.html>.
124. <https://www.dap-news.com/kh/ព័ត៌មានក្នុងប្រទេស/33335.html>.
125. <https://www.dap-news.com/kh/ព័ត៌មានក្នុងប្រទេស/33397.html>.
126. <https://www.dap-news.com/kh/ព័ត៌មានក្នុងប្រទេស/56926.html>.
127. <https://www.dap-news.com/kh/ព័ត៌មានក្នុងប្រទេស/59277.html>.
128. <https://www.vietnamplus.vn/viet-namcampuchia-phoi-hop-phong-chong-cuu-ho-cuu-nan-khu-bien-gioi/480751.vnp>.
129. <http://www.phnompenhpost.com/national/asean-treads-lightly-south-china-sea-observers-point-cambodias-support-beijing>.
130. <http://hrkhnews.com/?p=7099>.
131. Personnel communications from Merle Pribbenow, 8 August and 7 November 2017.
132. <http://timsach.com.vn/viewEBOOK_38_7503_hoi-ky-Tran-Quang-Co.html; http://vietsuky.wordpress.com/2012/12/01/220-ghi-chep-ve-campuchia-1975-1991-1/>.
133. Womack, *China and Vietnam*, pp. 235–36, 240.
134. <https://leminhkhai.wordpress.com/2017/08/21/revisiting-the-vietnamese-annexation-of-cambodia-3-king-chan-and-vietnam/>.

Indonesia

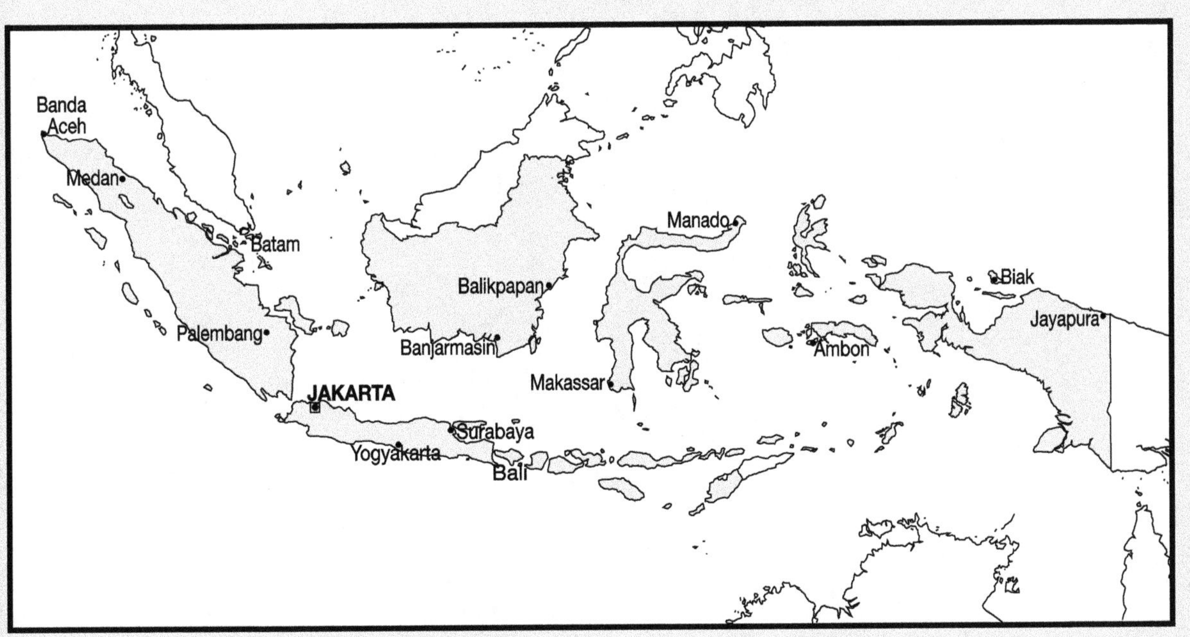

Banda Aceh
Medan
Batam
Palembang
JAKARTA
Yogyakarta
Surabaya
Bali
Banjarmasin
Balikpapan
Makassar
Manado
Ambon
Biak
Jayapura

INEQUALITY, NATIONALISM AND ELECTORAL POLITICS IN INDONESIA

Eve Warburton

As election season looms, President Joko Widodo's (Jokowi) political opponents have begun to craft their campaign message.[1] From mid-2017, Prabowo Subianto, Jokowi's closest rival, made an increasing number of public appearances. Campaign-style videos started to appear with greater frequency on his party's (Gerindra) social media pages. Gerindra's twitter profile, for example, was filled with content about economic inequality, emphasizing to followers that the richest 1 per cent of Indonesians own 49 per cent of the country's wealth.[2] In one video, posted in November 2017, Prabowo blames Indonesia's worsening economic inequality on a political elite who have abandoned the egalitarian spirit of Indonesia's 1945 Constitution.[3] Meanwhile, senior members of Gerindra, along with Jokowi's other detractors from Partai Keadilan Sejahtera (PKS), and conservative Islamic groups, accuse the Jokowi government of providing economic privileges to foreign business interests and Indonesian Chinese tycoons. Indonesia's Muslim masses, they intimate, have been excluded and left behind.

These claims of economic injustice, whether real or imagined, are typical of a populist political style. Prabowo ran on a similar platform during the 2014 presidential race, and lost. So, how vulnerable is Jokowi to this kind of narrative? To what extent might such nationalist and populist appeals have more traction with the electorate in 2019 than they did in 2014? Are exclusivist electoral campaigns and nationalist economic agendas becoming a permanent fixture of post-Suharto politics?

This chapter attempts to address these questions. It begins with a brief overview of populist politics and economic nationalism in the Indonesian context. It then progresses in three sections, each of which explores a major line of critique put

EVE WARBURTON is Visiting Fellow at the ISEAS – Yusof Ishak Institute.

forward by Jokowi's political rivals: (1) growth, foreign investment and the China problem; (2) resource nationalism and food sovereignty; and (3) socio-economic inequality. It argues that Jokowi's economic record has been mixed over the past three years, which exposes him to technocratic critiques about missed economic targets and poor policy execution. But he is also vulnerable to populist-nationalist attacks, which exaggerate the president's closeness to China and Indonesian Chinese tycoons and question his commitment to the prosperity of the *ummah*. In a fourth section, I look at Jokowi's attempt to adjust his economic message and undercut these critiques. The chapter closes by reflecting on scholarly debate about the conditions which have produced an upswing in populist politics and economic nationalism in Indonesia.

Populism and Economic Nationalism in Indonesia

Like many countries around the world, Indonesia has experienced an upswing in populist politics in recent years. Particularly since the 2014 presidential elections, leading analysts of Indonesian politics have identified new and competing forms of populism.[4] Populist politicians set out to challenge an existing politico-economic order by claiming it serves the interests of a narrow, corrupt and entrenched elite.[5] Populists mobilize popular grievances with the status quo, and paint themselves as political outsiders who can best defend "the people" against "crises, threats and enemies".[6] Mudde describes populism as an ideology that claims to represent the "pure people", and its ideological opposites are "elitism and pluralism".[7]

What does populism look like in the economic sphere? During the 1980s and 1990s, many scholars associated populism with "expansionary developmentalist economic policies" and welfare interventions.[8] Based primarily upon case studies from Latin America, economic nationalism was seen as a fundamental part of the populist agenda, too.[9] However, populists can also fuse their political strategy with neoliberal economic ideas, and as such there is no uniform set of populist economic policies.[10] Most analysts refer to populism as a political style, without attaching it to an economic ideology.

When it comes to Indonesia, however, populist political styles and movements have long been tied to statist and protectionist socio-economic ideas. The first president, Sukarno, presented a style of politics in which, according to Aspinall, "[p]opulism, along with nationalism, was the ideological centrepiece."[11] Hadiz observes a prominent place for "Islamic populism" in Indonesia's political history as well, which propagates the idea of an *ummah* that is economically aggrieved and constantly under threat from non-believers.[12] Both secular and Islamic forms of populism embraced protectionist economic ideas and expressed antagonism towards foreign actors.

In the contemporary post-Suharto period, Aspinall observes how:

> invocations of 'the people', condemnations of elite corruption, propagation of economic nationalism, and rhetorical hostility to capitalism and neoliberalism have all become the basic stuff of mainstream politics[13]

But it was not until 2014 that an explicitly populist style of politics once again rose to prominence. Mietzner characterized the 2014 presidential election as a race between two different kinds of populists: Jokowi was a polite, "technocratic populist", while Prabowo represented a neo-authoritarian brand of populism.[14] The overarching theme of Prabowo's campaign was that Indonesia's democracy and its economy had been stolen. The corrupt elite had allowed foreigners to exploit Indonesia's land, labour and resources at the expense of the people. Prabowo combined this political populism with a protectionist and nationalist economic platform that focused on natural resources and food sovereignty.[15]

Jokowi, on the other hand, offered a moderate brand of populism, and his economic nationalism was also less extreme. There was no aggressive rejection of the political or economic status quo. Instead, it was Jokowi's image as a political outsider, and a humble man of the people, that constituted his populist appeal.[16] Jokowi did not clearly articulate an economic agenda. Indeed, his entire campaign was, as described by Mietzner, a "piecemeal compilation of ideas and proposals, [with] no overarching message".[17] But, like Prabowo, he expressed a commitment to economic sovereignty and self-sufficiency, and he promised to overcome the socio-economic inequalities between Java and the outer regions. To the extent that he outlined a plan for redistribution, Jokowi promised the same kind of subsidized health and education programmes he had become famous for when governor of Jakarta. While lacking in detail, Jokowi's plan thus had a pro-poor and nationalist orientation.

Now, as the 2019 elections draw near, the president's economic achievements are coming under scrutiny. How has Jokowi's economic agenda evolved over the past three years, what has been the public's response, and what kind of critique have the president's detractors put forward?

Growth, Foreign Investment and the China Problem

During his first two years in office, Jokowi's focus on fast economic growth overshadowed his pro-poor and distributive agenda. The president spent much of his political capital marketing the government's state-led infrastructure boom and reforming the business investment climate. With funds freed-up by the removal of fuel subsidies back in 2014, the Jokowi administration allocated an unprecedented amount of money to expanding Indonesia's roads, ports and power stations.[18] The government prioritized over two hundred projects for completion by 2019. In an effort to speed up the process, Jokowi distributed many of the most strategic contracts to state-owned enterprises (SOEs), and provided them with budget funds and state loans.[19] The scale of the government's infrastructure plan meant that the private sector would need to make a significant contribution as well. The government estimated that 31 per cent of the financing would come from private investors, 50 per cent from the state budget, and 19 per cent from SOEs.[20]

Jokowi's other key economic programmes — like a tax amnesty initiative and a series of deregulation packages — sought to boost revenue and private investment to help sustain the infrastructure boom and motivate higher economic growth.[21] Economists and the business community welcomed Jokowi's reform priorities. For decades analysts had argued that aging transport and road infrastructure kept Indonesia from breaking free of the lower-middle-income trap.

With elections on the horizon in 2018 and 2019, however, Jokowi's political opponents stepped up their criticism of the government's record on growth, investment and infrastructure. The two parties in opposition, Gerindra and PKS, point regularly to Jokowi's missed targets and problems with project implementation. They claim the government has wasted state funds and clocked up reckless levels of debt in order to fund its infrastructure projects, the vast majority of which remain incomplete.[22]

Indeed, the implementation process has been less than ideal. President Jokowi admitted that in 2017 only about 9 per cent of its priority infrastructure projects were complete, 40 per cent were under construction, 5 per cent were still at the transaction stage, and the remaining 37 per cent were still being planned.[23] Although the infrastructure boom and deregulation packages were projected to boost economic growth, Indonesia's GDP growth rates remained stubbornly at around 5 per cent.

To be fair, compared to many countries, 5 per cent growth looked impressive. In 2016, Indonesia's GDP figures were higher than neighbouring Malaysia and Thailand. But Indonesia was eclipsed by Vietnam, Cambodia and Laos, who all achieved growth figures of over 6 per cent. Most importantly, Indonesia's GDP growth levels remained below the 7 per cent Jokowi consistently promised since coming to office.

The main line of critique that emerged from Jokowi's opponents, however, was framed in nationalist rather than technocratic terms. They accused the president of prioritizing foreign investors and putting growth before welfare and inequality. PKS and Gerindra argued, for example, that Jokowi's development projects disproportionately benefit foreign investors. In the rhetorical style typical of Jokowi's critics, one PKS legislator claimed that under Jokowi, Indonesia submits to "compradors, foreign capitalists, and corporations", and that foreign companies and foreign labour are reaping the rewards of Indonesia's infrastructure boom.[24] Deputy chairperson of Gerindra, Ferry Juliantono, told the press that:

> The government's priority to develop infrastructure is not right. Factories are built by foreigners, the workers are foreigners, and yet it's the public's money that is used for these projects, our people don't profit.[25]

China has featured prominently in this nationalist narrative. Critics accused the Jokowi government of relying heavily on capital and companies from China. Prabowo, opposition parties, and high-profile Islamic leaders made hyperbolic claims that Jokowi is "selling Indonesia off" to Chinese investors and giving jobs away to Chinese labourers.[26] Amein Rais, a founder of Partai Amanat Nasional (PAN) and head of the party's Dewan Kehormatan (Esteemed Council), was quoted often in the media, proclaiming the malign ambitions of Chinese investors and foreign workers.[27]

Direct investment from China has indeed increased in recent years, as has the volume of Chinese labour brought in to work on Chinese-financed construction projects.[28] Back in 2010, China was placed ninth in the top source countries for FDI into Indonesia; by 2016 it came in third place.[29] The panic about Chinese labour, however, appears to be seriously exaggerated. To put things in perspective, according to Indonesia's Foreign Investment Board, foreign workers of all nationalities still only constitute 0.1 per cent of the labour force in Indonesia.[30] The minister for manpower confirmed in a statement to the media that on average Indonesia had accepted only 14,000–16,000 Chinese workers a year between 2011 and 2016.[31]

So, to what extent might such a nationalist critique of Jokowi's development agenda, and its alleged dependence upon Chinese capital, resonate with the electorate? Recent opinion polls indicate a constituency for such nationalist and anti-Chinese narratives. For example, a survey conducted by the ISEAS – Yusof Ishak Institute in May 2017 revealed that China was the country least admired by Indonesians (at least of those included in the survey), and very few (27.7 per cent) felt Indonesia would benefit from close ties with the global superpower.[32] Around half of respondents wanted Chinese labour migration to be limited, and

26.6 per cent felt Chinese citizens should not be allowed to work in Indonesia at all. About a quarter of respondents (25.2 per cent) wanted a complete ban on Chinese investment, while 54 per cent felt investment should be limited.[33]

These polls suggest a level of disquiet within the electorate about the place of foreign — and particularly Chinese — investment and labour in the economy. Chinese investment is contentious in many countries in the region. Conflicting territorial claims, histories of war, and concerns over one-party communist rule have made China a controversial business partner for governments in North and Southeast Asia, as well as Australia.

In Indonesia, however, antagonism towards China is tied to a long history of racial prejudice against the Indonesian Chinese minority. Indeed, opposition to mainland Chinese influence in the Indonesian economy is often a thinly veiled attack on the economic dominance of Indonesian Chinese business tycoons. As such, nationalist rhetoric that censures Jokowi for cosying up to China frequently acts as a proxy for opposition to Indonesian Chinese business interests, who have long endured accusations of disloyalty because of their connections to Singapore, Hong Kong and mainland China.[34] The underlying claim is that Jokowi has overlooked the economic needs of the "pribumi", a term which loosely translates as "natives", but in practice signifies Muslim and non-Chinese citizens.[35]

To be sure, we should not read these opinion polls as evidence voters are convinced by sensationalist claims that Jokowi has sold the country to Chinese investors with nefarious designs. But the exclusivist rhetoric coming from some of Indonesia's political leaders appears to be tapping into, or even motivating, popular ambivalence about foreign and Chinese economic intervention.

Resource Nationalism and Food Sovereignty

In other economic arenas, however, Jokowi has largely insulated himself from nationalist attacks. Over the course of 2017, Prabowo resurrected the nationalist tropes he used back in 2014. His trademark claim was that Indonesia is "kaya tapi miskin" ("rich but poor"), because the country's natural riches have been exploited by foreigners rather than the Indonesian people. Prabowo blamed the theft of Indonesia's resources upon a greedy and corrupt elite. However, it is doubtful such appeals will provide leverage over President Jokowi in 2019. Jokowi has done much to bolster his nationalist credentials when it comes to the resource industries.

In the mining sector, for example, the Jokowi government introduced new regulations that compel foreign companies to divest their majority equity share after ten years of being in operation.[36] Under the guidance of his influential minister for state-owned enterprises Rini Sumarno, Jokowi also oversaw the establishment of a state-owned mining holding company.[37] The goal was to enable state miners to borrow more money, become more liquid, and take over lucrative foreign-owned projects. Jokowi has been particularly concerned with wresting control of the Grasberg gold and copper mine from Freeport McMoran, an American company which runs the oldest and most lucrative mine in the country.[38] Jokowi marketed these and other interventions in the resource sectors as a measure of his nationalist resolve. For example, at a conference organized by the Indonesia Ulama Council (MUI) in April 2017, Jokowi emphasized how he had facilitated the transfer of some of Indonesia's most strategic mining and hydrocarbon resources from foreign into Indonesian hands.[39]

Jokowi also introduced and maintained protectionist initiatives and trade barriers in an effort to reduce dependence upon foreign imports.[40] The president promised, for example, that Indonesia would achieve self-sufficiency in corn, rice, soybeans and sugar. By increasing subsidies for tractors, seeds, fertilizer and irrigation technology, Jokowi argued that Indonesia's farmers would produce more and eventually help wean Indonesia off foreign imports.[41] In a similar vein, Jokowi committed to reforming and expanding the domestic oil-refining sector in order to reduce Indonesia's reliance on the import of expensive fuel and petroleum products.[42] The net economic benefit of these nationalist interventions remains the subject of much debate, and many economists view them as counterproductive to Jokowi's goal of achieving 7 per cent growth.[43]

However, economic nationalism offers the president political capital. Jokowi's focus on resource ownership and food sovereignty protects him against the kind of nationalist campaign that Prabowo ran in 2014. That Jokowi's opponents have recently placed so much emphasis upon foreign and Chinese capital in the infrastructure sector indicates an awareness that nationalist mobilization around resource ownership and food sovereignty would be something of a blunt tool in 2019. Together, both trends reveal the political attraction of economic nationalism in the post-Suharto era, and the constraints that nationalist outbidding can place upon a government's economic agenda.

Socio-economic Inequality

Inequality, on the other hand, has proven a thorny political issue for the president. Indonesia has one of the highest rates of inequality in the world, and is second only to China in the Asia-Pacific.[44] The global commodity boom from 2003 to

2013 spurred Indonesia's impressive economic growth over this period. But the boom exacerbated the gap between rich and poor, as those at the upper end of the social stratum accrued more and more wealth. According to a recent Oxfam report, "the wealthiest 1 percent of the population owns nearly half (49 per cent) of total wealth".[45] When Jokowi came to office, the Gini coefficient, which measures inequality, was at an historical high of 0.41 (where 0 is perfect equality and 1 is the maximum level of inequality). Once commodity prices cooled after 2013, and Indonesia's economy slowed, there was a slight improvement in the Gini to 0.39 in 2017.

Since Jokowi came to power, and despite the downward trend in the Gini, inequality has become increasingly politicized. Jokowi's opponents frame the problem of inequality in ethno-religious terms. Former president Yudhoyono, Prabowo Subianto, and other high-profile elites have embraced a narrative of economic injustice that implicitly, and sometimes explicitly, blames Indonesia's growing income gap on the country's wealthy ethnic Chinese minority.[46] Even Vice President Jusuf Kalla has made public comments about the wealth of non-Muslim Indonesians and the economic plight of Muslim masses.[47] The president's detractors suggest that Jokowi has been unable or unwilling to address the gap between the poor Muslim majority and a wealthy, predominantly non-Muslim — or Chinese Christian — elite.

A series of Islamist mobilizations against Jakarta's Christian-Chinese governor revived and mainstreamed anti-Chinese narratives to a degree not seen during the post-Suharto era. The protests were spearheaded by Front Pembela Islam (FPI), a radical Islamic nationalist group, but enjoyed sponsorship from Prabowo and Yudhoyono; rumours circulated that Kalla was also involved. An unprecedented number of Indonesians took to the streets to protest against the governor, Basuki Tjahaja Purnama, known as Ahok, for allegedly making blasphemous statements about the Qur'an. The campaign proved highly successful.[48] Ahok lost the election decisively, and was then imprisoned for two years on blasphemy charges.

Ahok's blasphemy was not the only target of the Islamist mobilizations, however. As Mietzner et al. explain in a forthcoming study,[49] a second narrative of the mobilization was that Indonesia's *ummah* had been economically sidelined by a system that favoured non-Muslim and Chinese business interests. Protagonists depicted Ahok as an embodiment of this alleged ethno-religious inequality. Ahok was Jokowi's close political ally, so the protests were widely viewed as an attack on the president as well. Indeed, at the one year "reunion" of the anti-Ahok mobilizations that took place in December 2017, Islamist leaders and politicians from Gerindra, PKS and PAN focused their rhetoric upon the president. Amien

Rais, for example, closed his speech by imploring Jokowi not to "sell the country to foreigners or Indonesian Chinese".[50]

The Islamist protests and accompanying narrative of ethno-religious inequality disturbed the president for several reasons. First, post-election polls and analyses showed clearly that the mobilizations had moved public opinion. Ahok had been a popular incumbent with very high approval ratings; but he lost decisively, and exit polls showed that those who rejected Ahok overwhelmingly agreed he had blasphemed.[51] Of more concern, however, was that the mobilizations changed the way the electorate felt about non-Muslims in politics more generally. A poll taken in August 2017, over seven months after the mobilizations, showed that approximately 50 per cent of Muslim Indonesians felt non-Muslims should not be allowed to hold leadership positions within government (mayor, governor or president). This had increased by a margin of around 8 per cent on the year before.[52]

A third worrying trend for Jokowi is that Indonesians appear more likely to see inequality in ethno-religious terms since the Islamist mobilizations against Ahok. Mietzner et al.'s forthcoming study shows that, for years, polls indicated fewer and fewer Indonesians felt Muslims were economically worse off than non-Muslims — but that trend was reversed in 2017. The authors put forward a compelling case that the sudden shift in public opinion was a response to the nativist economic narrative that accompanied the anti-Ahok mobilizations. The lesson, according to Mietzner et al., is that where latent economic grievances exist, "political entrepreneurs" can deploy exclusivist narratives with the potential to change voters' preferences. While Jokowi is neither Christian nor Indonesian Chinese, his association with a pluralist political platform makes him vulnerable to attacks by conservative Islamic and nationalist groups, who now see that religious and nativist campaigns carry electoral weight.

Polls also indicate that many Indonesians are not impressed by the Jokowi administration's approach to inequality. A September 2017 poll by Indikator Politik Indonesia revealed that only 26 per cent of Indonesians felt the country was becoming more equal, while 48 per cent said inequality remained unchanged, and 22 per cent felt Indonesia was becoming more unequal.[53] On related economic questions, the survey found a minority of respondents believed Jokowi was doing a better job (than the previous year) at controlling the price of staple goods (34 per cent), providing enough jobs (30 per cent), and reducing poverty (32 per cent). In general, a large slice of Indonesians felt the economy was improving (43 per cent); but many also believed there had been no change at all (34 per cent), or that things were getting worse (18 per cent). (Though, to put this in perspective, President Yudhoyono received similar sorts of figures during his first term in office — until a few months prior to the 2009 election, at which point a direct cash transfer programme for the poor helped boost popular perceptions of his performance and the economy.)

After winning the 2014 elections, President Jokowi maintained his commitment to pro-poor policies, like subsidized health, education and social insurance programmes — indeed, he immediately increased funding for these sectors after coming to office. However, over much of the last three years, Jokowi's pro-poor agenda was eclipsed by an overemphasis on fast-paced developmental projects. The picture that emerged at the end of 2017 was one in which almost half of the electorate remained unconvinced that Jokowi was doing enough to reduce the gap between rich and poor, control the price of staples, and reduce unemployment. This was particularly concerning when viewed in the context of other opinion polls (presented in the first section above) that indicated striking levels of antagonism towards foreign investment and migrant labour, particularly from China, and an increase in the number of people that believed non-Muslims enjoy disproportionate economic wealth. These patterns of public opinion indicate fertile ground for the kind of populist and nationalist narratives emerging from Prabowo, PKS and Islamist groups.

Jokowi Adjusts

Jokowi clearly views a nationalist-populist campaign as a serious political risk. He and his staff spent much of 2017 reorienting the government's policy agenda to focus on programmes that deal with socio-economic inequality. For example, the government stepped up its marketing of land certification schemes for rural Indonesians, and the "Cash For Work" programme, which channels funds to village governments to provide wages for unemployed or underemployed citizens in return for low-skilled labour.[54] The idea is to provide land, work and cash to poor rural citizens, which will increase their purchasing power and close the income gap.

The decision to explicitly shift the economic message from growth to inequality was clearly expressed in the third annual report of the Presidential Staff Office (Kantor Staf Presiden, KSP), issued in October 2017:

> In this third year, the government focuses upon policies for achieving just equality for all Indonesians … because we do not want prosperity to be enjoyed only by some people or some groups of people. The focus of this third year is an extension of the first year in which the government focused upon building a firm foundation for national development by

> transforming economic fundamentals. This work continued into the second year, in which the government focused upon fast national development, including physical infrastructure, human resources, and improving economic competitiveness to compete with other countries.[55]

The government's decision to switch gears and refocus on socio-economic equality appeared to have a positive impact on public opinion. While a September 2017 Indikator survey found only 43 per cent of respondents felt Jokowi was doing enough to overcome inequality, this was a significant improvement on the previous year, when only 25 per cent of Indonesians were satisfied with the president's approach. Similarly, when it came to how respondents viewed the government's record on jobs, poverty and other key economic programmes, 2017 saw a notable uptick in public approval ratings compared to the same time in 2016.

These are comforting numbers for the president. But approval ratings do not translate directly into electoral support in Indonesia, as Mietzner and Muhtadi pointed out in their analysis of Ahok's loss in 2017.[56] And while by no means conclusive, existing polls and scholarly studies indicate that a campaign focused on inequality, identity and economic nationalism would resonate with many Indonesians, and pose a threat to Jokowi come 2019.

Much of this chapter has been concerned with the Jokowi administration's economic vulnerabilities. However, before closing, it is important to emphasize that President Jokowi remains in a strong political position. By late 2017 the president's approval ratings had stabilized at over 60 per cent since April of 2016.[57] In 2017 Jokowi also enjoyed a clear lead in the polls over Prabowo, his nearest rival.[58] Several of the government's economic programmes were well received by the public, too. In 2017, a solid majority of Indonesians felt the president had done a good job developing roads (72 per cent), improving health services (65 per cent), and expanding transport infrastructure (60 per cent), which is a striking reflection of where Jokowi directed much of his political and policy energy over the past three years.[59] Assertive interventions in the resource sectors and a sustained emphasis upon food sovereignty boosted the president's nationalist image. Jokowi also retained his reputation as a clean, unpretentious politician. As long as inflation remains low, and growth is steady, the president enjoys a strong electoral advantage.

However, as we have seen, aspects of Jokowi's economic agenda have become fodder for his rivals. The administration has so far failed to move Indonesia beyond 5 per cent growth, as Jokowi promised to do, and the majority of the government's priority infrastructure projects remain incomplete. More troubling for supporters of the government, is that populist-nationalist critiques of Jokowi's economic policies, and his record on inequality, would appear to resonate with and even structure popular anxieties about Chinese labour and investment, and non-Muslim wealth.

Conclusion

Observers are now grappling to explain why, at this particular juncture, Indonesia's politics has become more populist, and its economy more nationalist. What are the socio-economic or political conditions that have made populist-nationalist appeals such a prominent feature of Indonesia's contemporary political landscape? Similar questions are being asked about other democratic countries around the globe. Analysts observe a general disillusionment with liberal democracy, and growing scepticism towards free trade and liberal-market principles, both in established Western democracies and in younger democracies in Eastern Europe, Latin America and Asia.[60]

Some of the causal conditions identified in these other contexts are present in Indonesia, too. For example, cross-national studies suggest inequality feeds social resentment amongst the working class and the poor, making them "susceptible to anti-establishment, nativist, and xenophobic ... populist movements".[61] In Indonesia, we find evidence of public dissatisfaction with rising inequality and, back in 2014, there were also high levels of disillusionment with government. During the ten years of Yudhoyono's presidency, Indonesia enjoyed political stability, and a resource boom kept the economy moving at an impressive pace. But the gap between rich and poor grew, and corruption remained endemic. By the end of his time in office, President Yudhoyono's public approval ratings were on a downward trajectory. Under these circumstances it should come as no surprise that in 2014 Indonesians sought a populist outsider that represented something other than the status quo.

What, however, explains the particularly nativist kinds of political mobilization we have seen since 2014? Anti-Chinese activism has historically taken place during times of economic crisis in Indonesia. While Jokowi's economic agenda has failed to propel Indonesia to 7 per cent GDP growth, the president has still maintained economic stability and growth, and made significant investments in both infrastructure and welfare. It is curious, therefore, that nationalist-populist narratives have re-emerged under conditions of relative economic prosperity.

The driver, according to some experts, is political. In one instructive analysis of Indonesia's rising nationalist sentiment, Aspinall[62] suggests that the particular features of Indonesia's party system, where no "strong policy or ideological differences [exist] between major parties", have created conditions conducive to "nationalist outbidding" and the development of a new xenophobic political and economic discourse. In other words, the imperatives of electoral politics in Indonesia's patronage democracy have pushed political rhetoric further towards the extremes, making political populism, and particularly economic nationalism, a more persistent part of Indonesia's democratic landscape.

We can also point to the role of particular individuals and groups, who opportunistically enflame anti-foreign and anti-Chinese tensions for short-term political ends. Indeed, the elites who have deployed exclusivist and nationalist narratives since 2014 are primarily those who feel excluded from Jokowi's governing coalition, and who are dissatisfied with the president's pluralist and secular orientation.

In sum, there has been a striking rise in nativist discourse in Indonesia, and economic nationalism has persisted beyond the resources boom, bucking historical patterns of economic policymaking in Indonesia. Nationalist outbidding constrains the policy options available to economic managers as they try to manage inequality, boost productivity, and free Indonesia from the middle-income trap. And yet, somewhat ironically, the populist political climate makes sound economic management even more urgent, because, in the past, economic crises and high inflation have triggered outbursts of racially charged violence. The government's capacity to manage new nationalist-populist pressures is important, not for the president's re-election necessarily, but for Indonesia's broader political and economic stability.

Notes

1. Indonesia's regional elections are set for June 2018, and the presidential elections will take place in just over a year, in April 2019.
2. See, for example <https://twitter.com/Gerindra>.
3. The video can be viewed here: <https://twitter.com/Gerindra/status/932521015179059201>.
4. Marcus Mietzner, "Reinventing Asian Populism: Jokowi's Rise, Democracy, and Political Contestation in Indonesia", 2015 <http://www.eastwestcenter.org/publications/reinventing-asian-populism-jokowis-rise-democracy-and-political-contestation-in>; Edward Aspinall, "Oligarchic Populism: Prabowo Subianto's Challenge to Indonesian Democracy", *Indonesia* 2015, no. 99 (2015): 1–28; Vedi R. Hadiz and Richard Robison, "Competing Populisms in Post-Authoritarian Indonesia", *International Political Science Review* 38, no. 4 (2017): 488–502 <https://doi.org/10.1177/0192512117697475>.

5. Cas Mudde, "The Populist Zeitgeist", *Government and Opposition* 39, no. 4 (2004): 541–63 <https://doi.org/10.1111/j.1477-7053.2004.00135.x>.
6. Kurt Weyland, "Clarifying a Contested Concept: Populism in the Study of Latin American Politics", *Comparative Politics* 34, no. 1 (2001): 14 <https://doi.org/10.2307/422412>.
7. Mudde, "The Populist Zeitgeist", p. 543.
8. Weyland, "Clarifying a Contested Concept", p. 5.
9. Ronald Inglehart and Pippa Norris, "Trump, Brexit, and the Rise of Populism: Economic Have-Nots and Cultural Backlash", Harvard Kennedy School Faculty Working Paper Series, 2016; Weyland, "Clarifying a Contested Concept".
10. The term "economic populism" has often been used pejoratively by liberal economists to describe the economic blunders of Latin America's populists in the 1980s and 1990s, which were characterized by trade protectionism, huge budget deficits and unmanageable inflation. Rudiger Dornbusch and Sebastian Edwards, *The Macroeconomics of Populism in Latin America* (University of Chicago Press, 1991).
11. Aspinall, "Oligarchic Populism", p. 4.
12. Vedi R. Hadiz, *Islamic Populism in Indonesia and the Middle East* (Cambridge University Press, 2016).
13. Aspinall, "Oligarchic Populism", p. 4.
14. Mietzner, "Reinventing Asian Populism".
15. Ibid., p. 15.
16. Mietzner, "Reinventing Asian Populism", p. 45.
17. Ibid., p. 41.
18. Jamie S. Davidson, "Eminent Domain and Infrastructure under the Yudhoyono and Widodo Administrations", in *Land and Development in Indonesia: Searching for the People's Sovereignty*, edited by John McCarthy and Kathryn Robinson (Singapore: ISEAS – Yusof Ishak Institute, 2016); Siwage Dharma Negara, "Indonesia's Infrastructure Development under the Jokowi Administration", *Southeast Asian Affairs 2016*, edited by Malcolm Cook and Daljit Singh, pp. 145–65 (Singapore: ISEAS – Yusof Ishak Institute, 2016).
19. Eve Warburton, "Indonesian Politics in 2016: Jokowi and the New Developmentalism", *Bulletin of Indonesian Economic Studies* 52, no. 3 (2016): 297–320; Davidson, "Eminent Domain and Infrastructure".
20. PwC, "Indonesian Infrastructure: Stable Foundations for Growth", 2016 <https://www.pwc.com/id/en/cpi/asset/indonesian-infrastructure-stable-foundations-for-growth.pdf>.
21. Ibid.; Natasha Hamilton-Hart and Günther G. Schulze, "Taxing Times in Indonesia: The Challenge of Restoring Competitiveness and the Search for Fiscal Space", *Bulletin of Indonesian Economic Studies* 52, no. 3 (2016): 265–95 <https://doi.org/10.1080/00074918.2016.1249263>. Indonesia's ranking on the World Bank's Ease of Doing business index improved as a result of these reforms, and FDI into infrastructure

projects experienced a marked increase. At the same time, many analysts criticized the haphazard execution of the economic packages, which they believe have had a limited overall impact on an economy which continues to sit at 5 per cent GDP growth; World Bank, "Indonesia Continues Strong Pace of Reforms to Improve Business Climate: Doing Business", press release, 31 October 2017 <http://www.worldbank.org/en/news/press-release/2017/10/31/indonesia-continues-strong-pace-of-reforms-to-improve-business-climate-doing-business>; Harwanto Bimo Pratomo, "5 Serangan Pada Paket Kebijakan Ekonomi Yang Dibanggakan Jokowi", *Merdeka.Com*, 8 September 2017 <https://www.merdeka.com/uang/5-serangan-kritik-pada-paket-kebijakan-ekonomi-yang-dibanggakan-jokowi.html>; Jun Suzuki, "Widodo's Support Erodes as Economy Sags, Infrastructure Projects Stall", *Nikkei Asian Review*, 27 April 2017 <https://asia.nikkei.com/magazine/20170427/Politics-Economy/Widodo-s-support-erodes-as-economy-sags-infrastructure-projects-stall>.

22. Pratomo, "5 Serangan Pada Paket Kebijakan Ekonomi Yang Dibanggakan Jokowi"; Yusran Yunus, "Muhammadiyah Kritik Paket Kebijakan Ekonomi Jokowi-JK Belum Konkrit | Finansial", *Bisnis Indonesia*, 13 October 2015 <http://finansial.bisnis.com/read/20151012/9/481241/muhammadiyah-kritik-paket-kebijakan-ekonomi-jokowi-jk-belum-konkrit>; Kurnia Sari Aziza, "Gerindra Tolak Pengesahan APBN 2018, Ini Alasan-Alasannya", *Kompas*, 25 October 2017 <http://ekonomi.kompas.com/read/2017/10/25/212851326/gerindra-tolak-pengesahan-apbn-2018-ini-alasan-alasannya>.
23. Fedina Sundaryani, "Infrastructure Development on Track: Jokowi", *Jakarta Post*, 3 May 2017 <http://www.thejakartapost.com/news/2017/05/03/infrastructure-development-on-track-jokowi.html>.
24. Bimo Wiwoho, "PKS Nilai Rakyat Puas Pada Jokowi Karena Sering Beri Sepeda", CNN Indonesia, 7 October 2017 <https://www.cnnindonesia.com/nasional/20171006213040-32-246755/pks-nilai-rakyat-puas-pada-jokowi-karena-sering-beri-sepeda>.
25. Erwin Dariyanto, "Gerindra Kritik Prioritas Proyek Infrastruktur Jokowi", *Detiknews*, 2 August 2017 <https://news.detik.com/read/2017/08/02/003450/3582602/10/gerindra-kritik-prioritas-proyek-infrastruktur-jokowi>.
26. Rully Widayati, "Serbuan Pekerja Cina, DPR: Ini Merugikan", *Tempo*, 29 June 2015 <https://bisnis.tempo.co/read/679319/serbuan-pekerja-cina-dpr-ini-merugikan>; John McBeth, "Is Indonesia's Widodo in China's Pocket?" 11 December 2017 <http://www.atimes.com/article/indonesias-widodo-chinas-pocket/>.
27. CNN Indonesia, "Amien Rais Khawatir Indonesia Jadi Subordinat China", 5 September 2015 <https://www.cnnindonesia.com/nasional/20150904200421-32-76746/amien-rais-khawatir-indonesia-jadi-subordinat-china>; "Reklamasi Pulau Untuk Cina, Amien Rais Heran TNI Diam Saja", *Tribunnews.Com*, 2 November 2017 <http://www.tribunnews.com/nasional/2017/11/02/reklamasi-pulau-untuk-cina-amien-rais-heran-tni-diam-saja>.

28. Tao Kong and Pierre van der Eng, "Mixed Messages of Chinese Investment in Indonesia", *East Asia Forum*, 18 May 2017 <http://www.eastasiaforum.org/2017/05/18/mixed-messages-of-chinese-investment-in-indonesia/>.
29. Leo Suraydinata, *The Growing "Strategic Partnership" between Indonesia and China Faces Difficult Challenges*, Trends in Southeast Asia 2017, no. 15 (Singapore: ISEAS – Yusof Ishak Institute, 2017), p. 6 <https://www.iseas.edu.sg/images/pdf/TRS15_17.pdf>.
30. Dylan Amirio, "BKPM Focuses on Internal Reform to Enhance Climate", *Jakarta Post*, 21 February 2017.
31. "Is There a Significant Influx of Chinese Workers to Indonesia?" Global Indonesian Voices, 18 July 2016 <http://www.globalindonesianvoices.com/27144/is-there-a-significant-influx-of-chinese-workers-to-indonesia/>.
32. Diego Fossati, Hui Yew-Foong, and Siwage Dharma Negara, *The Indonesia National Survey Project: Economy, Society and Politics*, Trends in Southeast Asia 2017, no. 10 (Singapore: ISEAS – Yusof Ishak Institute, 2017) <https://www.iseas.edu.sg/images/pdf/TRS10_17%20(002).pdf>.
33. Polls also reveal anxiety about foreign labour in general, not just when it comes to workers migrating from China. In the ISEAS survey, for example, only 40 per cent of respondents agreed with the statement that Indonesia should be more open to migrant workers, while 40 per cent disagreed (the rest did not respond). A CSIS survey from November 2017 asked a slightly different question, and found much higher levels of antagonism towards foreign workers: just over 77 per cent of respondents aged under 30, and 76 per cent of those over 30 years old, viewed migrant labour as detrimental to the Indonesian economy; CSIS, "Ada Apa Dengan Milenial? Orientasi Sosial, Ekonomi dan Politik" 2 November 2017 <https://www.csis.or.id/uploaded_file/event/ada_apa_dengan_milenial____paparan_survei_nasional_csis_mengenai_orientasi_ekonomi__sosial_dan_politik_generasi_milenial_indonesia__notulen.pdf>.
34. Eve Warburton and Liam Gammon, "Class Dismissed? Economic Fairness and Identity Politics in Indonesia", *New Mandala*, 5 May 2017 <http://www.newmandala.org/economic-injustice-identity-politics-indonesia>/; Charlotte Setijadi, "Chinese Indonesians in the Eyes of the Pribumi Public", *ISEAS Perspective* 2017, no. 73 (27 September 2017) <https://www.iseas.edu.sg/images/pdf/ISEAS_Perspective_2017_73.pdf>.
35. "New Jakarta Governor Faces Backlash for Racially Tinged Speech", Reuters, 17 October 2017 <https://www.reuters.com/article/us-indonesia-politics-baswedan/new-jakarta-governor-faces-backlash-for-racially-tinged-speech-idUSKBN1CM0ZJ>.
36. Eve Warburton, "Resource Nationalism in Post-Boom Indonesia: The New Normal?" Lowy Institute, 27 April 2017 <https://www.lowyinstitute.org/publications/resource-nationalism-post-boom-indonesia-new-normal>.
37. "Mining Holding Company to Acquire Freeport's Shares", *Jakarta Post*, 30 November

2017 <http://www.thejakartapost.com/news/2017/11/30/mining-holding-company-to-acquire-freeports-shares.html>.

38. John McBeth, "Freeport under Multiple Guns in Indonesia", *Asia Times*, 2 November 2017 <http://www.atimes.com/article/freeport-multiple-guns-indonesia/>.
39. Eko Wicaksono, "Pemerintah Berhasil Nasionalisasi Aset Negara Yang Dikuasai Asing", *Liputan6*, 22 April 2017 <http://bisnis.liputan6.com/read/2928961/pemerintah-berhasil-nasionalisasi-aset-negara-yang-dikuasai-asing>.
40. Arianto Patunru and Sjamsu Rahardja, "Trade Protectionism in Indonesia: Bad Times and Bad Policy", Lowy Institute, 2015 <http://www.lowyinstitute.org/publications/trade-protectionism-indonesia-bad-times-and-bad-policy>.
41. Ina Parlina, "Jokowi Aims for Food Self-Sufficiency in Three Years", *Jakarta Post*, 27 December 2014 <http://www.thejakartapost.com/news/2014/12/27/jokowi-aims-food-self-sufficiency-three-years.html>.
42. Wicaksono, "Pemerintah Berhasil Nasionalisasi Aset Negara Yang Dikuasai Asing."
43. Patunru and Rahardja, "Trade Protectionism in Indonesia"; Ross Garnaut, "Indonesia's Resources Boom in International Perspective: Policy Dilemmas and Options for Continued Strong Growth", *Bulletin of Indonesian Economic Studies* 51, no. 2 (2015): 189–212 <https://doi.org/10.1080/00074918.2015.1061910>.
44. World Bank, "Indonesia's Rising Divide", 2015 <http://www.worldbank.org/en/news/feature/2015/12/08/indonesia-rising-divide>; Luke Gibson, "Towards a More Equal Indonesia", Oxfam, February 2017 <https://www.oxfam.org/en/research/towards-more-equal-indonesia>.
45. Gibson, "Towards a More Equal Indonesia", p. 2.
46. Warburton and Gammon, "Class Dismissed?"
47. "Kalla: Kesenjangan Di Indonesia Berbahaya Karena…", *Tempo*, 26 February 2017 <https://nasional.tempo.co/read/850391/kalla-kesenjangan-di-indonesia-berbahaya-karena>.
48. Marcus Mietzner and Burhanuddin Muhtadi, "Ahok's Satisfied Non-Voters: An Anatomy", *New Mandala*, 5 May 2017 <http://www.newmandala.org/ahoks-satisfied-non-voters-anatomy/>.
49. Marcus Mietzner, Burhanuddin Muhtadi, and Rizka Halida, "Entrepreneurs of Grievance: Drivers and Effects of Indonesia's Islamist Mobilization", forthcoming.
50. Aditya Fajar Indrawan, "Materi Pidato Amien Rais Di Reuni 212: Kecebong Dan Asing-Aseng", *Detiknews*, 2 December 2017 <https://news.detik.com/read/2017/12/02/091202/3751873/10/materi-pidato-amien-rais-di-reuni-212-kecebong-dan-asing-aseng>.
51. Mietzner and Muhtadi, "Ahok's Satisfied Non-Voters."
52. Lembaga Survei Indonesia, "Korupsi, Religiusitas, dan Intoleransi: Temuan Survei Nasional 16–22 Agustus", 2017, pp. 43–46.
53. Indikator Politik Indonesia, "Evaluasi Tiga Tahun Pemerintahan Jokowi-JK Dan Ejek Elektoralnya: Temuan Survei Nasional, 17–24 September", 2017, p. 26.
54. Hendra Kusuma, "Program Padat Karya Cash Jokowi Dimulai Januari 2018",

Detikfinance, 3 November 2017 <https://finance.detik.com/read/2017/11/03/193049/3712785/4/program-padat-karya-cash-jokowi-dimulai-januari-2018; Fedina Sundaryani and Ina Parlina, "Jokowi Pledges to Close Inequality Gap in 2017", *Jakarta Post*, 5 January 2017 <http://www.thejakartapost.com/news/2017/01/05/jokowi-pledges-to-close-inequality-gap-in-2017.html>.

55. KSP, "Laporan 3 Tahun Pemerintahan Joko Widodo – Jusuf Kalla", Kantor Staf Presiden, October 2017.
56. Mietzner and Muhtadi, "Ahok's Satisfied Non-Voters".
57. Indikator, "Evaluasi Tiga Tahun Pemerintahan Jokowi-JK Dan Ejek Elektoralnya", p. 12.
58. Ibid.
59. Ibid., p. 36.
60. Michael J. Boyle, "The Coming Illiberal Order", *Survival* 58, no. 2 (2016): 35–66 <https://doi.org/10.1080/00396338.2016.1161899>; Roberto Stefan Foa and Yascha Mounk, "The Signs of Deconsolidation", *Journal of Democracy* 28, no. 1 (2017): 5–15 <https://doi.org/10.1353/jod.2017.0000>.
61. Inglehart and Norris, "Trump, Brexit, and the Rise of Populism", p. 2.
62. Edward Aspinall, "The New Nationalism in Indonesia", *Asia & the Pacific Policy Studies* 3, no. 1 (2015): 72.

INDONESIA IN 2017: Jokowi's Supremacy and His Next Political Battles

Priyambudi Sulistiyanto

After successfully consolidating his power in his second year in office (2016), 2017 saw President Joko Widodo (Jokowi) gradually and consistently expand his power base to strengthen his political authority in Indonesia to the point that he was able to weaken opposition forces both in and outside parliament. Against predictions, he successfully reduced political tensions arising from the two high-profile events that occurred in early 2017: first, the defeat of the ethnic Chinese, Christian Governor of Jakarta, Basuki Tjahaja Purnama (Ahok) in the Jakarta election and, second, the two-year prison sentence handed to Ahok for blasphemy. Jokowi responded to these events decisively, with constitutional initiatives and political manoeuvres aimed at outlawing social and religious organizations deemed to be anti-Pancasila[1] and moving to limit the impact of outspoken critics in Jakarta and the countryside. At the grass-roots level, Jokowi visited and consulted with religious and community leaders across Indonesia to gain support for his efforts to reduce what threatened to become an increasing level of religious intolerance and hatred in Indonesian communities.

The Indonesian economy did not improve much, with growth remaining at around 5.1 per cent per annum. This was not enough to fully support Jokowi's ambitious infrastructure programmes, leading him to deploy available resources and funding inside and outside the country to ensure those programmes stayed on track. In terms of foreign policy, Jokowi continued to attract prominent international

---

Priyambudi Sulistiyanto is Senior Lecturer at the College of Business, Government and Law, Flinders University, Adelaide, Australia. He is also with the Centre for United States and Asia Policy Studies, Flinders University.

state visitors to Indonesia, and participated actively on the world stage in forums such as the G20, ASEAN and APEC meetings, and a visit to China to participate in the One Belt, One Road (OBOR) gathering organized by President Xi Jinping. The highlight of Jokowi's regional engagement was his quick response to domestic pressure to address the plight of the Rohingya refugees who became stranded along the Myanmar–Bangladesh border. Towards the end of 2017, his third year in office, Jokowi harvested the fruits of his efforts, with independent public opinion polls showing him to have an unprecedented level of support, making him, at this time, the most powerful and popular political leader in Indonesia.

This chapter will highlight key trends in Indonesia in 2017 in the areas of domestic politics, the economy and foreign policy. It will discuss the ways in which Jokowi navigated the complex Indonesian political landscape and stayed on top of the game. It will examine briefly the implications of local elections for governors across Indonesia in 2018 and consider the consequences for Jokowi's looming political battles in the 2019 presidential election of the arrest of Setya Novanto, the Chairman of the House of Representatives (Dewan Perwakilan Rakyat, DPR), and the appointment of Marshall Hadi Tjahjanto as the new Armed Forces Chief.

Domestic Political Developments

Spillovers from Mass Protests at the End of 2016

There was no doubt that in the last months of 2016 Indonesian politics was preoccupied with the drama that centred on the mass protests against Ahok on 4 November 2016 (which became known as the 4/11 protest) and on 2 December 2016 (the 2/12 protest). These mass protests in front of the Presidential Palace and in the vicinity of the National Monument (Monas), both involving more than a million people, were the largest political protests of the Jokowi presidency.[2] They were organized by a broad-based alliance of Islamic and social organizations called the National Movement of the Guardian of MUI Fatwa (Gerakan Nasional Pengawal Fatwa MUI, GNPFM) led by Bachtiar Nasir and Rizieq Shihab, the latter being also the leader of the radical Islamic Defenders Front (Front Pembela Islam, FPI). This alliance was established after the Indonesian Muslim Scholars' Council (Majelis Ulama Indonesia, MUI) issued a fatwa (a religious verdict) stating that Ahok had committed blasphemy in a speech made in September 2016. The case originated with a complaint made about a video clip that circulated on YouTube in which Ahok was seen citing the Qur'anic verse *Al Maidah* 51 to advise his audience in the Thousand Islands area in Jakarta Bay of the danger of being influenced by religion when making political decisions in the upcoming Jakarta election. The video clip was uploaded to YouTube by Buni Yani, who was not even in the audience and who later faced trial for copying and posting the controversial part of Ahok's speech on social media. Ahok was convicted based on this, though the clip that circulated was altered to portray his quoting of the Qur'an out of the context of his speech, which made his words appear more offensive to Muslim viewers. The mass protests that followed the finding against Ahok were the culmination of a growing desire among some camps in the Jakarta political elite and more broadly to see Ahok removed from office. Prominent participants in the protests included political leaders such as Fadli Zon (a member of parliament from Prabowo Subianto's Gerindra Party), Fahri Hamzah (a member of parliament from the Justice and Prosperous Party, PKS), and Amien Rais (a prominent politician from the National Mandate Party, PAN). Despite protest leaders promising peaceful demonstrations, in the last hours of the 4/11 protest a number of people were injured when radical students belonging to the Association of Indonesian Muslim Students (Himpunan Mahasiswa Islam Indonesia, HMI) clashed with anti-riot police officers who stopped them entering the Presidential Palace.[3]

The political atmosphere in Jakarta during this period was heated, with saturation print and electronic media coverage that revealed significant divisions of opinion. For example, *Republika* daily, TV One (owned by the Bakrie family) and the MNC television channel (owned by tycoon Hary Tanoesoedibyo) were in the anti-Ahok camp, while the *Jakarta Post*, *Kompas* daily and Metro TV (owned by media moghul Suryo Paloh) sided with him. This intensity of coverage also appeared in social media where supporters of both sides battled on Facebook, Twitter, Instagram and WhatsApp. The significance of social media battles in the Jakarta election cannot be underestimated, as Jakarta is an international social media capital, with millions of users.[4] Consequently, the spread of hatred and fake news became entangled with religion and identity politics in social media communities.

In everyday life, many in Jakarta and other parts of Indonesia (West Java, West Sumatra and Lombok, in particular) were drawn into a worrying situation in which religion and ethnicity cards were played to swell the ranks of anti-Ahok protesters. Large numbers of Muslims were mobilized by being persuaded that Ahok had to be punished for what he did and that those who supported Ahok were anti-*pribumi* (native Indonesian) and anti-Islam. Although diversity is protected in the Indonesian constitution, Ahok's Chinese ethnicity and Christianity made him a target for attack.

Jokowi's Counter Punches

In the aftermath of the 4/11 protest, Jokowi and Prabowo met briefly in the latter's residence in Hambalang, near Bogor (about sixty kilometres from Jakarta), to address the political tensions. They agreed that the protestors' demands had to be accommodated to avoid further political unrest in the lead-up to the Jakarta election. After the 2/12 protest, Jokowi responded carefully to the unprecedented political development. In the first instance he met directly with protesters and their leaders, together with his senior ministers, to persuade them that despite talk on the streets and on social media to the contrary, neither he nor his government stood in opposition to the Muslim majority; secondly, he agreed that the blasphemy case against Ahok should proceed; and thirdly, he reminded the public of the urgent importance of respecting and upholding diversity and Pancasila and therefore not using religion as a political tool.[5]

Meanwhile, on the ground, the police stepped up their response by bringing in for questioning a number of prominent political critics of the Jokowi government suspected of plotting to topple the government by directing protesters to the parliament building, similar to the scenario in the days prior to the fall of Suharto in 1998. These critics came from a variety of backgrounds and were prominent public figures, included the poet Ratna Sarumpaet, the pop singer Ahmad Dhani, the former military general Kivlan Zein, Rachmawati Soekarnoputri (sister of Megawati) and the political activist Sri Bintang Pamungkas. More significant was the questioning of Rizieq Shihab in a police station in Bandung, West Java. After his success in mobilizing a massive number of protesters, Rizieq was regarded as a "big imam" (*iman besar*) who positioned himself as a strong defender of and spokesperson for radical Islamic communities in Jakarta and neighbouring regions. His increased political profile saw him join the ranks of national-level political players, which was something he had wanted for a long time. However, this also put his activities and speeches on the government's radar and raised the eyebrows of other political elites in Jakarta, in particular where his radical views on Islam and on the relationship between Islam and Pancasila were concerned. Sukmawati Sukarnoputeri (also the sister of Megawati) lodged a complaint against Rizieq concerning a speech he had given in Bandung and other places in which he attacked Islam and non-Islamic faiths and also undermined the principles of Pancasila, which is an offence in Indonesia.[6] Others also brought complaints against Rizieq to police. In the end, however, there was insufficient evidence to charge him in court. Ironically, Rizieq then absconded after performing the hajj pilgrimage to Mecca, Saudi Arabia, and to date has not returned to Indonesia.[7]

Believing that the unhealthy political situation required a stronger and more organized response in order to maintain unity and security in Indonesia, the government introduced a legal instrument known as the Regulation in Lieu of Law No. 2/2017 on Mass Organisations (Peraturan Pemerintah Pengganti Undang-undang Organisasi Kemasyarakatan, Perppu Ormas), with the aim of outlawing social and religious organizations deemed against the national ideology of Pancasila and the 1945 Constitution. The first casualty was the Hizbut Tahrir Indonesia (HTI), which has many followers among the educated middle class and university students in Jakarta and West Java. This was due to the number of complaints from the public about HTI, which encourages followers to establish an Islamic caliphate in Indonesia and displays religious symbols (in flags and posters) in Arabic, which does not respect Indonesian sovereignty. In theory, other radical organizations with different ideological brands could be affected, but for the time being the HTI has been the main target. Other similar organizations, including FPI, could be affected in the future.

Next, the Jokowi government moved to establish the Pancasila working group headed by rising Muslim scholar Yudi Latief accompanied by nine advisors comprised of such eminent figures as Megawati Sukarnoputeri, former general Try Sutrisno, constitutional expert Mahfud M.D. and members of a range of religious organizations.[8] This working group was tasked to work with formal and informal educational institutions throughout Indonesia, campaigning on and re-educating the public about the importance of Pancasila. Ironically, it has been acknowledged that during the democratic era the status of Pancasila as the nation's guiding principles has been eroded or sidelined by other ideological views, including those of radical Islamic groups. Recognition of this has provided impetus for the government to actively promote public education about Pancasila, something that was similarly practised by Soeharto's New Order government.

In another move that had echoes of the New Order period, Jokowi started to communicate directly with ordinary people living worlds away from Jakarta. This was a hallmark of Soeharto's leadership style. On these regional visits, Jokowi would invite local people to participate in nationally broadcast stage-managed quizzes or competitions in which he would test their knowledge of the five principles of Pancasila, with the winners rewarded with prizes. He also visited grass-roots religious and community leaders, in keeping with his strong desire to bring *ulamas* or *kyais* (Islamic teachers/scholars) on side in the attempt to limit the potential for radical religious figures to gain footholds in Islamic boarding schools (*pesantren*) across Indonesia.

The Contest of Three Political Camps in the Lead-up to the Jakarta Election

As mentioned above, the divisions seeded by the 4/11 and 2/12 protests not only affected ordinary people but they were also clearly visible among the Jakarta elite, among whom rumours and accusations circulated regarding who had masterminded the protests and who had given them political and financial support. One name on everyone's lips was that of former president Susilo Bambang Yudhoyono (SBY), who, according to a report published by *Tempo*, had provided funding for the demonstrations. SBY categorically denied this in a press conference and demanded that senior government officials such as Vice-President Jusuf Kalla and the Coordinating Minister for Security and Law Affairs, Wiranto, clear his name. However, many continued to believe it was no coincidence that SBY was the focus of attention, because many in Jakarta believed he had acted to bolster the popularity of his eldest son, Agus Harimurti Yudhoyono (AHY), who had suddenly resigned from his military job to run against Ahok,[9] with Sylviana Murni (a senior public servant) as his running mate.

Another prominent politician rumoured to be behind the protests was Prabowo Subianto, a political rival of Jokowi in the 2014 presidential election. Many of his loyal Gerindra supporters and other followers participated in both the 4/11 and 2/12 demonstrations (many even travelling from other parts of Indonesia). The presence of Gerindra's Fadli Zon (one of Prabowo's trusted advisors) and other evidence on the ground suggested that Prabowo wanted to be seen as a "kingmaker" by supporting the alternative candidates in the Jakarta election. This became more obvious when Prabowo, together with his party, Gerindra, and other small political parties such as the Islamist PKS, threw their support behind Anies Baswedan and businessman Sandi Uno who were running against Ahok. The decision to back Anies Baswedan was made at the last minute, after Prabowo and SBY failed to reach an agreement on a suitably strong candidate to support against Ahok. There was speculation among the political elite that Vice-President Jusuf Kalla suggested that Anies Baswedan was the best choice among the available candidates.[10] The was proved when it appeared in public that Erwin Aksa — who is Jusuf Kalla's nephew — was also among the top advisers in the Anies–Sandi campaign team.[11]

Support for Ahok was to be found in Megawati Sukarnoputeri, former Indonesian president and the powerful chairwoman of the Indonesian Democratic Party–Struggle (Partai Demokrasi Indonesia–Perjuangan, PDI-P). It was well known that she supported Ahok in the Jakarta election and provided him with political and moral support when he was under intense pressure and fiercely attacked by his opponents during the campaign in the lead-up to the two-round elections.[12] In this period Ahok was accompanied by his running mate Djarot Saiful Hidayat (a PDI-P politician and former district head in Blitar, East Java). Megawati's strong political clout in Jakarta and PDI-P's large number of seats in the Jakarta parliament, together with support from the National Democratic party (Nasdem) led by Surya Paloh, and other parties such as Golkar (Golongan Karya) and Hanura (Hati Nurani Rakyat), meant that theoretically Ahok (who has good track records in Jakarta) and Djarot had the numbers to win the Jakarta election, in addition to the benefit of incumbency.

The political contest between these three political camps, with the direct and indirect influences of their respective patrons — SBY, Prabowo and Megawati — formed the backdrop for the Jakarta election.

The Jakarta Two-round Election: Ahok, Anies and AHY

The Jakarta election took place in two rounds: the first held on 15 February 2017 and the second on 19 April. Prior to the voting days the three contenders (Ahok–Djarot, Anies–Sandi and AHY–Sylviana) engaged in public debates to explain their respective programmes and ideas for the development of Jakarta over the next five years. These were televised nationally and, surprisingly, generated massive interest among Indonesians, both inside and outside the country. Of course, huge public interest also came from netizens in Jakarta and other parts of Indonesia. Because of this publicity, jokes circulated about the Jakarta election being "a local election with a taste of presidential election" (*pilkada dengan rasa pilpres*).[13] Surprisingly, on the voting days themselves, which were public holidays, Jakarta was calm and peaceful. From dawn, millions of people (about 7.1 million) went to polling stations in their neighbourhoods, queuing in a patient and dignified manner.[14] Predictions of possible riots or public disturbances were not borne out.

Each of the contenders hoped to win above 50 per cent of the total vote in the first round, but the actual distribution of votes saw Ahok–Djarot receive about 42.99 per cent, Anies–Sandi about 39.95 and AHY–Sylviana about 17.06 per cent.[15] Why did the Ahok–Djarot camp not win more than 50 per cent of the total vote in the first round? There are a few possible explanations. First of all, as mentioned earlier, public opinion about Ahok in the lead-up to the first round was swayed by relentless personal attacks on his ethnicity and religious background. This overshadowed the voting public's views on the programmes and policies he planned to deliver in Jakarta. Ahok's opponents were able to air their opinions continuously through various channels such as public forums, electronic media and social media, with the main goal of defeating Ahok at all costs.[16] Secondly, Ahok lost the support of some poor urban communities in Jakarta because of an uncompromising policy of removing squatters and poor families who lived along the rivers in metropolitan Jakarta. One of Ahok's programmes to clean up the Ciliwung River as a way of reducing the yearly floods in Jakarta created controversies, and reduced the number of his constituents. Thirdly, many Ahok supporters were members of the urban educated middle class, whose vote was shared with the Anies and AHY camps. Finally, Ahok relied heavily on volunteers to help him win the campaign in a situation where the machineries of the parties that supported him did not work hard enough on the ground to convince voters.

On the other hand, the 17.06 per cent of the vote won by the AHY–Sylviana camp in the first round can be regarded as an achievement for someone with no political experience. In a sense, however, AHY was "born-to-rule", coming as he does from the Yudhoyono family and possessing qualities valued in an Indonesian politician. He is smart, savvy and educated and grew up with strong military and intellectual traditions. There is no doubt that AHY had been groomed by his father and, having made his mark in this tough and nasty political contest in Jakarta, more opportunities for AHY in politics will likely open in the near future.

In the second round of the election, which was held on 19 April 2017, the Anies–Sandi camp won the majority of votes (about 57.96 per cent), with the vote for the Ahok–Djarot camp remaining at about 42.04 per cent.[17] It was very clear that those who voted for the AHY–Sylviana camp in the first round had given their votes to the Anies–Sandi camp in the second.[18] This is understandable, because the supporters of AHY–Sylviana shared similar aspirations to those who supported Anies–Sandi; they are educated, middle-class people with conservative and religious views. Secondly, as mentioned earlier, the constant use of anti-Chinese and pro-Islamic sentiments worked strongly in favour of the Anies–Sandi camp, which positioned itself in public debates as representing the interests of the majority Muslim population.[19] Thirdly, in the lead-up to the second round, controversial publicity appeared in the mainstream media and on social media about rice being distributed by PDI-P supporters in poor areas in return for votes, and this affected the credibility of the Ahok–Djarot camp.

The result of the second round changed the political landscape in Jakarta dramatically, because the Anies–Sandi win was not just about the defeat of the Ahok–Djarot camp but also about the political decline of Ahok, both for his alleged blasphemy and for what he stood for during the first term that he governed Jakarta. The blasphemy case went to trial and, after a lengthy legal process, he was given a two-year jail sentence. This was a severe blow for the supporters of Ahok, who saw his sentence as being politically motivated. However, for the anti-Ahok camp the sentence was overwhelmingly welcomed, and to a certain extent many were satisfied that he had received what he deserved. Meanwhile, the political implications of the rise of Anies Baswedan have yet to be revealed. One scenario is that, after running Jakarta for a while, Anies would be tempted to enter the presidential race in the future, if not soon in 2019 then perhaps more realistically in 2024.

The Economy: Slow Growth, Expensive Infrastructure Costs and Jokowinomics

After putting in place a new economics team in 2016 under the triumvirate of Coordinating Minister for Economic Affairs Darwin Nasution, Minister of Finance Sri Mulyani and Minister of National Planning Bambang Brodjonegoro, the Indonesian economy in 2017 improved its performance slightly, but was not as impressive as some other Asian countries. Indonesia's macroeconomic indicators are generally reasonably healthy, with economic growth around 5.1 per cent in the second quarter of 2017, an unemployment rate of 10.64 per cent, and poverty reduction at 10.64 per cent.[20] International financial institutions such as the World Bank, OECD and ADB praised the strong economic fundamentals of Indonesia, recognizing its capacity to increase growth in years to come while pointing out that more attention needed to be given to improvements in health, human resources and the social sectors. In the eyes of the international community, Indonesia's investment climate has improved slowly under the Jokowi government, which is a tribute to the introduction of a series of new economic packages and the effort to clean up the bureaucracy and eradicate corruption.

However, the bad news is that Indonesia has accumulated a high level of debt and the government's tax revenue did not improve much over 2016, despite the efforts made to promote a tax amnesty programme and corporate and income tax schemes. In 2017 Jokowi wasted no time in speeding up the roll out of his expensive and ambitious infrastructure projects all over Indonesia, including freeways and seaports in Sumatra, Sulawesi and Papua. The reality was that funding to the tune of $353 billion was required to finance these projects,[21] of which only 41.3 per cent was available from the national budget. The balance, therefore, had to be sourced from state-owned enterprises and private investors.[22]

The third year of the Jokowi presidency saw the term "Jokowinomics" come into use when referring to the particular economic approach of the president encapsulated in the *Nawacita* (nine national priorities, such as building up economies in both the centre and the regions, strengthening the rule of law and democracy, and "nation character building", to mention a few) that he promised to implement during his presidency. Prominent among these is Jokowi's determination to see Indonesia become a powerful maritime nation through the implementation of (costly) infrastructure projects in Java and across the archipelago, a priority that is slowly being understood and appreciated by the regional and international communities. In an interview, Jokowi argued that by developing infrastructure facilities across Indonesia, it will help to address the questions of equality and justice for the Indonesian people in the long run.[23] An opinion survey conducted by the Centre for Strategic and International Studies (CSIS) in September 2017 found Jokowi's public approval rating had risen to 68 per cent (compared to 66.5 per cent in 2016) and, more importantly, that public satisfaction with the economic situation was at 56.9 per cent (compared to 46 per cent in 2016). Satisfaction in the maritime sector was very high at 75.5 per cent (compared to 63.9 per cent in 2016).[24]

Foreign Policy: International Forums and Response to the Rohingya Crisis in Myanmar

In 2017 Jokowi moved with increased confidence on the international stage, improving on his performance in the first two years of his presidency. His attendance at international forums in 2017 was impressive. This has been significant for him personally because prior to becoming president he had little knowledge about and not much interest in international affairs. This was in contrast to his predecessor, SBY, who was known for his internationalist outlook. After taking up the presidency, however, Jokowi quickly learned the importance of international diplomacy and of participating in international forums, not just to assert his international credentials but also to reach out to potential investors. At the G20 and APEC meetings, the ASEAN 50th Anniversary, and China's One Belt, One Road forum in 2017, Jokowi wore the hat of national CEO, making and signing business deals with foreign governments, corporations and business partners.

The president made many visits to countries in the region for the purpose of inviting foreign investors to Indonesia. For example, in February 2017 Jokowi visited Australia to meet Prime Minister Malcolm Turnbull with the view to signing the first ever Indonesia–Australia Comprehensive Economic Partnership Agreement (IA-CEPA) by the end of 2017. A similar partnership agreement was achieved when Jokowi met Turkish President Recep Tayyip in the middle of the year. There was a flow of international dignitaries to Indonesia in 2017, with a visit from Japanese Prime Minister Shinzo Abe early in the year, followed by a high-profile visit from King Salman of Saudi Arabia in March, another strategic visit by United States Vice-President Mike Pence in April, and the South Korean President Moon Jae-in in November. These visits reinforced recognition of Jokowi's international standing and enhanced awareness in the international community that Indonesia is open for business.

A 2017 foreign policy engagement that surprised observers, both domestic and international, was Indonesia's quick response to the plight of almost a million Rohingya refugees stranded along the Myanmar–Bangladesh border. News about this humanitarian crisis, reported widely in the Indonesian media and across the region in June–August 2017, had resulted in domestic pressure to respond through both diplomatic and humanitarian channels. Jokowi acted decisively, dispatching his energetic Foreign Minister Retno Marsudi to Myanmar on a fact-finding mission in September, tasked with finding ways in which humanitarian action could be taken to assist those refugees living in camps along the border and prevent further regional crisis.

Reluctantly, Myanmar accepted the visit of Minister Retno Marsudi, who was able to convey Jokowi's humanitarian action plans to Myanmar's Foreign Minister Aung San Suu Kyi and other leaders such as Chief of Armed Forces, Senior General U Min Aung Hlaing and national security advisers. Minister Marsudi's visit resulted in the "4+1 Formula", which comprised four principles: restoring security and stability, maximum restraint and non-violence, protection for all citizens of Rakhine State and immediate access to humanitarian assistance, plus the suggestion that Myanmar immediately implement the recommendations of the Advisory Commission on Rakhine State presented to Aung San Suu Kyi by Kofi Annan in August 2017.[25] Jokowi's prompt response to the Rohingya crisis would appear to have been motivated by both a desire to address domestic demand for action, which came particularly from the Islamic community, and a readiness to show leadership in the region, especially as ASEAN had failed to respond to this humanitarian crisis.

Concluding Remarks

In his chapter on assessing Indonesia in 2016, Dirk Tomsa wrote that through consolidation efforts he made in that year, "Jokowi is clearly laying the groundwork for his re-election campaign in 2019".[26] It appears that towards the end of 2017 Jokowi has gone beyond consolidation of power and has strengthened his presidency even further. He has again ably navigated the complex domestic political environment in Indonesia, as evidenced in such areas as reducing the tensions that arose around Ahok in the Jakarta election, and also by countering the political opposition forces that tried to threaten his presidency. A clear sign of the strength of his presidency was seen in August, when a new election bill was passed in which the presidential threshold of 20 per cent of seats or 25 per cent of the popular vote was retained. This puts Jokowi in a strong position to fight in the 2019 election, because with his current popularity level being so high he will easily gain the support of 20 per cent of the legislature. The October passing of the new law governing social organizations (Undang-undang Ormas, No. 2/2017) was a further vote of confidence in Jokowi. A total of 317 members supported the government on this legislation, and only 124 opposed it.[27]

Nonetheless, the recent political developments of December 2017 must be noted here. First was the arrest of Setya Novanto, chairman of former ruling party Golkar and the Speaker of the House of Representatives, who was implicated in an e-ID corruption case. He was replaced by Airlangga Hartarto, who is also a Minister of Industry in the Jokowi government. This is significant for many reasons. Jokowi's support from Golkar would be crucial in the context of preparing for the 2019 election, because Golkar is the second-largest political party in parliament and it has many supporters in both Java and other parts of Indonesia. The second is the appointment of Marshall Hadi Tjahjanto as the new Armed Forces Chief, to replace General Gatot Nurmantyo, whom Jokowi has not had a good rapport with in past years. Many observers believe that Marshall Hadi Tjahjanto has been groomed by Jokowi and he is someone that Jokowi has more confidence and trust with simply because both of them have known each other for a long time, starting when Jokowi was still a Mayor of Solo municipality in 2010.[28] Consequently, by having both the police (under General Tito Karnavian) and the military (under Marshall Hadi Tjahjanto) under control, Jokowi would be able to consolidate two very important institutions able to manage domestic and external security matters in Indonesia in the lead-up to the 2019 election.

None of this means a 2019 election win is guaranteed. Moving into 2018 Jokowi will require all his political skill to ensure that the anti-Ahok camp does not slowly transform into an anti-Jokowi camp. While his counter punches have successfully reduced political tensions in 2017, he will need to come up with more comprehensive and sophisticated ways to stop the anti-Ahok camp from becoming an organized opposition force that could interfere with his chance of re-election. The politics of accommodation might be considered, particularly in addressing grievances about the income gap between rich and poor in Indonesia and the majority–minority issues (such as Muslim and non-Muslim, Chinese and non-Chinese, Indonesian and foreigners) aired by opposition groups (especially from the Islamic radical groups and opposition parties in parliament). However, the real test ahead for Jokowi is whether the candidates he supports will win in the local elections that will take place across Indonesia in 2018. If they can win in the politically important provinces of West Java, Central Java, East Java, North Sumatra, and Bali (where 80 per cent of Indonesia's total vote is concentrated), Jokowi's political fortune will be secured.

Notes

1. The constitutionally recognized national ideology of Indonesia, consisting of five principles.
2. The author was in Indonesia in October and November 2016. On the morning of the 4/11 mass protest, Jokowi visited development sites near the Jakarta airport and returned to the palace in the evening. Meanwhile, at midday on the day of the 2/12 mass protest, Jokowi, Vice-President Jusuf Kalla and senior ministers met with top protest leaders after conducting Friday prayer together at the National Monument.
3. "Jam-Jam Yang Mencekam", *Tempo*, 13 November 2016.
4. It is difficult to verify the precise numbers in Jakarta, but there were about 79 million users of social media across Indonesia in 2016. See <https://www.clickz.com/social-media-in-indonesia-big-numbers-with-plenty-of-room-to-grow/94062/> (accessed 19 December 2017>.
5. On Jokowi's views about Pancasila, see <https://news.okezone.com/read/2017/01/24/337/1599574/presiden-jokowi-dan-pimpinan-mpr-bahas-pemantapan-pancasila> (accessed 26 November 2017).
6. "Musim Laporan Imam Petamburan", *Tempo*, 29 January 2017.
7. "Salam Rizieq untuk Jokowi", *Tempo*, 9 July 2917.
8. "Jokowi Inaugurates Chief, Advisors of Pancasila Working Unit", *Jakarta Post*, 7 June 2017.
9. "Kabar Intelijen Yang Menyengat Cikeas", *Tempo*, 13 November 2016.
10. The author gathered these views from talking with journalists and observers in Jakarta on 15 February 2017.
11. See <http://koransulindo.com/ada-jusuf-kalla-di-balik-kemenangan-anies-sandi/> (accessed 15 November 2017).
12. "Laga Pemanasan Para Veteran", *Tempo*, 19 February 2017.
13. The author was in Jakarta to observe the first-round election on 15 February 2017.
14. "Siapa Melaju", *Koran Tempo*, 15 February 2017.
15. "New Ball Game Awaits Jakarta", *Jakarta Post*, 16 February 2017.
16. Dodi Ambardi, "Priming Isu dalam Pilkada Jakarta 2017", *Tempo*, 26 February 2017.
17. "Ibu Kota Menatap Era Baru", *Kompas*, 20 April 2017.
18. "Amunisi di Ronde Kedua", *Tempo*, 26 February 2017.

19. "Penghuni baru Balaikota", *Tempo*, 30 April 2017.
20. Badan Pusat Statistik, "Statistics Indonesia" <https://www.bps.go.id/QuickMap?id=0000000000> (accessed 20 October 2017).
21. "Beragam Alternatif Pembiayaan Infrastruktur", *Gatra*, 1 November 2017; See also Dikanaya Tarahita and Muhammad Zulfikar Rakhmat <https://thediplomat.com/2017/05/solving-indonesias-infrastructure-gap/> (accessed 19 December 2017).
22. "Infrastruktur Skema Pina", *Gatra*, 1 November 2017.
23. "Presiiden Republick Indonesia Joko Widodo, Saya Sudah Menghitung Semua Resiko", *Tempo*, 12 November 2017.
24. "3 Tahun Jokowi: Kenaikan Electoral dan Kepuasan Publik", *Laporan Survei CSIS*, 12 September 2016 <https://www.csis.or.id, downloaded 13/10/2017>.
25. The role of Foreign Minister Retno Marsudi was appreciated by the United Nations. See <http://www.thejakartapost.com/news/2017/09/21/indonesian-fm-retno-marsudi-receives-un-agent-of-change-award.html> (accessed 29 November 2017).
26. Dirk Tomsa, "Indonesia in 2016: Jokowi Consolidates Power", in *Southeast Asian Affairs 2017*, edited by Malcolm Cook and Daljit Singh (Singapore: ISEAS – Yusuf Ishak Institute, 2017), p. 160.
27. "Peta Anyar Pendukung Jokowi", *Gatra*, 1 November 2017.
28. See <https://www.voanews.com/a/new-indonesian-armes-forces-chief-seen-as-ally-of-president/4158382.html> (accessed 18 December 2017).

Laos

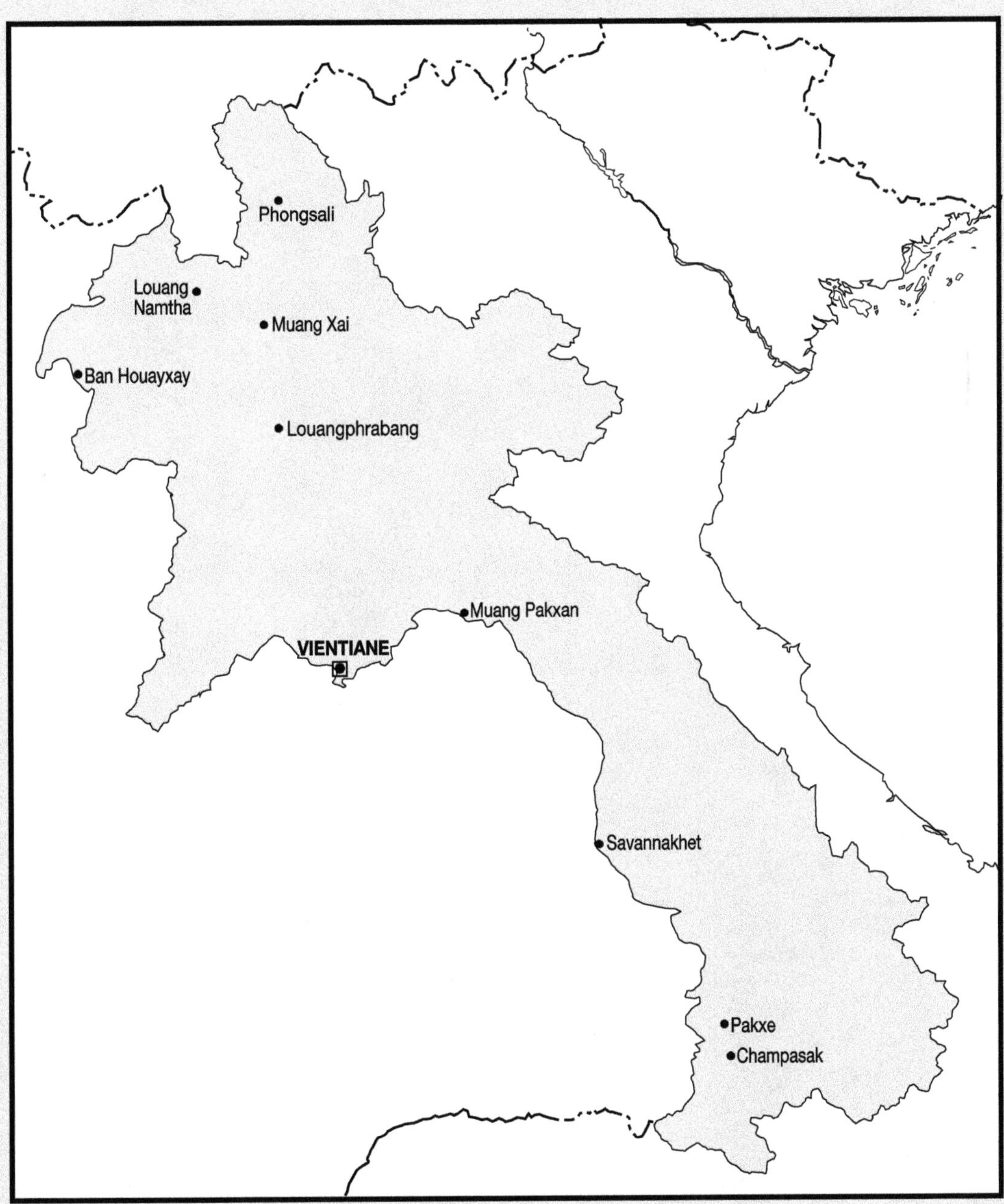

Phongsali
Louang
Namtha
Muang Xai
Ban Houayxay
Louangphrabang
Muang Pakxan
VIENTIANE
Savannakhet
Pakxe
Champasak

ON THE RIGHT TRACK? The Lao People's Democratic Republic in 2017

Oliver Tappe

The year 2017 was an important one to assess the performance of the new government of Laos. Prime Minister Thongloun Sisoulith tackled key problems of Lao governance and economy — most notably corruption and illegal logging — earning him both domestic and international approval. However, Laos is still facing numerous socio-economic challenges such as weak legal institutions, poverty, environmental degradation, and a civil society subdued.

According to the 8th Five-Year National Socio-Economic Development Plan (2016–20), Lao economic politics is focused on graduating from the status of being a least developed country (LDC), not least through mega projects like hydropower dams, mines and large-scale infrastructure projects — negative social and ecological side effects notwithstanding. China and many ASEAN countries compete in large-scale investment in these fields. The Lao–Chinese railway linking Kunming with Vientiane is a case in point.

This chapter gives an overview of political and economic tendencies in the Lao PDR at the beginning of the new five-year cycle.

The Tenth Party Congress and its Aftermath

The year 2017 saw widely noticed political decisions of the new Government of Laos. The government addressed key challenges mentioned in the 8th Five-Year National Socio-Economic Development Plan (2016–20), such as the fight against corruption, illegal logging, and uncontrolled investment. This raised cautious hopes

Oliver Tappe is Research Fellow at the Global South Studies Center, University of Cologne (Germany).

for more efficient and transparent governance. Prime Minister Thongloun Sisoulith gained a public image of a pragmatic and responsible politician. However, Laos still faces many problems: poverty and low education, environmental degradation, pressure on civil society, and the negative ecological and social impacts of hydropower dams and mining projects.

Meanwhile, the dynamic economic sector — with a growth of slightly below seven per cent in 2017 — dominated the Lao news and the political agenda. Large-scale investment projects such as hydropower dams, coal plants and, not least, the huge Lao–Chinese railway project indicate Laos' ongoing reliance on natural resources and increasing regional connectivity. The high social and environmental costs of the government's obsession with such mega projects became evident in 2017 as well. This chapter gives an overview of political and economic tendencies — and their social implications — in the Lao PDR.

In last year's country overview on Laos, Soulatha Sayalath and Simon Creak provided an insightful analysis of the Lao People's Revolutionary Party's "regeneration". This process, culminating in the reshuffle of the leadership at the Tenth Party Congress, demonstrated "not only the degree to which the party's structures and processes have been designed to maintain party power and stability, but also to ensure elite prerogatives are not unduly challenged".[1] Indeed, 2017 demonstrated the stability of the Lao party-state (*phak lat*) and the government's will to maintain control and order.

The replacement of retired president and secretary general Choummaly Sayasone (then 78 years old) with party-state veteran Bounnyang Vorachit (77; number one in the Politburo), and former prime minister Thongsing Thammavong (73) with Thongloun Sisoulith (72; number two in the Politburo), was certainly not a generation change. Yet, the rise of sons and daughters, nieces and nephews of the old "30-year-struggle" guard, as well as a new generation of well-educated technocrats within the ranks of the Central Committee, hint at a rejuvenation with simultaneous continuity within the party-state. Old family relations and patronage networks ensure the reproduction of the Lao political elite.

Continuity is probably best represented by the Politburo members Xaysomphone Phomvihane and Sonxay Siphandone, sons of the revolutionary heroes and party founding fathers Kaysone Phomvihane and Kamtay Siphandone. They also represent the powerful southern families (including the Sayasons and Vorachits) that for decades have paired political with economic power. Thongloun Sisoulith (his father-in-law was Phoumi Vongvichit, another LPRP founding father) and his confidants, including rising stars like Vice President Phankham Viphavanh and Foreign Minister Saleumxay Kommasith, hail from the revolutionary heartland in

Northeastern Laos. Finally, Pany Yathotou, president of the National Assembly and number three in the Politburo, is the daughter of the Hmong military leader Thao Touya.

Gradually, the post-1975 generation is taking over, still with inseparable kinship or patron–client ties to the old guard. As Martin Rathie, one of the few experts on Lao party-state politics, comments in a recent article:

> … the circles of power relate to groups who studied in the USSR, PRC, and SRV, those who were active in the Lao People's Revolutionary Youth Movement, those who have held and processed the dossiers of the Party rank and file at Km 6, those who cultivated investment ties while posted in foreign missions, those who have safeguarded land holdings and not been burnt by speculators, those who occupy executive positions in multiple company boards, and those who simply influence security forces and legal institutions with their social connections and financial largesse.[2]

This observation leaves no doubt that economic interests — from land property and resource control to the ability to draw investment — still shape the agenda of most elite families. This is particularly true for the lucrative logging business that used to be a key source of revenue for the Lao state and its ruling families. In recent years, excesses and collusion resulted in public resentment and increasing inquietude within the party-state leadership. For example, the involvement of former minister of finance Dr Nam Vinyaket (son of long-time Politburo member Samane Vinyaket) and his wife in illegal timber export deals had produced a veritable scandal.[3]

Thongloun seemed to take the fight against the excesses of nepotism and collusion seriously. An experienced politician — he already held the positions of minister of labour and social welfare, president of the State Planning Committee, minister of foreign affairs, and deputy prime minister — he combined an impressive party-state career with a modest appearance and good international standing. Even though his stricter policy against corruption, illegal logging and drug trafficking is mainly related to concerns of party legitimacy and social order, it has already given him the reputation of a "reformer".[4]

In many speeches, Thongloun directly addressed corruption and criticized the selfish behaviour of state cadres at all governmental levels. He stated, for example, that "we can have foreign investment but we must share the benefits", and "rising social inequality, and the perception that the nomenklatura and connected businessmen had retained the country's wealth for themselves, threatened the Party's legitimacy".[5] By giving his internal critique unusual publicity through Lao media, he clearly distanced himself from predecessors such as Somsavat Lengsavat, who had developed an ambivalent renown for his ability to attract Chinese investment in combination with personal enrichment. Thus, Thongloun's decisions should not be considered reforms but rather attempts to protect party-state power.

Against Corruption: PM Thongloun Sisoulith and the New Leadership

Thongloun's first year was characterized by responses to public resentment of corruption excesses and the drug trade, of scandals related to illegal logging business, and the problem of belated payments for civil servants' salaries. The number of decisions and orders in these fields was impressive. Apparently, the government had noticed increasing discontent from various sectors of Lao society. Shameless displays of wealth of a few, and growing social inequality in Laos created a problem of legitimacy that used to rely on constant economic growth and increasing prosperity for the so-called "Lao multi-ethnic people".

The year 2017 started with an order by the prime minister to prioritize civil servants' salaries.[6] In March, a highly symbolic act brought the new political stance to the fore: Fifteen luxury cars of party-state leaders were sold in a bidding process. This event followed a decision to replace BMW and Mercedes-Benz cars with cheaper brands in a bid to cut lavish spending on vehicles and related costs.[7] Recent (November 2017) conversations with Lao informants revealed a lasting impression of this spectacular move on the part of Thongloun that raised hopes that the new leadership would put an end to elite extravaganza and corruption.

Thongloun encouraged the Party and State Inspection Authority to investigate cases of corruption and embezzlement to further restore confidence in party-state governance. For 2016 alone, anti-corruption officials investigated 786 cases throughout fifteen ministries and government agencies, and reported that over 98 billion kip, 15 million baht, and US$2 million had been syphoned away through corruption. Bounthong Chitmany, deputy prime minister and chief of the Inspection Authority, warned that corruption in Laos eroded the influence and leadership of the party.[8]

In April 2017, Vice President Phankham Viphavanh stressed that organization directors will be dismissed if it is proved that their organizations or people under their supervision are corrupt. He made his point clear:

> Among the problems the Party has attached most importance to and that need urgent address is corruption, which is prevalent at all levels and in all groups of people in the Lao society today, especially corruption

> committed in the Party and government realms which continues to plague political stability and national security.... If this problem (corruption) remains unaddressed, it will have effects on the leading role of the Party and the national security.[9]

Another important political tendency in 2017 was the ongoing enforcement of "Prime Minister's Order No. 15 on Enhancing Strictness on the Management and Inspection of Timber Exploitation, Timber Movements and Timber Businesses" from 13 May 2016, issued by Thongloun less than one month after taking office. Before this, reports of rampant illegal logging and timber exports, the shameless exploitation of forest resources, and the collusion of local authorities entailed public resentment and the necessity for the central government to intervene.[10]

The ban seems to have had its intended effect, since exports of raw logs to Vietnam — the largest market, with its booming furniture industry — dropped from 321,718 cubic metres in 2015 to 36,060 cubic metres in 2016, and the export of sawn wood from 383,149 cubic metres in 2015 to 95,572 cubic meters in 2016.[11] In addition, sawmills and furniture factories in Laos came under closer surveillance, and Lao media reported numerous investigations and shutdowns.[12]

This certainly does not mean that deforestation in Laos is under control. On the contrary, environmental degradation and forest depletion continue at an alarming pace, not least with regard to the insufficient control of concession projects producing "conversion land" that can be easily logged. According to a recent World Bank report, forest depletion is "affecting forest-dependent households, leading to soil erosion and accelerated sedimentation of hydropower reservoirs, exacerbating weather-related risks, affecting wildlife populations and undermining the future growth of sectors like tourism and clean agriculture".[13]

This is also true for uncontrolled mining decimating forests and polluting rivers. While the mines operated by the two biggest mining companies in Laos, MMG Sepon and Phu Bia Mining — contributing around 95 per cent of government revenue from the mining sector[14] — might be considered as relatively well managed and monitored, numerous small mining concessions in remote upland regions cause severe environmental damage. In January 2016, a bomb attack on Chinese nationals working for a mining company in Xaysomboun Province hinted at local resentment and lack of government control.[15]

Another reason for local people's discontent — and anti-Chinese resentment — was the rapid expansion of banana plantations established by Chinese investors in northern Laos; especially the fatal consequences of the excessive use of toxic herbicides and pesticides (e.g., paraquat, a weedkiller banned in many countries), which left the authorities alarmed. Dramatic reports of poisoned rivers and forest products, and of severe illnesses related to poisoning, finally instigated the government to issue a ban on new concessions in 2016 and, since early 2017, even to close down farms.[16]

In recent years, Aroma banana became a boom crop in the Sino–Lao borderlands, not unlike the rubber boom in the 2000s that had transformed the agricultural landscape of northern provinces like Bokeo, Luang Namtha and Oudomxay. Lao peasants rented their farmland to Chinese investors for a good price (roughly the equivalent to full-time rice cultivation), and plantation workers — mostly from upland ethnic minorities such as the Khmu and Hmong — earned a good salary. Apparently a good deal for impoverished communities in northern Laos, the true cost in the form of environmental devastation and health risks soon overshadowed these cross-border arrangements.[17]

Besides this rare intervention against environmentally destructive practices, the Lao authorities also took steps towards more effectively fighting the rampant drug trade along the Mekong. In cooperation with the Thai police, drug "kingpin" Xaysana Keopimpha was arrested in January 2017. Lao media remained suspiciously silent about Lao authorities' links with Xaysana, who was known for his connections to celebrities and politicians on both sides of the Thai–Lao border.[18]

Given that even state authorities admitted direct involvement of party members and government officials in illegal activities in the timber and drug trafficking trades, time will tell whether more prominent names will emerge from the diverse investigations. However, the big families have probably marked out their claims already, and many dubious investment projects have delivered their yield in foreign bank accounts in past years. It remains to be seen if the new leadership will reassess some of the more disgraceful projects, such as badly planned hotel complexes and shopping malls in Vientiane.[19]

Also overshadowing some positive tendencies in Lao governance are the facts that the country is still far from a system of checks and balances or a free and functioning civil society. This became dramatically evident in the strict control of social media and some harsh reactions to public expressions of critique. In March 2016, three Lao workers were arrested for criticizing the government on Facebook while working in Thailand, and sentenced to long prison terms.[20] This indicates the oppressive and opaque nature of the state apparatus. Moreover, on 15 December 2017 the country faced a particularly sad anniversary: five years previously Lao NGO activist Sombath Somphone was abducted, and to date his whereabouts are unknown.[21] His case is a constant reminder of the precarious state of Lao civil society.

Laos in the Region: Investment, Mega Projects, Railway

In November 2017, I visited the construction site of the new Laos–China railway linking Vientiane with the Mohan–Boten border checkpoint. Following the road to Tha Ngon by the Nam Ngum River, the extent of so-called "development zones" and diverse businesses and factories revealed the economic dynamics in Vientiane Province, where some years ago the roads outside the capital were bordered mostly by rice fields. Five kilometres from Tha Ngon, the tracks of the new railway stretch towards the horizon, an endless row of concrete poles that promise to make the railway impervious to seasonal rainfall and other impacts. It is certainly a technological and logistical endeavour previously unseen in Laos.

The project is part of Beijing's Belt and Road Initiative, a massive investment programme dedicated to countless infrastructure projects throughout Asia, with estimated financing of almost a trillion U.S. dollars.[22] The railway in Laos will form part of the three thousand kilometres of rail running from China to Singapore. Behind the newly established Laos–China Railway Company stands the leading infrastructure builder and biggest construction company, by revenue, in Asia, the Chinese state-owned China Railway Group. Given China's experience with such infrastructure projects, most notably the railway in Tibet, it is not unlikely that the company will finish construction within five years as scheduled.

While China's regional interests are clear, it remains to be seen whether projects such as the China–Lao railway or Malaysia's US$13.3 billion East Coast Rail Link will yield mutual prosperity, or just a heavy burden of debt. For the Lao government, responsible for a 40 per cent share of the costs, the US$5.8 billion project is certainly a financial hazard (to put it in perspective, the country's GDP in 2016 was US$15.7 billion).[23] Mining concessions granted to China as security, and a large Chinese loan covering 65 per cent of Laos' share, will only increase Lao dependency on its big neighbour.[24]

The technical challenges of the railway linking Vientiane with the Mohan–Boten border checkpoint are impressive: 62.7 per cent of the 414-kilometre track consist of bridges (167, with a total length of 61.81 km) and tunnels (75,197.83 km).[25] Labour demand amounts to an estimated hundred thousand workers; predominantly Chinese and Vietnamese labour migrants.[26] And impressive progress was made in 2017. The Laos–China Railway Company on 31 March launched a campaign of "a 100-day of dry season working competition" to speed up clearing and construction, and to finish sidewalk reinforcement before the rainy season impedes construction. In less than six months, workers finished the construction of the foundations for nine bridge piles and eighty-six holes for the construction of forty-six tunnels.[27]

Besides environmental concerns, one of the major problems is resettlement — not least due to a buffer zone along the tracks reserved for Chinese business interests — and the question of adequate compensation. In a recent case, thirty families in Naxaithong District, Vientiane, had been displaced but could not afford to move because of belated compensation payments.[28] The government's negligence and harassment by construction companies and security forces do not help to create an atmosphere in favour of such investment projects. Adding to local resentment is the fact that often government members took advantage of their advance information, bought cheap farmland or forestland, cut and sold timber, and received compensation as soon as the land was declared a "development zone". This is also a general pattern in many of the so-called mega projects that the government sees as the future of Laos' economic prosperity.

Attracting foreign investment via mega projects is a pillar of Lao economic politics and key for the aims of the 8th Five-Year National Socio-Economic Development Plan: the reduction of poverty and graduation from LDC status.[29] According to the five-year plan, the government aims to "create a favourable legal framework and investment climate".[30] However, corruption, regulatory ambiguity, and the uneven application of law remain as disincentives to foreign investment. Chinese investors also complain about the lack of infrastructure, skilled labour, and opaque financial and institutional regulations. Thongloun's occasional pledges for the "rule of law" indicate that there are still considerable deficits.[31]

However, many Asian states provide large-scale investment in Laos, which offers a lens on Laos' regional relations. Besides the usual suspects — China, Vietnam and Thailand — increasingly, Malaysia and South Korea are financing diverse projects. The alleged competition for influence between China and Vietnam is still of concern for Western observers, even though Thongloun recently issued a decree to promote economic cooperation with both countries, which illustrates his policy to balance these two important partner countries.[32]

China is currently the largest investor and aims to expand investment and cooperation, as President Xi Jinping made clear on the occasion of his visit to Laos in November 2017. In a speech reprinted in the Lao daily *Vientiane Times*, he provided some numbers: China's total direct investment of projects exceeded US$6.1 billion (in several hundreds of projects related to infrastructure, hydropower, mining, manufacturing, and commercial agriculture), and bilateral trade reached US$2.1 billion. In addition, four hundred thousand Chinese tourists travelled to Laos in the first half of the year.[33]

A new tendency is Chinese investment in the health sector; namely, a US$90 million hospital project,[34] perhaps to dispel anti-Chinese sentiment fuelled by land dispossession tied to Chinese investment projects. At the same time, there is increasing interest among Lao students to learn Chinese with regard to business perspectives.[35] It is safe to say that last year's reshuffle of the Lao leadership does not indicate a move away from China. Xi Jinping's state visit left no doubt about the common economic interests of both countries.

However, Vietnam still remains a close political and economic partner, and the Lao government used the fortieth anniversary of the "Laos–Vietnam Treaty of Amity and Cooperation" to emphasize the "special relationship" between the two socialist brother countries, reminiscent of the joint struggle against France and the United States in the two Indochina Wars.[36] In a particularly telling speech at a reception for Lao Prime Minister Thongloun Sisoulith in Hanoi on 3 October 2017, Vietnam's General Secretary Nguyen Phu Trong stressed not only the significance of promoting trade and investment but also Vietnam's support for "national security" and the "reform process" of Laos, hinting at the ongoing advisory role of Vietnam's Communist Party for the Lao government and Thongloun's new policy.[37]

Thailand continues to be a major trading partner and buyer of electricity produced in Laos. Concerning its growing energy demand, Thailand is financing and building two particularly controversial mega projects in the border province of Xayaboury: the Hongsa Coal Plant and the Xayaboury hydropower dam, the first mainstream dam of the Mekong. By the middle of 2017, the much-criticized US$3 billion hydropower project was 70 per cent complete. Ecological concerns include declining fish stocks and changing water levels that seriously affect the livelihoods of Lao and Thai communities.[38]

Another ill-famed mega project is the Don Sahong Dam in southern Laos, one of eleven planned dams on the Mekong. Although this dam threatens Lao and Cambodian fishing grounds,[39] as well as the last populations of the Mekong dolphin, Cambodian Prime Minister Hun Sen joined his Lao counterpart Thongloun in an approving visit to the construction site.[40] Environmentalists thus cannot expect support from the respective governments. This is also true of Vietnam, who occasionally criticizes such projects as detrimental to the ecosystem of the Mekong delta but at the same time imports Lao hydropower.

The Don Sahong Dam is financed by Malaysia. It is only one of several large investment projects that make Malaysia the forth-largest foreign direct investor in Laos, behind China, Vietnam and Thailand. A Malaysian company holds concessions in the Savan-Seno Special Economic Zone (Savannakhet Province) with an investment value of US$132 million. The first dry port in the Lao PDR is going to be linked with the Vietnamese coast via a 220-kilometre double-track railway from Savannakhet to the Lao–Vietnamese border, another important railway project in Laos (somewhat overshadowed by the Laos–China railway).[41]

To sum up, the Lao government is still successful in ensuring a constant influx of foreign money, both direct investment and development aid (to which Japan and numerous countries of the European Union continue to add). However, some alleged solutions to the old problems of rural poverty and weak infrastructure create new problems, as illustrated by the environmentally detrimental effects of hydropower dams and commercial banana plantations. The feeling of dispossession both of rural communities affected by dam projects and residents of urban and peri-urban areas turned into "development zones" will continue to challenge the legitimacy of the Lao government. Yet PM Thongloun Sisoulith insists:

> Special attention must be attached to these [mega] projects to ensure they are implemented as planned and effectively as well as to the addressing of their impacts on local communities and environment to ensure these projects best benefit local people and improve their living standards so they will win the support of the local people.[42]

Outlook: On the Advent of "Visit Laos Year 2018"

On the occasion of the That Luang Festival, the most important religious — and increasingly commercial — festival in Laos, Prime Minister Thongloun Sisoulith announced on 30 October 2017 the launch of "Visit Laos Year 2018", in the presence of ministers, foreign diplomats, senior officials of Vientiane Capital, representatives of international organizations and Vientiane residents. According to the Minister of Information and Culture, this tourism campaign aims to boost currency reserves and the circulation of money in the country, and create more job opportunities in the service and production sectors, particularly agriculture and handicraft production.[43]

Supporting the recent anti-corruption campaigns, the Visit Laos initiative forms part of the government's agenda of fostering legitimacy or gaining the "support of the local people", in the words of Thongloun. Yet, the image of the Lao "happy people" as promoted by tourism agencies and Beerlao commercials is increasingly ambivalent. The negative social and ecological impacts already triggered by the recent land run and the above-mentioned investment projects have severe effects on many Lao communities that no anti-corruption or anti-logging decree can reverse. Even if the Lao PDR now witnesses a better standard of living for the majority of the population and arguably new opportunities for the younger generations, the concerns about dispossession, legal insecurity, environmental depletion (aggravated by climatic effects), and authoritarianism remain.

Thongloun's laudable initiatives notwithstanding, powerful patrimonial networks seem to have divided up the natural wealth of Laos and staked out their claims in various sectors of the economy, emblematizing increasing social inequalities. Lao PDR expert Martin Rathie asks the important question of whether the country will simply become "a façade for power plays between elite families like the RLG, or if the Party will take some radical steps to remain loyal to its historic legacy".[44] In 2017, Thongloun Sisoulith and his new government did not give a definite answer.

Notes

1. Soulatha Sayalath and Simon Creak, "Regime Renewal in Laos: The Tenth Congress of the Lao People's Revolutionary Party", in *Southeast Asian Affairs 2017*, edited by Daljit Singh and Malcolm Cook, pp. 179–200 (Singapore: ISEAS – Yusof Ishak Institute, 2017), p. 196.
2. Martin Rathie, "The History and Evolution of the Lao People's Revolutionary Party", in *Changing Lives in Laos – Society, Politics, and Culture in a Post-Socialist State*, edited by Vanina Bouté and Vatthana Pholsena, pp. 19–55 (Singapore: NUS Press, 2017), pp. 48–49.
3. "New Governor of Laos' Attapeu Province Pledges to Deliver Justice in Logging Scandal", Radio Free Asia, 30 November 2017 <http://www.rfa.org/english/news/laos/new-governor-of-laos-attapeu-province-pledges-to-deliver-justice-in-logging-scandal-11302017164315.html>.
4. David Hutt, "Is Laos' New Leader Really a Reformer?" *The Diplomat*, 26 April 2017 <https://thediplomat.com/2017/04/is-laos-new-leader-really-a-reformer/>.
5. Ibid.
6. Ibid.
7. "Leaders' Vehicles to Undergo Bidding Process Next Week", *Vientiane Times*, 3 February 2017. Rumours have it that the cars of the state president and the prime minister were sold to rich businessmen from Luang Prabang. For the Asian Development Bank, the turn towards curtailing spending has fostered cautious hope for financial consolidation of the deficient economy; *Asian Development Outlook Update, 2017*, p. 199 <https://www.adb.org/sites/default/files/publication/365701/ado2017-update.pdf>.
8. "Deputy Prime Minister to Stamp Out Corruption in Laos", *Laotian Times*, 19 January 2017 <https://laotiantimes.com/2017/01/19/corruption-in-laos/>; David Hutt, "Little Laos Tackles Big Corruption", *Asia Times*, 16 February 2017 <http://www.atimes.com/article/little-laos-tackles-big-corruption/>; "PM Declares 'Intolerance' of Corruption, Abuse of Power", *Vientiane Times*, 24 October 2017.

9. "Heads Will be Dismissed If Corrupt, says Vice President", Khaosan Pathet Lao, 19 April 2017 <http://kpl.gov.la/En/Detail.aspx?id=23787>. A specific aspect of corruption is overvalued development projects where corrupt officials cash the difference to the disadvantage of investors and state revenues; "Overvalued Development Projects Face Scrutiny", *Vientiane Times*, 12 December 2017.
10. A report by the World Wide Fund for Nature (WWF) leaked in October 2016 revealed great increases in illegal logging and discrepancies in timber export and import figures with China and Vietnam. It turns out that the value of Lao wood product imports reported by China and Vietnam exceeded the value of Lao exports by more than tenfold, indicating considerable collusion by local authorities. Particularly lucrative is so-called "conversion forestry": Logging in areas marked for the development of hydropower dams, mining operations, and other infrastructure projects — often used as an excuse for large-scale logging that otherwise would not be permitted under Lao law; "New Lao Prime Minister Issues Ban on Timber Exports", Radio Free Asia, 17 May 2016 <http://www.rfa.org/english/news/laos/new-lao-prime-minister-issues-ban-on-timber-exports-05172016152448.html>.
11. Hutt, "Little Laos".
12. "Bolikhamxay Shuts Down 17 Timber Factories", Khaosan Pathet Lao, 15 June 2017 <http://kpl.gov.la/En/Detail.aspx?id=25372>.
13. World Bank Group, *Lao People's Democratic Republic – Systematic Country Diagnostic*, March 2017, p. 81.
14. "Lao Government Consults Stakeholders on Draft Mining Law", Khaosan Pathet Lao, 4 October 2017.
15. Edward Wong, "Bombing in Central Laos Kills 2 From China", *New York Times*, 29 January 2016 <https://www.nytimes.com/2016/01/30/world/asia/laos-bombing-kills-chinese.html>.
16. Nirmal Ghosh, "Chemicals are Killing Laos' Farmlands", *Straits Times*, 16 April 2016 <http://www.straitstimes.com/asia/se-asia/chemicals-are-killing-laos-farmlands>; Prashanth Parameswaran, "What's Behind Laos' China Banana Ban?" *The Diplomat*, 14 April 2017 <https://thediplomat.com/2017/04/whats-behind-the-china-banana-ban-in-laos/>; "Luang Namtha Shuts Down Aroma Banana Farms", Khaosan Pathet Lao, 20 March 2017 <http://kpl.gov.la/En/Detail.aspx?id=23032>.
17. Brenda Goh and Andrew R.C. Marshall, "Cash and Chemicals: For Laos, Chinese Banana Boom a Blessing and Curse", *Daily Mail*, 12 May 2017 <http://www.dailymail.co.uk/wires/reuters/article-4497838/Cash-chemicals-Laos-Chinese-banana-boom-blessing-curse.html>; Arnaud Dubus, "The True Cost of Laos' Banana Plantations", *Southeast Asia Globe*, 10 February 2016 <http://sea-globe.com/laos-banana-plantations/>. For an insightful study on Lao banana plantations, corresponding networks of local middlemen, short-term land acquisition at the village level without involving the government, and the effects of rapid land use conversion and chemical pollution, see: Cecilie Friis and Jonas Ø. Nielsen, "Small-scale Land Acquisitions,

Large-scale Implications: Exploring the Case of Chinese Banana Investments in Northern Laos", *Land Use Policy* 57 (2016): 117–29.

18. Hutt, "Is Laos' New Leader Really a Reformer?"
19. The historical buildings of the National Museum and the National Library in Vientiane city are still projected for demolition to make way for such questionable investment projects. Since my last visit to Vientiane two years ago, some construction projects have not really made much progress due to financial problems; and the demand for office space and apartments had to have been overestimated, as the almost empty condominiums in the That Luang Marshes suggest; see: Oliver Tappe, "Forty Years of Lao PDR: What's Next?" *New Mandala*, 22 January 2016 <http://www.newmandala.org/forty-years-of-lao-pdr-whats-next/>.
20. "Three Lao Workers Handed Lengthy Jail Terms for Slamming Government Online", Radio Free Asia, 16 May 2017 <http://www.rfa.org/english/news/laos/sentences-05162017165950.html>.
21. Simon Creak, "Laos in 2013", in *Southeast Asian Affairs 2014*, edited by Daljit Singh, pp. 151–71 (Singapore: Institute of Southeast Asian Studies, 2014); Luke Hunt, "New Guard, Old Problems: What Sombath Somphone's Continued Disappearance Says about Rights in Laos", *The Diplomat*, 13 December 2017 <https://thediplomat.com/2017/12/new-guard-old-problems-what-sombath-somphones-continued-disappearance-says-about-rights-in-laos/>.
22. Tom Phillips, "The $900bn Question: What is the Belt and Road Initiative?" *The Guardian*, 12 May 2017 <https://www.theguardian.com/world/2017/may/12/the-900bn-question-what-is-the-belt-and-road-initiative>.
23. IMF, World Economic Outlook Database, October 2017.
24. Marimi Kishimoto, "Laos Merely a Bystander as China Pushes Belt and Road Ambitions", *Nikkei Asian Review*, 6 October 2017 <https://asia.nikkei.com/Politics-Economy/International-Relations/Laos-merely-a-bystander-as-China-pushes-Belt-and-Road-ambitions>; Tang Siew Mun, "Can China be a Considerate Power?" *ASEAN Focus* 2017, no. 6 (November 2017), pp. 6–7 <https://www.iseas.edu.sg/images/pdf/NOV_ASEANFOCUS_WEB.pdf>; Edgar Pang, "'Same-Same but Different': Laos and Cambodia's Political Embrace of China", *ISEAS Perspective* 2017, no. 66 (5 September 2017), pp. 1–7 <https://www.iseas.edu.sg/images/pdf/ISEAS_Perspective_2017_66.pdf>.
25. "Tunnel Boring for Laos–China Railway Expected in Coming Weeks", *Vientiane Times*, 21 March 2017.
26. Due to the shortage of skilled labour in Laos, labour migration is indispensable for large construction projects. For the railway construction, Oudomxay Province even issued a special law to register foreign migrants and offer them legal documentation and three-month work permits; "Oudomxay Legalises Foreign Workers", *Vientiane Times*, 12 October 2017.
27. "Chinese Companies Gearing Up as Construction of China–Laos Railway in

Full Swing", Xinhua, 29 August 2017 <http://news.xinhuanet.com/english/2017-08/30/c_136566266.htm>.

28. "Lao People Affected by Railway Project Still Waiting for Compensation", *Vientiane Times*, 6 December 2017.
29. "Govt Pushes for Development of Mega Projects", *Vientiane Times*, 9 December 2017; World Bank Group, *Lao People's Democratic Republic – Systematic Country Diagnostic*, March 2017; Ministry of Planning and Planning, *8th Five-Year National Socio-Economic Development Plan*, 2016, p. 165.
30. Ibid., p. 166.
31. Chen Qingqing and Ma Jingjing, "Chinese Firms Eye Laos Opportunities", *Global Times*, 12 November 2017 <http://www.globaltimes.cn/content/1074802.shtml>; "PM Urges Continued Addressing of Economic Difficulties", Khaosan Pathet Lao, 12 September 2017 <http://kpl.gov.la/En/Detail.aspx?id=27881>; World Bank Group, *Lao People's Democratic Republic.*
32. "Gov't Approves Guidance on Promotion of Cooperation with China and Vietnam", Khaosan Pathet Lao, 11 December 2017 <http://kpl.gov.la/En/Detail.aspx?id=30305>. Laos also avoids a clear position in the South China Sea conflict; see Pang, "Same Same but Different".
33. "China and Laos: Working Together for a Community with a Shared Future and Strategic Significance", *Vientiane Times*, 13 November 2017; See also: "Xi's State Visit Sees Laos' Investment Profile, Opportunities Rise", *Vientiane Times*, 20 November 2017; and Chen and Ma, "Chinese Firms Eye Laos Opportunities".
34. David Hutt, "China's Aid a Matter of Life and Death for Laos", *Asia Times*, 12 December 2017 <http://www.atimes.com/article/chinas-aid-matter-life-death-laos/>.
35. "TV, Beer and Railways – Bringing Laos and China Together", Xinhua, 16 November 2017 <http://news.xinhuanet.com/english/2017-11/16/c_136757338.htm>.
36. "Laos, Vietnam Celebrate Two Historic Days", Khaosan Pathet Lao, 18 July 2017 <http://kpl.gov.la/En/Detail.aspx?id=26339>.
37. "Vietnam's Party Chief Requests Stronger Vietnam–Laos Trade, Connectivity", Khaosan Pathet Lao, 4 October 2017 <http://kpl.gov.la/En/Detail.aspx?id=28537>.
38. International Rivers, "Mekong Mainstream Dams", n.d. <https://www.internationalrivers.org/campaigns/mekong-mainstream-dams>.
39. International Rivers, "Local Knowledge, Culture and Heritage: Collateral Damage of Mekong Dams", 23 October 2017 <https://www.internationalrivers.org/blogs/259/local-knowledge-culture-and-heritage-collateral-damage-of-mekong-dams>.
40. "PM Thongloun, Cambodian Counterpart Visit Don Sahong Project", Khaosan Pathet Lao, 11 January 2017 <http://kpl.gov.la/En/Detail.aspx?id=21056>. Not surprisingly, Hun Sen himself in September 2017 opened a dam downstream in Cambodia financed by China; Pascal Laureyn, "The Mekong, Dammed to Die", Inter Press Service, 14 November 2017 <http://www.ipsnews.net/2017/11/mekong-dammed-die/>.

41. "Lao–Malaysia Bilateral Relations at an All-time High Celebrating Malaysia's 60th National Day", Khaosan Pathet Lao, 11 September 2017 <http://kpl.gov.la/En/Detail.aspx?id=27846>.
42. "Gov't Approves Guidance on Promotion of Cooperation with China and Vietnam", Khaosan Pathet Lao, 11 December 2017 <http://kpl.gov.la/En/Detail.aspx?id=30305>.
43. "Visit Laos Year 2018 Launched along with That Luang Festival 2017", Khaosan Pathet Lao, 30 October 2017 <http://kpl.gov.la/En/Detail.aspx?id=29185>.
44. Rathie, "The History and Evolution of the Lao People's Revolutionary Party", p. 52.

Malaysia

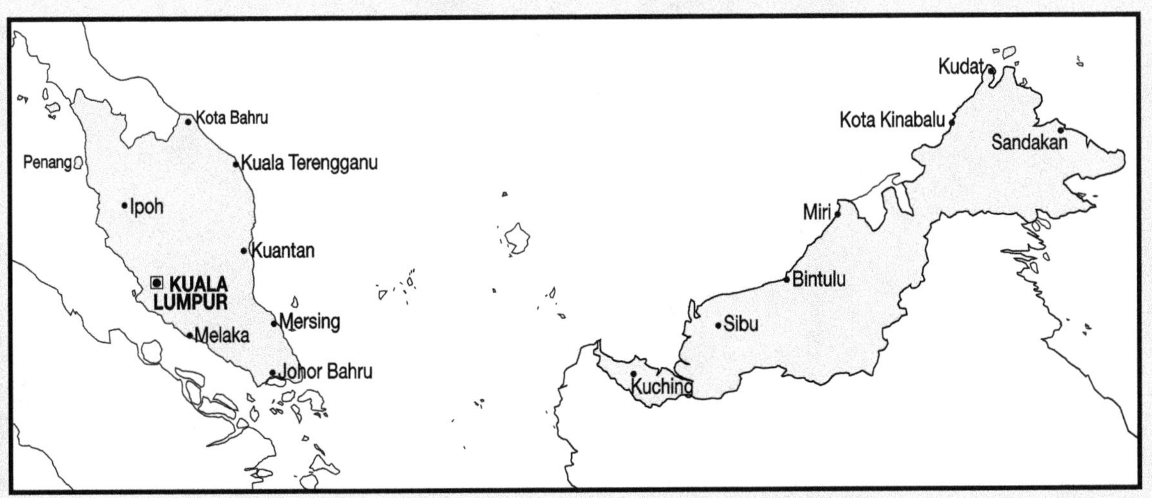

Kota Bahru
Penang
Kuala Terengganu
Ipoh
Kuantan
KUALA LUMPUR
Mersing
Melaka
Johor Bahru
Kudat
Kota Kinabalu
Sandakan
Miri
Bintulu
Sibu
Kuching

JOHOR AND TRADITIONALIST ISLAM: What This Means for Malaysia

Norshahril Saat

In a survey conducted by the ISEAS – Yusof Ishak Institute in May–June 2017, one may be alarmed by the level of conservatism and exclusivism expressed by the Malay respondents living in Johor.[1] For example, 89 per cent of the Malays believed that Malaysia is an Islamic state, and 75 per cent supported the implementation of *hudud* laws in Johor (punitive Islamic laws which include stoning, whipping and amputation as modes of punishment).[2] One would expect those living in the rural states of Kelantan, Terengganu and Kedah, the states which were once governed by conservative Islamic party PAS (Islamic Party of Malaysia), to demonstrate such views. Yet, these sentiments were expressed by Malays residing in the highly urbanized, modern state of Johor, which is ruled by a religiously moderate sultan and the Malay nationalist party, UMNO (United Malays National Organisation). Moreover, observers have regarded Johor as a bastion of moderate, cultural and Sufi (spiritual) Islam. Is Johor experiencing a wave of Salafism-Wahhabism? In this chapter, I argue that Johor is not undergoing the Salafism-Wahhabism that may be experienced in some other Malaysian states; yet, this does not necessarily translate into a less exclusivist mode of thinking among the masses.

One has to go back a century to understand the nature of Islam practised in Johor, and how its religious elites have warded off influences from the Middle East. Historically, Islam in the state was tied to the royal courts, and Sufism was the dominant mode of orientation. In 1916, Haji Abdul Karim Amrullah,[3] an Islamic religious scholar (ulama) from Sumatra, who was influenced by the reformist movement in the Middle East, made a sneering remark about the Mufti of Johor. "To become a Government Mufti in Malaya is a great glory", he said.

NORSHAHRIL SAAT is Fellow at the ISEAS – Yusof Ishak Institute.

"You have an official uniform, with a whole banana-comb of epaulettes on the shoulder, a *jubbah* [Arabian-style garment] embroidered with gold thread, a silk turban, and your own car. The *ra'ayat* [people] fear and obey you, eat the scraps from your table, your spat of *sireh* [betel leaf]. And if you want to get married … *Bismillah* [anytime with God's consent]."[4] Muftis are religious scholars whose role is to provide guidance to the Muslim community and issue fatwas (religious rulings). In Malaysia, muftis are appointed by the Malay Rulers. Ideally, an alim (singular for ulama) must not blindly serve the interest of ruling elites; instead, they must be pious individuals who protect the interests of the religious community. Haji Abdul Karim's harsh words showed that he must have felt strongly that the Johor Mufti of his time had been falling far short of those ideals.

Haji Abdul Karim and the then–Johor Mufti came from rival schools of thought.[5] Haji Abdul Karim was a key player in the reformist/modernist movement in Sumatra, which called for Indonesian Muslims to return to the fundamentals of the Qur'an and the Hadith (sayings and deeds of the Prophet Muhammad). The movement appealed for a "pure" Islam in Indonesia, one erased of local beliefs coloured with mysticism and irrationalism.

The reformists' position on theology, rituals and cultural practices was in fact quite similar to that held by Salafi-Wahhabi scholars. Salafism is a Sunni orientation that can be traced back to the theologian Ibn Taimiyyah (b.1263–d.1328). It urges Muslims to return to Islam's pristine past, and considers the first three generations after Prophet Muhammad's death as the ideal period for Islamic societies to copy. Salafis believe that ideas and scholarship generated by savants of these three generations should therefore be applied in contemporary social and political life. One of the main tenets of Salafism is its rejection of Islamic innovations. Its followers can, however, be either progressive or regressive in their religious outlook. For progressive Salafis, reliving the system of the first three generations after the Prophet means the upholding of its values and principles. They embrace modern social life and scientific knowledge, but promote ideals such as justice, gender equality and human rights. Some Salafis are even tolerant of Sufism, a religious experience that promotes spirituality and metaphysics. On the other hand, the Wahhabi interpretation of Salafism is a traditionalist one. This article uses the term Salafi-Wahhabi to describe this puritanical orientation. Founded in eighteenth century Arabia by Muhammad Ibn Abdul Al-Wahab,[6] Salafism-Wahhabism has been seeking to cleanse Islamic beliefs of "innovations", a teaching that when applied to the Malay world means the forbidding of rituals such as the *slametan* (mass prayers and communal feasting), participation in *tariqah* groups (Sufi groups engaging in devotional rituals such as rhythmic repetition of Allah's virtues), *ziarah kubur* (visits to graves of pious Muslims), and *maulid Nabi* (celebration of Prophet Muhammad's birthday). The Wahhabis considered these practices alien to the Prophet and his companions, and to be without basis in the Qur'an or Hadith. Ibn Abdul Al-Wahab and his followers destroyed many tombs, including those of key Muslim personalities and heroes.[7] Following in the footsteps of their ideologue, Salafism-Wahhabism in Southeast Asia has sought to end practices such as visits to tombs of pious Muslims and Sufi saints, which are common in the Malay world. The tenacity of Salafi-Wahhabis in Malaysia and Singapore has alarmed some academics in Malaysia and Southeast Asia, who believe that the ideology contributes to extremism and even terrorism.[8]

The Johor muftis, however, have always adopted what is known in the region as the *kaum tua* tradition. They condone the Sufi practices and rituals that Salafi-Wahhabis condemn. Historically, their role has always been tied to the royal house and to Malay aristocracy. Today, Johor still houses traditional *pondok* or *maahad* schools (boarding schools) that train religious teachers and *hafidz* (those who memorize the thirty chapters of the Qur'an by heart), and most are shaped by the Sufi tradition. The Islamic Religious Council of Johor today continues to allow many *tariqah* networks to practise.

Given the perceived rise of Salafi-Wahhabi ideas in Malaysia, one needs to ask whether Johor has managed to remain the bastion of *kaum tua*. I argue that Johor's religious discourse, at the least, remains strongly *kaum tua*. The Johor muftis seem crucial players in preventing Salafi-Wahhabi-oriented clerics from proselytizing in the state. Moreover, the overt intervention of Sultan Ibrahim Sultan Iskandar in the state's religious affairs means that its religious institutions are protected from encroachment by federal Islamic institutions, especially JAKIM (Department of Islamic Development). However, this sultan–mufti alliance does not necessarily mean that only progressive fatwas are passed in Johor. On many aspects — including women's role in society, religious minority rights, and intra-faith diversity — several of the fatwas or opinions passed by the Johor muftis are traditionalist in nature.

The Johor case does contribute fruitfully to the ongoing debate about countering extremism in Islam. Some analysts equate Salafism-Wahhabism to intolerance,[9] and Sufism to progress and as the remedy for terrorism.[10] The reality, however, is more complex. The Johor Islamic institution is also unique in Malaysia in portraying itself as the bastion of Sufism at a time when scholars are associating Malaysia with Arabization and Salafism-Wahhabism. Johor is also seen as a state that retains its Malay character effectively, led by a strong royal institution.

The Johor Islamic Religious Bureaucracy

As a rule, the Malay Rulers appoint all key positions in the Islamic institutions in their states (in contrast to the federal religious institution, JAKIM). This is in accordance with the Federal Constitution. The constitution of each state also maintains that the Ruler must be a person of Islamic faith, and that Islam is the official religion of all the states except Sarawak.[11] The Malaysian King (Yang di-Pertuan Agong) is the head of Islam for states that do not have a sultan — Malacca, Penang, Sabah, Sarawak, and the Federal Territories.[12] The key appointments in the religious bureaucracy include members of the Islamic Religious Council (Majlis Agama Islam Negeri) and the mufti, who is the ex-officio of the council, which has the important role of issuing fatwas. In many Muslim countries, fatwas are not legally binding. But in Malaysia, once a fatwa is published in the state gazette it is enforceable. The Ruler has the final say on whether a fatwa gets published or not.

A fatwa applies only to Muslims, and the maximum punishment for a sharia offence is a fine of five thousand ringgit (US$1,280), six strokes of the cane and three years' imprisonment. In late 2016, plans had been presented by the federal government, taking the lead from PAS president Abdul Hadi Awang, to harden shariah punishments by amending Act 355, or Syariah Courts (Criminal Jurisdiction) Act 1965. The federal Fatwa Committee of the National Islamic Council (JKF-MKI) consists of all the muftis and some other ulama. This body discusses issues of national concern, after which in some cases leads to a collective fatwa.

The state of Johor was in fact one of the earliest to delineate the powers of the Ruler, the Islamic Religious Council, and the mufti. In 1895, the Undang-undang Tubuh Kerajaan Negeri Johor (Johor State Constitution 1895) introduced new laws and departments into the administrative service. It spelt out the authority of the Sultan of Johor as the Head of Islam in the state, and his right to appoint members of the Majlis Agama Islam Negeri Johor (Johor Islamic Religious Council) and the mufti. The law declared Islam the religion of the state, and also introduced the Jabatan Agama Islam Johor (Islamic Department of Johor). It also specifies that all religious queries should be directed to the mufti, while the qadi (meaning either a judge, administrator or mediator) and his assistants will run the religious affairs of the state.[13] Most of these provisions remain to this day. Under section 4 of Enactment No. 16/2003, it is stated that "There shall be a body known as the 'Majlis Agama Islam Negeri Johor' to aid and advise His Majesty the Sultan in matters relating to the religion of Islam."[14] According to section 6 of the enactment, the council shall aid and advise the sultan on all matters relating to the religion of Islam in the state of Johor, except on matters of *Hukum Syarak* (jurisprudence) and administration of justice. It is the mufti who has authority over *hukum syarak*, while the administration of justice falls under the sharia courts.

The Majlis Agama Islam is presided over by eight members: the chairman, the vice-chairman, the state legal advisor, the state finance officer, the mufti (ex-officio), deputy mufti, Qadi Besar Johor (sharia court judge), and the chief assistant director of religious education. On matters relating to Islamic legal opinions, a separate fatwa body, chaired by the mufti, plays an important role.[15] According to section 48, a fatwa is prepared by the committee before it is presented by the mufti to the council, which will then discuss and make recommendations to the sultan. If royal assent is given, the council then instructs the state government to publish the fatwa in the gazette in *Jawi* (Malay written in Arabic script). This procedure means that a fatwa can become law without going to the state assembly.

In general, the Muslim community looks to the mufti for religious guidance. For queries on religious rulings, members of the religious community may call, email or write to the mufti department directly. The muftis also attend state and palace functions to recite prayers.

Johor Muftis Since the Nineteenth Century[16]

Generally, the earlier muftis were mostly involved in the administrative service. Apart from being judges, they were members of the state's Executive Committee (equivalent to ministers of the state government). Interestingly, the fifth mufti, Hassan Yunus, ran for office and became chief minister of Johor from 1959 to 1967. Also, the earlier muftis showed how the Arabs, particularly the "Syeds", played an important role shaping the religious discourse in Johor. The "Syeds" are well respected by the populace in the Malay world and in the Middle East for being descendants of Prophet Muhammad. Interestingly, the fourth mufti, an Arab, went into hiding during the Japanese Occupation, suggesting that he had worked closely with the colonial government. The dominance of Arabs in Johor's religious affairs also demonstrates the entrenchment of Sufi-oriented *kaum tua* ideology. Historically, the Hadrami Sufis (who came from the region that is today's Yemen) played a significant role in spreading Islam to the region.

Finally, most of the muftis received their early education in religious schools in the state, and later moved to Al-Azhar University in Cairo. Al-Azhar is the most prestigious institute of higher learning in the Islamic world. Though Al-Azhar is a traditionalist institution, its graduates are less sympathetic to

Salafism-Wahhabism compared to their counterparts in Saudi Arabia. To this day, Al-Azhar continues to discuss the different Islamic sects with its students, including schools that many Malaysian ulama consider deviant, such as Shiism and Mu'tazilite (rationalists).[17]

Mahathir's Strengthening of Federal Islamic Institutions

Although the Constitution declares that Islam is a state matter, federal Islamic institutions underwent massive upgrading in terms of infrastructure and powers under the Mahathir administration (1981–2003). In 1984, the Federal Territory Administration of Islamic Laws Enactment was passed to streamline the administration of Islamic laws in all states. The shariah courts were strengthened, and in the federal territory they were expanded into three levels: the lower court, high court and appeal court. In 1991 the shariah courts in the other thirteen states followed suit.

One of the key federal institutions that Mahathir upgraded was the Islamic Affairs Unit in the Prime Minister's Office, BAHEIS (Bahagian Hal Ehwal Agama Islam, Jabatan Perdana Menteri, Malaysia). In 1997 this became JAKIM. The body continues to serve as the secretariat of the National Islamic Council (Majlis Kebangsaan Bagi Hal Ehwal Ugama Islam Malaysia, or MKI) and handles, inter alia, research, fatwa management, the coordination of Islamic legal matters across all Malaysian states, and publishing. The MKI also hosts the aforementioned JKF-MKI. JAKIM also determines what constitutes the correct interpretation of Islam, censorship of publications, and halal certification. There have been instances when JAKIM prevented scholars from speaking in public events. JAKIM officials are known to be intolerant of those spreading pluralism, liberalism, feminism and Shiism. In October 2014, JAKIM forbade a roundtable discussion featuring Indonesian scholar Ulil Abshar Abdalla because he was seen as promoting liberal Islamic thinking. In another instance, JAKIM was proactive in banning books by laureate Faizal Musa (or Faizal Tehrani) for promoting Shiism. The extent of JAKIM's powers is in fact significant to such an extent that the Constitutional provision that Islam is a state-level matter is called into question.

In October 2016, JAKIM asked for its annual budget to be increased to a billion ringgit (US$225 million), something it claimed was needed to reflect its expanded role. The deputy minister in the Prime Ministers Department, Datuk Dr Aysraf Wajdi Dusuki, argued that JAKIM needed the extra amount in order to combat ISIS (Islamic State in Iraq and Syria), liberalism, pluralism, and LGBT (lesbian, gay, bisexual, and transgender) issues. JAKIM director-general Datuk Othman Mustapha further stated that part of the increment would be distributed to state Islamic religious departments.[18] This request was also strongly criticized by the Sultan of Johor.

Johor Muftis and the *Kaum Tua* Orientation

The official reason for expanding the power of the federal Islamic institutions has been the need for uniformity between state religious institutions. Mahathir was, however, also suspected of aiming to dilute the authority of the Malay Rulers. In truth, to make Islamic laws uniform across all states would be futile, because the muftis do not speak with one voice. They are factionalized between the *kaum tua* and *kaum muda* (modernists) orientations. States in the southern part of the peninsula such as Johor, Negeri Sembilan, Melaka, Pahang, and also northerly Perak, are more at home with *kaum tua* thinking, while others, especially Perlis, are oriented towards reform (both liberal and, at times, Wahhabi). In fact, some states with *kaum tua* orientation have prevented Dr Mohd Asri Zainul Abidin, the Mufti of Perlis, from speaking in their states. In 2010 he was detained for speaking without a permit in Selangor, and in February 2016 he was listed as one of sixteen speakers banned in Johor.[19] Another individual who is banned is UMNO politician Dr Fathul Bari Mat Jahaya, who is seen to hold Salafi-Wahhabi views.

Datuk Tahrir Samsudin, the current Johor Mufti, exhibits *kaum tua* thinking in many ways and, as with his predecessors, he is also sympathetic to Sufism. During my interview with him, Datuk Tahrir defended the *tariqah* groups in Johor, even though the religious department is keeping a close eye on them for departing from "true" Islamic teachings.[20] In fact, the mufti emphasizes his commitment to promoting *tariqah* groups in the state. He does not deny that Salafi-Wahhabi ideas are gaining traction in Malaysia, especially when these are propagated through the social media, but considers Johor the bastion of the Sunni tradition. He admits, though, that the arrival of Salafism-Wahhabism has led to some disunity in Johor.

The mufti also says that Johor ulama feel that since they inherited their religious traditions from pious Muslim scholars, they can never be misguided in upholding Sufism.[21] In April 2016, he presented a paper pointing out that Johor ulama should follow the methods of the earlier Johor Mufti, Datuk Syed Alwi Tahir al-Haddad, when issuing a fatwa, although this did not mean that the new fatwas should not differ from al-Haddad's.[22] Syed Alwi was mufti from 1934 to 1941 and 1947 to 1961, and wrote many fatwas condemning Wahhabism and the modernists.

The dominance of the *kaum tua* orientation is also seen in the publications of Johor's Islamic Religious Council. The Mufti Department of Johor runs an e-book series available for download by the public. The e-books contain anti-Salafi-Wahhabi ideas, as the discussion on two of these publications below demonstrates.[23] The first e-book is entitled *Sambutan Maulidur Rasul Bidáh Dhalalah?* (Celebration of the Prophet Muhammad's Birthday: A forbidden innovation?), written by Haji Jainal Al-Jauhari, chief executive of the Islamic Religious Council of Johor. The book was vetted by Nooh Gadot, the former mufti.[24] In essence, it attacks the Salafi-Wahhabi position that celebrating Prophet Muhammad's birthday is an innovation and un-Islamic. Jainal argues that the practice is allowed by the Sunni school of jurisprudence (Ahli Sunnah wal Jamaah), which is the only school allowed in Malaysia. He underscores how such celebrations could bring the religious community closer to the teachings of the Prophet. He claims that the celebration is an expression of happiness over the birth of the Prophet, and it has been practised by savants of the past, for example, under the rule of Salahuddin Al-Ayubi between 1171 and 1193. The celebration normally includes reciting verses from the Qur'an and singing praises to the Prophet, and would often end with a feast. The common practice in Malaysia is for a *maulid* to be accompanied by a procession. The book also points out that the celebration is Islamic and should be encouraged because it can unite Muslims and strengthen their faith.

Another e-book that reflects the mufti's Sufist thinking is written by Muhammad Fuad, entitled *Kepentingan Tariqah dan Tasawwuf* (The importance of *Tariqah* and Islamic spirituality).[25] The *tariqah* is a Sufi order that mainly teaches spirituality (*tasawwuf*) through *zikr* (chanting verses from the Qur'an or repeating praises to the Prophet). There are many such Sufi orders in Malaysia, including the Naqshabandiyah and Ahmadiyah Idrisiah. These are headed by *murshids* (spiritual leaders) and their followers pledge allegiance to their masters before becoming part of the group (*bai'ah*). Some *tariqah* groups promote mysticism, spirituality and metaphysics, practices that are also frowned upon by the Salafis-Wahhabis for the same reasons they are against celebrating the Prophet's birthday, i.e., that they are not found in the Qur'an and that these groups therefore practise innovations. The book supports the existence of *tariqah* groups in Johor mainly because these are within the spirit of the religion and are in accordance with the teachings of the Prophet.

Some scholars, including some from the West, posit that Sufism is a more tolerant orientation than Salafism-Wahhabism, and this has become an ever more dominant view after 9/11. Sufism is considered by them to be the solution to terrorism. But what we see is that the embracing of Sufism by the Johor muftis has not made them more progressive. In fact, they are basically traditionalists. Sociologist Robert Towler defines traditionalism as a mode of thinking that holds on to old ways, resists change and is marked by an unquestioning celebration of its own certainty.[26] Many views expressed by the previous mufti, Nooh Gadot, are traditionalist in essence. In 2006, Nooh Gadot published an article suggesting that the state come up with guidelines for how women should dress in public. He also said that although women can join the workforce, they have to prioritize their role as mothers.[27]

The Johor religious elite's traditionalism also leads to exclusivist thinking, especially on relations with non-Muslims. In 2014, Nooh Gadot was quoted in *Berita Harian* condemning opposition leader Anwar Ibrahim for allowing non-Muslims to use the term *Allah*. Malaysia has since the 1980s been debating whether the term *Allah* is exclusive to Muslims. Malay-speaking Christians, especially from Sarawak, have traditionally used the term in their Bible. According to Nooh Gadot, Anwar was disrespectful of the fatwa issued by fourteen Malaysian muftis in 1986 that claimed the term for exclusive use by Muslims.[28] Nooh Gadot continues to play an important religious role in Johor, and is a trusted ally of the sultan. Upon his retirement he was made Advisor to the Islamic Religious Council of Johor and to the Sultan.

Two other e-books warn Johor Muslims of the Shia and the "threat" of liberal Islam, and mirror the general trend among Malaysian religious elite that Shiism is a deviant ideology and that liberalism is a threat to Islam.[29] They call on those who harbour these trends of thought to repent. In truth, Sunni Muslims in many parts of the world have lived peacefully alongside the Shias. Moreover, many ulama around the world, including those in Indonesia, have pointed out that Shiism should be seen as part of mainstream Islam.[30]

The Sultan of Johor: Resisting Federal Intrusion

Johor muftis tend to participate in royal events. In March 2015 the mufti played an important role during the sultan's coronation ceremony. He placed a 1.6-kilogram crown — capped with sapphires, emeralds, rubies and diamonds and which included an Islamic crescent — on the sultan's head, performing a role similar to that played by the Archbishop of Canterbury during the coronation of a British monarch.[31] The same was done for Princess Raja Zarith Sofiah.[32] In March 2016 the mufti was also present at the sultan's birthday celebrations.[33] On 4 August 2016, he read the opening prayers for the sultan's grandson's birth rituals,[34] and in September 2016 allowed Muslims to join mass prayers for Bangsa Johor (the Johor Nation), which involved non-Muslims. At the end of the ceremony, participants went to the palace Istana Bukit Serene to release a hundred birds in accordance with Chinese customs.[35]

There have been instances when the sultan has publicly made a stand on religious issues. In late 2013 he was instrumental in reinstating the Islamic week starting 1 January 2014. This means that working days for the state are now between Sunday and Thursday. The rationale for this is to allow Muslims more time to complete their Friday prayers. Johor had in fact been practising this Islamic week since the colonial period, until it was reversed in 1993 by the chief minister of the state.[36] The sultan's reinstatement of Friday and Saturday as off-days boosted his image as a protector of Islam. In an exclusive interview with *The Star* in 2015, he iterated that it was he who was the authority of Islam in the state, and that JAKIM could only advise the religious councils. He explained that he had the final authority to appoint members to the religious council, and that only he could approve fatwas. To be sure, he had occasionally questioned fatwas and sought further clarification, and emphasized that JAKIM had no authority to meddle in the state's religious affairs. He also questioned JAKIM's request for a bigger budget and has asked for the breakdown of their spending at the Conference of Rulers' meeting.[37] Recently, the sultan also publicly criticized Malays for mimicking Arabs in their religious orientation. He urged them to stick to their culture: "If there are some of you who wish to be an Arab and practise Arab culture and do not wish to follow our Malay customs and traditions that is up to you. I also welcome you to live in Saudi Arabia."[38] It has also been noted that the sultan prefers to use Malay words such as "Hari Raya" (a day of celebration upon the completion of the fasting month) and "*buka puasa*" (breaking fast), instead of the recently popularized Arabic equivalents of "Eid al-fitr" and "*iftar*", respectively.[39]

In February 2016, while opening the Majlis Tilawah Al-Quran (Qur'an recitation competition), the sultan emphasized that members of the religious elite preaching in the state must obtain accreditation from the Islamic Religious Council of Johor. He added that even speakers who are popular and credible must respect this, because that has been the law since 1895, when the Ruler was established as the Head of Islam in the state.[40] Indeed, in May 2016, a popular preacher from Singapore, Ustaz Rasul Dahri, was fined five thousand ringgit (US$1,280) and jailed by the Islamic Religious Department of Johor for teaching there without proper accreditation.[41] He was also accused of spreading views that are not in line with the Sunni school of thought.

The sultan emphasized that Johoreans must be proactive in tackling both extremism and deviant teachings, and should therefore study religion from teachers recognized by the state. Interestingly, he positioned Salafi-Wahhabi teachings alongside Shia, liberalism and pluralism as deviant ideologies.[42]

Conclusion

Overall, there has been continuity in the religious and political behaviour of the Johor muftis. They remain committed to upholding Sufism, and are active in stopping Salafi-Wahhabi ideas from entering the state. Sufi values are promoted in the fatwas passed by the Islamic Religious Council, and through publications. The sultan's interventions in religious affairs also ensure that the Johor Mufti and the religious institutions under his charge are protected from federal encroachment. The Ruler acts as the gatekeeper for Johor Islamic identity, preventing Salafi-Wahhabi thinking from penetrating the state's religious discourse.

Nevertheless, being close to Sufism does not mean that Johor muftis have not expressed exclusivist tendencies. This is evident in their views towards women and to alternative discourses. What becomes clear in Johor is that the contestation between *kaum tua* and Salafism-Wahhabism has not ended, despite many decades of debate. In fact, it remains in the interest of the Johor Mufti to maintain Johor's reputation as the bastion of *kaum tua*.

Despite conservative and exclusivist trends shown by Johor Malays, the role of the sultan — who is the gatekeeper of Islam and Malay culture in the state — in ensuring the rights of non-Muslims and non-Malays are protected in the state, is key. The sultan has managed to thwart any attempts by conservative voices to push their agenda. For instance, the sultan publicly reprimanded a launderette located in Muar that only catered to Muslim patrons. The owner displayed a "Muslim-only" signboard, and the sultan, angered by this, decreed the sign be removed. The owner apologized.[43] Potential interfaith conflict might have been averted by the sultan's intervention; nonetheless, whether the sentiment on the ground follow the same path remains to be seen.

Overall, the Johor case calls for deeper reflections about the state of Islam in Malaysia. First, Johor is an urban and developed state, bordering Singapore. Yet, this does not mean that the religious discourse is progressive. Second, Islam in Johor is multilayered, with a moderate sultan at the apex but an increasingly conservative religious elite and masses. As it is, the sultan alone is able to thwart any conservative beliefs, because his role is delineated in the constitution. It only takes a populist ruler or politician who panders to the masses to alter the dominant religious outlook of the state. Third, conceptualizing Islam in Malaysia requires a rethinking, beyond the present Wahhabi-Salafi and Sufi dichotomy. Often, one considers the former as a threat and the latter as the solution. As the Johor case demonstrates, exclusivism applies to both orientations. Thus it is necessary to judge the impact of ideas on Malaysia's multiracial and multi-religious settings.

Acknowledgements

I wish to thank the Mufti of Johor, Sahibus Samahah Datuk Hj Mohd Tahrir Bin Dato' Kiyai Hj Samsuddin, for sharing his thoughts, and the Johor Archives for facilitating my research. Most parts of this chapter have been published as an ISEAS Trends in Southeast Asia, *Johor Remains a Bastion of Kaum Tua* (2017, no. 1).

Notes

1. The sample size was 1,003 respondents.
2. Norshahril Saat, "Johor Survey 2017: Attitudes towards Islam, Governance and the Sultan", *ISEAS Perspective* 2017, no. 83 (10 November 2017).
3. Haji Abdul Karim Amrullah is the father of the well-known Indonesian religious scholar Hamka.
4. William R. Roff, *The Origins of Malay Nationalism*, 2nd ed. (Kuala Lumpur: Oxford University Press, 1994), p. 67.
5. This rivalry between the *kaum tua* and the reformists extended to name-calling. Haji Abdul Karim's son, Hamka, also criticized the Johor Mufti for wrongly representing modernists (*kaum muda*) as "communists" and "stooges" of Christian missionaries in Indonesia. See Hamka, *Teguran Suci & Jujur Terhadap Mufti Johor* (Persatuan Muhammadiyah, 1958; repr., Shah Alam: Pustaka Dini, 2009).
6. Natana J. Delong-Bas, *Wahhabi Islam: From Revival and Reform to Global Jihad* (New York: Oxford University Press, 2004).
7. Ibid., p. 26.
8. See, for example, articles by Syed Farid Alatas, "Battle against Extremism within Islam", *Straits Times*, 5 April 2014; and Ahmad Fauzi Abdul Hamid, "ISIS in Southeast Asia: Internalized Wahhabism is a Major Factor", *ISEAS Perspective* 2016, no. 24 (16 May 2016).
9. See, for instance, the work by Khaled Abou El-Fadl, *The Great Theft: Wrestling Islam from The Extremists* (New York: HarperOne, 2005).
10. See Jason Webster, "Sufism: Natural Antidote to Fanaticism" <https://www.theguardian.com/books/2014/oct/23/sufism-natural-antidote-fanaticism-the-sufis-idries-shah> (accessed 8 December 2016); *Times of India*, "Sufism Can Act as Antidote to Terrorism: Arjun Meghwal" <http://timesofindia.indiatimes. com/city/jaipur/Sufism-can-act-as-antidote-to-terrorism-Arjun-Meghwal/ articleshow/54862205.cms> (accessed 8 December 2016).
11. Shad Saleem Faruqi, "The Malaysian Constitution, The Islamic State and Hudud Laws", in *Islam in Southeast Asia: Political, Social and Strategic Challenges for the 21st Century*, edited by K.S Nathan and Mohammad Hashim Kamali, pp. 256–77 (Singapore: Institute of Southeast Asian Studies, 2005), p. 274.
12. The position of the Yang di-Pertuan-Agong rotates among the nine Malay Rulers once every five years.

13. Hasnan Kasan, *Institusi Fatwa di Malaysia* (Bangi: Universiti Kebangsaan Malaysia, 2008), p. 26.
14. Enactment no. 16 of 2003, Administration of the Religion of Islam (State of Johor) Enactment 2003 <http://www2.esharia.gov.my/esharia/mal/portalv1/enakmen2011/Eng_enactment_Ori_lib.nsf/100ae747c72508e748256f aa00188094/a079fdb33f522cdf482576c000093a03?OpenDocument> (accessed 19 September 2016).
15. Prior to 1978 the power to issue religious opinions rested only with the Mufti. The Islamic Religious Council only acted as a rubber stamp. After 1978, the Johor government formed a fatwa-making body to assist the mufti, called Lujnah Fatwa. At any one time the body consists of not more than four clerics, and is chaired by the mufti. Hasnan Kasan, *Institusi Fatwa di Malaysia* (Bangi: Universiti Kebangsaan Malaysia, 2008), p. 26.
16. Azman, Zahari, Nur Salida, and Adel, *Biografi Mufti-Mufti Malaysia* (Negeri Sembilan: Universiti Sains Islam Malaysia, 2008), pp. 1–13.
17. M. Quraish Shihab, *Sunnah-Syiah: Bergandengan Tangan Mungkinkah?* (Ciputat: Lentera Hati, 2007), p. 3.
18. Aizyl Azlee, "JAKIM Says Will Comply with Johor Sultan's Demand for It to Explain RM1b Funding", *Malay Mail Online* <http://www.themalaymailonline. com/malaysia/article/jakim-says-will-comply-with-johor-sultans-demand-for-it-to-explain-rm1b-fun> (accessed 18 October 2016).
19. *Malay Mail Online*, "Mufti Perlis, exco Pemuda Umno dilarang ceramah di Johor" <http://www.themalaymailonline.com/projekmmo/berita/article/Mufti- perlis-exco-pemuda-umno-dilarang-ceramah-di-johor> (accessed 25 October 2016).
20. Interview with Sahibus Samahah Datuk Hj Mohd Tahrir Bin Dato' Kiyai Hj Samsuddin, 23 October 2016.
21. Interview with Sahibus Samahah Datuk Hj Mohd Tahrir.
22. Ibid. Datuk Tahrir disagrees with al-Haddad's fatwa on some issues.
23. See Jabatan Mufti Negeri Johor website <http://Mufti.johor.gov.my/v3/muatturun>.
24. Haji Jainal Al-Jauhari, *Sambutan Maulidur Rasul Bidáh Dhalalah?* (Johor: Majlis Agama Islam Negeri Johor, 2008).
25. Muhammad Fuad Kamaludin Al-Maliki, *Kepentingan Tariqah dan Tasawwuf* (Johor: Majlis Agama Islam Negeri Johor, 2008).
26. Robert Towler, *The Need for Certainty: A Sociological Study of Conventional Religion* (London: Routledge and Kegan Paul, 1986), pp. 90–91.
27. Nooh Gadut, "Pandangan Islam terhadap pencapaian wanita". In *Memahami Kedudukan Wanita dari Perspektif Islam*, edited by Siti Fatimah Abdul Rahman, pp. 19–36 (Kuala Lumpur: MPH and IKIM, 2006), pp. 34–35.
28. *Berita Harian*, "Dua Mufti lagi kecam Anwar", 19 February 2014.
29. Wan Adli Wan Ramli, *Bahaya Liberalisme dan Pluralisme Agama Terhadap Akidah Belia Muslim* (Johor: Majlis Agama Islam Johor, 2012); Jainal Sakiban, *Kebatilan Akidah Syi'ah* (Johor: Majlis Agama Islam Johor, 2012).

30. Norshahril Saat, "'Deviant' Muslims: The Plight of Shias in Contemporary Malaysia", in *Religious Diversity in Muslim-Majority States in Southeast Asia: Areas of Toleration and Conflict*, edited by Bernhard Platzdasch and Johan Saravanamuttu, pp. 359–78 (Singapore: Institute of Southeast Asian Studies, 2014).
31. Francis E. Hutchinson and Vandana Prakash Nair, *The Johor Sultanate: Rise or Re-Emergence?* Trends in Southeast Asia 2016, no. 16 (Singapore: ISEAS – Yusof Ishak Institute, 2016), pp. 15–16.
32. *Bernama*, "Istiadat Kemahkotaan Berlangsung Gilang Gemilang", 23 March 2015.
33. *myMetro*, "Tanda taat setia", 24 March 2016.
34. *Berita Harian*, "Sultan Johor hadiri majlis akikah cucunda", 4 August 2016.
35. *Berita Minggu*, "Ribuan rakyat jayakan Program Gabungan doa bangsa Johor", 18 September 2016.
36. Francis and Nair, *The Johor Sultanate*, p. 18.
37. Wong Chun Wai and Nelson Benjamin, "Johor Ruler: I'm Above Politics", *The Star*, 27 December 2015 <http://www.thestar.com.my/news/nation/2015/12/27/johor-ruler-im-above-politics-the-interest-of-the-rakyat-always-comes-first/> (accessed 27 December 2015).
38. *Straits Times*, "Johor Sultan to Malays: Stick to Your Own Culture", 25 March 2016.
39. *MalaymailOnline*, "Stop Aping Arabs, Johor Sultan Tells Malays", 24 March 2016 <http://www.themalaymailonline.com/malaysia/article/stop-aping-arabs- johor-sultan-tells-malays> (accessed 3 November 2016).
40. Badrul Kamal Zakaria, "Pendakwah ke Johor perlu tauliah MAIJ", *Berita Harian*, 24 February 2016.
41. "Pendakwah S'pura dipenjara di Johor", *Berita Harian*, 7 May 2016.
42. Ahmad Fairuz Othman, "Sultan Johor: Learn Islam from Those with Credentials", *New Straits Times*, 31 March 2016.
43. *The Star*, "Launderette Owner Apologises over Muslim-Only Signboard", 27 September 2017.

MALAYSIA IN 2017: Strong Economic Growth amidst Intense Power Struggle

Faisal S. Hazis

Malaysia was in election mode in 2017 as many were expecting Prime Minister Najib Razak to call a snap election to take advantage of a seriously divided opposition. The upcoming election will be a win or bust battle for Najib, as he attempts to reverse consecutive slides in the number of seats won by the ruling Barisan Nasional (BN) in recent general elections, amid concerns among voters about bread and butter issues. Meanwhile, the new opposition coalition, Pakatan Harapan (PH), made former prime minister Mahathir Mohamad its chairman, to lead the challenge against BN and Najib. Mahathir's comeback provides a boost to an opposition that has been plagued by inter- and intra-party schism. Nonetheless, without the largest Malay opposition party — Parti Islam SeMalaysia (PAS) — in its fold, Pakatan has a difficult, if not impossible, task to unseat the BN. As the year came to a close, Najib solidified his grip both on his party, the United Malays National Organisation (UMNO), as well on the administration, leading to optimism within the party about the upcoming election. However, the UMNO leader kept the whole nation guessing about the election date up to the year-end. The embattled premier looks set to stretch the current parliament close to its full five-year term, which expires on 24 June 2018. When finally called, the election will be one of the country's fiercest ever political battles, pitting Najib against his former mentor, Mahathir.

Despite the intense power struggle, Malaysia's economy was on a strong growth trajectory in 2017. The unexpected growth was driven by strong domestic

Faisal S. Hazis is Associate Professor and Head of the Centre for Asian Studies at the Institute of Malaysian and International Studies (IKMAS), Universiti Kebangsaan Malaysia.

demand and strengthening exports. Another positive trend in Malaysia's economy in 2017 was the strengthening of the ringgit, which had been undervalued for quite some time. However, critics argued that the solid economic numbers did not reflect the reality on the ground, as many Malaysians, especially the lower income group, were struggling to cope with the rising cost of living. Another alarming trend in the Malaysian economy was the government's spiralling debt burden, caused by an exponential increase in operating expenditures.

On the diplomatic front, Prime Minister Najib Razak faced mounting domestic criticism for being too pro-China, consequently undermining Malaysia's sovereignty and its status as a middle power.[1] The premier tried to silence his critics by reaffirming the country's long-standing relations with the United States so as to balance China's growing influence. At the regional level, Malaysia was confronted with the Rohingya crisis that has led to a massive influx of refugees into the country. Weak leadership and ASEAN's non-interference policy prevented Malaysia from taking a more effective role in resolving the crisis.

This chapter discusses the key trends in Malaysia through 2017. First, it looks at the fractious political struggle that destabilized the country and further divided its people. It also looks at the strong economic growth recorded in 2017 but the limited impact that it had on the people, particularly the lower income group. And, finally, this chapter examines Malaysia's attempt to reposition itself as a middle power after a barrage of domestic criticism over the government's perceived pivot to China.

Intense and Divisive Power Struggle

The BN, and its predecessor, Perikatan (Alliance), have ruled Malaysia since independence in 1957 — that is more than six decades of uninterrupted rule. Throughout this period the ruling party easily secured a two-thirds parliamentary majority (except in 1969) and dominated almost all state elections. However, its electoral dominance was seriously challenged in the last two elections. In the 2008 election it lost its traditional two-thirds parliamentary majority and five state governments (out of thirteen states) — its worst electoral showing since 1969. In the subsequent 2013 election, the BN lost more ground when the opposition secured a majority of the popular vote and continued to deny the ruling party's two-thirds parliamentary majority. On top of that, the BN lost seven more parliamentary seats and three states.

In the last two elections, the ruling BN's popularity declined significantly as a huge section of the electorate demanded change from pro-elite to pro-people economic policies, from race-based politics to an inclusive form of politics, from corrupt government to clean and efficient government, and from an authoritarian regime to a democratic system. The call for change came from all segments of voters, but the core support for the opposition came from urban and non-Malay voters.[2] Thus, the opposition needs to move the Malay ground in order to capture federal power in the looming general election. Another key factor in contributing towards the vote swing in the last two elections was the strategic choices made by the opposition elites to work together in order to unseat the BN.[3] Prior to 2008 the ruling government could maintain its hold on power because the opposition elites failed to form organizational structures that could effectively challenge it.[4] However, the opposition managed to overcome this flaw and formed a viable coalition, known as Pakatan Rakyat, comprising three major opposition parties: Parti Keadilan Rakyat (PKR), PAS and the Democratic Action Party (DAP). The coalition contested against the BN in 2008 and 2013, producing unprecedented results for the opposition in an electoral system that has been consistently labelled as free but not fair.[5]

The power struggle continued unabated and intensified after the 2013 election as the next general election loomed closer. Malaysians must go to the ballot box by August 2018 to elect the federal government and the respective state governments. But election fever had already hit the country in late 2016 and further intensified in 2017. The call for a snap election was triggered mainly by the collapse of Pakatan Rakyat after the biggest Malay opposition party, PAS, left the coalition in 2015. However, the rationale for an early election was not only motivated by the opposition split; Najib also wanted to take advantage of the strong economic growth in 2017 and the consolidation of UMNO after the expulsion of his critics from the party. To the embattled premier, success at the polls will be defined by whether the BN can increase the 132 parliamentary seats it currently holds and prevent the new opposition coalition, PH, from winning more states beyond the 2 it currently holds.

It had been a difficult few years for Najib, who had been attacked both at home and abroad in the wake of graft allegations involving RM2.6 billion (US$700 million) found in his personal bank accounts. The money allegedly came from state investor 1Malaysia Development Berhad (1MDB). Najib, who headed 1MDB's board of advisers, has denied all wrongdoing, saying the funds were a legal political donation and that he did not take any money for personal gain.[6] In August 2017, the Najib administration had to deal with the latest revelations from the U.S. probe into the 1MDB scandal. The U.S. Department of Justice alleged that an estimated US$4.5 billion was siphoned from the state firm and used to buy luxury properties, a yacht, artworks and jewellery.[7] Yet, despite the opposition's nationwide road show — dubbed "Anti-Kleptocracy Roadshow" — to revive the scandal in Malaysian minds, Najib was still able to shrug off these allegations.[8] Najib's visit to the White House in September 2017 further silenced his critics who had said he was a wanted man there.[9]

The scandals, however, did not let up in 2017, as Malaysians were exposed to a long list of revelations of fraud, abuses of power, and impropriety involving several state agencies. The year 2017 will probably be remembered as the year of the Federal Land Development Authority (FELDA) — for all the wrong reasons. Once internationally hailed as a successful example of a rural poverty eradication programme in a developing country, the agency in 2017 gained a reputation for shady land deals, bad business decisions, and leadership tussles.[10] The various controversies that had been brewing among its subsidiaries came to a head when FELDA chairman Mohd Isa Samad was replaced and investigated for corruption. Isa was also chairman of the agency's plantation arm, FELDA Global Ventures (FGV), and non-executive director at FELDA Investment Corporation (FIC). In July, the Malaysia Anti-Corruption Commission (MACC) opened investigations into FIC's purchase of a four-star hotel in the affluent Kensington district of London. FIC had allegedly bought the property in December 2014 for £60 million (RM330 million), a figure allegedly far above the market price.[11] The MACC also looked into FIC's purchase of a hotel in Kuching for RM160 million but which was worth RM50 million.[12] Another FELDA bombshell was dropped before the end of 2017, when the titles for four parcels of the agency's land in Jalan Semarak, Kuala Lumpur, worth RM270 million, were transferred under dubious circumstances.[13]

Another scandal that haunted the Najib administration in 2017 was the shady property purchases made by Majlis Amanah Rakyat (MARA). Exposés by online news portal *Malaysiakini* alleged that MARA officers defrauded millions by buying property in Melbourne through middlemen.[14] MARA paid A$41.8 million (RM138 million) to buy Thrush Cross Land Holdings Ltd., a US$2 shell company incorporated in the British Virgin Islands, because of a building in Melbourne the company purportedly owned. In January 2013, five months after MARA bought the shell company, Thrush Cross Land paid the actual owner A$23.5 million for the twelve-storey building. On 19 July 2013, top officials of MARA Inc. mortgaged the property to raise money to buy another building in Melbourne — Dudley House. The transaction is also being investigated for fraud, corruption and money laundering.[15]

BN's scandalous year continued with the Johor State Executive Council's land scandal that broke in March 2017. The former Housing and Local Government executive committee chairman Abdul Latif Bandi, his son, and real estate consultant Amir Shariffuddin Abdul Raub were charged with 21 counts of money laundering and 33 counts of receiving RM30.3 million in bribes.[16] The bribes were allegedly paid by property developers to have bumiputra housing lots converted to non-bumiputra ones at a rate lower than the 7.5 per cent charge required to change the status of bumiputra lots.

In December 2017, former Sabah Water Department deputy director Teo Chee Kong was charged with 146 counts of laundering RM32 million in one of MACC's biggest cases.[17] Teo was detained along with other department officials on suspicion of misappropriation of project funds. MACC confiscated jewellery, handbags, cars, land titles and other items worth around RM114 million, along with RM53.7 million in cash found in their possession. MACC said it was its biggest ever seizure of cash.[18]

Apart from scandals, the Najib administration also had to deal with growing public discontent over the rising cost of living. Although Najib regularly boasted of Malaysia's strong GDP, many Malaysians were worried over the economy.[19] Based on the 2017 Merdeka Center survey, the top three concerns among Malaysian voters are inflation (62 per cent), corruption (40 per cent) and the lack of job opportunities (15 per cent). Whether it is a problem of perception or not, BN leaders had admitted that the cost of living and a slowing economy were the key concerns for Malaysian voters heading into the 2018 election.[20]

With endless scandals and public concern over the rising cost of living, Najib and his government's popularity continued to plunge in 2017. Based on Merdeka Center surveys, the public perception of the federal government declined significantly, from a 50 per cent favourable rating in August 2013 to 30 per cent in October 2017.[21] Meanwhile, Najib's popularity rating suffered an even sharper decline, from 62 per cent in August 2013 to 35 per cent in October 2017.[22] Thus, to maintain its grip on federal power, the BN had to resort to its old, tested strategies of suppressing dissent and cajoling the electorate by evoking ethno-religious nationalism,[23] prosecuting opposition leaders and government critics,[24] manipulating the redrawing of electoral boundaries,[25] and deploying various patronage programmes.[26] Consequently, the intense power struggle further divided an already fragmented Malaysian society along racial, religious and party lines.[27]

Despite the declining popularity of both Najib and his administration, there was still uncertainty whether the opposition could win federal power, as they themselves faced leadership problems and factional fights. The biggest problem was the exclusion of the biggest Malay opposition party, PAS, from the main opposition coalition, PH. Unlike in the 2008 and 2013 elections, the opposition parties are seriously divided and fragmented as they head to the next general election. Apart from PH, there are at least two other opposition coalitions: Gagasan Sejahtera and United Sabah Alliance (USA). Established in August 2016, Gagasan Sejahtera comprises PAS, Parti Ikatan Bangsa Malaysia (IKATAN), Pan-Malaysian Islamic Front (BERJASA), Parti Cinta Malaysia (PCM) and Parti Harapan Malaysia (PHM). Meanwhile, USA is made up of all the local Sabah parties that reject any form of cooperation with national opposition parties. As of December 2017, the USA members were Parti Solidariti Tanah Airku (STAR), Sabah Progressive Party (SAPP), Parti Harapan Rakyat (Harapan) and Parti Perpaduan Rakyat Sabah (PPRS). The two opposition coalitions are not expected to make much headway in the coming election, but their presence will definitely affect PH's chances in 52 marginal parliamentary seats throughout the country.

The spirit of the opposition was lifted a little in the middle of 2017, when Mahathir Mohamad was picked to lead PH to unseat Najib and the BN. The former prime minister and UMNO president for twenty-two years, until 2003, quit the party in 2015 and set up Parti Pribumi Bersatu Malaysia (PPBM) in September 2016. In March 2017, PPBM was accepted as a component of PH, alongside PKR, DAP and Parti Amanah Negara (AMANAH). Following this, Mahathir was appointed chairman of PH in July, with PKR's Anwar Ibrahim being made the coalition's de facto head and PKR president Wan Azizah Wan Ismail appointed as its president.[28] Under Mahathir's aggressive drive, PH is making headway in a few states, especially Kedah and Johor.

Despite lower approval ratings and being tainted by scandals, 2017 was a relatively good year for Prime Minister Najib Razak. It had been an uncomfortable few years for Najib, with the 1MDB scandal and public unhappiness over runaway inflation, stagnant wages and unaffordable homes. But he seems to have weathered the storm. As 2017 came to an end, Najib was arguably at his strongest since BN's narrow victory in 2013. Hence, Najib is widely expected to win the next election, mainly due to a divided opposition and the redrawing of electoral boundaries, which critics say favours the government.

Strong Growth but Minimal Trickle-Down Effect

Despite the intense political struggles, Malaysia's economy had defied all expectations to grow well above 5 per cent over three quarters in 2017, driven by strengthening domestic demand and a boom in exports. The economy recorded a strong growth of 6.2 per cent in the third quarter of 2017, the best since the second quarter of 2014.[29] Many had anticipated moderate growth in 2017, but none had expected it to accelerate at such a pace.

At the start of 2017, cautious sentiments prevailed in forecasts about the Malaysian ringgit, which was by far the worst performing currency in Asia, losing nearly 5 per cent against the dollar. The drop happened after U.S. President Donald Trump's election win in November 2016 and a hike in U.S. interest rates, which led to a foreign fund outflow from emerging markets.[30] Although Malaysian exports were gaining traction during the period, the weakening currency made it difficult to keep optimism alive. In March 2017, the consumer price index rose to an eight-year high of 5.1 per cent on higher fuel costs, which raised concerns about living costs and business expenses.[31]

Thus, it came as a surprise when the first quarter results in May 2017 revealed economic growth of 5.6 per cent, surpassing the consensus of a 4.8 per cent expansion.[32] The ringgit also strengthened by 3.7 per cent against the greenback from RM4.988 in January, while inflation averaged 4.3 per cent in the same quarter.[33] Stronger exports and improved commodity prices lifted corporate earnings during the first three months of 2017, as the majority of the nearly a thousand listed firms on the local bourse reported better profits and earnings year-on-year.[34]

Despite the positive outlook, external risks (U.S. Federal Reserve rate hikes, elections in Europe, and China's slowdown) forced analysts to maintain a cautious stance on the Malaysian economy.[35] A Reuters poll projected second quarter growth to slow on weaker private consumption.[36] However, Malaysia's economy grew at its fastest pace in over two years in the April–June period at 5.8 per cent, driven by domestic demand and resilience in exports. The third quarter continued to surprise the market, with economic growth of 6.2 per cent — one of the fastest in Asia — as all major sectors of the economy expanded.[37]

Despite this notable performance, the majority of Malaysians felt they were struggling to make ends meet. A national survey on economic hardship indicators by pollster Merdeka Centre in 2017 found that two-thirds of those surveyed said economic issues comprising worries over the rising cost of living, economic hardship, jobs and other related matters topped their concerns. This cut across all ethnic groups.[38] The survey also indicated that between one and two in every ten Malaysians were cutting back on essentials such as food in order to make ends meet. The weak ringgit has had a big impact on the price of food — especially processed food and beverages — which makes up 74.3 per cent of Malaysian household spending.[39] In 2017 the ringgit strengthened against the U.S. dollar, but it was still far from RM3.80 to the dollar.

The Merdeka Center survey also found that 40 per cent of respondents had delayed or were unable to make payments on utility bills, such as electricity or telephone bills, with more than 60 per cent of the Malay, Indian and bumiputra communities encountering such problems, while only 20 per cent of Malaysian Chinese reported problems with paying utility bills. On debt, 22 per cent said they have taken on new liabilities in the form of personal loans or charges on credit cards, while 11 per cent reported needing to sell or pawn possessions to meet expenses. Respondents who were reported to have skipped meals in order to make ends meet stood at 15 per cent.[40] Commenting on how some people are not feeling the effects of economic growth, economist Dr Muhammad Abdul Khalid said this is due to sustained cost-of-living pressures, especially on the lower-income groups, and concerns over employment opportunities.[41] He added, "we need to look at it in totality, we need to look at an economic policy that can create better paying jobs, we need to look at industries that can generate high value added, we need to relook our education policy to train our people to be more productive".[42]

The trickle-down effect was not being felt, simply because there was uneven growth in the various sectors of the economy. Critics argue that only certain public and private sectors contributed to Malaysia's strong growth in 2017, including government expenditure, infrastructure, construction, information technology and exports.[43] And as the growth was not broad-based, it did not benefit the public, especially those in the lower income group.

Another worrying trend in 2017 was spiralling government debt. In 2017, government debt was about 53 per cent of GDP, a significant hike from the 41 per cent of 2008.[44] Due to excess spending, the Malaysian government's debt has grown an average of 10 per cent a year over the past ten years to reach RM687.43 billion in September 2017, from RM266.72 billion in 2007.[45] A major part of the debt spiral is due to operating expenditure growing an average of 6 per cent a year over the past ten years, to RM219.91 billion in 2017 from RM123.1 billion in 2007. According to prominent economist Jomo K.S., "such government spending is needed to sustain growth, but all too often, has been abused to fund large-scale projects for crony companies with 'kickbacks' for key decision makers. The growing burden of such debt is inevitably borne by taxpayers."[46]

External Relations

Pivot to China?

On the diplomatic front, the biggest challenge for Malaysia is its perceived pivot to China. The perception that Malaysia is snubbing the United States and embracing

China stems from the investigation by the U.S. Department of Justice (DOJ) into the 1MDB scandal that implicates Prime Minister Najib Razak. The U.S. Federal Bureau of Investigation (FBI) started its investigation into the 1MDB scandal just a few months after an exposé by news portal Sarawak Report and British newspaper the *Sunday Times* in 2015.[47] In 2016 the DOJ filed a civil lawsuit to recover more than US$1 billion from people close to Najib and 1MDB. In the lawsuit, a high-ranking government official who had control over 1MDB was referred to as "Malaysian Official 1" (MO1), and mentioned over thirty times. MO1 was alleged to have received around US$681 million (RM2.797 billion) of stolen money from 1MDB.[48] About two months later the Malaysian government confirmed that the MO1 mentioned in the DOJ's civil suit was actually Najib, but clarified that the premier is not being implicated in the probe.[49] In 2017 the DOJ filed two more civil lawsuits to recover US$100 million and US$450 million, respectively, from the people linked to the 1MDB scandal, bringing the total identified stolen proceeds to US$4.5 billion. The 1MDB lawsuits are the largest action brought by the DOJ's Kleptocracy Asset Recovery Initiative, giving Malaysia headlines around the world for the wrong reasons.[50] Najib responded by saying that 1MDB was not directly implicated in the lawsuits; instead, he questioned the unprecedented publicity given to the civil suits, which were "usually low key".[51]

Thus, when Najib's administration attempted to strengthen Malaysia's relations with China, critics interpreted the move as an attempt to snub the United States and embrace China. This perception was further amplified when the Chinese government allegedly bailed out 1MDB, which had amassed RM42 billion (US$12.18 billion) in debt.[52] In 2015, China General Nuclear Power Corp. bought 1MDB's power unit, Edra Global Energy, for RM$17 billion (US$4.1 billion), while China Railway Engineering Corp. bought a stake in a key 1MDB development project in the capital, Kuala Lumpur, for RM12.4 billion (US$3 billion).[53] And in 2016 it was reported that China had been approached to help 1MDB pay off US$6.5 billion debt to an Abu Dhabi Investment arm.[54] These reports raised serious questions over the cost of China's bailout of 1MDB. The flurry of Chinese investments — mainly in infrastructure and property development projects — in the last couple of years has compounded this fear. In 2016, not long after the purported bailout of 1MDB by China, Najib returned from a state visit there with about US$34 billion worth of deals, including Malaysia's first major military purchases from China.[55] The Chinese investments in Malaysia ballooned further in 2017 when Najib signed nine MOUs worth RM30 billion with Chinese companies. Among the notable Chinese projects in Malaysia are the US$100 billion Forest City in Johor, the US$13 billion East Coast Rail Line, the US$10 billion Melaka Gateway project, the US$2.92 billion Kuala Linggi International Port, the US$3 billion Samalaju Industrial Park Steel Complex in Sarawak and the US$900 million Kuantan Port Expansion.

In 2017, China had overtaken Singapore as the largest real estate investor in Malaysia. Chinese companies had invested more than US$2.1 billion in Malaysia's real estate between 2014 and 2016, compared with US$985 million by Singaporean companies.[56] Although trade and investment from China helps to boost the Malaysian economy, some critics pointed out that the flurry of Chinese investments could undermine the country's sovereignty, because they are acquiring "national strategic assets" such as land, ports and cities.[57]

Najib dismissed the claims that his administration is selling Malaysia to China as opposition propaganda. The premier argued that FDI from Japan is much higher than China and yet nobody is claiming that his administration is selling Malaysia to Japan.[58] Najib's nemesis, Mahathir, was responsible for the influx of Japanese investments since the 1980s when he was the prime minister. In seeking to further allay the concern raised by his critics that Malaysia is pivoting to China, the Najib administration sought to strengthen Malaysia's economic and strategic partnership with the United States under newly elected President Trump. In September 2017, Najib met Trump at the White House. Among the top issues discussed during the visit were trade deals, investment pledges and security issues. There is no doubt that the visit itself was a feat within the context of Malaysia–U.S. bilateral relations. The last time Malaysia was granted a White House visit was in 2004, under former premier Abdullah Badawi, and this was Najib's first-ever White House visit since coming to power nearly a decade ago. The initial forecast for Malaysia–U.S. relations under Trump seemed to be rather gloomy, with Malaysian policymakers worrying about the implications of a so-called America First foreign policy, with the U.S. withdrawal from the Trans-Pacific Partnership (TPP), the Trump travel ban and the continuing investigation of the 1MDB scandal by the DOJ. Yet, as the Trump administration's Asia policy began to take shape, convergence in interests on several areas such as trade and regional security eventually paved the way for Najib's White House visit.

Prior to Najib's visit, critics, both at home and abroad, lambasted the United States for inviting a tainted leader like Najib. Opposition leader Mahathir accused the United States of taking sides in the looming general election, while another top Malaysian opposition leader, Lim Guan Eng, went overboard by calling Trump "stupid". The American media also gave Najib negative publicity ahead of his visit to the White House. The *Washington Post* published a scathing op-ed about the similarities and differences between Najib and Trump as a "nationalist with authoritarian tendencies". The *Wall Street Journal* even called upon the White House to cancel the visit because it was a mistake to help a tainted leader like Najib, while CNN ran a headline that read "Trump meets Malaysia leader under investigation by his Justice Department". Despite the negative publicity, Najib had the final laugh by making the high-profile visit to the White House, thus dismissing the claims that he is a wanted man in the United States on account of the 1MDB scandal. With the high-profile visit, Najib could finally tell Malaysians that 1MDB is a non-issue, thus burying his biggest scandal for good before going into the 2018 election.

The perception that Malaysia is pivoting to China has been much exaggerated and is not grounded in reality. Historically, Malaysia has a long and robust relationship with the United States that spans more than six decades. Malaysia–U.S. relations became a little bit rocky towards the end of the Obama administration due to the 1MDB scandal, but still remained strong. Malaysia considers the United States an important trade and political partner, while the United States sees Malaysia as a vital ally in its fight against terrorism, and also its attempts to balance China's influence in Asia. Thus, Malaysia would not abandon its Western friend just because it receives huge investments from its rival, China. Najib needed help in bailing out 1MDB and China was willing to lend a hand. So, naturally, the premier would turn to China. But, for geopolitical reasons, Najib will not abandon the United States. He knows that he will need U.S. support in neutralizing China's presence in the region, especially when the latter is aggressively pushing its One Belt One Road (OBOR) initiative and its claims in the South China Sea. Nonetheless, the concerns raised by many quarters over Chinese investments in Malaysia should not be dismissed. Sceptics want Najib to manage the investments transparently, a trait that is absent from his approach in administering the country. If the premier fails to do this, the perception that Malaysia is pivoting to China will persist.

North Korea

Another significant development in Malaysia's foreign relations in 2017 was the diplomatic spat between Malaysia and North Korea. It was sparked by the assassination of Kim Jong-nam, the half-brother of North Korean despot Kim Jong-un, at Kuala Lumpur International Airport on 13 February, which the United States, South Korea and Malaysia claim was ordered by the North Korean leader.[59] Kim Jong-nam was supposedly assassinated because he was viewed as a threat to Kim Jong-un's rule. The assassination brought into focus the lesser-known

Malaysia–North Korea diplomatic ties, which have a long history. The two countries established diplomatic ties on 30 June 1973, during the period when Malaysia started to embrace the policy of non-alignment under Prime Minister Abdul Razak.[60] Malaysia is one of fewer than thirty countries to have an embassy in Pyongyang, and it is the only country whose citizens can enter North Korea without a visa. Malaysia also had trade relations with North Korea, but the volume was quite small. Nonetheless, bilateral trade between the two countries had increased from RM7.77 million in 2014 to RM22.7 million in 2015, but dropped to RM18.89 million in 2016.[61] The drop was due to lower exports from Malaysia to North Korea despite a significant increase in imports, totalling RM8.2 million.

However, Kim Jong-nam's murder damaged the long-standing relations between the two countries. In September 2017, Malaysia banned its citizens from travelling to North Korea. Malaysia also stopped its trade with North Korea ahead of sanctions by the United Nations and the United States on North Korea in September. The falling out between Malaysia and North Korea came about when the Malaysian authorities wanted to launch an investigation into the killing of Kim Jong-nam, including carrying out an autopsy, while North Korea wanted the body to be returned immediately to Pyongyang. The strained relations were made worse when the North Korean ambassador in Malaysia accused Malaysia of colluding with "hostile forces" in order to harm Pyongyang.[62]

Terrorism

Another notable feature in Malaysia's foreign relations in 2017 was the country's continued participation in the global movement against terrorism. In May, Malaysia was invited to join more than fifty Muslim countries in the Arab-Islamic-American Summit to discuss the issues of security and stability. The summit was also attended by U.S. President Donald Trump, who was making his maiden foreign trip after taking office in January 2017. Ironically, Trump's election campaign had been marked by anti-Muslim rhetoric, but he toned down this rhetoric at the summit, saying he was not there to lecture or impose the American way of life on anyone.[63] Initiated by Saudi Arabia in conjunction with Trump's state visit to the Middle Eastern country, the Riyadh summit called for close coordination over issues of common interest, starting with doubling joint efforts to combat extremism and terrorism. The summit also pledged to deploy 34,000 troops to support operations against terrorist groups in Iraq and Syria.[64]

In November, Malaysia participated in the Islamic Military Counter Terrorism Coalition (IMCTC) meeting in Riyadh led by Saudi Arabia. The IMCTC is a forty-one-member pan-Islamic anti-terrorism coalition founded in Riyadh in December 2015. That Malaysia was among those invited to this meeting was yet another illustration of the Southeast Asian state's cultivation of closer ties with Riyadh, as well as its broader counterterrorism cooperation with external partners.[65] However, some quarters in Malaysia have questioned the country's close cooperation with Saudi Arabia in combating terrorism, since the Middle Eastern country is propagating puritan Salafi-Wahhabi Islamic doctrines that have allegedly been responsible for the radicalization of Islam in Malaysia.[66] It is argued that the Saudi's version of Islam is responsible for moulding an exclusivist, supremacist and intolerant mindset among Muslims, thus it would be odd for Malaysia to embrace Saudi Arabia and partake in its so-called fight against terrorism.

The Rohingya Crisis

Malaysia was confronted with one of the biggest humanitarian crises in the region, with the killing of thousands and the displacement of almost half a million ethnic minority Rohingya by the Myanmar army. The United Nations described the military offensive in Rakhine state, which provoked the exodus, as a "textbook example of ethnic cleansing".[67] Myanmar's military, on the other hand, said it was fighting Rohingya militants and denied targeting civilians. In the last few years, before the latest crisis in 2017, thousands of Rohingya were making perilous journeys out of Myanmar to escape communal violence or alleged abuses by the security forces. The latest exodus began on 25 August 2017 after Arakan Rohingya Salvation Army (Arsa) militants attacked more than thirty police posts.[68] The Rohingyas fled after Myanmar troops, backed by local Buddhist mobs, responded by burning their villages and attacking and killing civilians. Malaysia was quite vocal in condemning the killings and warned that the crisis might lead to security threats, since extremist groups like ISIL might take advantage of the displaced Rohingyas to recruit them to their ranks.[69] Malaysia had also sent humanitarian aid for Rohingya refugees in Bangladesh. There are also more than 56,000 Rohingyas living in Malaysia who are registered with the United Nations High Commissioner for Refugees.[70] But Malaysia and the rest of ASEAN look powerless in resolving the conflict. Despite bringing up its concerns at ASEAN meetings more than seven times in 2017, Malaysia has yet to see any quick solution to the crisis. It needs the backing of the United Nations and major powers, especially China and India, to intervene in the crisis and put more pressure on the Myanmar government. Ironically, ASEAN's code of non-interference benefits the Myanmar government as the Rohingya crisis persists.

Conclusion

Malaysia went through yet another challenging year in 2017 as the political struggle between the ruling BN and the opposition intensified. The intensity is expected to be even greater in 2018, since elections will finally be called and the contesting parties will unleash all their energy, resources and "tricks" to win power. If the BN recaptures its traditional two-thirds parliamentary majority and wins one or two opposition-held states, Najib's position will be further consolidated and the ruling party's grip on federal power further strengthened. After a big defeat, the fragmented opposition will find it difficult to pick themselves up to continue the struggle to bring about regime change. The opposition coalitions might disintegrate and Malaysia might see a prolonged period of BN rule.

But, if the opposition wins (an unlikely prospect due to the opposition split), Malaysia will go through many more testing years, as the transition from a BN to PH government might face administrative hiccups, bureaucratic challenges and intra-party issues. The BN, especially UMNO, might also transform itself after a heavy defeat and offer a fresh alternative to Malaysian voters. The political struggle is expected to be even greater after that. Consequently, the intense and divisive struggle will tend to adversely affect Malaysia's economic growth and foreign policy as manifested in 2017.

Notes

1. In international relations, the term *middle power* refers to a state that wields less influence on the world stage than a superpower. Various scholars, such as Johan Saravanamuttu (2010) and Mustafa Izzuddin (2007), contend that Malaysia exercises middle-power diplomacy.
2. Johan Saravanamuttu, "A Tectonic Shift in Malaysian Politics", *March 8: Eclipsing May 13* (Singapore, Institute of Southeast Asian Studies, 2008).
3. Faisal S. Hazis, "Competitive Elections and Regime Stability in Malaysia", unpublished paper, 2017.
4. Howard, Marc Morje, and Philip G. Roessler, "Liberalizing Electoral Outcomes in Competitive Authoritarian Regimes", *American Journal of Political Science* 50, no. 2 (2006): 365–81.
5. Freedom House, "Freedom in the World 2017: Malaysia", 2017.
6. *New Straits Times*, "Najib on RM2.6 billion: My Conscience in Clear", 8 December 2015.
7. *The Guardian*, "More Than S1 billion Deposited in Malaysian Prime Minister's Account – Report", 1 March 2016.
8. *Malaysiakini*, "Anti-Kleptocracy Roadshow May Not Lead to Extra Votes", 1 July 2017.

9. *New Straits Times*, "Najib Makes His Mark in White House Visit", 17 September 2017.
10. Bloomberg, "Felda Global Ventures on Mission to Fix Image as Graft Scandal Cools", 29 December 2017.
11. *Malaysian Insight*, "MACC Investigates FELDA's London Hotel Purchase", 14 July 2017.
12. *The Star*, "MACC Now Investigating FIC Purchase of Kuching Hotel", 27 July 2017.
13. *Malaysian Insight*, "Najib Cannot Wash His Hands of Felda Land Scandal, Says Settlers' Group", 24 December 2017.
14. *Malaysiakini*, "How MARA Lost RM60m in Property Deal Down Under", 29 November 2017.
15. Ibid.
16. *The Star*, "Ex-Johor Exco Latif Bandi, Two Others Charged for Money Laundering RM35.7 million", 14 June 2017.
17. *The Star*, "Teo Slapped with 146 Charges", 14 December 2017.
18. *Malaysian Insight*, "Ex-Sabah Water Department Deputy Director in Graft Scandal to be Charged", 12 December 2017.
19. *Straits Times*, "Voters' Gripes about Rising Prices a Key Malaysia Election Issue", 5 June 2017.
20. Ibid.
21. Merdeka Center, "Socio-Political Developments in Malaysia", November 2017.
22. Ibid.
23. *South China Morning Post*, "Religion, Race, Politics: What's Causing Malaysia's Great Divide", 27 August 2017.
24. Free Malaysia Today, "Graft Charges a Federal Weapon to Silence Sabah Rights Advocates", 11 December 2017.
25. Reuters, "Malaysia PM Gets Likely Boost with Electoral Boundaries Ruling", 18 December 2017.
26. *Malaysian Insight*, "Ahead of Budget 2018, Najib Offers RM3 billion Election Goodies", 4 October 2017.
27. *South China Morning Post*, "Religion, Race, Politics: What's Causing Malaysia's Great Divide", 27 August 2017.
28. *Straits Times*, "Mahathir Named Chairman, Anwar Named De-Facto Leader of Pakatan Harapan", 14 July 2017.
29. *The Star*, "Robust Economic Growth", 18 November 2017.
30. *International Business Times*, "Malaysian Ringgit, Asia's Worst Performing Currency, to Fall Further in 2017", 5 January 2017.
31. *The Star*, "Malaysia's CPI Up 5.1% on Year in March, Hitting 8-year High", 19 April 2017.
32. *The Star*, "Malaysia's Economy Expands at 5.6% in Q1", 19 May 2017.
33. Bernama, "2017 Recovery Year for Ringgit, BNM Measures Place in Check", 30 December 2017.

34. Malaysian Reserve, "Malaysian Economy Defies all Expectation in 2017", 22 December 2017.
35. *Deloitte Insights*, "Malaysia: Subdued Growth Prospects for 2017", 28 March 2017.
36. Reuters, "Malaysia Second Quarter GDP Growth Seen Slowing on Weaker Private Consumption, Reuters Poll", 15 August 2017.
37. *The Edge*, "2017 Year in Review: Riding on Economic Recovery", 29 December 2017.
38. *Sun Daily*, "Survey: 15% of Malaysians Skipping Meals to Survive", 30 November 2017.
39. *The Star*, "Stronger Economy but Purchasing Power Eroding", 21 November 2017.
40. *Malay Mail Online*, "Survey: Malaysians Not Better Off Economically Despite Macro Upswing", 24 November 2017.
41. Syed Jaymal Zahiid, "Feeling the Pinch? It's Not Just Because of Higher Cost of Living", *Malay Mail Online*, 8 August 2017.
42. Ibid.
43. Ibid.
44. Jomo K.S., "Malaysia's Debt Problem", *Malaysian Insight*, 24 October 2017.
45. *The Edge*, "Malaysia's Spiralling Debt Burden", 6 January 2018.
46. Jomo K.S., "Malaysia's Debt Problem".
47. Reuters, "FBI Launches Investigation into Malaysian State Fund 1MDB: WSJ", 20 September 2015.
48. Reuters, "US Justice Department Files Lawsuits in Connection with 1MDB Probe", 20 July 2016.
49. *Malaysiakini*, "MO1 is Najib, but Why Didn't DOJ Name Him, Asks Rahman Dahlan", 1 September 2016.
50. *Malaysiakini*, "Yacht, Diamonds, and More in DOJ's Latest 1MDB Filing", 16 June 2017.
51. *Malay Mail Online*, "Najib: 1MDB Not Directly Involved in US DOJ Suit", 29 July 2017.
52. *Straits Times*, "Most of 1MDB's Debts Settled with Asset Sale: Najib", January 2016.
53. *South China Morning Post*, "Has China Offered to Bail Out Malaysia's 1MDB?: At What Cost?", 7 December 2016.
54. *Straits Times*, "Chinese Deals in Malaysia under Scrutiny", 7 May 2017.
55. *South China Morning Post*, "Has China Offered to Bail Out Malaysia's 1MDB?
56. *Financial Times*, "China Overtakes Singapore as Biggest Investor in Malaysia Property", 27 March 2017.
57. *Asia Times*, "Chinese 'Taking Over' Malaysia in 20 Years, Politicians Warns", 6 May 2017.

58. *Malaysian Insight*, "Najib Slams Claims that Government is Selling Malaysia's Sovereignty to Beijing", 23 January 2018.
59. *The Star*, "Malaysia Has Halted All Imports from North Korea", 13 October 2017.
60. Mustafa Izzuddin, "Reviewing Malaysia's Relations With North Korea", *ISEAS Perspective* 2017, no. 30 (8 May 2017).
61. *The Star*, "Bilateral Trade with North Korea Has Grown over the Years", 24 February 2017.
62. Channel NewsAsia, "North Korea Warns Malaysia for Forcing Post-mortem on Kim Jon Nam", 18 February 2017.
63. *New Straits Times*, "Riyadh Summit Reaffirms Urgent Need for Closer Cooperation, Moderation in Combating Terrorism", 22 May 2017.
64. Asharq Al Awsat, "Royadh Declaration Announces Reserve of 34,000 Soldiers to Back Terrorism Fight", 21 May 2017.
65. "What's Malaysia Role in the New Islamic Anti-Terror Coalition", *The Diplomat*, 28 November 2017.
66. *The Star*, "The Radicalisation of Islam in Malaysia", 28 August 2016.
67. United Nations, "UN Human Rights Chief Points to 'Textbook Example of Ethnic Cleansing' in Myanmar", *UN News*, 11 September 2017.
68. BBC, "Myanmar Rohingya: What You Need to Know About the Crisis", 16 January 2018.
69. *The Telegraph*, "Malaysia Warns Rohingya Crisis Could Lead to ISIL Attacks in Burma", 12 September 2017.
70. *The Star*, "Malaysia to Help Bangladesh Deal with Rohingya Issue", 10 September 2017.

Myanmar

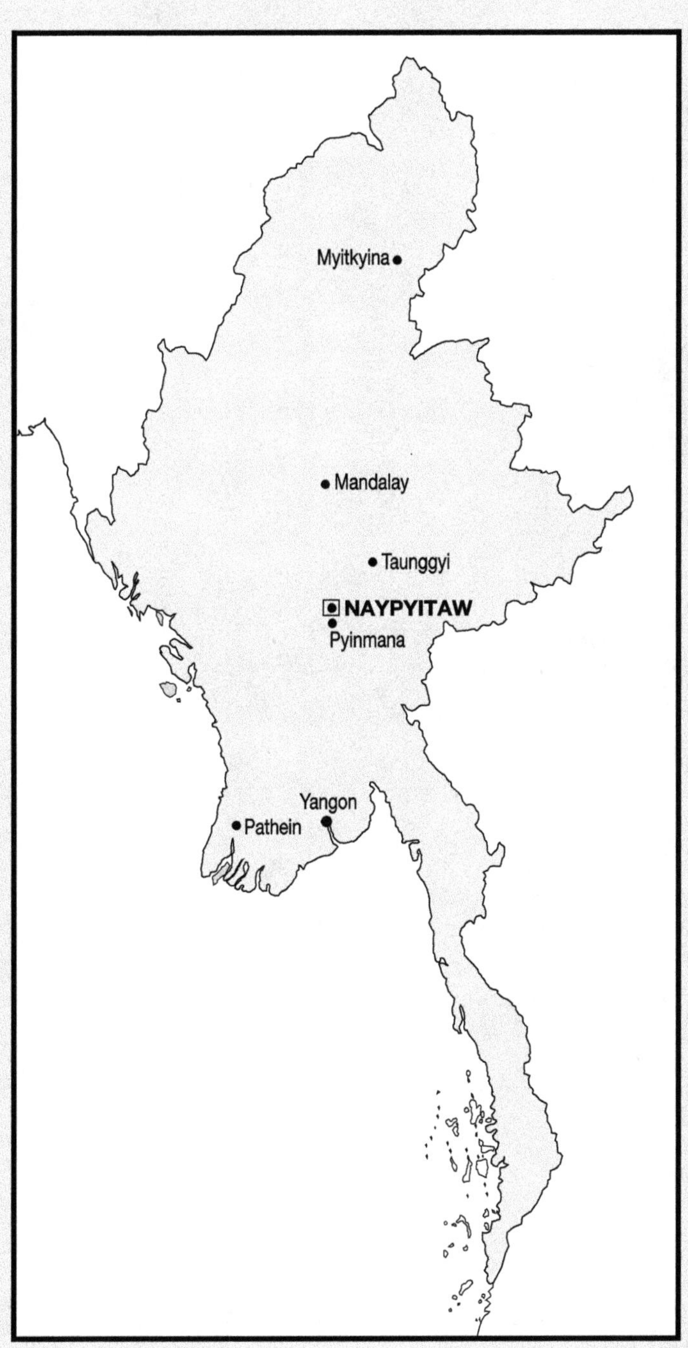

Myitkyina
Mandalay
Taunggyi
NAYPYITAW
Pyinmana
Yangon
Pathein

STABILITY AND EXPECTATIONS: Economic Reform and the NLD Government

Aka Kyaw Min Maw

The people of Myanmar overwhelmingly voted in the 2015 general elections to usher in a historic change for the country. As a majority of the citizens hoped, the major opposition party, the National League for Democracy (NLD), won a majority of the vote. As a result, for the very first time, the people of Myanmar were able to witness a civilian government. The date of the election, 8 November 2015, marked a historic moment for Myanmar, and engendered great expectations among the public that reform would accelerate under the new administration.

Winning over 80 per cent of the vote, the NLD was able to form the government. The new administration, led by president U Htin Kyaw, commenced on 1 April 2016. The beginning of the journey for the new administration was quite rocky, as it had to boost an economy that had contracted in the difficult fiscal year[1] (FY) 2015/16, affected as it was by natural disaster and lower commodity prices. As a first step in its economic reforms, in July 2017 the new government released a twelve-point economic policy agenda, covering all the important sectors.[2] The twelve-point agenda, though generally positively received, was criticized for a lack of clarity, priorities or specifics.[3]

The most significant economic reform of the year was the Myanmar Investment Law 2016. This was enacted in October 2016 and its implementation rules were published in March 2017. It replaces Foreign Investment Law 2012 and the Myanmar Citizens Investment Law 2013 with a consolidated law that provides a level playing field for both foreign and domestic investors. In addition, it will streamline internal procedures. However, there has been a delay in enacting

Aka Kyaw Min Maw is an independent economic consultant based in Yangon, Myanmar.

another important piece of legislation for the country — the new Myanmar Companies Act, the most anticipated legislation for 2017. The act was approved by President U Htin Kyaw in the first week of December 2017. Hence, the NLD government failed to enact this important legislation during its first year as part of its economic reform agenda. This may have led to lower investments for the government's first year.

The first year of the NLD administration, FY 2016/17, witnessed a slower than expected[4] growth rate of 5.9 per cent — lower than the average 7.3 per cent growth rate of the previous administration. The low growth rate was not the only disappointment: FY 2017/17 saw foreign direct investment (FDI) commitments of only US$6.65 billion, 30 per cent lower than the previous year. Nonetheless, the economy can be seen to be in a better situation when other indicators are assessed. The government managed to keep the inflation rate at 6.7 per cent, significantly lower than the 10 per cent of the previous year, and the fiscal deficit was reduced to 3 per cent of GDP compared to the previous fiscal year's 4.4 per cent. The lower fiscal deficit helped reduce the Central Bank of Myanmar's (CBM) financing requirements and inflationary pressure. In addition, the trade deficit narrowed to US$5.21 billion in FY 2016/17, 4 per cent lower than the US$5.44 billion deficit of FY 2015/16, contributing to reduced pressure on the current account deficit.

Major economic indicators provide a mixed picture on the economic performance of the government. As pessimistically mentioned in the media, the economy slowed under the current government — not badly, but just at a moderate rate. Besides slower growth and lower FDI commitments, other indicators suggest that the economy is still in good health. A few significant regulatory reforms were accomplished, whilst details on the twelve-point economic policy agenda have not yet been released. The new government therefore had some accomplishments as well as witnessed some failures in terms of its plans to accelerate economic reform in its first year. The sections that follow will analyse in detail the recent economic developments and evaluate key reform efforts in order to assess whether the NLD government was able to fulfil the hopes of its citizens.

Macroeconomic Performance

Part of the blame for the slower FY 2016/17 growth rate goes back to the previous year. In fact, it was a difficult year for Myanmar due to both internal and external pressures. Internal pressures surged in the second quarter of FY 2015/16 as Cyclone Komen hit, resulting in widespread flooding, impacting negatively on the productivity of the agricultural sector.[5] The economy was further weakened by lower global commodity prices — the external pressure. Given these challenges, the last year of the U Thein Sein administration saw the lowest growth rate, at 7 per cent, in four years. The implication was that the new government had to take over responsibility when the economy was turning in a different direction. However, it is largely contingent on the government to set the economy in the right direction by exploiting the relevant policy tools and setting priorities.

Real GDP Growth and Inflation

Figure 1 shows the real GDP growth rate and sectoral[6] growth rates and demonstrates how the economy continued to grow at a slower rate in FY 2016/17. Significant contraction in the agriculture sector, at 0.4 per cent, was the main contributor to the slower growth of FY 2016/17, along with slower growth in the services sector. Only the industry sector grew at a faster rate than in FY 2015/16. The available data[7] tells us that the contraction in the agricultural sector was mainly due to the decrease in the production of beans and pulses.[8] The industry sector slowly recovered from the contraction of industrial output in FY 2015/16 due to a decline in gas prices, the sharp deceleration of the construction sector and the lower output of food processing firms affected by Cyclone Komen. Hence, it should not be a surprise that the economy grew at a slower rate after a challenging FY 2015/16. The consumer price index (CPI) increase declined to 6.7 per cent in FY 2016/17, compared with 10 per cent in FY 2015/16 (Figure 2). The relatively lower overall CPI was due mainly to relatively low and stable non-food price inflation, while food price inflation fluctuated during FY 2016/17, with a spike between December 2016 and February 2017 due to imported processed food.[9] During the four-year period, a spike in food price inflation can be observed in FY 2015/16 — this was largely to do with the flooding caused by Cyclone Komen, and exchange rate depreciation.[10] FY 2016/17 was able to recover from food price inflation, leading to a moderate overall inflation rate.

Foreign Direct Investment

With the slower growth rate in FY 2016/17, FDI commitments were also lower, at US$6.65 billion (30 per cent lower than FY 2015/16). In fact, FY 2015/16 received the highest FDI commitments from investors for the whole period of the previous administration. A sharp drop of FDI commitments in FY 2016/17 was partly due to lack of commitments in the oil and gas sector (Figure 3). Indeed, the previous government enjoyed a huge amount of FDI commitments in the oil and gas sector in its last two years, as shown in Figure 3. Another

FIGURE 1
Real GDP Growth and Growth Rate by Sector

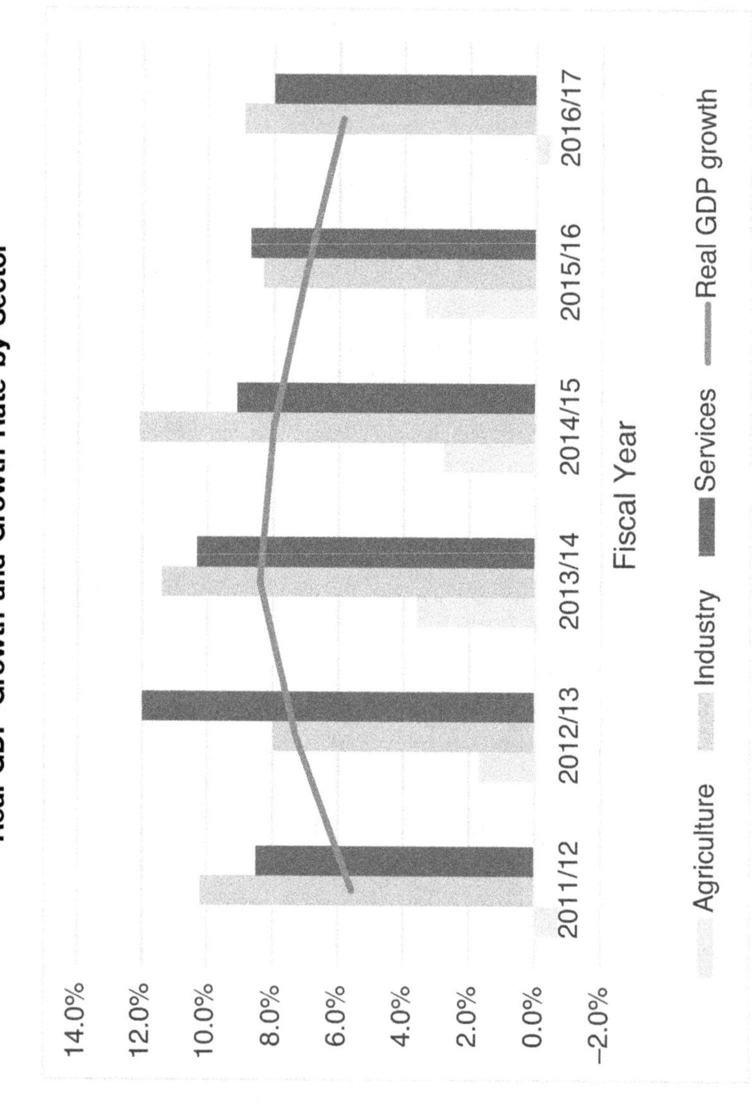

Source: *Myanmar Statistical Year Book 2015*, and *Myanmar Economic Monitor*, October 2017.

FIGURE 2
Inflation Rate

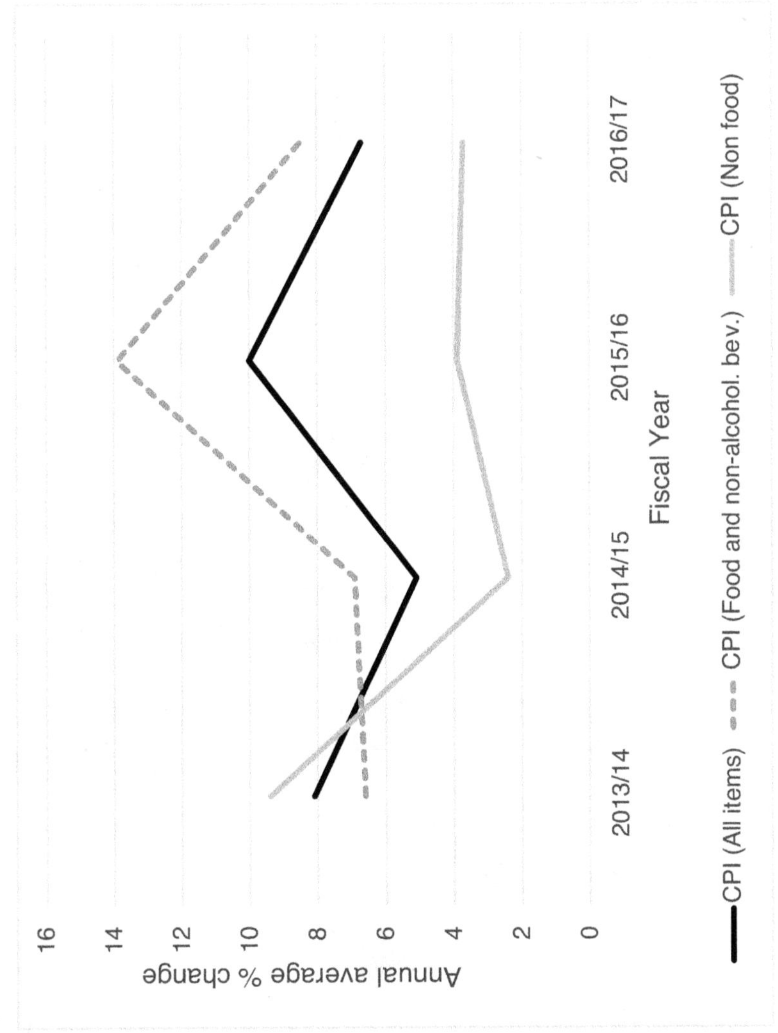

Source: *Myanmar Economic Monitor*, October 2017.

FIGURE 3
FDI Commitments by Sector

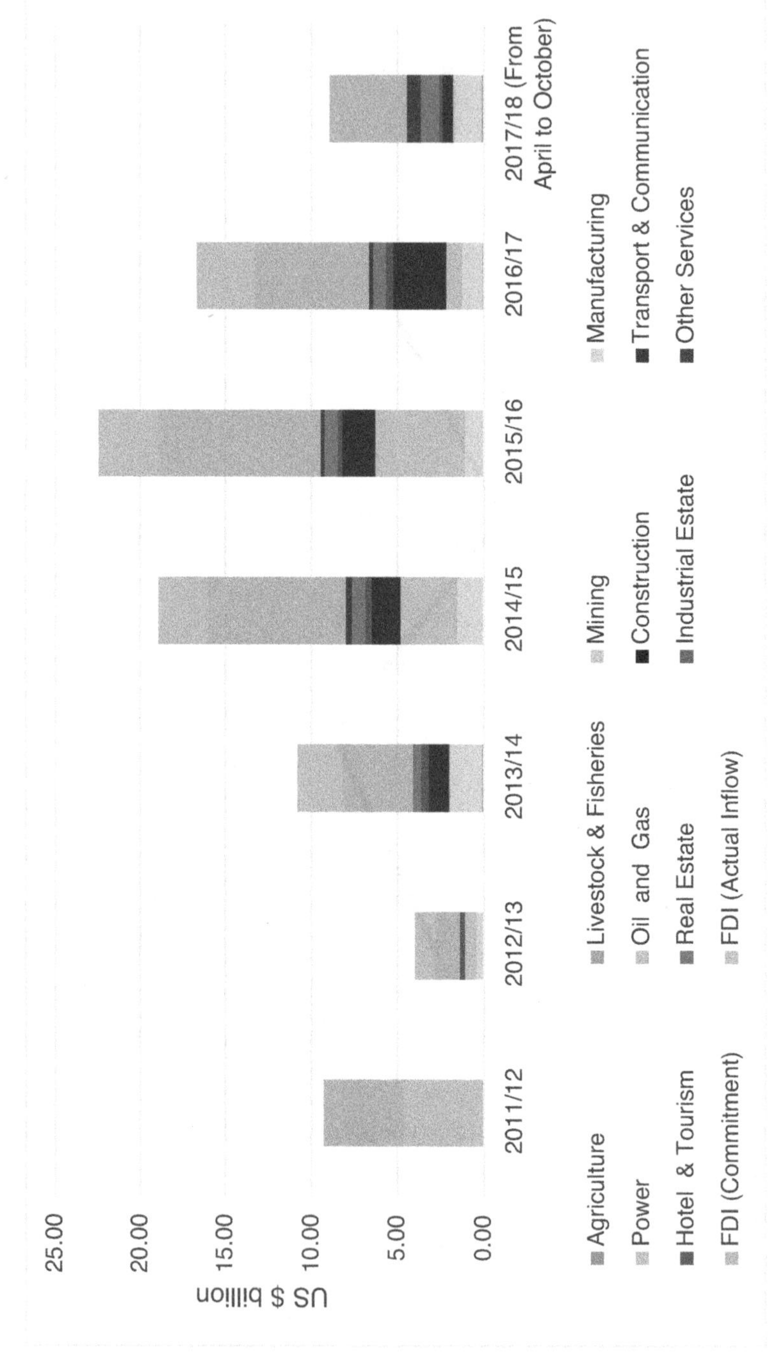

Source: Department of Investment and Company Administration (DICA).

possible explanation for lower FDI commitments could be a reflection of a natural slowdown after high commitments in the past three years, as noted by the World Bank.[11] Given the challenges in getting actual FDI inflow data, it was estimated, using the IMF's BOP statistics, to have declined by 2 per cent, from US$3.44 billion in FY 2015/16 to US$3.37 billion in FY 2016/17 (Figure 4). Even though a huge discrepancy between FDI commitments and actual inflow can be observed, both indicators suggest the same story — that the FDI trend went upward from FY 2012/13, reached its peak in FY 2015/16 and slowed down in FY 2016/17.

Trade

Even though the challenges faced in FY 2015/16 exposed the new government to slower growth and lower FDI inflows, exports recovered from the previous year's decline. Based on official figures, exports increased by 8 per cent in FY 2016/17 compared to FY 2015/16, but remained lower than in FY 2014/15 (Figure 5). The World Bank[12] notes that the slower recovery of exports in FY 2016/17 could be due to a surge in garment exports, offsetting lower exports of natural gas that have dominated Myanmar's export composition for a long time. Along with the increase in exports, imports also increased in FY 2016/17, but only by 4 per cent — lower than the increase in exports. This led to a narrower trade deficit in FY 2016/17 of US$5.21 billion — 4 per cent lower than the deficit for FY 2015/16.

Fiscal Operations

The decreased trade deficit helped the economy reduce the current account deficit to 5.3 per cent of GDP in FY 2016/17, lower than the 7.2 per cent of FY 2015/16. Other factors that affected the decline in the current account deficit of FY 2016/17 were increased service exports and incoming transfers, including grant aid. Along with a narrowed current account deficit, FY 2016/17 enjoyed a balance of payments surplus of 1.4 per cent of GDP, up from the 0.8 per cent of the previous year due to lower FDI inflows and a reduced current account deficit (Table 1). Driven by the current account deficit, the value of the Myanmar kyat against the U.S. dollar depreciated by 3 per cent in FY 2016/17 compared to FY 2015/16, but its fluctuations were fewer, with a standard deviation of 75.98 for daily exchange between the U.S. dollar and kyat, compared to the 83.64 of FY 2015/16.[13]

Fiscal performance in FY 2016/17 was better than the previous year, since the overall fiscal deficit was at 3 per cent of GDP, an improvement over the

FIGURE 4
FDI Commitments and Actual Inflow

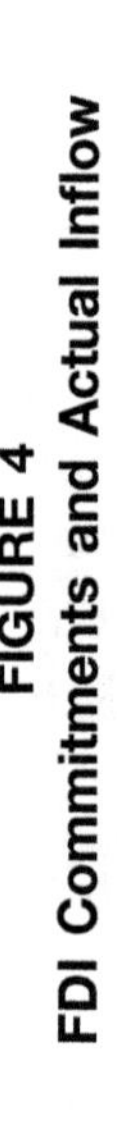

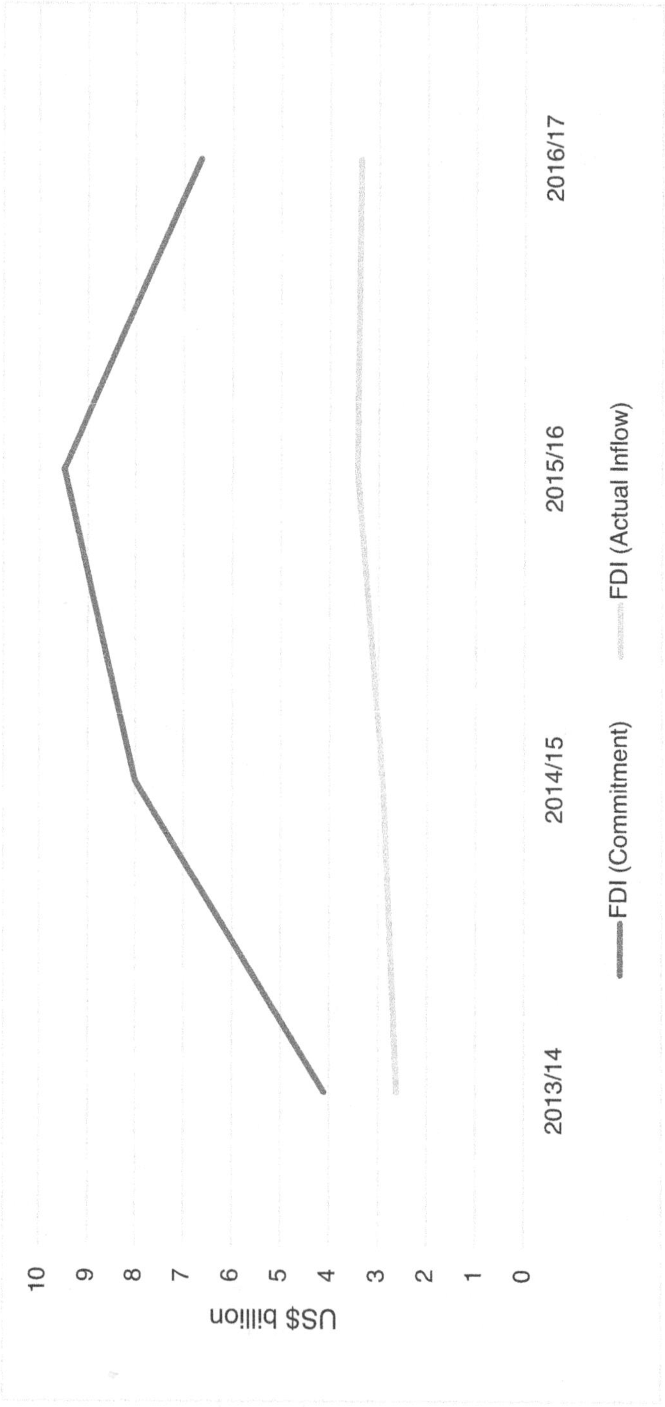

Source: DICA and IMF BOP Statistics.

FIGURE 5
Exports, Imports and Trade Balance

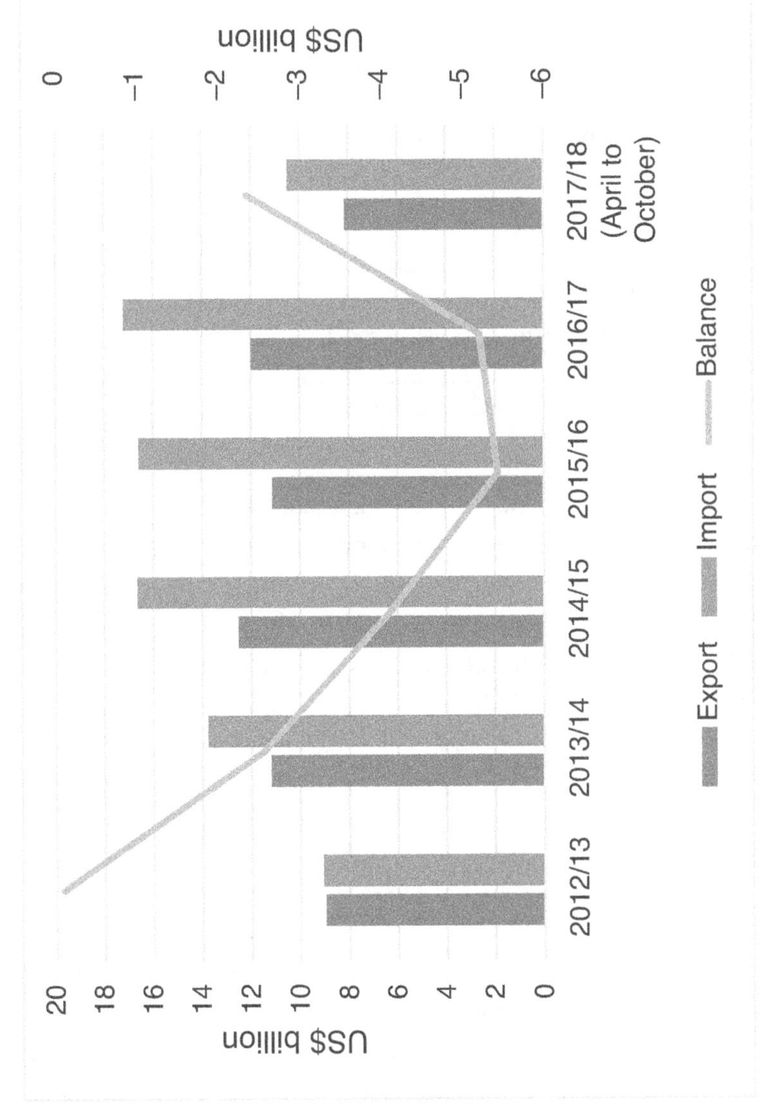

Source: Ministry of Commerce (MOC).

TABLE 1
Balance of Payments (% of GDP)

	2013/14	*2014/15*	*2015/16*	*2016/17*
Current account	**–3.8**	**–5.5**	**–7.2**	**–5.3**
Trade balance	–3.6	–6.2	–9.0	–8.5
Exports	15.7	18.6	17.1	16.8
Imports	19.3	24.7	26.1	25.3
Services balance	0.9	1.8	1.9	1.4
Primary income balance	–3.4	–4.8	–4.2	–3.5
Secondary income balance	2.3	3.7	4.2	5.3
Capital account	**0.0**	**0.0**	**0.0**	**0.0**
Financial account	**8.3**	**7.1**	**7.7**	**7.4**
Direct investment	–4.3	–6.9	–7.1	–5.8
Portfolio investment	0.0	0.0	0.0	–0.1
Other investment	–3.9	–0.2	–0.6	–1.4
Net errors and omissions	**–2.1**	**1.1**	**0.2**	**–0.7**
Overall balance	**2.4**	**2.7**	**0.8**	**1.4**

Source: *Myanmar Economic Monitor*, October 2017.

previous year's 4.4 per cent. Improvement in the fiscal balances of both state economic enterprises (SEE) and the union government contributed to narrowing public sector fiscal deficit (Figure 6). In addition, government spending was reduced and revenue expanded in FY 2016/17. Fiscal performance is detailed in Table 2. The government expanded its tax base in FY 2016/17 to finance its fiscal deficit (Figure 7), and this effort helped reduce financing and inflationary pressure on the CBM.

Public Perception

With the slower growth rate of 5.9 per cent, the economy remained stable in FY 2016/17 following the difficult FY 2015/16, thanks to no major external or internal economic threats during the year. Public perceptions of economic performance complement the major economic indicators. According to the 2017 Public Opinion Survey of the International Republican Institute (IRI), a healthy majority of the people are satisfied with the country, as 63 per cent of respondents perceive the current economic situation as going well, even though there has been a decline in the positive perception of the economic situation between 2014 and 2017. People also tend to perceive that their economic situation would get better in the future, as 55 per cent of respondents indicated an improved economic situation and 26 per cent that they were in the same situation. The economy is the top priority for

FIGURE 6
Fiscal Balance (share of GDP)

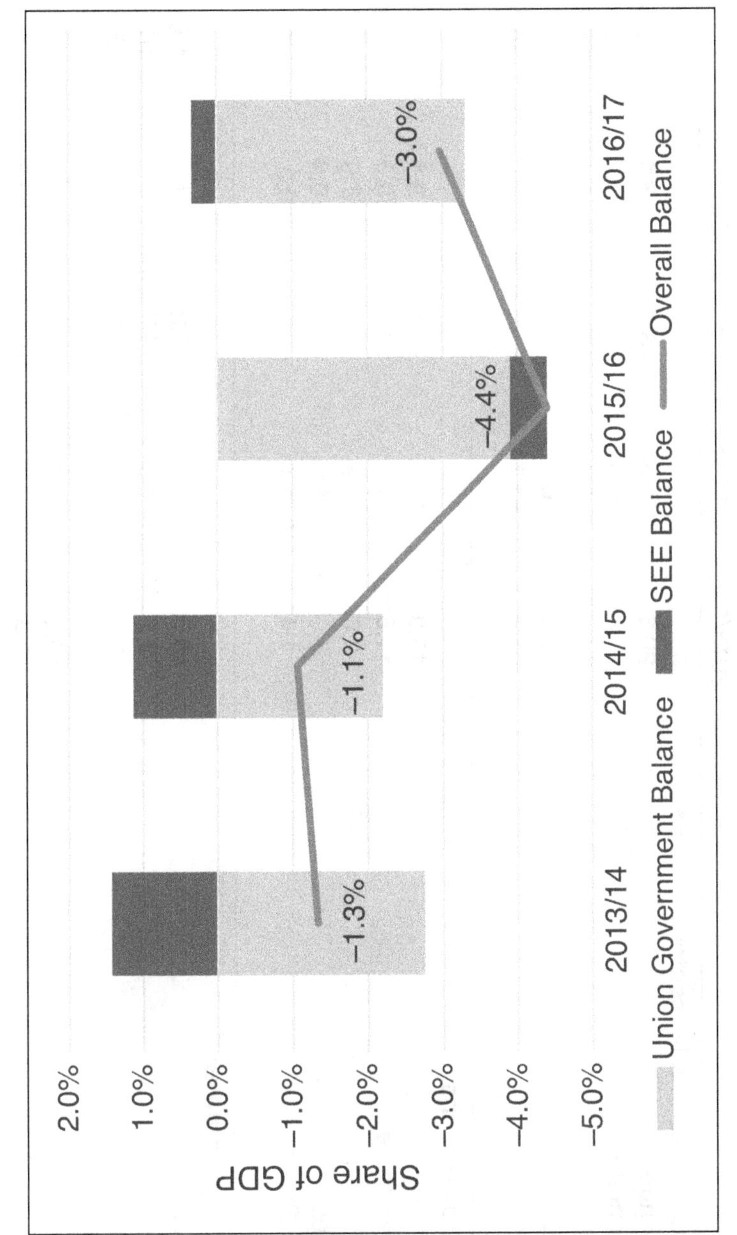

Source: Myanmar Economic Monitor, October 2017.

TABLE 2
Fiscal Operations (% of GDP)

	2013/14	*2014/15*	*2015/16*	*2016/17*	*2017/18*
Consolidated public sector					
Revenue	**20.3**	**22.3**	**18.7**	**18.1**	**22.6**
Expenditure	**21.7**	**23.4**	**23.1**	**21.1**	**28.9**
Recurrent	14.0	16.4	16.9	16.1	21.8
Capital	7.6	6.9	6.2	5.0	7.1
Balance	**–1.3**	**–1.1**	**–4.4**	**–3.0**	**–6.3**
SEE operations					
Revenue	**13.0**	**12.6**	**10.1**	**9.1**	**10.1**
Expenditure	**11.6**	**11.5**	**10.6**	**8.8**	**11.2**
Recurrent	9.6	9.9	9.3	7.9	9.7
Capital	2.0	1.5	1.3	0.9	1.5
SEE Balance	**1.4**	**1.1**	**–0.5**	**0.3**	**–1.0**
Union government					
Revenue	**10.3**	**12.4**	**11.2**	**11.1**	**15.1**
Tax	6.7	7.0	6.7	7.1	10.2
Non-Tax	3.4	5.1	4.1	3.6	3.9
Grants	0.3	0.3	0.4	0.4	1.0
Expenditure	**13.1**	**14.6**	**15.2**	**14.4**	**20.3**
Recurrent	7.4	9.3	10.3	10.3	14.8
Capital	5.7	5.4	4.9	4.1	5.6
Union government balance	**–2.8**	**–2.2**	**–3.9**	**–3.3**	**–5.2**

Note: Figures for FY 2017/18 are forecasts.
Source: *Myanmar Economic Monitor*, October 2017.

FIGURE 7
Tax Revenue (share of GDP)

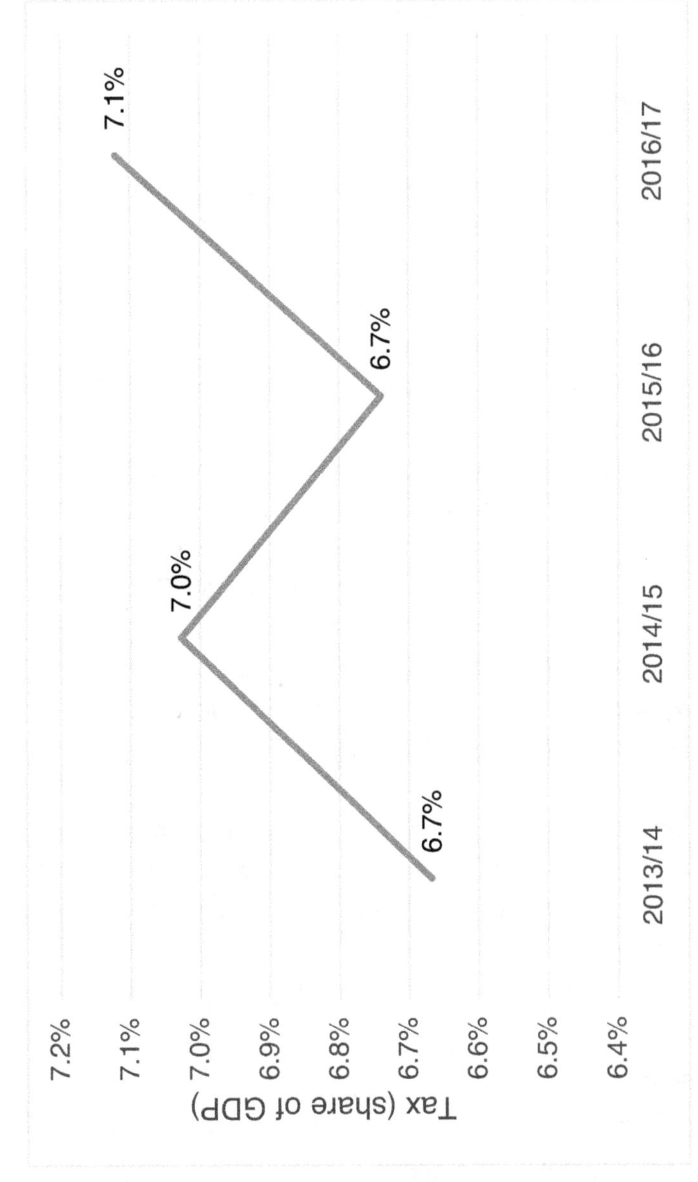

Source: *Myanmar Economic Monitor*, October 2017.

the public, followed by ethnic/sectarian conflict, development/infrastructure, and social services. Among economic matters, the top priorities that people would like to see addressed are jobs and inflation.[14]

Economic Reform and Achievements

Given the pressure of high expectations, the NLD government attempted a raft of reforms in FY 2016/17. These were as follows:

1) The revised company registration fee of the Directorate of Investment and Company Administration (DICA) in June 2016;
2) Release of the twelve-point economic policy agenda of the Ministry of Planning and Finance (MOPF) in July 2016; enactment of the 2016 Myanmar Investment Law in October 2016;
3) Financial sector reforms, including Myanmar's first-ever Treasury bond auction in September 2016;
4) Enactment of the new investment law in October 2016;
5) The launch of the Myanmar Automated Cargo Clearance System (MACCS) by the Customs Department in November 2016;
6) Establishment of the National Trade Facilitation Committee (NTFC) as part of World Trade Organization Trade Facilitation Agreement (WTO-TFA) commitments in December 2016;[15]
7) Issuance of investment rules in March 2017 leading to the new investment law becoming effective on 1 April 2017.

Along with reforms, several achievements were also observed. A significant one was the removal of economic sanctions and the restoration of trade benefits by the United States in October and November 2016. As mentioned in the previous section, the lower inflation rate, lower current account deficit and the decline in the budget deficit were achievements of the government in FY 2016/17.

DICA's Revised Registration Fees

As part of MOPF's hundred-day plan, DICA imposed revised registration fees for both private limited companies and listed public companies. The purpose of this reform was to encourage small and medium enterprises to be registered companies at their initial stage, and to scrutinize the listed companies intending to conduct actual business operations. Effective from 1 June 2016, the new registration fees are 500,000 and 2,500,000 kyat for private limited companies and listed public companies, respectively. Previously, both types of companies were charged 1,000,000 kyat. In addition, the company registration extension fee was reduced from 50,000 to 30,000 kyat. Fees for other services[16] such as change of company name or change of authorized capital were increased to offset possible income loss from the new, lower company registration fees. Even though it is a minor reform, DICA believes the step is in line with government efforts to promote local and foreign investment and the expansion of businesses. The change is also in line with policy number 7 (enabling private sector growth) of the twelve-point economic policy agenda.

The Twelve-Point Economic Policy Agenda

As a very first step towards economic reform, the NLD government released its twelve-point economic policy agenda. It was a much-welcomed effort by the government as it covered a broad range of economic issues and targeted specific areas such as infrastructure and job creation to bring about development, with the overall objective to achieve national reconciliation, balanced economic development, skilled human capital, and a people-centred economic system. The twelve-point policy agenda is the backbone of the NLD government's plans to accelerate economic reform for the country.

The Myanmar Investment Law (MIL)

The 2016 Myanmar Investment Law can be considered the most important reform made by the NLD government during its first year. Bringing the Foreign Investment and Myanmar Citizens Investment Law together, the MIL provides a level playing field for domestic and foreign investors. This will help Myanmar attract more FDI in the future. According to the new law, only businesses that fall into one of the restricted categories[17] will require Myanmar Investment Commission (MIC) permits. Businesses outside of these categories need only apply for MIC endorsement. The advantage of MIC endorsement is that the application process could be faster than applying for a permit.[18] The new investment regime delegates state/region investment committees to provide endorsement for smaller investments, which will reduce the workload of the MIC and DICA.[19] As the new law only came into effect on 1 April 2017, it did not have an impact on FDI inflow/commitments for FY 2016/17. However, this major reform will certainly bring in foreign investment in coming years.

Financial Sector Reforms

The most significant financial sector reform for the year was the first-ever Treasury bond auction, successfully held in September 2017.[20] This was a major financial sector reform move for the new government. With the Treasury bond auction, the Central Bank can manage the fiscal deficit more efficiently, rather than through CBM financing. According to Turnell,[21] CBM financing, following a sequenced reduction, would reach zero per cent after FY 2018/19. Other reform related to the financial sector included a change to the insurance market to allow foreign companies entry to it, CBM exchange rate reform, and an interbank market mechanism to replace the current daily auction mechanism.

In addition, regulations related to modernizing the financial infrastructure were introduced in FY 2016/17. Regulations enabling non-financial institutions to provide mobile financial services were introduced in April 2016.[22] Alongside this, regulation on the Credit Information Reporting System was adopted by the CBM in March 2017, laying the ground for credit reporting companies, such as credit bureaus, to be established and operated.[23] New prudential regulations for private banks, including stricter capital requirements and liquidity ratios, came into force a few months into FY 2017/18 to implement the Financial Institution Law (2016).[24] Hence, along with these reforms, better financial services are expected in the future.

Trade Facilitation Reform

In November 2016, with assistance from the Japan International Cooperation Agency (JICA), the Myanmar Customs Department launched the Myanmar Automated Cargo Clearance System (MACCS), a key step in customs modernization and one which will help push for further reform in trade facilitation. The use of MACCS streamlines the cargo clearance process as it significantly reduces the amount of manual document checking, replacing this with an automated document verification process.[25] The system is currently used in the Yangon area and is expected to expand to land-border areas in 2018.[26] The MACCS is not just a part of trade facilitation reform but is also in line with the government's economic reform policies (number 4, prioritizing physical and IT infrastructure, and number 7, enabling private sector growth).

In addition to this, continuous efforts in trade facilitation have been observed. In December 2016, the National Trade Facilitation Committee (NTFC) was established as part of the World Trade Organization Trade Facilitation Agreement (WTO-TFA) that Myanmar ratified in December 2015.[27] The establishment of the

NTFC is crucial for Myanmar to be able to implement the WTO-TFA, which will bring a significant improvement to Myanmar's economy through improved trade. This was accomplished during the first year of the NLD government. Further reforms to liberalize trade, such as reducing the export and import negative lists[28] and developing new trade and customs laws, are ongoing.

U.S. Sanctions Lifted

In October 2016 the United States terminated the national emergency with respect to Myanmar and, as a result, financial and economic sanctions administered by the U.S. Department of the Treasury's Office of Foreign Assets Control, which had been in place since 1997, were lifted.[29] This led to (1) the ending of the ban on imports of Myanmar jade and rubies to the United States; (2) reducing regulatory burdens on U.S. banks to do business in Myanmar; and (3) relaxed compliance with the State Department's Responsible Investment Reporting Requirements for U.S. investors. In addition, effective 13 November 2016, the United States restored access for Myanmar to its Generalized System of Preferences (GSP), which allows developing countries to export about five thousand products duty-free. The removal of sanctions and the restoration of GSP will help Myanmar diversify export destinations and bring in U.S. investments. Given the current small amount of Myanmar's exports to the United States — US$244 million in 2016[30] — while significant improvement is likely over time, any short-term impact is less likely to be seen. As the removal of sanctions is likely to reduce transaction costs for U.S. investors, the first half of the current fiscal year saw significantly higher investment commitments from the United States — about US$129 million for the first half of FY 2017/18 compared to an average of US$4.65 million over the previous six fiscal years. Hence, the lifting of sanctions will have positive implications for the country, though these are more likely to be felt over the longer term.

Disappointments

The twelve-point economic policy agenda can also be considered as a disappointment, even if it was a great effort by the government. The government failed to release prioritized policy areas and specific strategies or policy tools for implementing the agenda in FY 2016/17. As the agenda is broad, it would be easier for the government to set priorities for implementation, as targeted results from some policies would take longer than other policies, given the capital and infrastructure constraints of Myanmar.

For instance, formulating policies to increase foreign investment mentioned in policy number 7 could be accomplished faster than policy number 8, to do with building environmentally sustainable cities, given investment-related legislation had already progressed when the NLD government took office. In addition, some policies in the twelve-point economic agenda can complement each other; for instance, policy number 7 (increased foreign investment) and policy number 4 (prioritizing basic infrastructure), since increased investment in infrastructure will foster a stronger economy.

The government's delay in releasing detailed economic strategies and priorities could have contributed to lower FDI commitments and inflows.[31] Another example of the slow pace of government is the new Myanmar Company Act, approved[32] just recently by the president. Along with the new investment law, this company act is crucial for bringing in investments and developing Myanmar's private sector. In addition, the government needs a better public relations strategy to keep the public aware of the progress of economic reform. For instance, the public is not sure whether the government will publish details of the twelve-point policy and implementation plan. Hence, major disappointments in relation to the performance of the government in its first year were due to the slow pace of implementation and the poor communication of its policy agenda.

Since its priorities have been national reconciliation and the peace process, the NLD government has seemingly neglected economic reform.[33] In a speech on the occasion of the one-year anniversary of the government,[34] State Counsellor Daw Aung San Suu Kyi spoke mainly about peace and national reconciliation. Whilst the importance of infrastructure and job creation was mentioned in her speech, the focus was on peace and national reconciliation. Indeed, given the prevalence of historically rooted civil war and conflict in the country, the peace and national reconciliation process are of course important. However, this should not lead to a reduced focus on economic reform. In fact, economic reform should be pursued in parallel to political reform, as even the twelve-point economic policy agenda notes that the government's objective is to achieve national reconciliation through an economic framework. Neglecting the economy will further retard the growth of the economy in the future and deepen people's disappointment.

Conclusion

Given that FY 2015/16 was a challenging year, both the IMF and World Bank forecast the growth rate for FY 2016/17 to be slower, at 6.3 and 6.5 per cent, respectively, lower than FY 2015/16. However, the actual growth rate for FY 2016/17 was even lower than these projections, so in this respect it might be justifiable to blame the government for not being able to drive economic growth in line with expectations. However, the economy was stabilized in the first year of the government, even with the slower growth rate and lower FDI commitments. Weak performance in growth rate and FDI can be offset with lower inflationary pressure, lower budget deficit and lower current account deficit. Moreover, the public perception of economic performance is still generally positive.[35]

The most significant reform in FY 2016/17 was the new investment law. Reforms in the financial sector were also achievements for the new government. These legal and regulatory frameworks will be crucial for the government to boost FDI inflows and for the development of the private sector. However, weakness of the government was observed in the course of its first year. The most significant weakness was a lack of clarity in setting priorities for economic policies, along with delays in passing and enacting important legislation; for instance, the late approval of the new Myanmar Company Act and financial sector regulations, which came into force eighteen months after the passage of the Myanmar Financial Law 2016. In addition, it can be a frustrating situation when the government seemingly gives precedence to other initiatives over economic ones.

Despite slower economic growth, Myanmar's economy is projected to recover and grow at 6.4 per cent in FY 2017/18.[36] However, the government will need to prioritize achieving quick wins in the short-term to boost public confidence in the economy. Otherwise, the NLD government will likely face a loss of popularity among the public, which might carry a high price. Besides setting priorities for the economy, the government also faces political risk due to conflict in Northern Rakhine, which might have a negative impact on FDI inflow as it could affect foreign investor perceptions. Hence, the government also needs to carefully handle this issue, along with its economic priorities. To sum up, even though one year is still early to judge the NLD government, the condition of the economy was not as bad as depicted by the media, given the stabilized economic performance. The government suffered from the high expectations of the public and the business community. Setting economic priorities and the release of detailed economic policy can help the government better meet these high expectations and stimulate the economy in the future.

Notes

1. Myanmar's fiscal year begins in April and ends in March of the following year.
2. See <http://themimu.info/sites/themimu.info/files/documents/Statement_Economic_Policy_Aug2016.pdf for twelve-point economic policy of Myanmar>.
3. See, for example <https://www.mmtimes.com/business/21664-nld-12-point-economic-

policy-announcement.html and https://www.wsj.com/articles/myanmar-government-releases-economic-policy-goals-without-specifics-1469799645>.

4. Myanmar's GPD growth rate for FY 2016/17 was projected at 6.5 per cent and 6.3 per cent by the World Bank and the IMF, respectively. See the World Bank's Myanmar Economic Monitor (MEM) December 2016 and the IMF's 2016 Article IV consultation February 2017.
5. Agriculture growth was estimated to decelerate at 2 per cent for FY 2015/16. However, official estimates showed that it accelerated at 3.4 per cent, slightly higher than the previous year. This unexpected increase in agricultural growth for FY 2015/16, contrary to the effects of Cyclone Komen, was due to higher outputs of beans and pulses, offsetting a decline in rice production. For more details, see the World Bank's Myanmar Economic Monitor (MEM) October 2017.
6. Three main sectors contribute to GDP production: agriculture, industry and services. The agriculture sector is comprised of agriculture, livestock and fishery, and forestry; the industry sector is comprised of energy, mining, processing and manufacturing, electric power, and construction; and the services sector is comprised of transportation, communications, financial institutions, social and administrative services, rental and other services, and trade.
7. USDA estimated that the output for beans and pulses declined by 2.4 per cent in FY 2015/16 compared with FY 2014/15.
8. World Bank, *Myanmar Economic Monitor: Capitalizing on Investment Opportunities*, October 2017.
9. Ibid.
10. World Bank, *Myanmar Economic Monitor*, May 2016.
11. World Bank, *Myanmar Economic Monitor: Capitalizing on Investment Opportunities*, October 2017.
12. Ibid.
13. Reference exchange rate of the Central Bank of Myanmar.
14. International Republican Institute, Survey of Burma/Myanmar, public opinion survey, Center for Insights in Survey Research, 2017.
15. <http://www.myanmarinsider.com/government-agencies-and-the-private-sector-to-be-devised/>.
16. For the complete list of new registration fees, see <http://dica.gov.mm/en/news/announcement-revised-registration-fees-company-registration-and-other-company-related-matters>.
17. Under section 36 of the Investment Law, investors wishing to conduct businesses that: "(i) are strategic to Myanmar; (ii) are capital intensive; (iii) may have a large potential impact on the environment or local community; (iv) utilise state-owned land or property; or (v) are otherwise designated by the Government, will need to submit a proposal to the MIC for an MIC Permit".

18. <http://www.nationmultimedia.com/business/New-Myanmar-investment-law-is-the-right-move-30295067.html>.
19. Allen & Overy, *Myanmar's New Investment Regime*, 2017.
20. <https://www.mmtimes.com/business/22644-bankers-satisfied-with-first-treasury-auction.html>.
21. Sean Turnell, "Myanmar Macro-Economy 2017: Taming Dragons, Finding Tigers", presentation in Yangon, Myanmar, August 2017.
22. <https://www.mmtimes.com/business/technology/19851-mobile-money-regulations-released.html>.
23. <http://www.mizzima.com/business-domestic/ifc-and-myanmar-central-bank-promote-new-credit-reporting-regulation>.
24. <https://frontiermyanmar.net/en/central-bank-enacts-long-awaited-finance-regulations>.
25. World Bank. "Diagnostic Trade Integration Study: Opening for Business", 2016.
26. <https://www.mmbiztoday.com/articles/maccs-border-trade-system-launch-myawaddy-gate-next-year>.
27. <http://www.myanmarinsider.com/government-agencies-and-the-private-sector-to-be-devised/>.
28. Negative list refers to items requiring export/import licences.
29. <https://www.whitecase.com/publications/alert/us-terminates-burma-sanctions-program-accompanied-limited-fincen-relief>.
30. <https://ustr.gov/countries-regions/southeast-asia-pacific/Burma>.
31. For instance <https://www.ft.com/content/f7bda5bc-e150-11e6-8405-9e5580d6e5fb> and <https://www.wsj.com/articles/suu-kyis-myanmar-problem-wheres-the-economy-1501752602>.
32. <https://www.mmtimes.com/news/myanmar-companies-act-approved.html>.
33. A famous tycoon in Myanmar urges the government to focus on the economy. See <https://www.reuters.com/article/us-myanmar-investment/myanmar-tycoon-says-economy-neglected-by-suu-kyis-government-idUSKBN19R28V>.
34. <http://www.statecounsellor.gov.mm/en/node/798>.
35. International Republican Institute (IRI), "Survey of Burma/Myanmar Public Opinion Survey", Center for Insights in Survey Research, April 2017.
36. World Bank, *Myanmar Economic Monitor: Capitalizing on Investment Opportunities*, October 2017.

MYANMAR IN 2017: Crises of Ethnic Pluralism Set Transitions Back

Mary P. Callahan

The challenges of ethnic pluralism dominated Myanmar's landscape in 2017, with the long-simmering discord in Rakhine State escalating to large-scale violence and an unprecedented exodus of refugees, just as the government's peace negotiations with ethnic armed groups ground to a standstill. Entering her second year in office, State Counsellor, National League for Democracy (NLD) leader and Nobel Peace Prize laureate Aung San Suu Kyi promised to rule "Together With the People" for development, peace and reconciliation.[1] As the year wore on, she faced widespread international criticism for how she and the Defence Services managed the evolving Rakhine State crisis, while domestic popular support grew around the Rohingya issue and regional allies — especially China — rallied behind the military and the State Counsellor. It was a retrograde year for the history books. The feel-good narrative about Myanmar's remarkable transitions was replaced with the kind of denunciations by UN officials and others of "ethnic cleansing" and "crimes against humanity" reminiscent of military rule from 1988 to 2011.

First Anniversary Woes

Late March marked the NLD's one-year anniversary of the historic and peaceful transfer of power from one political party to another — the first since independence from Britain in 1948. For all its flaws, the 2008 constitution established a degree of predictability and a structure of government largely accepted in principle by

---

MARY P. CALLAHAN is associate professor in the Jackson School of International Studies at the University of Washington in Seattle, Washington.

both the army and the newly empowered democracy movement led by the NLD. Thanks to reforms begun in 2011, thousands of people have used their new political freedoms to vent frustrations, expose abuses and demand action.

By late March, grumbles of discontent were heard as observers noted the NLD had accomplished little more than a reduction in the number of ministries, but notably had made few policy moves in the direction of improving the economy, increasing jobs, offering crucial services, building infrastructure or resolving the violence that plagued the western and northeastern parts of the country. When the majority of the electorate voted for the NLD in 2015, it was likely a vote against the old dictatorship and in support of the democracy movement. However, it was also an expression of desire for material progress. Identifiable, concrete signs of improvement in everyday lives had not yet materialized by the anniversary-mark, nor through the rest of 2017.[2]

On 30 March, in a televised address on the state of the union, State Counsellor Aung San Suu Kyi reacted defensively: "I have said since the beginning that I would try my best", continuing, "if people think my best effort is not enough for them and if there are any other persons or organizations who can do better than us, we are ready to step back".[3] Domestic pressure aside, she was likely stung by a barrage of one-year anniversary criticisms coming from the West, particularly over her inability or unwillingness to intervene on behalf of Rohingya victims of clearance operations carried out by the military in Rakhine State.

The fact that the NLD won only nine out of nineteen seats in the 1 April by-election suggested to some observers that the party's popularity had declined, particularly in minority ethnic areas. However, it should be noted that the party only lost two seats it held before. Six of the seats the NLD did not win were in two conflict-affected townships in Shan State, where elections had not previously taken place for security reasons and where support for the Shan party was very strong. Elsewhere, the victory of U Aye Maung, leader of the Arakan National Party — the main Rakhine Buddhist political party — in a Pyithu Hluttaw seat brought to Naypyitaw an experienced, hard-line political operative who has promoted Rakhine nationalist views in the parliament and beyond.

Background to the Rakhine/Rohingya Crisis of 2017

Rakhine State has long been home to tensions between Buddhist and Muslim communities, and these pressures have periodically erupted into deadly violence.[4] At the heart of the tensions are three axes of deeply felt grievances. Along all three lie multifarious disputes over identity, land, historical narratives, and economic underdevelopment. On the first axis of tension, Buddhist Rakhine ethnic nationals have long felt mistreated by Bamar majority elites and state leaders. This sense of discrimination was stoked by Aung San Suu Kyi's decision in 2016 to place an NLD appointee in the Rakhine State Chief Minister post, despite the state-level legislative victory of combined Rakhine ethnic parties. A second axis of tension lies between Rakhine Buddhists and Muslims, but especially those Muslims who identify or are identified by the category, "Rohingya". Prior to the 2017 crisis, Buddhists probably constituted sixty per cent of the 3.3 million in Rakhine State, with Muslims making up about thirty-five per cent.[5] Rohingya have long been denied citizenship rights, and Rakhine–Rohingya communal violence — most recently in 2012 — has particularly scarred the communities of the three northwestern-most townships: Maungdaw, Rathedaung and Buthidaung. Finally, the third axis of tension is between Myanmar Buddhists generally and this same Rohingya community. For the vast majority of Myanmar people, there is no such thing as a "Rohingya", and this group of people are called "Bengali", to reflect the illegal-immigrant status widely associated with them.

The origins of the 2017 crisis date to 9 October 2016, when a group that identified itself as Harakah al-Yaqin ("The Faith Movement") launched synchronized attacks on three Border Guard Police garrisons in northern Rakhine State. Renaming itself in English as the Arakan Rohingya Salvation Army (ARSA) in March 2017, the militants claimed to stand on behalf of oppressed Rohingya.[6] Apparently led by its military commander on the ground, Ata Ullah, ARSA has repeatedly insisted it had no links to terrorist groups, and assured the safety of civilians from non-Muslim communities. In demands circulated on videos, its focus was on Rohingya civil and political rights. Likely taken to some degree by surprise, the military responded to those October attacks, and subsequent clashes in November, with disproportionate force. As a result of the violence and widely reported atrocities committed against civilians, upwards of seventy thousand Rohingya fled to camps in Bangladesh.

The UN Office of the High Commissioner on Human Rights on 3 February issued a highly condemnatory "flash report". Two weeks later came the report of an Aung San Suu Kyi–appointed investigation, led by Vice President Myint Swe, which found no evidence that the Defence Services committed any crimes against civilians.[7] In March 2017 the UN Human Rights Council in Geneva decided to establish an international Fact Finding Mission to investigate allegations of crimes against humanity by the military in northern Rakhine State and other human rights issues in the country.[8] Myanmar indicated that it would not cooperate with the investigation and still has not done so to date.[9] In a rare April 2017 televised interview, Aung San Suu Kyi denied "ethnic cleansing [was] going on. I think ethnic cleansing is too strong an expression to use for what is happening", although there was "a lot of hostility" present in Rakhine State. The State Counsellor said: "It is Muslims killing Muslims as well, if they think they are co-operating with the authorities."[10]

Subsequent to the post–October 2016 crackdown, the military did not manage to eradicate ARSA militants, who continued to recruit followers from rural villages throughout northern Rakhine State. They prepared new foot soldiers for later attacks by teaching them how to produce improvised explosive devices (IEDs), bring in other recruits, and act as cells in a small, but widening, anti-government movement.[11] In the lead up to the August 2017 attacks, dozens of Rohingya who served the government as village headmen, hundred-household heads, and possibly informers were killed, likely at the hands of ARSA, which wanted to raise the costs of collaborating with its enemy, the Myanmar military and state.[12]

The Kofi Annan Commission

Prior to the 2016 attacks and the military response, State Counsellor Aung San Suu Kyi had attempted to get in front of the Rohingya, Rakhine and citizenship issues when she appointed former UN Secretary General Kofi Annan to run an Advisory Commission on Rakhine State made up of domestic and international members. In March 2017, the commission, which had no mandate to investigate the violence that post-dated its formation, issued interim recommendations in Yangon, largely embraced by State Counsellor Aung San Suu Kyi's government. The final report, issued in Yangon by Kofi Annan himself on 24 August, expanded on the interim recommendations.[13] It recognized the formidable historical and political obstacles to improving conditions for all in Rakhine State, but still proposed, among other suggestions, a review of the 1982 Citizenship Law, which in implementation has denied not only citizenship to Rohingya but also basic human rights. The report also called for Rakhine-based Muslims to be granted freedom of movement and access to political rights, as well as social services, education and livelihood assistance.

Given the considerable legitimacy Kofi Annan brought to the process, Western capitals and human rights organizations largely aligned and continue to align with his commission's recommendations. State Counsellor Aung San Suu Kyi's response to the final Kofi Annan report was to welcome it and promise to set up a committee to implement the commission's proposals. A statement from her office on 25 August read, "We hope to set out a full roadmap for implementation in the coming weeks."[14] The military response to the Annan Commission report was less sanguine. A statement from the Commander-in-Chief's office cited "factual errors and unfair attitudes" in the report, defended the 1982 citizenship law and the way it has been implemented, and warned, "If Rakhine ethnics do not accept it [the report], it will face difficulty to solve the problems."[15]

The 2017 Crisis

Only hours after Kofi Annan publicly presented the final recommendations of his commission's report in Yangon, ARSA launched a second round of coordinated attacks, early on 25 August, against as many as thirty police posts and an army garrison in northern Rakhine State. Armed with *dah* (knife blades), farm tools, and rudimentary IEDs, the attackers were said to have killed twelve or more members of the security forces.[16] ARSA cells in villages across northern Rakhine were activated in the early hours that day, and messaged via WhatsApp to mobilize male villagers to join in the attacks. Hundreds of villagers responded to that call, only to be met with significant police and military firepower. According to the government, 371 attackers were killed.[17] The military once again unleashed a disproportionate campaign of violence, first against the villages that had sustained ARSA attacks, and then in areas adjacent and remote. Local Rakhine civilians were also armed to accompany or supplement soldiers. In at least some well-documented cases — such as the village of Tula Toli — civilians were attacked, women raped, men shot and homes systematically burned down.[18] Satellite footage confirms widespread burning; both Aung San Suu Kyi and the military claimed it all occurred at the hands of ARSA, while human rights groups who interviewed survivors blamed the military and Rakhine ethnonationalists. Attacks by the police and military or fear of such attacks, as well as threats and vigilante action by local Rakhine villagers, led to the flight of hundreds of thousands of Muslims from northern Rakhine to Bangladesh. UN and international non-governmental organizations (INGOs) were forced to withdraw assistance services from northern Rakhine State in early September. As time wore on, still more Rohingya ran away from areas distant from the violence out of fears for personal security and because of collateral damage to markets and social relations that prevented people from carrying on their lives.

The crisis represents not only the largest-ever violent displacement of the Rohingya but is also one of the fastest refugee exoduses in modern global history. It has also radically re-made the demographics of Rakhine State. More than eighty per cent of the Rohingya population of northern Rakhine State has now fled to

Bangladesh, and the exodus continues. Many of their villages were completely destroyed, and despite the 23 November conclusion of a Bangladesh–Myanmar memorandum of understanding for repatriation, prospects for the voluntary return of a majority of close to eight hundred thousand refugees in the short- or medium-term appears extremely low.[19]

Several international reports suggest atrocities and abuses were widespread. For example, the Office of the UN High Commissioner for Human Rights released its 11 October report from its "rapid response mission" (13–24 September) to Cox's Bazar, Bangladesh. It found that the Myanmar military armed Rakhine Buddhist groups who carried out "the destruction of Rohingya villages in northern Rakhine State, and other serious human rights violations committed in the aftermath of the 25 August attacks … in a well-organised, coordinated, and systematic manner".[20] Amnesty International issued a report on 18 October titled " 'My World Is Finished': Rohingya Targeted in Crimes against Humanity in Myanmar". The report states that "the military has carried out a campaign of violence that has been systematic, organized, and ruthless", which it says amounts to crimes against humanity under the Rome Statute of the International Criminal Court.[21] U Zaw Htay, spokesman for the government, used his Facebook platform to deny all such charges and instead claimed that Myanmar was the victim of a "fake news" campaign.

As it has with most challenges it faces, the Suu Kyi–led government responded by appointing deliberative bodies to initiate top-down changes. On 9 October, via the President, the Committee for the Implementation of the Recommendations on Rakhine State was appointed and chaired by the Minister for Social Welfare. Its remit is to implement the recommendations of both the Kofi Annan–led Advisory Commission and the domestic Maungdaw Region Investigation Commission, which the prior year had probed into the military's response to the 9 October 2016 ARSA attacks. In her 12 October speech to the nation about the Rakhine Crisis, Suu Kyi announced the formation of the Union Enterprise for Humanitarian Assistance, Resettlement, and Development in Rakhine (UEHRD).[22] An amorphous "public-private partnership", this committee is chaired by Aung San Suu Kyi, the vice-chair is the Minister for Social Welfare, and the Chief Coordinator of the UEHRD is Myanmar university professor Aung Tun Thet. The UEHRD is intended to coordinate and implement humanitarian, resettlement, and development activities in Rakhine State. Funds of about US$14 million have been solicited from the local private sector, but it is unlikely that any Western government donor or multilateral organization will contribute. These actions come up significantly short of what will likely require a massive logistical repatriation operation costing in the hundreds of millions of dollars.

International Reactions to the Rakhine Crisis

Reactions from regional allies such as China and India have been supportive of Myanmar's sovereign claims to protect itself, while the United Nations and Western nations have been defensive and critical. Defensive, because only days after the ARSA attacks, the State Counsellor's Office issued a statement alleging that INGO staff may have been collaborating with ARSA and reiterated a claim that World Food Programme (WFP) supplies had been diverted to ARSA.[23] Other accusations of ARSA support ensued. The claims were condemned by the U.S. ambassador to Myanmar as "absurd" and by the UN High Commissioner for Human Rights as "irresponsible", and who went on to say that "unsupported allegations against international aid organizations place their staff in danger and may make it impossible for them to deliver essential aid".[24] Subsequent statements and developments suggest Myanmar's 2017 rift with the United Nations will not mend anytime soon.

After the crisis began, UN Secretary-General António Guterres repeatedly expressed his concern over the plight of Rohingya Muslims in Rakhine.[25] He took the unusual step of writing to the UN Security Council on this issue in September. In remarks to the media, he called what was taking place in Myanmar "ethnic cleansing".[26] For the first time in nine years, the Security Council — which includes China and Russia — agreed upon a statement on Myanmar; it "expressed concern about reports of excessive violence during the security operations and called for immediate steps to end the violence in Rakhine, de-escalate the situation, re-establish law and order, ensure the protection of civilians".[27] The UN Fact Finding mission presented its first oral update to the UN Human Rights Council in Geneva in mid-September, warning that Rohingya had faced "major atrocities" and had been the subject of "dehumanizing propaganda" and noting "reports of landmines being planted on the border with Bangladesh that are maiming and killing those trying to escape the violence, including children".[28]

As UN–Myanmar relations continued to deteriorate, State Counsellor Daw Aung San Suu Kyi withdrew from her trip to New York for the UN General Assembly, which she was due to address on 20 September; Vice-President-2 Henry Van Thio spoke instead. On 19 September, in lieu of her General Assembly speech, the State Counsellor delivered a televised, English-language speech to the international diplomatic corps in Naypyitaw.[29] She condemned all human rights violations and expressed concern for the suffering of all those caught up in the conflict, but the speech did not convey a sense of urgency, nor did it contain any indication that the government understood the seriousness of the moment.

The UN Security Council met both informally and formally in open session on the Rakhine crisis throughout late 2017 and, on 6 November, adopted a Presidential Statement that demanded international humanitarian access to northern Rakhine; the Myanmar government condemned the statement as unhelpful.[30] The UN General Assembly's Third Committee adopted a resolution on 16 November requesting the Secretary-General to appoint a Special Envoy, although Suu Kyi's government may refuse to cooperate with any such appointment.[31]

Beyond the United Nations, on 19 September, the United Kingdom announced it was suspending training programmes for the Myanmar military.[32] The following day the Defence Services issued a statement indicating that the UK had required the five officer trainees from Myanmar currently attending courses there to return home, and that Myanmar would never again send trainees to the UK.[33] On 16 October, the EU Council of Foreign Ministers decided at its meeting to suspend visits of Myanmar military officers to Europe, to review all defence cooperation, and hinted at the possibility of more formal sanctions in the future.[34] On 23 October, Prime Minister of Canada Justin Trudeau appointed a Special Envoy to Myanmar, Bob Rae, former Premier of Ontario, tasked with "engaging in diplomatic efforts to address the crisis".[35] On 15 November, U.S. Secretary of State Rex Tillerson visited Myanmar, where he requested an independent investigation into "credible reports of widespread atrocities" and committed the United States to taking action against any individuals responsible. He said he did not think broad-based economic sanctions were advisable at this time: "We want Myanmar to succeed … I have a hard time seeing how [broad sanctions] help resolve this crisis [but] targeted sanctions on individuals very well may be appropriate."[36] Two bills were submitted to the U.S. Congress in November that reimpose precisely these targeted sanctions via the Specially Designated Nationals and Blocked Persons (SDN) List, as well as other conditions.[37]

In Myanmar, all these developments have been met with popular hostility. Interfaith rallies and demonstrations have been held in several cities to show support for Aung San Suu Kyi and to express dissatisfaction with international "interference". A November visit by Pope Francis drew crowds in the tens of thousands, but every word was scrutinized for any possible usage of the word, "Rohingya", which he studiously avoided in his messages of peace, reconciliation and tolerance.

Buddhist Nationalism

With deep roots in Myanmar's political history, Buddhist nationalism in Myanmar has become noticeably more prominent, demanding and popular in recent years.

The lifting of military junta controls on free expression and assembly led to populist mobilization of hard-core and deeply felt grievances about Buddhism being under siege from the forces of modernity, globalism and Islam. Myanmar's rapid uptake of cellular phones enabled proponents of a new and virulent Islamophobia to fill social media with nationalist hate-speech-laden narratives. A wave of anti-Muslim violence swept across the country, beginning in Rakhine State in 2012 then spreading across the country the following year.

Rakhine State, with its internal divisions, is a natural breeding ground for anti-Islamic feelings, but also because it is home to a long-held national myth that underlies fears that Buddhism and Buddhists have been at risk of being overrun. The myth of the "western gate" portrays the Bangladesh border as the last line of defence protecting the pure, Theravadda Buddhism of Myanmar. If the gate breaks, the tens of millions of Muslims from Bengal will overrun not only Myanmar but also mainland Southeast Asia, much as is narrated to have occurred centuries ago in island Southeast Asia. Since the transition in 2011, nationalist Buddhist forces have been at times highly organized (e.g., in the 969 and later Ma Ba Tha movements, meetings and rallies) and at other times relied upon social media for the spread of popular nationalist monks' sermons and to stoke fears and hatred of Muslims.[38]

Hence, the attacks by ARSA tapped into the deep-seated fears of nearly all Myanmar Buddhists. In the national mythology, the attacks constituted a breach of the "western gate", resulting in widespread rallying around the military and the government for their defence of the nation and religion. The publication of anti-Rohingya hate speech in state media and social media expanded after the attacks, as did sermonizing by prominent Buddhist monks. As the crisis grew in Rakhine State, anti-Muslim sentiment heightened and spread. The crisis and the intense international criticism that resulted has boosted not only Ma Ba Tha but also a xenophobic nationalism more broadly conceived.[39]

A poignant example came on 30 October, when perhaps the most revered Myanmar monk, Sitagu Sayadaw, delivered a sermon to military officers at a training college in Kayin State. In it he preached unity between the military and monkhood. He then recounted a fifth-century fable from Sri Lanka commonly used in Myanmar to justify the use of violence in defence of the faith. Killing non-Buddhists, the tale suggests, is justified, as the latter are not "fully human". No guilt is to be borne for killing such people, thus there is a religious justification for the mass killing of non-Buddhists. "Our soldiers should bear that in mind and should serve in the military, I would urge", he said.[40] The sermon was live-streamed on the Internet and clips of this particular section went viral on social media.

Deterioration in the Peace Process

Over 2017, the government-led peace process in relation to ethnic armed groups continued to deteriorate, with no obvious progress in the formal negotiations and a realignment of armed organizations that gives formerly excluded groups along the northern border with China ultimate sway over whether any progress will unfold.[41]

The formal process is anchored around the Nationwide Ceasefire Agreement (NCA) signed on 15 October 2015 by the government, army and eight ethnic armed organizations. It provides for a union-level peace conference (UPC, branded by Aung San Suu Kyi as the "Panglong-21st Century Peace Conference") to be held every six months. The opening conference was held in August 2016; the next one was not held until 24–29 May 2017 and the UPC scheduled for late 2017 has been pushed back into 2018. The delays have been due to planning and communication challenges as well as declining faith in the process on the part of ethnic armed organization (EAO) signatories and non-signatories to the NCA, and probably the Defence Services. Several working groups around different sectors were established as part of the political dialogue and seven subnational dialogues were held, but throughout 2017 there has been no clear vision for connecting these to follow-on steps in the formal process.

What has emerged in recent years is the polarization in conflict dynamics roughly between signatories, mostly located in the southeast, and the non-signatories, particularly those located in the northeast. In the southeast, many armed groups signed the NCA in 2015 and few violent clashes have occurred since. There, the two non-signatory groups — the Karenni National Progressive Party and the New Mon State Party — indicated in 2017 a willingness to sign the NCA, pending certain conditions. But their willingness was less a sign of the vitality of the peace process or a vote of confidence therein, but rather recognition of the strategic reality that small armed groups have no real alternative to the NCA.

However, even among signatories, frustration and anger mounted throughout 2017 as they perceived that the government and the army delayed significant progress in developing a proper peace agreement out of the NCA. In particular, NCA groups in Rakhine and Shan State were denied permission to hold the subnational dialogues — part of the Panglong process — in their chosen areas.[42] For example, in the lead-up to the May UPC, requests by the Committee for Shan Unity (CSSU) to hold a Shan dialogue in Taunggyi or Panglong towns were rejected, likely by the army. A subsequent attempt at a Shan dialogue in Chiangmai, Thailand was blocked when the Myanmar embassy in Thailand asked the Thai government to withhold permission. Said General Yawd Serk of the signatory, the Restoration Council of Shan State: "They (Myanmar authorities) might not want peace because what we have been doing is to promote unity among the ethnic groups which is actually helping the Myanmar government. We talk with groups that the Myanmar government does not have access to and are talking to encourage all groups to sign the NCA."[43]

Among non-signatories in the southeast, the NCA lost traction with NCA-sympathetic groups when — without any authorization from armed groups — Aung San Suu Kyi's spokesman announced immediately after her March State of the Union address that five EAOs would sign the NCA. These armed groups and their constituencies, which of all non-signatories were most committed to the NCA as the vehicle for moving peace negotiations forward, had not been informed such an announcement was to be made and were angry that they were being manipulated. None have subsequently signed.[44]

Northern Dimensions of the Conflict

In the north and northeast, by contrast, the civil wars continued unabated throughout 2017. Fighting along the China border escalated considerably in 2016, with attacks by EAOs on government-held towns and military offensives against key EAO bases through 2017. The most dramatic escalation occurred in northeastern Shan State on 6 March when at least thirty people were killed after MNDAA (Myanmar National Democratic Alliance Army) troops — some dressed in police uniforms — launched a surprise attack against police and military posts in Kokang.[45] Although the Defence Services declared the territory recaptured a couple of weeks later, this outbreak represented the worst violence in Kokang region since dozens died in the 2015 fighting that led to thousands fleeing into China.[46]

In conflict areas of Kachin State and northern Shan State, civilian populations found themselves at risk as the warfare continued. In one prominent case, the Defence Services arrested two Kachin pastors, Nawng Latt and Gam Seng, on Christmas Eve 2016 in Mong Ko, northern Shan State. The Ministry of Defence accused them of acting as "financial-supporter, informer, recruiter, [and] rumor-monger" for ethnic armed group offensives in November and December.[47] News reports suggest the two men had helped journalists to report on the conflict in Mong Ko and Muse, sites of heavy fighting between the Burma Army and an alliance of northern Shan State–based armed anti-state groups. In October 2017, the pastors were sentenced to multi-year prison terms, having been found guilty of all charges brought against them, including under the "unlawful association act".[48]

Just as the most significant fighting has occurred in the north and northeast, it is from therein that the strongest, most important new negotiating force has emerged. The largest armed group, the United Wa State Party, convened two summits of EAO leaders in February and April 2017. Participants included Wa, the Mongla Group and the Shan State Army-North, along with the Northern Alliance, which had been formed in November 2016 and included four armed groups from Shan State. These were the Ta'ang National Liberation Army, Myanmar National Democratic Alliance Army, Arakan Army and Kachin Independence Army. Notably, although the Northern Alliance groups have been involved at times in intense attacks, no fighting has occurred with the Wa and Mongla groups, whose bilateral ceasefires have broadly held since 1989 and were reaffirmed in 2011. The Wa-sponsored summits rejected the Nationwide Ceasefire Agreement (NCA) framework, calling for a new approach and for all negotiations to be held collectively with the seven armed groups, with the latter represented by a new political body called the Federal Political Negotiation and Consultative Committee (FPNCC).[49] The government has rejected demands for multilateral negotiations.

The Union Peace Conference

In late April, as the May UPC drew near, its potential looked grim. The United Nationalities Federal Council, the largest group of non-signatories, which still included the Kachin Independence Organisation, saw little value in participating in the peace conference, having been offered only observation spots. The UNFC ultimately did not attend. Even among signatories, there was fractiousness, as the RCSS (Restoration Council of Shan State) announced it would not sign anything, given the government's and army's blockage of its CSSS dialogue. Only at the last minute did the UPC result in any identifiable breakthrough, in terms of attendance, and that came through the last minute, high-wire intervention of China's special envoy, Sun Guoxiang. Sun coaxed the army and government to allow all seven members of the FPNCC — including three never before permitted by the military in the negotiations — to participate as a unit, to receive protection from legal redress, and to be considered "specially invited guests" who could submit papers. On the day before the UPC opened, FPNCC leaders agreed and boarded a Chinese government aircraft and flew to Naypyitaw.[50] The breakthrough, while symbolic, held little import for the conduct of the UPC. FPNCC representatives attended the lavish opening ceremony and dinner, but were banned from taking part in the plenary or breakout sessions over the next few days. They flew back to Kunming two days before the UPC ended.

The UPC was organized around forty-one "principles", said to have been submitted out of the seven subnational dialogues held around the country and compiled by working committees of the Union Peace Dialogue Joint Committee (UPDJC), which is chaired by Aung San Suu Kyi and made up of representation from government, legislature, military, political parties and armed groups. At the opening session, State Counsellor and UPDJC Chair Suu Kyi promised that "peace and stability will enable our nation to realise its potential as a strong, prosperous democratic federal Union" as the necessary "resolution to our country's long-running armed conflicts".[51] On the final day, the UPC agreed in the plenary session on an undebated set of thirty-seven "principles" for a future peace agreement. The latter is said to provide for the state to be a federal democracy.

Yet UPC debates ran far from smoothly.[52] The government and army countered demands for self-determination and the possibility for states to have their own constitutions with the requirement that they reject any possibility of secession. As the International Crisis Group notes, "This failure to achieve what should have been an acceptable compromise — state constitutions are a longstanding demand of ethnic communities and no group wishes to secede — highlighted deficiencies in the process and lack of trust."[53] Furthermore, the principles that were agreed were pushed through the plenary without discussion.

International Relations

Peace process and Rakhine State developments in 2017 suggest that there has been a major shift in the role of outside actors in Myanmar. Formerly, the peace process was a domestically driven effort, albeit with physical plant, travel, capacity building and other activities funded by Western governments, the European Union and Japan. From 2011 to 2015, many Western INGOs played a prominent role supporting both the government and the anti-state groups in preparations for negotiations. The Western/Japanese-funded nature of the peace process had long alarmed China, as did the escalation of fighting along the China border in 2016–17. That all this was unfolding at a time when the government of President Thein Sein was very actively courting Western approval and attention further troubled China.

Things have since changed. The government of Aung San Suu Kyi enjoys what appears to be an ever-friendlier relationship with Beijing and to some degree has distanced itself from Western/Japanese funding and INGOs. Beyond China's growing influence in the peace process, by virtue of its relationship with the now-powerful FPNCC groups, Western criticism of both the military and Aung San Suu Kyi have been accompanied by renewed Chinese commitment to both. Commander-in-Chief Min Aung Hlaing was met with an honour guard reception upon his arrival in Beijing in November 2017.[54] Aung San Suu Kyi travelled to China for a "working visit" a week later, her second of the year.[55] At the same time, Myanmar and China have started negotiations at the highest levels on the Belt and Road Initiative and potentially related infrastructure projects, as China's stated aim is to radically upgrade connectivity across Myanmar from Yunnan to the Bay of Bengal. China's envoy Sun Guoxiang and Foreign Minister Wang Yi have shuttled between Naypyitaw, Kunming and Bangladesh to meet government and armed organizations on matters related to the peace process and the Rakhine crisis. Where these negotiations lead will likely have a major impact on the future of Union peace conferences or a peaceful solution to the situation in Rakhine State.

Domestic Politics

Politically dominant after its landslide election in 2015, the National League for Democracy suffered a serious blow on 29 January when U Ko Ni, senior NLD constitutional lawyer and advisor to Aung San Suu Kyi, was assassinated outside Yangon International Airport. One of the most high-profile Muslim voices in the country, U Ko Ni had just arrived back from an experience tour to Indonesia with a cross-section of senior Buddhist and Muslim figures involved in Rakhine State affairs. The trip was aimed at learning about overcoming inter-religious tensions. Two were arrested, but the alleged mastermind remains at large in a killing that — as the International Crisis Group concluded — had "all the appearances of a hate crime".[56]

Elsewhere, beyond the NLD, other political figures and parties have their eyes trained on 2020, for the next general elections. In March 2017, 88 Generation leader U Ko Ko Gyi held a two-day seminar that brought together many intellectual, media and civil society leaders to discuss a wide range of political, economic and social affairs. The intent appeared to be to prepare for the launching of an alternative democratic political party, the "Four Eights Party", which was registered in December.[57] Among ethnic nationality parties, which fared poorly in 2015 in large part because they could not unify ethnic loyalty around single parties, there are moves afoot to remedy that problem with mergers of active parties. In June, after five years of trying to do so, two Chin State–based parties — the Chin National Democratic Party and the Chin Progressive Party — agreed to merge.[58] In November, the All Mon Region Democracy Party (AMDP) and the Mon National Party (MNP) took early steps towards a possible merger.[59] Although a proper merger between the Shan Nationalities Democratic Party (SNDP) and the Shan Nationalities League for Democracy (SNLD) made little progress, the two agreed on discussing the 2020 elections at a convening of the Committee for Shan State Unity (CSSU) — a coalition of the SNDP, SNLD, Shan ethnic armed organizations (EAOs), civil society groups and women and youth organizations.[60] In a countercurrent, the only successful 2015 merger, which brought together the Arakan League for Democracy and the Rakhine National Democratic Party to combine forces in the Arakan National Party, frayed in 2017. On 8 January 2017, former leaders of the ALD declared their departure from the ANP to re-register with the Union Election Commission.[61] While the ANP held on, the ramifications of the resignation of U Aye Maung, its leader, on 27 November remain unknown.[62]

Finally, 2017 has seen continued tension between the government and the military, on the one hand, and the media, on the other. Periodic protests have erupted against continued use of Section 66(d) of the 2013 Telecommunications Law for criminal prosecutions of individuals for peaceful communications on Facebook. It is widely seen to have been used to stifle criticism of the authorities. Parliament amended the law, which provides for up to three years in prison for "extorting, coercing, restraining wrongfully, defaming, disturbing, causing undue influence or threatening any person using a telecommunications network", in August 2017 in only a minor fashion, with the only significant change being the allowance of bail for those charged.[63] According to Human Rights Watch, at least seventy-one people are known to have been charged for online defamation under the law.[64]

The high profile arrests of eleven journalists have further raised concerns that the government is restricting rather than expanding the freedom of the press.[65] On 26 June, Ko Lawi Weng of *The Irrawaddy*, also known as Thein Zaw, and *DVB* reporters Ko Aye Naing and Ko Pyae Bone Aung were arrested for covering a Namhsam ceremony held by the TNLA marking International Day against Drug Abuse and Illicit Trafficking.[66] After facing possible five-year prison terms under the colonial-era Unlawful Associations Act, the court eventually dropped the charges against the three men on 15 September.[67] On 27 October, Myanmar police arrested two foreign journalists and two Burmese nationals after they flew a drone over the parliament building in Naypyitaw.[68] The four — two of whom work for Turkish state media — were charged with the import and export of "restricted or banned goods" (the drone) without obtaining a licence, as well as offences under the 1934 Aircraft Law.[69] On 12 December, two Reuters journalists, Wa Lone and Kyaw Soe Oo, were arrested under the Official Secrets Act for possession of internal military documents related to the Rakhine conflict. The arrests prompted international condemnation, with the United States, the United Kingdom, European Parliament and the UN Secretary General demanding their release.[70]

Notes

1. "State Counsellor Daw Aung San Suu Kyi's Speech on the Occasion of the One Year Anniversary of the Government (30 March 2017)", *Global New Light of Myanmar*, 1 April 2017 <http://www.myanmargeneva.org/NLM%202017/04%20April%20 2017/1_April_17_gnlm.pdf>.
2. A 2017 public opinion poll commissioned by the International Republican Institute showed that sixty per cent of respondents considered that their "personal economic situation" had stayed the same or worsened over the previous twelve months. Center for Insights in Survey Research, "Survey of Burma/Myanmar Public Opinion, March 9–April 1, 2017", Yangon: International Republican Institute, 2017.
3. From Aung San Suu Kyi's 30 March State of the Union Address, quoted in Nyein Nyein, "State Counselor Pledges to Try Harder to Earn Public's Support and Trust", *The Irrawaddy*, 31 March 2013 <https://www.irrawaddy.com/news/burma/state-counselor-pledges-try-harder-earn-publics-support-trust.html>.
4. For background, see International Crisis Group, "Myanmar: The Politics of Rakhine State", Report 261/Asia (Brussels: International Crisis Group, 22 October 2014).
5. Republic of the Union of Myanmar, "The 2014 Population and Housing Census, The Union Report: Religion", vol. 2-C (Naypyitaw: Ministry of Labour, Immigration and Population, July 2016).
6. "Rohingya 'Army' Stresses Right to Self-Defence in First Statement", *Frontier*, 29 March 2017 <https://frontiermyanmar.net/en/rohingya-army-stresses-right-to-self-defence-in-first-statement>.
7. OHCHR, "Report of OHCHR Mission to Bangladesh: Interviews with Rohingyas Fleeing from Myanmar Since 9 October 2016, Flash Report", 3 February 2017 <http://www.ohchr.org/Documents/Countries/MM/FlashReport3Feb2017.pdf>; President's Office, "Investigation Commission Writing Full Report on Maungtaw", 20 February 2017 <http://www.president-office.gov.mm/en/?q=briefing-room/news/2017/02/20/id-7298>.
8. Office of the High Commissioner on Human Rights (OHCHR), "Human Rights Council Decides to Dispatch a Fact-Finding Mission to Myanmar to Establish Facts on Violations, Especially in Rakhine State", 24 March 2017 <http://www.ohchr.org/EN/NewsEvents/Pages/DisplayNews.aspx?NewsID=21443&LangID=E>.
9. Michael Peel, "Suu Kyi Rejects UN Probe into Myanmar Violence", *Financial Times*, 3 May 2017 <https://www.ft.com/content/a2c7c410-2fbc-11e7-9555-23ef563ecf9a>.
10. Fergal Keane, "Myanmar: Aung San Suu Kyi Exclusive Interview", BBC News, 5 April 2017 <https://www.youtube.com/watch?v=MFEEmdKbqBE&t=29s>.
11. Carlos Sardiña Galache, "Inside View of Myanmar's Rohingya Insurgency", *Asia Times*, 31 October 2017 <http://www.atimes.com/article/inside-view-myanmars-rohingya-insurgency/>.
12. International Crisis Group, "Myanmar's Rohingya Crisis Enters a Dangerous New

Phase", Report 292/Asia (Brussels: International Crisis Group, 7 December 2017), p. 2.

13. Advisory Commission on Rakhine State, "Interim Recommendations", March 2017 <http://www.rakhinecommission.org/app/uploads/2017/03/Advisory-Commission-Interim-Report.pdf>; Advisory Commission on Rakhine State, "Towards a Peaceful, Fair and Prosperous Future for the People of Rakhine: Final Report of the Advisory Commission on Rakhine State", August 2017 <http://www.kofiannanfoundation.org/mediation-and-crisis-resolution/rakhine-final-report/>.
14. Republic of the Union of Myanmar, Office of the State Counsellor, "Statement by the Office of the State Counsellor on the Final Report of the Advisory Commission on Rakhine State", 24 August 2017, published in the *Global New Light of Myanmar*, 25 August 2017 <http://www.myanmargeneva.org/NLM%202017/08%20August%202017/25_Aug_17_gnlm.pdf>.
15. A report on the 24 August 2017 meeting between Kofi Annan and Commander in Chief, Senior General Min Aung Hlaing is carried in "In Accord with Myanmar Saying, 'Make a Record Durable and Reliable' Written Records are More Profound and Must be Correct and Flaw-Free", *Myawaddy*, 24 August 2017 <http://www.myawady.net.mm/index.php/news/headline/item/2057-in-accord-with-myanmar-saying-"make-a-record-durable-and-reliable"-written-records-are-more-profound-and-must-be-correct-and-flaw-free>.
16. Wa Lone and Shoon Naing, "At Least 71 Killed in Myanmar as Rohingya Insurgents Stage Major Attack", Reuters, 25 August 2017 <https://www.reuters.com/article/us-myanmar-rohingya/at-least-71-killed-in-myanmar-as-rohingya-insurgents-stage-major-attack-idUSKCN1B507K>.
17. "Humanitarian Aid Provided to Displaced People without Discrimination", *Global New Light of Myanmar*, 6 September 2017, p. 7.
18. Amnesty International, " 'My World is Finished': Rohingya Targeted in Crimes against Humanity in Myanmar" (London: Amnesty International, 2017). Other sources have presented compelling evidence in support of Amnesty's findings about the victimization of Tula Toli's residents, such as Oliver Slow, "The Destruction of Tula Toli", *Frontier*, 30 November 2017 <https://frontiermyanmar.net/en/the-destruction-of-tula-toli>.
19. David Scott Mathieson, "Rohingya Repatriation Risky Business for Myanmar", *Asia Times*, 19 October 2017 <http://www.atimes.com/article/rohingya-repatriation-risky-business-myanmar/>.
20. UNOHCHR, "Mission Report of OHCHR Rapid Response Mission to Cox's Bazar, Bangladesh, 13–24 September 2017", Geneva, 11 October 2017 <http://www.ohchr.org/Documents/Countries/MM/CXBMissionSummaryFindingsOctober2017.pdf>.
21. Amnesty International, " 'My World' ", p. 6.
22. See the UEHRD website at <http://rakhine.unionenterprise.org>.
23. Office of the State Counsellor, Information Committee, "State Counsellor Office Information Committee's Statement Regarding Extremist Terrorists", 30 August

2017 <http://www.statecounsellor.gov.mm/scoicen/information-committee-news/state-counsellor-office-information-committees-statement-regarding>.

24. Both are quoted in Rik Glauert, "US Ambassador Rejects Govt Implication of Aid Agencies in Rakhine Attacks", *The Irrawaddy*, 31 August 2017 <https://www.irrawaddy.com/news/burma/us-ambassador-rejects-govt-implication-of-aid-agencies-in-rakhine-attacks.html>.
25. Office of the United Nations Secretary-General, "Statement Attributable to the Spokesman for the Secretary-General on Myanmar", 28 August 2017 <https://www.un.org/sg/en/content/sg/statement/2017-08-28/statement-attributable-spokesman-secretary-general-myanmar>.
26. Reuters Staff, "U.N.'s Gutteres Calls on Myanmar to End Violence, Urges Aid", Reuters, 13 September 2017 <https://www.reuters.com/article/us-myanmar-rohingya-un/u-n-s-guterres-calls-on-myanmar-to-end-violence-urges-aid-idUSKCN1BO2AI>.
27. UN Security Council statement, quoted in Michelle Nichols, "U.N. Chief, Security Council Call on Myanmar to End Violence", Reuters, 13 September 2017 <https://www.reuters.com/article/us-myanmar-rohingya/u-n-chief-security-council-call-on-myanmar-to-end-violence-idUSKCN1BO0B1>.
28. Marzuki Darusman, "Statement by Mr. Marzuki Darusman, Chairperson of the Independent International Fact-Finding Mission on Myanmar", 19 September 2017 <http://www.ohchr.org/EN/NewsEvents/Pages/DisplayNews.aspx?NewsID=22099&LangID=E>.
29. Aung San Suu Kyi, "State Counsellor's Speech on Government's Efforts with Regard to National Reconciliation and Peace", *Global New Light of Myanmar*, 20 September 2017 <http://www.myanmargeneva.org/NLM%202017/09%20September%202017/NLM_170920.pdf>.
30. UN Security Council, "Security Council Presidential Statement Calls on Myanmar to End Excessive Military Force, Intercommunal Violence in Rakhine State", 8085th Meeting, SC/13055, 6 November 2017 <https://www.un.org/press/en/2017/sc13055.doc.htm>.
31. Michelle Nichols, "U.N. States Call for End to Myanmar Military Operations", Reuters, 16 November 2017 <https://www.reuters.com/article/us-myanmar-rohingya-rights/u-n-states-call-for-end-to-myanmar-military-operations-idUSKBN1DG0FQ>.
32. "UK Suspends Aid for Myanmar Military", BBC News, 19 September 2017 <http://www.bbc.com/news/uk-41326179>.
33. "Tatmadaw: 'We Will Never Again Send Trainees to Britain'", *Global New Light of Myanmar*, 20 September 2017 <http://www.myanmargeneva.org/NLM%202017/09%20September%202017/NLM_170921.pdf>.
34. European Council, "Myanmar/Burma: Council Adopts Conclusions", press release, 16 October 2017 <https://www.consilium.europa.eu/en/press/press-releases/2017/10/16/myanmar-burma-conclusions/#>.
35. Office of the Prime Minister of Canada, "Prime Minister Appoints the Honourable Bob Rae as Special Envoy to Myanmar", 23 October 2017 <https://pm.gc.ca/

eng/news/2017/10/23/prime-minister-appoints-honourable-bob-rae-special-envoy-myanmar>.

36. Rex Tillerson, "Joint Press Availability with Burmese State Counsellor Aung San Suu Kyi", *FedWatch USA*, 15 November 2017 <http://www.fedwatchusa.com/?p=21650>.
37. The Senate bill is entitled, "The Burma Human Rights and Freedom Act of 2017", available online at <https://www.mccain.senate.gov/public/_cache/files/0af489c7-691c-40cd-b1f3-55a178ad614d/burma-human-rights-and-freedom-act-of-2017-11-2-17.pdf>. The House of Representatives bill is entitled, "Burma Unified through Rigorous Military Accountability Act (BURMA) of 2017", available online at <https://democrats-foreignaffairs.house.gov/sites/democrats.foreignaffairs.house.gov/files/Taiwan%20Leg.pdf>.
38. International Crisis Group, "Buddhism and State Power in Myanmar", Report No. 290 (Brussels: International Crisis Group, 5 September 2017) <https://www.crisisgroup.org/asia/south-east-asia/myanmar/290-buddhism-and-state-power-myanmar>.
39. Thant Myint-U, "Myanmar's Resurgent Nationalism Shapes New Political Landscape", *Nikkei Asian Review*, 5 October 2017 <https://asia.nikkei.com/Viewpoints/Thant-Myint-U/Myanmar-s-resurgent-nationalism-shapes-new-political-landscape>.
40. Mratt Kyaw Thu, "Tatmadaw, Sangha and Government Must Work Together, Sitagu Sayadaw Says in Sermon to Officers", *Frontier*, 1 November 2017 <https://frontiermyanmar.net/en/tatmadaw-sangha-and-government-must-work-together-sitagu-sayadaw-says-in-sermon-to-officers>.
41. For an overview of the process, see International Crisis Group, "Building Critical Mass for Peace in Myanmar", Asia Report No. 287 (Brussels: International Crisis Group, 29 June 2017).
42. Htet Naing Zaw, "National-Level Dialogue Delays Troubled Panglong Conference", *The Irrawaddy*, 1 November 2017 <https://www.irrawaddy.com/news/burma/national-level-dialogue-delays-troubled-panglong-conference.html>.
43. "CSSU Meeting in Chiang Mai during July 20–22 Cancelled following Myanmar Protest", Thai PBS, 22 July 2017 <http://englishnews.thaipbs.or.th/cssu-meeting-chiang-mai-july-20-22-cancelled-following-myanmar-protest/>.
44. For an analysis of the statement, see Sai Wansai, "UNFC and State Counselor Aung San Suu Kyi's Desperate Move", Shan Herald Agency for News, 2 April 2017 <http://english.panglong.org/2017/04/02/unfc-and-state-counselor-aung-san-suu-kyis-desperate-move/>.
45. "Deadly Clashes Hit Kokang in Myanmar's Shan State", Aljazeera, 7 March 2017 <http://www.aljazeera.com/news/2017/03/deadly-clashes-hit-kokang-myanmar-shan-state-170306143633608.html>.
46. "Tatmadaw Troops Occupy MNDAA's Outposts", *Global New Light of Myanmar*, 24 March 2017 <http://www.moi.gov.mm/moi:eng/?q=news/24/03/2017/id-10308>.
47. Ministry of Defence Statement, quoted in Lawi Weng and Rik Glauert, "Missing Kachin Pastors Confirmed Detained by Army", *The Irrawaddy*, 20 January 2017

<http://www.irrawaddy.com/news/burma/missing-kachin-pastors-confirmed-detained-by-burma-army.html>.

48. Ibid.; Ye Mon and Andrew D. Kaspar, "Two Kachin Pastors Given Lengthy Prison Terms for Role in Muse Conflict", Democratic Voice of Burma, 27 October 2017 <http://www.dvb.no/news/two-kachin-pastors-given-lengthy-prison-terms-role-muse-conflict/78081>.
49. See its website at <http://fpncc.org/fpncc/>.
50. Lun Min Mang, "Three More Rebel Groups to Join Union Peace Conference", *Myanmar Times*, 24 May 2017; ICG, "Building Critical Mass".
51. State Counsellor Daw Aung San Suu Kyi's speech at the Opening Ceremony of the Union Peace Conference – 21st Century Panglong 2nd Session, *Global New Light of Myanmar*, 25 May 2017, p. 4.
52. Nyan Hlaing Lynn and Oliver Slow, "Mixed Results at Latest Panglong Peace Conference", *Frontier*, 30 May 2017 <https://frontiermyanmar.net/en/mixed-results-at-latest-panglong-peace-conference>.
53. ICG, "Building Critical Mass", pp. i–ii.
54. Li Jiayao, "Senior Chinese Military Official Meets with Myanmar Guest", *China Military Online*, 23 November 2017 <http://eng.chinamil.com.cn/view/2017-11/23/content_7839949.htm>.
55. "State Counsellor in China for Working Visit", *Global New Light of Myanmar*, 1 December 2017, p. 1.
56. International Crisis Group, Myanmar Assassination Shows Urgent Need for Unity against Hate Crimes", 29 January 2017 <https://www.crisisgroup.org/asia/south-east-asia/myanmar/myanmar-assassination-shows-urgency-burmese-unity-against-hate-crimes>; see also Wai Moe, Mike Ives and Saw Nang, "Brazen Killing of Myanmar Lawyer Came after He Sparred with Military", *New York Times*, 2 February 2017 <https://www.nytimes.com/2017/02/02/world/asia/myanmar-ko-ni-lawyer-constitution-military.html?_r=0>.
57. Nyein Zaw Lin and Chan Wai Soe, "Activists Meet to Establish Political Party", *Eleven Media*, 31 March 2017 <http://elevenmyanmar.com/politics/8575>; Chan Thar, "88 Generation to Register New Four Eights Party by Year End", *Myanmar Times*, 18 December 2017 <https://www.mmtimes.com/news/88-generation-register-new-four-eights-party-year-end.html>.
58. "Two Chin Parties Agree to Merger", *Democratic Voice of Burma*, 16 June 2017 <http://www.dvb.no/news/two-chin-political-parties-agree-merger/76084>.
59. "Two Mon Parties Agree to Continue Talks about Merging", *Mon News*, 10 November 2017 <http://monnews.org/2017/11/13/two-mon-parties-agree-to-continue-talks-about-merging/>.
60. Nyein Nyein, "Political Outfit Appeals for Unified Shan State Party", *The Irrawaddy*, 30 October 2017 <https://www.irrawaddy.com/news/burma/political-outfit-appeals-unified-shan-state-party.html>.

61. Ye Mon, "Eyeing 2020 Comeback, Rakhine's ALD Party Regroups", *Myanmar Times*, 10 January 2017 <https://www.mmtimes.com/national-news/24472-former-ald-prepares-to-restart-the-party.html>.
62. "ANP Leadership Will Meet to Discuss Resignation of Party Chair Aye Maung", *Democratic Voice of Burma*, 30 November 2017 <http://www.dvb.no/news/anp-leadership-will-meet-discuss-resignation-party-chair-aye-maung/78661>.
63. Shoon Naing, Yimou Lee, "Myanmar Retains Tough Clause in Communications Law Despite Call for Repeal", Reuters, 18 August 2017 <https://www.reuters.com/article/us-myanmar-media/myanmar-retains-tough-clause-in-communications-law-despite-calls-for-repeal-idUSKCN1AY13J>.
64. Human Rights Watch, "Burma: Repeal Section 66(d) of the 2013 Telecommunications Law, Joint Statement by 61 Human Rights Organizations", 29 June 2017 <https://www.hrw.org/news/2017/06/29/burma-repeal-section-66d-2013-telecommunications-law>.
65. San Yamin Aung, "Timeline: Journalists under Attack", *The Irrawaddy*, 15 December 2017 <https://www.irrawaddy.com/news/burma/timeline-journalists-attack.html>.
66. Nyan Hlaing Lynn, "Journalists Arrested in Shan State to Face Unlawful Association Charges", *Frontier*, 28 June 2017 <https://frontiermyanmar.net/en/journalists-arrested-in-shan-state-to-face-unlawful-association-charges>.
67. Saw Yamin Aung, "Court Drops Charges against Three Journalists", *The Irrawaddy*, 15 September 2017 <https://www.irrawaddy.com/news/burma/court-drops-charges-three-journalists.html>.
68. "Foreign Journalists Charged after Flying Drone near Myanmar's Parliament", *The Guardian*, 29 October 2017 <https://www.theguardian.com/world/2017/oct/29/myanamar-foreign-journalists-charged-flying-drone-parliament>.
69. Htet Aung Khant, "Journalists Charged for Bringing Drone into Myanmar", VOA News, 16 November 2017 <https://www.voanews.com/a/journalists-charged-drone-myanmar/4119218.html>.
70. Reuters Staff, "Factbox: International Reaction to Arrest of Reuters Reporters in Myanmar", Reuters, 17 December 2017 <https://www.reuters.com/article/us-myanmar-journalists-factbox/factbox-international-reaction-to-arrest-of-reuters-reporters-in-myanmar-idUSKBN1EB0NX>.

Philippines

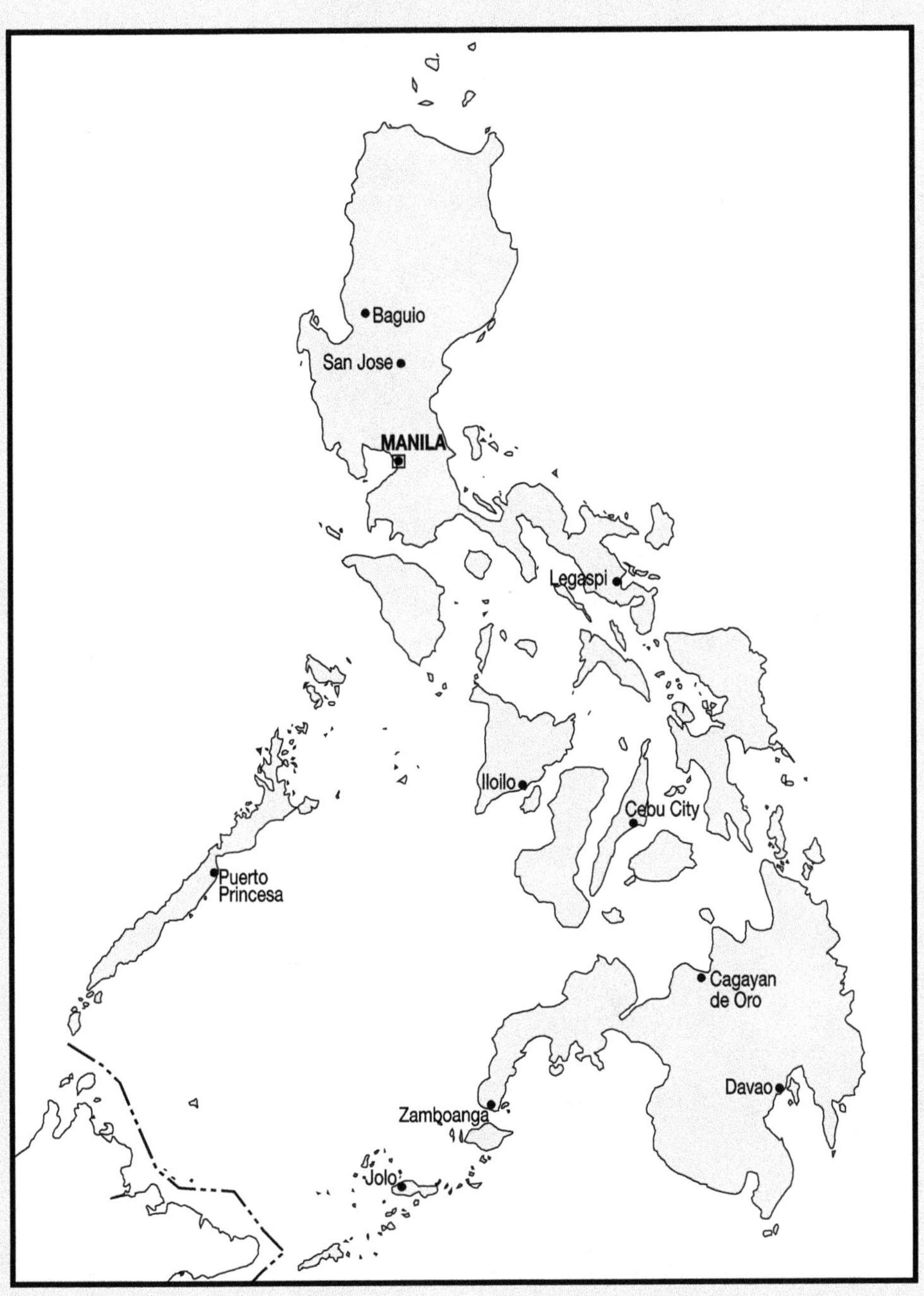

THE PHILIPPINES IN 2017: Turbulent Consolidation

Malcolm Cook

At the end of 2017, President Rodrigo Duterte and his administration finished in a stronger position than at the beginning of the year, as did the Philippine economy. This was the case despite 2017 being a turbulent year, even by Philippine standards.

Marawi City, the largest city in Muslim Mindanao, was taken over for months by a coalition of ISIS-inspired local and regional terrorists. A fifth of the country ended the year under martial law, while the rest of the country remained under an indefinite state of emergency declared in September 2016. The Philippine National Police were twice removed from the crusade-like war on drugs, due to gruesome deaths of apparently innocent foreigners and children, and then reinstated. The Philippine government suspended peace talks with the communist insurgents, started them again, then suspended them again and reclassified the Communist Party of the Philippines and its armed wing, the New People's Army, as terrorist groups. Congress' Commission on Appointments knocked back the largest number of cabinet appointments made by any president (five). According to President Duterte, China threatened war if the Philippines exercised its maritime rights in the West Philippine Sea.[1]

In *Southeast Asian Affairs 2017*, Aries A. Arugay from the University of the Philippines analysed the socio-political reasons for President Duterte's surprise "outsider" victory in the May 2016 presidential elections.[2] His victory was truly a populist watershed moment in the country's post-Marcos democratic development. Joseph Franco from the S. Rajaratnam School of International Studies in Singapore and a former Philippine soldier deployed to Mindanao dissected President Duterte's

---

Malcolm Cook is Senior Fellow at the ISEAS – Yusof Ishak Institute, Singapore. He formerly taught at the Ateneo De Manila University in the Philippines.

new and often contradictory approach to the insurgency in Muslim Mindanao and the terrorist groups it continues to spawn.[3]

Building on these two chapters, this year's Philippine country overview contends that 2017 was a year of political consolidation for President Duterte and his administration. The year saw much of the potential for change and a new style of government promised by President Duterte's May 2016 victory, for good and bad, be turned into political reality. The chapter begins by looking at developments in national politics and how the president's political position strengthened and his prerogative was wielded over the year. Second, it briefly covers worrying developments in the three main internal security concerns: the president's national war on drugs, the entrenched nationwide communist insurgency, and the insurgency in Muslim Mindanao and its terrorist dimensions. Then, it looks at the uncertain development of an "independent" foreign policy, with particular attention given to Philippine relations with China, Japan and the United States. The final section looks at the country's robust economic performance and major economic reform success and their political benefits.

National Politics

President Duterte is unique in Philippine presidential history. He is the first president from Mindanao (the most distant part of the country from Metro Manila) and the first president to come to the office directly from a local government position (mayor of Davao City). Befitting this unique background in local politics far from the national political elite in Metro Manila, President Duterte has adopted a particularly mayoral approach to the presidency.[4] This approach, echoing Donald Trump's approach to the presidency in the United States of America, rails against any constraint, even if legal or constitutional, to his personal political prerogative.

This intensely personal, brusque and often confrontational approach to the highest political office has been well received by a large majority of the electorate. According to the well-respected Social Weather Stations' quarterly polls on trust and support for the president, President Duterte entered office with the highest level of trust, finished his first year with the highest rating and maintained the highest ratings over the first quarter of his single six-year term of any president polled. In December 2017, eighteen months into his iconoclastic and bloody term in office, 71 per cent of adults polled were satisfied with the president, while only 13 per cent were not.

Belying the stereotypical views of populist outsider leaders, President Duterte's popularity is strongest among the most educated and the wealthiest, as well as those aged 25–44 years old, urban residents and males. His approval ratings are strongly positive across all sub-sections of the population. In the last poll of 2017, only one demographic sub-category expressed a presidential dissatisfaction rate above 20 per cent (18–24 year olds at 22 per cent) and one sub-category a satisfaction rate below 67 per cent (those in Luzon outside Metro Manila at 64 per cent).[5]

Aided by this strong and consistent presidential popularity and the fluid and ephemeral nature of Philippine party politics, the Duterte administration was able to enhance its historic super-majority in the House of Representatives and majority in the Senate.[6] After the May 2016 congressional elections, the Liberal Party (headed by President Aquino, Mar Roxas who had finished second to Duterte in the presidential election and Leni Robredo who won the vice-presidential election) was the largest party in the House of Representatives, with over a hundred members, and in the Senate. PDP-Laban, the party that Duterte ran under, had fewer than ten members in the House. Yet, at the beginning of 2017, these positions had switched, with the Liberal Party having only 32 members in the House of Representatives out of 296 sitting members. Only 5 of these Liberal Party members chose to join the "magnificent 7" members of the official opposition, while 27 remained with the PDP-Laban-led super majority.

By mid-year, the 5 of these 27 Liberal Party members had chosen to switch parties to PDP-Laban. Deputy Speaker Miro Quimbo, the highest-ranking Liberal Party member in the House and part of the PDP-Laban-led super-majority, rationalizes the choice of the large majority of his party mates to switch to PDP-Laban by noting that,

> Being part of the administration party protects their districts in a number of ways. First, you are able to get the national government's support for your district needs in terms of social and infrastructure programs. You feel a certain degree of certainty that being part of the administration party ensures that you are closer to the kitchen, so to speak.... This aspect of politics, we never really experience in Metro Manila because of the media's active role. But in the provinces, based on stories of my colleagues, the PNP (Philippine National Police), AFP (Armed Forces of the Philippines), and the Comelec (Commission on Elections) can make or break a candidate.[7]

Led by Speaker Pantaleon Alvarez in the House of Representatives and Senate President Koko Pimentel — both from PDP-Laban and from Mindanao — the Duterte administration strengthened its already dominant legislative position. Liberal Party senators who participated in the EDSA anniversary,[8] which was deemed an opposition rally by Duterte supporters, lost their sought-after positions on Senate committees, even though they were nominally part of the PDP-Laban-led Senate majority.[9] In the House of Representatives' deliberations on the 2018 budget, funding was stripped from projects supported by members of the opposition for their districts.[10] This funding is seen as vital for representatives' re-election chances.

The president and his supporters inside and outside government adopted a maximalist view of the presidential mandate in line with President Duterte's mayoral approach. Any criticism, real or deemed, was interpreted as an unjustified attack on the president and his mandate, which called for retribution. January began with Justice Secretary Vitaliano Aguirre II publicly musing that criticisms of President Duterte's lethal war on drugs were part of an opposition destabilization plot. The Director General of Philippine National Police, Ronaldo "Bato" de la Rosa, oversaw an investigation into whether such a far-fetched plot was real.[11]

On 30 January, the Executive Director of the Anti-Money Laundering Council, Attorney Julia Bacay-Abad, resigned after a number of foul-mouthed presidential tirades against the council.[12] Later, President Duterte would insinuate without evidence provided that Bacay-Abad was the mistress of Senator Antonio Trillanes IV, a fierce opposition critic of the president. Senator Trillanes rejected this slur as false.[13] In late May, President Duterte fired the chairperson of the Dangerous Drugs Board after he cited Dangerous Drugs Board figures on drug addiction in the Philippines that were much lower than those used by the president to justify his war on drugs.[14] The incriminating board statistics were based on a nationwide survey. Those used by the president are not.

Major media organizations deemed to be at the forefront of critical reporting on the Duterte administration were a main focus of presidential criticism in 2017, particularly the Inquirer Group that prints the *Philippine Daily Inquirer*, the top-rated television station ABS-CBN (previously shuttered by President Marcos during the martial law period), and the influential online news portal *Rappler*. The Inquirer Group restarted negotiations to sell a controlling share in the firm to Ramon Ang, a business leader with close ties to the president. President Duterte has repeatedly threatened not to renew ABS-CBN's broadcast licence due in 2020.[15] During his second State of the Nation Address on 24 July, President Duterte, going off-script, attacked *Rappler* for being 100 per cent foreign-owned, a claimed unconstitutional ownership status that *Rappler* has repeatedly rejected as untrue.

The Duterte administration's criticism and actions against sources of authority and legitimacy beyond their control reached a new worrying level in November when impeachment hearings against Chief Justice Maria Lourdes Sereno, who questioned the conduct of the war on drugs, began. In December, an impeachment case against Ombudsman Conchita Carpio-Morales was filed with the House of Representatives. Both Sereno and Carpio-Morales were appointed to their positions prior to the Duterte administration. Sereno's predecessor as chief justice, Renato Corona, himself was impeached in 2012.

Internal Security

Internal security was a major focus of President Duterte's campaign for the May 2016 presidential election and a sharp point of differentiation between him and the other candidates. The militant left strongly supported him for his promise to seek a final peace agreement with the communist insurgency. The leaders of the Moro Islamic insurgency in Muslim Mindanao publicly supported him for his promise to deliver a peace agreement to this most troubled part of the country. A large number of voters, particularly in urban areas, strongly supported his call for a nationwide war on drugs reminiscent of the one he carried out as mayor of Davao City. Yet, at the end of 2017, each of these three internal security concerns were in worse positions than when President Duterte took office.

War on Drugs

Since coming to office, the war on drugs has been President Duterte's signature issue that he has expended the most time and political capital on. In 2017, the international and local opposition to the war on drugs reached higher levels, which led to temporary tactical retreats and reforms. Internationally, on 31 January, Amnesty International published a damning report on the war on drugs claiming that the thousands of deaths linked to this campaign may constitute crimes against humanity.[16] Two months later, Human Rights Watch issued a similar gory report entitled *License to Kill* claiming that the Philippine National Police were culpable in many extrajudicial killings.[17] Not surprisingly, the Duterte administration rejected the findings of both reports. Secretary of Justice Aguirre went so far as to contend that there could be no crimes against humanity, as drug lords and drug pushers were not part of humanity.[18]

While international criticism of the war on drugs was brushed off, two murders by police officers led to unprecedented local criticism that triggered a presidential response. By early 2017, the case of a South Korean businessman, Jee Ick-joo, abducted from his home and strangled to death by members of a police anti-drug unit on 18 October 2016, became an international sensation that overwhelmed police efforts to brush it under the carpet or claim it was an isolated event. On 25 January, Chief Justice Sereno asserted that the unsolved killings associated with the war on drugs undermined justice reforms.[19] At the same time, Senate hearings into the conduct of the war on drugs were reopened and aired publicly, with strong criticism of the conduct of the police not limited to opposition senators. On 29 January, the president ordered the immediate dismantling of all police anti-drug units, ordered a cleansing of the police before they could rejoin the war on drugs, and transferred leadership of this campaign to the much smaller Philippine Drug Enforcement Agency. "Scalawag" police officers implicated in the war on drugs were then redeployed to Muslim Mindanao, against the wishes of Senate President Pimentel.[20]

A month later, on 28 February, President Duterte allowed the Philippine National Police to rejoin the war on drugs, still under the formal leadership of the Philippine Drug Enforcement Agency. This reinstatement was ordered with no evidence provided of the scope or success of the ordered internal cleansing operation beyond the assurances by the police leadership that its ranks had been cleansed. These assurances proved incorrect, as in August and September a number of cases of teenagers killed in very mysterious circumstances as part of the war on drugs surfaced and again overwhelmed police and administration efforts to suppress the public outrage they caused. President Duterte again ordered the police to withdraw from the war on drugs. A move he again reversed in early December.

The conduct of the police in the war on drugs sparked the largest and most consistent opposition against the Duterte administration in 2017 and did impose some short-term costs. The Catholic Bishops Conference of the Philippines, the peak body of the Catholic Church in the country, issued two pastoral letters criticizing the war on drugs and its heavy death toll among the poor. The first letter issued on 5 February and read out in all churches referred to a "reign of terror" among poor communities. On 12 February, the Quezon City Court of Appeals elevated the temporary restraining order protecting survivors of the war on drugs and their families from police retribution issued by the Supreme Court into a permanent restraining order. A week later, a Catholic lay organization organized a large number of anti-war-on-drugs "Walks of Life" around the country that were endorsed by the clergy. The media storm around the killings of the teenagers was certainly a major factor in an 18 per cent drop in net satisfaction with the president in the quarterly Social Weather Stations' poll conducted in September. By December, the president had recaptured the majority of this lost ground.

Communist Insurgency

At the beginning of his term, President Duterte, a self-avowed socialist and student of communist leader "Joma" Sison, went strongly against the grain and appointed three members of his cabinet upon the recommendation of the militant left, engaged directly with Joma Sison, and released nineteen communist leaders from jail as a sign of goodwill before the recommencement of peace talks. The start of 2017 suggested that this new against-the-grain approach may be bearing fruit. The third round of peace talks was scheduled to begin in mid-January in Rome and the Armed Forces of the Philippines had issued a new operation plan focused on hunting down Islamist terrorists and seeking cooperation with the communists.[21]

Yet, the third round of negotiations showed few signs of progress before they were suspended by the Duterte administration. Manila alleged that the New People's Army had violated their unilateral ceasefire in a clash that led to the death of an insurgent on 21 January in southern Mindanao. A further clash in early February in southern Mindanao led to the death of three soldiers. President Duterte used this as the pretext to cancel the peace talks, informally label the New People's Army terrorists, and call for the re-arrest of the nineteen leftist prisoners he had earlier released. By April, heads had cooled enough for the fourth round of talks to be held in the Netherlands in which a joint ceasefire, long a government condition for progress in the peace talks, was agreed upon.[22]

The fifth round of peace talks though lasted only two days before the government again withdrew. On 23 May, President Duterte proclaimed martial law and the lifting of the writ of habeas corpus across all of Mindanao to address the terrorist threat emanating from Muslim Mindanao. The government claimed that the New People's Army used the period when the police and army in Mindanao were focused on the terrorist threat and siege of Marawi to break the new joint ceasefire and intensify attacks on government targets.[23] Among the twelve key tasks identified by the Armed Forces of the Philippines under martial law are efforts to degrade the New People's Army. The communist insurgency (along with the war on drugs) was used as part of the government's justification for the extension of martial law across Mindanao until the end of 2017.[24] On 13 December, martial law across Mindanao was extended again for a further twelve months.

The apparently final breakdown of peace talks with the communist insurgency and the return to a military-first approach could carry a longer-term political cost for President Duterte and his administration. The militant left, led above ground by the Makbayan grouping that is represented in the House of Representatives, strongly supported Duterte during the election campaign and his early months in office. Yet, a number of government actions and policies — including the rejection by the Commission on Appointments of the three cabinet members recommended by the militant left, the war on drugs, and the burial of President Marcos in the Cemetery of Heroes — have led the militant left to question the wisdom of this support and to criticize the administration. The breakdown of peace talks and the military crackdown on the New People's Army will make any further support or non-opposition to the Duterte administration more difficult.

Moro Insurgency[25]

As with the communist insurgency, 2017 began hopefully for efforts to end the Moro Islamic insurgency in Muslim Mindanao. In mid-January, President Duterte agreed with the assessment of the Armed Forces of the Philippines that martial law was not required to address current internal security threats, including that from Islamist terrorists.[26] The president did warn though that Mindanao was being contaminated by ISIS ideology. In March, the new, expanded Bangsamoro Transition Council met for the first time to redraft a more inclusive Bangsamoro Basic Law. This law would legalize the Comprehensive Agreement on the Bangsamoro signed in early 2014. This landmark agreement aimed to provide a final political solution to the Moro insurgency that has contributed to the Autonomous Region of Muslim Mindanao being the poorest and most violent part of the country.

The Armed Forces of the Philippines and President Duterte reversed their January assessment on 23 May after a failed attempt to arrest terrorist leader Isnilon Hapilon in Marawi City, the largest city in the Autonomous Region of Muslim Mindanao and the heart of Islam in the Philippines. The failed attempt led the Maute Group from the Marawi City region and Isnilon Hapilon and his Abu Sayyaf followers to lay siege to large parts of Marawi City in an attempt to establish an ISIS beachhead in Southeast Asia and have the southern Philippines designated as an ISIS province.[27]

President Duterte, while on a visit to Russia with most of the senior military and police leaders, immediately declared martial law and lifted the writ of habeas corpus across all of Mindanao for a period of sixty days as allowed for under the Constitution. Despite the extra powers granted by martial law and public assurances that the Maute Group–led network would be defeated swiftly, the Marawi siege lasted until mid-October, displacing hundreds of thousands of people and destroying large parts of Marawi City. The ability of the Maute Group–led network to quickly seize large parts of Marawi City and defend it for months underlined serious intelligence shortcomings and the continuing severity of the terrorist threat in and emanating from Muslim Mindanao. If the massive rehabilitation operation in Marawi City is not carried out carefully and in respect to local Maranao concerns, the already deep alienation of the Maranao community based around Marawi City will worsen.[28]

The Marawi siege in act, and likely in consequence, was a blow to the peace process in Muslim Mindanao. The leaders of the Moro Islamic Liberation Front, the main insurgent group that has been involved in peace talks with Manila for two decades, have repeatedly claimed that the slow progress of and very uncertainty of the Bangsamoro Basic Law was dangerous and counterproductive. The lack of visible progress undermined the legitimacy of the Front in Muslim Mindanao and made the appeals of local terrorist groups like the Maute Group and of ISIS more attractive to frustrated Moro youth.[29] In January 2015, a botched police raid to apprehend a Malaysian terrorist in Muslim Mindanao led to the death of forty-four police special forces officers. This incident stopped the legislative progress of the Bangsamoro Basic Law during the last eighteen months of the Aquino administration. The Marawi siege, and President Duterte's push for a federal state, could serve the same damaging function for the revised Bangsamoro Basic Law. When tabled in the House of Representatives and Senate, the new Bangsamoro Basic Law failed to gain sponsors and was omitted from the list of priority bills released soon after the State of the Nation Address.

While the political effects of the Marawi siege on the peace process in Muslim Mindanao are likely to prove detrimental, the national political and foreign relations impacts of the siege are more positive. On the national front, the image of the Armed Forces of the Philippines and of martial law has been burnished. The presidential declaration of martial law on 23 May and the two further extensions received strong legislative support in both houses of Congress. The Supreme Court's strong majority ruling in favour of the first declaration provides a very permissive precedent on the presidential prerogative to declare martial law.

While the initial 23 May declaration sparked, for many, dark memories of the abuses of martial law during the Marcos dictatorship, the conduct so far of the armed forces under martial law in Mindanao have quelled these fears. This could ease the ground for further extensions of martial law in Mindanao and beyond. The communist insurgency is nationwide in scope and can easily be represented as an act of rebellion. President Duterte's declaration on 17 October that Marawi City had been liberated may well have contributed to his improved ratings in the opinion polls as well.

Foreign Policy

The Marawi City siege also had a major and largely positive impact on Philippine relations with its closest Southeast Asian neighbours, the country's only treaty ally the United States, and China. The presence of terrorists from other parts of maritime Southeast Asia in Marawi and fears of an ISIS node in Southeast Asia led to new forms of counterterrorism cooperation between the Philippines, Malaysia and Indonesia. This despite the ongoing territorial dispute between Malaysia and the Philippines over Sabah.

In early 2016, the Philippines, Indonesia and Malaysia agreed to a framework for coordinated maritime patrols to counter piracy in the Celebes Sea emanating from the islands of Muslim Mindanao. The Abu Sayyaf Group had been linked to a growing number of incidents involving Indonesian and Malaysian vessels plying trade with Mindanao. This framework was activated during the Marawi siege and the first trilateral maritime and air patrols were conducted to help staunch the movement of terrorists between the three countries. The Philippines' chairing of ASEAN in 2017 helped coordinate regional and international support for the reconstruction of Marawi and counterterrorism efforts. The Marawi siege and its legacies were a major focus of discussion during the November ASEAN Summit in Manila.[30] The regional salience of the terrorist threat and the Marawi siege, helpfully for President Duterte, deflected attention away from the South China Sea maritime rights disputes between China and five ASEAN member states.

Responses to the Marawi siege also helped highlight the strict limits of President Duterte's strong rhetorical commitment to an "independent" nationalist Philippine foreign policy. In the early months of his presidency, this new phrase seemed to be code for sharply reduced security relations with the United States (the Philippines' only treaty ally and largest source of remittances and foreign direct investment) and much closer and subservient relations with China (the Philippines' largest source of imports and an unlawful infringer of Philippine maritime rights in the West Philippine Sea). However, it was American counterterrorism support during the Marawi siege that proved instrumental in "tilting the balance" in favour of the government, according to the Philippine ground commander.[31] In response, the Philippines and the United States will enhance their schedule of bilateral military exercises in 2018, after President Duterte had ordered them to be sharply downscaled in 2017.

The Marawi siege also led to a new milestone in Philippine–China relations, as China donated a number of rifles and ammunition to the Philippine army and police. President Duterte incorrectly claimed that one of these Chinese rifles had been used in the killing of Isnilon Hapilon near the end of the Marawi siege. The Department of National Defense later clarified that the rifle used had been an American one.[32]

This pattern of Philippine–China relations of new cooperative milestones, presidential enthusiasm and pushback from the Armed Forces was replicated at the general level in 2017 as well. As the leader chairing ASEAN in 2017, President Duterte and the Department of Foreign Affairs were central to the much shorter and anodyne comments on the South China Sea disputes contained in the Chairman Statements at the end of the two ASEAN Summits. The president and the Department of Foreign Affairs reacted mildly to continued Chinese militarization of its artificial islands in the West Philippine Sea while the two countries recommenced talks on joint resource development in the West Philippine Sea. In April, upon a request from China, President Duterte cancelled a planned visit to Pag-asa island in the West Philippine Sea.[33]

The Department of National Defense and its Secretary Delfin Lorenzana (also from Mindanao) was more actively critical of China's unlawful activities in the West Philippine Sea. In mid-January, Lorenzana issued a formal statement expressing the view that China's militarization of its artificial islands in the West Philippine Sea was "very troubling".[34] Two weeks after the president had cancelled his planned trip to Pag-asa island, Lorenzana himself visited and promised to improve its aging facilities.[35]

President Duterte has continually justified his embrace of China by arguing it was necessary for better economic relations with Asia's leading power and key to his "Build, Build, Build" infrastructure push. The U.S. government was not a major financier of infrastructure, whereas China, particularly under the Belt and Road Initiative, promised to become Asia's leading source of infrastructure financing.

In 2017 the Philippine economy benefitted from this diplomatic embrace of China. In January, the Department of Tourism reported a 250 per cent increase in daily requests for tourist visas from China, while the Chinese ambassador predicted that one million Chinese tourist may visit the country in 2017. Tourist arrivals for the first ten months of 2017 support this one million claim, as tourist arrivals from China had reached 810,807, close to a 40 per cent increase over the same period in 2016.[36] President Duterte was invited to and attended the Belt and Road Forum in Beijing in May, where he met both President Xi Jinping and Premier Li Kejiang.[37] Such high-level meetings undoubtedly contributed to China's enhanced commitment to Philippine infrastructure development, symbolized by the agreement reached in June for China to fund through a grant the building of two bridges in Metro Manila.[38]

President Duterte's independent foreign policy has not been a hindrance to improved Philippine–Japan relations. The year began with a visit by Prime Minister Abe to President Duterte's family home in Davao City. Instead, Japan, already the leading country of foreign infrastructure financing in the Philippines, has improved its position. This choice by Tokyo undoubtedly has been influenced by the ongoing rivalry between Japan and China for Southeast Asian infrastructure projects. In late March, Japan agreed to fund three rail projects in the Philippines worth $8.8 billion.[39]

Philippine Economy

Aided by favourable regional and international conditions, the Philippine economy continued to be the strongest economy in maritime Southeast Asia in relation to GDP growth. According to the Philippine Statistics Authority, GDP growth in 2017 is estimated at 6.7 per cent, only slightly below the 6.9 per cent growth in 2016 and well above the 6.1 per cent growth recorded in 2015. In 2017, agriculture bounced back into positive growth after slumping in 2016, while construction continued to be the strongest growing sector in the economy.

The Philippines' macro-economic indicators continued to be positive. From January to September 2017, exports expanded by a robust 11.2 per cent in year-on-year terms, while imports grew by 10.6 per cent. The country's public debt to GDP ratio continued its decline, as did the debt-servicing burden to exports ratio. Inflation was at a higher level in 2017 than in 2016 but still fell well within the central bank's inflation target range of 2–4 per cent.

The end of 2017 saw President Duterte sign into law the first and most important of five tax reform laws that are at the centre of his administration's economic plan. The so-called TRAIN law lowers personal income tax rates and compensates for this lost revenue with increased taxes on vehicles, fuel, sugared drinks, the mining sector and others and a reduction in tax write-offs and write-downs. Finance officials estimate it will have a one-off upward effect on inflation in 2018.[40] The passing of the TRAIN law took a long time and was the source of fierce lobbying in the House and Senate. President Duterte, before passing it into law, removed some of the tax-reducing lobbying effects written into the law by Congress. The next tax reform scheduled for passage into law in 2018 will seek to lower corporate income tax and jettison more tax write-offs and write-downs.

The passage of the TRAIN law was the most significant legislative achievement in 2017, bolstering market confidence in the Philippines and in the Duterte administration's economic team. If the Duterte administration is able to pass all of its planned tax reforms they will amount to the most comprehensive tax reform effort in decades.

There is a close correlation between the sustained period of rapid economic growth in the Philippines since 2010 and improved satisfaction with the president and with both chambers of Congress. Both President Aquino and President Duterte, despite being very different leaders, have maintained public satisfaction levels far above any of their post-Marcos predecessors. In a similar vein, approval ratings for both the House of Representatives and Senate since 2010 have been markedly higher.[41] A similar trend can be discerned when people are asked about their personal economic outlook.[42] It seems that as long as the economy is doing well and people feel that their economic situation will likely improve, the happier they are with their politicians.

Looking Forward

The fact that President Duterte remained extremely popular throughout 2017, despite its domestic political turbulence and significant internal security setbacks, strongly suggests that he will remain very popular in 2018. The positive global, regional and domestic economic outlooks for the year ahead further bolster this prediction. The year 2018 should see the Duterte administration's push to revise the 1987 Constitution to introduce a federal system of government and a parliamentary form of government take centre stage. This could well test the president's ability to translate sustained high levels of approval into popular support for his reform agenda, as constitutional revisions require a plebiscite. The push to reform corporate taxation could see even more intense lobbying of the House and Senate by affected business interests. If there is no visible progress on the peace processes with the communist insurgents or in Muslim Mindanao in the year ahead, then further internal security problems are likely. The year 2018 promises to be as turbulent and challenging for the Philippines as 2017.

Notes

1. "DFA Urged to File Protest over China's War Threat", *Rappler*, 21 May 2017 <http://www.rappler.com/nation/170516-dfa-urged-protest-china-war-threat>. The West Philippine Sea is the official name for the Philippines' exclusive economic zone in the South China Sea.
2. Aries A. Arugay, "The Philippines in 2016: The Electoral Earthquake and Its Aftershocks", in *Southeast Asian Affairs 2017*, edited by Daljit Singh and Malcolm Cook, pp. 277–96 (Singapore: ISEAS – Yusof Ishak Institute, 2017).

3. Joseph Franco, "Uncertainty in Duterte's Muslim Mindanao". in *Southeast Asian Affairs 2017*, edited by Daljit Singh and Malcolm Cook, pp. 297–311 (Singapore: ISEAS – Yusof Ishak Institute, 2017).
4. For more insight into this unique mayoral approach, see "Mayor or President?", *Philippine Daily Inquirer*, 30 June 2017 <http://opinion.inquirer.net/105232/mayor-or-president> and Malcolm Cook, "Ignoring the Curve: President Duterte's First Year in Office", *ISEAS Perspective* 2017, no. 44 (28 June 2017) <https://www.iseas.edu.sg/images/pdf/ISEAS_Perspective_2017_44.pdf>.
5. All data for these two paragraphs was taken from Social Weather Stations, "Fourth Quarter 2017 Social Weather Survey", 22 December 2017 <https://www.sws.org.ph/swsmain/artcldisppage/?artcsyscode=ART-20171222105042>.
6. For more on the weak nature of political parties in the Philippines, see Julio C. Teehankee, "Clientelism and Party Politics in the Philippines", in *Party Politics in Southeast Asia: Clientelism and Electoral Competition in Indonesia, Thailand and the Philippines*, edited by Dirk Tomsa and Andreas Ufen, pp. 186–214 (New York: Routledge, 2003) <https://books.google.com.au/books?hl=en&lr=&id=aQxflEvYWSkC&oi=fnd&pg=PA186&dq=Philippines,+party+politics&ots=5NNgbR0unJ&sig=ye_sZNvZmpoPihDrrT055nq7lWE#v=onepage&q=Philippines%2C%20party%20politics&f=false>.
7. Cited in Mara Cepeda, "Being 'Dilawan' in the Duterte-controlled House", *Rappler*, 14 June 2017 <https://www.rappler.com/newsbreak/in-depth/172182-liberal-party-dynamics-house>.
8. EDSA is the acronym for the main arterial road bisecting Metro Manila where, in February 1986, hundreds of thousands of Filipinos protested peacefully and successfully to end the Marcos dictatorship after a fraudulent vote count.
9. Patricia Lourdes Viray, "LP Senators Ousted from Majority, Committee Posts", *Philippine Star*, 27 February 2017 <http://www.philstar.com/headlines/2017/02/27/1676278/lp-senators-ousted-majority-committee-posts>.
10. D.J. Yap, "Alvarez Tells 24 Solons Who Got No Funding: That's Life", *Philippine Daily Inquirer*, 21 December 2017 <http://newsinfo.inquirer.net/954026/alvarez-tells-24-solons-who-got-no-funding-thats-life>.
11. Bea Cupin, "Grand Conspiracy against de la Rosa, Duterte?", *Rappler*, 23 January 2017 <http://www.rappler.com/newsbreak/inside-track/159224-conspiracy-duterte-dela-rosa>.
12. Chrisee Dela Paz, "Anti-Money Laundering Council Head Resigns", *Rappler*, 30 January 2017 <https://www.rappler.com/business/159981-julia-abad-resigns-amlc-head>.
13. Nestor Corrales, "Duterte: Bank Records Given to Trillanes by His 'Mistress' Abad of AMLC", *Philippine Daily Inquirer*, 4 October 2017 <http://newsinfo.inquirer.net/935586/duterte-trillanes-mistress-bank-account-abad-amlc-anti-money-laundering-council>.

14. Jodesz Gavlian, "Duterte 'Fires' DDB Chair: You Do Not Contradict Your Own Gov't", *Rappler*, 24 May 2017 <https://www.rappler.com/nation/170839-duterte-fires-ddb-benjamin-reyes-contradict-government>.
15. Trisha Macas, "Duterte Threatens to Block Renewal of ABS-CBN's Franchise", *GMA News*, 27 April 2017 <http://www.gmanetwork.com/news/news/nation/608650/duterte-threatens-to-block-renewal-of-abs-cbn-s-franchise/story/>.
16. "If You Are Poor, You Are Killed: Extrajudicial Killings in the Philippines' War on Drugs", Amnesty International, 2017 <https://www.amnesty.org/en/documents/asa35/5517/2017/en/>.
17. "License to Kill: Philippine Police Killings in Duterte's War on Drugs", Human Rights Watch, 2017 <https://www.hrw.org/sites/default/files/report_pdf/philippines0317_insert.pdf>.
18. Camille Elemia, "Aguirre to Amnesty Int'l: Drug Lords, Pushers Are 'Not Humanity' ", *Rappler*, 1 February 2017 <http://www.rappler.com/nation/160165-aguirre-amnesty-international-drug-lords-not-humanity>.
19. "Sereno: Extrajudicial Killings a Setback in Judicial Reforms", *Rappler*, 25 January 2017 <http://www.rappler.com/nation/159477-sereno-extrajudicial-killings-setback-judicial-reforms>.
20. Bea Cupin, "Pimentel to PNP: Stop Sending Bad Cops to Mindanao", *Rappler*, 31 January 2017 <http://www.rappler.com/nation/160121-pimentel-dela-rosa-pnp-bad-cops-mindanao>.
21. Carmela Fonbuena, "AFP Chief: Reds Should Work with Military in New Campaign Plan", *Rappler*, 9 January 2017 <http://www.rappler.com/nation/157788-armed-forces-philippines-dssp-kapayapaan>.
22. "Timeline: The Peace Talks between the Government and the CPP–NPA–NDF, 1986–Present", *GMA News*, 6 December 2017 <http://www.gmanetwork.com/news/news/specialreports/634324/timeline-the-peace-talks-between-the-government-and-the-cpp-npa-ndf-1986-present/story/>.
23. Karlos Manlupig, "Gov't: Peace Talks with NDF to Continue in the Future, But…", *Philippine Daily Inquirer*, 29 May 2017 <http://globalnation.inquirer.net/157436/govt-peace-talks-ndf-continue-future>.
24. Carmela Fonbuena, "Martial Law Also Aims to Crush NPA, Drug Syndicates", *Rappler*, 3 July 2017 <https://www.rappler.com/nation/174582-martial-law-communist-insurgency-war-on-drugs>.
25. Dennis Quilala will deal with the Marawi siege and its place in the history of political violence in the Philippines in greater detail in the following chapter.
26. Trisha Macas, "Duterte: No Martial Law, But It Could Be Done Quietly If Needed", *GMA News*, 18 January 2017 <http://www.gmanetwork.com/news/story/596237/news/nation/duterte-no-martial-law-but-it-could-be-done-quietly-if-needed>.
27. "Maute Plans to Raise ISIS Flags at Lanao Capitol, Marawi City Hall to Declare 'Wilayat' ", *GMA News*, 27 May 2017 <http://www.gmanetwork.com/news/news/

nation/612374/maute-plans-to-raise-isis-flags-at-lanao-capitol-marawi-city-hall-to-declare-wilayat/story/>.

28. Ted Khan Juanite, "Marawi Rehab Face Complex Challenges", *Manila Times*, 10 December 2017 <http://www.manilatimes.net/marawi-rehab-faces-complex-challenges/367765/>.
29. Carmela Fonbuena, "MILF, Maute Group Battle for Legitimacy", *Rappler*, 5 July 2017 <https://www.rappler.com/newsbreak/in-depth/174531-milf-maute-group-peace-process-marawi-crisis\>.
30. Dharel Placido, "Terrorism Dominated ASEAN Summit Talks, Says Duterte", *ABS-CBN News*, 14 November 2017 <http://news.abs-cbn.com/news/11/14/17/terrorism-dominated-asean-summit-talks-says-duterte>.
31. Phil Stewart and Manuel Mogato, "U.S. Touts Military Ties in Philippines as Duterte Courts Russia, China", Reuters, 24 October 2017 <https://www.reuters.com/article/us-asia-mattis-philippines/u-s-touts-military-ties-in-philippines-as-duterte-courts-russia-china-idUSKBN1CT0TH>.
32. Ian Storey, "End of Siege Underscores Critical Importance of US–Philippine Alliance", ISEAS Commentaries, 30 October 2017 <https://www.iseas.edu.sg/medias/commentaries/item/6469-end-of-marawi-siege-underscores-critical-importance-of-usphilippine-alliance-by-ian-storey>.
33. Paterno Esmaquel II, "Duterte Cancels Plan to Raise Flag in Spratlys", *Rappler*, 13 April 2017 <http://www.rappler.com/nation/166812-philippines-duterte-cancels-plan-raise-flag-spratlys>.
34. "China's Sea Militarization 'Very Troubling' – PH Defense Chief", *Rappler*, 17 January 2017 <http://www.rappler.com/nation/158671-china-sea-militarization-troubling-philippines-defense>.
35. Carmela Fonbuena, "PH Plans for Pag-asa to Test Duterte's Friendship with China", *Rappler*, 27 April 2017 <http://www.rappler.com/newsbreak/in-depth/167612-lorenzana-pag-asa-island-duterte-china>.
36. "Visitor Spending up, Chinese Tourists Now 2nd Biggest Market – DOT", *GMA News*, 11 October 2017 <http://www.gmanetwork.com/news/lifestyle/travel/629158/visitor-spending-up-chinese-tourists-now-2nd-biggest-market-dot/story/>.
37. "Duterte: China 'Sincere' about Commitments to PH", *Rappler*, 16 May 2017 <http://www.rappler.com/nation/169955-duterte-china-sincere-commitments-philippines>.
38. Tina G. Santos, "China to Fund 2 New Metro Bridges", *Philippine Daily Inquirer*, 23 June 2017 <http://newsinfo.inquirer.net/908021/china-to-fund-2-new-metro-bridges>.
39. Ben O. de Vera, "Japan to Fund 3 Rail Projects", *Philippine Daily Inquirer*, 31 March 2017 <http://business.inquirer.net/227106/japan-fund-3-rail-projects>.
40. Ben O. de Vera, "3-Step Oil Excise Tax Eyed", *Philippine Daily Inquirer*, 19 January 2017 <https://business.inquirer.net/223156/3-step-oil-excise-tax-hike-eyed>.
41. "Fourth Quarter Social Weather Survey", Quezon City: Social Weather Stations,

28 December 2017 <https://www.sws.org.ph/swsmain/artcldisppage/?artcsyscode=ART-20171228170154>.

42. "Third Quarter Social Weather Survey", Quezon City: Social Weather Stations, 13 December 2017 <https://www.sws.org.ph/swsmain/artcldisppage/?artcsyscode=ART-20171213112417>.

NARRATIVES AND COUNTER-NARRATIVES: Responding to Political Violence in the Philippines

Dennis Quilala

Political violence has defined Philippine politics for decades. It has been used by different agents in order to achieve their political goals. In local politics, bosses and warlords have included it as part of their repertoire to remain in power. Non-state actors like the communist New People's Army and the different Moro (Muslim Filipino) groups have used violence as leverage in peace negotiations. Terrorists and criminal groups also use violence to achieve material and non-material goals. The national government struggles to have a monopoly on the legitimate use of violence in some areas, including Mindanao. The lack of resources also undermines the ability of national security forces to keep local warlords and non-state armed actors in check. As a result, groups that use political violence thrive in some areas of the Philippines.

It is important for the Philippine state to assert its monopoly of the use of legitimate violence to suppress armed non-state actors. This is well understood by the new Philippine president. In the first State of the Nation Address of Rodrigo Duterte, he promised to strengthen the Armed Forces of the Philippines and the Philippine National Police. He also called for lifestyle checks among members of the security forces to ensure that they do not have corrupt members. These are prerequisites in Duterte's declaration of war against terrorism, criminality and illegal drugs. While the promise of this war on criminality, drugs and terrorism was

DENNIS QUILALA is Assistant Professor in the Department of Political Science of the University of the Philippines.

a reason for Duterte's successful election campaign, human rights groups and the international community have been critical of the government's implementation of the programme after more than seven thousand people have died in the process. An ensuing war against the communist party, which Duterte declared a terrorist group, will most likely increase the number of casualties.

Moreover, in the first year of the Duterte presidency, the use of political violence by terrorist groups in occupying the city of Marawi in the southern island of Mindanao has been touted by International Alert[1] as a new form of vertical conflict (i.e., a conflict between the national government and a non-state armed actor). Marawi City was declared liberated from terrorist groups by Duterte in October 2017, after four months of fighting. According to the Philippine military, the conflict dragged on because they have yet to develop urban warfare capabilities and because the terrorist groups were well prepared. Meanwhile, hundreds of thousands of civilians have been displaced and a large part of the city of Marawi will be uninhabitable until it can be rehabilitated.

Terrorism in the Philippines and Southeast Asia is not something new. The Philippine Congress has passed legislation that aims to address the threat of terrorism. Engagement with regional and international actors has been incessant in order to improve the capabilities of the security forces. These efforts, however, have not been enough. Therefore, to argue that political violence waged by non-state armed groups could be dealt with by similar responses done in the past by the Philippine government would contribute to the narrative that political violence in itself is the solution to these problems. This chapter will argue that political violence, particularly terrorism and internal armed conflicts in Mindanao, have not been properly addressed in the Philippines. A counter-narrative is necessary. It is further argued that a strategy towards the prevention of extremism needs to be crafted, and that the involvement of the community is necessary to address terrorism in the Philippines. The peace strategy with the different armed groups should also be more inclusive. Narratives have to be adjusted and counter-narratives have to be asserted.

New Terrorism(?), Old Responses

Terrorism has been identified by the Philippine government as one of the major security threats in the Philippines. The Philippine National Security Policy 2011–2016 (NSP 2011–2016) under the Benigno Aquino administration and the Philippine National Security Policy 2017–2020 (NSP 2017–2020) under the Duterte administration see terrorism as a hindrance to the economic potential of the Philippines. Moreover, the NSP 2011–2016 recognizes the international links of terrorist groups and also the motivation of a terrorist group to attack urban areas like metropolitan Manila. As a security issue, terrorism and the complications it brings are not new. It is therefore expected of government to prepare for effective responses and prevent terrorist attacks. The siege of Marawi points to the weakness of the security sector in the Philippines to prevent terrorist attacks and respond more effectively to such occurrences. It is important to be critical of how the Duterte administration responded to Marawi and how it proposes to respond to terrorist attacks in the future.

The Maute group and the Abu Sayyaf group led the siege of Marawi City. They have been involved in previous terrorist acts, including bombings of cities and criminal activities like kidnapping and piracy. The leaders of these groups have pledged allegiance to the Islamic State in Iraq and al-Shaam (ISIS), but there is no evidence that ISIS has recognized this. It is, however, argued that ISIS has encouraged supporters who could not go to Syria or Iraq to go to Mindanao and help the local groups. While terrorist activities from these groups are not new, the attempt to occupy Marawi resembles the "statization" of ISIS in Syria and Iraq. This distinguishes ISIS from al-Qaeda,[2] and this is probably what the terrorist groups wanted to achieve in occupying Marawi. The occupation of territories by armed groups, however, is also not new in the Philippines. The Moro National Liberation Front–Misuari faction attempted to occupy the City of Zamboanga in September 2013, and the supporters of Sulu Sultan Jamalul Kiram III attempted to occupy Lahad Datu in Sabah in February 2013.

The rise of extremism in Mindanao is also not unexpected. The chair of the Moro Islamic Liberation Front (MILF) Peace Panel with the Philippine Government Mohaqher Iqbal warns of the rise of extremism in Mindanao. According to him, this is due to the perceived discrimination against Muslims in the Philippines. As such, he has called for the immediate passage of the Bangsamoro Basic Law (BBL) by the Philippine Congress.[3] The rise of extremism is seen as an expression of discontent with the slow development of the peace process. The threat of terrorism then was used to pressure the Philippine Congress to immediately pass the BBL. This threat is still being used to hasten the passage of the BBL. While there is no proof offered to link the non-passage of the bill to terrorism, it might be an admission on the part of the MILF that it has limitations in mobilizing support for the peace process from all Moros. As such, the peace that may result from the peace process with the MILF may not be sustainable.

The Philippine government also recognizes the rise of extremism in Mindanao and has moved to prevent it. In response to the siege of Marawi City, Duterte declared martial law across the whole of Mindanao, particularly because of the history of violent activities of the Maute, including an attack on a military outpost in February 2016 and the Marawi jailbreak in August 2016. In the report of Duterte to the Philippine Congress, he justified the declaration of martial law by arguing that Mindanao has been a "hotbed of violent extremism". He argued the declaration of martial law would help in preventing the establishment of an ISIS *wilayat*, or province, in the Philippines. The Philippine Congress did not revoke its declaration of martial law in Mindanao and has also extended it until 31 December 2018. The Supreme Court of the Philippines also declared that the proclamation of martial law has factual basis and is therefore constitutional.

Terrorism in the Philippines is not something new, nor is it unexpected. After the 9/11 attacks in the United States, Southeast Asia was considered the "Second Front" of the war against terror. The Philippines was not only engaged by the United States but also by other regional actors, like Australia, in order to ensure that it would not be the weakest link in the fight against terror. At that time, aside from the presence of the Abu Sayyaf group, the MILF was seen by the United States as an international security threat. Moreover, since then, there was fear that terrorist groups in the Philippines had links to Jemaah Islamiyah and al-Qaeda. The international connection of the terrorist groups in the Philippines is well entrenched. It is because of this that international cooperation is important in responding to terrorism.

The United States, through Operation Enduring Freedom–Philippines, became active in the security situation in Mindanao. From 2001 to 2014 the United States assisted the Philippine military against local terrorist groups and other transnational terrorists. According to RAND, the operations resulted in the capture of terrorist leaders, reduced enemy attacks, reduced the freedom of movement of enemies, and decreased popular support for the enemies.[4] The RAND report also noted the increased capacity of the Philippine security forces; however, it also noted the need to improve how military operations are conducted, so as to reduce collateral damage.

The Association of Southeast Asian Nations (ASEAN) also responded to the international threat of terrorism by signing the 2001 ASEAN Declaration on Joint Action to Counter Terrorism. In this document, the ASEAN states committed to strengthen their respective national mechanisms to combat terrorism and to deepen cooperation among front-line law enforcement agencies and in intelligence exchange. Beyond this document, states in Southeast Asia have made progress in arresting key regional terrorists, particularly those who belong to Jemaah Islamiyah. It is from these arrests that regional law enforcement learned of the plan to establish a *wilayat* in Southeast Asia. The goal of the terrorist groups in Marawi to establish a *wilayat* has its roots in the early 2000s. At best, it has been a revived regional project by the different terrorist groups in Southeast Asia.

In the Philippines, the Philippine Congress passed Republic Act Number 9372, or the Human Security Act of 2007. It defined acts of terrorism and established rules that would guide the Philippine government in the fight against terrorism. With court authorization, the law allows law enforcement officers to conduct surveillance against suspected terrorists. In addition, the Philippines also passed Republic Act 10168, or the Terrorism Financing Prevention and Suppression Act of 2012, to limit the flow of financial support to terrorists. These two laws strengthen the capacity of the state to respond to terrorism.

In a sense, the Philippines and the region were ready to respond to the challenges of terrorism. The Philippine legal framework empowers the government to aggressively respond to terrorists, and it does not lack regional and international support. So why did Marawi happen? How was it possible for a group of identified terrorists to be able to prepare for such an attack, and for it to last for months? How is it also possible for foreign terrorists to get into the Philippines and to support local terrorist groups?

Duterte admitted and agreed to what security experts had been saying, that the Marawi siege was the product of the failure of the intelligence agencies.[5] This explains why the military operations against the Maute group dragged on for months, the deaths of hundreds of terrorists, and the displacement of hundreds of thousands of residents. The initial assessment of the intelligence agencies was that the military would have control of Marawi within sixty days. It was not only in the assessment of the siege itself, however, that the military agencies failed. The leaders of the terrorist groups were identified terrorists, who, by law, could have been under surveillance by the Philippine government using the Human Security Act. The alleged financial support by ISIS could also have been prevented by the Terrorism Financing Prevention and Suppression Act of 2012. It was not simply a failure of intelligence, but the inability of the state to use mechanisms that could have prevented such a terrorist attack. As Duterte has promised to support the security forces with the necessary hardware for their mission against drugs, criminality and terrorism, it is also important to ensure that the security forces know how to use existing legal mechanisms to thwart such threats. The effective and consistent use of these mechanisms would limit the available actions of individuals who want to use violence for political ends. Institutions in the Philippines need to be strengthened in order to respond more effectively against terrorism and prevent terrorist attacks.

The Philippine government should also look into the sources of the weapons of terrorist groups. The NSP 2011–2016 has identified the trafficking of small arms in Southeast Asia as a security threat that enables groups to threaten national and regional security. Unfortunately, this concern could not be found in the NSP 2017–2020. It is important for the Philippine government to prevent the entry of illegal weapons to the Philippines and to ensure the monitoring of those who apply for gun licences. These weapons enable political actors to use violence against the state and cause injury to civilians. The control of the ownership and transfer of such weapons would weaken the capacity of terrorists to launch attacks. Aside from preventing future attacks by stopping such weapons entering the Philippines, it is imperative for law enforcers to be made accountable for the presence of the huge haul of weapons found in Marawi as reported by the Philippine military. Weapons dealers should also be brought to justice.

The presence of foreign terrorists in Marawi is also an indication of the failure of the sharing of intelligence among the member states of ASEAN and with intelligence agencies beyond the region. The military has reported the presence of Indonesians and Malaysians in Marawi who could have already been flagged as terrorists by the Indonesian and Malaysian intelligence agencies. Was such information shared with their Filipino counterparts? We could expect trust issues among the intelligence community in Southeast Asia to be minimal, given the history of cooperation among them at various levels. There is continuous exposure of security personnel in regional activities, including military exercises, human development activities, conferences, and even in conflict monitoring such as the case of the International Monitoring Team in Mindanao. This, however, may not be the case. The regional documents on cooperation against terrorism may have been just grandiose plans that failed implementation. States in Southeast Asia could not afford to work alone against security threats that do not recognize borders. The Philippines could not respond sustainably against terrorism on its own.

It is also important to note that, with the expected demise of ISIS plans to control parts of Syria and Iraq, security experts have been informing states about the return of foreign terrorist fighters from Syria and Iraq to their countries. There are about five hundred foreign terrorist fighters from Southeast Asia who might return. Some may have even participated in Marawi. States seem to be silent as to any strategy regarding such foreign terrorist fighters.

The Bureau of Immigration of the Philippines should be made accountable for the entry of so many foreign terrorists. The agency's capacity against terrorism should also be developed. The borders of the Philippines with other states are definitely porous, but this is a challenge to improve the Philippine's capacity to secure its borders. The initiative of Indonesia, Malaysia and the Philippines to jointly patrol their shared borders is a positive development, but, beyond this, each state must also develop its own capacity to effectively protect its sovereignty.

With the transnational nature of the terrorist threat, it is important to improve cooperation on terrorism among the countries of Southeast Asia. The case of Marawi tells us that, while the attack occurred in Marawi, extremism in Southeast Asia is not limited to Mindanao. States beyond the region should also be involved, especially in the case of foreign terrorist fighters.

The Philippine government has attracted international support as a result of the Marawi siege. There have been pledges to support the rehabilitation of the city, and the United States and Australia have vowed to support the Philippine military in its counterterrorism efforts. The United States would continue training the Philippine military and develop their capacity against terrorism.[6] This was an interesting initiative, given Duterte's vocal hostility towards the United States. Australia also vowed to support counterterrorism efforts in the Philippines, capped by a visit of Australian Defence Minister Marise Payne to the Philippines. The support would include the training of Philippine military personnel in urban warfare.[7]

The Armed Forces of the Philippines and the Philippine National Police definitely require international support to develop their capacity against terrorism. They must also learn how to acquire and share intelligence information regarding terrorism with the international community. However, it is not enough. We know that since the early 2000s, these two forces have been the recipients of international assistance against terrorism. Other institutions need to be strengthened and may need international support. The capacity of various governmental agencies like the Bureau of Immigration and the Central Bank need to be improved in order to limit the capacity of terrorists to plan and launch attacks. The Philippine government, however, should not stop at just improving its own capacity against terrorism. There is much more that needs to be done.

Towards a More Inclusive Peace Process

In a systematic comparison of al-Qaeda and ISIS, an expert opined that these terrorist groups have flourished in conflict areas.[8] So, while extremism can be found all throughout Southeast Asia, Marawi offers conducive conditions for a terrorist attack since it is at the centre of a conflict area. The lack of effective governance might have made it into an attractive base for terrorist groups based not only in the Philippines but also in the region. It also provides the best excuse for the struggle against discrimination and injustice, as people are not free due to the continuing armed conflict. Sustainable peace in Mindanao is important in preventing future terrorist attacks. The peace process with the MILF needs to be inclusive to include other groups in Mindanao.

The Benigno Aquino administration successfully signed the Comprehensive Agreement on the Bangsamoro (CAB) with the MILF in 2014. It was hoped that Congress would have passed the BBL before Aquino's term ended in 2016. The draft law, however, met opposition from those who believed that parts of it were unconstitutional and that it was not inclusive. The biggest hurdle to its passage though was the carnage that occurred in Mamasapano in 2015, where police special action force officers died together with civilians and members of other non-state armed groups. It then became political suicide for members of Congress to support a draft law that could result in a duplication of the Mamasapano incident.

The Aquino administration gave the MILF special attention in the peace process. While consultations with different groups were conducted, it was clear that the peace process was primarily driven by the interests of the MILF. For example, Aquino called the Autonomous Region in Muslim Mindanao (ARMM) a failed experiment. The ARMM was one of the products of the peace agreement between the Fidel Ramos administration and the Moro National Liberation Front (MNLF). By declaring the ARMM a failed experiment, it meant that the negotiations with the MNLF would be disregarded and that the negotiations with the MILF would be considered the primary solution to the armed conflict in Mindanao. The MNLF–Misuari faction responded with the attempted siege of Zamboanga City. This attempt was a manifestation of the dissatisfaction of the MNLF-Misuari faction in the peace process. The Aquino administration went on to prioritize the interests of the MILF.

Aside from the dissatisfied Moro groups, there is also fear from indigenous (*lumad*) groups in the ARMM that their rights would not be protected by the 2014 draft of the BBL. These groups have called for the inclusion in the draft law of the recognition of the Indigenous Peoples Rights Act of 1997, which protects and recognizes their rights. There are no indications that these groups will take up arms to protect their rights. However, it is important that their concerns are taken into consideration so that violence entrepreneurs will not take advantage of their marginalization in the peace process. It is also possible that the MILF's continued negotiations with the government have marginalized other groups. Possible evidence of this is the separation of the Bangsamoro Islamic Freedom

Fighters from the MILF. It may also be true of other extremist groups who do not perceive of the MILF as representing their interests.

The CAB and the draft BBL received wide support from government, members of civil society, the academe, and the international community. However, there are also indications that, while hundreds of consultations were conducted, many important groups and sectors have been marginalized by the process. While the MILF and even the government argue that the non-passage of the BBL could result in the rise of extremist groups, its passage might also result in the taking of arms by groups marginalized in the process.

If the aim is to make Mindanao a place hostile to terrorist groups, it is important that the peace process in Mindanao be more inclusive. This means that the MILF should not be the only Moro voice in the process, regardless of the support it receives from civil society and the international community. It is important that the various Moro groups settle their own differences. The indigenous groups, while small in number, must be protected by the national government and any future regional government. Crafting the peace that Mindanao deserves would have a lot of negative implications for terrorism.

The Counter-narratives

The peace process between the Philippine government and the two Moro armed groups has been based on the assumption that the Philippine government controlled by "Christian Filipinos" has marginalized the Moro minority. While this might have been true during the Marcos administration under the 1972 Philippine Constitution and when the Moro groups were formed, institutions have changed with the 1987 Philippine Constitution. The 1987 Philippine Constitution recognizes cultural diversity and local government autonomy. It even compels the Philippine Congress to draft laws to constitute autonomous regions for Muslims in Mindanao and the Cordilleras in Luzon. While discrimination might still occur, this does not particularly target a specific group. Moreover, any Filipino discriminating against another will not be protected based solely on his or her religion. It is important that we have an updated narrative on the dynamics of Filipinos, Moros and other groups in the Philippines.

In relation to this updated narrative, the Philippines also needs to develop counter-narratives against various forms of extremism in the Philippines. For extremist groups based on religion, the state needs to cooperate with religious leaders, who are in the best position to provide those counter-narratives. While the counter-narratives could be developed by experts, they usually have limited capacity to inform the people about their ideas. It is therefore imperative to include the media and the education sector in order to disseminate these counter-narratives.

Terrorism and armed conflicts are issues where the national government has important roles to play. However, it is not the sole responsibility of the national government to solve these issues. This government-only narrative should be replaced with an assertion that everyone has a role to play in resolving political violence in the Philippines.

The role of local governments in security and conflict resolution has not been maximized in the Philippines. Local governments have knowledge of the sources of local political violence and, potentially, the solution to these causes. Local governments also have the role of delivering basic social services, which, if implemented properly, would reduce political violence due to grievances. There are cases in the Philippines where local government involvement in resolving armed conflicts and preventing terrorism could be exemplars of ending political violence from non-state armed groups. It is for this reason that it is also important to demand accountability from the local governors of Marawi and the regional government for what happened to Marawi.

The communities and individuals must also be involved in countering terrorism, preventing violent extremism, and resolving armed conflicts. This is possible when socialization agents like schools, religious institutions and media teach tolerance, cultural sensitivity and dialogue. Building a culturally competent citizenry is a sustainable way of preventing political violence. The government would also multiply its eyes and ears on the ground with the involvement of the community against terrorism.

Conclusion

Violence is a political tool that can be used to achieve one's political goal. Terrorism and armed conflict are just two manifestations of political violence in the Philippines. The Marawi siege in 2017 has been an example of a terrorist act that is connected to the armed conflict in Mindanao. Terrorism is not something new to the Philippine government, but the response to the Marawi siege was found wanting. It is not enough for the national government to just respond militarily. It is important to cooperate with the international community, especially in intelligence sharing and counterterrorism training. However, the Philippine government needs to go beyond this traditional view of solving political violence. While the dominant narrative is for the national government to respond by enhancing its ability to monopolize the legitimate use of force, it is also important to identify the roles of other political actors, including local governments, religious leaders and individuals. Everyone has a role to play in eradicating terrorism and in resolving armed conflicts.

Notes

1. International Alert Philippines, *Guns, Drugs, and Extremism: Bangsamoro's New Wars* (Philippines: International Alert, 2017).
2. Mohammad-Mahmoud Ould Mohamedou, "ISIS and the Deceptive Rebooting of Al Qaeda", GCSP Policy Paper 2014/5-August 2014.
3. John Unson, "BBL Seen to Sway Muslims from Extremism, Fanaticism", *Philippine Star*, 19 May 2015 <http://www.philstar.com/headlines/2015/05/19/1456471/bbl-seen-sway-muslims-extremism-fanaticism>.
4. Linda Robinson, Patrick Johnston, and Gillian Oak, *U.S. Special Forces in the Philippines, 2001–2014* (Santa Monica: Rand Corporation, 2016).
5. Trisha Macas, "Duterte Admits Failure of Intelligence in Marawi City", GMA News Online, 24 July 2017 <http://www.gmanetwork.com/news/news/nation/619295/duterte-admits-failure-of-intelligence-in-marawi-city/story/?tag=sona2017>.
6. Ron Gagalac, "US Envoy Reiterates Support for PH Counter-terror Efforts", ABS-CBN News, 26 September 2017 <http://news.abs-cbn.com/news/09/26/17/us-envoy-reiterates-support-for-ph-counter-terror-efforts>.
7. Prashanth Parameswaran, "Australia's New Philippines Counterterrorism Role Takes Shape", *The Diplomat*, 25 October 2017 <https://thediplomat.com/2017/10/australias-new-philippines-counterterrorism-role-takes-shape/>.
8. Mohammad-Mahmoud Ould Mohamedou, "ISIS and the Deceptive Rebooting".

Singapore

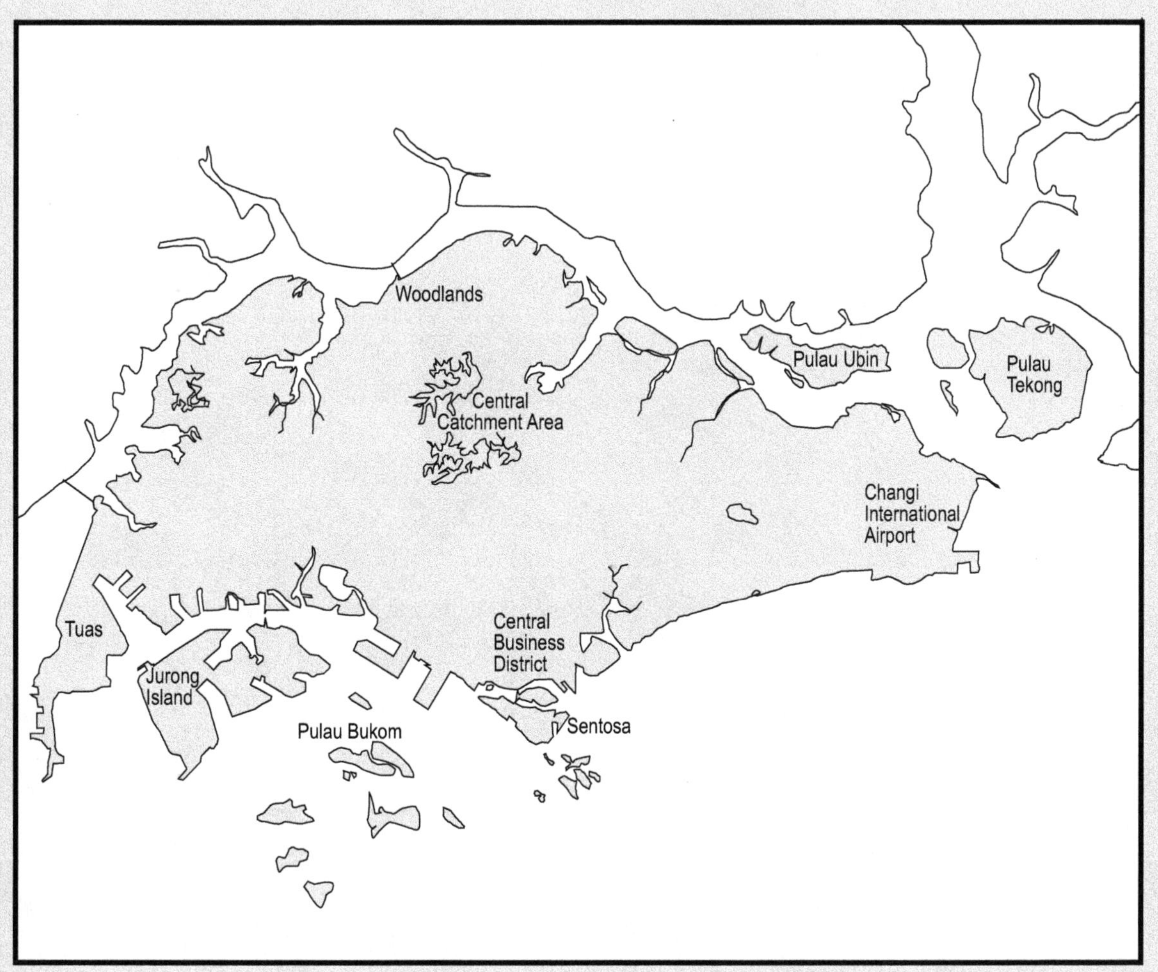

Woodlands
Central Catchment Area
Pulau Ubin
Pulau Tekong
Changi International Airport
Tuas
Jurong Island
Central Business District
Sentosa
Pulau Bukom

SINGAPORE IN 2017: Testing Times, Within and Without

Shashi Jayakumar

Presidential Election

An amendment to the constitution in November 2016 reserved the office of the president for a particular ethnic group if a representative of that group had not been president for five consecutive terms. Other changes also tightened the criteria for those seeking the post: candidates from the private sector must have been the chief executive of a company with at least $500 million in shareholders' equity (up from $100 million) on average for the most recent three years.[1] Subsequently, in February 2017, Parliament amended the Presidential Elections Act (PEA). The key part of the amendment meant that President Wee Kim Wee is considered to have served the first presidential term in Singapore. Given that President Wee and subsequent holders of the office were from the Chinese or Indian communities, the 2017 Presidential Election would be reserved for a member of the Malay community.

A legal challenge was mounted by former PAP MP Dr Tan Cheng Bock, who in 2011 had come within a whisker of the presidency. Tan submitted that President Wee Kim Wee, unlike his successors, was not elected by Singaporeans and did not serve six-year terms. Therefore, the five presidential terms should only be counted from the term of President Wee Kim Wee's successor, Ong Teng Cheong (1993–99). If Tan's argument held, this would have made the 2017 Presidential Election an open one that any individual could have contested. Tan, who stated that the reason for his challenge was to give Singaporeans a choice, saw this application at the High Court dismissed, prompting him to appeal to the Court of Appeal, which also rejected his application, in August 2017.

SHASHI JAYAKUMAR is Head of the Centre of Excellence for National Security at the S. Rajaratnam School of International Studies (RSIS). He also holds the appointment of Executive Coordinator, Future Issues and Technology, at RSIS.

Three candidates from the Malay community put themselves forward. One was Halimah Yaacob, former Speaker of Parliament and widely seen as the government's candidate. The other two hopefuls were Farid Khan, chairman of a marine services firm, and Salleh Marican, chief executive of a listed property company. The Presidential Elections Committee (PEC) found that Khan and Marican did not meet the requirement of having led a company with an average shareholder equity of $500 million in the three most recent years. The rejection of their eligibility by the PEC meant that Halimah Yacob was declared president by walkover on 13 September 2017.

Halimah Yaacob was of course Singapore's first female president — this achievement also has a backstory of personal success through extremely humble origins. Although there was in the media and online space recognition of her abilities and qualifications, there was also a significant amount of ground chatter that the changes made concerning eligibility and minority representation had been made to foil the presidential aspirations of Dr Tan Cheng Bock. Another criticism was that the PAP government's pushing through the constitutional changes and amendments to the PEA went against Singapore's foundational meritocratic ethos. Online commentary and discussion on social media suggested frustration at being denied the chance to vote in the election.[2] On 16 September 2017, two days after Halimah Yacob's swearing in, several hundred individuals gathered at Hong Lim Park in protest at what they saw as the government's handling of the issue and the subsequent walkover. Also present were some opposition politicians, but the show stealer was Tan Cheng Bock, ostensibly there to "share the frustrations of other Singaporeans at being deprived of voting".[3]

The entire debate also opened uncomfortable questions about the very nature of race and ethnicity in Singapore. The constitutional amendment concerning minority eligibility of someone from the Malay community stipulates a Malay as "any person, whether of the Malay race or otherwise, who considers himself to be a member of the Malay community and who is generally accepted as a member of the Malay community by that community". These definitions tended to blur when faced with ground reality. Farid Khan was listed as a Pakistani on his identity card, while Mohammed Salleh Marican (whose father was Indian) is an Indian Muslim. Marican was criticized by some quarters of the community for not being fluent in Malay, after his fumbling during an interview conducted outside the Elections Department. Halimah herself has Indian lineage — her father was Indian Muslim.

It is not entirely certain if the government had foreseen in every respect the divisive debate within the Malay community on what exactly was meant by "Malayness". The entire debate seemed to go against the intention of the scheme — which seemed to be to cement multiracialism. On issues raised by the discussion on race and reserved elections, Law and Home Affairs Minister K. Shanmugam said that "The fact that we were able to talk about it, debate it ... in a way it helps strengthen the overall multiracial fabric."[4]

When it came more generally to the tightening of eligibility criteria, it is clear that the government had been keenly aware that there would be a negative blowback, and that the PAP could end up paying a political price. From the leadership's point of view, however, notwithstanding that the government had to have guardrails in place to ensure multiracialism, this was not something that could be deferred for future generations of leaders to solve.[5]

OxleyGate

On 14 June 2017, the two younger siblings of Prime Minister Lee Hsien Loong, Dr Lee Wei Ling and Lee Hsien Yang, issued a public statement that they had lost confidence in their brother, PM Lee. This marked the beginning of the public aspect of a full-on rift within Singapore's first family.

The discerning observer could perhaps be forgiven for thinking issues had been simmering within the first family in one form or another for some time. Indeed, some signs of disagreement had been publicly visible as early as 2015, when Dr Lee and Lee Hsien Yang, as executors of their father's estate, had tried to gain control of their father's Oral History Transcripts — interviews conducted in the early 1980s — a bid dismissed by the High Court in 2016. There was a further episode in April 2016, when Lee Wei Ling, seemingly upset by state-led efforts to commemorate her late father, published email exchanges which saw her calling PM Lee a "dishonorable son" attempting to "establish a dynasty".

The public statement on PM Lee had in some way to do with a similar set of issues — the legacy of the late PM Lee Kuan Yew — but in terms of the effect it had on the body politic, it was of a different order of magnitude altogether. On the surface, the root cause appeared to be differing interpretations and intentions over the family home at 38 Oxley Road. Dr Lee and Lee Hsien Yang said that PM Lee had wanted the house preserved for political reasons, and for his political gain, all this against the wishes of the late Lee Kuan Yew. In response, PM Lee gave a rebuttal and in turn put forth misgivings over the preparation of the late Mr Lee's will. PM Lee was concerned especially about the "demolition clause", including what was to be done with 38 Oxley Road if the house could not (say, by decision of Singapore's leaders) be demolished.

This clause had reappeared in Mr Lee's final will (after a period where Lee had appeared to accept that the government would not allow the house to be demolished). Lee Hsien Yang noted that the government — and specifically the ministerial committee tasked with looking into the issue — was interested solely in challenging the validity of the demolition clause. There were also allegations — not substantiated — about the abuse of state power and use of state organs against them (Lee Hsien Yang said he would leave Singapore for the "foreseeable future") and other allegations posted on social media about PM Lee and his wife Ho Ching wanting to use Mr Lee's legacy to further their own ambitions for their son, Li Hongyi. Subsequent exchanges, including claim and counterclaim, were played out over the press and social media involving, amongst other things, the release of personal emails and correspondence involving (inter alia) the late Mr Lee.

PM Lee issued a statement and a video apology in June, rendering an apology to the people of Singapore that the dispute had affected Singapore's reputation and Singaporeans' confidence in the government. He made a ministerial statement to clear the air — and to refute, inter alia, the allegations of abuse of power — on 3 July 2017. This was followed by parliamentary debate on the issue.[6]

The public was initially gripped by every detail of the saga, but eventually there seemed some broad sense, as people tired of the issue, that Singapore's first family should settle the issue as families did — away from public scrutiny. There seemed at one point the possibility that matters might head to a truce of sorts, with an agreement by Lee Hsien Yang and Lee Wei Ling not to post on the issue on social media.[7] But on the whole it seems likely that this was only a temporary hiatus, with even PM Lee stating in an interview on 20 October that he was "not sure if the issue is solved".[8]

The odds that the issue might face further public airings shortened considerably when it became clear that the younger generation was being drawn into the affair. Lee Hsien Yang's son Li Shengwu stated on Facebook that his family had become "increasingly worried about the lack of checks on abuse of power", also commenting on Singapore's "pliant court system". He subsequently declined to fully comply with a request from the Attorney-General's Chambers (AGC) that he delete the post and issue a written apology. In August, the High Court gave the AGC permission to commence contempt of court proceedings against Li Shengwu. At the time of writing, the AGC is proceeding in a contempt of court case against him, a junior fellow at Harvard University, with Li's lawyers contending that the court order allowing the AGC to serve papers on their client in the United States should be set aside.

The entire saga had brought quite unprecedented speculation to bear directly on Singapore's first family, together with (inevitably) speculation on the part of foreign media and academic commentators (including those not particularly well-disposed to Singapore) choosing to give their own interpretations on the saga.[9] The resilience of Singapore, and the confidence in it, had been affected. And as PM Lee observed, the open airing of a private family matter meant damage to the legacy of the late PM Lee Kuan Yew.[10]

Government and Politics

The year 2017 saw lawsuits filed by Pasir Ris–Punggol Town Council (PRPTC) and Aljunied–Hougang Town Council (AHTC) against Workers' Party (WP) chief Low Thia Khiang, party chairman Sylvia Lim and assistant secretary-general Pritam Singh. The lawsuits concern the circumstances surrounding the setting-up of FM Solutions & Services (FMSS), its eventual appointment as managing agent of the now-defunct Aljunied–Hougang–Punggol East Town Council (AHPETC), and past payments made by the town councils to FMSS and a related service provider between 2011 and 2015 while the WP was managing AHPETC from 2013 to 2015. Independent audits flagged the need to investigate whether potential criminal offences, including criminal breach of trust, had been committed and should be investigated. The lawsuits sought to show that the WP figures (as town councillors) had breached their fiduciary duties and made allegedly improper payments to contractors.

The potential seriousness of the charges did not appear to have cast too much of a dampener on the sixtieth anniversary celebrations of the WP in November 2017. There was, however, something of a surprise at this occasion: Low, 61, made it known that he would not be contesting the post of secretary-general at the next party election (likely to be held in 2018).[11] There was speculation that the ongoing lawsuits might have had a hand in Low's decision, but Low would only volunteer that the move had been made to make way for new blood in the WP's ranks.[12]

The PAP, too, was in a transitional phase of renewal. Changes to the cabinet and other positions in the leadership in April 2017 saw several younger politicians appointed as Senior Ministers of State and two individuals promoted to the level of full minister: Josephine Teo and Desmond Lee.[13]

News of a more surprising exit from the top ranks came in September when it was announced that Tan Chuan-Jin, Minister for Social and Family Development, once seen as a core member of the fourth-generation political leadership, would resign his position to take up the position (on the nomination of PM Lee) as Speaker of Parliament, a position vacated by Halimah Yacob in August when she resigned to contest the presidential election. The role of Speaker (which cannot be filled by an individual who is at the same time a political office holder) was seen as an important but largely ceremonial one. PM Lee stated that Chuan-Jin remained an important member of his team, albeit in a different role, and much was made of Tan Chuan-Jin stepping into an enhanced, "Speaker-plus" role.[14] This did little, however, to scotch the coffee-shop talk that this was a demotion of sorts as well as a sign that Tan was out of the running for the top job.

The issue of choosing Singapore's fourth prime minister and successor to PM Lee was increasingly occupying the media, netizens and people at large. Quizzed by CNBC in a widely noted interview in October on whether he was ready to step down after the next election, PM Lee said that he was ready, with the caveat he needed to make sure "somebody is ready to take over from me". Lee has been clear that the younger generation of leaders have to come to a consensus as to who should lead, and has made it known that his successor is likely already a cabinet member, but he has given away few clues about who that might be.[15]

Against this was a level of curiosity (tinged with anxiety) on the part of Singapore watchers, and at the grass-roots level, as to who PM Lee's successor would be.[16] This had to do in part with the fact (acknowledged by some of the main actors involved) that this was a very different succession scenario compared to the elevation of Goh Chok Tong (1990) or Lee Hsien Loong (2004). Both had had considerable time at the top ranks before their ascensions, and were considered seasoned political hands. Lee Hsien Loong's successor would have a considerably shorter runway, with the public having a similarly short runway in terms of getting to know the future PM.[17]

Even leaders close to the apex evinced some anxiety. Emeritus Senior Minister Goh Chok Tong weighed in on the issue at the close of the year, saying in a social media post in December that he would like to see the "urgent challenge" of the fourth-generation leadership settled. Goh (who in 1984 had been chosen by his peers to succeed PM Lee Kuan Yew) went as far as to suggest that he hoped that the current cohort of leaders could settle the issue within six to nine months, allowing PM Lee to formally designate his potential successor before the end of 2018.[18]

If 2017 closed with a degree of anxiety over the succession issue, the opening of 2018 saw the fourth-generation leadership going some way to allaying concerns. On 4 January, sixteen fourth-generation cabinet ministers and office holders (including Ong Ye Kung, Chan Chun Sing and Heng Swee Keat, the three thought to be in serious contention for the premiership) issued a response of sorts, acknowledging the pressing nature of the issue but stating also that the team of younger ministers "would settle on a leader from amongst us in good time". What seemed surprising, perhaps, was that Ong Ye Kung (Minister for Higher Education and Skills) appeared at this time to rule himself out, saying that he had another, unnamed, individual in mind for the top job.[19] This would suggest that just Heng Swee Keat and Chan Chun Sing remain in contention. Whether this is indeed the case or whether further surprises remain in store will become clearer at some point in 2018, when PM Lee intends to carry out a major cabinet reshuffle. The likelihood is that even if this reshuffle does not contain an outright anointing, there will be a strong indication of PM Lee's preferred successor — and the individual chosen by his peers to take Singapore into the next lap.

Foreign Policy

PM Lee had had a very good relationship with then American president Barack Obama, having made a state visit in 2016 and being honoured by a state dinner celebrating the strength of the bilateral relationship on that occasion. PM Lee's six-day official working visit to the United States in October 2017 at the invitation of President Donald Trump was important in terms of getting acquainted with the United States' unpredictable new leader, and in keeping Singapore in the minds of American policymakers at an uncertain period in global affairs.

Lee's meeting with Trump produced some standard niceties, with Lee noting that both sides reaffirmed the strength of the half-century-long relationship and the substantial cooperation in the defence and security and (not least) economic spheres. To underscore this, at the White House meeting, both President Trump and PM Lee witnessed Singapore Airlines' signing of a US$13.8 billion deal with Boeing. During the course of the visit, President Trump accepted PM Lee's invitation to visit Singapore sometime in 2018.

It was also important to get President Trump and his administration to keep their minds on Asia, and Southeast Asia specifically. Speaking at a November Manila summit commemorating forty years of dialogue relations between ASEAN and the United States, PM Lee (as prime minister of the incoming country chair of ASEAN in 2018) told President Trump that his attendance at the summit was a positive step pointing to expanded relations, and that Singapore looked forward to continued support from the United States.

ASEAN

In the course of symbolically taking over the ASEAN chairmanship from the Philippines in Manila during the ASEAN Summit, PM Lee outlined Singapore's approach and key priorities as chair. Singapore, Lee said, would seek to ensure the group promotes and upholds a rules-based regional order. It would focus on the twin themes of "resilience" and "innovation". The scope would encompass dealing with emerging security challenges, including cyber security, transnational crime and terrorism. This would also involve finding innovative ways to leverage digital technologies and equip citizens of ASEAN member states with skills and capabilities.

"Small States"

Singapore's diplomacy — indeed the very nature and purpose of it — also came under the spotlight from a wholly different source in July, when the dean of the Lee Kuan Yew School of Public Policy, Kishore Mahbubani, published an opinion piece in the *Straits Times* dealing — on the face of it — with the ongoing economic and diplomatic blockade of Qatar by some of its neighbours. Mahbubani said that one lesson for Singapore was that "small states must behave like small states", especially now that Mr Lee Kuan Yew (by Mahbubani's account, Singapore's only globally respected statesman who could comment freely on the affairs of other countries) had passed on. Mahbubani's view attracted opprobrium from a range of notable individuals, including current and former Singapore diplomats and even a government Minister (K. Shanmugam).[20] Implicitly, rejection also came, although in a more nuanced way, from Foreign Minister Vivian Balakrishnan.[21] Mahbubani was forced to defend his views (but not backpedal), stating that his piece was criticism against statements made by senior officials which had caused missteps in Singapore's external relations, but he had not meant his piece to be an attack on PM Lee (which was the reading taken by many).[22]

Malaysia

In February, Malaysia applied to the International Court of Justice (ICJ) to review its May 2008 judgment that awarded sovereignty over Pedra Branca and its surrounding waters to Singapore. The original ICJ judgment was final and without appeal, but Malaysia's application was made under a statute of the ICJ that allows application for a revision of judgement when new facts have been unearthed. Malaysia appears confident that such facts have indeed been discovered. Public statements from the Singapore side have appeared measured but equally confident, and a "comprehensive rebuttal" was filed with the ICJ in October. The next step in the case is for the two sides to present oral arguments to the ICJ, on dates yet to be fixed.[23]

It has not escaped the attention of some observers that a general election will take place in Malaysia sometime during 2018. PM Lee himself has remarked that the Malaysian election "may have something to do" with the fresh Malaysian application to the ICJ. Some Malaysian leaders and officials bristled at such a suggestion.[24] Whatever plot twists follow, however, and even if Pedra Branca becomes Malaysian electoral fodder, it seems unlikely that both countries will allow the issue to mar a period of excellent ties. PM Lee's very good personal relations with Malaysian PM Najib aside, there have been several bilateral accomplishments over the course of 2017. These include progress made in plans and discussions for cross-border connectivity between the two countries through two projects of immense scale: namely, the Kuala Lumpur–Singapore High Speed Rail, to be completed by 2026, and the Johor Bahru–Singapore Rapid Transit System Link, to be operational by 2024.

The Economy

Topline figures for the economy held up reasonably well, with several sectors showing a modest recovery over 2016. In the third quarter of the year the economy grew 5.2 per cent, the fastest in nearly four years. In an upward revision, PM Lee in his New Year's message bringing in 2018 said that the economy grew by 3.5 per cent (echoing earlier MTI statements that the economy was expected to grow by 3–3.5 per cent in 2017, against the initial estimate of 2–3 per cent).[25] Manufacturing (in particular electronics, biomedical engineering and precision engineering) was the main support for overall growth in 2017, but services (in particular financial services, retail and information and communications) also contributed, leading government agencies to state that the overall recovery was one not simply measured in pace but also in breadth.[26] In the statements associated with the third-quarter forecast, there were, however, points from MTI that denoted, if not concern, at least the sense that the pace of growth would moderate into 2018 (with, for example, growth in key external demand markets such as China and the eurozone likely to ease).[27]

It was partly in recognition of challenges lying ahead that the government convened a high-powered committee — the Committee on the Future Economy (CFE) — in early 2016 to chart out Singapore's long-term growth trajectory.[28] The thirty-member CFE, headed by Finance Minister Heng Swee Keat, reported in February 2017. Some of the observations in the final report might have seemed somewhat underwhelming: taking steps to ensure that the economy remained open and connected globally, and equipping the workforce with deep skills and an attitude that embraced lifelong learning. But as was made clear, the committee (made of five cabinet ministers, with the remaining twenty-five being individuals drawn from diverse parts of the private sector) never intended to prescribe miracle pills for the economy. The aim was a longer-term blueprint mapping out the transformation of the economy. Core parts included keeping adult workers relevant in an age of technological disruption. An important beginning had been made, the report noted, through the SkillsFuture movement. For businesses, upping innovation was emphasized. Here, targeted recommendations were made for SMEs (which make up the bulk of Singapore enterprises) in terms of helping them build up their digital capabilities — an area that the report notably went into more detail than the CFE's predecessor, the Economic Strategies Committee (ESC; 2009–10).

For the near-term, 2018 may well bring with it some degree of belt-tightening, given the need to tackle future challenges — not least the ageing population.[29] Finance Minister Heng Swee Keat said that government expenditure on healthcare is expected to "rise quite sharply" in the next three to five years and beyond, while Prime Minister Lee Hsien Loong has said tax increases are not a matter of if, but when, given investments in infrastructure and social spending.[30]

SMART Nation

The CFE report mentioned SMART Nation or the use of smart technologies 19 times; "innovation" featured approximately 150 times in the 130-page report. These two — innovation and technological advancement — are the *sine qua non* in taking the economy to the next level. But not all of the journey to SMART Nation status will be smooth sailing. PM Lee in his 20 August 2017 National Day Rally speech observed that Singapore has the "right ingredients" to be a Smart Nation (a vision unveiled by Lee himself in 2014) but needed "to do much better" to create a SMART Nation.[31]

Getting government agencies to interface better is clearly a priority. A few months earlier, wide-ranging organizational changes in the agencies (and personnel) responsible for getting Singapore to SMART Nation status had taken place. These developments involved chiefly a centralization under the Prime Minister's Office (PMO), which saw the Smart Nation and Digital Government Office (SNDGO) formed under it, with staff drawn from the Smart Nation Programme Office (SNPO) in the PMO as well as other government departments. In addition, the

Government Technology Agency (GovTech), a statutory board under the Ministry of Communications and Information (MCI) was placed under the PMO as the implementing agency of SNDGO. Together, SNDGO and GovTech would form the Smart Nation and Digital Government Group (SNDGG) in the Prime Minister's Office.

The announced rationale behind these changes was to "enable the Government to be more integrated and responsive" in the nation's Smart Nation and Digital Government (SNDG) strategy and processes. The revamped government SMART Nation organizational architecture is a high powered — and many-layered — one. The SNDGG is overseen by a ministerial committee chaired by Deputy Prime Minister (DPM) Teo Chee Hean. Dr Yaacob Ibrahim, Minister for Communications and Information, will be Deputy Chairman and Minister-in-charge of Cybersecurity and the Info-communications Media Development Authority of Singapore (IMDA). The other members of the Ministerial Committee are Dr Vivian Balakrishnan, Minister-in-charge of the Smart Nation Initiative, Ong Ye Kung (who will champion Public Service innovation) and Dr Janil Puthucheary (Senior Minister of State, Ministry of Communications and Information and Ministry of Education), appointed Minister-in-charge of GovTech.[32]

Some SMART Nation efforts were already in some respects starting to bear fruit. The SNDGO revealed that initiatives in the pipeline included developing common QR codes for Singapore, to make it easier for consumers and small businesses to receive money through common integrated platforms, with MAS and banks here also working with industry partners on simplifying e-payments for merchants, thus going some way to address PM Lee's concerns. SNDGO also revealed that the National Environment Agency (NEA) will be embarking on the adoption of e-payments at hawker centres.

What was apparent in 2017 was the fact that technological disruption brings real world effects, and that in some cases, rather than freewheeling adoption, the platforms (if not the technology) would have to be brought under the regulatory ambit. For example, amendments to the Road Traffic Act in February meant that private-hire car drivers, including those under the ride-sourcing operators Uber and Grab, would now be required to obtain a vocational licence. This would also go some way to address concerns that ordinary taxi drivers could not compete on the same playing field as private-hire cars.

The regulatory regime appears reasonably well prepared to adapt to further developments — with measured calibration to disruption being the goal rather than outright rejection. But, given the sheer pace of change, whether the regime has the luxury of doing so at its own time and pace is less clear.

Transport

Disruption of a more conventional but depressingly familiar kind marred 2017, with train disruptions becoming a regular occurrence. At the nub of the issue was SMRT's inability to get to grips with the multitude of engineering and technical woes plaguing it. In some cases, people were at fault; in others, systems. Apart from delays which could be classed as the more run-of-the-mill variety, two incidents stand out.

The first was flooding on the North–South Line on 7 October, which caused service disruptions across that day and the next, lasting some twenty hours in all. A quarter of a million commuters were affected.[33] Preliminary investigations revealed that a water pumping system malfunction resulted in flooding between Bishan and Braddell stations, with two float switches controlling the pump system at Bishan failing to kick in. Transport Minister Khaw Boon Wan's initial comment that the SMRT maintenance team had "failed us" was swiftly overshadowed by revelations that maintenance works for the Bishan pump system had not been properly carried out since December 2016. It appeared that some key individuals had been party to the falsification of maintenance records to show that maintenance had taken place when actually it had not.

Worse was to come. On 15 November a train collision took place at Joo Koon station on the East–West Line. A stalled train was hit by another, injuring thirty-six people. SMRT's Twitter account initially referred to the accident — the second train-to-train collision (after one in 1993) — as a "train fault", also referring to the crash as an incident that saw one train that "came into contact" with another. Following extensive investigations the LTA announced that a "software logic issue" with a new signalling system, coupled with a "confluence of failure conditions", had been the root causes. LTA said that failure conditions arose as a result of complications from operating two signalling systems concurrently on a single line. The French company that supplied the new signalling system for the East–West Line acknowledged its responsibility for the incident and has apologized to the public. Transport Minister Khaw Boon Wan acknowledged that commuter confidence would inevitably be affected by the incident, but he said that overall, progress would be made in reliability and he was confident that these improvements would be visible to commuters.[34]

Whether things will look up from 2018 remains to be seen. The incidents in 2017 triggered a public debate — played out in the press and social media — on issues concerning responsibility and SMRT's corporate culture. After the flooding incident, several individuals in SMRT's maintenance team faced disciplinary action and suspensions, with some also having their employment terminated.[35]

SMRT CEO Desmond Kuek took full responsibility and apologized to commuters affected.[36] MRT chairman Seah Moon Ming (flanked by Kuek and other senior members of SMRT management) at a press conference bowed to apologize for the incident as well.

Despite efforts (since major breakdowns affected the MRT in 2011) to emphasize maintenance and reliability, SMRT CEO Desmond Kuek acknowledged after the 2017 flooding incident that "deep-seated cultural issues" remain within the company that need more time to root out.[37] However, increasingly, questions were being asked (particularly in the realm of online socio-political commentary) about Kuek himself — whether, in position since October 2012, he had been given enough time to rectify the issues and whether he should make way for someone else.[38]

Threats Seen...

A threat assessment report issued by the Ministry of Home Affairs in June laid bare the magnitude of the terror threat to Singapore, making it clear that the threat level was the highest it had been in recent years. The report — arguably the most important public-facing document on the terror threat since the 2003 Jemaah Islamiah White Paper — revealed that ISIS elements had plotted two attacks in Singapore. Perhaps more importantly, the report noted that in the age of ISIS, there had been a quickening in the pace and tempo of radicalization. Formerly, it would take around twenty-two months for people to become radicalized. But this has now been cut to nine months. Telling data was adduced to support this: while eleven individuals were detained under the preventive Internal Security Act (ISA) between 2007 and 2014, the period 2015–17 saw fourteen radicalized individuals detained, some of whom had planned to join ISIS.

For the first time, a Singaporean featured in ISIS propaganda videos. In his appearances in September and December, this individual, Megat Shahdan Abdul Samad, alias Abu Uqayl (hitherto completely unknown to the public, but apparently known to the security services), urged fighters to come to the region to undertake jihad.[39] New *types* of individuals in Singapore were coming under the thrall of ISIS, with women beginning to feature in the ranks of the radicalized. One 22-year-old female infant-care assistant became the first woman detained in Singapore for radicalism. She had planned to make the trip with her young child to join ISIS.[40]

Given the nature of the threat, government officials have unsurprisingly for some time been open in acknowledging that it is a matter of "when, not if" a terrorist attack takes place in the country. The issue is not simply prevention, but shoring up resilience for day-after scenarios. The key government initiative in this respect is SgSecure, the nationwide call to arms launched in 2016 (in part a refresh of the decade-old Community Engagement Programme). In its report card on SgSecure, launched at the one-year mark of the SgSecure movement, the Ministry of Home Affairs gave updates on how many individuals and households SgSecure had reached, with additional details on the ramping up of the scale and frequency of emergency preparedness exercises. Work still needs to be done. In his remarks marking one year of SgSecure, Home Affairs Minister K. Shanmugam noted that while it had "some success" in raising awareness, there is "some way to go" in ramping up preparedness, and in getting people to "take ownership and prepare themselves". "I think a lot of people are not mentally tuned to preparedness."[41] Shanmugam noted that the national SGSecure movement is shifting gears, from raising public awareness of the threat of terror attacks to raising the level of "preparedness" among the population.

The year 2017 also saw the government making renewed efforts against intolerance, the feedstock of extremism. In June, at a closed-door dialogue with various faith and community groups, PM Lee drew attention to extremist and exclusivist religious teachings entering the mainstream in countries elsewhere. Lee warned of the dangers of exclusivist views taking root in Singapore, and the weakening effect it would have on racial harmony.[42] The government also made it a particular point to show that external influencers supporting hate speech, or the denigration of other faiths, will have no place in Singapore. In one case, two well-known preachers, Ismail Menk and Haslim Baharim, preachers with known hard-line views against other religions, and against multiculturalism, were prevented from entering Singapore, after earlier having been engaged to preach on a religious-themed cruise departing and ending in Singapore in November.[43] Their barring came soon after two Christian preachers known to have made negative comments of other religions were prevented from entering Singapore to preach.[44]

With Law and Home Affairs Minister K. Shanmugam stating that the Ministry of Home Affairs is looking at further tightening restrictions on foreign preachers who do not share Singapore's values of religious harmony, it seems likely that 2018 will see further preventive measures, with some taking the legal form.[45] Shanmugam had also given indications that, more generally, laws concerning hate speech or actions that could upset religious sensitivities will be strengthened, with amendments to the Maintenance of Religious Harmony Act in the works to deal with "segregationist teachings".

...And Unseen

Another type of threat, perhaps less visible but equally insidious, reared its head sporadically in 2017. In February, the Ministry of Defence announced that one of its servers had been breached, with the details of some eight hundred national servicemen compromised. Keeping with past practice, no fingers were directly pointed, but the language of official pronouncements on the issue strongly suggested that a state actor was responsible. This follows other attacks against other government agencies, including the Ministry of Foreign Affairs (2014) and other unnamed public agencies, as well as sophisticated advanced persistent threat (APT) attacks against academic institutions known to work with the government.[46] In its inaugural report on the cyberthreat landscape in Singapore, the Cyber Security Agency (CSA) noted that attacks have become more sophisticated. Attacks, the report revealed, have targeted not just government agencies. Ransomware attacks against other sectors, including the healthcare sector, have also featured.[47] Key concerns of the authorities, revealed in the CSA Cybersecurity Awareness Survey released in February, are uneven levels of cyber hygiene and awareness, with one finding (out of several that would give the authorities cause for concern) being that a third of those surveyed do not manage their passwords securely.[48]

Straightforward cyberattacks are not the only concern. A different type of threat — fake news and disinformation campaigns — has increasingly reared its head worldwide in this post-truth era. In May, a study by BBC Global News found that eight in ten Singaporean news consumers are concerned about fake news, the highest among five places — the others being Australia, Malaysia, Hong Kong and India — in the Asia Pacific which were surveyed.[49] Real world effects of fake news were in abundance, from, for example, unfounded rumours on social media that someone was given a hefty fine for leaving used tissue behind at a public eating place, to (in a more serious vein) false allegations against the police, leading Law and Home Affairs Minister K. Shanmugam to decry these "completely false, made up, trumped up" attacks against the police, noting that they also dumbed down discourse.[50] Shanmugam suggested that a law against fake news and misinformation was in the works.[51] This may still eventuate in 2018, but the authorities appear determined to move in a calibrated fashion, with early January 2018 seeing the news (following a parliamentary debate on the issue) that a select committee of MPs would first be set up to study the issue, consult widely, and make recommendations.[52]

Experience around the world has shown in recent years that fake news and disinformation can be part of wider, state-sponsored subversion campaigns and influence operations. This was brought home in August 2017 when a professor at the Lee Kuan Yew School of Public Policy, Huang Jing (an American citizen of ethnic Chinese origin), had his permanent residence status revoked for allegedly being an agent of a (unnamed) foreign country. According to the Ministry of Home Affairs, in an unusually detailed statement, Huang Jing had worked with intelligence agents from that country, and engaged prominent and influential Singaporeans, providing them with what he claimed was "privileged information" about the foreign country to influence their opinions in favour of that country. The ministry noted how Huang Jing gave supposedly "privileged information" to an unnamed senior member of the LKY School, who duly conveyed this to senior public officials who were in a position to direct Singapore's foreign policy, in an attempt to cause the Singapore Government to change its foreign policy. However, the government declined to act on the information.[53]

Conclusion

Singapore will not lack challenges in the next phase of its growth trajectory. These will include economic headwinds, socio-demographic challenges brought on by an ageing population, and a workforce buffeted by the pace and intensity of technological disruption. Threats in the security sphere will abound, too. Some, such as terrorism, have been present for some time, while others such as cyber and adjunct hybrid threats are of somewhat newer vintage, with potential aggressors themselves honing their methods. The next generation of Singapore's leadership tasked to navigate the nation safely through these waters has, on the face of it, all the attributes to do so. They have been chosen and sieved out through a thoroughly rigorous, meritocratic process; can boast the technocratic skills to govern the nation; and will, for a time at least, have the mentorship of older-generation leaders — not least PM Lee himself. The individual eventually chosen to succeed to the premiership by his peers will by their estimation have the undoubted mettle to do the job. Whether this mettle will first be tested by external challenges or by issues pertaining to the inner resilience of Singapore society is, at this stage, impossible to tell. It might be one or the other, or perhaps even both.

Notes

1. For the (stringent) requirements for candidates with a public sector background, see *Eligibility Criteria and the Presidential Elections Committee ("PEC")* <http://www.pmo.gov.sg/sites/pmo2/files/02%20-%20Eligibility.pdf>. Candidates with a public sector background are required to have previously held office (in one of a number of select positions) or served as the chief executive of a key statutory board or government

company for at least three years. The Presidential Election Committee also can at its discretion approve candidates not fulfilling these requirements if satisfied that the individual has the experience and ability to effectively carry out the functions and duties of the office of President.

2. For a sampling, see The Online Citizen, "No Longer the Singapore That I Was Once Proud Of", 13 September 2017 <https://www.theonlinecitizen.com/2017/09/13/no-longer-the-singapore-that-i-was-once-proud-of/>.
3. Nur Asyiqin Mohamad Salleh, "Hundreds Take Part in Silent Protest against Reserved Election at Hong Lim Park", *Straits Times*, 16 September 2017 <http://www.straitstimes.com/politics/hundreds-take-part-in-silent-protest-against-reserved-election-at-hong-lim-park>.
4. Elgin Toh, "Reserved Elections 'Critical as President Serves Unifying Role': Shanmugam", *Straits Times*, 9 September 2017 <http://www.straitstimes.com/politics/reserved-elections-critical-as-president-serves-unifying-role>.
5. Tham Yuen-C., "Reserved Presidential Election was Right Thing to Do: PM Lee Hsien Loong", *Straits Times*, 29 September 2017 <http://www.straitstimes.com/singapore/reserved-presidential-election-was-right-thing-to-do-said-pm-lee-hsien-loong>; Lianne Chia, "Govt Prepared to Pay Political Price over Changes to Elected Presidency: Chan Chun Sing", Channel NewsAsia, 8 September 2017 <http://www.channelnewsasia.com/news/singapore/govt-prepared-to-pay-political-price-over-changes-to-elected-9199326>.
6. PM Lee, in giving his account of the saga and his rebuttal to the allegations made against him, said he was reluctant to take his siblings to court as it would "besmirch" his parents' names and prolong the dispute. See Ministerial Statement on "Alleged Abuse of Power on 38 Oxley Road" at the Parliamentary Sitting on 3 July 2017 by Prime Minister Lee Hsien Loong <http://www.pmo.gov.sg/newsroom/ministerial-statement-pm-lee-hsien-loong-alleged-abuse-power-38-oxley-road>.
7. "Oxley Road: Lee Hsien Yang, Lee Wei Ling Will Stop Posting Evidence on Social Media – Full Text of Statement", *Straits Times*, 6 July 2017 <http://www.straitstimes.com/singapore/oxley-road-lee-siblings-issue-joint-statement-in-response-to-parliament-session>.
8. Seow Bei Yi, "Family Feud Stuns Nation", *Straits Times*, 18 December 2017 <http://www.straitstimes.com/singapore/family-feud-stuns-nation>.
9. See, for example, Chun Han Wong, "Singapore, a Model of Orderly Rule, is Jolted by a Bitter Family Feud", *Wall Street Journal*, 14 July 2014 <https://www.wsj.com/articles/first-family-feud-shakes-up-singapore-1500051573>; and Bhavan Jaipragas, "Siblings of Singapore PM Fear for Their Safety, Accusing Him of Harassment and Thrashing Lee Kuan Yew's Values", *South China Morning Post*, 14 June 2017 <http://www.scmp.com/week-asia/politics/article/2098224/siblings-singapore-pm-fear-their-safety-accusing-him-harassment>.
10. Lee Hsien Loong, Ministerial Statement on "Alleged Abuse of Power on 38 Oxley

Road", Parliamentary Sitting, 3 July 2017 <http://www.pmo.gov.sg/newsroom/ministerial-statement-pm-lee-hsien-loong-alleged-abuse-power-38-oxley-road>.

11. Danson Cheong, "Low Thia Khiang Will Step Down as Workers' Party Secretary-General Next Year", *Straits Times*, 3 November 2017 <http://www.straitstimes.com/politics/low-thia-khiang-will-step-down-as-wp-secretary-general-next-year>.
12. For analysis, see Elgin Toh, "WP Chief Low Thia Khiang to Step Down: Why Has He Chosen to Act Now?", *Straits Times*, 5 November 2017 <http://www.straitstimes.com/politics/why-has-low-chosen-to-act-now>.
13. Teo was appointed Minister in the Prime Minister's Office, and Second Minister in the Ministry of Manpower. Mr Desmond Lee was appointed Minister in the Prime Minister's Office.
14. PM Lee Hsien Loong, Facebook post, 5 September 2017 <https://www.facebook.com/leehsienloong/photos/a.344710778924968.83425.125845680811480/1593633260699374/?type=3&theater>.
15. CNBC, "CNBC Transcript: Lee Hsien Loong, Prime Minister of Singapore", 19 October 2017 <https://www.cnbc.com/2017/10/19/cnbc-transcript-lee-hsien-loong-prime-minister-of-singapore.html>.
16. See Bhavan Jaipargas, "Why Singaporeans Are Anxious to Know Who Will Replace Prime Minister Lee Hsien Loong", *South China Morning Post*, 4 November 2017 <http://www.scmp.com/week-asia/politics/article/2118357/singapores-burning-question-who-will-succeed-lee-hsien-loong>.
17. Ibid.
18. <https://www.facebook.com/MParader/photos/a.584664768242860.1073741858.182873625088645/1954246467951343/?type=3&theater>; Elgin Toh, "ESM Goh Chok Tong Says Settling 4G Leadership an Urgent Challenge, Hopes Next PM Can Be Designated 'Before 2018 Ends'", *Straits Times*, 31 December 2017 <http://www.straitstimes.com/politics/esm-goh-says-settling-4g-leadership-is-an-urgent-challenge-hopes-next-pm-can-be-formally>.
19. Tham Yuen-C. and Seow Bei Yi, "4G Ministers Say They Will Pick a Leader 'In Good Time'", *Straits Times*, 4 January 2018 <http://www.straitstimes.com/politics/4g-ministers-say-they-will-settle-on-a-leader-in-good-time-ong-ye-kung-says-he-has-someone>.
20. Chew Hui Min, "Prof Kishore Mahbubani's View on Singapore's Foreign Policy 'Deeply Flawed': Ambassador-at-large Bilahari Kausikan", *Straits Times*, 2 July 2017 <http://www.straitstimes.com/singapore/prof-kishore-mahbubanis-view-on-singapores-foreign-policy-deeply-flawed-ambassador-at>.
21. Danson Cheong, "As a Small Country, Singapore Has to Be Friends with Everyone, But at Times It Needs to Advance Its Own Interests", *Straits Times*, 17 July 2017 <http://www.straitstimes.com/singapore/as-a-small-country-singapore-has-to-be-friends-with-everyone-but-at-times-it-needs-to>.

22. *Today*, “Kishore Reiterates: S’pore’s Statements Must Be More Prudent”, 3 July 2017 <http://www.todayonline.com/singapore/kishore-reiterates-spores-statements-must-be-more-prudent>.
23. Elgin Toh, “Singapore is ‘Confident’ of Its Case on Pedra Branca, Files Rebuttal to Malaysia: MFA”, *Straits Times*, 31 October 2017 <http://www.straitstimes.com/politics/singapore-is-confident-of-its-case-on-pedra-branca-files-rebuttal-to-malaysia-mfa>.
24. Channel NewsAsia, “UMNO Youth Condemns PM Lee’s ‘Irresponsible’ Comments on Pedra Branca”, 20 November 2017 <https://www.channelnewsasia.com/news/singapore/umno-youth-condemns-pm-lee-s-irresponsible-comments-on-pedra-9422258>.
25. See Lee Hsien Loong, New Year Message for 2018, “A Strong Foundation for the Future”, 31 December 2017 <http://www.pmo.gov.sg/newsroom/2018-new-year-message-pm-lee-hsien-loong>; and Ministry of Trade and Industry Singapore, “MTI Forecasts GDP to Grow by ‘3.0 to 3.5 Per Cent’ in 2017 and ‘1.5 to 3.5 Per Cent’ in 2018”, press release, 23 November 2017 <https://www.mti.gov.sg/NewsRoom/Pages/MTI-Forecasts-GDP-to-Grow-by-3.0-to-3.5-Per-Cent-in-2017-and-1.5-to-3.5-Per-Cent-in-2018.aspx>.
26. Vivien Shiao, “Singapore Economy Grows 5.2% in Q3, Beating Expectations; 2017 Forecast Raised to 3–3.5%”, *Straits Times*, 23 November 2017 <http://www.straitstimes.com/business/economy/singapore-economy-grows-52-in-q3-beating-expectations-2017-forecast-raised>; Vivien Shiao, “Singapore Economy Grows 4.6% in Q3; Beats Expectations”, *Business Times*, 13 October 2017 <http://www.businesstimes.com.sg/government-economy/singapore-economy-grows-46-in-q3-beats-expectations>; Tang See Kit, “Singapore’s 2018 Economic Growth Likely to ‘Moderate’ from This Year: MAS”, Channel NewsAsia, 27 October 2017 <https://www.channelnewsasia.com/news/business/singapore-s-2018-economic-growth-likely-to-moderate-2017-gdp-9348276>.
27. Tang, “Singapore’s 2018 Economic Growth Likely to ‘Moderate’ ”.
28. Lee Min Kok, “What You Need to Know about the Committee on the Future Economy”, *Straits Times*, 9 February 2017 <http://www.straitstimes.com/singapore/what-you-need-to-know-about-the-committee-on-future-economys-report>.
29. *Straits Times*, “Singapore’s Demographic Time Bomb: Number of Old People Will Match Number of Young for First Time Next Year, Says UOB Analyst”, 6 December 2017 <http://www.straitstimes.com/business/economy/singapore-will-reach-critical-demographic-crossroad-in-2018-says-uob-economist>.
30. Salma Khalil, “Govt Spending on Healthcare to Rise Sharply in Next 3–5 Years: Heng Swee Keat”, *Straits Times*, 6 December 2017 <http://www.straitstimes.com/singapore/health/govt-spending-on-healthcare-to-rise-sharply-in-next-3-5-years-heng-swee-keat>; Lianne Chia, “As Singapore’s Spending Needs Grow, Raising Taxes is Inevitable: PM Lee”, Channel NewsAsia, 19 November 2017 <https://www.channelnewsasia.com/news/singapore/as-singapore-s-spending-needs-grow-raising-taxes-is-inevitable-9420086>.

31. PM Lee Hsien Loong, National Day Rally speech, 20 August 2017 <http://www.pmo.gov.sg/national-day-rally-2017>.
32. Prime Minister's Office, "Formation of the Smart Nation and Digital Government Group in the Prime Minister's Office", 20 March 2017 <http://www.pmo.gov.sg/newsroom/formation-smart-nation-and-digital-government-group-prime-minister's-office>.
33. Charissa Yong, "10 MPs to Ask Transport Minister Khaw Boon Wan about MRT Tunnel Flooding Incident in Parliament", *Straits Times*, 3 November 2017 <http://www.straitstimes.com/singapore/10-mps-to-ask-transport-minister-khaw-boon-wan-about-mrt-tunnel-flooding-incident-in>.
34. *Today*, "Joo Koon Train Collision: Khaw Chides Signalling System Provider Thales", 21 November 2017 <http://www.todayonline.com/singapore/joo-koon-train-collision-khaw-chides-signalling-system-provider-which-could-have-done>.
35. At the time of writing, thirteen employees (several holding senior managerial positions) had been held responsible. C.K. Tan, "SMRT Sacks 8 Staff, Holds 5 Others Responsible for Falsification of Anti-flooding System Maintenance Records", *Stomp*, 28 November 2017 <http://stomp.straitstimes.com/singapore-seen/smrt-sacks-8-staff-holds-5-others-responsible-for-falsification-of-anti-flooding>.
36. Channel NewsAsia, "SMRT Takes 'Full Responsibility' for Tunnel Flooding, Says CEO Desmond Kuek", 16 October 2017 <https://www.channelnewsasia.com/news/singapore/smrt-takes-full-responsibility-for-tunnel-flooding-says-ceo-9315322>.
37. Adrian Lim, "SMRT Maintenance Staff Bonuses Will Be Affected following Lapse Which Led to Oct 7 Tunnel Flooding", *Straits Times*, 16 October 2017 <http://www.straitstimes.com/singapore/transport/smrt-maintenance-staff-bonuses-will-be-affected-following-lapse-which-led-to-oct>.
38. See, for example, Belmont Tay, "Calls for SMRT CEO Desmond Kuek to Quit Grow Louder", *Mothership*, 6 November 2017 <https://mothership.sg/2017/11/smrt-ceo-desmond-kuek-step-down/>.
39. Joanna Seow, "Singaporean ISIS Fighter Shown Executing Man in Video", *Straits Times*, 31 December 2017 <http://www.straitstimes.com/singapore/singaporean-isis-fighter-shown-executing-man-in-video>.
40. Danson Cheong, "Radicalised Female Infant Care Assistant from PCF Sparkletots Detained under ISA for Pro-ISIS Activities", *Straits Times*, 12 June 2017 <http://www.straitstimes.com/singapore/radicalised-female-infant-care-assistant-from-pcf-sparkletots-detained-under-isa-for-pro>. A second woman, a 38-year-old housewife, also intended to join the group in the conflict zone. Danson Cheong, "Two Singaporeans, One a Woman, Detained under ISA for Terror-Related Activities", *Straits Times*, 9 November 2017 <http://www.straitstimes.com/singapore/two-singaporeans-one-a-woman-detained-under-isa-for-terror-related-activities>.
41. Wong Pei Ting, "SGSecure to Shift Focus from Raising Terror Awareness to

Preparedness", *Today*, 28 September 2017 <http://www.todayonline.com/singapore/sgsecure-shift-focus-raising-terror-awareness-preparedness>.

42. Channel NewsAsia, "Singapore Must Strengthen Trust between Different Faiths amid Terror Threat: PM Lee", 24 July 2017 <https://www.channelnewsasia.com/news/singapore/singapore-must-strengthen-trust-between-different-faiths-amid-9058660>.
43. Tham Yuen-C., "2 Foreign Islamic Preachers Barred from Entering Singapore for Religious Cruise", *Straits Times*, 30 October 2017 <http://www.straitstimes.com/politics/two-foreign-islamic-preachers-barred-from-entering-singapore-for-religious-cruise>.
44. Ibid.
45. Channel NewsAsia, "Government to Tighten Rules against Hate Speech, Extremist Teachings: Shanmugam", 3 October 2017 <https://www.channelnewsasia.com/news/parliament/government-to-tighten-rules-against-hate-speech>; Valerie Koh, "Cyber Attack on S'pore Public Organisation Was by State-Sponsored Group: CSA", *Today*, 14 September 2017 <http://www.todayonline.com/singapore/cyber-attack-spore-public-organisation-was-state-sponsored-group-csa-extremist-9275006>.
46. *Today*, "NUS-NTU Hack: Other Recent Cyber Breaches in Singapore", 12 May 2017 <http://www.todayonline.com/singapore/recent-cyber-security-attacks>; *Straits Times*, "Hackers Broke into NUS, NTU Networks in Search of Government, Research Data", 12 May 2017 <http://www.straitstimes.com/singapore/hackers-broke-into-nus-ntu-networks-in-search-of-government-research-data>.
47. Valerie Koh, "Cyber Attack on S'pore Public Organisation Was by State-Sponsored Group: CSA", *Today*, 14 September 2017 <http://www.todayonline.com/singapore/cyber-attack-spore-public-organisation-was-state-sponsored-group-csa>.
48. Cyber Security Agency Press Release, "CSA Releases Key Findings from First Cybersecurity Public Awareness Survey", 15 February 2017 <https://www.csa.gov.sg/news/press-releases/csa-releases-key-findings-from-first-cybersecurity-public-awareness-survey>.
49. A separate study by a respected private sector survey company found that 42 per cent of Singaporeans "regularly wonder if the news they read is fake", with six in ten saying the issue worries them. See Kelly Ng, "In an Era of Fake News, the Truth May Not Always Be Out There", *Today*, 2 June 2017 <http://www.todayonline.com/singapore/big-read-era-fake-news-truth-may-not-always-be-out-there>.
50. Ibid.
51. Chan Luo Er, "New Laws on Fake News to be Introduced Next Year: Shanmugam", Channel NewsAsia, 19 June 2017 <https://www.channelnewsasia.com/news/singapore/new-laws-on-fake-news-to-be-introduced-next-year-shanmugam-8958048>.
52. The green paper issued by the Ministry of Communications and Information and the Ministry of Law on 5 January 2018 (just before the parliamentary debate) gives a sense of government thinking. It is available at <https://www.mlaw.gov.sg/content/dam/

minlaw/corp/News/Annexe%20A%20-%20Green%20Paper%20on%20Deliberate%20Online%20Falsehoods.pdf>.

53. Royston Sim, “LKY School Professor Huang Jing Banned, Has PR Cancelled, for Being Agent of Influence for Foreign Country”, *Straits Times*, 4 August 2017 <http://www.straitstimes.com/singapore/lky-school-professor-huang-jing-banned-has-pr-cancelled-for-being-agent-of-influence-for>; for the official ministry statement on the issue, see Ministry of Home Affairs, “Cancellation of Singapore Permanent Residence (SPR) Status – Huang Jing and Yang Xiuping”, press release, 4 August 2017 <https://www.mha.gov.sg/newsroom/press-releases/Pages/Cancellation-of-Singapore-Permanent-Residence-Status-Huang-Jing-and-Yang-Xiuping.aspx>.

SINGAPORE–CHINA RELATIONS: Building Substantive Ties amidst Challenges

Lye Liang Fook

Singapore is extremely small compared to China on a range of indicators such as geographical size, population strength, natural resource endowment and economic scale. Despite this huge asymmetry, Singapore has been able to develop a substantive relationship with China. On its part, China also sees value in engaging Singapore in a number of areas.

In fact, the two countries interact and cooperate in many fields ranging from economics, business, the arts, culture, education and the environment to military cooperation (that has progressed from bilateral land-based to naval exercises). This relationship is also manifested at many levels ranging from government-to-government ties involving the top leaders to people-to-people exchanges of tourists and students. Over the years, bilateral relations have not only deepened in existing areas but have also broadened into new areas such as financial cooperation and legal and judicial matters.

Perhaps even more notable has been the establishment of three government-to-government projects over the years which are in line with the development priorities and needs of the two countries. By working hands-on on common projects, the two countries are able to share and benefit from each other's experiences as well as best practices from around the world. Moreover, each of these projects is overseen by a high-level bilateral cooperation mechanism that ensures progress is being made on a regular basis. Such a mechanism also provides a regular platform for the leaders and officials of the two countries to interact and get to know each other better. It would be rather unusual for China to have such a mechanism with a small country like Singapore unless it saw value in the relationship.

Lye Liang Fook is Senior Fellow at the ISEAS – Yusof Ishak Institute, Singapore.

Going forward, there are broader factors at play that have affected and could increasingly affect the dynamics of this bilateral relationship. Foremost among them is the strategic realignment of forces between China and the United States, which small states like Singapore will have to adjust to. When China–U.S. relations are stable, there will be more room for small states to manoeuvre. However, when there is tension in China–U.S. ties, there will be greater pressure on small states to take sides. Moreover, China has certain expectations of how small countries like Singapore ought to conduct themselves, and it has made this known in no uncertain terms. On its part, Singapore, as a small country, has always stressed the sanctity of principles such as the rule of law and the resolution of disputes through legal means rather than the "might is right" approach.

From Turbulent Times to Better Relations

Before diplomatic ties were established, Singapore and China stood on opposing sides of the political and ideological spectrum. In the 1950s, 1960s and even 1970s, China lent moral and material support to communist insurgency movements in Southeast Asia that threatened to overthrow the post-colonial governments in these countries. Singapore was among the Southeast Asian countries that were particularly vulnerable following its separation from Malaysia in 1965 and the intractable challenges of economic survival and nation-building.

Unlike its Southeast Asian counterparts, the Singapore government had to grapple with the additional challenges of assuaging the concerns of its Malay neighbours that Singapore would not come under China's sway or become a "third China", given its predominant ethnic Chinese population.[1] At that time many ethnic Chinese in Singapore had a strong attachment to their country of origin, i.e., the People's Republic of China (hereafter China), and had little sense of a Singapore national identity. To foster such an identity, Singapore since independence has practised multiracialism and multilingualism so that its citizens would not think of themselves as exclusively a Chinese, an Indian or a Malay, but as a Singaporean first. Equally important, Singapore made a political decision to be the last country in ASEAN to establish diplomatic relations with China.

Despite its political and ideological differences with China, Singapore adopted a pragmatic approach and maintained economic and trade relations with China. For instance, when Malaysia's relations with China deteriorated during the period when Singapore was a part of Malaysia from 1963 to 1965 and the Bank of China branch in Singapore faced the prospect of forced closure, the Singapore government resisted pressure from the central government in Malaysia and kept the branch open. When Singapore became independent in August 1965, the Singapore government decided that the branch would be allowed to continue operating. The Bank of China hailed this decision as beneficial to the development of friendly relations.[2]

Equally significant, in the 1950s and 1960s when China's trade with Indonesia, the Philippines and Thailand was either seriously disrupted or banned altogether, China's trade with Singapore continued uninterrupted.[3] In fact, for several decades from 1950 to 1990, Sino–Singapore trade was conducted in the absence of a formal diplomatic framework.[4] Bilateral trade in the early 1970s hovered around S$700 million to S$800 million, with the balance of trade in China's favour.

Following the fallout with the Soviet Union in the late 1960s and the détente with America in the early 1970s, Beijing saw the need to improve its ties with the countries in Southeast Asia. Beginning in the second half of the 1970s, Beijing began to reduce its ties with the insurgency movements in Southeast Asia and ended its support for them thereafter. It established diplomatic relations with Malaysia (in May 1974), the Philippines (June 1975) and Thailand (July 1975). Although Singapore did not establish formal ties, it went on to improve relations with China. S. Rajaratnam became Singapore's first minister to visit China, in March 1975.[5] His visit paved the way for Singapore Prime Minister Lee Kuan Yew's trip to China in May 1976 where Lee met with Chairman Mao Zedong.[6] Although the meeting with Chairman Mao did not amount to a "substantive conversation", due to the latter's frail health, Lee was of the view that the Chinese side had extended a courtesy to the Singapore delegation through such a meeting to signal that China considered Singapore important enough.[7]

Another significant milestone in bilateral relations was reached when Vice-Premier Deng Xiaoping made his first and only official visit to Singapore in November 1978, to reciprocate Lee's visit of 1976. During his visit, Deng held detailed and frank discussions with Lee, and the two got to know each other on a personal basis. They exchanged views on the geostrategic environment, particularly the threat posed to the world by the Soviet Union, and how China could improve its relations with the countries in Southeast Asia. Deng was also unexpectedly impressed by Singapore's socio-economic progress since its independence in 1965. Deng told Lee that he was "glad he had come and seen Singapore again after 58 years".[8] He remarked that Singapore had undergone a "dramatic transformation" and congratulated Lee, who replied that "Singapore was a small country with two and a half million people". In response, Deng sighed and said, "If I had only Shanghai, I too might be able to change Shanghai as quickly. But I have the whole of China!"[9]

At the end of his visit, after Deng had boarded the plane to depart, Lee said to his colleagues that Deng's staff were going to get a "shellacking", as Deng had witnessed a Singapore that "his brief had not prepared him for". Sure enough, after Deng's visit, articles in the *People's Daily*, the main newspaper of the Communist Party of China, took a different line and portrayed Singapore in a positive light. No longer seen simply as "running dogs of the American imperialists", Singapore was described as a "garden city worth studying for its greening, public housing and tourism".[10] Another indication of Deng's positive impression of Singapore was his speech in October 1979 when he mentioned how Singapore had utilized foreign capital to generate revenue for the state and income for the workers, and promoted the growth of the service sectors.[11] To Deng, Singapore was a vivid example of a country that had done well after independence. More importantly, Singapore's experience could provide a reference for China.

Before arriving in Singapore in November 1978, Deng had visited Thailand and Malaysia. His impression of Southeast Asia before the tour was that it was a backward region, as this was the view of many Chinese leaders of the day. But among the three countries he visited, Singapore was said to have left the deepest impression on him.[12] What he saw in Singapore and the frank discussions he had had with Lee had "in some way convinced Deng to open up China". Lee also told Deng that "if Singaporeans, who were descendants of illiterate, landless peasants who had to leave China, could do it, then China with its progeny of scholars, mandarins and literati who had stayed home could certainly do it".[13] In other words, Singapore had shown China that it was possible to achieve a high level of socio-economic development under a strong and capable leadership. More precisely, a market economy was compatible with a one-party dominant state.

Singapore left such an indelible impression on Deng that he mentioned Singapore in his 1992 *Nanxun* speech when he sought to jump-start economic reforms in China following the 1989 Tiananmen incident and the 1991 collapse of the Soviet Union. In his *Nanxun* speech, Deng said that "Guangdong should catch up with Asia's four dragons (Hong Kong, Singapore, South Korea and Taiwan) in 20 years, not only in economics but also in social order and social climate. China should do better than these countries in these matters."[14] In particular, Deng mentioned that "Singapore enjoys good social order. They govern the place with discipline. We should tap their experience and learn how to manage better than them."[15] Deng's particular reference to Singapore opened the political window for Singapore and China to cooperate further. It sparked off "Singapore fever" in China and led to numerous visits by Chinese delegations to Singapore. In 1992 alone, more than four hundred delegations from China came to Singapore. They wanted to better understand how Singapore had established good social order alongside rapid economic growth.[16]

However, it was unclear how much these visiting Chinese delegations could benefit from the Singapore experience, as they merely studied isolated aspects of the Singapore system, such as its housing, labour, the airport and industrial parks, and their stay only lasted a few days. They were thus unable to get a full picture, much less understand the underlying philosophy behind the Singapore system. To overcome this shortcoming, Lee believed that the best way to transfer Singapore's economic and public administration experience — i.e., its software — to China was to have officials from both sides work jointly on a project. Hence, the idea of the Suzhou Industrial Park was conceived for Singapore to share its experience in planning, implementing and administering an integrated new town with industrial, commercial and residential sectors.

On its part, Singapore's leaders had since the late 1980s and early 1990s actively pushed regionalization, i.e., exhorting its businesses to venture into regional markets to develop a second wing to augment Singapore's small domestic market. In a speech to cadres of the ruling People's Action Party (the ruling party in Singapore) in 1992, Lee cited the success of Taiwan, Hong Kong and South Korea in building economies outside their geographical boundaries. He commented that these newly industrializing economies had "two wings with which to take flight. With only one wing, Singapore will stay on the ground and not get airborne."[17] The Suzhou Industrial Park provided a means for Singapore businesses to go overseas, as well as for the Singapore government to share its software experience with China.

A Substantive, Broad-Based Relationship

The personal rapport and deep mutual respect that Lee and Deng struck in their initial encounter in 1978 and thereafter strengthened through subsequent encounters in the 1980s helped to lay a strong foundation for the development of Singapore–China relations.[18] Today, China and Singapore enjoy a multifaceted relationship with cooperation and interaction on many fronts and at several levels.

One of the important anchors is their ever-expanding and deepening trade and investment ties. As mentioned earlier, bilateral trade between the two countries hovered around S$700 million to S$800 million in the early 1970s. In 1990, the year diplomatic ties were established, the figure for bilateral trade was S$5.2 billion. By 2016, bilateral trade had increased more than twentyfold to reach $117.2

billion (see Figure 1). In 2013, China overtook Malaysia to become Singapore's largest trading partner and has retained this position ever since.

According to China's customs statistics, Singapore's trade with China in 2015 amounted to US$79.5 billion, occupying third spot among ASEAN member states, after Malaysia at US$97.3 billion and Vietnam at US$95.8 billion (see Figure 2).

In terms of investment, China has been Singapore's top investment destination since 1997. In 2015, Singapore's cumulative investment in China was US$121 billion, almost eight times the figure of US$15.7 billion in 2001 when China joined the World Trade Organization. Furthermore, over the years the gap between Singapore's top investment destination of China and its second-largest investment destination of Hong Kong has widened. In 2015, the country's investment in China was US$121 billion, more than double the figure of US$52.7 billion for Hong Kong. Even more significant for a small country, Singapore has been China's largest investor since 2013 (see Figure 3).

With regard to tourism, the number of tourist arrivals from China to Singapore has increased over the years. Chinese tourist arrivals in Singapore crept upwards to the seventh position in 1998, third position in 2002 (overtaking Malaysia and Australia) and second position in 2003 (overtaking Japan). It remained in the second position after Indonesia for several years. In 2016, despite the downturn in bilateral relations, the number of Chinese tourist arrivals hit a record high of 2.86 million, growing 36 per cent from 2015 and almost closing the gap with tourist arrivals from Indonesia at 2.89 million (see Figure 4). Chinese tourists also ranked top in tourism receipts for the second consecutive year since 2015.[19] In 2017, the number of Chinese tourist arrivals to Singapore exceeded for the first time those to Indonesia.

Cultural exchanges between the two countries cover various aspects. China's dance troupes and bands have been a regular feature at the annual Chingay Parade and River Hongbao that celebrates the Lunar New Year and the cultural diversity of Singapore. In 2009, Singapore's Asian Civilisations Museum collaborated with China's Palace Museum to stage a well-received local exhibition known as "The Kangxi Emperor: Treasures from the Forbidden City". Most recently, in June 2017, Singapore's National Heritage Board and China's Palace Museum signed a five-year memorandum of understanding (MOU) for collaboration in areas such as exhibition and loan exchange, curatorial and conservation staff exchange, collections management and conservation, and retail opportunities.[20]

In addition, the China Cultural Centre, that further promotes bilateral arts and cultural exchange, was officially opened during President Xi Jinping's state visit to Singapore in November 2015. Designed by local architect Liu Thai Ker,

FIGURE 1
Singapore–China Total Trade (1990–2016)

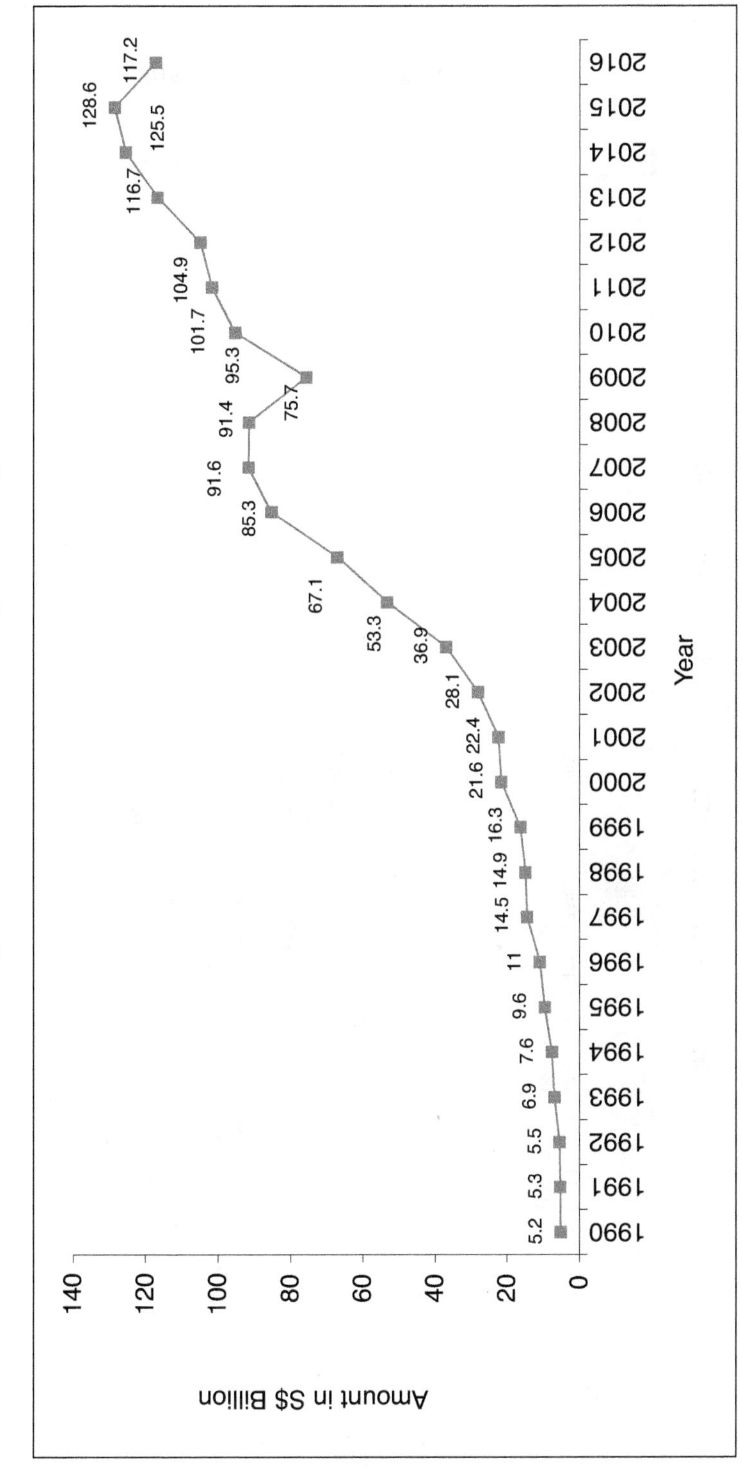

Source: Yearbook of Statistics, Singapore (various issues).

FIGURE 2
China's Trade with ASEAN-5 and Vietnam (2000–2015)

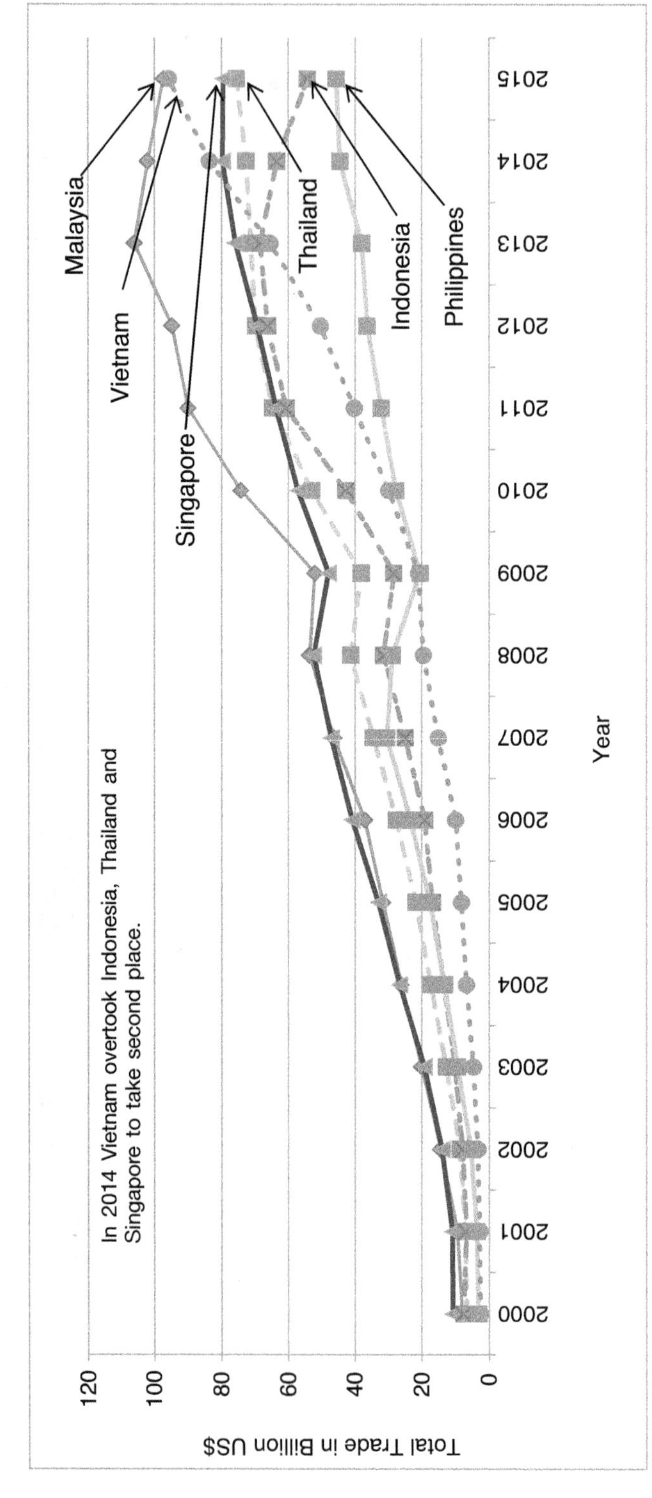

Source: China Statistical Yearbook, China (various issues).

FIGURE 3
Singapore's Cumulative Direct Investment Abroad (2003–15, Top 8*)

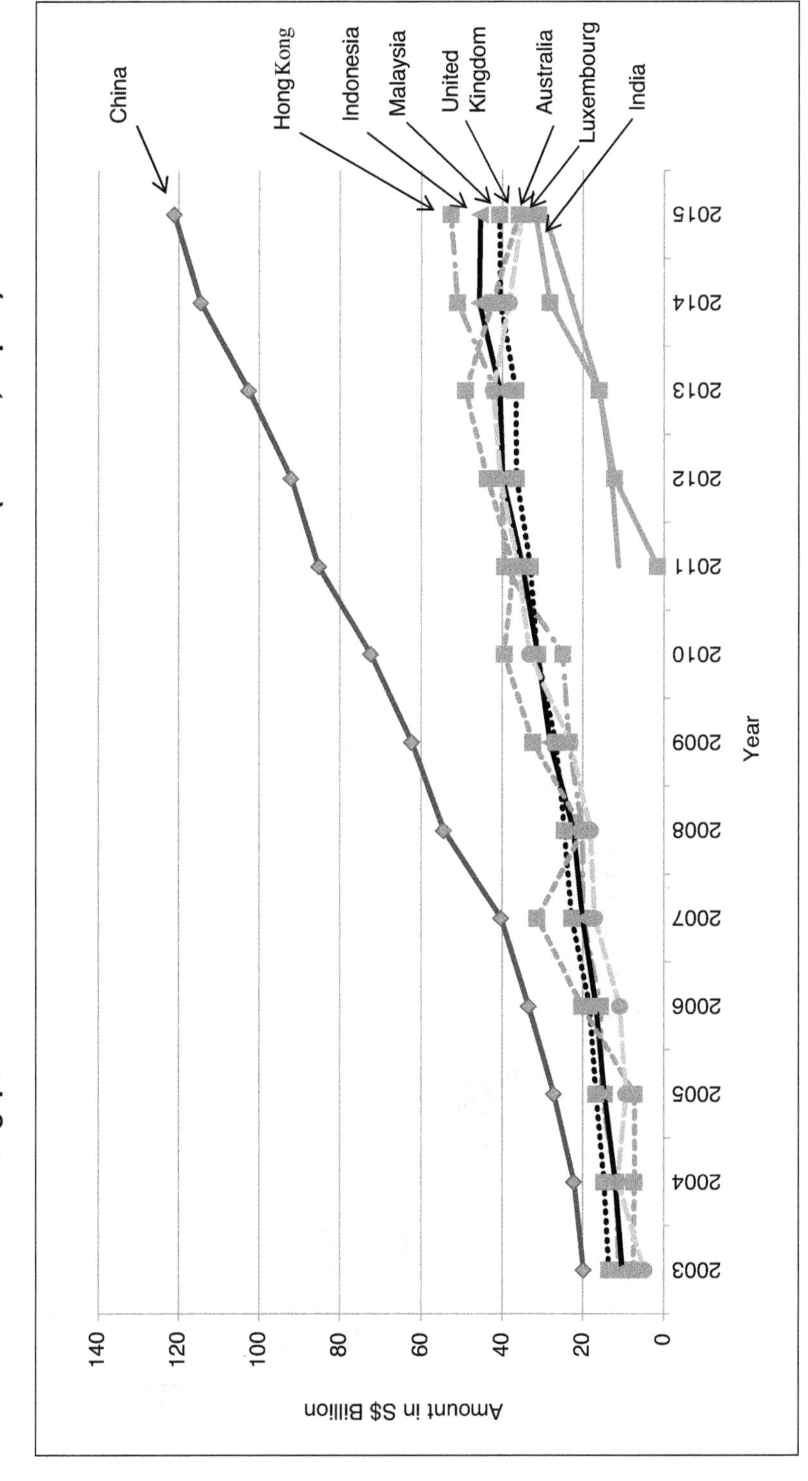

Note: * Minus the Caymen and Virgin Islands.
Source: Yearbook of Singapore Statistics (various years).

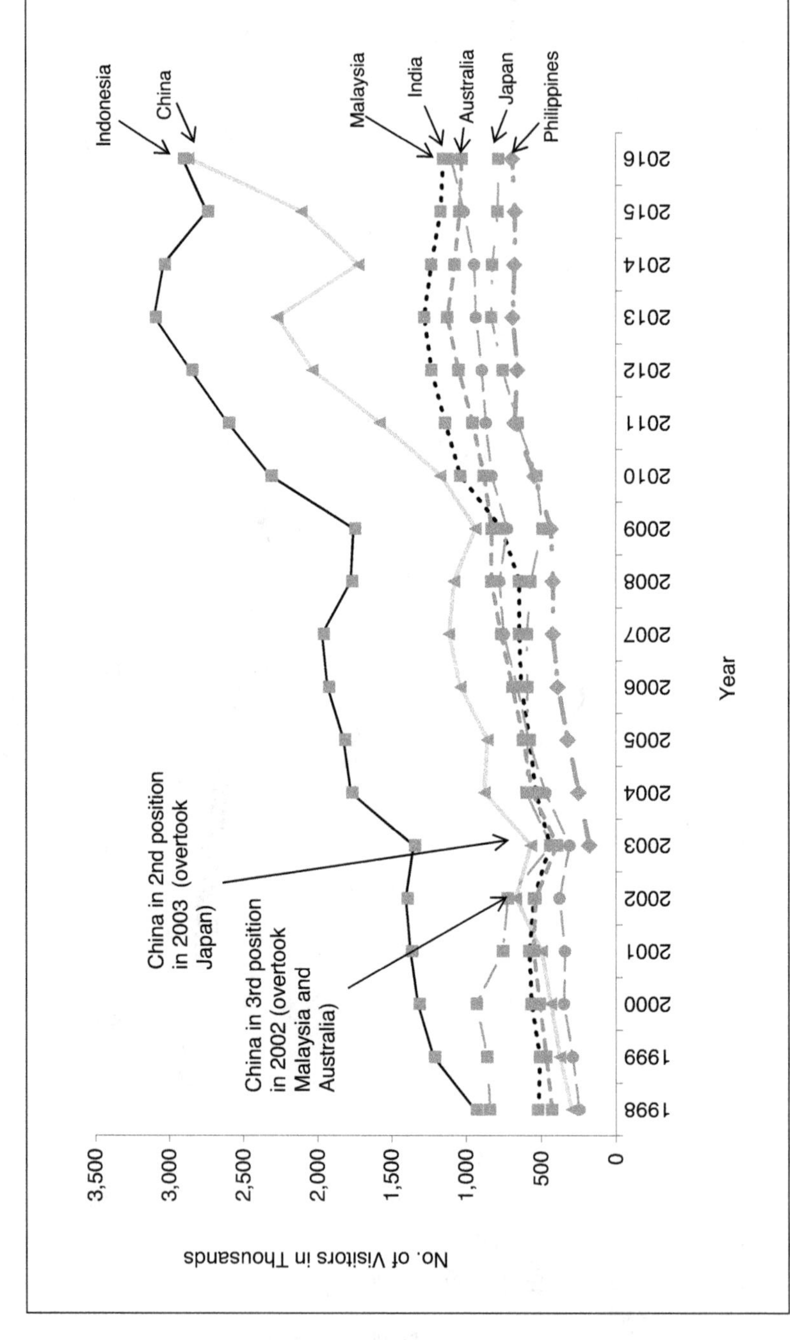

FIGURE 4
Top Seven Visitor-Generating Markets for Singapore (1998–2016)

it is the first such centre in the world.[21] Cultural interactions between Singapore and China are not confined to the people-to-people level. Singapore is among a handful of countries to have received a pair of giant pandas, considered China's national treasure, in 2012. The Singapore zoological authorities are trying hard to bring the relationship between the pair of pandas to the next level by getting them to breed.

More significantly, Singapore is an early and active supporter of China's Belt and Road Initiative (BRI). It was among the first batch of countries to sign the MOU to establish the Asian Infrastructure Investment Bank (AIIB) in Beijing in October 2014. The AIIB is a key financial platform to fund BRI projects around the world. Through its membership of the AIIB, China can leverage on Singapore's strength as a regional financial centre to raise funds for the various BRI projects. Currently, China's investments in Singapore alone amount to about one third of its total investments in BRI countries. Furthermore, Singapore's investments in China accounted for 85 per cent of total inbound investments from BRI countries.[22]

Among the countries along the BRI route, Singapore is somewhat different in that it is not a major recipient of BRI projects, given its already developed economy and relatively good infrastructure network. Instead, Singapore is in a good position to provide key services required by other countries, such as financing solutions (as mentioned above), legal and consulting services, and the provision of human resource training for other countries to manage BRI projects and raise the requisite capital.

In line with this thrust, the Singapore Business Federation and China Enterprises Association launched the BRI Connect Platform (an online and offline network) in August 2017 that aims to provide its members an avenue to share information on the latest developments on the BRI, provide market analysis and intelligence, conduct feasibility and evaluation studies, assist in project investment and financing, offer legal and arbitration consultation, set up online and offline BRI project-matching activities, promote the development of talent capability and showcase successful BRI stories.[23] In addition, the two countries have also embarked on legal and judicial cooperation in 2017 that provides avenues for businesses to resolve commercial disputes arising from the expanded economic opportunities under China's BRI. Singapore also looks forward to working with China on e-commerce and has invited China to put in a strong bid for the Kuala Lumpur High Speed Rail project.

Singapore has in fact bucked the general trend of countries hosting BRI projects from China to investing in China. The most iconic example of this is the third government-to-government project known as the Chongqing Connectivity

Initiative, where the focus is on developing businesses and networks in areas such as information and communication technology, aviation, transport and logistics, and financial services. This project, launched during President Xi's state visit to Singapore in November 2015, is positioned as "the key priority demonstration project" of China's three important development strategies; namely, the BRI, Western Region Development and Yangtze River Economic Belt.[24]

There are two other government-to-government projects that Singapore and China are involved in. The first is the Suzhou Industrial Park that began in 1994. Despite encountering initial difficulties, the Suzhou Industrial Park is today a leading industrial park known not only for its economic achievements but also its clean, green and liveable environment. The second project is the Tianjin Eco-city of 2008 that is geared towards creating a sustainable urban and environmentally friendly living environment. For each of these projects, a high-level joint steering council led by the deputy prime ministers of the two countries drives progress by sharing each other's experiences as well as best practices from elsewhere. At the same time, such high-level mechanisms provide a platform for the leaders of the two countries to meet regularly to promote understanding and rapport.

Not Altogether Smooth Sailing

From time to time, Singapore–China relations have run into difficulties. These difficulties can be attributed to a number of factors, including the ongoing strategic shift in power between China and the United States, and the implications of this shift for small states like Singapore; China's rise and its expectations of how smaller states like Singapore ought to respond to its rise; and China's perception that Singapore has encroached on its interests, such as its claims to the South China Sea and the "One China" policy on Taiwan.

In recent years there has also been a growing sense of national sentiment and pride in China that has not taken lightly to perceived slights by Singapore. At times, Chinese officials would lend credence to such sentiments by asserting that the actions of a particular country have hurt the feelings of the 1.3 billion people of China, and that that particular country would have to bear all the consequences arising from this. It is not uncommon to find each of these factors or a combination of these factors at play when there is a downturn in bilateral relations.

In 2016, Singapore–China relations hit their lowest point. The key incidents are outlined here:

- In April 2016, two senior Singaporean diplomats reportedly accused China of meddling in ASEAN's internal affairs and even attempting to divide ASEAN after Chinese Foreign Minister Wang Yi announced that China had reached a four-point consensus with Brunei, Cambodia and Laos on the South China Sea issue. In response, Chinese Vice-Foreign Minister Liu Zhenmin asserted that China's intentions had been misunderstood and that China had sought clarification from Singapore on the accusation levelled by the diplomats.

- In June 2016, a joint foreign ministers' press conference that was supposed to involve Wang Yi and his Singapore counterpart Vivian Balakrishnan — after a special ASEAN–China Foreign Ministers' Meeting in Yunnan — ended up with only a solo media appearance by the Chinese minister. The meeting was originally supposed to discuss ASEAN–China relations, the implementation of the Declaration on the Conduct of Parties in the South China Sea and hold consultations on the Code of Conduct, but it was bogged down by disagreements over the South China Sea issue.
- In September 2016, a robust exchange ensued between the Singapore Ambassador in Beijing and the editor of the hawkish Communist Party publication, *Global Times*, over what was perceived to be Singapore's sole attempts (when in fact it was ASEAN's efforts) to revise the paragraphs on Southeast Asia (that contained references to the South China Sea issue) in the Non-Aligned Movement Summit's final documents.
- In November 2016, the Hong Kong's Customs and Excise Department seized nine Terrex infantry carrier vehicles belonging to the Singapore Armed Forces while they were in transit at Hong Kong's Kwai Chung Container Terminal. Capitalizing on this incident, China's foreign ministry spokesperson Geng Shuang was reported to have said that the Chinese government is "firmly opposed to any forms of official interaction between Taiwan and countries that have diplomatic relations with us, military exchanges and cooperation included".[25] In China's view, Singapore had contravened the "One China" policy by maintaining military exchanges and ties with Taiwan.

Of the four incidents above, the first three concerned the South China Sea issue while the fourth is related to Taiwan. A primary reason why the South China Sea issue loomed large in Singapore–China relations in 2016 was because this was the same year that the arbitral tribunal issued its award on the case lodged by the Philippines against China in 2013. Before, during and after the arbitral tribunal issued its award in July 2016, China was closely monitoring the responses of other countries and organizations to this award, including ASEAN member states, and took proactive steps to prevent ASEAN or its member states from lending any form of support to the award.

From the perspective of a small state, Singapore has publicly stated on various occasions the sanctity of principles for small states, such as freedom of navigation and the rule of law in the conduct of foreign relations and in resolving disputes. It has further stated its firm opposition to the "might is right" approach. Singapore's approach stood in stark contrast to China's preference for the South China Sea issue to be resolved away from the media glare and only involving the parties directly concerned. As a result, the Chinese government and public regarded Singapore as deliberately going against China's interests by constantly playing up the South China Sea issue, even though Singapore was not a claimant state. In addition, they felt that Singapore was not as neutral as it had professed to be in its capacity as the coordinator of ASEAN–China relations.

Another reason why relations hit a nadir in 2016 was China's belief that Singapore had chosen to side with America against China. Various Chinese sources have interpreted the fact of U.S. littoral combat ships and P-8A Poseidon maritime surveillance aircraft operating out of Singapore in the South China Sea as hard evidence of Singapore leaning to the side of the United States to "contain" China.

More tellingly, a *Global Times* article took issue with Singapore Prime Minister Lee Hsien Loong's remarks at a White House state dinner in August 2016 where he commended U.S. President Barack Obama for his "leadership and decision to rebalance to Asia" which has won "America new friends and strengthened old partnerships, including with Singapore".[26] The article criticized Prime Minister Lee for praising Obama's "rebalance to Asia-Pacific" strategy and for his claim that all Southeast Asian countries welcome America engaging in such a rebalancing. The article opined that as the "rebalancing to Asia-Pacific" strategy was essentially a sword pointed at China, Prime Minster Lee had obviously taken sides by articulating these words. The article went on to assert that Singapore wanted to take possession of everything. While toying with "balancing", it would occasionally jab China, which, at the very least, has led ordinary Chinese to feel very uncomfortable.[27]

This is not the first time that Singapore's use of the word "re-balancing" or "balance" has irked China. Several years ago, in October 2009, at a dinner hosted by the U.S.–ASEAN Business Council in Washington DC, Minister Mentor (MM) Lee Kuan Yew reportedly told his audience that "the size of China makes it impossible for the rest of Asia, including Japan and India, to match it in weight and capacity in about 20 to 30 years. So we need America to strike a balance."[28] Comments from Chinese netizens in response to MM Lee's use of the word "balance" came fast and furious, especially after *Global Times* and other Chinese media channels gave it prominent coverage. More specifically, the word "balance" was carried in *Global Times* and other media channels to mean that the United States should "counteract" China's rise or the United States should be involved in Asian affairs as a "check against" China or, worse, even to "contain" China. Comments by Chinese netizens ranged from the mild, such as "Singapore trusting the US more than it trusts China", that MM Lee had treated the Chinese as outsiders although they had treated Singaporeans as "among their own", to the highly critical view that "Singapore is America's Beachhead in Containing China".[29]

Already in 2009 Chinese netizens had reacted strongly to MM Lee's use of the word "balance". At that time a different China was already emerging due to its new-found sense of confidence as it came relatively unscathed through the 2008 world economic crisis that adversely affected the United States and Europe. A key difference between then and now is that China today is far stronger and influential than it was in 2009. It has a higher expectation of how smaller states ought to behave or conduct themselves in developing relations with China. It is also more sensitive to perceived slights by other countries. Another equally important difference is that a different generation of leadership is at the helms in Singapore and China. In Singapore, a post–Lee Kuan Yew era of leaders has to grapple with a China that accords greater priority and attention to its relations with other big powers than with a small country like Singapore. China's leaders are apparently also less receptive of what current Singapore leaders say about China, especially if such views are deemed to be critical of China. Chinese President Xi has replaced China's low-profile orientation with a foreign policy that is more in line with that of a major power. These are the current realities that Singapore will have to contend with.

Fortunately, Singapore–China relations appear to have recovered from the unhappy episodes of 2016. In February 2017 the two countries resumed their high-level Joint Council for Bilateral Cooperation (JCBC) Meeting, which was postponed from the year before, led by the deputy prime ministers of the two countries. The JCBC oversees the joint steering councils that drive the progress of the three government-to-government projects. Prime Minister Lee Hsien Loong also met with President Xi Jinping in China in September 2017 and reaffirmed the strong friendship built by succeeding generations of leaders on both sides. The visit came just before China held its all-important 19th Party Congress in October 2017.

Going forward, the contours of Singapore–China relations will continue to be determined by broader factors beyond Singapore's control, particularly the state of U.S.–China relations and the shift in relative power between the two that will determine the room to manoeuvre for small states like Singapore, and China's increasing pressure on small states to take into account its growing interests. Singapore's response has been to reiterate its willingness to seek close and friendly ties with as many countries as possible. It continues to advocate a "consistent, honest and reliable" approach in managing its relations with other countries and has stated that if this approach sometimes gets it into a "slightly warmer soup with either China or the US, so be it". It has even said that it is prepared to take "short-term penalties" in order to maintain its long-held position as "honest brokers who say the same thing and can be relied on".[30]

These words may sound harsh but they underpin Singapore's foreign policy that is guided by principles, transparency and predictability. They form the very basis of Singapore's independence and sovereignty. They need not necessarily work against China's interests, as China itself has benefitted greatly from an open and rules-based world order. China has even singled out "sovereign equality" — regardless of whether a country is big or small, rich or poor — as the most important norm governing state-to-state relations and the cardinal principle observed by the United Nations and other international organizations.[31] In this sense, China could find much value in Singapore being a reliable, consistent and honest partner.

Conclusion

The huge asymmetry between Singapore and China has not prevented the two countries from developing a friendly and substantive relationship in many areas and at various levels. The early generation of leaders — namely, Lee Kuan Yew and Deng Xiaoping — were instrumental in laying a firm foundation for the pragmatic development of relations which succeeding generations of leaders have continued to build upon. In addition, the small size of Singapore and its socio-economic achievements and effective governance have made it an attractive partner for China. The two countries continue to identify new areas in which to collaborate, such as in finance, in judicial and legal matters, and in e-commerce and infrastructure. The three government-to-government projects reflect how the two countries have shifted the nature of collaboration in line with their development needs. Certainly, relations between Singapore and China are bound to hit bumps from time to time. Singapore's principled approach may appear to be at odds with China's penchant to use a combination of power and other means. Yet, this difference is not strategic in nature. The two countries have continued to expand and deepen cooperation.

Notes

1. "Kuan Yew 'Dispels' Third China Idea about S'pore", *Straits Times*, 12 April 1966, p. 12.
2. "'Thank You' to Lee from Bank of China Chief", *Straits Times*, 15 August 1965, p. 10.
3. Indonesia broke off diplomatic ties with China in April 1967 when President Sukarno came into power and ties were only resumed in August 1990. The Philippines suspended trade ties with China in 1949 after the People's Republic of China was formed and established diplomatic relations with China in June 1975. Similarly, Thailand joined the Philippines (and the United States) in suspending trade ties with China during the Cold War. It only established diplomatic ties with China in July 1975. Malaysia normalized relations with China in May 1974, becoming the first ASEAN country to do so. Singapore was the last among the ASEAN countries to establish diplomatic ties with China, on 3 October 1990.
4. John Wong, "Sino–Singapore Relations: Looking Back and Looking Forward", in *Singapore–China Commemorative Souvenir in Celebration of the 10th Anniversary of the Establishment of Diplomatic Relations between the Republic of Singapore and the People's Republic of China* (Singapore: Grenadier Press, 2000), p. 74.
5. On this trip, Minister Rajaratnam was accompanied by Lee Khoon Choy, then Senior Minister of State for Foreign Affairs, three officials (Joseph Koh, Foreign Ministry desk officer and secretary of the delegation; Howe Yoon Chong, Port of Singapore Authority and Development Bank of Singapore Chairman; and I.F. Tang, Economic Development Board Deputy Chairman) and five Singapore newsmen. See "Raja Sees the Sights in Canton after Train Journey", *Straits Times*, 13 March 1975 and "It All Began at a Dinner in New York...", *Straits Times*, 14 March 1975.
6. Lee Kuan Yew could not meet Zhou Enlai during his visit in May 1976 as the latter had passed away in January 1976.
7. Lee Kuan Yew, *From Third World to First: The Singapore Story, 1965–2000* (New York: HarperCollins, 2000), p. 582.
8. In 1920, Deng had transited in Singapore for two days while he was en route to France.
9. Lee, *From Third World to First*, pp. 667–68.
10. Ibid., p. 668.
11. Ibid., pp. 668–69.
12. This view was expressed by Lü Yuanli, director of the Singapore Research Centre at Shenzhen University. See "Deng–Lee Meeting Depicted in China TV Serial", *Straits Times*, 27 August 2014 <http://www.straitstimes.com/news/asia/east-asia/story/deng-lee-meeting-depicted-china-tv-serial-20140827> (accessed 1 December 2017).
13. Mr Goh Chok Tong, then Senior Minister of State for Finance, was present at the historic meeting between Lee Kuan Yew and Deng Xiaoping in Singapore in November 1978.

See "Speech by Mr. Goh Chok Tong, Senior Minister, at the Singapore–Guangdong Development Forum" (in Guangzhou), Prime Minister's Office Singapore, 24 March 2009 <http://www.pmo.gov.sg/mediacentre/speech-mr-goh-chok-tong-senior-minister-singapore-guangdong-development-forum-24-march> (accessed 1 December 2017).

14. Lee, *From Third World to First*, p. 714.
15. Shenzhen Propaganda Department, ed., *Deng Xiaoping yu Shenzhen: 1992 Chun* [Deng Xiaoping and Shenzhen: Spring 1992] (Shenzhen, Haitian chubanshe, 1992), p. 9.
16. John Wong, "China's Fascination with the Development of Singapore", *Asia-Pacific Review* 5, no. 3 (Fall/Winter 1998): 51–63.
17. "SM: Singaporeans Must Now Build Up External Economy", *Straits Times*, 16 November 1992. See also remarks by then Deputy Prime Minister Lee Hsien Loong in "Walking with Two Legs", *Straits Times*, 9 November 1992.
18. Lee has described Deng as a "great statesman", a "giant among world leaders" and who had "saved China" with his open-door policy. Lee added that "without him, China could have been like the Soviet Union. Instead, China would become a huge heavyweight nation in 30 years." See "A Giant among World Leaders", *Straits Times*, 21 February 1997.
19. "Singapore Achieves Record Tourism Sector Performance in 2016", Singapore Tourism Board Tourism media release, 14 February 2017 <https://www.stb.gov.sg/news-and-publications/lists/newsroom/dispform.aspx?ID=696> (accessed 1 December 2017).
20. The MOU was signed during Minister for Culture, Community and Youth Grace Fu's visit to China in June 2017. See "The National Heritage Board, Singapore, Signs Inaugural Memorandum of Understanding with the Palace Museum, China", Singapore's National Heritage Board media release, 16 June 2017 <https://www.nhb.gov.sg/~/media/nhb/files/media/releases/new%20releases/media%20release%20on%20nhb-pm%20mou%20signing.pdf> (accessed 1 December 2017).
21. In November 2010, when Vice President Xi Jinping visited Singapore to commemorate the twentieth anniversary of the establishment of diplomatic ties, he officiated at the ground-breaking ceremony for the China Cultural Centre with Senior Minister Goh Chok Tong.
22. "The One-Belt One-Road Initiative: Impact and Implications", Speech by Mr K. Shanmugam, Minister for Home Affairs and Minister for Law, Singapore's Ministry of Home Affairs website, 28 August 2017 <https://www.mha.gov.sg/newsroom/speeches/Pages/Asia-Economic-Forum-on-The-One-Belt-One-Road-Initiative-Impact-and-Implications.aspx> (accessed 1 December 2017).
23. "SBF and China Enterprises Association jointly launched the 'BRI Connect' Platform at Singapore Regional Business Forum 2017", Singapore Business Federation website <http://www.sbf.org.sg/singapore-business-federation-and-china-enterprises-association-jointly-launched-the-bri-connect-platform-at-singapore-regional-business-forum-2017> (accessed 1 December 2017). The Singapore Business Federation has a network

of twenty-four thousand companies, while the China Enterprises Association has a membership of five hundred companies.

24. "Joint Statement between the People's Republic of China and the Republic of Singapore on the Establishment of an All-Round Cooperative Partnership Progressing with the Times", Singapore's Ministry of Foreign Affairs website, 7 November 2015 <https://www.mfa.gov.sg/content/mfa/media_centre/press_room/pr/2015/201511/press_20151107.html> (accessed 1 December 2017).
25. "Foreign Ministry Spokesperson Geng Shuang's Regular Press Conference", China's Ministry of Foreign Affairs website, 25 November 2016 <http://www.fmprc.gov.cn/mfa_eng/xwfw_665399/s2510_665401/t1418891.shtml> (accessed 4 December 2017).
26. "Toast Speech by Prime Minister Lee Hsien Loong at the White House State Dinner", Prime Minister's Office Singapore, 2 August 2016 <http://www.pmo.gov.sg/newsroom/toast-speech-prime-minister-lee-hsien-loong-white-house-state-dinner> (accessed 4 December 2017).
27. "Shan Renping: Zhongguo ying tiliang Xinjiapo, yeyao huachu dixian" [Shan Renping: China should understand Singapore, it should also draw its bottom-line], *Global Times*, 4 August 2016 <http://opinion.huanqiu.com/shanrenping/2016-08/9262616.html> (accessed 5 December 2017).
28. "MM Calls on US to Retain Key Role in East Asia", *Straits Times*, 29 October 2009.
29. "Li Guangyao de yanlun baolu Xinjiapo shi Meiguo weidu Zhongguo de qiaotoubao" [Lee Kuan Yew's remarks reveal that Singapore is America's beachhead in containing China], *Zhonghuawang luntan*, 4 November 2009 <http://military.china.com/zh_cn/critical3/27/20091104/15689477.html> (accessed 10 June 2011).
30. "S'pore Consistent in Ties with China, US: Vivian", *Straits Times,* 14 May 2017.
31. "Work Together to Build a Community of Shared Future for Mankind", Speech by President Xi Jinping, Xinhuanet, 19 January 2017 <http://news.xinhuanet.com/english/2017-01/19/c_135994707.htm> (accessed 5 December 2017).

Thailand

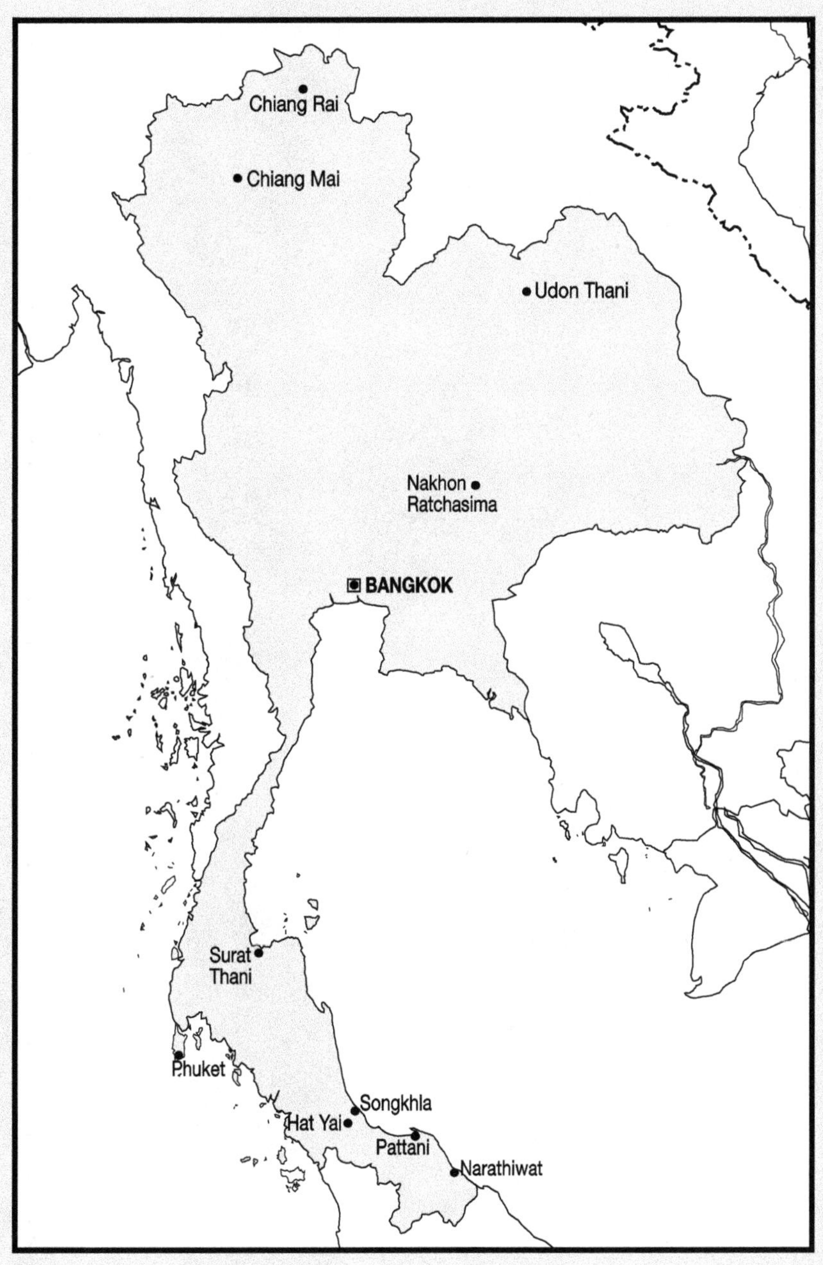
Chiang Rai
Chiang Mai
Udon Thani
Nakhon Ratchasima
BANGKOK
Surat Thani
Phuket
Songkhla
Hat Yai
Pattani
Narathiwat

THAILAND IN 2017: Stability without Certainties

Pongphisoot Busbarat

Thailand in 2017 has been relatively stable, despite the fact that a decade-long political struggle has not come to an end. In fact, a widely anticipated process of national reconciliation has never taken place; hence, tensions between contending groups will continue to challenge Thailand in the immediate and long-term future. Despite this there were several important factors in 2017 that helped contain the conflict and which, in turn, maintained the stability of the military government. Such stability has, first and foremost, been preserved by restrictions on political freedom in the kingdom. The death of King Bhumibol in October 2016 and the year-long period of mourning, during which political activities were deemed inappropriate and socially unacceptable, further silenced opposition voices.

However, with the military holding power and the political bargaining between elites in different factions still unsettled, uncertainties cloud the future of Thai democracy. Illustrative of such uncertainties is the case of the charges against former prime minister Yingluck Shinawatra in the latter half of 2017 for negligence in regard to the rice-pledging scheme. The fact that Yingluck managed to flee the country in September added uncertainty to the future of the pro-Thaksin front and its leadership.

On the economic front, Thailand's economy experienced slow growth. Some policies were launched to stimulate the stagnant economy, in particular the Thailand 4.0 model, with the aim of upgrading Thailand to an innovative economy. However, it is unclear whether these policies will work as intended. The country's low economic performance has gradually affected all levels of the population, particularly the middle-class and the poor. Income disparity between the haves and have-nots remains a major challenge to Thailand's attempts to step up to a high-income economy.

Pongphisoot Busbarat is Visiting Fellow at the ISEAS – Yusof Ishak Institute, Singapore.

Regarding foreign relations, China is still an important factor in Thailand's foreign policy. Since the early period of the military government, when the junta sought international support amid strong criticism from Western nations, the country's reliance on China has continued. And while October saw the normalization of Thai–U.S. relations, tensions could resurface in the future, especially on trade issues. While the direction of Thai–U.S. ties remains unclear, Thailand will face difficulty in balancing Beijing's influence. After all, Thailand still relies on China for assistance with its economic recovery, so it cannot reduce the latter's heavy influence on policy calculations.

Moving Towards Controlled Democracy

For more than a decade, during the post–Cold War era, Thailand was one of the most vibrant democracies in East Asia. The military's attempt to return to politics in the early 1990s faced popular resistance, resulting in the new 1997 Constitution that strengthened mechanisms for checks and balances, improved the efficiency of the executive branch and broadened civil, political and human rights.

While the 1997 Constitution led to positive development in Thai politics, it quickly tilted the power balance away from the establishment towards a new political group led by former prime minister Thaksin Shinawatra. This structural change arguably induced a decade-long political crisis in the kingdom. Thaksin and his political circle gained popular support based on populist policies which attracted the underprivileged population, especially in the rural parts of the country. As a result, the establishment and the urban middle class felt threatened and attempted to weaken Thaksin's political legitimacy through judicial activism against him, his family and his political parties. Political struggle loomed large throughout the decade since 2005 between the anti-Thaksin group, or the Yellow Shirts, and the pro-Thaksin group, the Red Shirts. The colour-coded politics brought protests and counter-protests to the streets of central Bangkok that paralysed the city many times. The military intervened by staging two coups, first in 2006 and again in 2014.

Prolonging the Military's Role in Politics

Unlike coups of the past, the 2014 coup leaders under the name of the National Council for Peace and Order (NCPO) show a determination to control the future of Thai politics for a prolonged period. Both the delayed timeframe for a new election and political engineering in the new constitution, which passed a referendum in August 2016, may suggest the military's political intentions.

After returning from his visit to the White House in the first week of October 2017, Prime Minister Prayut announced that elections would be held in November 2018. However, this timeframe seemed to be unattainable. Although the National Assembly passed the laws related to the election at the end of January 2018, they need to go through a review process by the Election Commission. If approved, the law will be signed by the king and announced in the Royal Gazette by the end of June 2018. A 90-day window period will be left until the end of September. After that, the election will be held within 150 days. Therefore, if everything goes smoothly, the election should be realized by February or March 2019 at the latest. If there is any interruption in the process or any problem — in the judgement of the junta — it will cause a delay to the election. Such a delay would not be impossible, considering the previous experience of the first drafting of the constitution when it failed to receive approval from the National Assembly in September 2013. The start of a new drafting process helped prolong the tenure of the military government until now.

In an interview in early December 2017, Thai army chief and secretary of the NCPO General Chalermchai Sithisart mentioned that the current situation may not be suitable for any political activities. His opinion was given in reference to the seizure of a large quantity of illegal weapons in Chacheongsao province at the end of November 2017, which the Thai authorities later claimed were connected to some segments of the Red Shirts.[1] Moreover, many observers and political parties were worried that if the NCPO did not allow political parties to start their activities by 5 January 2018, they may have insufficient time to fulfil the requirements of the new political party law, hence being at risk of being disqualified for the election.[2] There are possibilities, therefore, that the election might be delayed if the military cannot ensure the result will be in its favour.

Despite possible delay, there were also signs at the end of December 2017 and in the New Year that the above election road map may be on track. General Prem Tinsulanonda, chairman of the Privy Council, informed Prayut that, despite having fewer supporters, he would be able to regain public support due to his determination to serve the people.[3] Several days after that, Prayut started calling himself a "politician"[4] — a career he had previously dubbed as "dirty" and "corrupt". This might suggest that he was sending a signal to the public that it was highly possible for him to be directly involved in politics after the election. However, it remains to be seen in what capacity he would be involved.

Moreover, there has been increasing pressure towards the Prayut government that may signal its declining popularity. The public, even among Prayut's supporters, has questioned the political legitimacy of the ruling regime following a scandal involving Deputy Prime Minister General Prawit Wongsuwan over his undeclared luxury wristwatches. Political activists have started to call both for Prawit to step down and for the election to be announced soon. These developments could remind Prayut that the longer he holds on to power the less he will benefit from the new politics after the election. Such a realization may influence him to keep the election within the timeline.

Embedding Military Influence

Looking at the legal architecture in the new constitution, it seems that the military will influence Thai politics and the policies of the future governments for quite some time. Significantly, the new constitution will retain the power of the current junta leaders in several aspects. Firstly, it empowers the NCPO to appoint members of the Senate, which will have veto power over the House of Representatives. Moreover, the constitution also allows the possibility of having an unelected prime minister. It opens several channels through which political parties can nominate a non-elected individual for the position. Therefore, the NCPO will be able to exercise its influence in the future legislature, especially through the Senate. There is also the possibility that Prayut or another coup leader could be nominated as the next prime minister.

The new constitution is built on another iron wall; that is, it is difficult to amend, and the Senate plays an important role in the amendment process. The process consists of four steps. First, a motion for amendment needs to be passed by at least a fifth of the members of the House of Representatives or of both houses combined who are present at the time of the vote. Once the motion is endorsed, the draft amendment needs approval in principle from at least half of the members of both houses who are present. It also requires the support of a third of the members of the Senate. The next step will be to vote for the individual amendments, each of which requires a majority vote in parliament to pass. The final approval needs to receive a *yes* vote from half of the members of both houses present at the time of voting. However, the *yes* vote must also meet two other criteria: firstly, it has to come from twenty per cent of the members of all political parties whose members do not hold the positions of prime minister, spokesperson of the House of Representatives and its deputies; secondly, it must also be from one third of the members of the Senate present at the time of the vote. Considering these requirements, any amendment to the new constitution would be near impossible, especially when the Senate is under the influence of the NCPO.

Apart from the political architecture that will retain the military's power in the future, the current regime also intends to shape the policy direction of future governments by embedding the so-called Twenty-Year National Strategy (2017–36) into the constitution. The National Strategy covers six aspects, including security, competitive enhancement, human resource development, social equality, environmentally green growth, and readjustment and development of the public sector.[5] On the surface the framework of the National Strategy seems to benefit Thailand's future development. Prime Minister Prayut had stated that Thailand needs a strategy that will improve and strengthen the Thai economy and overcome the middle-income trap.[6]

However, critics suggest that the process of drafting the National Strategy was opaque and did not involve public opinion or participation. The cabinet directly appointed the committee responsible for drafting it. The committee members consisted of seventeen members of the NCPO and another seventeen selected experts[7] who wield political and economic power, including members of the military and businessmen. The details of the National Strategy have not been revealed to the public for feedback or debate, with the committee only having published a thirty-five page summary document. At the end of September 2017, the committee unveiled the members of six subcommittees tasked with preparing concrete plans under the six strategic aspects.

The new constitution also stipulates that the National Strategy will be enforced under the law. This means the National Strategy will become the overarching policy framework for Thailand for the next twenty years. It would likely limit the ability for political parties to initiate or propose any policy to their voters. Any new government would also be required to announce its policies to parliament and allocate the budget in accordance with the National Strategy. Although there are no specific penalties for not complying with the National Strategy, non-compliance could be interpreted as violating the constitution, leading to motions against the government.

Continued Suppression of Political Freedom

Voices of political dissent have continued to be suppressed and the role of the military in Thai politics has been further entrenched. Although the military has achieved stability by prohibiting mass political gatherings, Thai politics is by no means static. After all, political grievances and tensions did not vanish in the wake of the 2014 military coup. There are still signs of civil resistance and unease within the pro-democratic movements. However, during the past year the military has continued to suppress these political activists, including anti-military individuals and pro-Thaksin propaganda.

The Thai authorities have continued to threaten and silence political opinion. Amid the political crisis, the lèse-majesté law and Computer Crime Act have become legal tools used by the military and other political factions to curb the activities of their opponents. The legal process under the lèse-majesté law is conducted behind closed doors, and the police normally refuse bail. The use of the lèse-majesté law and Computer Crime Act have not only created fear in Thai society but have also led to the sense that the monarchy under the new constitution is an untouchable institution. It also prompts suspicion that law enforcement agencies have violated and compromised citizens' privacy and rights, often through their ability to access any individual's social media such as Facebook and Line messengers.

Between 2016 and 2017, the case of Mr Chatuphat Bunphathararaksa (also known as Phai Daodin) was prominent. In December 2016, the police charged Phai under the lèse-majesté law and the Computer Crime Act for sharing on his Facebook page a BBC news article which contained "inappropriate" analysis about King Vajiralongkorn. The police denied Phai's bail several times. The court eventually sentenced him to five years' imprisonment, but halved this when he later pleaded guilty to the charge. In mid-April 2017 the Ministry of Digital Economy and Society also warned the public not to follow the Facebook pages of three outspoken critics of the military and monarchy; namely, Somsak Jiamthirasakul, Pavin Chachavalpongpun, and Andrew MacGregor Marshall. The Ministry claimed that, according to the Computer Crime Act, it could pursue legal charges against those who followed or shared the posts of these critics.[8]

The Military and the Monarchy

The death of King Bhumibol in October 2016 added uncertainties to the future of Thailand. Despite the fact that the royal transition took place relatively smoothly, it is still unclear whether the new reign will command the influence and respect as the fulcrum of national unity to the same extent as the late king.

King Bhumibol, who came to the throne at an early age, had time to cultivate a close, symbiotic relationship with the military. Since the 1960s the palace benefited from the support of the military in reviving its status following the end of absolute monarchy in 1932. Between the 1960s and the end of the 1980s, Thailand was mostly ruled by military leaders. This political structure was a part of nation-building that provided stability amid the communist threats of the Cold War. Thailand's survival after the fall of the Indochina countries to the communists also justified the military's self-perception as the prime protector of the national holy trinity — the nation, the religion (Buddhism) and the monarchy. The Thai military, therefore, maintains its status and role beyond the concept of military professionalism, which promotes a restricted role of the military in defending the nation against external threats.

The deteriorating health of the late king before his passing posed a challenge to Thailand's stability amid the political struggle. This factor became part of the pretext for the military's intervention in May 2014 and its incentive to remain in power for the foreseeable future. The military and its allies wanted to ensure that the royal transition was uninterrupted and that the military was guaranteed its role in politics. In order to secure these objectives, the military made compromises with the palace. For instance, the military amended the constitution and laws related to palace affairs according to the suggestions of the new king, including the appointment of the regent[9] and the centralized power of the palace in managing its wealth.[10] At the same time, the dedication of the military government in 2017 to the royal cremation of the late king in October 2017 has symbolized to the public the continuity of the military–monarchy axis. The military has enjoyed public recognition of its ability to manage the grandiose plan for the late king's funeral. This success helped boost acceptance of the military among the Thai public.

However, it remains uncertain how the relationship between the military and the palace will evolve. The late king spent a lot of effort throughout his seventy years in building his charisma and networks across elite groups, hence gaining soft power and respect. The new monarch, however, has adopted a relatively different approach to convey how his wishes and demands should be met. Some ordinances have been initiated by the palace, including issues related to the king's prerogatives, the removal and appointment of palace staff and the royal guard, and even some minor issues related to new military practices, such as a new salute design or strictly short hairstyle. All in all, the relationship between the two parties currently shows no conflict on the surface, which in turn helps stabilize the military's role in politics. However, the reign is still new. It is uncertain how this relationship will develop in the long run, especially to what extent the military may agree with the way in which the palace broadens its role and power more explicitly.

Yingluck's Trial and Implications for Thai Politics

Another politically important episode in Thailand took place in August 2017, regarding the trial of former prime minister Yingluck Shinawatra for negligence in relation to the rice-pledging scheme during her tenure. The Thai Supreme Court was scheduled to read the verdict on 27 August 2017, but Yingluck did not show up in court. Her lawyer claimed she was suffering from Meniere's disease and requested for a delay of the reading, but did not produce a medical certificate for this. The court objected to the request, rescheduled the reading to 27 September and prepared an arrest warrant. On 27 September the court eventually sentenced Yingluck to five years' imprisonment in absentia. It appeared that she had already fled the country before the first court hearing, to reunite with her brother, former prime minister Thaksin Shinawatra, in Dubai. The media reported that she later went to the United Kingdom to seek political asylum.[11]

Increased Legitimacy of the Military

Yingluck's flight turned out to be beneficial for the military government, as it can justify to the public that she had committed a wrongdoing, in turn legitimizing its rule. Had Yingluck decided to stay, neither a positive nor a negative verdict would have benefited the government, as either would have strengthened the unity of the pro-Thaksin Red Shirts movement. A negative verdict would have deepened the Red Shirts' grievances about perceived injustice and would have set a stronger tone against the military. But if Yingluck had been found not guilty, this would have added confidence to their political position. Her disappearance therefore surprised the public, especially the Red Shirt supporters who had come to the court on the morning of 27 August 2017. It would be interesting to know what motivated her to flee Thailand, when her fight through the justice system of the previous two years had unified millions of her supporters amid the junta's suppressive laws against dissent and political mobilization. Some observers speculated that the government may have known in advance about her plan to escape, but allowed it to happen.[12]

Impact on Political Parties

While Yingluck's flight helped strengthen the military's position, it demoralized the Red Shirt movement and led to a leadership vacuum in the Pheu Thai Party. There are no candidates who possess a similar charismatic style of leadership who could lift the party's profile and command the Red Shirt's allegiance. Without Thaksin or Yingluck, the Pheu Thai Party has no unifying figure able to garner the same level of support for the next election. There is speculation that Sudarat Keyuraphan, a former deputy leader of Pheu Thai, will step in, as she is likely to be more moderate and acceptable to the junta.[13] Despite the weaker position of Pheu Thai, this incident may help simmer positive developments for the party and the Red Shirts. Certainly, this could be the case if they can develop a strong political ideology and a broad-based political platform that is not dependent on the Shinawatras beyond symbolic figureheads.

While the pro-Thaksin faction faces leadership disarray in the wake of Yingluck's flight, the case has reassured the anti-Thaksin group's direction. The People's Democratic Reform Committee (PDRC) and its supporters (also largely associated with the previous Yellow Shirts movement) feel vindicated for their campaigns, the basic cue of which was that corruption loomed large in the Shinawatra administrations. Their support for military intervention in 2014 can be touted as having helped to cleanse Thailand's dirty politics. Some of the former PDRC leaders have indicated their intention to either set up their own party or to return to the Democrat Party to contest the next election. With this development, it remains to be seen whether the Democrats' hope to be a leading party in the next coalition government will be affected by the split of the PDRC. The Democrats' leverage is based on their strong link to the PDRC and some in the establishment.

Some military leaders have recently signalled the possibility of setting up a political party to contest the election. Deputy Prime Minister General Prawit Wongsuwan stated in a media interview that this option could be pursued if necessary.[14] However, the following three scenarios would oblige the next prime minister and the coalition government to arrange for political deals after the next election. First, the junta leader is nominated by political parties to be the prime minister. Second, the military sets up its own political party and co-opts other parties to form a coalition government with a junta leader as prime minister. Third, the junta may choose to influence politics from behind the scenes through the Senate. In early January 2018, just a week after General Prayut dubbed himself a politician, General Prawit also endorsed the idea that the former should be a candidate for the position of prime minister after the election.[15] The two major parties, Pheu Thai and the Democrat Party, have also suggested the idea of forming a coalition to prevent an outsider — meaning someone from the military — from becoming prime minister.[16] This is still uncertain, considering their longstanding antagonism throughout the decade, especially between their mass bases, and the Democrats' close ties with some military leaders.

Implications for Public Policy

The most significant aspect of Yingluck's case is that it will impact future administrations. On the positive side it will prompt politicians to be more cautious about future public policy formulation and implementation. Any misconduct or corruption could land them in trouble, as with Yingluck and the other government officials involved.

However, there are several drawbacks. Fear will prevent intellectual leadership from emerging in the political scene; hence, there will be less innovative policies. The policies may not be responsive to the real needs of the majority of the population, as they will need to be framed in conjunction with the Twenty-Year National Strategy. Consequently, this development will roll back the Thai political system into the hands of the bureaucracy and technocrats, whose institutional objective is to preserve the status quo rather than encourage innovation.

Moreover, the politicization of the judiciary will further intervene in the executive branch in the future. The success of judicial interventions in recent decades has set this trend; ironically, ever since Thaksin came to office. Thaksin's overwhelming support based on his landslide victory in 2001 may arguably have influenced the verdict of the Constitutional Court in his favour during his case pertaining to hiding assets. The role of the court thereafter has been significant, especially throughout the decade-long political conflict. The court has disbanded political parties, dismissed a few prime ministers, as well as prevented certain policies from being implemented.

Stagnant Economy with Uncertain Prospects for Growth

While the military may have achieved political and judicial manoeuvrability under its rule, its ability to stimulate economic growth is perhaps a different story. Economic management has become a major challenge for the military's legitimacy, as observers compare the economic performance of the military government to that of elected governments.

Slow Growth and Lack of Confidence

Thailand has experienced low GDP growth since the military took power. The annual growth rates were recorded at 0.9 per cent, 2.9 per cent and 3.2 per cent in 2014, 2015 and 2016, respectively, and the forecast for 2017 is roughly 3.5 per cent.[17] It is noteworthy that Thailand's GDP growth rates plummeted during the unstable period of political crisis after the 2005 coup but recovered when an elected civilian government restored some political stability. Notably, the GDP growth steadily dropped after the political crisis in 2008, and the suppression of the Red Shirts demonstration also resulted in negative growth of –0.69 per cent in 2009 during the Abhisit government. The growth rate spiked to 7.5 per cent in 2010 when political stability was sustained and the prospect of a new election looked promising. Although the Yingluck government faced the challenge of devastating floods throughout the central plain and Bangkok after winning the July 2011 election, growth picked up to 7.2 per cent in 2012.

In 2017, the World Bank reported that the Thai economy had gained some momentum, with an expected growth rate of around 3.5 per cent, mainly due to external demand from the recovery of the world economy. However, the Thai economy still faces challenges and uncertainties. Increasing corporate and household debt (80 per cent of GDP) resulted in banks reducing credit and lending, as well as low levels of confidence among domestic consumers and investors. Coupled with increasing protectionism and lower growth in major economies such as China, Europe and the United States, Thailand's economic expansion is still limited, despite global demand improving. It is therefore interesting to note that despite political stability low growth has become the new normal under the military government.

The government launched several economic stimulus packages to help boost the economy. It introduced a "shopping for the nation" campaign for three weeks in late November 2017 to stimulate domestic consumption. The campaign allowed individuals who purchased designated goods and services below 15,000 baht to qualify for personal income tax deductions.[18] However, analysts assessed that the impact was relatively small. The campaign only benefited 7 per cent of taxpayers, and a lack of consumer confidence in the economy still limited their consumption to regular purchases.

In late September 2017, the government introduced a State Social Welfare Scheme targeting low-income earners. Under this scheme, the beneficiaries are grouped into two categories: those with an annual income lower than 30,000 baht and those with an income between 30,000 and 100,000 baht. They are eligible for a cash card worth 300 or 200 baht per month, respectively. The card is also loaded with separate allowances, including 500 baht for the Bangkok transit system, 500 baht for provincial buses, 500 baht for trains, and 45 baht for cooking gas.[19] The Finance Ministry is considering increasing the household allowance to 500 baht in the future. The extension of social welfare will impact government expenses and eventually put pressure on the government to increase its revenue, by both increasing the effectiveness of tax collection and expanding the tax base. The government recently announced it will increase value-added tax from 7 per cent to 9 per cent in October 2018 and that it is also considering an e-commerce tax.

Socio-economic Conditions

As a result of slow growth, the unemployment rate in 2017 had increased to 1.2 per cent, from 1 per cent in 2016.[20] Thailand's unemployment rate is usually at a low level due to the high transferability of the labour force between agricultural and non-agricultural sectors. In the second quarter of 2017, the unemployment rate in the non-agricultural sector had increased due to slow expansion in private investment in the industrial and service sectors. At the same time, a better climate and improved prices in agricultural products in early 2017 also gave more incentives for agricultural production. Despite the positive aspects of labour absorbability across sectors, this nature of the Thai economy shows that a large proportion of the labour force, roughly 33 per cent, remains in the agricultural sector. However, this sector's share of GDP accounted for only approximately 8.34 per cent in 2016, and around 8.8 per cent in the first half of 2017.

What implications does this structure have for Thailand's socio-economic prospects? First and foremost, a significant proportion of the Thai population still operate in low-income and lower-productivity sectors. Almost 10 per cent of the population is defined as poor, and the income gap between the top 20 per cent and the bottom 20 per cent is around ten times.[21] A survey in 2015 showed that the North and Northeast regions have the lowest monthly income per household in the kingdom, at approximately 19,000 and 21,000 baht, respectively. The monthly household income in the greater Bangkok metropolitan area is around 41,000 baht, much higher than the national average of 27,000.[22] Therefore, income disparity in Thailand remains a critical challenge.

Moreover, a large pool of labour in low productivity sectors also implies the presence of a significant number of low-skilled workers. An assessment conducted by the Office of the National Economic and Social Development Board suggested that Thailand has made slow progress in education and training. The majority of the labour force, or roughly 45 per cent, receive only primary education, while less than 9 per cent have vocational education that is crucial for industrial upgrading.[23] Thailand therefore faces the challenge of the middle-income trap as it fails to transform to a high-income economy. Tackling this problem has therefore become a major economic policy objective for the current government.

Prospects for the Thailand 4.0 Project

In the long run, the government will focus on its "Twenty-Year National Strategy" as a large umbrella to achieve its goals, under which the idea of "Thailand 4.0" specifically serves economic purposes.[24] The government initiated this economic model as a platform to solve the problem of the middle-income gap. The core of the model is a knowledge-based economy, emphasizing research and development, science and technology, creative thinking and innovation. The model focuses on five key industries: biotech food and agriculture, bio-medicine, robotics and mechatronics, digital technology, and high-valued and creative services.

Thailand 4.0 was implemented by setting up the Eastern Economic Corridor (EEC) in Thailand's eastern seaboard. The government expects the EEC to attract and support investment in the aforementioned priority areas, hence becoming an important centre for trade, investment, regional transportation and a strategic gateway to Asia. The EEC covers the three provinces of Chachoengsao, Chonburi and Rayong. This area is already the country's major industrial and export zone and is equipped with the necessary infrastructure, including Thailand's largest deep-sea port at Laem Chabang. U-Tapao International Airport is also being upgraded to become the country's third major aviation hub, as the two existing airports in the Bangkok area are almost reaching capacity. Moreover, the ongoing Thai–Chinese high-speed railway project will also extend from Bangkok to this area at a later stage. The government, therefore, has high hopes of attracting more Chinese investment into this economic zone by promoting the EEC as a hub for regional connectivity within Beijing's infrastructure project, the Belt and Road Initiative (BRI).

Despite the new economic strategy to boost investment, some foreign investors are not confident that this project will be fruitful. Japan, as the largest foreign investor in Thailand, seems doubtful of the project's potential. Although Japan remains the biggest investor in Thailand, it has gradually reduced its investment by more than half since 2013, from nearly 350 billion baht to 120 billion baht in 2016.[25] Analysts point to several internal factors for the reduction of Japanese FDI, one of which is Thailand's unfolding political disunity, which is a major concern as it has the potential to bring instability in the future. Thailand's ageing population also affects the country's workforce and the economy. At the same time, Japanese investors now have more options in Thailand's neighbouring countries, with lower wages and younger populations.[26] The big challenge for the government, therefore, is to seek ways to manage the new economic strategy in order to improve the confidence of foreign investors and to slow down capital flight.

Foreign Relations: Improvement, but Still Imbalanced

The main focus of Thailand's foreign relations in 2017 was on its relations with China and the United States. It is indisputable that China and the United States are two major powers in Thailand's foreign policy calculations, and Thailand has traditionally managed to maintain good relations with both countries. However, Thai foreign policy posture lost a fine balance between the two following the 2014 military coup. Understandably, the strong reactions from Western nations against the military government have pushed Bangkok to rely more on Beijing, not only to benefit from China's economic expansion but also from its political support in the international community.

Inescapable Dependence on China?

However, Thailand's increasing dependence on China also means that Beijing can assert its influence over Thai policymaking to a certain degree. The case of the Thai–Chinese high-speed railway project is a good example.

Beijing's irritation over the slow progress of the project was revealed in the lack of an invitation for Prayut to attend the BRI Summit in Beijing in May 2017, despite a seemingly cosy relationship between the two countries since the 2014 coup. The official explanation, however, avoided linking the lack of invitation to the delay of the railway project. The Thai foreign minister explained that the Chinese government had already invited Prayut to the 9th BRICS Summit in Xiamen in September, therefore his attendance was unnecessary at this time. However, if one looks at the wider context, the link is highly possible.

The project has been delayed since 2010, when both countries agreed to a joint venture on a high-speed railway project connecting Thailand with another high-speed railway from Yunnan province to Laos. The delay was mainly due to the change of government during the political crisis in Thailand. There had been new hopes for the project as the military government, which had close ties with China, came into power. To the surprise of the public, the Thai and Chinese premiers announced at the Lancang–Mekong Cooperation Summit on 22–24 March 2016 in Hainan Province that Thailand would finance the project domestically and China would only invest a 60 per cent share in the rail system and train operations. A lengthy negotiation process continued on other technical issues, including material standards and the use of Chinese labour to construct the railway.

However, it is interesting to observe that Thailand sped up the process to approve the project a few months after the BRI Summit. Considering the failure to reach agreements over the past three years, the eighteenth meeting, which was held ten days after the BRI Summit, nearly reached a conclusion. The Thai Transport Ministry agreed to clear up the legal bottleneck in the project regarding the use of Chinese personnel and materials, which contravened Thai laws. In mid-July the prime minister eventually exercised his prerogative under section 44 in the interim constitution to bypass all the legal obstacles. Essentially, it exempts Chinese engineers and architects from taking Thai professional licence exams and allows the use of up to 25 per cent of Chinese materials. The nineteenth meeting in early July concluded that the construction would start in October 2017. Considering how speedily these agreements were reached, it is likely Chinese leaders had employed diplomatic pressure to influence Thailand's decision-making.[27]

Improved Ties with the United States

The inauguration of Donald Trump as U.S President in 2017 heralded a breakthrough for Thai–U.S. relations. In March 2017, President Trump made phone calls to the leaders of three Southeast Asian countries — the Philippines, Singapore and Thailand — with invitations to visit Washington. Bangkok embraced the invitation. The prime minister initially planned to visit Washington at the end of July but it was postponed to 2–4 October 2017.

Upon his return, General Prayut announced his achievement in cementing Thai–U.S. relations. Regaining international recognition from Western nations, especially the United States, had been a major foreign policy objective for the military government. And there had been earlier attempts to restore bilateral ties towards the end of the Obama administration. For example, Prayut had restated Thailand's interest in joining the Trans-Pacific Partnership (TPP) after attending the ASEAN–U.S. Summit in February 2016. However, the momentum waned because of the U.S. presidential election campaign and Thailand's decision-making processes.

The normalization of Thai–U.S. relations brought about several changes. Firstly, it marked a pragmatic approach between the two nations as longstanding security allies. Trump's invitation reaffirmed Thailand's strategic importance to the overall U.S. strategy in Southeast Asia. Secondly, the return to normal contacts between the two nations offered a chance for Bangkok to readjust its foreign policy position after heavily relying on China for political recognition since 2014.

In exchange for U.S. recognition, however, Thailand has pursued a "shopping diplomacy" — making promises to buy more American products and invest in the United States.[28] The list includes lifting the ban on importing American pork, and purchases of American arms, coal and Boeing aircraft. This exchange certainly justifies the United States' change in approach to the military regime, as it serves President Trump's "America First" campaign. However, critics worry that U.S. approval of the regime and the abandonment of the human rights issue in its foreign policy would worsen the state of human rights and democracy in Thailand.[29]

Despite the fact that Thai–American relations have returned to normal, it is still a challenge for Thailand to maintain its footing on the tightrope, and the country may still face uncertainty with the U.S. card. As long as Thailand is under authoritarian rule, political legitimacy will always be a thorn in Bangkok's flesh. As a smaller power, democratic deficit is a liability, not leverage, to Thai foreign relations, especially with liberal democracies. Moreover, it is unclear whether the U.S. Congress and other interest groups will try to restrain the White House from improving diplomatic ties with Thailand. After all, U.S. law prohibits the executive branch from providing full military assistance to foreign governments that came to power by way of a military coup.

Bangkok may face this uncertainty as long as the military is still in power. Thailand may not be able to readjust its position with Beijing as easily as optimists have expected. In contrast, Bangkok may have to give more reassurances to China that its renewed ties with Washington will not be at the expense of Thai–China relations. More policy concessions to China may be seen to help secure trust and support, especially when Thailand's economic recovery may heavily depend on China. It will eventually complicate Thailand's foreign policy if the tension between China and the United States is intensified in the future.

Conclusion

It can be seen from the above discussion that 2017 has potentially set the course for Thailand for the years to come. Politically, despite uncertainties regarding the election timeframe, the military government may not be able to resist domestic and international pressure to restore the democratic system. Thailand will be heading towards a new election by at least early 2019. However, politics will reflect a new power-sharing in which the military explicitly establishes its major role, both in the legislature through the Senate and in policies through the enforcement of the Twenty-Year National Strategy.

It remains to be seen, however, how widely this power-sharing structure will be accepted and able to provide long-term stability. As the political contestation since the mid-2000s is still unfolding, the new structure may not be legitimate in the eyes of a large group of people, therefore possible tensions and conflicts cannot be ruled out in the future. Such political tension may intensify if the new rules become major obstacles to improving Thailand's economic performance and social well-being. In such a case, the new political economy will exacerbate existing socio-economic problems, especially poverty and inequality. Such political and socio-economic conditions have the potential to lead to a new round of power struggle.

It is apparent that the Thailand 4.0 model aims to revitalize and sustain the kingdom's economic vibrancy and to address the abovementioned socio-economic issues. The current policymakers have eyed China and have tried to synchronize their plans and connectivity with China's megaprojects, particularly the Belt and Road Initiative. Certainly, this strategy will benefit Thailand as long as China's economic performance remains high. This also puts Thailand at risk of being overdependent on China and makes the Thai economy vulnerable to future shocks. Economic diversification may help ameliorate this risk. Thailand will need to maintain and secure cooperation with its traditional economic partners such as Japan, the United States and European and Asian countries, while seeking new partners for more economic opportunities. When the path towards democracy becomes clear, confidence from foreign investors will likely resume to help Thailand achieve its policy objectives.

Economic diversification will also enhance Thailand's ability to recalibrate its foreign relations with external powers. Although relations with the United States improved in 2017, relations with its European counterparts are still at a low ebb. With democratic restoration in the future, Thailand would likely be able to resume its regular contacts with them. However, a major impediment in the future may be Thailand's poor record on human rights and freedom of expression. Considering the fact that the power of the military will remain strong, attempts to silence political opposition may continue through the implementation of the draconian law of lèse-majesté and the Computer Crime Act. This situation will not only tarnish the kingdom's international reputation but will also worsen Thailand's relations with liberal democracies.

Notes

1. "Lekha Ko.So.Cho. Lan Yang Mai Plot Lok Kanmueang Yam Chap Awut Yong Puan Pi 57" [NCPO secretary says it is not time to unlock political restrictions, repeated that the confiscation of weapons linked to political chaos in 2014], *Thairath* <https://www.thairath.co.th/content/1143397> (accessed 4 December 2017).
2. "Suriyasai Khat Plod Lok Lacha at Luean Lueak Tang Pai Pi 62" [Suriyasai suspects the delay in unlocking political restrictions may postpone the election to 2019], *Bangkok Biznews* <http://www.bangkokbiznews.com/news/detail/783749> (accessed 4 December 2017); aof, "Adit Ko.Ko.to. Chi Phak Kanmueang Siang Thuk Yup Hak

Maithan Wela Chi Ko.so.Cho. Plot Lok Kanmueang" [Former secretary-general of the election commission points out political parties risk being disbanded if they can't process in time; calls the NCPO to lift the ban on political activities], *Prachachat*, 3 December 2017 <https://www.prachachat.net/politics/news-82044>.

3. "PM's Support Ebbing, Says Prem", *Bangkok Post*, 29 December 2017 <https://www.bangkokpost.com/news/politics/1387322/pms-support-ebbing-says-prem>.
4. " 'I'm Just a Politician,' Prayut Says", *The Nation*, 4 January 2018 <http://www.nationmultimedia.com/detail/politics/30335332>.
5. Thai Government, "Rang Krop Yutthasat Chat Raya 20 Pi (Pho.so. 2560–2579)" [Twenty-year national strategy framework draft (2017–36)] (Bangkok: Office of the Prime Minister, 2016) <http://dl.parliament.go.th/handle/lirt/475208>.
6. "Yutthasat Chat 20 Pi Khue Arai? Khaochai Kan Baep Yoyo" [What is the twenty-year national strategy? Understand it in summary], *iLaw* <https://ilaw.or.th/node/4570> (accessed 6 November 2017).
7. Ibid.
8. "Nueng Thotsawat Khadi 112 Tonthi 2: 'Khwam Plaek Mai' Lang Ratthaprahan Lae Ratchasamai Mai" [A decade of section 112 charges: 'New aspects' after the coup and the new reign], *Prachatai* <https://prachatai.com/journal/2017/11/74132> (accessed 17 November 2017).
9. "Thiap Mattra to Mattra Ratthathammanun Chabap Phan Prachamati Kap Chabap Kaekhai Lae Prakat Chai" [Compare section by section between the draft constitution that passed the referendum and the one with new amendments that is promulgated], BBC Thai, 6 April 2017 <http://www.bbc.com/thai/thailand-39514040>.
10. Ratchakitchanubeksa, "Praratchabanyat Chat Rabiap Sapsin Fai Phramahakasat Pho.so.2560" [The management of the crown treasury act 2017], Pub. L. No. 134/75 Kor (2017) <http://www.ratchakitcha.soc.go.th/DATA/PDF/2560/A/075/1.PDF>.
11. "Government in Dark on Yingluck Plans to Seek UK Asylum", *Bangkok Post* <https://www.bangkokpost.com/archive/government-in-dark-on-yingluck-plans-to-seek-uk-asylum/1337359> (accessed 8 November 2017).
12. "Roitoe Chi 'Yinglak' Phen Ok Nok Prathet Khue 'Thang Ok' Thi Di Thisut Samrap Kho.so.Cho." [Reuters points out that Yingluck's escape from the country is the best 'way out' for the Junta], *Manager Online* <http://www.manager.co.th/Around/ViewNews.aspx?NewsID=9600000088029> (accessed 8 November 2017).
13. "Thitinan Pongsudhirak: Thailand Needs to Escape Its Political Cul-de-Sac", *Nikkei Asian Review* <https://asia.nikkei.com/magazine/20171019/Viewpoints/Thitinan-Pongsudhirak-Thailand-needs-to-escape-its-political-cul-de-sac> (accessed 7 November 2017).
14. "Thot Rahat Tang 'Phak Tahan' Kap Kan Pan Krasae Ching Tua Prayut?" [Decoding the setup of 'military party' and the speculation of grabbing Prayut?], BBC Thai, 7 November 2017 <http://www.bbc.com/thai/41896399>.

15. "Prawit Backs Prayuth as Post-Election Prime Minister", *Khaosod English*, 11 January 2018 <http://www.khaosodenglish.com/politics/2018/01/11/prawit-backs-prayuth-post-election-prime-minister/>.
16. Pravit Rojanaphruk and Senior Staff Writer, "Thai Political Enemies Weigh Alliance to Defeat Junta", *Khaosod English*, 28 November 2017 <http://www.khaosodenglish.com/politics/2017/11/28/thai-political-enemies-weigh-alliance-defeat-junta/>.
17. Asian Development Bank, "Thailand: Economy", 28 September 2017 <https://www.adb.org/countries/thailand/economy>.
18. "Cabinet Approves End-Year Tax Break for Shoppers", *The Nation*, 7 November 2017 <http://www.nationmultimedia.com/detail/breakingnews/30331071> (accessed 4 December 2017).
19. "Welfare Card Scheme Will Help Poor Pay for Basic Needs", *The Nation*, 31 August 2017 <http://www.nationmultimedia.com/detail/national/30325331> (accessed 4 December 2017).
20. "Phawa Sangkhom Thai Q1/2560 Khon Wang Ngan Sungsud Nai Rop 7 Pi Suanthang Chidiphi-Tae Mi Khwamsuk Andap 2 Khong Asian" [Social condition in Q1/2017, highest unemployment rate in 7 years reversing the trend in GDP – Yet, Thailand ranks second in ASEAN for happiness], *ThaiPublica*, 26 May 2017 <https://thaipublica.org/2017/05/nesdb-social-outlook-q1-2560/>.
21. Fiscal Policy Office, "Kwam Yakchon" [Poverty] <http://www.fpo.go.th:81/StatisticData/table.php> (accessed 15 November 2017).
22. National Statistics Office, "Raidai Raichai Khruaruen Lae Chamnuan Khruareun" [Household income and expenditure and number of households] <http://service.nso.go.th/nso/web/statseries/statseries11.html> (accessed 15 November 2017).
23. Office of Economic and Social Development Board, "Kamlang Raengngan Ruam (Ayu 15 Pi Khuen Pai) Chamnaek Tam Radap Kansueksa Thi Samret Thua Ratcha-Anachak Pi Pho.so.2544-2560" [Total labour force (from 15 years old) categorised according to the level of education around the kingdom from 2001 to 2017] <http://social.nesdb.go.th/SocialStat/StatReport_Final.aspx?reportid=542&template=2R2C&yeartype=M&subcatid=7> (accessed 15 November 2017).
24. Government Public Relations Department, "Thailand 4.0 Policy to Transform the Thai Economy" <http://thailand.prd.go.th/mobile_detail.php?cid=4&nid=3784> (accessed 15 November 2017).
25. Bank of Thailand, "Nguen Longthun Doi Trong Chak Tang Prathet Chamnaek Tam Prathet" [Foreign direct investment categorized by countries] <http://www2.bot.or.th/statistics/ReportPage.aspx?reportID=653&language=th> (accessed 20 November 2017).
26. Ryan Hartley, "Junta Reforms Doing Nothing to Assuage Thai Investment Flight", *East Asia Forum*, 14 November 2017 <http://www.eastasiaforum.org/2017/11/14/junta-reforms-doing-nothing-to-assuage-thai-investment-flight/>.

27. Pongphisoot Busbarat, "China's 'Shame Offensive': The Omission of Thailand's Prime Minister from the Belt and Road Initiative Summit 2017", *ISEAS Perspective* 2017, no. 54 (19 July 2017).
28. Pongphisoot Busbarat, "Shopping Diplomacy: The Thai Prime Minister's Visit to the United States and Its Implications for Thai–US Relations", *ISEAS Perspective* 2017, no. 78 (20 October 2017).
29. John Sifton, "Another Week, Another Autocratic Leader Visiting Trump's Washington", Human Rights Watch, 1 October 2017 <https://www.hrw.org/news/2017/10/01/another-week-another-autocratic-leader-visiting-trumps-washington>.

HAUNTED PAST, UNCERTAIN FUTURE: The Fragile Transition to Military-Guided Semi-Authoritarianism in Thailand

Prajak Kongkirati

The National Council for Peace and Order (NCPO) junta led by General Prayuth Chan-ocha came to power on 22 May 2014 after it toppled the elected government of Yingluck Shinawatra, sister of former prime minister Thaksin. This coup returned Thailand to military authoritarian rule similar to that of strongman Field Marshall Sarit Thanarat's in the late 1950s and early 1960s. Prayuth's premiership brought back the old model of "Thai-style democracy" in which the royal–military alliance dominates politics with an ultra-conservative discourse. Since the coup, the military has established itself as the new ruling elite by enhancing its scope of power, budget and size. It has also sought to maintain its dominance by weakening majoritarian democracy and undermining the influence of political parties and civil society through constitutional design. This chapter explains an attempt of the Prayuth administration at restructuring Thai political order through various institutional mechanisms in order to prolong military power.

During the Cold War period, military rule was the most common form of non-democratic regime. Between the end of the Second World War and the beginnings of the third wave of democratization, militaries have intervened in approximately two-thirds of the more than one hundred non-Western states. And in the late 1970s militaries controlled the governments in about a third of these countries.[1] However, since the end of the Cold War, the phenomenon of

---

PRAJAK KONGKIRATI is Assistant Professor and Director of the Direk Jayanama Research Centre and Head of the Government and Politics Department, Faculty of Political Science, Thammasat University, Thailand.

military coup and military government has gradually disappeared and become anachronistic. Only a handful of poverty-stricken countries still encounter political intervention from the army and military coups. Thailand is currently the only country in Southeast Asia being governed under military rule. This striking fact points to the necessity of closely examining the roles and politics of the military in Thailand's transition.

Consolidating Military Power

Instead of pursuing a power-sharing mode like the previous coup governments in 1991 and 2006, the current ruling junta led by General Prayuth and General Pravit Wongsuwan aims to consolidate and entrench military power in the political system for the long term. They aim to re-centralize the state structure by increasing the duties and power of the military at the expense of civil society and elected forces. The new political structure is designed to control majoritarian democracy by blunting the power of political parties. The 2017 charter, promulgated on 6 April 2017, Chakri Day, established a bicameral National Assembly consisting of an elected House of Representative (500) and an appointed senate (250). The term of the lower house is four years, while that of the senate is five. In the first five years the NCPO has authority to handpick a 250-member senate, with six seats reserved for the security forces: army, navy, defence, police, supreme commander, and defence ministry permanent secretary. The senate is also granted power to nominate and vote to decide who would be the prime minister in a joint session with the lower house.[2]

The NCPO leaders claim that the appointed senate will carry out their "20 year national reform strategic plan". They also argue that the incorporation of the security forces into the senate will prevent military coup attempts.[3] Besides the junta-appointed senate, many empowered independent organizations (election commission, constitutional court, anti-corruption commission, ombudsman, etc.) will function as veto mechanisms that can check and disqualify the elected government.

Another significant institutional mechanism created to weaken majoritarian democracy is the newly designed electoral system. The junta-appointed constitutional drafting commission, led by Meechai Ruchupan, has changed the electoral system from a mixed-member majoritarian system (MMM) with 375 single-seat constituencies and 125 party-list seats to a so-called mixed-member apportionment system (MMA). Under the MMA system, there are 350 constituency seats and 150 party-list seats. Instead of casting two separate votes (one for a candidate and one for a party list), under the new system voters can cast only one vote and that vote will count as both a vote for the chosen candidate and simultaneously a vote for that candidate's party for the party-list seat calculation. The total share of seats of any party is determined by the total number of votes that party receives nationwide via the constituency vote. This electoral system is a tweaked version of the German-style mixed-member proportional system (MMP), and is rarely used anywhere else in the world. It will make the Thai party system more fragmented, and it will be more difficult for any party to win a clear majority. A weak coalition government would thus be a likely outcome. It also hurt the major parties and the small parties, but helped the medium-sized parties. According to Allen Hicken and Bangkok Pundit, who ran a simulation using 2011 election results to test the effects of the new system, they found that Pheu Thai will be the biggest loser under this system, as their seats will be reduced from 265 (53 per cent) to only 225 (45 per cent). Meanwhile, according to the simulation, the Democrats will receive roughly the same number of seats under the new system. The biggest winners are the medium-sized parties like Bhum Jai Thai, Chart Pattana Pheu Paendin, and Chart Thai Pattana, who perform well in the constituency competition.[4] This has a significant implication, as there is a widely shared belief that the junta plans to co-opt these medium-sized parties in the new election. With the support of medium-sized parties and the 250 votes from the junta-appointed senate, they can decide who will be the prime minister.[5]

Overall, Meechai's constitution is designed to give greater power to an unelected elite minority: the army, the judiciary, and independent organizations. An elected government and executive leader can easily be disqualified. The government's use of the budget will be monitored and constrained by independent organizations. The implementation of policies will be constrained by various unelected institutions. Moreover, government cannot implement any policies that contradict the twenty-year national reform strategic plan laid out by the NCPO. The electoral mandate of the voters will be less meaningful in deciding who should govern. It does not matter much which party — the Democrats or Pheu Thai — wins the election, because the elected government will be placed under the control of unelected minority elites, with the military at the top of the power structure.

With the army's institutionalized power embedded in the constitution, military elites have designed new mechanisms to seize power without resorting to a military coup. The institutional design created by the 2017 charter could thus be characterized as military-guided semi-authoritarianism. Through the institutional (mis)design, the military elites "tame" the majoritarian democracy. All in all, the army maintains their position as the dominant power, while other institutions and political forces are weak and less united.

New Reign, New Political Order

In the new era of transition after the royal succession in October 2016, the relationship and power structure between the royalty and the military is changing. Without the late King Bhumibol Adulyadej, the long-established political order centred on a charismatic and popular monarch loyally served by the army could not be sustained. The new political order in the post–King Bhumibol era has not yet been clearly established. The military does not want a power vacuum to occur at this fragile time of historic transition. The army intervened in politics in May 2014 to ensure that this transition would be orderly and peaceful. The military, as the traditional political force, stepped in during the fragile time of royal succession to be a new ruler who dictates the distribution of power in the new reign. Consequently, the military is in the process of creating new relationships with other social and political forces.

Following the coup the military has sought to establish itself as a hegemonic ruler, dominating power in the long term and not allowing others access to this power or to form an alternate elite group. We can clearly see this in the budget, in increased privileges, increased salaries, increased troops, an expansion of the situations in which military power can be used, the placing of military personnel in charge of state enterprises as well as independent organizations, and, most importantly, enshrining this power within the constitution. From the 2014 coup to 2017, military generals marshalled to control the lucrative state-owned enterprises (SOEs). Currently, forty SOEs now have military personnel as their board members (a 100 per cent increase from the pre-coup era) and sixteen enterprises have military generals as their board presidents (a fivefold increase from the civilian administration before the coup).[6]

"Military Party": Historical Patterns and Future Prospects

On 10 October 2017, Prime Minister Prayuth Chan-ocha announced that Thailand will hold a general election in November 2018. At Government House, the junta chief told a group of reporters that, "around June we will announce the date for the next election. Then in November we will have an election."[7] It is important to note that this is not the first time that the NCPO has set an exact date for the election. At least twice in the past the junta has announced election dates which were subsequently postponed citing security concerns and the claim that a return to democracy would stir up the polarized conflicts and lead to street violence. Therefore, it would not be unusual if this new schedule for the general election were pushed back again.

Another interesting political move from the Prayuth government took place in early November 2017, when Prayuth posed a set of six political-related questions to the public for their response. The first two questions were the most telling. They asked the Thai people, "Do we need new political parties or new politicians for the people to consider in the next general election?". And, "Does the NCPO have the right to support a political party?"[8] This set of public questions clearly revealed the political intentions of the junta, and unequivocally signalled that the junta aspires to retain power after next November's election. To gain power through an election, the NCPO has two options to consider: seeking support from existing political parties, or setting up their own party to contest in the election.

Why does the NCPO need to have political parties to support them in parliament after the election? There are two apparent reasons. The first is that, according to the 2017 constitution, the prime minister will be selected through vote in a joint session of the upper and lower houses. As the NCPO already has 250 appointed senators under its control, it still needs an additional 125 votes from members of parliament in the lower house for one of the NCPO leaders to ascend to the position of prime minister. The second reason is that whilst the senate has the power to select the prime minister, it has no authority to vote should a motion of no confidence be called. This means that whilst the NCPO-appointed senators could help a junta leader like Prayuth become prime minister, they could not protect him from being disqualified. To secure its power, the NCPO has no other option but to have allied parties in the house. For this reason it is rather certain that Thailand will witness military-backed parties in the next election.

When asked by a journalist whether he would set up a political party, Prayuth did not categorically deny that he would. Prawit Wongsuwan, the deputy prime minister, however, made it clear that "when necessary, it [the party] needs to be set up".[9] One of Prayuth's classmates from military cadet school, Colonel Suchat Chantarachotkul, is prepared to create a party to support Prayuth in the next election, as he explained:

> Today I still could not see who would be a good prime minister except General Prayuth. Even though he has not yet talked about his political future, but in the future we must have someone to be a prime minister. Assumed that it is him, it is impossible for him to be a prime minister

> without support in the parliament. So we have to assemble people and set up a party in advance to support him.[10]

Apart from Prayuth's military friend, Paiboon Nititawan, a provocative senator appointed by the military to its reform council and a staunch opponent of Thaksin, said he would set up a party to propel Prayuth to become the next prime minister. His party's 117 founding members consist of retired generals, royalists, conservative senators, and former Yellow Shirt leaders. Paiboon said the country needs a good person to ensure that the reforms put in place by the junta get carried out, and he strongly believes that that person is General Prayuth.[11] Paiboon's party will undoubtedly be one of those to compete for votes to back up the junta in the coming election. Another important player in the next election will be Anutin Charnvirakul, the former chairman of Sino-Thai Engineering & Construction Pcl, Thailand's third-biggest building firm, and the leader of the Bhumjaithai party. His party is the third-largest party, winning 34 seats in the 2011 election, and it has a stronghold in the lower northeast. The new electoral system was designed by the junta-backed committee to benefit medium-sized parties like Anuthin's Bhumjaithai in the hope that these parties could form a coalition and help Prayuth, or another NCPO leader, becoming premier. This explains why the leaders of medium-sized parties strongly supported the draft constitution in the referendum.[12]

A military-backed party is not new in Thailand. As a country that has witnessed frequent coups and military regimes since the revolution from absolute monarchy to constitutional monarchy in 1932, several coup leaders have sought to sustain their power through military-backed parties. The following section explains the historical development, success and failure of military parties in the past, with the aim of shedding light on the current military politics in Thailand.

Two Models of Military Party: Bureaucratic and Nominee Party

The military parties of Thailand can be divided into two main types: bureaucratic and nominee party. The first model was a prototype created by powerful military figures in the late 1950s. It was a party headed by military generals which employed manpower and mobilized resources from the bureaucratic machine. The whole bureaucratic organization was utilized to make campaigns, collect votes, and, if necessary, manipulate the electoral results in favour of the military party. It was a party of the military for the military. The second model was developed later, in the 1990s, by coup leaders who understood the changing social context. Instead of creating a party based on bureaucracy and army organizations, they financially and logistically supported political parties led by civilians to work on their behalf. The purpose was the same as for the first model, to help one of the coup leaders to become prime minister.

Bureaucratic Party Model: From Phibun to Thanom

The exemplary case of a military bureaucratic party is the Serimanangkasila Party created by Field Marshall Phibun in 1955. The rationale behind the creation of this party was to use it as a power base for the then prime minister Phibun. After the 1947 coup, power struggles shifted to rivalries among the three major military leaders: Prime Minister Phibun, police chief Phao Sriyanond, and army general Sarit Thanarat. They established political parties to attack their enemies. Phibun and Phao founded the Serimanangkasila Party in 1955, in preparation for the 1957 general election, mobilizing extensive government resources to back party activities. Several cabinet members and leading bureaucrats joined the party as committee members, and the middle and lower rank officials acted as party staff. The separation between state and political party was completely blurred.[13] Sarit was officially the deputy head of this government-backed party, but he also created his own party, called Sahaphum, to tacitly sabotage Phibun and Phao. Like his enemies, Sarit mobilized the state machinery to endorse his party.[14]

Evidence from the 1957 election, which occurred under military rule, provides important lessons for today's Thailand, as it shows the pitfalls the military parties encountered, and their negative consequences for political development. The February 1957 election, known as "the dirty election", was regarded as the most corrupt vote in Thai history.[15] This election was held when Premier Phibun wanted to enhance the legitimacy of his long-standing rule, both domestically and internationally (particularly with the United States). Also, Phibun expected that the democratic credentials gained from the election would give him greater leverage over other elite factions. To make the election appear legitimate, the Phibun government allowed some competition.

To ensure a decisive victory, government leaders mobilized state networks to support Serimanangkasila candidates, competing with twenty-two other parties for 160 parliamentary seats. Shortly before the dissolution of the house, the government dispensed largesse (over a hundred million baht) for building infrastructure and provided goods to people in opposition-strong provinces. Government leaders campaigned for their provincial party members using public money. Leading bureaucrats, especially those from the Ministry of Interior ordered local officers to canvass votes for the Serimanangkasila Party. Civil servants became the government's so-called *Huana Nuai Khum Siang* (chief vote controllers).[16] These local officers were responsible for gathering local residents for meetings and instructing them to vote for the government-supported party. Their main slogan was, "Our country will develop if you elect Serimanangkasila Party".[17] Government-controlled television and radio stations allocated a large amount of airtime for Serimanangkasila campaign advertisements; access by opposition parties to public channels was restricted.

When their regular campaigning was deemed insufficient, the government deployed police and soldiers to intimidate voters. They coerced opposing candidates to withdraw from the competition or to stop campaigning. Some journalists were also targets of the government.[18] Furthermore, the government employed many dirty tactics on election day to distort the electoral results. Officials manipulated the electoral rolls, disenfranchising a large number of opposition supporters. False registrations abounded. In some villages, residents' names were wiped from the list, and those of people who were deceased were added.[19] At the polling stations, officials permitted "ghost voters" to cast ballots repeatedly for the Serimanangkasila Party. Officials also stuffed ballot boxes with ballot papers pre-filled for the Serimanangkasila Party. Electoral fraud occurred most heavily in the vote-counting process. In some precincts, government poll officers intentionally turned off the lights to change the tallies. In Bangkok, where the opposition parties, particularly the Democrats, were very strong, vote counting was delayed for two days. With the early vote counted in 8 districts (out of 13), tallies showed the Democrats leading the government candidates. But when the official results were announced the Democrats won only 2 seats, and the Serimanangkasila candidates won the other 6. Phibun was the winner, with the highest number of votes. Nationwide, the Serimanangkasila Party won 86 seats (out of 160), more than half of the assembly, but clearly not a landslide victory. The Democrat Party, the runner-up, grabbed 30 seats, with the other seats distributed among small parties.[20]

The government's brazen electoral fraud led to student protests. On 2 March 1957, university students led a march, joined by Bangkok voters and opposition politicians, denouncing the government party and accusing it of rigging the results. The protesters called for a nullification of the election result and the holding of a new general election. The protests ended with the storming of Government House. Following this incident the Phibun government's legitimacy deteriorated sharply. Using electoral fraud and civil unrest as pretexts, Sarit staged a coup on

16 September 1957, toppling the Phibun government and introducing a military absolutist regime. The Sarit administration (1958–63) revoked the constitution and ruled the country by military decrees, banning all political parties, civic associations, and elections.[21]

After Sarit died, power passed to his political heir, Thanom Kittikachorn, who continued the military regime for another decade. Thanom called for an election in 1969 under growing domestic and international pressure, since the country had had no election for eleven years. Thanom and his subordinates established the Sahaprachathai Party (United Thai People's Party) to contest in the election. The Sahaprachathai Party was a replica of the Serimanangkasila Party, and the 1969 campaign was a rerun of the 1957 "dirty" election. Government electoral fraud and malpractice were pervasive as the government-backed Sahaprachathai Party won the election using the same old tactics. Government officials intimidated student volunteer groups who tried to file complaints about voting irregularities. The Thanom administration had learned well enough from the 1957 election to rig the vote more subtly this time. Military elites were unified and had dominant control over the system, therefore no post-election protests occurred. However, despite the heavy use of state resources and illegal tactics, the Sahaprachathai Party won only 74 seats (out of 219), less than half of parliament. The Democrat Party, the runner up, secured 55 seats, and the remaining 90 seats were divided among small parties. Viewed in this light, the military failed to consolidate their power through the election. With no absolute control in parliament, Thanom dissolved the assembly two years later in a self-staged coup, the event that led to the mass protests which ended military rule in October 1973.[22]

Nominee for Military: From the 1991 to the 2006 Coup

When the army leaders, who called themselves the National Peace Keeping Council, staged a coup in February 1991, their leaders realized that the old model of creating a military party based on the bureaucratic apparatus was no longer viable, as the social context had changed dramatically. The extra-bureaucratic forces — i.e., elected politicians, business groups, and civil society — were stronger than their counterparts of the past, and they demanded more open politics. The 1991 coup leaders planned to maintain their power by drafting a new constitution to restore military power in the political system through the Senate and an unelected prime minister. The changing international political environment, plus Thailand's strong connection to the globalized economy, however, made it difficult for junta leaders to continue to govern the country without a legitimate election. Therefore, the coup makers called for a general election in March 1992, one year after the coup. Moreover, the coup leaders were aware that it would appear illegitimate to create a political party headed by military generals. So, instead of establishing their own political party, they supported a group of politicians in creating a nominee party for them, called Samakheetham (United Dharma).

Leading up to the election, the junta coerced many leading politicians to join the Samakheetham party in exchange for acquitting them of corruption charges.[23] These troubled politicians had no option but to join the party, and shortly afterwards their corruption charges were cancelled and their frozen assets were released. With a combination of state machinery, military interference, and the electioneering skills of veteran politicians, the Samakheetham party won the election. It was far from a landslide victory though. The Samakheetham party secured only 79 seats (out of 360), and was forced to form a coalition government with other parties. General Suchinda Kraprayun, a coup leader, assumed the premiership, breaking the promise he made to the public when he staged the coup that he would not be involved in politics after the election. Suchinda also appointed many corrupt politicians to his cabinet in exchange for political support. Students, opposition parties and civil society organizations organized a mass demonstration demanding Suchinda's resignation. The coalition government of Suchinda lasted for only two months. In May 1992, with intervention from the palace, Suchinda had to step down after facing street protests in Bangkok.[24] This demonstrated that though the nominee party of the military could win at the polls, it lacked legitimacy, and thus could not govern the country smoothly.

The Samakheetham model was revived for the 2007 election by the army leaders who had toppled Thaksin in the 2006 coup. The 2007 election was the first electoral contest after the September 2006 coup, and it was held under the new constitution. The military supported several parties led by former TRT faction leaders who had left Thaksin after the 2006 coup. These parties — the most notable being the Pheu Pandin Party — were nominee parties of the military. The military-backed Pheu Pandin Party presented itself as a compromise party, an alternative to the two main parties, the Democrats and the People's Power Party (Palang Prachachon Party; PPP). It included former members of Thaksin's party as well as some of his political rivals.

The 2007 election witnessed major interference on the part of the military. Security officials used martial law to disperse rallies, search the houses of candidates and their vote canvassers, and detain party supporters. A report by the Asian Network for Free Elections (ANFREL), an international election-monitoring body, concluded that the existence of martial law "undoubtedly created a climate of fear where freedom of expression and assembly was curtailed".[25] The interference by the army in this election was clear. General Sonthi Boonyaratklin, a coup leader and deputy prime minister, made several public comments against Thaksin and the PPP. Moreover, the independent monitoring body found evidence of military interference in the electoral process in many districts. For example, in Chiang Rai, army personnel were told by their commanders to vote for the main rival of Thaksin's PPP.[26] The military threatened and blocked the PPP's vote canvassers, and allowed other party's vote canvassers to carry on regardless.[27] After the election, many PPP opponents — surprised at winning — attributed their victory to army support.[28]

Despite strong support from the coup leaders, all the nominee parties of the military failed to win many seats; the Pheu Pandin Party won only 24 seats, while the PPP and the Democrats won 233 and 165, respectively. This reflected the pattern of voting behaviour that emerged in Thailand after the 1997 Constitution, in which most Thai voters (more than 80 per cent) cast votes for only two major parties — the Thaksin-allied party and the Democrats. Since 1997, Thailand had clearly moved towards a two-party system, where the party policies, brand and ideology have played decisive roles in winning votes.[29] The campaigns of the military-backed parties, on the other hand, such as the Pheu Pandin, have still relied mainly on personality, patronage and intimidation, which led to their failure.

Fragile Politics: The Military, Party Politics and the Next Election

After the coup the military returned to the centre of the Thai political scene as the ruling elite. Their efforts at embedding their power in the constitution, state organizations and societal sphere have been systematic, as described at the beginning of this chapter. The fact that the military leaders invested their time and energy in institutionalizing their power in the political landscape of the post-Bhumibol era shows that they will not return to the barracks anytime soon. In the design of the constitution, the Prayuth administration has devised a strategic plan to move Thailand towards semi-authoritarianism guided by the military. As mentioned, there is a strong possibility that the NCPO will set up or tacitly support political parties to contest in the coming election to ensure that Prayuth and his colleagues will return to control the country after the election. From the institutional legacies of the past, the NCPO and Prayuth have a choice of two models to adopt. One option is to set up a military party led by top brass, based on the bureaucratic machine of the likes of the Serimanangkhasila and Sahaprachathai parties. The second option is to back a nominee party headed by civilians to win votes for them, as was the case with the Samakheetham and Pheu Pandin parties. As of now, there have already been political moves, both from military officers and politicians, to establish parties to support Prayuth in the next general election. So one may expect to see both types of military-backed parties running in the coming polls.

Nevertheless, it is important to note that even though the 2017 Constitution has already been promulgated, the NCPO will remain in power — with its absolute power vested in the controversial Article 44 — until the new cabinet assumes power. The implication is, that, prior to the new election, the NCPO can exercise its power to postpone or cancel the election if they believe they will not be able to dictate the outcome.

Moreover, considering the experience of military involvement in past elections, Thailand's political future is heading towards uncertainty and unstable politics. The history of military-backed parties provides us with three main lessons. First, the involvement of military-backed parties has tended to make the elections unfree and unfair, as witnessed in 1957, 1969, 1992 and 2007. Second, the army leaders have no skill in party management or electioneering. The military-backed parties have never achieved a landslide majority win, and they have constantly had difficulty in disciplining their party members. Given the two-party system dominated by Pheu Thai and the Democrat Party, the nominee parties of the military are unlikely to win a significant amount of votes in the coming election. Lastly, the electoral misconduct and manipulation by the army has had a tendency to lead to public outcry and mass protests, as witnessed in 1957 and 1992. Taking the historical pattern into account, one cannot expect to see a smooth return to democracy for the next election. An unruly election, the resurgence of street protests, and a short-lived coalition government are more plausible outcomes for Thailand in 2018.

Notes

1. Nordlinger, E.A, *Soldiers in Politics: Military Coups and Governments* (Englewood Cliffs, NJ: Prentice-Hall, 1977), p. 6.
2. After five years the senate will be appointed by a selection committee comprised of nominated professional groups.
3. *Khaosod*, 17 March 2016, p. 1. According to the original draft, the senate could not vote to select the prime minister. However, the NCPO inserted a second referendum question at the last minute, asking voters to decide whether the senate should have the power to select the premier in a joint session with the lower house. In the

referendum the majority of voters approved the senate's power to select the premier. This paves the way for a potential non-elected MP premier, who would likely be a junta general or nominee.

4. Allen Hicken and Bangkok Pundit, "The Effects of Thailand's Proposed Electoral System", 9 February 2016 <http://www.thaidatapoints.com/project-updates/theeffectsofthailandsproposedelectoralsystembyallenhickenandbangkokpundit>.
5. *Kom Chad Luek*, 19 May 2016 <http://www.komchadluek.net/news/sport/227926>; *Post Today*, 14 April 2016 <http://www.posttoday.com/politic/426538>.
6. "Three Years of the Coup: Military Officers Controlling the State Enterprise over the Reform Promise", BBC Thai, 5 June 2017 <http://www.bbc.com/thai/thailand-40121632>.
7. "Thai Junta Sets Firm Date for Election after Many False Starts", Reuters, 10 October 2017 <https://www.reuters.com/article/us-thailand-politics/thai-junta-sets-firm-date-for-election-after-many-false-starts-idUSKBN1CF0M5>.
8. "PM's 6 Questions 'Designed to Rile Critics'", *Bangkok Post*, 10 November 2017 <https://www.bangkokpost.com/news/politics/1357619/pms-6-questions-designed-to-rile-critics>.
9. BBC Thai, 7 November 2017 <http://www.bbc.com/thai/41896399>.
10. Ibid.
11. "EC Turns Down Paiboon's Bid to Form Party", *The Nation*, 1 December 2017 <http://www.nationmultimedia.com/detail/politics/30332992>.
12. *Kom Chad Luek*, 19 May 2016 <http://www.komchadluek.net/news/sport/227926>; Reuters, "Thai Politician Eyes Kingmaker Role as Election Plotting Starts", 30 November 2017 <https://af.reuters.com/article/worldNews/idAFKBN1DU106>.
13. Singhakhom (pseudonym), *Khui fueang rueang kanlueaktang* [Talking of elections] (Bangkok: Aksonsat, 1968), pp. 292–93.
14. Montri Chenvidyakarn et al., *Phakkanmueang Thai Yuk Mai* [New era of Thai political parties] (Bangkok: Krungthai, 1969), pp. 1–48.
15. Chongkon Krairoek, *Sinlapa lueaktang* [Arts of electioneering] (Bangkok: Praphansan, 1974).
16. In Thai Studies literature, the most common name for a vote broker who gathers votes for candidates during a campaign is *vote canvasser*, which translates from the Thai *hua khanaen*. Prior to 1969, commentators used a few terms interchangeably, with *Huana Nuai Khum Siang* being one of them.
17. Kriengsak Phitnakha, *Lueaktang sokkaprok* [Dirty elections] (Bangkok: Asia, 1974), pp. 102–21.
18. Thongchai Saengpradap, "Kansueksa priapthiap phakkanmueang thai: Sueksa chapho korani phak Serimanang kha sila kap phak sa ha pracha thai" [A comparative study of Thai political parties: A comparison between the Serimanangkhasila Party and the Sahaprachathai Party] (MA thesis, Chulalongkorn University, 1974), pp. 90–94.

19. Chumsai Chaiwat, "Botbat thang kanmueang khong phon tamruat ek phao si ya non pho so 2490–2500" [The political role of Police General Phao Siyanon, 1947–1957] (MA thesis, Chulalongkorn University, 1995), p. 133.
20. Prasert Patthamasukhon, *Ratthasapha thai nai rop si sip song pi (2475–2517)* [Thai Parliament in 42 Years, 1932–1974] (Bangkok: Chumnumchang, 1974), p. 866.
21. See Thak Chaloemtiarana, *Thailand: The Politics of Despotic Paternalism* (Bangkok: Social Science Association of Thailand, 1979).
22. Prajak Kongkirati, "Thailand: The Cultural Politics of Student Resistance", in *Student Activism in Asia: Between Protest and Powerlessness*, edited by Meredith Weiss and Edward Aspinall (University of Minnesota Press, 2012), pp. 234–41.
23. After the coup the junta established a commission to investigate and prosecute top provincial politicians on corruption charges. During the investigation, their assets were frozen.
24. William A. Callahan, *Imagining Democracy: Reading "The Events of May" in Thailand* (Singapore: Institute of Southeast Asian Studies, 1998).
25. ANFREL (Asian Network for Free Elections), "Post-Election Summary Report", 25 December 2007 <http://blog.nationmultimedia.com/anfrel/2007/12/28/entry-1>.
26. Human Rights Watch, "Thailand: Military Interference Undermines Upcoming Elections", 20 December 2007.
27. Interviews with several vote canvassers, Phrae and Buriram, January and September 2010.
28. See, in particular, the cases of Democrat candidates in Nakhon Sawan; Prajak Kongkirati, "Bosses, Bullets, and Ballots: Electoral Violence and Democracy in Thailand 1975–2011" (PhD dissertation, Australian National University, 2013), pp. 163–67.
29. Prajak, Kongkirati, "The Rise and Fall of Electoral Violence in Thailand: Changing Rules, Structures and Power Landscapes, 1997–2011", *Contemporary Southeast Asia* 36 no. 3 (2014): 386–416.

THAILAND'S SOUTHERN INSURGENCY IN 2017: Running in Place

Matt Wheeler

The year 2017 marked the fourteenth year of a renewed insurgency that has roots in the post–Second World War wave of national-liberation movements, a legacy of Siam's annexation of the Patani region at the start of the twentieth century.[1] Beginning in the 1960s, and waged at a low level through the 1970s to the 1990s, the insurgency re-emerged with unprecedented intensity at the start of the new millennium.[2] Malay nationalist groups cast their fight as one for liberation from Thai rule and for national self-determination. The main militant group, Barisan Revolusi Nasional Melayu–Patani (Patani–Malay National Liberation Front; BRN), founded in 1960, built a clandestine network of cells in the southernmost provinces during the 1990s. Since the beginning of 2004, militants have continually staged ambushes, bombings and assassinations, but at a slowing pace over the past several years. Deep South Watch, an NGO that monitors violence in the region, estimates that almost seven thousand people have been killed. Violence has declined over the past several years, and in 2017 reached its lowest point since 2004; the insurgency claimed 235 lives, compared to 309 in 2016 and a peak of 892 in 2007.[3]

Violence has been largely confined to the provinces of Pattani, Narathiwat and Yala and four southeastern districts of Songkhla: Chana, Nathawi, Saba Yoi and Thepa.[4] This region of approximately 13,500 square kilometres is home to two million Thai citizens. Roughly eighty-four per cent of the population are Muslims who speak Malay as their first language, the remainder almost entirely Thai or Sino-Thai Buddhists. In contrast to the previous year, there were no insurgent attacks outside of the southernmost provinces in 2017.

MATT WHEELER is Senior Analyst, South East Asia, at the International Crisis Group.

Peace Dialogue

Thailand's military junta, the National Council for Peace and Order (NCPO), took power in a May 2014 coup. The military had been hostile to a peace dialogue process with BRN initiated by the Yingluck Shinawatra government in February 2013. Known as the Kuala Lumpur Process and facilitated by Malaysia, it collapsed after just three plenary meetings, but it marked the first time that a Thai government had publicly committed to negotiating a settlement with those who had taken up arms against the state. In spite of the army's scepticism of the earlier dialogue, the NCPO turned to reviving a dialogue with militants in late 2014, six months after seizing power. Prime Minister's Office Order 230/57 of November 2014 set out mechanisms, including a peace-dialogue panel, to undertake talks with Malay-Muslim militant groups. Malaysia agreed to serve again as facilitator.

In March 2015, representatives of five militant groups established the Majilis Syura Patani (Patani Consultative Council, MARA Patani) as a vehicle for dialogue with Bangkok. MARA Patani nominally unites five groups: BRN, Barisan Islam Pembebesan Patani (Islamic Liberation Front of Patani; BIPP), two factions of the Patani United Liberation Organisation (PULO), and Gerakan Mujahidin Islam Patani (Patani Islamic Mujahidin Movement).[5] MARA Patani's unproven capacity to control fighters in southernmost Thailand is a continuing cause of doubts and criticism of the process. Only BRN is known to command significant numbers of fighters. The top positions in MARA Patani are held by professed BRN members — Awang Jabat is chairman, Sukri Hari delegation chief, and Ahmad Chuwo a steering committee member. However, BRN's senior leaders have not endorsed their participation, and BRN has repeatedly declared that it is not participating in the process. BRN sources say these MARA delegates were senior BRN figures but were suspended after joining MARA Patani; their participation in MARA is freelance.[6] Supporters of the process argue it is still early in a process that remains in a trust-building phase and that, as the dialogue shows progress, BRN will eventually join. But the issue of BRN's participation cannot be sidestepped. As an army officer in the Deep South observed about the dialogue process: "We are fighting BRN, but talking to MARA."[7]

Many military officers and senior bureaucrats opposed the dialogue process under the Yingluck government, concerned that the public nature of the process could legitimize the militants and internationalize the conflict. The NCPO sought to distinguish its dialogue effort from the Yingluck government's process by labelling its goal *santisuk*, which conveys the idea of well-being, rather than "peace" (*santipap*), which suggests an existing state of war. The government seeks to minimize the political nature of the conflict, referring to the militants as "those who think differently from the state".

In late March 2016, after two plenary meetings and three rounds of technical talks, the Thais and MARA reached preliminary agreement on an eight-point Terms of Reference (TOR) document that would allow for official talks. But in late April, the army abruptly transferred Major General Nakrob Bunbuathong, secretary for the Thai dialogue team, and the Thai panel declined to sign the TOR. Panel chief General Aksara Kerdpol said Bangkok needed to review the TOR, and questioned MARA Patani's standing to engage in official talks with Bangkok. Prime Minister Prayuth Chan-ocha expressed irritation with the process, which he called a legacy from the Yingluck government. After coordinated bombings in tourist areas of peninsular Thailand in August 2016, the government returned to dialogue with MARA Patani.

Safety Zones

The Thai government has demanded a reduction in violence since the outset of dialogue. The Thais passed a document on "safety zones" to MARA Patani through the facilitator in early 2016, before Nakrob was ousted.[8] When meetings resumed in September 2016, the two sides agreed on — but did not sign — a version of the TOR and consented to discuss safety zones. Joint technical teams for safety zones met for the first time in late October 2016. At a second meeting on 22 November 2016, MARA Patani submitted three proposals: immunity for MARA representatives in Thailand, release of "political prisoners", and cancellation of a proposed coal power plant in Thepa district, Songkhla province. At a third meeting, the two sides agreed to forward a draft General Framework on Safety Zones for consideration by the full dialogue teams, known as the Joint Working Group (JWG).[9] At the end of 2016, Abu Hafez said that a pilot safety zone would likely be implemented in the first half of 2017.[10]

On 22 February 2017, Major General Sitthi Trakulwong, secretary of the Thai dialogue delegation, announced that the two sides had agreed to establish safety zones "to show their good faith".[11] They re-affirmed the General Framework on Safety Zones at a Joint Working Group meeting on 28 February, but signed no agreement. The framework provides for five districts to be designated as safety zones, two each in Yala and Narathiwat and one in Pattani. One district is to be designated as a pilot safety zone. A Joint Action Committee, including representatives of MARA, the government, civil society organizations and the local community, would be formed to monitor the safety zone for six months and serve as a clearinghouse for investigations of violent incidents.

The announcement of a breakthrough on safety zones appeared to spur a reaction from BRN. A spate of attacks took place in late February through early April. On 2 March, police in Thepa district found the bodies of a married couple whose car had been stolen and rigged with a hundred kilogram improvised explosive device (IED). The vehicle was discovered near a police post before the bomb could be detonated. On 3 March, gunmen ambushed a local official in Ruesoh district, Narathiwat, killing four, including a four-year-old boy, sparking nationwide outrage and earning condemnation from MARA Patani.[12] On 3 April, roughly thirty militants fired more than five hundred rounds at a police booth in Yala, an attack recorded on closed-circuit television. The provincial police chief said it was the largest attack in many years.[13] Aksara announced a briefing for the media on 16 March, in part to dispel the popular notion that the dialogue process caused the violence.[14]

At this briefing, Major General Sitthi said that there were two criteria for selecting districts to serve as safety zones: they must have violent incidents, and the militants must be able to control those perpetrating violence there.[15] He added that there would be a limit of three violent incidents per month; if the Joint Action Committee could not identify the culprits, the safety zone would be scrapped. As Sitthi explained, "The delineation of a safety zone is one measure of testing mutual trust between the government and the dissidents, which, at present, is not quite there yet."[16] Abu Hafez of MARA Patani responded to Sitthi's comments, denying that rules or procedures had been agreed and insisting that further discussions were required, but he concurred that safety zones would serve to gauge the level of cooperation between the Thai government, MARA Patani and local people. Abu Hafez explained that the safety zones are not ceasefires, but mechanisms to protect the civilian population and to provide an environment for open political discussion and popular participation.[17]

BRN's Words and Deeds

BRN's senior leadership changed in early 2017. The group's reputed spiritual leader, Sapaeng Basor, alias Ustaz Shafie Baso, died in Malaysia on 10 January, just three months after being named chairman of the BRN's governing council. According to media reports, Abdullah Wan Mat Noor, aka Dulloh Waemanor, succeeded Sapaeng on 17 January.[18] A BRN member discounted speculation in the Thai media that the change of leadership would mark a shift to more aggressive insurgent operations: "BRN is a secret organization and it is very difficult for anyone to discover the real inner workings of the party especially in terms of the leadership.... Our leadership is not comprised of specific or prominent individuals but is rather a collective leadership, i.e. a council."[19]

In a statement released on 10 April, its first since October 2015, the BRN's Information Department reiterated three preconditions for its participation in talks: First, peace dialogue must be based on voluntary willingness to resolve the conflict, and must include "participation of third parties (international community) as witnesses and observers"; second, the mediator should be "credible", "impartial", and without conflicts of interest; third, "The negotiation process should be designed clearly by the negotiating parties and agreed upon before the start of negotiation."[20] The statement did not break new ground, but flagged BRN's willingness to talk, even as it rejected the existing process between Bangkok and MARA Patani. It also demonstrated BRN's burgeoning understanding of the need to employ an idiom other than violence and to shape a message aimed at the international community.[21]

The statement is notable not only for its rarity and substance but also because BRN issued it in the midst of an unannounced, ten-day unilateral suspension of hostilities. From 8 to 18 April, there were no insurgent attacks in the southernmost provinces. As if to emphasize BRN's command and control, coordinated attacks across the region bracketed this interlude. On the night of 6–7 April, militants carried out a wave of attacks in nineteen districts across the four provinces, with bombs damaging some fifty-two electricity pylons, causing blackouts in Pattani. The operations also included arson and small arms attacks. There were no casualties. On 19 April, between 19:30 and 20:30, insurgents launched thirteen attacks across the region, seven attacks in Narathiwat, and three each in Pattani and Songkhla provinces. Insurgents targeted security-force outposts and checkpoints in hit-and-run raids with grenades and small arms fire, wounding eight people. Two insurgents were killed in Saba Yoi district, Songkhla, when the bomb they were transporting detonated prematurely. The short period between the attacks of 6–7 and 19 April represented an unusually fast tempo for such large-scale, coordinated operations, which in the past had been separated by months.[22]

Persistent questions about BRN's ability to control insurgents and whether or not BRN can effect a ceasefire appeared to have been answered. BRN's Abdul Karim Khalid told a foreign journalist on the day the statement was released, "It is a common matter in the process of negotiations everywhere to prove certainty [by ceasing operations]. That is a simple matter, and BRN does not take it as an objection."[23] In an interview with BBC Thai in September, a BRN spokesman identified as "Yusuf" declared that BRN implemented the April ceasefire, "because we understand that resolving the problem depends on the trust of both sides. We demonstrated that we can control our forces."[24]

Insurgent attacks resumed with a vengeance on 27 April, when militants killed six paramilitary rangers in an ambush in Reusoh, Narathiwat, and set fire to the corpses. On the afternoon of 9 May, a large bomb exploded in front of the Big-C hypermarket in Pattani. A smaller bomb preceded the second blast, which wounded some sixty people, mostly Malay-Muslim civilians, including more than a dozen children; twenty-one people were hospitalized. There were no fatalities. The Big-C attack broke from precedent in causing indiscriminate Malay-Muslim casualties and provoked widespread revulsion in the region. MARA Patani condemned the attack. Security forces killed two suspects in the bombing in July. On 16 August, militants attempted an audacious, but poorly planned, operation, stealing six vehicles from an auto dealership in Nathawi district, Songkhla, immediately rigging them with IEDs, and deploying them. Three of the vehicles were abandoned, at least one after running out of fuel. Two successfully detonated in Pattani, one injuring four soldiers and the second causing no casualties. The sixth vehicle was stopped at a checkpoint; security forces shot and killed the driver. Authorities attributed this operation to new recruits, indicating that militant recruitment and indoctrination continue in spite of a decline in violence.

Bangkok's Ambivalence about Dialogue

The initial Thai response to the 10 April BRN statement was dismissive. Officials said that if BRN had any problems related to the dialogue process they should raise them with Malaysia. The demands for international observers and impartial mediation inevitably excite Thai fears about internationalizing the conflict and opening the door to foreign intervention leading to a plebiscite. Prayuth said that there was no need for foreign involvement: "Why? Our country cannot resolve our problem? If they (international community) are involved (in the peace process), will they understand the problem?"[25]

BRN's April statement and ceasefire may nonetheless have prompted re-evaluation within the NCPO. On 28 June, then deputy defence minister General Udomdej Sitabutr, a former army chief who then headed the NCPO's committee for resolving southern problems, told reporters that he had discussed with Prime Minister Prayuth the issue of whether or not Thailand had the right partner at the dialogue table. He added that General Aksara had been asked to discuss this issue with Ahmad Zamzamin bin Hashim, the Malaysian facilitator.[26] Zamzamin reportedly met with Dulloh Waemanor repeatedly over the next several months, but failed to bring BRN into the dialogue.[27] Udomdej's comments were a rare instance of a senior official publicly expressing misgivings about the process, and seemed to indicate recognition of the need to engage directly with BRN. But this did not lead to observable overtures to BRN or evident change in the Thai approach. Udomdej's remarks reportedly "irked" Aksara, who maintained that MARA's BRN members speak for BRN, and any militants seeking to speak to the Thai government should work through the facilitator Malaysia and MARA Patani.[28]

In July, General Aksara said that the Thai side was in the final stages of selecting one district of the five proposed by MARA Patani as the site for the pilot safety zone, but subsequent rounds of technical-team meetings failed to produce agreement. After technical meetings on 11–12 September ended abruptly, both sides traded blame for the lack of progress. Aksara asserted that MARA Patani was not ready to move forward on a safety zone, and MARA responded that details "especially from the Thai side" remained to be addressed.[29] While these details were not specified, it is likely that the issue of immunity for MARA Patani members was a sticking point. The Justice Ministry reportedly opposed granting immunity to Ahmad Chuwol and Shukri Hari, both of whom fled Thailand in 2007 while on bail, fearing that such a move would create a precedent.[30] Media reports suggested that a scheduled late-September meeting of the technical teams was cancelled and that the dialogue was suspended, which Aksara denied.[31] In mid-December, Aksara said that the JWG would soon convene to review the technical teams' joint assessment of the safety zone and that there had been progress on establishing a "safe house" where the Joint Action Committee would meet.[32] The year ended without any announcement of which district would serve as the pilot safety zone.

The dialogue process under the NCPO is burdened by a fundamental ambivalence about talks with the militants. On one hand, the government understands that there is a public relations benefit to engaging in talks, which demonstrate to locals and the international community an effort to use "peaceful means" to resolve the conflict. On the other hand, the military government has not signed the TOR and is apprehensive about any action that it believes might legitimize the rebels. A pamphlet issued by the Thai delegation in July makes this point explicit, describing a traditional negotiation process in which two parties "balance tradeoffs which eventually lead to a win-win solution". It concludes, "This concept cannot be applied to resolve problems of southern border provinces because we are the Government exercising a sovereign power to ensure territorial integrity."[33]

The government instead conceives of the conflict as a "misunderstanding" in which "those who think differently from the state" must be reconciled to the political status quo. As Prime Minister Prayuth explained in January 2017, "We are negotiating for peace. We are not at war, or talking with an opponent, as some media outlets have said. We simply have different thoughts."[34]

This ambivalence is also reflected in officials' insistence that the Thai government does not, and will not, talk with those who use violence to pressure the government, which would seem to contradict the purpose of a peace dialogue.[35] For Bangkok, the utility of dialogue is not as a mechanism of compromise, but rather as a means to isolate the militants from a population weary of violence. Aksara said that the government's "peaceful means … will result in loss of approval for those who use violence and cause them to cease violence against the people".[36]

BRN's rejection of the current dialogue process has apparently created differences of opinion within the Thai government on how best to proceed. Aksara has steadfastly maintained that the BRN members in MARA Patani speak for the organization, and insisted that no media or analysts have access to the "real" BRN. But National Security Council secretary General Wanlop Rugsanoh has described safety zones as a means to determine whether MARA Patani are the "real people": "If they can [deliver a ceasefire], we can be confident about who we are speaking with."[37] Aksara argues that BRN must work through the existing process, but some officials are reportedly pushing to establish direct talks with BRN.[38] The Thai dialogue panel's July pamphlet complained of "fixation with an old theory" by officials maintaining "secret contact with certain groups/factions/sides of people with different views and [bringing] proposals from those groups to pressure the Government".[39] There were rumours of mooted talks between BRN and Thai officials to be held in a third country in 2018.[40]

Government Policy: More of the Same

While the dialogue process generated little more than unmet expectations, the government continued with its conventional efforts to prevail over the insurgents without introducing political change. The new *Administration and Development Policy for Southern Border Provinces 2017–2019*, issued by the National Security Council, cites the late king's formula of "reaching out, understanding, and developing" as its guiding principle and recapitulates longstanding desiderata: foster economic development, improve the justice system, pursue dialogue with all concerned parties, and strengthen coordination among government agencies.

The military has claimed success in its programme to encourage insurgent surrenders — "Bring the People Home" — with more than 4,500 alleged militants turning themselves in since 2012. Fourth Army Region commander Lt General Piyawat Nakwanich personally received one surrendered militant in a media-soaked event in Yala province in February, ferrying the wanted man away in a helicopter. The programme came under scrutiny after some of the Big-C bombing suspects were revealed to be alumni.[41] The army also rolled out an initiative to bring all 262 sub-districts in the region into its security grid, ensuring that sub-district chiefs receive the same alerts as security forces and integrating them into operations at the local level.[42] The government is justly pleased with the decline in violence, but some officers believe that it has as much to do with militant calculations as government countermeasures.[43]

The centrepiece of the government's policy approach was a three-year economic development plan dubbed the Triangle of Stability, Prosperity, and Sustainability in the Deep South, approved by the cabinet in 2016, including five billion baht (US$155 million) for infrastructure projects in the three provinces through 2020. It entails model projects for one district in each of the three southernmost provinces: sustainable tourism in Betong, Yala; agricultural industries in Nong Chik, Pattani; and international trade and logistics in Sungai Kolok, Narathiwat. The 2018 budget includes a total of 13.25 billion baht (US$410 million) for the Deep South.[44] Since 2004, the government has spent roughly 330 billion baht (US$10 billion) on security operations and economic development. The impact of this spending has been attenuated by graft and local perceptions of paternalistic, top-down development planning. Corruption prevents much of this budget from reaching the grass roots. In August, a government fact-finding committee announced that preliminary review of four development projects, spurred by local complaints, found evidence of official graft.[45]

At the end of November, Prime Minister Prayuth led his cabinet ministers in a "mobile cabinet" meeting in Songkhla and Pattani, intending to showcase the Triangle of Stability, Prosperity, and Sustainability. The cabinet meeting was overshadowed by protests against a proposed coal-fired power plant in Thepa. Scuffles broke out as protestors tried to deliver a letter to the prime minister in Songkhla town. Six protestors were injured. Sixteen people were arrested and face charges of illegal public gathering.[46] MARA Patani issued a statement expressing support for the protestors and calling on the Thai government to respect the wishes of the people of Thepa.[47] Prime Minister Prayuth said plant construction would proceed. The clash in Songkhla and the NCPO's intransigence highlighted a contradiction in the government's refrain of "peaceful means": political activity remains illegal under junta orders and the government does not countenance free speech or popular political participation.

Conclusion

Throughout 2017, the government and MARA Patani both said talks would continue in spite of insurgent violence. Dialogue team representatives on both sides were publicly sanguine, but the process showed little progress. Bangkok has not signed the TOR, nor committed to anything more than periodic, informal meetings with MARA Patani in Malaysia. The failure to establish a pilot safety zone in 2017 lends weight to perceptions that the dialogue process as it is currently configured is sterile. The trend of declining violence is likely to reinforce the military government's reluctance to engage in substantive dialogue, and encourage use of military means with the aim of reducing violence to nuisance levels. Such an approach may succeed for a period of time, but failure to address longstanding political and cultural grievances through political decentralization promises prolonged unrest.

Notes

1. "Patani" refers to the pre-annexation sultanate, which corresponded roughly to the current conflict zone. "Pattani", with two *t*'s, is the transliteration of the Thai province name.
2. The current phase of the insurgency is usually dated to the 4 January 2004 raid on an army base in Narathiwat Province, in which militants killed four soldiers and stole more than four hundred small arms, but it may arguably be traced to 24 December 2001, when militants staged simultaneous attacks on five police checkpoints across Narathiwat, Pattani and Yala provinces, killing five policemen and a local defence volunteer.
3. "Death Toll in Thailand's Southern Conflict Hits Record Low", *Straits Times*, 27 December 2017.
4. In this chapter, "southernmost provinces" and "Deep South" refer to the three provinces and four Songkhla districts. "Southern border provinces" is a translation from Thai and by convention signifies Narathiwat, Pattani and Yala, though Pattani does not border Malaysia.
5. The two factions of PULO in MARA Patani are PULO-MKP (Majilis Kepimpinan Pertubuhan; Party Leadership Council) headed by Kasturi Makhota, and PULO-DSPP (Dewan Syura Pimipinan Pertubhuan; Consultative Council Leadership Party). A third faction, PULO-4P (Pertubuhan Persatuan Pembebesan Patani; Patani United Liberation Organization) headed by Samsudin Khan, did not sign the founding agreement and withdrew from MARA in June 2015.

6. International Crisis Group Briefing, *Southern Thailand's Peace Dialogue: No Traction*, 21 September 2016, p. 5.
7. Interview, army officer, Narathiwat, February 2017.
8. Abu Hafez Al-Hakim, "Two Years of Peace Dialogue: A Small Step Forward", Deep South Watch, 24 December 2016 <https://www.deepsouthwatch.org/node/9977>.
9. "Southern Thailand Safety Zone to be Trialled in 2017, Says Council Rep", Bernama, 25 December 2016.
10. Abu Hafez Al-Hakim, "Two Years of Peace Dialogue".
11. "Thai Army Claims Breakthrough Pact with Separatists in Restive South", Reuters, 22 February 2017.
12. "Violence Flare Up in Southern Thailand Cast a Shadow on 'Safety Zone' Deal", Bernama, 3 March 2017; "Mara Patani Denounce Fatal Attack", *Bangkok Post*, 6 March 2017.
13. "'Biggest Insurgent Attack in Years' in Thai South Wounds 12 Police", Reuters, 3 April 2017.
14. "Aksara Reports to 'Big Tu' on Talks with 'Mara Patani'" (in Thai), *Khom Chad Leuk*, 13 March 2017.
15. "Agreement on Southern Border Safety Zone" (in Thai), *Matichon*, 17 March 2017.
16. Araya Poejar and Razlan Rashid, "Thailand Places Cap on Violent Acts as Condition for Deep South Ceasefire", Benar News, 17 March 2017.
17. Ibid.; Interview, Abu Hafez, MARA Patani, Malaysia, 24 April 2017.
18. "Ex-headmaster Becomes Top BRN Rebel Leader in Deep South: Thai Officials", Benar News, 20 March 2017.
19. Anthony Davis, "South Thailand: War Drums before Fig Leaves", *Asia Times*, 10 April 2017.
20. Barisan Revolusi Nasional Patani Melayu, press release, 10 April 2017.
21. Rungrawee Chalermsripinyorat, "More Savvy BRN Seeks Foreign 'Aid'", *Bangkok Post*, 18 April 2017.
22. Davis, "South Thailand: War Drums".
23. Liston P. Siregar, "Main Muslim Rebel Group of Southern Thailand Ready to Negotiate" (in Indonesian), BBC Indonesia, 11 April 2017.
24. "BRN Declares no Ceasefire until Thai Government Engages in Bilateral Peace Talks" (in Thai), BBC Thai, 29 September 2017.
25. "Refer Demands to Malaysia, Thai Separatist Group Told", Bernama, 11 April 2017.
26. Pimuk Rakkanam, "Thailand Weighs Adding More Parties to Southern Peace Talks", Benar News, 28 June 2017.
27. "Behind the Scenes of the Safety-Zone Failure: MARA Patani Counters the Thais, Peace Talks Continue" (in Thai), *Naew Na*, 18 September 2017.
28. Don Pathan, "Thailand Eyes Next Moves in Southern Peace Talks", *Nikkei Asian Review*, 17 August 2017.

29. "Gen Aksara: Continued Violence in Deep South Won't Obstruct Peace Talks", Thai PBS, 16 September 2017; Media Statement, MARA Patani, 18 September 2017 <https://www.deepsouthwatch.org/node/11304>.
30. Don Pathan, "Deep South Peace Talks: Car-Jacked?" Benar News, 5 September 2017.
31. Wassana Nanuam, "Peace Talks 'Remain on Track'", *Bangkok Post*, 2 November 2017.
32. "Army–Academics Exchange Ideas on Realising Dream of Peaceful South" (in Thai), *Matichon*, 17 December 2017.
33. Peace Dialogue Panel, *The Peace Dialogue Process in Southern Border Provinces*, Office of the Peace Panel Secretariat, Internal Security Operations Command, Bangkok, July 2017, p. 8.
34. Rapee Mama, "'Significant Progress' in Deep South Peace Talks, Thai PM Says", Benar News, 6 January 2017.
35. "Thailand Won't Let Southern Rebels Sway Peace Talks through Violence: Chief Negotiator", Benar News, 29 September 2017; Peace Dialogue Panel, *The Peace Dialogue Process*, p. 9.
36. "Dialogue Makes Progress, Ready to Specify Safety Zone in the 3 Southern Border Provinces" (in Thai), *Krungthep Thurakit*, 30 September 2017.
37. "New Security Threats: Viewpoint of NCPO's NSC Secretary" (in Thai), *Thai Post*, 3 December 2017.
38. "'Peace Dialogue': Success Comes at Cost of Retaliation" (in Thai), *Thai Post*, 14 October 2017.
39. Peace Dialogue Panel, *The Peace Dialogue Process*, p. 19.
40. Maryam Ahmad, "Violence in Thai Deep South Reached Record Low in 2017", Benar News, 26 December 2017.
41. Wassana Nanuam, "Bomb Blast Link to Rehab Scheme Spurs Isoc Probe", *Bangkok Post*, 18 May 2017.
42. Don Pathan, "Thai Military Launches Tambon Defense Initiative in Deep South", Benar News, 22 September 2017.
43. Interview, army officer, Narathiwat, February 2017.
44. Wassana Nanuam, "Govt to funnel B13bn into Far South Ills", *Bangkok Post*, 19 October 2017.
45. Mariyam Ahmad, "Thailand: Panel Will Probe Graft Complaints in 4 Deep South Projects", Benar News, 18 August 2017.
46. "Thai Police Arrest 16 Protesting against Coal-Fired Power Plant", Reuters, 28 November 2017.
47. MARA Patani, media statement, 28 November 2017 <http://www.marapatani.com/2017/11/28/kenyataan-media-media-statement/>.

Timor-Leste

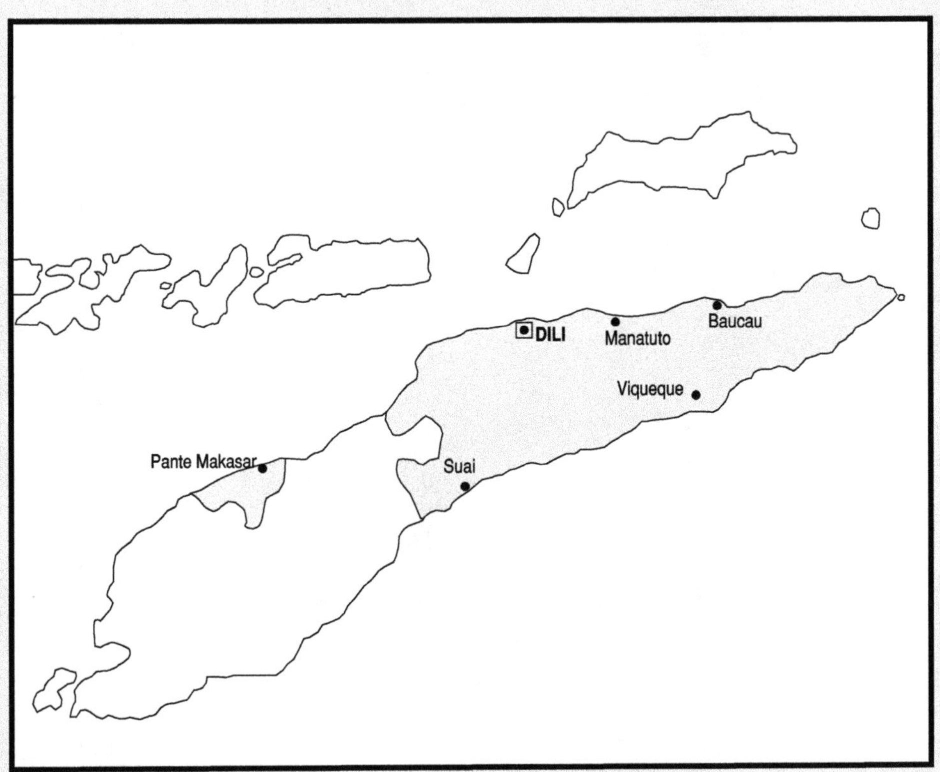

TIMOR-LESTE IN 2017: A State of Uncertainty

Rebecca Strating

Timor-Leste enters 2018 facing an uncertain future on a number of political and economic fronts. This review focuses on three issues: first, the progress of the Timor Sea negotiations with Australia in 2017; second, Timor-Leste's bid for ASEAN membership; and finally, the processes and outcomes of the presidential and parliamentary elections. By the year's end, the events of 2017 relating to these key issues have left Timor-Leste's political situation in an indeterminate state.

An agreement between Australia and Timor-Leste on resolving the long-running dispute over hydrocarbon resources and maritime boundaries in the Timor Sea will be integral to the short- and medium-term economic viability of the Timorese state. While the apparent resolution of the maritime boundaries dispute has been viewed as a moral victory, we currently know little about where the boundaries will be located or the specifics of the special regime that will govern the lucrative but contested Greater Sunrise gas field. How these negotiations will alter Timor-Leste's plans to develop oil industrialization capabilities also remain unknown. On the second major international relations issue — ASEAN membership — Timor-Leste finishes the year once again unsuccessful in its pursuit of joining the organization, as the current member states remain doubtful about the country's economic and diplomatic capacities. This again leaves Timor-Leste's membership prospects in suspension, and, consequently, its identity status as a Southeast Asian state remains ambiguous.

In terms of domestic politics, Timor-Leste held the third set of presidential and parliamentary elections since its independence in 2002. As such, the elections provided some important insights into democratic consolidation, and were widely regarded as well run. The national parliament elections in particular produced surprise outcomes and led to a peaceful change of government, replacing the

Rebecca Strating is Lecturer of Politics at the Department of Politics and Philosophy at La Trobe University, Melbourne, Australia.

sixth government of "National Unity" that comprised a cosy coalition between the two major parties, CNRT and FRETILIN. Subsequent to the election, the formation of new coalitions between political parties rendered obsolete those observations that oppositional politics had ended. The description by Dennis Shoesmith in *Southeast Asian Affairs 2017* of Timor-Leste as a "consociational" and "controlled" democracy that had ostensibly replaced conflict with consensus has now been supplanted, as a parliamentary majority opposition has emerged that threatens the authority of the new FRETILIN-led minority government.[1] Now, instead of no opposition, there may to be too much, highlighting the fluidity of the domestic political context. Timor-Leste's new government has been unable to pass its national agenda through parliament, potentially setting the scene for a constitutional crisis and, perhaps, new elections.

The Timor Sea dispute

In regards to the long-running Timor Sea dispute between Australia and Timor-Leste, the year started with a bombshell. In January 2017 the states released a joint press release that revealed their agreement to terminate the 2006 *Treaty on Certain Maritime Arrangements in the Timor Sea* (CMATS). The CMATS was a controversial treaty originally designed to distribute revenues derived from Greater Sunrise. It was ultimately unsustainable because many Timorese viewed the deal as unfair. An earlier 2003 International Unitisation Agreement (IUA) positioned nearly 80 per cent of the field in Australia's territorial waters, yet the CMATS agreement mandated a 50:50 split in Greater Sunrise revenues. The CMATS also set aside two key sticking points: the delimitation of maritime boundaries and the development of Greater Sunrise. On the latter, Timorese leaders wanted a pipeline built to carry the gas to an onshore processing plant on the south coast of Timor-Leste. However, the venture partners, headed by Woodside, considered the pipeline unviable and consequently shelved production of the field. Consequently, Timor-Leste began pursuing delimitation of relevant maritime boundaries and employing legal proceedings to dissolve the CMATS. Australia, meanwhile, was steadfast in its support for retaining the treaty. Thus, the news of CMATS' demise was viewed by many as a significant win for Timor-Leste. In mid-January it became evident that the quid pro quo for Australia acquiescing to the dissolution of CMATS was Timor-Leste's commitment to dropping the two international legal proceedings that it had initiated against Australia. This was a risky foreign policy strategy for Timor-Leste, as the IUA that locates most of the field in Australian waters remains active.

The January decisions resulted from the United Nations Compulsory Conciliation (UNCC) proceedings Timor-Leste initiated under Annex V of the United Nations Convention on the Law of the Sea (UNCLOS). The UNCC is not a court or an arbitral tribunal: it was provided for under UNCLOS to assist states to reach amicable settlements of maritime disputes. Meetings between representatives of Timor-Leste and Australia in Copenhagen, Singapore and elsewhere were scheduled to run for one year from September 2016. A commission of five conciliators was scheduled to produce a non-binding report in October 2017 to assist bilateral negotiations. However, conciliation proceedings deviated from this agenda as talks remained ongoing. On 30 August 2017 a press release revealed details of another apparent "breakthrough" in the negotiations in what would become known as the "Copenhagen Agreement".[2] It released vague details of an agreement package. Both states had agreed to the central elements of a maritime boundary delimitation, but the agreement also addressed "the legal status of the Greater Sunrise gas field, the establishment of a Special Regime for Greater Sunrise, a pathway to the development of the resource, and the sharing of the resulting revenue". The news of an agreement in maritime boundary delimitation was particularly significant because Australia had steadfastly supported the moratorium on boundaries.

While some supporters believed the deal had vindicated Timor-Leste's risky foreign policy approach, others saw it as another chapter of Australia "bullying" Timor-Leste into unfair deals. It was possible to glean from the "Copenhagen Agreement" that while Timor-Leste was able to negotiate a maritime boundary with Australia, it had to compromise on its claims to the entire Greater Sunrise gas field. At the time of writing, the "central elements" for delimitation have not been made public. It seems likely that the agreement would conform to median-line principles under UNCLOS, but what exactly the "median line" entails will differ from Timor-Leste's public interpretation wherein Greater Sunrise falls in its territorial waters. A treaty text is ready to be signed, but much of what happens now depends on whether a development plan can be agreed upon. This negotiation is not a straightforward bilateral discussion between Australia and Timor-Leste, as it is largely between Timor-Leste and the commercial venture partners. Any deal will therefore need to be economically viable. Hence, much depends upon how wedded Timorese negotiators are to the pipeline, which was a particular ambition of former prime minister and Timor-Leste's lead negotiator Xanana Gusmão. The pipeline is a potent symbol of Timor-Leste's pursuit of sovereignty, economic justice and economic development. While much has been made of Timor-Leste's purported foreign policy victories, the evidence suggests that it enters 2018 uncertain about whether the development negotiations will succeed. On 26 December, a press release declared the intentions of parties to sign the boundary treaty and settle on a development plan by March 2018. Given the gap between Timor-Leste and the venture partners about what constitutes a commercially viable plan, this timeline may prove to be overly optimistic.[3]

This issue has significant flow-on effects for other sectors. A development arrangement for Greater Sunrise is central to the short- and medium-term economic viability of Timor-Leste. Timor-Leste remains one of the most oil-dependent states in the world. The oil revenues from the earlier 2002 Timor Sea Treaty (TST) furnish around 90 per cent of Timor-Leste's state budget and around 80 per cent of its GDP. The 2017 state budget of $1.38 billion for 2017 was largely derived from oil and gas revenues, and was only slightly lower than the $1.562 billion of the 2016 budget.[4] For the majority of the maritime area under question — the Joint Petroleum Development Area (JPDA) — possession means little in material terms unless there are untapped hydrocarbon resources that have not yet been found. The TST that governs the JPDA mandated a 90:10 revenue split in Timor-Leste's favour. While Australia received rights to pipe the oil to Darwin for processing, the field is expected to run dry in the early 2020s. Timor-Leste's 2011 Strategic Development Plan committed Timor-Leste to developing its oil refinery industries. The centrepiece was the Tasi Mane project on the south coast, which was criticized by observers as a "fantasy" and a "white elephant". In 2017 the IMF advised that any frontloading of capital must be limited and prioritized. It also noted that non-oil GDP had slowed by 3 per cent due to lower governmental spending and a slowdown in economic activity. The petroleum fund has again declined from over US$16 billion to US$15.8 billion.[5]

As the state has already compromised on complete control of Greater Sunrise, a new FRETILIN government (if it remains in power) will need to adjust the previous government's ambitions for Tasi Mane. Timor-Leste's long-term economic viability will rely upon diversifying the economy away from reliance on oil and gas in order to avoid the "resource curse". However, for the immediate future, an agreement on Greater Sunrise is urgent, particularly because the state plays a significant role in the economy. Even with the oil and gas revenues, the poverty rate in 2017, according to the United Nations Development Programme, remains at around 50 per cent.[6] An austerity programme induced by dwindling oil revenues would be disastrous for the livelihoods of many people, the economy as well as internal security, which has been largely bolstered by state welfare payments in the form of "buying the peace".[7] Any deal on development will ultimately need to have broad support across the spectrum of Timorese political elites to succeed in the future, particularly as domestic politics in Timor-Leste is facing a potential end to the stability of recent years (discussed below).

ASEAN

The second major foreign policy issue for Timor-Leste was in a similar state of uncertainty at the end of 2017. Successive governments have regarded accession into the Association of Southeast Asian Nations (ASEAN) as the cornerstone of Timor-Leste's foreign policy. The 2011 Strategic Development Plan envisaged that Timor-Leste would be an ASEAN member state by 2015. The SDP also aspired for Timor-Leste to become recognized as having expertise in "economic development, small-nation management, good governance and aid effectiveness and delivery" by 2020. As part of Timor-Leste's foreign policy approach, it has developed a narrative of "fragile state exceptionalism" that seeks to inculcate its self-image as a development success story, reflected in the phrase, "from fragility to resilience".[8] In March 2011, Timor-Leste unsuccessfully applied for formal membership to ASEAN when Indonesia was chair. The key challenge for Timor-Leste has been the ability to prove to the current ASEAN member states that it has the capacity to meet its membership obligations, particularly the English language requirements for the high number of meetings and dialogues held yearly.

The year 2017 was particularly significant for Timor-Leste in terms of its ASEAN membership efforts. It began with some promising signs. First, in 2016, three independent studies on the implications of Timor-Leste's accession to ASEAN's political, economic and sociocultural pillars were completed. The first two studies found that Timor-Leste's human resources needed "capacity-building" to "boost economic growth and skills". Yet it was also said that Timor-Leste would be permitted to participate in more ASEAN meetings. Second, Timor-Leste was given responsibilities in ASEAN. In 2016 it held the ASEAN People's Forum (APF) for Southeast Asian civil society when the chair — Laos — was reluctant to do so. Finally, and most importantly, the chair for 2017 was the Philippines, a state that has been publically supportive of Timor-Leste's desire to join the organization. Philippine representatives were reportedly "very keen to bring the region's young democracy into its embrace".[9] The combination of public support from powerful members of ASEAN — including de facto leader Indonesia — and increasing involvement and embeddedness in the architecture of the organization meant that there was optimism about Timor-Leste becoming its eleventh member.

And yet, despite these positive signs, Timor-Leste's progress stalled. The 2017 ASEAN foreign ministers' Joint Communiqué "welcomed Timor-Leste's participation in relevant ASEAN activities within the context of its need for capacity building".[10] The language of "capacity building" is similar to the ASEAN 2016 Joint Communiqué, indicating that very little has changed regarding Timor-Leste's application. A report by the ASEAN Coordinating Council Working Group on the membership bid is under way.[11] While the general feeling among the commentariat is that Timor-Leste's chances of joining ASEAN remain strong, the crucial players are the ten member states, who all have to agree to its accession as part of the consensus-oriented "ASEAN way" of decision-making. By the end of 2017 it was increasingly clear that Timor-Leste would not be admitted into ASEAN. There are media reports that ASEAN states had reached a decision to deny Timor-Leste's admittance in 2017, with "no breakthrough on the horizon".[12]

Interpreting the signals can be difficult, but it is important to focus on what the states have done rather than what they say. In this regard, the collective actions suggest that the ASEAN states continue to be wary of admitting a fragile new member into the association. ASEAN's chair in 2018 is Singapore, the most vocal opponent of Timor-Leste's membership. This could mean a loss of momentum for Timor-Leste's campaign and perhaps an indefinite delay. Singapore was concerned that Timor-Leste would burden ASEAN with requests for financial support and hinder the progress of ASEAN economic community building.

A key question, then, is whether Timor-Leste will likely need intervention in the future. Will it be a drain on ASEAN resources, particularly if Timor-Leste does not reach an agreement with Australia on the Greater Sunrise gas field? Will a weak Timor-Leste provoke an intervention into Southeast Asia? Given Timor-Leste's previous reliance on five UN missions, including a lengthy Australian-led intervention from 2006 to 2012, these are important considerations for ASEAN states. Given the current political instability (detailed below), it seems the decision of ASEAN to hold off on membership was prescient. In terms of Timor-Leste's pursuit of ASEAN membership into the future, much will depend upon its domestic political circumstances, as the current instability constitutes a potential threat to its state-building success narrative.

Elections in 2017

In 2017, Timor-Leste held its third set of elections since it achieved independence in 2002. The vote for the president was held in March, and parliamentary elections were held in July. For the past decade, Timorese politics has been dominated by two major parties — the Revolutionary Front for an Independent East Timor (FRETILIN) and the National Congress for Timorese Reconstruction (CNRT). Since February 2015, when Xanana Gusmão stood down as prime minister, Timorese politics has largely been defined by a coalition between the parties, as the Sixth Government of "National Unity"/"National Inclusion" — with FRETILIN's Dr Rui Araujo as prime minister — replaced the CNRT-led government. A key consequence of this arrangement was the absence of a strong parliamentary opposition, so then-president Taur Matan Ruak took up the mantle of holding the coalition government to account by using his post to become the de facto opposition. A key assessment when considering the nature of democracy is how opposition and cooperation are permitted and negotiated in the body politic. As many competitive authoritarian regimes have done before, Timorese politicians drew upon cultural relativism to justify the coalition as a transition from a Western-style "belligerent" democracy to a more "culturally appropriate" style of "consensus democracy".[13] As Feijo points out, while there is room in democratic political institutions for consensus and bipartisanship to operate, "inclusive" government does not necessarily contribute to "national unity", as strong executives "may be the other side of the coin of a weak state".[14] It was widely anticipated by commentators that the coalition would continue after the 2017 parliamentary elections.[15] These predictions failed to consider the dynamic nature of East Timorese politics, as the personal power of elites, the lack of institutionalization of democratic behaviour and the absence of clearly delineated ideological and policy preferences among parties establishes a fluid political environment.

In March, former FRETILIN resistance leader Francisco "Lú-Olo" Guterres was elected president. Of the 70 per cent of eligible Timorese who voted, Lú-Olo received 57.1 per cent of votes, ahead of former minister of state, coordinator of social affairs and minister of education in the sixth government, António da Conceição of the Democratic Party (PD), who attained 32.50 per cent of the vote. Unlike in 2007 and 2012, Lú-Olo's achievement of a simple majority avoided a second run-off election. CNRT also supported Lú-Olo, which hinted at the continuance of the political unity between the two parties in the lead-up to the parliamentary elections.

Timor-Leste held its parliamentary elections on 22 July 2017, with key election issues revolving around the economy, corruption, maritime boundaries, and the distribution of oil revenues. In a positive sign for democratic consolidation, Timor-Leste's elections were ably conducted by its electoral institutions, the National Elections Commission (CNE) and the Technical Secretariat for Election Administration (STAE), and the two sets of elections were recognized as free, fair and mostly absent of political violence.[16] The voter turnout of around 75 per cent (close to the average of 77.53 across ten elections) highlighted the ongoing popularity of electoral participation among the Timorese.[17] CNRT expected it would again receive the highest number of votes, like in 2012, followed by FRETILIN. The two parties achieved almost identical results. As the party most closely linked to the resistance movement against Indonesia, the FRETILIN loyal voter base came out in force, with the party obtaining a plurality of 29.87 per cent of the vote and 23 seats of the 65 available. In contrast, the CNRT party, led by former resistance leader Xanana Gusmão, came in second with 29.46 per cent of the vote and only 22 seats. Both parties experienced a drop in support: FRETILIN lost 2 seats while CNRT lost 8 seats.

However, as Aspinall, Hicken, Scambary and Weiss note in a forthcoming article in the January edition of the *Journal of Democracy*, FRETILIN's vote has remained relatively consistent across the 2007, 2012 and 2017 elections as a consequence of its visible, well-organized campaigning at the grass-roots level. While in government, CNRT benefited from excessive spending of oil wealth, and as a party it relies heavily on the charismatic legitimacy of Gusmão. Its reliance on the figure of Gusmão and its patronage machinery, however, proved much less successful in the 2017 election campaign than in 2012, when it was able to form and lead a coalition government.

Rather than continue the alliance between FRETILIN and CNRT as the second party, Gusmão shocked observers by announcing that CNRT would not replicate the "National Unity" government, but would instead fill the role of parliamentary opposition. Even though there was less than half a per cent difference between them, FRETILIN's higher vote count foiled CNRT's expectation that it would be elevated into leadership position. While Gusmão "retired" his prime ministership in 2015, he continued to hold powerful formal positions in government, including as the minister for planning and strategic development — a key portfolio with expansive control over state resources — and the lead negotiator for the Timor Sea dispute. While he continues to wield considerable influence in Timorese politics, the drop in support for CNRT suggests that his personal charisma was not enough to consolidate loyalty within the electorate to the same extent as FRETILIN.

The collective 10-seat loss for the two major parties signalled the emergence of new forces in Timorese politics that were able to capitalize on voter disillusionment and changing demographics. Three other parties joined FRETILIN and CNRT in parliament. The newly established People's Liberation Party (PLP), led by former president Taur Matan Ruak, was created to establish opposition to the two main parties. Although it was not able to challenge the two major parties for supremacy, it presented a credible third-party alternative, with 10.6 per cent of the vote and 8 seats. The PD, which has played the third-party role in Timorese politics since independence, attained 9.8 per cent of the vote and 9 seats, one less than in 2012. The elections also established a new player in Timorese politics, the KHUNTO Party (translated as Enrich the National Unity of the Sons of Timor). KHUNTO won 6.4 per cent of the vote in Timor-Leste's proportional representative system, which translated into 5 seats. According to Aspinall and Scambary, KHUNTO is unique insofar as it is not connected to the leaders of the independence movement, and its support base is derived from martial arts groups (which they described as "important social institutions among young people") as well as disenfranchised rural voters who are denied a share of the largesse distributed via networks of patronage.[18] They say that KHUNTO's success was due to its efforts to engender trust in the context of widespread corruption, which indicates that the fragile consensus upholding the political community may be eroding.[19] For a time it appeared that this new youth-oriented party would play kingmaker by joining a coalition with FRETILIN and PD.

Beyond the introduction of KHUNTO to the political landscape, Timorese politics remains dominated by an elite that has been trading plum political roles since independence in 2002. New prime minister Mari Alkatiri was the first prime minister from 2002 until 2006, when he was forced to resign in disgrace. Opposition leader Xanana Gusmão was the first president in 2002, and prime minister from 2007 to 2015. Jose Ramos-Horta, former foreign minister, president and acting prime minister is also back in cabinet as minister of state. The issues of generational change and the challenges of transitioning politics away from former leaders of the resistance who have now consolidated their place as political elites has not been resolved or substantially altered since the 2007 elections.

In September 2017, the KHUNTO party walked away from a deal it had struck with FRETILIN, causing the government to lose its parliamentary majority. At the time of writing, the coalition of FRETILIN and PD holds 30 of 65 seats, 5 seats shy of what it needs to form government. The three opposition parties call themselves the "Parliamentary Majority Alliance" (PMA). In the absence of a clear majority, the president's first choice is to appoint the party with a plurality. Yet, Prime Minister Alkatiri's legitimacy has been questioned by the PAM as unconstitutional on the grounds that the coalition government does not have majority rule.[20] This reflects alternative interpretations of the constitution. Sections 109 and 112 of the constitution require the government to submit a national programme to parliament, with dismissal of the government occurring if the programme is rejected two consecutive times.[21] The FRETILIN government's policy programme has currently been rejected once by the national parliament, putting it at risk of dismissal if it is rejected again.

The Programme of the Seventh Constitutional Government presented to parliament was based on four pillars: the social sector, infrastructure development, the economic sector, and good governance and institutional reform, focusing on education, health, employment and the economy.[22] However, the agenda mostly describes only a very general set of objectives and values for the next five years of governance, and very little in terms of specific policies, measurable outcomes or budget prioritization for achieving its ambitions. The commitments generally align with the ambitious 2011–2030 Strategic Development Plan, implemented under the CNRT-led government. The aim of transforming Timor-Leste into a high-middle-income economy by 2030 with an educated, healthy and secure population remains. The objections of the PMA to the document were similarly vague. According to civil society monitoring group La'o Hamutuk, "[d]uring the debate, most of the objections by opposition MPs were very general, or to the existence and alleged instability of a government whose coalition did not include parties with a majority of Parliamentary votes."[23] The PMA also released an alternative platform, reflecting its desire to form government, and the national agenda was voted down along party lines, with thirty-five voting against it.

The constitution is ambiguous on whether President Lú-Olo must call early elections or allow CNRT to attempt to form a majority government. Section 106:1 of East Timor's constitution states "[t]he Prime Minister shall be designated by the political party or alliance of political parties with parliamentary majority and shall be appointed by the President of the Republic, after consultation with the political parties sitting in the National Parliament."[24] The PMA has argued that they should be allowed to form government. It sent the president a letter saying they were "willing to present an alternative government solution" to ensure "peace, stability and development".[25] The PMA represents 42 of the 65 seats, so could feasibly form a coalition government. This is reminiscent of the constitutional crisis that emerged after the 2007 elections, in which FRETILIN argued it had a plurality and should have been allowed to form a minority government. Then-president Jose Ramos-Horta requested that CNRT — who did not hold the plurality but held majority cross-party support — form government.[26] In opposition, FRETILIN declared the new government unconstitutional and illegitimate, and the central committee threatened to boycott parliament and support a civil uprising. By moving CNRT into opposition after the 2017 elections, Gusmão gambled that FRETILIN would be unable to form a coalition government with the other parties represented in parliament, opening pathways to CNRT leadership or new elections.

At time of writing, there are several potential pathways that government in Timor-Leste might take: FRETILIN and PD might last a full five-year term as a minority government if it can pass its national programmes, or it might persuade an opposition party to join them in a majority coalition. Alternatively, CNRT and the opposition parties may be given an opportunity to govern. If PMA gets an opportunity to replace the FRETILIN government, its capacities to provide sustainable government may be undermined by the friction between the PLP and CNRT, their different electoral promises, and Taur Matan Ruak's blistering criticisms of the CNRT while president. In his review for *Southeast Asian Affairs 2017*, Shoesmith reasonably predicted that Taur Matan Ruak would "be no ally of Xanana Gusmão" in 2017 and beyond.[27] On the other hand, it is wise to avoid thinking that politicians are overly wedded to any particular ideology or programme in Timorese politics.

It is most likely, however, that new elections will be held in 2018. According to the electoral law, the date of elections must be declared sixty days in advance, and Section 100 of the constitution mandates that the National Parliament cannot be dissolved until six months after the elections.[28] Consequently, it may not be until May before a stable government may be formed. This would delay budget rectification and add considerable strain on Timor-Leste's already fragile economy.[29] The government may also be dismissed if a vote of no confidence is passed in the national parliament, making governing in the minority an unstable prospect.[30]

If a constitutional crisis were to eventuate, this would reflect one of the pitfalls of Timor-Leste's system of closed-list proportional representation in a unicameral parliament. While proportional representation electoral systems promote coalition governments, these are inclined to provide less stability than two-party majoritarian systems that tend to be produced by preferential voting systems. Less than 60 per cent of the vote went to the major parties in the 2017 parliamentary elections, and more than 10 per cent of votes were lost as a number of minor parties did not meet the threshold to enter parliament of 4 per cent of the total vote. Furthermore, Timor-Leste did not have a government for almost one month, as ministers were not inaugurated within the fifteen days mandated by the national constitution. The "interim government" made up of the 2012–17 government also illegitimately extended its expired mandate.[31]

There are also fears of political instability, as the current political context is reminiscent of the 2006 political crisis, during which Alkatiri was forced to resign as prime minister. In a concerning article written in October 2017, security monitor Fundasaun Mahein reported that growing anxiety among the Timorese was "causing people to flee the perceived threat of conflict. Every day, increasing numbers of people board buses bound for the rural districts, indicating a desire to escape the political tensions in Dili. Even more disturbingly, more and more people are exiting Timor-Leste altogether, either by airplane or across the land frontier with Indonesia."[32] On the one hand, the return of opposition politics is welcomed, because this is viewed as a necessary condition for democracy. However, the cost of the return of an opposition is a loss of stability, and the potential emergence of political violence and fear that has marred Timor-Leste's society in the recent past. The State Rectification Budget was again presented to the National Parliament in December and was rejected for a second time. Thus, the most probable pathway seems to be new elections held in March 2018.

Conclusion

The Timorese political situation in 2017 ended in flux. The three domestic and international issues canvassed in this review expose the ongoing political and economic fragilities experienced by Timor-Leste as a small new state. While there have been positive signs in the Timor Sea dispute and Timor-Leste's ASEAN membership status, by years end, progress on both fronts remained uncertain. The unknown factor in the Timor Sea dispute remains whether the venture partners and Timor-Leste can strike a deal on a development plan for Greater Sunrise; in particular, reaching an agreement on the pipeline. If a development plan cannot be settled upon, this could have consequences for the treaty text of the maritime boundary delimitation and put at risk the progress made throughout the UNCC proceedings. Ultimately, a hasty deal will need to be struck in order to head off the urgent economic challenges facing the state. Meanwhile, Timor-Leste's application to become an ASEAN member state has stalled, which means that its place in the region and its identity as a Southeast Asian nation remains ambiguous. Finally, at the time of writing, the new FRETILIN minority government has been unable to pass its national programme or budget through the National Parliament. At this stage it seems most likely that this political impasse will lead to fresh elections in 2018. A constitutional crisis in 2018 may have consequences for the consolidation of democratic state institutions in Timor-Leste, as well as for short-term economic prospects and internal security.

Notes

1. Dennis Shoesmith, "Timor-Leste in 2016: Redefining Democracy", *Southeast Asian Affairs 2017*, edited by Daljit Singh and Malcolm Cook, pp. 387–406 (Singapore: ISEAS – Yusof Ishak Institute, 2017).

2. Permanent Court of Arbitration, "Conciliation between the Democratic Republic of Timor-Leste and the Commonwealth of Australia", press release, Copenhagen, 1 September 2017.
3. Permanent Court of Arbitration, "Conciliation between the Democratic Republic of Timor-Leste and the Commonwealth of Australia", press release, The Hague, 26 October 2017.
4. Government of Timor-Leste, "Government's 2017 General State Budget presented to National Parliament", press release, 24 November 2016 <http://timor-leste.gov.tl/?p=16825&lang=en>.
5. International Monetary Fund, "IMF Staff Completes 2017 Article IV Consultation Mission to Timor-Leste", 6 October 2017 <http://www.imf.org/en/News/Articles/2017/10/06/pr17390-imf-staff-completes-2017-article-iv-consultation-mission-to-timor-leste>.
6. United Nations Development Programme, "Timor-Leste" <http://www.tl.undp.org/content/timor_leste/en/home.html>.
7. Craig Valters, Sarah Dewhurst, and Juana de Catheu, *After the Buffaloes Clash: Moving from Political Violence to Personal Security in Timor-Leste*, Development Progress Case Study Report (London: Overseas Development Report, 2015), pp. 13, 22.
8. Rebecca Strating, *The Post-Colonial Security Dilemma: Timor-Leste and the International Community* (Singapore: Institute of Southeast Asian Studies, forthcoming).
9. Kavi Chongkittavorn, "Will Timor-Leste Finally Join ASEAN in 2017?" *Reporting ASEAN* <http://www.aseannews.net/will-timor-leste-finally-join-asean-2017a/>.
10. ASEAN, "Partnering for Change, Engaging the World", Joint Communiqué of the 50th Foreign Ministers' Meeting, Manila, 5 August 2017.
11. ASEAN, "Turning Vision into Reality for a Dynamic ASEAN Community", Joint Communiqué of the 49th Foreign Ministers' Meeting, Vientiane, 24 July 2016.
12. Nikkei Asian Review, "ASEAN to Discuss Next Month Admitting East Timor as New Member", 12 November 2017.
13. Agio Pereira, "Timor-Leste Transforming Belligerent Democracy into Consensus Democracy", *Tempo Semanal*, 26 January 2014.
14. Rui Graca Feijo, "A Long and Winding Road: A Brief History of the Idea of a 'Government of National Unity' in Timor-Leste and its Current Implications", State, Society and Governance in Melanesia discussion paper 2016/3, Australian National University, 2016, pp. 1, 14–15.
15. See, for example, Khoo Ying Hooi, "After Timor-Leste's Election, a Young Democracy Looks Forward", *The Diplomat*, 25 July 2017; Iriana Ximenes, "The Big Winner of Timor-Leste's Parliamentary Elections? The Country Itself", *The Diplomat*, 16 June 2017.
16. International Republican Institute, "Timor-Leste's Parliamentary Elections: Voters Demonstrate Commitment to Democracy; Election Day Logistics Need Improvement"

<http://www.iri.org/resource/timor-leste%E2%80%99s-parliamentary-elections-voters-demonstrate-commitment-democracy-election-day>.

17. Inter-parliamentary Union, "Timor-Leste National Parliament" <http://archive.ipu.org/parline-e/reports/2369_E.htm>.
18. Edward Aspinall and James Scambary, "Fighting Corruption with Spiritual Power in East Timor", *New Mandala*, 3 November 2017.
19. Ibid.
20. "CNRT Party Questions New Government Model", *Independente,* 22 September 2017 <https://www.independente.tl/en/national/cnrt-party-questions-new-government-model>.
21. Constituent Assembly, *National Constitution of Timor-Leste*, sections 109 and 112.
22. Government of Timor-Leste, *Meeting of the Council of Ministers of October 4 2017*, press release, 4 October 2017 <http://timor-leste.gov.tl/?p=18847&lang=en>.
23. La'o Hamutuk, *Timor-Leste Seventh Constitutional Government* <https://www.laohamutuk.org/misc/gov7/17VIIGov.htm>.
24. Constituent Assembly, *National Constitution of Timor-Leste*, section 106:1.
25. Lindsay Murdoch, "East Timor's Opposition Threaten Newly Sworn-In Minority Government", *The Age*, 7 October 2017.
26. Rebecca Strating, *Social Democracy in East Timor* (Abingdon, UK: Routledge, 2016).
27. Shoesmith, "Timor-Leste in 2016", p. 396.
28. Constituent Assembly, *National Constitution of Timor-Leste*, section 100.
29. "Timorese Minority Government Faces First Test Next Week in Parliament", *Lusa*, 13 October 2017 <https://www.laohamutuk.org/misc/gov7/LusaMinorGovTest13Oct2017en.pdf>.
30. Constituent Assembly, *National Constitution of Timor-Leste*, sections 111, 112 1(e, f).
31. Fundasaun Mahein, *The Post-Election Situation: Between Constitutionality and Arbitrary Rule*, 25 August 2017.
32. Fundasaun Mahein, *Conflicting Constitution Interpretations Spread Fear of Instability*, 25 August 2017.

Vietnam

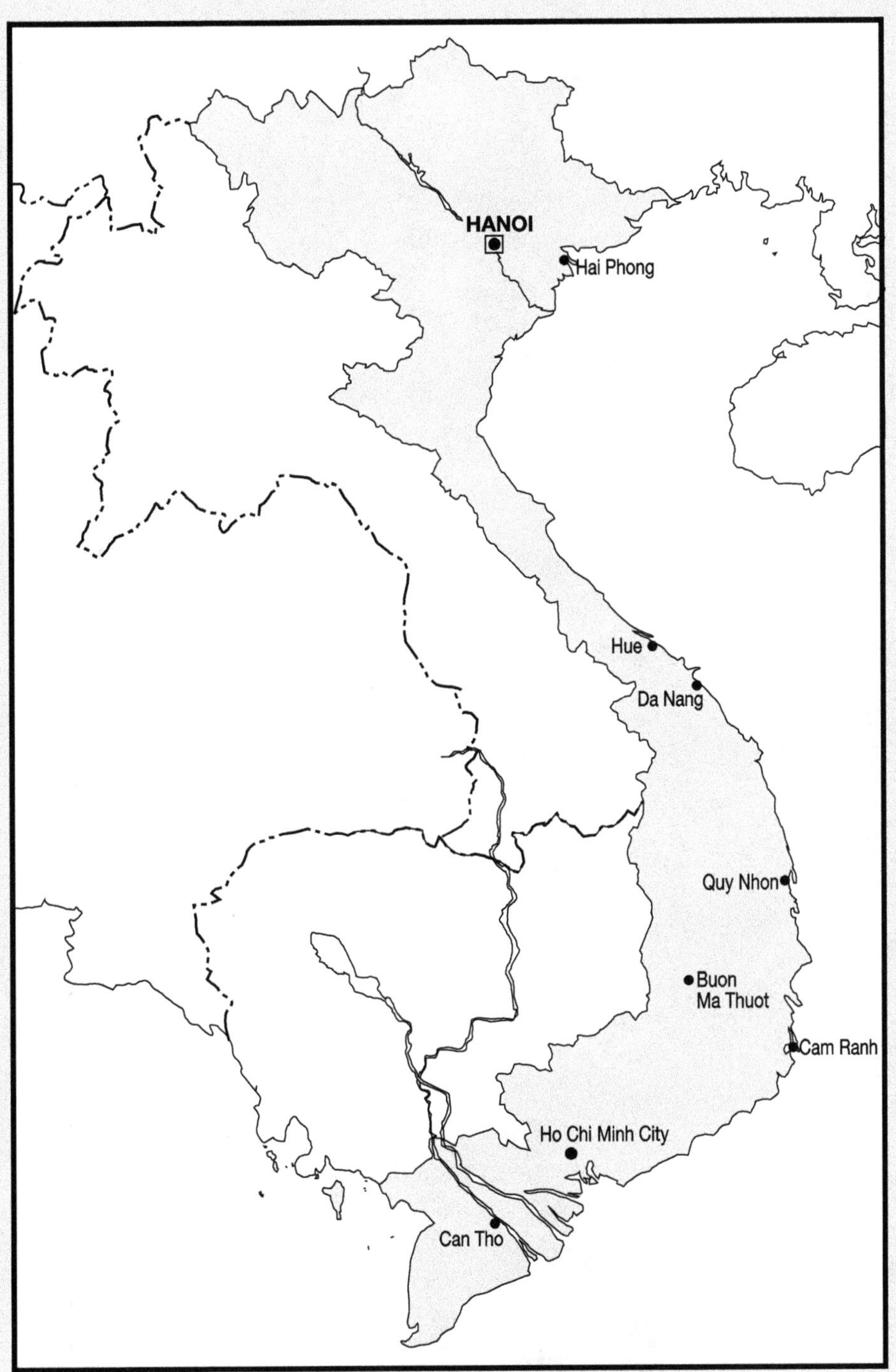
HANOI
Hai Phong
Hue
Da Nang
Quy Nhon
Buon
Ma Thuot
Cam Ranh
Ho Chi Minh City
Can Tho

VIETNAM IN 2017: Power Consolidation, Domestic Reforms, and Coping with New Geopolitical Challenges

Nguyen Manh Hung

Three distinct characteristics of Vietnam's development in 2017 were the consolidation of power in the hands of the Communist Party of Vietnam (CPV) and its leadership, politico-administrative reforms, and fashioning a foreign policy to deal with a worsening external environment.

Consolidation of Power

The process of consolidation of power in the hands of the party and its leadership began after the CPV's Twelfth National Party Congress in January 1916. It picked up steam and led to several high-profile trials and a major purge in 2017.

This process included three elements: a campaign against corruption, efforts to rebuild and strengthen the party, and a crackdown on dissidents.

Anti-corruption Campaign

The Twelfth National Party Congress of the CPV resulted in a victory for the party's General Secretary Nguyen Phu Trong over Prime Minister Nguyen Tan Dung, and of the party over the state. Immediately after the congress, Trong moved to consolidate his power and that of the party, placing his supporters in the top positions of all the important commissions of the Central Committee, bringing control of the fight against corruption back to the party's Central Committee on

---

NGUYEN MANH HUNG is Professor Emeritus of International Relations at George Mason University and Non-resident Senior Associate of the Southeast Asia Program at the Center for Strategic and International Studies, USA.

Corruption Prevention and Fighting (CCCPF), and renewing the anti-corruption campaign.[1] In 2017, Trong's position was further strengthened by the addition of two of his supporters — head of the Central Department of Internal Affairs Phan Dinh Trac and director of Ho Chi Minh National Institute of Politics Nguyen Xuan Thang — to the party secretariat, and the ousting from the Politburo of Dinh La Thang, a powerful protégé of former prime minister Nguyen Tan Dung.

The anti-graft campaign began with a move against the "biggest case" of economic corruption involving Vietnam Construction Joint Stock Commercial Bank (VNCB), where the bank's CEO Pham Cong Danh and his associates were charged with embezzlement and loss totalling over 401 million dollars.

On 24 January, Ho Chi Minh People's High Court upheld the lower court's 30-year prison sentence given to Pham Cong Danh and the prison sentences of between 19 and 22 years given to three other former executives of the bank.

Investigations of Pham Cong Danh eventually led to two major developments. In April, the party Central Control Commission recommended to the Politburo and the Central Committee to consider disciplinary measures against Dinh La Thang, member of the Politburo and party secretary of Ho Chi Minh City. Thang was accused of committing "very serious mistakes and violations" while leading Petro Vietnam between 2009 and 2011. He was subsequently removed from the Politburo and his position in Ho Chi Minh City and was reassigned to the unimportant position of deputy head of the Central Economic Commission.

Thang's demotion from the Politburo was unprecedented. Before Thang, Nguyen Co Thach and Tran Xuan Bach had been removed from the powerful Politburo for political reasons (Thach for his opposition to China, Bach for his demand for political pluralism); Thang was the first to be removed for being implicated in corruption.

After Thang, the Politburo took a decisive and risky action. On 23 May it issued regulations concerning the inspection of supervision over the declarations of assets of about a thousand top officials, including members of the Politburo, the secretariat, the Central Committee, and provincial standing committees, regardless of whether the person held a current position or had retired. This was tantamount to a declaration of war against the ill-gotten assets of most of those associated with former Prime Minister Dung.[2]

On 31 July, at a meeting of the CCCPF, committee chair Nguyen Phu Trong urged the committee to focus on pending cases with a view to bringing them to conclusion, "especially the cases of Ha Van Tham and Trinh Xuan Thanh".[3] Ha Van Tham, the founder of Ocean Bank, was charged with embezzlement and abuse of power. Trinh Xuan Thanh, former chairman of PetroVietnam Construction Joint Stock Company (PVC), had fled to Germany after being charged of "intentionally violating regulations on economic management causing serious consequences" and causing around $150 million in losses at PetroVietnam (PVN), but he was eventually kidnapped and brought back to Vietnam to stand trial.

Thanh's arrest was expected to lead to further charges and dismissals. His case led to the dismissal of Deputy Trade Minister Ho Thi Kim Thoa, former executive of Dien Quang Lamp Company. She was charged with several wrongdoings at the company and acting against procedures when promoting Thanh from a staff member to the deputy chief of the Party's Steering Committee at the Ministry of Industry and Trade. Her ex-boss Vu Huy Hoang was also dismissed retroactively for the same reason from his former position as Minister of Industry and Trade as well as former party secretary.[4]

The next day, banking tycoon Tram Be, former vice chairman of Sacombank, and Phan Huy Khang, former general director of the bank, were taken into custody for "deliberately violating state regulations on economic management, causing severe consequences". Tram Be was accused of colluding with Pham Cong Danh and accomplices in sending money to Sacombank to guarantee and pay off debts for six companies set up by Danh to borrow money from Sacombank, causing total losses of over US$79 million for VNCB.[5]

The height of the campaign against the banking sector and Petro Vietnam came in September. On 8 September, former deputy governor of the State Bank of Vietnam Dang Thanh Binh was placed under investigation for his alleged negligence in the financial loss at VNCB, which cost the state budget more than US$401 million. Earlier, the ex-VNCB chairman, Pham Cong Danh, was sentenced to thirty years in jail in January for his major role in the case.[6]

On 28 September, in a high-profile mass trial of fifty-one officials, Ha Van Tham was sentenced to life imprisonment and former Petro Vietnam chairman Nguyen Xuan Son was sentenced to death.

Trong has claimed that the anti-graft campaign has become "a movement, a trend of the entire society" that no one can resist. He compared the movement to a "blazing furnace" that would burn even the freshest of firewood.[7]

Before the year ended, a bombshell was dropped. On 8 December, Dinh La Thang, a powerful former Politburo member, former secretary of Ho Chi Minh City and close associate of former prime minister Nguyen Tan Dung, was arrested. Interestingly, on the same day, the government announced the publication of *Vung Buoc Tren Con Duong Doi Moi* (Moving steadily on the road of *Doi Moi*), General Secretary Trong's book on socialist-oriented *doi moi* and strengthening the party.

Trong has reached the point of no return. More heads are expected to roll. If he should stop, he would confirm the suspicion of sceptics that the current campaign was only designed to "hit corruption from the shoulders down", and the legitimacy that Trong hoped to restore to the party would be further lost. If he persists, he will meet stronger and more dangerous resistance. But if he succeeds, the power of the party over the state and society will be firmly established, and Trong may become the most powerful general secretary of the CPV since the establishment of the Muoi–Anh–Kiet ruling triumvirate following the 1991 Seventh National Party Congress.

Party Rebuilding and Strengthening

The campaign to rid the party of incompetent and undesirable elements started with two major decisions. First, on 4 May, as chairman of the CCCPF, General Secretary Trong formed eight inspection groups to investigate twenty provincial party committees where there were denunciation letters regarding corruption and serious economic wrongdoings. Second, to avoid mistakes in personnel matters "like the cases of Trinh Xuan Thanh and Vu Huy Hoang", on 16 May the Politburo established five inspection teams to examine the processes of appointment, promotion and rotation of officials of ten provincial executive committees and the party personnel committees of five central ministries.[8]

On 14 August the Politburo, for the first time, issued concrete criteria for holding leadership positions, as well as criteria to evaluate them. According to the Politburo, top officials must display "no corruption or opportunism … and be determined to push back against the degeneration in political ideology"; they must have "absolutely no ambition for power", "not let relatives and acquaintances benefit from their positions" and should lead "an honest, modest, sincere, transparent, simple and generous life".[9] It is difficult to believe that such an ideal model of officials could be achieved.

The campaign led, in addition to those of Vu Huy Hoang and Ho Thi Kim Thoa, to the dismissal of Vo Kim Cu, former party secretary and provincial chief of Ha Tinh province. It also imposed disciplinary measures on Nguyen Xuan Thien, member of the Central Committee and former party secretary of Binh Dinh City; Le Huu Loc, Thien's deputy and city mayor; Tran Cong Chanh, party secretary of Hau Giang province; Huynh Minh Chac, former member of the Central Committee and Hau Giang's party secretary; Tran Xuan Anh, party secretary; and Huynh Duc Tho, mayor of Danang City.

Suppressing Dissent

The year 2017 was not a good one for human rights activists in Vietnam. A report of Human Rights Watch on 18 June said Vietnamese bloggers and rights activists were being "beaten, threatened and intimidated with impunity". It highlighted thirty-six incidents between January 2015 and April 2017 in which unknown men in civilian clothes beat rights campaigners and bloggers.[10]

In the 2017 World Press Freedom Index, Reporters Without Borders described Vietnam (175th) and China (176th) as "the world's biggest prisons for journalists and bloggers". Vietnam was only five places ahead of North Korea in the index, the world's worst violator of press freedom.[11]

This prompted U.S State Department spokesperson Heather Nauert to complain, in a press briefing on 29 June, that the trend of increased arrests and convictions of peaceful protests was "deeply troubling".

The CPV has been battling political dissidents who have demanded democracy and questioned the legitimacy of the communist system since the Seventh National Party Congress in 1991, after the collapse of communist regimes in Eastern Europe and Russia. The first generation of dissidents was led by disillusioned legendary revolutionaries such as Tran Do, former head of the CPV Commission on Culture, Literature and the Arts; and Hoang Minh Chinh, former director of the Institute of Marxism-Leninism. Those leaders had political base in the party and were more dangerous, but now they have gone. Next came party intellectuals and experts, many of whom banded together in the Institute of Development Studies (IDS). After the dissolution of the IDS in 2009 they operated as lone voices and saw their impact weakened. With the advent of the Internet, blogging and Facebook, a new group of younger, tech-savvy bloggers and political activists emerged to advocate human rights and democracy. This was the group that the new CPV leadership had to deal with.

A new crackdown took place in January 2017. Between 11 and 21 January, police arrested three human rights activists on charges ranging from "conducting propaganda against the state" under article 88 of the penal code to "abusing the rights to freedom and democracy to infringe upon the interests of the State" under article 258.[12]

As of August, at least fifteen people have been arrested — "more than any year since a crackdown on youth activists in 2011".[13]

The 30 July crackdown involved the arrest of four human rights defenders, all members of the Brotherhood for Democracy and former prisoners of conscience: Nguyen Trung Ton, Nguyen Bac Truyen, Pham Van Troi and Truong Minh Duc. While all had previously been convicted and jailed for conducting propaganda against the state, this time they were charged under article 79 of the Penal Code for "carrying out activities aimed at overthrowing the people's administration", which could carry the death penalty.[14]

With harsh measures in the face of weakened international condemnation, the CPV in 2017 has succeeded in its efforts to contain political dissent. There were no big demonstrations, a lot of arrests, and silence from well-known activists, such as worker's rights activist Le Thi Cong Nhan and human rights lawyer Le Quoc Quan, since their releases.

Political and Administrative Reforms

Vietnam's economy grew just 5.1 per cent in the first three months of the year, prompting many economists to maintain that the 6.7 per cent growth target set by the government for 2017 was unrealistic.[15] This gloomy prediction was contradicted by the surge to 7.46 per cent growth by the third quarter of the year and the government's relative success in reducing the state budget deficit.[16] However, continued budget deficit and public debt estimated to be close to 65 per cent of GDP for the 2017–18 period remained serious problems for Vietnam's economy.[17] These problems were compounded by the fact that from July 2017 Vietnam has not been able to draw on official development aid at preferential terms, while those loans accounted for a whopping 98 per cent of its foreign loans.[18]

To deal with these problems, the government took measures to cut red tape, streamline the bureaucracy, clean up the banking system, reform the state-owned enterprises (SOEs), and carry out political reform.

Setting the Stage

As soon as he was elected, Prime Minister Nguyen Xuân Phuc, in his inaugural address on 7 April 2016, committed to transform the "command government into an enabling government (*chính phu kien tao*)" which was "honest (*liêm chinh*) and worked for the people and for businesses".[19] The concept of *chinh phu kien tao* was first introduced by former prime minister Nguyen Tan Dung in 2014, aimed at specifying the "relationship between the state and the market" in a socialist-oriented market economy, but the policy was never seriously implemented.

As prime minister, Phuc moved rapidly to carry out his commitment to create favourable conditions for business development. The first meeting between the prime minister and businesses, with the theme "Vietnamese Businesses – Driving Force in National Economic Development", was held in Ho Chi Minh City on 29 April 2017 with the participation of five hundred businessmen. Two weeks later, on 16 May, the government issued resolution number 35/NQ-CP to support and develop businesses to the year 2020. Ministries and other government agencies were instructed to modify regulations to help business to develop.

Despite problems in the economy that Phuc's supporters blamed on the previous administration, the new administration persisted in setting the 6.7 per cent growth rate as the goal of the economy for 2017. To achieve this goal, a series of highly publicized conferences and meetings — attended by hundreds of businesses and experts from both home and abroad — were organized to showcase the government's determination and to mobilize the support and participation of the private sector in developing the economy.

At the fifth plenum of the CCP, on 5–10 May, the Central Committee resolved to pursue three objectives: "completing the socialist-oriented market economy institution; continuing to re-organize, renovate and improve the efficiency of State-owned enterprises; and develop the private economy into an important driving force of the socialist-oriented market economy". Following the plenum, a meeting between the prime minister and private businesses was held on 17 May 2017 in Hanoi on the theme "Walking together with Private Business". This meeting was followed by a seminar on "Economic Management toward an Enabling Government" on 23 June, and the Vietnam Private Sector Forum (VPSF) on 31 July.

In addition to promotional efforts, on 28 July Prime Minister Phuc formed an Economic Advisory Board, consisting of prominent experts currently working in Vietnam as well as in foreign countries, to advise him on economic development strategy, plans, projects and policy for the medium and long term.

Cutting Red Tape

To provide a favourable environment for investment, one of the most important factors is the reduction of regulations and paperwork. In June, Prime Minister Phuc instructed various government ministries and offices to create the "most favourable conditions" for investment and eliminate "unnecessary investment requirements".[20]

Pursuant to the prime minister's instruction, the Ministry of Industry and Trade decided, in September, to reduce and simplify investment requirements within the jurisdiction of the ministry for the 2017–18 period. This decision cut 675 investment requirements, the largest cut in the history of the ministry. After the cut, only 541 investment requirements remained.[21]

Perhaps the most important measure to simplify paperwork was government resolution 112/NQ-CP tabled on 30 October 2017 abolishing the registration book (*so ho khau*) to manage and control people's place of residence. If implemented, this resolution would give the people greater freedom of movement, save them the burden of paperwork, and significantly reduce opportunities for corruption.

Streamlining the Bureaucracy

Streamlining the bureaucracy began with restructuring the SOEs and reducing their number and importance in the national economy through privatization. For the 2017–10 period, the government set the goal of privatizing 127 SOEs, 44 of which were to be completed in 2017. The result was disappointing. According to the Ministry of Finance, by the end of September, approvals of privatization programmes had been given to only 34 SOEs, of which a mere 11 had completed their privatization programmes.[22] The chairman of the SOE Reform and Renovation Committee, Central Institute for Economic Management, Pham Duc Trung, singled out "nepotism and self-interests" as the major causes blocking the privatization process.[23]

More sensitive was the need to streamline the political system. An article in *Quan Doi Nhan Dan* (People's Army) on 30 March highlighted the resolution of the Twelfth National Party Congress to "renovate and complete the reorganization of the party ... merging into one a number of positions and streamlining the whole political system". It complained that "our administrative system is too cumbersome and overlapping with 2.7 million salaried employees" whose number should be reduced.[24]

The goal of streamlining and reorganization was not only to avoid duplication and waste and save money but was also to make the government more efficient and strengthen the leadership of the party over the government.[25]

At the local level, Quang Ninh province began a pilot project to merge the positions of party secretary and chairman of the people's committees at the district and village levels, as well as the merging of party and government functions at various agencies and offices.[26]

At the cabinet level, the Interior Ministry was in the process of drafting a decree regulating the reorganization of offices and agencies under provincial and city people's committees, and making suggestions for merging a number of offices.[27]

Previously, on 4 March 2017, in an online conference on Party Organizing and Building which saw the participation of many Politburo and Central Committee members, "several participants" suggested experimenting with merging the position of party secretary and people's committee chairman in several provinces.[28]

More important was the proposal to merge the positions of general secretary and state president. Former deputy director of the National Assembly Office, Nguyen Si Dung, argued that the merging of those positions would end the overlap of functions between the party and the state.[29]

The sixth plenum meeting in October decided reorganization on the safe side. In a closing speech, General Secretary Nguyen Phu Trong stated that the party should "give priority to develop and implement issues that have received clear and strong approval by the Central Committee", and insisted on implementing the model whereby the party secretary also cumulated the position of chairman of the people's committee "at districts and villages where conditions permitted".[30]

Call for Concurrent Political Reform

Steps taken so far have been limited to administrative reform. Commenting on the need for political reform, Dr Pham Quy Tho of the Institute of Policy and Development, Ministry of Planning and Investment, insisted that the key issue was the "transition from collective to individual ownership". An enabling government could only succeed if its institutional reform in the economy was carried out in parallel with institutional reform in politics. To him, laws must be changed to guarantee private ownership, equality between economic sectors and components, and "civil, economic and political rights, such as freedom of association, freedom of information, the right to demonstrate and peaceful expression ... together with personal responsibilities must be regulated by law in a civilized manner".[31]

Even bolder was the demand of Nguyen Trung, former president of the Vietnam Academy of Social Sciences and member of the advisory boards of former prime ministers Vo Van Kiet and Pham Van Khai. In "A Heart-Felt Petition" on 27 September 2017, he argued that "the CPV as it is has failed in every reform attempt, even only partial reforms"; that the CPV must abandon Marxism-Leninism, for "totalitarianism will lead to the danger of 'being overthrown by the people, or social alienation leading to system collapse and disaster for the country;' that the party must battle alienation, corruption, and foreign influence; it must transform itself into a party of the people to carry out peaceful and democratic reform to save the country from current dangers".[32]

So far, Trung's appeal has fallen on deaf ears.

Coping with the New Geopolitical Environment

Vietnam continued to carry out its proclaimed policy of "multilateralization and diversification" of its foreign relations and practice a soft balancing act among the major powers, particularly between the United States and China, to protect its national sovereignty and territorial integrity as well as to promote economic development.

The success of this policy depends on two important factors: the presence and credible commitment of the United States to serve as a counterweight to the increasing assertiveness of China, and ASEAN unity to provide Vietnam with some sort of bargaining power in dealing with major powers.

Both these factors were put to serious test by the accession to power of President Rodrigo Duterte in the Philippines and President Donald Trump in the United States.

Duterte's Bombshell

In recent years the Philippines had been Vietnam's strongest ally and supporter among the ASEAN countries in opposing China's aggressiveness in the South China Sea. The Philippines had the advantage of being a treaty ally of the United States. And it had won the case it had brought to the Permanent Court of Arbitration (PCA) against China's "nine-dash line". These two factors indirectly benefited and strengthened Vietnam's bargaining position. The election of Duterte to the presidency in the Philippines changed this favourable situation dramatically.

To the disappointment of many, Duterte decided to ignore the Philippines' legal victory at The Hague and set aside the PCA award. Worse yet, he distanced the Philippines from the United State and leaned towards China in the hope of gaining economic benefits and possible concession in its territorial dispute with China.

Duterte's policy had a negative effect on ASEAN unity, another goal of Vietnam's foreign policy. When the 30th ASEAN Summit met in Manila in April 2017 under the chairmanship of the Philippines, Vietnam had to fight hard to have included in the final communiqué the terms "concerns expressed by some ministers" on land reclamation and militarization in the South China Sea, but failed to get the mention of the need for a "legally binding" code of conduct in the disputed waters to put a stop to "unilateral actions".

There was also no mention of the international tribunal ruling in The Hague which dismissed most of China's claims to the South China Sea. Even the phrase "serious concern", which has repeatedly appeared in ASEAN statements regarding maritime spats in previous years, was visibly absent.[33]

Having lost the support of Cambodia, Laos and the Philippines on the issue of the South China Sea, Vietnam turned increasingly to other Southeast Asian countries for support, particularly Indonesia for its size and Singapore for its diplomatic skill and influence within ASEAN and among the big powers.

The Trump Surprise

Relations between Vietnam and the United States had improved markedly under the Obama administration. The Obama administration's pivot to Asia and its military deployment in the Asia-Pacific emboldened ASEAN and Vietnam to stand up to Chinese aggressiveness in the South China Sea. Vietnam increasingly looked to the United States not only as an important factor in its economic development but particularly as a reliable partner and a restraining force against China's aggressive activities in the South China Sea.

The election of Donald Trump to the presidency of the United States put a temporary hold on such progress and introduced uncertainty in the future of U.S.–Vietnam relations. In the beginning, the Trump administration seemed to take a tougher stand on the South China Sea. Whilst campaigning for the presidency, Trump criticized China over island building, currency manipulation, and trade. His secretary-of-state designate Rex Tillerson, during his confirmation hearing, declared that China's building of islands and putting military assets on those islands was "akin to Russia's taking of Crimea". He further added: "We're going to have to send China a clear signal that, first, the island-building stops and, second, your access to those islands also is not going to be allowed."[34]

On the military side, U.S. freedom of navigation operations (FONOP's) were conducted in a more aggressive manner, inside twelve miles of the islands, and in the form of "freedom of navigation operations", not as "innocent passages".[35]

However, subsequent statements and actions of the administration gave Vietnam concerns about U.S. intentions. First, it was difficult to make sense of the discrepancy between the statements of Trump's policy advisers and those of the president himself. While his military advisers tried to assure its Asian allies and partners of U.S. commitment, the president decided to pull out of the Trans-Pacific Partnership (TPP) and complained about unfair trade deals. While Tillerson visited China and talked about the need to build "mutual respect" and strive for "win-win" cooperation, the president was tweeting criticism of China. But when Tillerson criticized China for "undermining the international rule-based system" and its "provocative actions in the South China Sea", this hard position was undermined by Trump's actions during his own visit to China where he lavished praise on Chinese President Xi and cited the "special chemistry" between him and Xi.

Then there was concern that Trump's seeming lack of attention to or deep understanding of Asia, and his overemphasis on North Korea and his attempt to cajole China into helping to resolve the North Korean nuclear issue, may lead him to neglect other issues in Asia. This was evidenced by the fact that as of November 2017, eleven months into his presidency, Trump has not appointed an assistant secretary for East Asian and Pacific Affairs, and the position of U.S. ambassador to South Korea remained unfulfilled. This neglect emboldened China and resulted in a tepid U.S. reaction when China forced Vietnam to stop oil drilling at the Vanguard bank, which falls clearly within Vietnam's exclusive economic zone and continental shelf and barely touches China's nine-dash line.

American failure to react to a clear violation by China of international law, which America had vocally supported, led Bill Hayton to complain about "The week Donald Trump lost the South China Sea".[36] Before Trump's trip to China, a FONOP conducted by USS *Chafee* on 3 October only came "close to but not within" the disputed Paracel Islands, an apparent de-escalation of FONOPs.[37] This apparent deference to China prompted Panos Mourdoukoutas to suggest "To Stop Kim Jong-Un, China Needs a Big Price: The South China Sea".[38]

In addition to Trump's well-known unpredictability, his administration's policy towards China introduced uncertainty in the future of U.S.–Vietnam relations and renewed Vietnam's fear of possible collusion between the United States and China at its expense.[39]

Adjusting to New Realities

The changing regional and international environment created by the policies of Duterte and Trump presented a new strategic challenge to Vietnam's foreign policy. While the external environment has changed, China remains a constant threat to Vietnam's national sovereignty and territorial integrity, particularly in the South China Sea. Given the power asymmetry between China and Vietnam, the only way to deal with this threat is for Vietnam to improve its own defence capability and seek a counterweight to China, particularly from the United States and, failing that, from other powers.

Vietnam and the United States

The electoral victory of Donald Trump in November 2016 was a shock to many experts and leaders of the world, including those in Vietnam. Concerns over the reliability and credibility of the new U.S. administration did not negate the indispensability of U.S. presence and commitment to peace, security, and the rule of law in the South China Sea. Vietnam has to do its best to maintain good relations with the United States, elicit its support, and encourage it to engage in the Asia-Pacific region. In this area, Vietnam has achieved some small successes.

After intensive lobbying efforts, Vietnam's prime minister Nguyen Xuan Phuc was among the first of world leaders to make a congratulatory phone call to the newly elected U.S. president, and the first ASEAN leader to be invited to meet with Trump in the United States, where he announced the signing of commercial agreements worth US$12 billion with U.S. companies.[40] In return, Trump hailed Vietnam for helping to create jobs for Americans and Phuc for doing a "fantastic" job as prime minister of Vietnam.

The joint U.S.–Vietnam statement declared,

> As a Pacific power with widespread interests and commitments throughout the Asia Pacific, the United States shares many important interests with Vietnam. The two leaders emphasized that many opportunities lie ahead for United States–Vietnam relations, including increasingly enhanced political, diplomatic, economic and trade ties, and ever-growing cooperation in the areas of science and technology, national defense and security, education, people-to-people exchange, humanitarian and war legacy issues, as well as regional and international issues of mutual concern.

Phuc also received a pledge from Trump of "support for … Vietnam in successfully hosting APEC 2017" and "to visit Vietnam and [to attend] the APEC Leaders' meeting in November", which ultimately he did.

In the field of military cooperation, the joint statement announced

> The two leaders pledged to strengthen bilateral defense ties under the 2011 Memorandum of Understanding (MOU) on Advancing Bilateral Defense Cooperation and the 2015 Joint Vision Statement on Defense Relations. Prime Minister Nguyen Xuan Phuc expressed interest in acquiring more defense equipment from the United States, including additional Coast Guard cutters.

When Vietnam's Defence Minister Ngo Xuan Lich visited the United States in August following a spat with China two months earlier and met with his counterpart, General Mattis, he was promised a strong defence relationship, shared interest in freedom of navigation in the South China Sea and, more importantly, a visit of an aircraft carrier to Vietnam the following year — the first such visit since the end of the Vietnam War in 1975.[41]

Vietnam and Japan

To hedge against the lack of strong U.S. commitment, Vietnam has tried to strengthen relations with other regional powers which share its concerns about Chinese behaviour in the South China Sea, such as India and particularly Japan, whose prime minister was among the first leaders in East Asia to visit Trump and whose country is the most important ally of the United States in Asia.

In 2017, Vietnam–Japan relations picked up speed and there seemed to be some coordination between the two countries to engage the United States and save the TPP.

Prime Minister Shinzo Abe was the first world leader to meet and play golf with Donald Trump after his election as president of the United States. His visit was followed three months later by Vietnam's Prime Minister Nguyen Xuan Phuc as the first ASEAN leader to be invited to meet with Trump in the United States.

One month before Abe's visit to the United States, he visited Vietnam, where he declared support for Vietnam's efforts to "enhance its maritime law enforcement capability" and promised concessionary loans for Vietnam to buy six new patrol boats. He also stressed the importance of the TPP. Almost immediately after Phuc met with Trump in the United States he went to Japan to talk with Abe, where he declared Vietnam always gave "top priority" to cooperative relations with Japan and will do its best to "elevate the ties to new height".[42] They both agreed to "bolster their security ties through Japanese-funded projects including the upgrading of Vietnamese coastal patrol capabilities, defense equipment and technology transfer" amid concerns about China's increasingly assertive activity in regional seas. They declared that they share a "deep concern over the complex developments" involving China in the South China Sea. They urged China — without referring to it by name — to avoid taking action to change the status quo and escalate regional tensions.[43]

In a joint statement, Japan and Vietnam reaffirmed the importance of the TPP trade pact and agreed to pursue it despite the withdrawal of the United States. The two leaders agreed to cooperate in discussions among the eleven remaining TPP members to bring the agreement into force. Their labour eventually resulted in the announcement at the APEC summit of an agreement on "core elements" of a revised multilateral trade agreement among the eleven original countries minus the United States, known as TTP-11, or Comprehensive and Progressive Agreement for Trans-Pacific Partnership (CPTPP).

Vietnam and India

India is the only major power whose relations with Vietnam are not tainted by past conflicts. For years, India has been a loyal supporter of Vietnam, but her military relations with Vietnam had been limited by India's policy of non-alignment. The rise of China and her aggressive behaviour in the South China Sea and around India's periphery has brought India and Vietnam closer.

Vietnam's concern over the staying power of the United States and its possible grand bargain with China has motivated it to seek closer relations with India. To Vietnam, the size of India's territory and population and its conflict and rivalry with China makes it an attractive regional counterweight to China. This perspective is strengthened by the fact that India has chosen Japan, another regional power, as its "maritime security partner", and shared its concern with Japan over the importance of the South China Sea shipping lane.[44]

Under Prime Minister Narendra Modi, India's policy of "Look East" turned into "Act East", and its "strategic partnership" with Vietnam was elevated to a "comprehensive strategic partnership" during Modi's visit to Hanoi in September 2016. Since then, India has been expanding its military training, technology sharing, joint exercises, and exchanges of experts with Vietnam. The fact that both India and Vietnam bought Kilo-class submarines and Sukhoi fighters from Russia made India an ideal training centre for Vietnamese sailors and pilots.

In January 2017 it was reported that there was "active discussion" for the possible sale of an Akash surface-to-air missile system to Vietnam. Previously, India has offered Brahmos supersonic cruise missiles and Varunastra anti-submarine torpedoes to Vietnam.[45]

In June, Vietnam granted Indian oil firm ONGC a two-year extension to explore oil bloc 128, part of which was in China's "nine-dash line". A senior official of ONGC was reported as saying that "interest in the bloc was strategic rather than commercial", given that oil development there was seen as "high-risk with only moderate potential". He added, "Vietnam also wants us to be there because of China intervention in the South China Sea."[46]

Towards the end of the year, in October, the ninth political consultation and sixth strategic dialogue at the deputy ministerial level between Vietnam and India was held in Hanoi. Both sides agreed to foster collaboration and committed to "work closely with each other and other countries to ensure a strategic security environment". India affirmed its support for Vietnam in improving defence capability, training in English for soldiers, transferring defence technologies and providing defence credit.

Vietnam and ASEAN

In August, CPV General Secretary Trong visited Indonesia to mend fences after two recent maritime stand-offs in the waters around the Natuna Islands in the South China Sea. Trong and the Indonesian president agreed "to speed up negotiations on the limits of the EEZs between the two countries". In a keynote speech in

Jakarta, Trong emphasized the need for "consultation and consensus" for "unity and solidarity within ASEAN" and the importance of "ASEAN centrality".[47]

Vietnam also hosted a three-day visit of Malaysian Foreign Minister Datuk Seri Anifah Aman. The two countries reaffirmed their commitment to the 2015 Malaysia–Vietnam Strategic Partnership. In the area of defence and security cooperation, the two sides stressed the importance of cooperation between navies, including sharing information on strategic, military and security issues.

Vietnam and Singapore

Among ASEAN countries, Singapore occupies a special place in Vietnam's foreign policy. Vietnamese leaders admire Singapore's development model, appreciate its support for Vietnam's cause, and respect its diplomatic skill and influence among the major powers, as well as its role in promoting ASEAN unity and centrality. After two years under the successive chairmanships of two countries under Chinese influence — Laos and the Philippines — the forthcoming ASEAN chairmanship by Singapore in 2018 provides the hope and opportunity to restore a certain degree of ASEAN centrality and influence.

Vietnam–Singapore relations are perhaps the best and most trusting bilateral relations between a communist and non-communist country in Southeast Asia. In 2017, two events highlighted this trusting and cosy relationship: the five-day visit of the Singapore Navy's RSS *Endurance* to Cam Ranh Bay from 17 February, followed by the visit of Singapore's Prime Minister Lee Hsien Loong to Hanoi from 21 to 24 March 2017. The RSS *Endurance* was also the first international naval ship to visit Cam Ranh Bay, on 17 March 2016, after Vietnam's biggest international seaport went into operation on 8 March that year.

During the visit of PM Lee the two sides pledged to foster cooperation in many fields, including economics, trade, investment, politics, people-to-people exchange, personnel training, and defence and security. Prime Minister Lee promised that Singapore would continue to assist Vietnam in personnel training; support Vietnamese firms in their bid to join the global market and supply chains, while considering the setting up of high technology industrial parks; help Vietnam develop smart cities, facilitate start-up firms, especially in science-technology, capital access and management capacity, and encourage linkages with some major cities of Vietnam, including Ho Chi Minh City and Da Nang.

Vietnam and China

Despite the talks of "managing and control disputes, expanding military and security cooperation, and coordinating on global issues" during General Secretary Nguyen

Phu Trong's visit to China in January 2017, the South China Sea remained a bone of contention between Vietnam and China, but changes in the international environment have weakened Vietnam's leverage against Chinese pressure.[48]

Vietnam continued its strategy of soft balancing between the major powers to restrain China's further encroachment. In addition, its leaders had to navigate between popular Vietnamese antipathy towards China and the realities of big power geopolitics. They had to accommodate China when needed, but could not afford to be perceived as pro-China.

Duterte's pivot to China and Trump's deference to China gave China greater freedom to impose its will in the South China Sea without effective resistance. China continued to impose unilateral fishing bans. It ignored the PCA award and was bolder in enforcing its claims within the nine-dash line. China succeeded in preventing the Philippines from building shelters for its fishermen on a sandbar at Sandy Cay Bank and in forcing Vietnam to stop drilling for oil at block 136/3 near the Vanguard Bank.

In June, General Fan Changlong, vice chairman of China's Central Military Commission, abruptly cut short his visit to Vietnam, reportedly to protest news of the drilling.[49] He might also have angered Vietnamese leaders by stating to their faces in closed-door meetings that the South China Sea islands were Chinese territory since ancient times.[50] Again, in August, China cancelled a meeting between its foreign minister and the Vietnamese foreign minister on the sidelines of the ASEAN Foreign Ministers Meeting in Manila because of Vietnam's insistence on the inclusion in the joint communiqué of the concern of some countries over "land reclamation on disputed islands". Yet, at the same time, China considered it to be within its right to reinforce launch sites for surface-to-air missiles on three of its man-made atolls in the South China Sea: Fiery Cross, Mischief Reef, and Subi Reef.[51]

Under the circumstances, Vietnam had to resort to a strategy of "cooperating and struggling".[52] In struggling, Vietnam sought but failed to make the "agreed framework" of the code of conduct between ASEAN and China in the South China Sea legally binding to "put a stop to unilateral action".[53] It continued to raise verbal protests against Chinese activities to consolidate its control over disputed territory, such as its decision to start live-fire military drills near the Paracel Islands from 29 August until 4 September. In cooperating, visits to China were made by all three top Vietnamese leaders — party general secretary, state president, prime minister — in 2017; and officials from both countries made regular visits to each other. Trade continued to expand. China was the largest exporter of goods to Vietnam compared to any other country in Southeast Asia. Vietnam's exports to China jumped nearly 43 per cent to $13 billion in the first half of 2017. Chinese tourist arrivals soared 60 per cent to nearly 1.9 million in the same period, to account for approximately one third of foreign visitors.[54]

After the spat in June which was resolved by the concession by Vietnam, bilateral relations began to improve. Liu Yunshan, member of the Chinese Politburo Standing Committee, made the first fence-mending visit to Vietnam in September. Liu counselled that the two parties had a "shared destiny", that there was great potential for bilateral economic cooperation, and that the stable development of bilateral ties would help to "solidify the ruling position of the two parties". In return, Vietnam's Prime Minister Nguyen Xuan Phuc suggested that the two countries should strive to maintain peace and stability in the South China Sea and avoid all activities that could increase tension.[55] Between Liu's visit in September and President Xi's state visit to Vietnam in November, a meeting to discuss border defence issues was held on 23–24 September at the border of the two countries between the vice chairman of China's Central Military Commission Fan Changlong and Vietnam's defence minister Ngo Xuan Lich. On 31 October, Hoang Binh Quan, head of the CPV Central Commission for External Affairs and special envoy to General Secretary Nguyen Phu Trong made a visit to China to congratulate Xi on his re-election as general secretary of the CCP and expressed the wish that both sides would strive to further develop traditional friendship and a comprehensive strategic cooperative partnership.[56] In November, before Xi went to Vietnam to attend the APEC summit, Chinese assistant foreign minister Chen Xiaodong announced that national leaders of the two countries have had many "deep, frank" discussions on maritime issues and that they had reached an "important consensus". Vietnam's deputy prime minister Pham Binh Minh put out a statement saying that he had proposed during a meeting with Chinese foreign minister Wang Yi that the two countries "resolve disputes based on common sense and international law".[57] The year concluded with the first state visit to Vietnam on 12 November by Xi Jinping since his re-election as general secretary of the CCP. On the sidelines of the APEC summit in Danang, the Chinese leader received agreement from Prime Minister Phuc to "align their development initiatives" — the China-proposed Belt and Road Initiative and Vietnam's "Two Corridors and One Economic Circle" plan. Phuc stressed the upgrading of Vietnam–China relations as the "priority of Vietnam's foreign policy", and hoped to enhance cooperation with China in many fields.[58]

Given these economic ties, if the United States gradually retreats from its leadership role in the Asia-Pacific, the prospects of Vietnam escaping from the Chinese embrace (*thoat trung*) does not look very bright.

Notes

1. For more details, see Nguyen Manh Hung, "Continuity and Change under Vietnam's New Leadership", *ISEAS Perspective* 2016, no. 50 (13 September 2016).
2. Bui Quang Vom, "Tran Huyet Chien Cuoi Cung" [The all or nothing final battle] <https://boxitvn.blogspot.com/2017/06/tran-huyet-chien-cuoi-cung.html#more>.
3. *Voice of Vietnam*, 31 July 2017 <http://www.bbc.com/vietnamese/vietnam-40776964>.
4. *Tuoi Tre News*, 11 February 2017 <https://tuoitrenews.vn/society/39505/vietnam-deputy-minister-in-spotlight-as-huge-personal-assets-discovered>.
5. *Vietnamnet*, 2 August 2017 <http://english.vietnamnet.vn/fms/business/183078/former-executives-of-sacombank-kept-in-custody-for-investigation.html>.
6. *Tuoi Tre News*, 8 September 2017 <https://tuoitrenews.vn/news/society/20170908/former-state-bank-of-vietnam-deputy-governor-placed-under-investigation/41497.html>.
7. *Vietnamnet*, 1 August 2017 <http://vietnamnet.vn/vn/thoi-su/chong-tham-nhung/lo-nong-len-roi-thi-cui-tuoi-vao-cung-phai-chay-387640.html>.
8. *Bao Moi*, 15 May 2017 <https://baomoi.com/bo-chinh-tri-lap-5-doan-kiem-tra-ve-cong-tac-can-bo/c/22280938.epi>.
9. *VNExpress*, 15 August 2017 <https://e.vnexpress.net/news/news/vietnam-tells-officials-to-avoid-graft-and-live-modestly-3627759.html>.
10. *Human Rights Watch*, "No Country for Human Rights Activists, Assaults on Bloggers and Democracy Campaigners in Vietnam" <http://www.hrw.org/report/2017/06/18/no-country-human-rights-activists/assaults-bloggers-and-democracy-campaigners>.
11. *2017 World Press Freedom Index* <https://rsf.org/en/2017-world-press-freedom-index-tipping-point>.
12. Human Rights Watch, 27 January 2017 <https://www.hrw.org/news/2017/01/27/vietnam-new-wave-arrests-critics>.
13. <https://www.reuters.com/article/us-vietnam-arrests/trump-factor-weighs-as-vietnam-intensifies-crackdown-on-dissidents-idUSKBN1AI0LF>.
14. *Time*, 31 July 2017 <http://time.com/4880162/vietnam-dissidents-arrested-crackdown/>.
15. Forbes, 5 April 2017 <https://www.forbes.com/sites/ralphjennings/2017/04/05/asias-economic-icon-vietnam-is-suddenly-facing-slower-growth-in-2017/#c013b739395b>.
16. Forbes, 28 September 2017 <https://www.bloomberg.com/news/articles/2017-09-29/vietnam-s-economy-expands-at-faster-pace-in-third-quarter; and *Vietstock*, 30 September 2017 <http://en.vietstock.vn/2017/09/adb-applauds-vietnam-on-reducing-deficit-37-295375.htm>.
17. *Radio Free Asia*, 29 September 2017 <http://www.rfa.org/vietnamese/in_depth/vietnam-public-debt-how-the-government-resolve-ha-09292017154330.html>.
18. *Vietnamnet*, 2 June 2017 <http://english.vietnamnet.vn/fms/business/179643/finance-ministry--public-debt-to-reach-record-high-in-2017.html>.
19. BBC, "Giai ma 'chinh phu kien tao' cua Thu tuong Phuc", 2 May 2017 <http://www.bbc.com/vietnamese/forum-40058517; See also "Thu tuong cua hanh dong" http://thutuong.chinhphu.vn/Home/Thu-tuong-cua-hanh-dong/20167/25151.vgp>.

20. *Viet Times*, 15 July 2017 <http://viettimes.vn/chinh-phu-yeu-cau-cat-giam-dieu-kien-kinh-doanh-khong-can-thiet-129957.html>.
21. *Vietnam Finance*, 21 September 2017 <http://vietnamfinance.vn/diem-nhan-kien-tao-bo-cong-thuong-cat-thang-675-dieu-kien-kinh-doanh-20170921181922881.htm>.
22. Quan Doi Nhan Dan, 27 September 2017 <https://baomoi.com/34-doanh-nghiep-co-phan-hoa-trong-9-thang-dau-nam-2017/c/23390337.epi>.
23. Tuoi Tre, 28 June 2017 <https://tuoitre.vn/doanh-nghiep-nha-nuoc-de-truc-loi-nen-kho-doi-moi-1339677.htm>.
24. *Quan Doi Nhan Dan* (People's Army), 30 March 2017 <http://www.qdnd.vn/thuc-hien-hieu-qua-nghi-quyet-trung-uong-iv-khoa-xii-cua-dang/nhat-the-hoa-de-tinh-gian-bo-may-503453>. See also Saigon Giai Phong, 15 September 2017 <http://www.sggp.org.vn/thi-diem-nhat-the-hoa-va-viec-doi-moi-he-thong-chinh-tri-467971.html>.
25. *Vietnamnet*, 27 March 2017 <http://vietnamnet.vn/vn/thoi-su/chinh-tri/doan-giam-sat-qh-me-mo-hinh-nhat-the-hoa-cua-quang-ninh-363624.html#inner-article>.
26. Ibid.
27. *Vietnamnet*, 31 March 2017 <http://vietnamnet.vn/vn/thoi-su/chinh-tri/bo-noi-vu-de-xuat-hop-nhat-mot-so-so-364428.html#inner-article>.
28. *Nguoi Lao Dong*, 4 March 2017 <https://news.zing.vn/de-xuat-nhat-the-hoa-bi-thu-kiem-chu-tich-tinh-post725690.html>.
29. Nguyen Si Dung, "Ngay Quoc Khanh, nghi gi ve bieu tuong doan ket, vai tro chu tich nuoc" [On National Day, thinking about the symbol of national unity, the role of the state president] <http://trandaiquang.org/ngay-quoc-khanh-nghi-ve-bieu-tuong-doan-ket-vai-tro-chu-tich-nuoc.html>.
30. *Nguoi Lao Dong*, 11 October 2017 <http://nld.com.vn/thoi-su/tong-bi-thu-bi-thu-huyen-xa-co-the-kiem-chu-tich-huyen-xa-20171011112572325.htm>.
31. Pham Quy Ngo, "Giai ma 'Chinh phu kien tao' cua Thu tuong Phuc' " [Decipher Prime Minister Phuc's "enabling government"], BBC, 27 May 2017 <http://www.bbc.com/vietnamese/forum-40058517>.
32. <http://www.viet-studies.net/NguyenTrung/NguyenTrung_KienNghiTamQuyet.html>.
33. Richard Heydarian, "China a 'Clear Winner' at Asean Summit", *South China Morning Post*, 12 August 2017 <http://www.scmp.com/news/china/diplomacy-defence/article/2106441/china-clear-winner-asean-summit>.
34. Reuters, 11 January 2017 <https://www.reuters.com/article/us-congress-tillerson-china/tillerson-says-china-should-be-barred-from-south-china-sea-islands-idUSKBN14V2KZ>.
35. In May 2017 the USS *Dewey* conducted a freedom of navigation operation within twelve miles of Mischief Reef in the Spratly Islands. In July the USS *Stethem* operated within twelve miles of Triton island in the Paracel Islands. Again, in August, the USS *McCain* came within twelve miles of Mischief Reef.

36. Bill Hayton, "The Week Donald Trump Lost the South China Sea, *Foreign Policy*, 31 July 2017.
37. *Business Insider*, 11 October 2017 <http://www.businessinsider.com/uss-chafee-south-china-sea-fonop-2017-10>.
38. Forbes, 7 September 2017 <https://www.forbes.com/sites/panosmourdoukoutas/2017/09/07/to-stop-kim-jong-un-china-needs-a-big-prize-the-south-china-sea/#25784b4c6df1>.
39. For detailed discussion of Vietnamese thinking on this issue, see Nguyen Manh Hung, *The Politics of the United States–China–Vietnam Triangle in the 21st Century*, Trends in Southeast Asia 2015, no. 21 (Singapore: ISEAS – Yusof Ishak Institute, 2015), pp. 24–25.
40. Reuters, 4 June 2017 <http://www.reuters.com/article/us-usa-vietnam-analysis/vietnams-white-house-lobbying-coup-secures-strategic-gains-idUSKBN18V0AC>.
41. Reuters, 8 August 2017 <https://www.reuters.com/article/us-usa-vietnam-military/vietnam-wins-u-s-defense-pledges-as-tension-with-china-grows-idUSKBN1AP010>.
42. *Vietnam News*, 6 June 2017 <http://vietnamnews.vn/politics-laws/377874/pm-viet-nam-gives-top-priority-to-relations-with-japan.html#C2fEwJsLvyQ6l2Zx.99>.
43. *Seattle Times*, 6 June 2017 <https://www.seattletimes.com/nation-world/japan-vietnam-to-bolster-maritime-security-cooperation/>.
44. For more detailed analysis, see Madhuchanda Ghosh, "India's Strategic Convergence with Japan in the Changing Indo-Pacific Geopolitical Landscape", *Asia-Pacific Bulletin*, no. 392 (16 August 2017).
45. *Times of India*, 9 January 2017.
46. Reuters, 6 June 2017 <https://www.usnews.com/news/world/articles/2017-07-06/vietnam-renews-india-oil-deal-in-tense-south-china-sea>.
47. *Strait Times*, 24 August 2017 <http://www.straitstimes.com/asia/se-asia/indonesia-vietnam-settle-recurring-maritime-standoffs-in-south-china-sea>.
48. Bloomberg, 12 January 2017 <https://www.bloomberg.com/news/articles/2017-01-12/vietnam-recalibrates-after-trump-duterte-combo-upsets-strategy>.
49. *South China Morning Post*, 22 June 2017 <http://www.scmp.com/news/china/diplomacy-defence/article/2099560/pla-general-skipped-south-china-sea-meeting-during>; Prashanth Parameswaran, "Nixed China-Vietnam Meeting Highlights Illusion of South China Sea Calm", *The Diplomat*, 22 June 2017.
50. *China Military Online*, 19 June 2017 <http://www.scmp.com/news/china/diplomacy-defence/article/2099560/pla-general-skipped-south-china-sea-meeting-during>; *New York Times*, 21 June 2017.
51. *Washington Post*, 23 February 2017.
52. Carl Thayer, "Vietnam's Strategy of 'Cooperating and Struggling' with China over Maritime Disputes in the South China Sea", *Journal of Asian Security and International Affairs* 3, no. 2 (2016) 200–20.

53. Reuters, 29 April 2017 <https://www.cnbc.com/2017/04/29/asean-firms-up-s-china-sea-stance-as-beijing-lobbies-over-statement.html>.
54. Reuters, 1 September 2017 <https://www.reuters.com/article/us-vietnam-china/despite-strains-vietnam-and-china-forge-closer-economic-ties-idUSKCN1BC3S2>.
55. *U.S. News and World Report*, 19 September 2017 <https://www.reuters.com/article/us-vietnam-china/despite-strains-vietnam-and-china-forge-closer-economic-ties-idUSKCN1BC3S2>.
56. *Vietnam News*, 31 October 2017 <http://vietnamnews.vn/politics-laws/416590/chinese-party-chief-receives-vietnamese-party-leaders-special-envoy.html#Qs8FFCFRAr69HYzx.99>.
57. Reuters, 3 November 2017 <https://www.cnbc.com/2017/11/03/south-china-sea-china-says-it-resolved-dispute-with-vietnam.html>.
58. *China Daily*, 12 November 2017 <http://www.chinadaily.com.cn/world/2017-11/12/content_34427936.htm>.

FORCE MODERNIZATION: Vietnam

Carlyle A. Thayer

During the period 2012–16, Vietnam was the tenth-largest importer of arms globally.[1] This is an impressive figure given that Vietnam ranked thirty-seventh in the world in terms of its gross domestic product (GDP) in purchasing power parity terms[2] and forty-eighth in the world in nominal terms.[3] This chapter discusses why Vietnam made such large arms purchases, what specific weapon systems and platforms it acquired and for what purpose.

States procure arms for a variety of reasons: to defend themselves from perceived threats, to develop capabilities to suit specific needs, to acquire modern military technology, to gain prestige and to modernize their existing weapons and platforms.[4] Force modernization (or defence modernization) may be conceptualized as two distinct yet interrelated processes. The first consists of reconditioning and upgrading existing stocks of weapons and platforms with new technology. The second process involves the acquisition of more modern sets of platforms and weapon systems to meet new roles and missions.

This chapter focuses on force modernization in Vietnam from the mid-1990s to the present and is divided into seven parts. Part 1 provides a brief historical overview of the Vietnam People's Army until the early 1990s when the conflict in Cambodia ended. Part 2 discusses naval modernization as a response to new security challenges in the South China Sea in the post–Cambodian conflict period. Parts 3 and 4 examine the modernization of the air defence air force and land force, respectively. Part 5 focuses on Vietnam's development of a national defence industry to support force modernization. Part 6 presents an overview of Vietnam's defence budget. Part 7 evaluates Vietnam's force modernization programme.

CARLYLE A. THAYER is Emeritus Professor at the School of Humanities and Social Sciences, The University of New South Wales, Canberra at the Australian Defence Force Academy.

Part 1: Historical Overview

The Vietnam People's Army (VPA) was founded on 22 December 1944 as a small guerrilla force. Within ten years it had grown into a regular army of 80,000 grouped into seven infantry divisions equipped with heavy artillery and 320,000 grouped into independent regiments and battalions at the regional and local level, largely armed by China.[5] These combined forces defeated the French in the First Indochina War, 1946–54.

After partition in mid-1954, the VPA was reorganized along conventional lines for the defence of North Vietnam. During this period, and especially during the Vietnam War (1965–75), the VPA expanded to include air, air-defence and coastal naval forces. During this period the Soviet Union overtook China as Vietnam's main provider of "big ticket" weapons and platforms. During the 1970s, the VPA was organized into multi-division corps units equipped with battle tanks and long-range artillery. This force spearheaded a major offensive in 1975 that led to the collapse of the Republic of Vietnam (South Vietnam) and the formal reunification of the country as the Socialist Republic of Vietnam.

In late 1978, the VPA invaded Cambodia in response to increased cross-border attacks by the Khmer Rouge. In early 1979, China, an ally of the Khmer Rouge, responded by launching a punitive attack on northern Vietnam. For the next decade, a quarter of a million VPA forces remained in defensive positions along the northern frontier to repel a second Chinese attack, while VPA forces in Cambodia conducted a protracted counter-insurgency campaign. The VPA expanded in numbers to 1.26 million to become the fifth-largest army in the world at that time after the Soviet Union, China, the United States and India.[6]

In 1987, Vietnam's leaders assessed that their counter-insurgency efforts in Cambodia had made sufficient progress that they could accelerate the withdrawal of military forces and commence a major demobilization of their large standing army. In September 1989, Vietnam withdrew all formed military units from Cambodia. Between mid-1987 and late 1990, 600,000 troops, or nearly half of the standing army, was demobilized.[7]

Vietnam's withdrawal from Cambodia set the stage for a comprehensive political settlement of the Cambodian conflict in October 1991 and the normalization of Vietnam's relations with China the following month. These two events led to an unprecedented period of peace. Vietnam, however, now faced new security challenges that necessitated the modernization of the VPA to carry out new roles and missions. There were two main drivers behind this process: changes in the international legal regime and the emergence of maritime disputes between Vietnam and an assertive China.

In July 1994, Vietnam ratified the United Nations Convention on the Law of the Sea (UNCLOS). UNCLOS came into force in November of that year. Under the Law of the Sea, Vietnam, as a coastal state, was entitled to a twelve nautical mile territorial sea and a two hundred nautical mile exclusive economic zone (EEZ) drawn from its coastline. In order to exercise sovereignty over its territorial sea and sovereign jurisdiction over the resources in its EEZ, Vietnam had to develop the requisite capabilities not only to monitor this large maritime area but also to enforce its sovereignty against unauthorized intrusions.

In 1992, China's National People's Congress passed a Law on Territorial Sea and Contiguous Zone that laid claim to sovereignty over the Paracel and Spratly islands. This brought China into conflict with Vietnam, which also claimed sovereignty over the two archipelagos.[8] In 1994 and 1996, Vietnam and China became embroiled in a series of maritime confrontations when the Crestone Energy Corporation, a U.S. company, began exploring for oil under a contract awarded by China in the Vanguard Bank claimed by Vietnam.

In sum, changes in the international legal regime and contingencies in the South China Sea were the main drivers behind Vietnam's initial efforts at force modernization. The following sections explore force modernization for each branch of the Vietnam People's Army and national defence industry during two phases: the initial phase from the mid-1990s to 2005 and a second phase from 2006 to 2015, when priority was given to the modernization of the Navy (*Quân chủng Hải quân*), Air Defence Air Force (*Phòng không Không quân*), technical surveillance (*Trinh sát kỹ thuật*), electronic warfare (*Tác chiến điện tử*), and information systems (*Thông tin liên lạc*).[9] In 2015, Vietnam's leaders concluded that sufficient progress had been made to shift priority to the modernization of the army. These developments are discussed in turn below.

Part 2: Naval Modernization

Vietnam began the first phase of force modernization during the mid to late 1990s when it began upgrading its legacy naval and air fleets and procuring naval and air platforms and weapon systems.[10]

During the first phase of force modernization, Vietnam signed a series of agreements on arms sales and servicing with the Russian Federation. Russia soon became Vietnam's major source of "big ticket" military weapons and equipment. In 1994, a memorandum of understanding on arms sales was signed. Between 1996 and 1999, Vietnam took delivery of four modified *Tarantul* guided missile fast patrol craft from Russia.[11] These ships were armed with twin launchers for anti-ship missiles, manually operated surface-to-air missiles (SAMs), and close-in weapon systems (CIWS). In 1998, Vietnam and Russia signed a framework agreement for continuing arms sales and support.

Vietnam also turned to the Ukraine, Belarus, India and other countries for assistance in modernizing its navy. For example, in 1997 Vietnam acquired two *Yugo*-class midget submarines from North Korea that it subsequently refitted. This acquisition represented the first step in implementing Vietnam's long-standing interest in developing an undersea-warfare capability.[12]

A major turning point in defence cooperation between Vietnam and Russia took place in February–March 2001, when the two countries agreed to raise bilateral relations to a strategic partnership during the visit by President Vladimir Putin. This was Vietnam's first such agreement. Under its terms, Hanoi and Moscow agreed to "strengthen their co-operation in military supplies to meet Vietnam's security demands".[13] Later the following year, Vietnam procured two *Svetlyak*-class coastal patrol boats armed with CIWS.

Under the terms of a Defence Cooperation Agreement (DCA) signed in March 2000, India agreed to assist Vietnam by repairing and upgrading its existing stock of Soviet-era *Osa*-II fast attack missile craft and *Petya*-class anti-submarine corvettes. In June 2005, the Indian Navy donated 150 tons of spares to Vietnam for these frigates and fast attack craft. Three years later, the Indian Navy donated five thousand essential spares to Vietnam to keep its *Petya* frigates operational. In 2015, India offered Vietnam a $300 million line of credit to purchase warships built in Indian dockyards. A year later, Vietnam's Border Guard and India's Larson & Toubro Ltd. signed a contract for the construction and delivery of four ocean patrol vessels under a $100 million line of credit offered in 2014. Subsequently, India offered to sell heavyweight torpedoes to Vietnam.

In 2006, Vietnam commenced a ten-year naval modernization programme by signing memoranda of understanding (MOU) and defence cooperation agreements (DCA) with a variety of foreign states. Vietnam sought assistance, services and equipment acquisitions in six major areas: the storage, maintenance and upgrading of existing military equipment; modernization of platforms and equipment for the army, navy and air force; modernization of Vietnam's national defence industry; maritime logistics capacity in the South China Sea; mitigating the effects of natural disasters, notably flooding and storm damage, and search and rescue at sea; and, finally, training for future involvement in UN-endorsed peacekeeping operations.

The second phase of defence modernization was signalled in 2006[14] when Vietnam placed an order with Russia for the construction of two *Gepard*-class frigates, Vietnam's first modern surface combatants. During the following decade Vietnam also acquired modern coastal defence systems, restructured its domestic shipbuilding industry and upgraded its technology, and created two new branches — a naval aviation unit and a submarine brigade.

The Vietnamese navy has responsibility for coastal defence. In the 1980s it took delivery of the 4K44 Redut (SS-N3 Shaddock) and 4K51 Rubezh (SS-N-2 STYK) coastal anti-ship missile systems. During the second phase of naval modernization, Vietnam acquired two K-300P (Bastion) coastal defence systems equipped with the *Yakhont* (SS-N-26 Strobile) anti-ship cruise missile between 2009 and 2011. This system is now operating in tandem with the Cold War–era legacy coastal defence systems. Between 2014 and 2016, Vietnam also took delivery of one hundred AccuLAR guided rockets and one hundred EXTRA guided rockets from Israel for coastal defence.

Between 2008 and 2016, Vietnam acquired eight *Tarantul*-5 (*Molniya*-class) guided missile fast attack craft armed with more advanced anti-ship missiles, manually operated surface to air missiles and CIWS. Two were purchased from Russia and six were assembled in Vietnam. Between 2011 and 2012, Vietnam took delivery of six more *Svetlayk*-class coastal patrol boats and commissioned into service two *Gepard*-class guided missile frigates armed with Kh-35E anti-ship missiles. In 2016–17, Vietnam added four more *Gepards* to its surface fleet, two outfitted for anti-submarine warfare.

In 2013, Vietnam placed an order for two SIGMA-9814 frigates from Damen in the Netherlands and acquired missiles for these ships from France, including forty MICA beyond-visual-range air-to-air missiles, twenty-five MM-40-3 Exocet anti-ship missiles and two VL-MICA-M surface-to-air missiles. Three years later it was reported that Vietnam opted to purchase the newer and larger SIGMA-10514.

In 2013, Vietnam stood up its first naval aviation branch by transferring Kamov Ka-27/28 helicopters from the Air Force's 954th Brigade. These helicopters were then sent to the Ukraine for upgrading. Vietnam also acquired three Canadian DHC-6-400 Twin Otter transport aircraft between 2012 and 2013 and three DHC-6-400 Guardian maritime patrol aircraft in 2014.

No development was more significant than Vietnam's acquisition of six *Varshavanyka* or enhanced *Kilo*-class conventional submarines in the period 2013–17. Crews for these submarines received training in Russia and India. The submarines are armed with heavy torpedoes and anti-ship and land-attack cruise missiles.[15]

By 2016, Vietnam's navy had been transformed from an inland and coastal brown-water fleet to a green-water one capable of operating in the South China

Sea. Vietnam's navy developed the capability to not only monitor its EEZ and protect key offshore oil and gas platforms but also to project power into the South China Sea to defend occupied features. Vietnam's navy also developed a modest deterrent to China's People's Liberation Army Navy.

Part 3: Air Defence Air Force Modernization

Vietnam modernized its air defence air force in parallel with naval modernization by upgrading existing inventories and procuring modern multi-role jet aircraft, armed with advanced missiles, capable of missions over the South China Sea.[16]

Air Force

In the first phase of modernization Vietnam cast its net wide for suppliers. Between 1996 and 1998, Russia upgraded thirty-two single-seat *Sukhoi* Su-22M4 and two twin-seat Su-22UM3 ground-attack aircraft. Under the 2000 DCA between India and Vietnam, India overhauled Vietnam's war-legacy fleet of MiG-21 combat aircraft and provided training assistance for Vietnam's technicians and pilots. Later, in October 2006, India supplied Vietnam with spare parts for its MiG-21s.

Between 1996 and 2006, Ukraine sold Vietnam ten L-39 trainers, six MiG-21 UMs, and eight Su-22s.[17] Later, Ukraine was contracted to upgrade these aircraft so they could mount anti-ship missiles. In 2004, Vietnam acquired five SU-22 UM3 aircraft from the Czech Republic, including spare parts and ammunition. Two years later, Vietnam purchased forty second-hand Su-22M4 fighter-bombers from Poland.[18] In 2015, Vietnam retired its fleet of MiG-21s. Russia has offered to sell its MiG-35 as a replacement.

Vietnam's air force entered a new phase of modernization when it procured seven Su-27SK (Flanker B) single-seat air superiority fighters, three Su-27UBK (Flanker C) two-seat trainers, and two additional Su-30Ks between 1995 and 1998. The Su-27s were later upgraded so they could operate the Kh-31 (AS-17) anti-ship missile and the *Vympel* Kh-29 (AS-14) and Kh-59M (AS-18) air-to-surface missiles.

After having gained experience with the Su-27, Vietnam next acquired thirty-six Su-30MK multi-role all-weather jet fighters. The first four were delivered in 2004, twenty Su-30s were acquired between 2010 and 2012, and the final batch of twelve was received in 2014–16. Vietnam upgraded its Su-30s so they could operate the Kh-29, Kh-31 and Kh-59MK air-to-surface missiles.

Air Defence

At the same time as Vietnam was acquiring a new generation of fighter aircraft, it also modernized its air defence and surveillance systems.

In May 2002, Vietnam and Ukraine signed a three-year agreement on military technical cooperation, including the development of naval test facilities and arms co-production. Under the terms of this agreement, Ukraine upgraded Vietnam's radar and communications systems as well as surface-to-air missiles. In 2005, Russia delivered to Vietnam two batteries of the highly advanced S-300PMU1 air defence system comprising twelve launchers and sixty-two missiles in total. The S-300 is regarded as one of the world's most effective all-altitude regional air defence systems. It has been recently reported that Russia is offering Vietnam the newer P-400 air defense system.

Intelligence, Surveillance and Reconnaissance (ISR)[19]

In 2012–13, Vietnam procured four Ukranian *Kolchuga* passive early warning radar systems capable of identifying and tracking land, sea and air threats. In 2013–16, Vietnam purchased five air search radar systems: two from Israel (EL/M-2288 AD STAR), two from the Ukraine (ST-68 *Tin Shield*), and one French Coast Watcher 100 air and surface radar system. In 2016, Vietnam took delivery of one Israeli SPYDER MR short and medium range air defence system; four additional systems are on order.

In 2016, Vietnam took a major step forward in ordering or acquiring four distinct ISR systems.

The first system was the VNREDSat satellite from France's Airbus Group. Also in 2016, the Indian Space Research Organisation agreed to finance a satellite tracking and imaging centre in Ho Chi Minh City and Japan's NEC and Mitsubishi Electric Corporations agreed to develop an ASNARO-2 high resolution Earth observation satellite to Vietnam's specifications.[20]

India's satellite tracking centre will be capable of accessing real time imagery from India's earth observation satellites that cover China and the South China Sea. Although India's satellites are primarily aimed at gathering scientific, environmental and agricultural information, analysts say the enhanced imaging technology can be used for military purposes.[21]

Second, Vietnam also began to acquire unmanned aerial vehicles (UAVs) through overseas procurements and domestic production. For example, in 2009–11, Vietnam placed an order for the Israeli Obiter-2 and Obiter-3 UAVs to assist in targeting for its Israeli coastal defence systems. In 2014–15, Vietnam took delivery of several Grif-K tactical drones from Belarus.

In May 2013, Vietnam flight-tested six indigenously built drones. But it was only in late 2015, with design assistance from Belarus, that Vietnam was able to successfully produce its first high-altitude long-endurance UAV, the HS-6L, with a range of four thousand kilometres and endurance of up to thirty-five hours.

Third, in May 2016, Vietnam placed an order for two Airbus DS C-295 airborne early warning and control (AEW&C) aircraft.

Fourth, in January 2017, Vietnam took delivery of one Pluto Plus unmanned underwater vehicle (UUV) from Italy's Gaymarine Electronics. This UUV will be used in tandem with its *Sonya*- and *Yurka*-class minesweepers.

Coastguard

In 2008, Vietnam elevated the status of its maritime police (now renamed in English as the Vietnam Coast Guard, or VCG) to an armed service under the joint command of the Ministry of National Defence and Vietnam People's Army Navy. The VCG was given responsibility for law enforcement, search and rescue and sovereignty protection over the territorial sea and EEZ off Vietnam's extended coastline.

In order to execute these roles the VCG moved to upgrade its maritime surveillance capabilities, which, at that time, comprised two Polskie Zaklady Lotnicze (PZL) M28 *Skytruck* short take-off and landing aircraft and four PZL *Swidnik* W-3RM *Anakonda* maritime search and rescue helicopters equipped with Wescam forward-looking infrared turrets. In 2008, Vietnam signed a contract with the Swedish Space Corporation for the purchase of three Spanish-manufactured EADS-CASA C212 Series 400 maritime patrol aircraft equipped with MSS 6000 side-looking radar.[22] In 2014–15, Vietnam took delivery of three twin-turboprop EADS CASA C-295. The C-295 is a tactical military transport aircraft manufactured in Spain by Airbus Defence and Space.

Between 2010 and 2016 the number of ships in the VCG over five hundred tons grew from thirty-nine to fifty-five, of which five were over a thousand tons. A major driver of the VCG's expansion was the mid-2014 crisis when China parked the *Haiyang Shiyou* 981 mega-oil drilling platform in Vietnam's EEZ.[23] China's actions precipitated a six-week maritime confrontation between the VCG and the Vietnam Fishery Surveillance Force and China's mixed armada of naval ships, coastguard vessels, tugboats, and fishing craft.

As a result of this crisis, in June 2014, Vietnam's National Assembly approved $756 million in funding for the construction of seven vessels: two 2,400-ton

Damen DN 2000–class patrol vessels, one 2,900-ton multipurpose logistics and transport ship; and four TT-400 patrol boats. In 2017, Vietnam took delivery of the 3,250-ton former United States Coast Guard *Morgenthau*, a Hamilton-class cutter. Vietnam is expected to place an order for at least one more ship of this class. In summary, the VCG is acquiring heavier ships for extended patrols in the South China Sea.

Part 4: Ground Force Modernization

In the initial phase of defence modernization, the main focus on the army was on refurbishing and upgrading its artillery, infantry fighting vehicles (IFV) and main battle tanks (MBT). In April 2001, for example, military factory Z-751 in Ho Chi Minh City undertook a modest overhaul of about fifty former U.S. M113 armoured personnel carriers (APC) by utilizing spare parts obtained through commercial sources and weapons stocks captured at the conclusion of the Vietnam War. Negotiations to purchase T-80 tanks from Russia fell through for lack of funding.

In May 2002, Vietnam and the Ukraine reached a three-year agreement on military-technical cooperation under which the Ukraine upgraded Vietnam's armour and artillery forces and armaments production. In 2005, Vietnam investigated the possibility of acquiring up to seventy Soviet-era T-54 and T-55 MBTs from Finland or 150 second-hand T-72 MBTs from Poland, but no sales eventuated. In 2006, Vietnam purchased two light armoured vehicles from Israel.

In December 2015, Lieutenant General Vo Van Tuan, Deputy Chief of the General Staff, stated that Vietnam's army had officially commenced a ten-year modernization programme. In early 2015, for example, Vietnam acquired the KZKT-7428 heavy tank transporter for the T-90 MBT. India was contracted to upgrade the thermal sights and fire control systems of Vietnam's stocks of Soviet-era armoured vehicles and T-54 and T-55 tanks. Vietnam was also reported to be in the market for eighteen CAESAR 155 mm self-propelled howitzers.

In 2016, in the first "big ticket" arms purchases for the ground force, Vietnam took delivery of the first batch of ten Guardian APCs manufactured in the United Arab Republic by the International Armored Group and, more significantly, announced the purchase of sixty-four modern T-90S/SK MBTs from Russia.[24]

Part 5: National Defence Industry

In January 2011, the Political Report to the Eleventh National Congress of the Communist Party of Vietnam identified modernization of the armed forces and the national defence industry as one of five key national objectives for the period

2011–16. The goals of defence modernization were "to further push the development of defense and security technology industry … to strengthen scientific research in military and security capable of defeating hi-tech wars from enemy forces …[and ensuring] that the armed forces incrementally have access to modern equipment with priority being given to the navy, air force, security, intelligence, and mobile police forces".

In his address to the eleventh congress, Lt. Gen. Ngo Xuan Lich, head of the Vietnam People's Army's General Political Department, identified "armaments, ammunition and technical means" as key priorities. Speaking on the sidelines of the congress, General Phung Quang Thanh, Minister of National Defense, included electronic and technical reconnaissance among the priorities for defence intelligence. Later in 2011 the Politburo adopted a resolution on "Building and Developing Defence Industry to 2020 and Beyond".[25]

According to Vietnam's 2014 Defence White Paper, priorities for the defence industry included the maintenance, manufacture, improvement and upgrading of weapons and equipment.

As noted above, Vietnam signed a number of MOUs and DCAs with its strategic partners and other states. These agreements usually contained clauses on bilateral national defence industry cooperation in five priority areas: promotion of defence research and technology transfer; co-production of weapons; maintenance, upgrading and repair; technical support; and personnel training.

Vietnam also has promoted national defence industry cooperation with its Southeast Asian neighbours. For example, Vietnam supported a Malaysian proposal to promote defence industry cooperation among members of the Association of Southeast Asian Nations (ASEAN). Vietnam and Indonesia have discussed co-producing fixed-wing transports, maritime surveillance aircraft and multi-role helicopters. Vietnam has approached Singapore for assistance in the safe storage of ordnance and munitions. Vietnam and the Philippines have discussed cooperation in the manufacture of various types of unspecified military equipment.

With respect to the modernization of Vietnam's national defence industry, two developments are noteworthy: the expansion and upgrading of Vietnam's shipbuilding industry and the co-production of missile systems.

Domestic Shipbuilding

In early 2008, Vietnam and Russia signed a contract for the delivery of several naval and coastguard ship-building kits and related weapon systems. These kits were assembled in Vietnam at the Hong Ha shipyard in Hai Phong and Ba Son shipyard in Ho Chi Minh City. The Hong Ha shipyard successfully produced

Vietnam's first 400-ton TT-400TP-class gunboat, which was commissioned in 2012; three other gunboats of the same class were commissioned between 2012 and 2014.[26]

In October 2011, President Truong Tan Sang made a state visit to India and requested Indian assistance to modernize the port facilities at Nha Trang.[27]

In 2013–14, under the terms of a co-production agreement, Vietnam and Russia assembled one KBO 2000/BPS 500 missile patrol boat at the Ba Son shipyard. This vessel failed to meet the technical requirements of Vietnam's navy and the project was terminated. However, by the end of 2016, Vietnam successfully assembled six *Tarantul*-5 (*Molniya*-class) guided missile fast attack craft at the Ba Son shipyard.

In 2015, the original Ba Son shipyard was sold off and redeveloped as a housing area. A new Ba Son shipyard is presently being constructed in Ba Ria-Vung Tau. It is expected to have the capacity to build ships displacing 500 to 2,000 tons and repair naval ships displacing up to 5,000 tons. There are reports that Vietnam will attempt to build two *Gepard*-class frigates when Ba Son becomes fully operational in 2018.

As noted above, the HD 981 crisis in 2014 was a major driver to expand the capabilities of the Vietnam Coast Guard through domestic production. In October 2016, the National Assembly approved a long-term VCG modernization programme that included the domestic construction of eight 1,500-ton TT-1500 offshore patrol vessels, four 2,200-ton DN 2000–class cutters and four 4,300-ton Damen DN 4000–class multi-role patrol vessels. These ships will be built at the Song Thu Shipyard in Da Nang with support from the Damen Group of the Netherlands.

Co-production of Missiles

Vietnam has sought offset agreements involving technology transfers in several of its arms procurement contracts.[28] In February 2002, the Russian defence enterprise LOMO announced that it reached a contract with Vietnam to assist in the transfer of technology so Vietnam could produce the Igla (SA-18 Grouse) low-altitude surface-to-air missile. Four years later, during the second phase of defence modernization, Russia and Vietnam reached agreement on technical assistance in the production of *Yakhont* (SS-N-26 Strobile) ship-to-ship missiles. In February 2012, it was announced that Russia and Vietnam would co-produce three versions of the Kh-35 Ural-E (SS-N-25 Switchblade) anti-ship missile to be deployed on aircraft, helicopters, ships and fired from coastal batteries.[29] Vietnam also has sought a licence to produce the Russia–India manufactured BrahMos anti-ship cruise missile.[30]

Currently, Vietnam is capable of maintaining and repairing existing stocks of naval and air weapons and platforms, depot-level reverse engineering of aircraft spares, assembling patrol boats from kits, building light aircraft,[31] constructing patrol boats and larger ships, co-producing a variety of missiles through technology transfer, and, most recently, manufacturing indigenous UAVs.

Part 6: Defence Budget

Vietnam's defence budget is closely tied to economic growth.[32] Since 1990, Vietnam has been one of the fastest growing economies in the world, averaging 6.4 per cent in the 2000s.[33] Its GDP in constant U.S. dollars rose from $99 billion in 2008, to $116 billion in 2010 to $193 in 2015. Defence spending averaged 2.89 per cent of GDP between 2006 and 2015, ranging from a high of 5.2 per cent in 2006 to a low of 2.0 per cent in 2011. In the five-year period ending in 2015, defence spending averaged 2.2 per cent of GDP.

Vietnam's defence budget as a percentage of nominal government spending averaged 9.89 between 2006 and 2015, with a high of 19.9 per cent in 2006 and a low of 6.9 per cent in 2010, reflecting the impact of the global economic crisis. Vietnam's defence budget as a percentage of nominal government spending averaged 7.76 for the five-year period ending 2015.

Vietnam's official defence budget, calculated in U.S. dollars (constant and exchange rate 2015), averaged $4.28 billion over the period 2006–15 and averaged $3.94 billion over the five-year period ending in 2015. It is estimated that Vietnam's defence budget will reach $5 billion in 2017 and rise to $6.2 billion by 2020.[34]

Part 7: Conclusion

Changes in the international legal regime and Chinese assertiveness in the South China Sea in the 1990s motivated Vietnam to embark on the modernization of its naval and air defence air force to develop capabilities to respond to likely contingencies in the maritime domain. This chapter traced two phases of force modernization, the first from the mid-1990s to the end of 2005 and the second from 2006 to the present. During the second phase, Vietnam moved from refurbishing and upgrading existing stocks to acquiring "big ticket" platforms such as missile attack craft, frigates, enhanced Kilo-class submarines, multi-role jet fighters, advanced radars, modern air defence and ISR systems, coastal defence missiles and new armoured fighting vehicles and main battle tanks. At the same time, Vietnam modernized its national defence industry to maintain and repair these new weapons and platforms, co-produce a variety of missiles and build larger and more capable warships.

Despite these impressive efforts to modernize its armed forces, Vietnam will face at least eight major interrelated challenges to create an effective modern joint fighting force.

First, Vietnam needs to maintain high economic growth in order to meet current operating costs, maintain expensive platforms such as the Kilo submarines, and to procure new platforms and weapons. Vietnam has set the target of 7 per cent growth of GDP per annum.

Second, Vietnam must overcome what Derek Grossman has called the legacy of army parochialism that has cast a shadow over the emergence of the navy as a separate co-equal service.[35]

Third, Vietnam must promote the effective integration of technology and systems acquired from diverse sources, such as radar and missiles.

Fourth, Vietnam needs to further develop the interoperability of its army, navy and air defence air force into an effective joint force by conducting innovative exercises.

Fifth, Vietnam must gain experience in conducting military operations in the maritime domain, including improving its capabilities in amphibious operations, mine sweeping, anti-submarine warfare, and acquiring acoustic signatures for its Kilo submarines.[36]

Sixth, Vietnam needs to gain experience in high-tech warfare by developing its newly acquired ISR assets for battlefield awareness and targeting, particularly for the land attack cruise missiles purchased for its Kilo submarines.

Seventh, Vietnam must articulate a national defence strategy, maritime strategy and military doctrine to guide the development of an effective and modern joint force.[37]

Eighth, Vietnam must continually revamp its system of professional military education and training to keep up with changes in technology and the creation of a joint force.[38]

Notes

1. A. Fleurant, P.D. Wezeman, S.T. Wezeman, and N. Tian, *Trends in International Arms Transfers, 2016*, SIPRI Fact Sheet, February 2017 <https://www.sipri.org/sites/default/files/Trends-in-international-arms-transfers-2016.pdf>. Vietnam's main sources were Russia (88 per cent), Belarus (3.5 per cent) and the Ukraine (2.8 per cent).
2. United States Central Intelligence Agency, "Vietnam", *World Fact Book*, 3 January 2018 <https://www.cia.gov/library/publications/the-world-factbook/geos/vm.html>.

3. International Monetary Fund, *World Economic Outlook*, October 2006 <http://statisticstimes.com/economy/projected-world-gdp-ranking.php>.
4. C.A. Thayer, *Trends in Force Modernization in Southeast Asia*, Working Paper no. 91 (Canberra: Peace Research Centre, Research School of Pacific Studies, The Australian National University, September 1990).
5. B.B. Fall, *The Viet Minh Regime: Government and Administration in the Democratic Republic of Viet Nam* (New York: Institute of Public Relations, 1956), p. 81.
6. "East Asia and Australasia – Vietnam", International Institute for Strategic Studies, *The Military Balance 1987–88*, pp. 14, 33, 145 and 175–76.
7. C.A. Thayer, *The Vietnam People's Army under Doi Moi*, Pacific Strategic Papers (Singapore: Institute of Southeast Asian Studies, 1994), p. 23.
8. In January 1974, China seized control of features in the Paracels occupied by the Army of the Republic of Vietnam (ARVN). The following year, VPA Special Forces similarly evicted ARVN forces from features in the Spratlys prior to the fall of Saigon. In March 1988, Chinese naval forces seized Fiery Cross and South Johnson reefs from Vietnam.
9. Bạch Dương, "Được ưu tiên hiện đại hóa, Lục quân VN sắp thay đổi lớn về chất" [Priority to modernisation: The army is about to change dramatically], Soha.vn, 22 December 2015 <http://soha.vn/quan-su/duoc-uu-tien-hien-dai-hoa-luc-quan-vn-sap-thay-doi-lon-ve-chat-20151222003129668.htm>.
10. C.A. Thayer, "Force Modernization: The Case of the Vietnam People's Army", *Contemporary Southeast Asia* 19, no. 1 (1997): 1–28; N.H. Son, "Vietnam: A Case Study in Naval Modernization", in *Naval Modernisation in South-East Asia: Nature, Causes and Consequences,* edited by G. Till and J. Chan, pp. 127–30 (New York: Routledge, 2014); Z. Abuza and N.N. Anh, "Vietnam's Military Modernization", *The Diplomat*, 28 October 2016 <https://thediplomat.com/2016/10/vietnams-military-modernization/>; and Alex Vuving, "Tracking Vietnam's Force Build-Up in the South China Sea", Asia Maritime Transparency Initiative, Center for Strategic and International Studies, 3 November 2017 <https://amti.csis.org/tracking-vietnams-force-build-south-china-sea/>.
11. Unless otherwise noted, data on Vietnam's arms acquisitions have been taken from the Stockholm International Peace Research Institute's Arms Transfer Database for the period 1990–2016 <http://armstrade.sipri.org/armstrade/page/trade_register.php>.
12. In the late 1980s, Vietnam expressed an interest in obtaining two or three Kilo-class submarines from the Soviet Union. Reportedly, a crew was in training when the Soviet Union collapsed and the programme was terminated.
13. Quoted in C.A. Thayer, *Vietnam People's Army: Development and Modernization*, Armed Forces Lecture Paper Series Paper no. 4 (Bandar Seri Begawan: Sultan Haji Hassanal Bolkiah Institute of Defence and Strategic Studies, 2009), p. 11.
14. T.M. Vu and N.T. Phuong, "Naval Development in Vietnam", in *Naval Modernisation in Southeast Asia*, edited by G. Till and A.S. Ristian, pp. 93–94 (London: Palgrave Macmillan, 2017).

15. C.A. Thayer, "Submarine Acquisition in Vietnam", in *Naval Modernization in Southeast Asia*, Part Two, *Submarine Issues for Small and Medium Navies*, edited by G. Till and C.S.L. Koh, pp. 109–118 (London: Palgrave Macmillan, 2018).
16. Abuza and Anh, "Vietnam's Military Modernization"; and Vuving, "Tracking Vietnam's Force Build-Up".
17. In 1980, Vietnam acquired the first of twenty-four Aero Vodochody L-39C jet trainers from Czechoslovakia. In mid-2008, Vietnam acquired four second-hand L-39s from the Czech Republic and ten new Yak-52 basic trainers from Rumania to replace the aging inventory in its air training division.
18. According to Government of Australia, Department of Defence, Defence Intelligence Organisation, *Defence Economic Trends in the Asia-Pacific 2007*, p. 22 <http://www.defence.gov.au/dio/documents/DET_07.pdf>.
19. Abuza and Anh, "Vietnam's Military Modernization".
20. "Japan to Export Earth Observation Satellite to Vietnam", Vietnam News Agency, 20 September 2016 <http://english.vov.vn/economy/japan-to-export-earth-observation-satellite-to-vietnam-331560.vov>.
21. S. Miglani and G. Torode, "India to Build Satellite Tracking Station in Vietnam That Offers Eye on China", Reuters, 25 January 2016 <https://www.reuters.com/article/us-india-vietnam-satellite/india-to-build-satellite-tracking-station-in-vietnam-that-offers-eye-on-china-idUSKCN0V30B3>.
22. "CASA C212-400 para la Guardia Costera Vietnamita", *Zona Militar*, 5 June 2008 <https://zona-militar.com/foros/threads/casa-c212-400-para-la-guardia-costera-vietnamita.12149/>.
23. Vuving, "Tracking Vietnam's Force Build-Up".
24. N.T. Phuong, "What Will New Russian Tanks Mean for Vietnam's Military?" *The Diplomat*, 27 July 2017 <https://thediplomat.com/2017/07/what-will-new-russian-tanks-mean-for-vietnams-military/>.
25. P. Nguyen, "Vietnam's Rising Geopolitical Profile is Driving a Military Sea Change", *Nikkei Asian Review*, 17 November 2016 <https://asia.nikkei.com/magazine/20161117-INCOMING/Viewpoints/Phuong-Nguyen-Vietnam-s-rising-geopolitical-profile-is-driving-a-military-sea-change>.
26. TT-400TP. TT is a Vietnamese abbreviation of *Tuần Tra*, or patrol, and TP is an abbreviation for *Tàu Pháo*, or gunboat.
27. S. Dikshit, "Vietnam's Plea Puts South Block in a Predicament", *The Hindu*, 9 November 2011.
28. These missiles were produced by the Soviet Union in the 1950s.
29. The Vietnamese name for this missile is KCT-15; Douglas Barrie and Tom Waldwyn, "Vietnam Paddles its Own *Kayak*", International Institute for Strategic Studies, *Shangri-La Voices*, 5 June 2016 <http://www.iiss.org/en/shangri-la%20voices/blogsections/2016-588c/vietnam-paddles-its-own-kayak-46c1>.
30. R. Johnson, "India is Preparing to Sell BrahMos Supersonic Cruise Missiles to Vietnam", *Business Insider*, 20 September 2011.

31. Between June 2003 and September 2005, Vietnam manufactured three A-41 (VNS-11) three-seat amphibious aircraft for use in search and rescue and forestry patrols.
32. The discussion in part 6 is based on Government of Australia, Department of Defence, Defence Intelligence Organisation, *Defence Economic Trends in the Asia-Pacific 2016* <http://www.defence.gov.au/dio/documents/DET_16.pdf>; see also Abuza and Anh, "Vietnam's Military Modernization".
33. "Vietnam GDP", *Trading Economics* <https://tradingeconomics.com/vietnam/gdp>.
34. IHS Jane's, "Defense Budget Overview", *Jane's Sentinel Security Assessment: Southeast Asia*, 25 July 2016, p. 1.
35. D. Grossman, "Can Vietnam's Military Stand up to China in the South China Sea?" *Asia Policy* (National Bureau of Asian Research) 13, no. 1 (2018): 123–24.
36. C. Koh, "Vietnam's Quest for a Greenwater Navy", *The Diplomat*, 18 March 2016 <https://thediplomat.com/2016/03/vietnams-quest-for-a-greenwater-navy/>; C.A. Thayer, "Vietnam: Evaluating its Fleet of Six Kilo-class Submarines", *Thayer Consultancy Background Brief*, 25 February 2017 <http://www.viet-studies.net/kinhte/Thayer_VN_subs.pdf>, and C.A. Thayer, "Vietnam: Acoustic Signatures and Kilo Submarines", *Thayer Consultancy Background Brief*, 8 May 2017 <https://www.scribd.com/document/348493131/Thayer-Vietnam-Acoustic-Signatures-and-Kilo-Submarines>.
37. Vu and Phuong, "Naval Development in Vietnam", p. 104; Abuza and Anh, "Vietnam's Military Modernization"; S.S. Wu, "The Development of Vietnam's Sea-Denial Strategy", *Naval War College Review* 70, no. 1 (2017): 143–61; and A.D. Ton, "Vietnam's Maritime Security Challenges and Regional Defence and Security Cooperation", *Soundings* (Sea Power Centre, Royal Australian Navy), forthcoming 2018.
38. P. Nguyen, "High Ambitions, Tall Orders for Vietnam's Military", *Nikkei Asian Review*, 2 November 2016 <https://asia.nikkei.com/Viewpoints/Phuong-Nguyen/Phuong-Nguyen-High-ambitions-tall-orders-for-Vietnam-s-military>.

www.ingramcontent.com/pod-product-compliance
Lightning Source LLC
Chambersburg PA
CBHW061831260326
41914CB00005B/957

* 9 7 8 9 8 1 4 7 8 6 8 3 6 *